CLIVE OF PLASSEY

ROBERT, BARON CLIVE OF PLASSEY
From a portrait by Nathaniel Dance
in the National Portrait Gallery

CLIVE OF PLASSEY

A BIOGRAPHY

BY

A. MERVYN DAVIES

NEW YORK

CHARLES SCRIBNER'S SONS

1939

TO

STRUTHERS *and* KATHARINE BURT

with profound admiration and deep affection

PREFACE

I MAKE NO APOLOGY for following my study of Warren Hastings with a companion work on Clive. It would have been more logical of course if I had taken Clive first, but that was not the order of my interest. There is an unquestioned lack of a satisfactory full-dress life of Clive, as of most other leading figures of British-Indian history. This lack I have tried to supply, at the same time giving to the subject a modern critical interpretation somewhat at variance on many points with that of previous writers. Because of the fact that presentations of Clive have tended in recent years to become stereotyped, a fresh and different view of him may not be unwelcome. I wish only to assure the reader who has well-formed views of his own that my conclusions have not been reached by making facts fit into a preconceived theory : they arise out of a close and unprejudiced study of all the available evidence and a prolonged study of the character and personality of Clive himself.

All biographers like to make a claim to " new material." I cannot make that claim, but I hope that I shall be considered to have made fuller use of " old material " than has previously been made. The Clive papers in the possession of Lord Powis have twice been examined and largely published. Whether or not anything of importance has been overlooked I am not in a position to say, as I have not been given access to them, but I found some interesting unpublished items in the extensive transcriptions from them that Sir George W. Forrest made and which are now in the India Office records. I had hoped to be able to examine the Strachey papers, perhaps the only source of possible new light on Clive still available, and had considerable correspondence with their present owner about them, but he has plans of his own in respect to them which we shall hope to see carried out in due course. All historical students are under a deep debt of gratitude to S. C. Hill for the work that he did on the Orme MSS. and that admirable collection of documents *Bengal in* 1756–1757, of both of which I have made full use.

There is now only one real *lacuna* in our story and that is

Lawrence Sulivan.   There is a splendid opportunity for research in unearthing his personal history and unravelling his important part in East India Company politics.   By making the best use of available material I have given the fullest treatment hitherto accorded him.

A word of warning is necessary regarding my treatment of quoted passages from contemporary letters and documents, in which I have not been consistent.   Whether or not to retain the original spelling, punctuation and liberal use of capitals of the originals is an insoluble problem for historians and biographers ; the arguments either way seem equally strong.   My own solution of it has been to transcribe some letters exactly, so that the uninitiated may appreciate their elegancies, while modernizing the rest for the sake of greater ease of reading, without of course in any way disturbing their sense.   Much of the same difficulty arises over the spelling of Indian words, old and modern usage varying widely.

For the rest I have taken as my aim the one that Professor Trevelyan has in our own day made his own, with such magnificent results : that the same book should make its appeal both to the general reader and to the historical student.

As in the previous volume I am indebted to Mr. W. T. Ottewill of the India Office for much kind help.   Miss L. M. Anstey has been of great assistance in following up some lines of research.   I am also grateful to Dr. W. D. Howe for his criticisms and suggestions, to Mr. G. P. Borglum for consenting to read the proofs, and to the British Library in New York for their assistance in obtaining for me books not easily available on the western side of the Atlantic.   Sir Evan Cotton and Dr. Sophia Weitzman have kindly given me the benefit of their wide knowledge of the subject, though I acquit them of any responsibility for my views.

January, 1939.   A. M. D.

CONTENTS

CONTENTS

NOTE : The numbers inserted in the text refer to the authorities cited. In order to avoid defacing the text with numerous footnotes the authorities have been listed at the end of the volume.

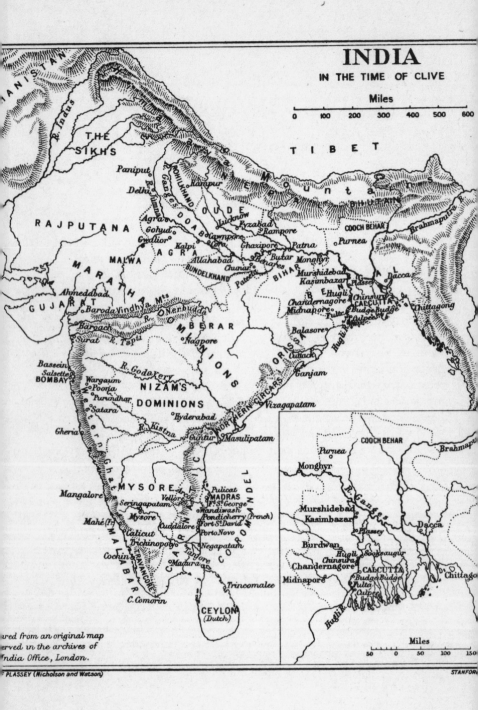

INDIA
IN THE TIME OF CLIVE

Miles

AFGHANISTAN

R. Indus

THE SIKHS

RAJPUTANA

MALWA

MARATHA

GUJARAT

Ahmeddbad

Baroda

Vindhya Mts

Baroach

Surat

R. Tapti

R. Nerbudda

Bassein

Salsette

BOMBAY

Wargaum

Poona

Purundhar

Satara

Gheria

NIZAM'S

DOMINIONS

R. Godavery

R. Kistna

Hyderabad

Guntur

Masulipatam

Vizagapatam

MYSORE

Mangalore

Vellore

Mahé (Fr.)

Mysore

Seringapatam

Cuddalore

Calicut

Trichinopoly

Cochin

TRAVANCORE

Madura

MALABAR

C. Comorin

CEYLON
(Dutch)

Trincomalee

Panipat

Delhi

R. Jumna

Agra

Gohud

Gwalior

Kalpi

AGRA

Allahabad

BUNDELKHAND

ROHILKHAND

Rampur

DOAB

R. Ganges

OUDE

Lucknow

Fyzabad

Cawnpore

Cora

Rampore

Ghazipore

Benares

Chunar

Pateli

Buxar

Patna

Monghyr

BIHAR

NEPAL

MOUNTAINS

TIBET

BHUTAN

COOCH BEHAR

Purnea

R. Brahmaputra

Murshidebad

Kasimbazar

Plassey

Dacca

BENGAL

Hugli

Chandernagore

Midnapore

Chinsura

CALCUTTA

Budge Budge

Culpee

Fulta

Chittagong

Balasore

Hugli R.

Cuttack

ORISSA

Ganjam

NORTHERN CIRCARS

BERAR

Nagpore

CARNATIC

COROMANDEL

Pulicat

MADRAS

Ft. St. George

Wandiwash

Pondicherry (French)

Fort St. David

Porto Novo

Negapatam

Tanjore

Western Ghats

Inset map

COOCH BEHAR

Purnea

Monghyr

R. Ganges

Brahmaputra

Murshidabad

Kasimbazar

Plassey

Dacca

Burdwan

Hugli

Chinsura

Chandernagore

CALCUTTA

Sooksaugur

Budge Budge

Midnapore

Fulta

Culpee

Chittagong

Hugli R.

Miles

50   0   50   100   150

...ared from an original map
...erved in the archives of
...India Office, London.

PLASSEY (Nicholson and Watson)   STANFORD

CLIVE OF PLASSEY

INTRODUCTION

I

"The History of Heroes is the History of Youth"
BENJAMIN DISRAELI

ALL PEOPLES CHERISH the memory of their heroes. They are part of the national inheritance woven into the very warp and woof of national consciousness. That the tradition is not always historically true matters little. The legend is more important than fact. The hero is above truth.

History knows very little about King Arthur, yet he is one of the most important personalities in English history. Even if it were to be proved that he never existed, the learned of the profession alone would take note of the fact, and it would still remain true that, though he never existed, he still lives in the minds and imaginations of the people that inhabit his island. Legends have a reality, a truth, and a power all their own.

Happy is the lot of the historian and biographer when legend and historical fact happen to coincide ; when in pursuit of his object he does not have to tear down images in the national temples of honour.

Clive, so far as he has been a hero, is the hero of youth rather than maturity. To boys he has an irresistible appeal that would seem to extend to the boy in grown men. In fact, one has the feeling that most of the books that have been written about him have been written by men—none has been written by a woman !—in memory of their own youth. Arcot and Plassey ! These adventures stir emotions in the blood such as will not easily settle. They remain even when the writer is brought up against the hard and discomforting facts of the hero's later life. How often they must have wished that he had met a hero's death, like Wolfe, upon the field of his greatest victory ! Yet even so, even though they had to tell of the remaining seventeen years of his

A

I

life, the glamour of youthful exploits still spreads its lustre, the hero keeps his pedestal, managing, though less often than before, to strike correct heroic attitudes. A soberer, less romantic note has to be struck as the " heaven-born general " gives place to the statesman and administrator. But the change is only superficial. Clive, the hero of Arcot and Plassey, remains. Indeed, he becomes *Clive of India* !

And then at last, in the due course of time, he receives the final apotheosis when the legend is translated into a successful stage and film play, which does the utmost that man can do to make him a romantic figure cast in true heroic mould. Between Henty's juvenile story *With Clive in India* and the play *Clive of India* there is no vital difference of view. Action, colour, romance are the ingredients of both.

But there is, and always has been, another view of Clive. One that may be called the historians' view in contrast to the romanticists' and biographers'. Neither the older school of historians of British India, represented by James Mill, nor the most modern, represented by Messrs. Thompson and Garratt, has been dazzled by his undeniably fine military qualities and feats. They have used other criteria for judgment than valour and have been concerned with other considerations than partiality for one man. Lacking that biographical temptation, they have arrived at conclusions strikingly different from the former. A number of virtues attributed to the hero do not appear in their pages.

There are, in fact, two Clives in literature and popular thought, two quite different traditions. And each has about the same weight of authority behind it. Each stems from his own lifetime, though from different sources, and each has had its adherents. As much evil was spoken of Clive during his lifetime as good, as much attention was centred on the alleged ill-deeds of the later years as on the heroisms of the earlier. Few men have known the same extremes of applause and opprobrium. To his own generation he was as much villain as hero.

It is interesting to read the " Reflections on the Life and Death of Lord Clive " that Thomas Paine published in the *Pennsylvania Magazine* (March 1775). The Reflections took the shape of a homily against avarice and ambition, a mystery play showing the inevitable fate attending wickedness. Clive is depicted at the close of his life envying chimney-sweeps and beggars, wishing he could change places with them. Words are put into his mouth :

" Could I unlearn what I've already learned—unact what I've already acted—or would some sacred power convey me back to youth and innocence, I'd act another part—I'd keep within the vale of humble life, nor wish for what the world calls pomp." And Paine's conclusion is : " As an emblem of the vanity of all earthly pomp, let his monument be a globe, but be that globe a bubble ; let his effigy be a man walking round it in his sleep ; and let fame and the character of a shadow inscribe honours on the air."

Thus we have two quite different conceptions of Clive, and the wide gap between them has never yet, in the popular mind at least, been filled. It is our business to try to fill that gap, to examine both traditions, and see where the real truth lies.

It will generally be found in such cases that the truth lies somewhere in between. So we believe it to be in the case of Clive. One tradition belongs especially to his youth, the other to his manhood, and both have equally strong elements of truth in them. There was once a hero, and there was once a man, though never the wicked man of Paine's imaginings, who might have uttered such a prayer. On the one hand his life may be read as a homily in praise of manly virtues, of courage, zeal, vigour, enterprise, and boldness ; on the other, it may be read as a homily against worldly ambition and love of power. Of such diverse materials was his life made.

Our task, then, is one of synthesis and reconciliation, to show that there were not two Clives but one, who partook of both natures.

II

The tradition of Clive the hero in its purest form is embedded in a rock that is hard to split. That rock is Orme.

What Hakluyt is to the Elizabethan mariners Orme is to Clive. That is to say, his *History of the Military Transactions of the British Nation in India* is the one indispensable contemporary account of Clive's military career. And in default of other accounts, except for one or two that merely supplement it, it has been for the historian almost a case of *aut* Orme *aut nihil*. As his dependability has been generally recognized, the result has been that what we read in most subsequent histories is little more than a paraphrase of his work.

But though Orme is indispensable he is not necessarily

infallible, and one of the questions we have to ask ourselves is whether there are any grounds for doubting the strict accuracy of his narrative, his impartiality, and the soundness of his judgment. In order to answer this question we must first see how he came to write his history ; the kind of man he was ; and the nature of his relations with Clive.

The two men entered the East India Company's service at Madras in the same year, though Robert Orme was three years Clive's junior, having come out to Calcutta at the age of thirteen apprenticed to a firm of merchants.[1] Within a short time we find them in partnership carrying on private trade between Madras and Bengal, and naturally when Clive took up soldiering his partner took care of his affairs.

The desire to be the chronicler of the wars of the English and French seems to have taken early possession of Orme and to have arisen from a natural admiration for the exploits of his friend. He had a literary bent and his companions had already dubbed him Cicero and employed him to write their letters.[2] So he began to make records of each military event as it occurred and to obtain from Clive accounts of earlier episodes in the war. When Clive returned home Orme accompanied him, and both used their time successfully in furthering their ambitions. Orme had by now prepared an early draft of his history and passed it around among prominent men. It obtained him the favour of Lord Holdernesse, Secretary of State, so that within a year he was on his way back to Madras as Member of Council. Clive soon followed him, and when he left to go on the Bengal expedition Orme again took care of his interests.

Their co-operation seems to have been very close. Orme proposed Clive for the command of the expeditionary land force, and when Orme evinced ambitions to succeed to the Governorship of Madras, Clive, who had the prior claim as Deputy-Governor of Fort St. David, wrote, as a consequence of his triumph at Plassey, to say that he was no longer a rival.[3] On Orme's return to India he had begun seriously to study Thucydides, his chosen model, and to collect additional materials from the principal performers. Clive sent him numerous memoranda which formed the body of his work.[4] It was Orme's experience that purely military men were seldom able to give coherent accounts of their own doings, for which reason he leaned heavily upon Clive, whose accounts were notably clear and succinct.

4

In writing to Clive he called it *his* history and said that it must be written at *his* elbow ; which seems to prove that though it was a general history of the war its real object was to celebrate Clive's martial exploits.[5]   That he appears to have been obligated to Clive financially is not an irrelevant point to consider in this connection.[1]

Orme's Indian career came to a sudden end in 1759. He showed himself in an unfortunate light by consenting to send private reports about his colleagues to the Company's chairman at home.   When the fact was discovered he naturally incurred their bitter enmity.   The Governor accused him of corruption and he was forced to resign.[6]   By going home shortly before Madras was besieged by Lally he incurred the further charge of cowardice.   Altogether he quitted the service under a heavy cloud.   The rest of his life was spent in retirement in England, where he redeemed his reputation by his literary work.[7]

When Clive joined him in England the following year their collaboration on the history was resumed.   Clive went over the proofs of the first volume, which brought the story down to the end of Dupleix's war.   It is that volume, published in 1763, which is the foundation of whatever there is of legend in Clive's reputation as a soldier and peerless hero.

The odd, or perhaps significant, thing about the publication of that volume is that the reception given to it was not at all what its author had expected.   Although he had celebrated the gallant deeds of other people besides Clive, none of these gentlemen, with the exception of Captain Dalton, Clive's intimate friend, thought that justice had been done him !   They were, in fact, so lukewarm in their appreciation that Orme was doubtful whether to continue.[8]

One reason for this lack of enthusiasm was probably that Clive was at that date ceasing to be a popular hero.   The tide of feeling was turning against him.   And there may consequently have been a great deal of scepticism about Orme's portrayal of him as a supreme military genius.

Some of this scepticism we may ourselves share.   A civilian himself, Orme seems to have had all of a civilian's passionate admiration for those of his colleagues who were distinguishing themselves in the field of war, and most of all, naturally, for his friend and partner only three years older than himself.   It is easy

---

[1] See his letter to Clive, Oct. 22, 1757, p. 249, below.

to see how anyone as young as—Orme only twenty-one at the time—would be quite carried away by the dazzling splendour of such a feat as the defence of Arcot. Nor is it to be doubted that Clive, with his more than ordinary ambitiousness, was fully as pleased to have the story written up in the way it was.

In plain terms, what we suspect is that, consciously or not, Orme had given birth to a legend and that there were people in England who recognized it as such and, therefore, withheld their admiration from his book. And what makes us suspect this the more is the positive fact that Orme's account does not always tally with the evidence contained in his papers.

On this point we cannot do better than to quote the late S. C. Hill, who calendared the Orme Collection now in possession of the India Office :

" It would appear that Orme's admiration of Clive's early exploits developed a tendency to exaggerate—at any rate in the first volume—his merit and to give him the whole credit for the success of battles and operations at which he was present even in a subordinate capacity. Thus he ascribes to his initiative the attack upon Arcot, though this expedition was first suggested by that least military of Indian princes, Muhammad Ali, Nawab of the Carnatic, who was in dire need of money and knew that the Arcot district was very rich, and though Clive himself was so ignorant of the political value of his achievement that he was saved from the fatal mistake of a retirement only by the remonstrances of Saunders and Pigot. So also Orme ascribes to Clive the bold and risky crossing of the Coleroon which resulted in the defeat of Auteuil and the surrender of Law, whereas the idea was most probably that of Lawrence, the force dispatched being placed under Clive only because of his reputation amongst our Indian allies. Evidently Orme never recognized, as Clive himself did, how much Clive owed to the military example and teaching of Lawrence. Dazzled, like the native chiefs, by Clive's capture and defence of Arcot, he expected everything from his hero. In 1751 he wrote to Stephen Law : ' This military genius is too well known to us and too much dreaded by the enemy not to let us expect that if he goes to Trichinopoly matters must be concluded immediately.' Fortunately for the English, Lawrence returned to India in time to take command of the expedition."[9]

When one gets past Orme's first volume the scenery of Clive's life undergoes a subtle but profound change. It broadens considerably—Orme is no longer our only authority—but also loses its ecstatic quality. The farther one goes the harsher do the configurations become. It is as though youthful illusions, Orme's along with the rest, have been dispelled and when seen in the hard light of reality and from a maturer standpoint Clive no longer appears either a military genius or a hero. As Orme progressed with his story he felt less and less relish for his task. And at the end he left it unfinished. He himself dated the beginning of his disillusionment from the events in Bengal of April 1757, which led up to Plassey and Clive's revolution.[10] One notes a change in his attitude to Clive which is reflected both in his writing and their personal relations. Their friendship ends. And one is left wondering how far its influence while it lasted had extended.

In other words, what we have to bear in mind in interpreting Clive's career, particularly the earlier part of it, is the importance of the personal equation. If the Clive that conducted the campaign of Plassey does not seem upon examination quite the same faultless figure as the one who defended Arcot, it seems more reasonable to seek the explanation in Orme than in any actual deterioration of Clive's military genius. If Plassey proves his fallibility, the deduction we draw is that that fallibility more nearly represents the truth about him than the earlier apparent infallibility, and we have accordingly tried to make our interpretation of his earlier career harmonize with the facts revealed by the later event.

The common mistake made has been to do just the opposite—to make the facts about Plassey fit into the previously conceived notion of Clive derived from Orme. According to this view, it is almost unimaginable that he should make a mistake, be completely at a loss how to act, or be less master of a situation than some of his officers. But in order to hold such a view it is necessary to ignore or gloss over a number of inconvenient facts. The known facts of this campaign happen to be far more numerous than those of the earlier ones and to come from other sources than Clive himself. For this reason the account of it that we can piece together is likely to be far more accurate. For the first time Clive had regular army officers under his command who not only knew their business and were in a position to criticize his conduct but were able afterwards to make their views known. Except for Lawrence, with his big-hearted liking for Clive, none of his fellow officers in the Carnatic had known even as much about the art of war as he. Those early campaigns had been fought by amateurs and recorded by a civilian. At Calcutta and Plassey Clive was, for the first time, subjected to the real test of performing under the critical eyes of professionals, and there is reason for thinking that he himself came to realize only too well his own deficiencies as a master of war. My own view is based on this belief.

Once started along this track the legendary elements in the story naturally continue to grow. If one succeeds in fitting Plassey into the picture it is easy to fit much more into it. If one imagines him as " a heaven-born general," it is not difficult to imagine him too as a heaven-born statesman. One ray of genius is sufficient to colour the entire view. It is this view that presents Clive to us as " a man of boundless devotion and charity, as a soldier of dauntless courage, as a sound and brilliant commander of victorious armies, as a wielder, by sympathy, of great influence over alien races, as a statesman who, by the power of an unfaltering will, founded a mighty empire."[11] And at the end, as the victim of all the hatred and odium that can sometimes come upon a man from having too faithfully, diligently, and heroically done his duty. So the story closes appropriately upon a note of martyrdom.

Such, in brief, is the heroic tradition and the way it has developed out of the pages of Orme, where it was first given birth.

III

It remains to indicate something of the nature of the bridge we propose to build between this traditional view of Clive and the other so different in every way.

Clive, as we see him, was a thoroughly typical man of his century, exemplifying to a high degree most of its particular virtues and vices. The virtues were principally vigour, enterprise, originality, initiative, courage, boldness, self-confidence ; all springing from an essential virility of thought, action, and expression. The vices may be summed up as those of unrestrained egotism, producing a voracity for wealth, power, and position the like of which has seldom been seen in English history.

We talk a lot to-day of our " system of private enterprise " and the need for preserving, or abolishing, it. Seen in the light of Clive's age it no longer exists. It began its decline, in England at least, not long after his death and died early in the nineteenth century.

So much was that an age of private enterprise that every important achievement and advance was the work of individuals. Governments and corporate bodies were sunk in torpor and wound around by the twin cords of red tape and private interest, whilst the general level of human living and thinking was as far below the standard of to-day as the level reached by a few was above it. The variety of type of person and achievement among those few is what makes the age so fascinating to the student of human nature. Untrammeled human nature in operation may not always be an inspiring spectacle in the eyes of the moralist or those possessed of a strong social sense, but it cannot fail to be absorbingly interesting and instructive. It enables us to see some of the heights to which man can rise and the depths to which he can fall. Both heights and depths are exemplified in Clive's career, and both, as we shall see, were caused by the same traits in his character and the same circumstances of his life ; corollaries, in fact, of his nature.

It was, moreover, a heartless, unfeeling age, with little or no sympathy for human suffering, little or no regard for one's fellow men. It cannot be called cruel or bloodthirsty, like previous ages, but rather, insensible. Though the lot of all common humanity was appallingly hard, it would have been considered bad form in a gentleman to call attention to the fact or trouble himself in the matter. Life with all that it had in store in the shape of fortunes, positions, titles, and comforts was for the privileged few, who could take them each for himself without caring for his neighbour. Those who failed to seize the opportunity, whether from moral scruple or delicacy, were regarded by most of their class as fools or madmen. In fact, in moral scruples of any kind, except those of a most conventional and domestic nature, the age was notably deficient. In these respects, too, Clive was typical of his generation.

The chief impression I have derived from studying Clive's career against this background is one of tragedy rather than romance. I see tragedy in preparation in his childhood. I suspect far more than I can actually see in the years of upbringing and in the early years in India. I tell myself, what is the literal truth, that what we actually know about him during those years is not a hundredth part of what we need to know in order to know the whole story. And I suspect that if we did know the whole story we should see much more clearly than we do the elements that were to cause the ultimate tragedy, because reason tells me that they were always present. His whole life I see as cut to a single pattern, his early triumphs paving the way for his later defeats, with the same qualities of mind and character producing both. Thus there appears an inevitability in his final tragedy, and it is that inevitability that gives his life its true dramatic quality, not the glamorous quality that it has assumed in the hands of romantic writers.

The youthful hero was fading away even before the great wealth came that finally obliterated him. His successes did not make him humble, but proud ; did not sweeten his nature, make him more kindly and generous, but more ambitious, more sensitive to slights, more avid of recognition, more intolerant of opposition. His overweening pride was insatiable and it became almost impossible for other men to esteem him as highly as he wished. Those, Stringer Lawrence, Robert Orme, his Madras comrades, who had loved the gallant youth could not love the mature man that emerged out of him, nor could the public continue to extend to him its admiration. Both love and admiration vanished as the years went by, and envy and hate more and more took their places.

For us the chief interest of his life is to trace that transition and to analyse its causes. We see a marked difference between the kind of enemies that all men in public life must make and the kind that Clive made, these latter being the products largely of his own peculiar nature and his own acts. It is this difference of view that distinguishes our interpretation of his life from certain other ones that conform to the heroic tradition. Clive was hated. That is the outstanding fact of the concluding years of his life. And we ask ourselves, Why ? How far was it his own fault ? In answering these questions I have tried to take a judicial attitude, identifying myself neither with him nor with his enemies.

Anyone who makes such an attempt is entitled to ask for the indulgence of his critics, because it is beset with tremendous difficulties. Those years reeked with controversy of the bitterest sort and it is sometimes practically impossible to arrive at definite conclusions, and not always can one be sure of being entirely just. The contemporary evidence consists in large measure of controversial pamphlets better suited to the purposes of verbal warfare than of history. And Clive was always in the forefront of the strife, giving and receiving blows of equal lustiness.

Yet the attempt to steer a straight course without partiality for Clive seems well worth while. Without important new material that would radically alter the accepted story of his life—something not to be expected at this date—the most that a biographer can offer is a fresh interpretation of his subject. A changed viewpoint frequently leads to as interesting results as new facts, and assuredly a viewpoint that does not throw all Clive's enemies out of court as perjured, worthless witnesses is a new one !

There is another consideration. If Clive has had his advocates, most of those with whom he was at odds have not. Many of them are too unimportant for biographical attention. Their honour and reputation rest mainly in the hands of Clive's biographers, and too often, as it seems to me, they have suffered in consequence. They are the under-dogs of our story, and I have tried to redress the balance a little in their favour.

Many hands helped to establish British ascendancy in India. It is not fair that to one man should go more of the credit than clearly belongs to him. And even to those who opposed its establishment and all the steps taken in that direction, justice should be done, particularly by our own generation, which is not very enamoured of the glories of imperialism. Let it readily be granted that Clive stood head and shoulders above everyone else, but let it also be granted that he sometimes strained himself to attain that additional height, and that he was not above pushing others to one side so that he could stand in solitary splendour ! We are not dealing with a hero or a demi-god, but a human being with great qualities and great weaknesses, whose life was a record of great achievement gained at the price of great suffering and sacrifice, physical, moral, and spiritual, both to himself and to others.

Chapter One

THE EXILE

"Myself I know that exiles feed on hope"

AESCHYLUS

I

ON MAY 31, 1744, as night fell, a lone East-Indiaman dropped her anchor in Madras roads on the Coromandel Coast of India. It was the *Winchester*, 500 tons, Captain Gabriel Stewart, six months overdue from England. Around her lay other ships of the East India Company's fleet which had long since arrived. The event caused excitement in the little colony ashore, as such events always did. It signified letters from home, news, new faces, a welcome break in the weary monotony of existence. Also the *Winchester*, like her consort the *Princess Louisa,* which had sailed with her from the Company's dockyard in the Thames on March 10, 1743, had been given up for lost. And lost she had nearly been several times during the course of her fifteen months' voyage. Her tale of adventures included the time when she had actually seen her consort hopelessly wrecked in a storm on one of the Cape Verde islands, and another when she had gone aground herself on the treacherous Brazilian coast.

That latter had been a particularly trying experience. After refloating the ship her company had to spend five weary, perilous months waiting for the winter storms to subside sufficiently for them to bring her to a harbour where she could be repaired, and then she had had to be refitted from stem to stern—work that had taken four months more. Finally she had spent another three and a half months at sea before at last completing her voyage.

A common enough occurrence, and one worth recording at this distance of time only because among her passengers happened to be a young man named Robert Clive.

As the burning sun rose next morning a desolate scene was spread out before the eager eyes of the eighteen-year-old youth waiting to land. A mile or two from the ship, which was

12

anchored in an open roadstead, lay the low, barren coast, with no sort of harbour to extend a welcome. It was not the most propitious time of year for new-comers, with their memories of England's green and pleasant land, to make their first acquaintance with this far outpost of trade. A scorching sun had long since burnt up every bit of verdure in the landscape, leaving nothing but a few palm-trees to break the appearance of utter aridity. Nor was there anything to betoken the existence of a European settlement except the shipping in the roads and the little fort with the English flag flying from its staff.

Landing was an adventure in itself. The catamarans dashed perilously through the surf with their loads of passengers and freight, which they deposited at the sea-gate of the fort.

Acquaintance with his new home was for young Clive a matter only of a few minutes. Fort St. George was a puny structure 400 yards long and a hundred wide, lying so close to the water's edge that in stormy weather the great seas washed its very walls. All it had in the way of defences was a high wall with ramparts planted with antiquated cannon and, on the landward side, a broad ditch partly dry. It had been built a hundred years before at a cost of only Rs. 23,000, and the highest estimate of a sufficient garrison for it was one hundred men. Inside its close confines were some fifty buildings, for the most part lofty, airy, and well-constructed, which housed the 400 European inhabitants of the settlement. On the south side stood the English church, with the Portuguese church opposite. The warehouses, go-downs, the main factory building, where Clive was to live with the rest of the junior servants, and the houses of the chief officials accounted for the remainder. Upon leaving the fort a short walk took one to the bounds of the settlement, the circumference of which was only four miles. A mile to the northward lay the " Black Town," a noisome place, dark, evil-smelling, miserably mean and squalid. Westwards were a few " garden houses " belonging to the Governor and the senior merchants. Beyond these lay nothing but a vast plain, broken here and there by a few gaunt mounds of earth, beautiful and fertile only when the seasonal rains had renewed its life. Far away, like low clouds on the horizon, there was a distant line of hills that marked the boundary between the plains of the Carnatic and the well-watered up-lands of Mysore, the real hinterland of India.

The youth who stepped ashore was not a prepossessing sight. He was stoutly built for his height, which was medium, and his heavy features made him anything but good-looking. In manners he was awkward, in temper morose. The long voyage had played havoc with his slender wardrobe. Such clothes as had not been ruined by salt water or worn out he had outgrown, and most of what he wore had been bought from fellow-passengers. He had fallen overboard in a rough sea at Pernambuco and nearly drowned (he had, in fact, only been saved by the lucky circumstance that the captain was able to throw him a rope and a bucket from the cabin window), and in this misadventure he had lost his hat, wig, and shoes with his only pair of silver buckles.

Nor did his misfortunes end with the voyage. He had come to a place where introductions were indispensable. He bore a letter of recommendation to the Governor, Mr. Morse, and another to Mr. Benyon, the gentleman to whose care he had been consigned, but when he presented himself to the Governor and enquired for Mr. Benyon he was told that he had embarked for home four months before. Having no other introductions he was left without anyone feeling the slightest personal responsibility for his welfare. He carried with him a bag of silver dollars which he was to have given to Mr. Benyon to be expended on his behalf. Instead, he had to take it himself and make the best use he could of it. Converted into the local currency it amounted to 137 pagodas, the equivalent of £54. It was all he had. When he had paid for his purchases on shipboard and bought himself all that he needed to restock his wardrobe and furnish his room, he had nothing left ; nor did he dare run into debt because of his employers' strict rule against it. He was a penniless youth without friends in a none too friendly place. His salary as a writer amounted only to £5 a year.

He was desperately homesick. Although he had been fifteen months on the way, there was no letter from home to greet him upon arrival, as he might have expected, and the season for arriving ships was almost over. The earliest he could expect to hear, when it was past, would be in six months.

The little settlement sweated in the intense heat and sank into relative inactivity. Day succeeded day when there was almost nothing to do and no relief to be found. Discipline, however, was strict and the routine rigid as in a school. Reveille at dawn, morning service in the church, breakfast, the writers taking all their meals together in the big refection room ; then came the business of the day, the dealings with the native traders, the purchase and sale of wares, the book-keeping, the packing and storing of goods in the warehouse to await the arrival of the ships ; dinner at twelve, followed by a long siesta, after which the writers received instruction in the native tongue ; then—but this only in busy seasons—business again from four till sundown, a brief time for relaxation, the evening service, supper, and the day was done.

What need was there for recreation ? Where could it be had ? There were taverns and other less reputable places in the black town. There was plenty of gambling and drinking. But Robert Clive was not much inclined that way. Where were the green fields and shady woods, rambling lanes and friendly cottages, where an English youth used to his native Shropshire could wander after working hours, or the many streets, byways, and curious sights of a large city ? There was no healthy way in which to relieve the monotonous boredom of his days, nothing to look at but the country boats riding the heavy surf that eternally broke on the lonely shore, nowhere to walk but along a strip of sandy, shelving beach, no shade from the merciless sun but that of a few palm-trees and the hot roofs of the houses themselves.

He fell ill, so ill that he was not expected to live. Everybody in the colony went down with fever, and twelve of the fifty servants of the Company died during the six months following his arrival, most of them young men like himself. He had been very ill as a child, when only a strong constitution had pulled him through. There now had begun the process that was to sap that constitution. He counted it good fortune to have survived at all. He and his comrades in exile were there to make money, nothing else, and the price even the luckiest of them paid was, too often, ruined health.

September came, bringing with it news of the outbreak of war with France and the fear of attack from the nearby French settlement at Pondichéry. There was no knowing now what ships might be held up or what treasured packets might fall into French hands. In time of war these distant outposts might be cut off for months at a time while hostile cruisers played havoc with their commerce.

The lonely, homesick youth wrote a long and painful letter home to tell of all his adventures and misadventures. " Honoured

Sir," he began. He tried to put a brave face on things, not wishing his parents to feel any anxiety on his account. He pretended that he was enjoying life and finding everything satisfactory. He expressed the hope that he would be able, if it pleased God to preserve his life, to provide for himself and be of service to his family. Did his mother or his sisters want any silks, stuffs, tea, or calicoes? But first he had to explain to a possibly irate father, and at great length, how he had come to put him at an added expense, how he had been unfortunate as well as careless, how there had been some miscalculation of his requirements for a tropical country, what damage could be done to linen garments by the native methods of washing clothes, and how outrageously he had been overcharged on his purchases by the captain of the *Winchester*. All this and much more he recounted with proper filial respect to a father of whom he evidently stood in some fear. He thanked him for all that he had done for him and made earnest promises of being worthy of his confidence and of behaving with sobriety and diligence. The only requests he made were for a loan that he might advantageously use in trading, recommendations to some of his superiors, the use of his father's influence to get him transferred to Bengal as being a more advantageous station, and some books. Books! Knowing nobody and with time hanging heavily on his hands, reading was the only diversion left to him. He added a further pathetic little request: " A little news would be also very agreeable to me."

October brought the north-east monsoon, when fierce gales that frequently reached hurricane force beat upon this coast, forcing all shipping to flee for shelter as far away as the Hugli river in Bengal and Trincomali in Dutch Ceylon ; for along the whole 1200-mile length of the Coromandel Coast of India there was not a single harbour.

Then, at last, December came, ushering in the season for arriving ships from England, a pleasant season this, of cool air and sea breezes and fleecy clouds gliding softly along a sky of perfect azure, the season when home-sick youth searched the far horizon for white sails betokening news from home, letters from loved ones.

And now the sails are sighted ! Five East-Indiamen are coming in under convoy of two of His Majesty's warships. The excitement in the little settlement is intense. Everybody runs to the seaward wall. It seems hours while the fleet wears in to its anchorage. Never in his life, declares Bob, had he enjoyed such real happiness as upon sight of these five ships : " Not all the riches of the Indies could have satisfied my desires more fully than news of my native country."

But when the greetings were over and the mail at last distributed, it was found that he, Robert Clive, alone in the colony had received nothing ! " It seems fortune had elevated me to this high summit of expectation that I might in a greater degree experience so heavy a disappointment. In short, I was the only sorrowful person in Madras." There was still a chance that he would receive something by two late arrivals, one of which had lost its main-mast west of the Cape, the other not yet reported. Yet even so, it would still remain true that almost three years would have passed since he had left England and last had news of his family.

Such was the ordeal to which Clive was subjected upon his arrival at the scene of his future glory. No wonder that he wrote to one of his cousins expressing doubt about the worthwhileness of such an existence ! No wonder the sacrifices seemed to him so much greater than any possible advantage that might accrue. No wonder that he added that he had not enjoyed a single happy day since he left his native country !

His wretchedness was greater than that of most of his fellows because his handicaps were greater. His personality was most unsuited to this kind of life. He admitted it himself when he said that, unacquainted as he was with anyone in the settlement, he lacked the assurance to introduce himself without being asked, and referred to himself as a solitary wretch. For he was anything but sociable, being proud, reserved, intractable, morose, extremely self-centred, totally lacking in social graces. He was inclined to be sullen when in a bad humour and had to be gratified in order to be put into good spirits. Life at this settlement was like that of all such isolated and confined communities and, to be tolerable, demanded of its members a cheery good humour, an easy comradeship, and a readiness to subordinate personal emotions and grievances to the common good. Consequently, he could hardly have been at first other than an unpopular addition to their numbers. The one thing he needed most was to have one of the senior merchants take a personal interest in him and draw him out of himself. Lacking that aid, he shut himself away from his fellows, a victim of homesickness, loneliness, and frustrated desires.

B

II

The youth of Robert Clive is a tempting subject for speculation. As one by one the lines of the future man emerge out of the mist of obscurity, we naturally want to see them in process of formation. The formative age is, perhaps, the most interesting part of biography, and all too often, unfortunately, it is the age about which least is known. The biographer of Clive is perhaps a little better off in this respect than many of his fellow-workers the early years of whose subjects sometimes present a complete blank. Yet a little knowledge may be more tantalizing than none at all. It may plunge us into endless surmise from which we may emerge very little the wiser. If the key-pieces of a puzzle are missing, there is little to be gained in trying to guess their likeness.

We have a fairly clear picture of the youth of eighteen as he faced life in its most unattractive guise, and we shall see how with the aid of fortune he came to solve his problem by moulding circumstances to his will. What we cannot determine exactly is how his character developed along those particular lines, how far they were innate and how far acquired. Were some of his characteristics the result of a defence mechanism working to offset the unfavourable influences of his upbringing? His moroseness, for instance, self-centredness, intractability? No definite answer can be given, but the facts about his early life are full of suggestion. They seem to suggest particularly that whatever the child's nature may have been, whether normally bright, cheerful and happy or already faintly overcast by a congenital disposition towards melancholia, later influences were wholly unfavourable to it and strong enough to blight a nature as sensitive as his. Nor is it at all difficult to see from them how the youth who stepped off the *Winchester* could have been produced, quite apart from hereditary considerations.

He was born on September 29, 1725, to Richard Clive, Esq., of Styche, in Shropshire, and his wife Rebecca, soon becoming the eldest son in a family whose large and rapid growth was to outstrip the father's ability to support and educate it and the mother's to give it proper care and attention. His father, a country squire by inheritance, a lawyer by profession, was an indifferent man of business, whose patrimony of £500 from the rent-roll of his Shropshire estate was inadequate for his needs.

Styche, the ancient black-and-white timbered house which had been the family home for three centuries, was already falling into disrepair when Robert was born. He being the heir, there would normally have been no need for him to be sent abroad to seek his fortune. That fate was usually reserved only for younger sons for whom the father could make no provision. He would have stayed at home, entered his father's profession, or, if there had been sufficient funds, bought himself a commission in the army, aspired to enter Parliament. That Robert was sent abroad plainly indicates, first, that the father was extremely hard-pressed financially and, secondly, that he could see no hopeful prospect at home for his son.

There are two possibilities. Either Robert had completely failed to fulfil parental hopes and was being cut adrift to sink or swim on his own, or the parents saw a chance to extricate themselves from their difficulties through Robert's success in India. There are passages in the letter he wrote his father after his arrival that suggest the second may be the true interpretation. He certainly shows a strong sense of responsibility towards his family and a firm resolve to succeed. May not that sense weighing upon him have been one of the factors that depressed his spirits ? May not that have been one of the motives that drove him so fiercely on to success ? It is indeed true that the first use he made of his fortune was to help his family. And if he had cause to resent the way he had been treated by his parents he never betrayed the fact by word or deed.

He had an honourable and not undistinguished lineage. The family had owned Styche since the day in the fifteenth century when James Clyve of Huxley, in Cheshire married the heiress of John Stuche of Stuche, thereby greatly improving the Clive family fortunes.[12] Since then he could count among his ancestors the Sir George Clyve who was Irish Chancellor of the Exchequer under Queen Elizabeth, and his son Ambrose, Fellow of St. John's College, Cambridge, and, more especially, Ambrose's son Robert, his namesake's great-great-grandfather, who had gone to his father's college at Cambridge, studied law at Lincoln's Inn, entered Parliament as member for Bridgenorth, risen to some prominence in the Civil War, when he became a member of the Committee of Safety of 1643, a colonel in the Parliamentary Army, and one of the sequestrators of Royalist estates in Shropshire. So the blood in him was sturdy as well as gentle. The nearness of the turbulent Welsh border is a factor not to be over-looked ; the border country bred a vigorous, self-reliant race.

Few boys have known pleasanter natural surroundings than those of Styche Hall.   Set deeply away from the rambling lanes of a quiet countryside and far back from any highway, approached unpretentiously by three long driveways that wind their way through fields and appear to lead nowhere, it stands upon a slight undulation of the plain of Shropshire, looking towards the small town of Market Drayton two miles away.   A quiet old town this, with a sequestered look about it as though for centuries it has lain off the beaten track of English history and so been able to pursue its function of supplying the physical, spiritual, and intel-lectual needs of a farming community, centuries old, with a minimum of interference from the disturbing hands of progress. Outside one of the gates of Styche Park is the tiny hamlet of Moreton Say, where is the church in which Lord Clive was to be buried.   Surely a placid enough setting for the beginning of a singularly tempestuous life !

" Quiet and Slumber ;—'twas not so in life ! "

But it seems as though he may not have spent much of his child-hood at home.   Perhaps he made too many demands upon his mother, occupied as she was with later arrivals, many of whom died in infancy.   At the age of three he was taken from home to visit his maternal aunt, Mrs. Elizabeth Bayley, at Hope Hall, Manchester, and it was while he was there that we get the first vivid picture of him.

He was taken desperately ill.   For weeks he lay at death's door, with the fever returning again and again.   On Christmas Eve he seemed better and his anxious relatives were cheered by his cross-ness, which seemed to them a natural sign of recovery.   At last, a month later, he came downstairs, very thin and emaciated, but otherwise normal, " very merry and good as it is possible," pos-sessed of a prodigious appetite, and able to run about and chatter continually and ask incessant questions.   Obviously the normal child !   But he already showed signs of an unusual desire and aptitude for bending people to his will, and his first conquests were his indulgent uncle and aunt.   Right well did the future ruler know the uses to which illness could be put in chaining his nurses to his bedside and making them gratify his childish whims ! Only when he was well again did he suffer his aunt " with some reluctance " to leave the house.

The Manchester house was his second home, " the centre of all his wishes," as he described it from India ; and it may well be that it was the one place where he received real affection and understanding. When he was seven his uncle wrote to his parents :

" I hope I have made a little further conquest over Bob, and that he regards me in some degree as well as his Aunt Bay. He has just had a fine new suit of clothes, and promises by this reformation to deserve them. I am satisfied that his fighting (to which he is out of measure addicted) gives his temper a fierceness and imperiousness that he flies out upon every trifling occasion, for this reason I do what I can to suppress the heroic that I may help patience. I assure you, Sir, it is a matter of concern to us, as it is of importance to himself, that he may be a good and virtuous man to which no care of ours shall be wanting."

Here, we might hazard a guess, is the real Robert Clive before schools and India laid their rough, crabbed hand upon him. An affectionate child, strong-willed but full of natural charm, with apparently none of those disagreeable traits that were so painfully evident when he arrived in India. It is the only authentic record we have of his personality during his first eighteen years.

A legend has grown up about his boyhood, the legend of a reprobate, a wild, undisciplined boy whom none could control or tolerate, the leader of a gang of mischievous spirits ; and by some the legend has been accepted as representing the whole truth about his character. It was because he was that kind of boy, they say, that he became the conqueror of India, or, as a recent writer puts it, " a neglected rod altered the history of three nations."[13] [1] Yet the legend has a minimum of substantial fact to support it : nothing more, in fact, than a neighbourhood tradition and a harmless anecdote or two about a boy who played tricks on local shopkeepers who offended him. In the hands of romantic writers it has been exaggerated and elaborated to a ridiculous extent. All the weight of evidence and probability is against it. He could not, we conceive, have been a reprobate in his boyhood unless his character underwent a complete and startling change as he approached manhood, and of that there is no evidence. As

[1] If there was anything that was *not* neglected by parents and schoolmasters in the eighteenth century, it was surely the rod !

applied to his known behaviour in India, the word is entirely inappropriate.

That is not to say that some of his elders may not have thought of him in that light. What he may have appeared to be in the eyes of a possibly unsympathetic father, unimaginative schoolmasters, and stupid townsfolk and what he actually was may have been quite different things. It is much more likely that he was a neglected, misunderstood, and unappreciated child than that he was in any way depraved. Said the wise Dr. Johnson, " I am always on the young people's side when there is a dispute between them and the old ones."

One fact alone seems to show the baselessness of the legend. Because he went to four schools the inference has been drawn that he was expelled from one, if not two, of them.[1] Yet the progression was a perfectly usual one from elementary school up to business school. And if he failed, as seems certain, to give satisfaction to his teachers, it does not necessarily follow that he was, as Macaulay called him, a dunce. By the school's standards, perhaps, but not by any others. In fact, we can safely put the blame for the failure of Robert Clive as a pupil upon his pedagogues, particularly in view of all that we know about English schools at that time.

Elementary schools were usually taught by persons whose chief qualification was their own unfitness for any other occupation. The ungraded classes were crowded together in one room and instruction was limited to the three Rs—reading, writing, and religion—the fourth, arithmetic, being frequently omitted because it was too difficult for the teacher. Robert seems to have been more fortunate, in that he found in Dr. Eaton a teacher who was able to make the famous prediction that if the lad should live to be a man and be given an opportunity for the exercise of his talents few names would be greater than his.[15] Only a rare teacher could be as discriminating as this, especially with the kind of boy who is not a natural scholar. But Robert's good fortune must have ended when he left Lostock Hall in Cheshire. Being a gentleman's son he had to have a public-school education, and to prepare him for this ordeal he was sent to the local grammar school at Market Drayton, where, we are told, the Rev. Dr. Burslem was " eminently skilled in the Latin tongue "—which is

---

[1] According to local tradition he was also a pupil for a time at Shrewsbury School, but his name does not appear on the school register.[14]

probably all that need or could be said about him. The grammar schools of that day served only one purpose, which was to instil into their victims, by methods more akin to torture than to love, the rudiments of Latin. " Empty walls without scholars," they have been called, " and everything neglected but the receipt of salaries and endowments." The hours of study were from 6 a.m. to 11 a.m. and 1 p.m. to 5.30 p.m. Any pupil who did not take kindly to this discipline was quite certain to be beaten and abused.[16]

To complete his " education " he passed on at the age of twelve to boarding school. At Merchant Taylors' School in London he found more empty walls without scholars. That school was by no means unique in combining a cramped and noisy site, where the boys had only a small paved court to play in, with obsolete customs and methods. The poet Cowper, a contemporary of Warren Hastings at the neighbouring school of Westminster, drew a vivid picture of conditions in his day, not likely to be at all different from those encountered by Clive. He described the wild excursions and fierce fights, even the open rebellions of the boys. There was a complete lack of organized games, comfort, and supervision and a plenitude of bad language, bad food, neglect, brutality, and heavy drinking. So that if a boy escaped from this environment without being permanently impaired physically, spiritually, and morally, he was made of very superior stuff.[17]

Clive was made of superior stuff, but damage may well have been done to him, nevertheless—damage that his early years in India only accentuated. Under the saner, happier modern system of education his whole life might have been different. He would not then have had to endure the drudgery and torture of having Latin daily drilled into him by the use of the cane. He would have had a healthy outlet—healthier than mischief—at the right age for his abounding energies and natural abilities as a leader. He might have learnt how to get along with his fellows on a fair give-and-take basis. He might have learnt the value of team work. He might not have been thrown back so completely upon himself and have become so absorbed in his own ambitions and desires. And, therefore, egocentricity might not have become so pronounced a part of his character.

The hard, unfriendly world of school and India could seriously affect a proud, sensitive, impecunious lad. It could knock cheerfulness and amiability out of him. It could make him put up a wall of cold reserve against all his fellows except the few whom he knew as intimates. It could make him hard, aggressive, excessively self-reliant, compelling him to put away the softer side of his nature for purely domestic use. It could make him, if the fire of ambition burned within him, acutely miserable yet grimly resolved to seize any chance that came to him and exploit it to the utmost. Owing to these circumstances Clive's whole world became a world built on selfishness.

If there was an element of tragedy in his youth this was it, and the shadow of it never left him. It lengthened and deepened as the years went by, as success came, bringing with it more and more occasions for ill-will. A disposition soured and warped in youth could not become sweet and generous again, no matter how much success might shine upon it.

So the legend disappears. We see, instead, a reckless, repressed lad showing off before his scared but admiring companions and the gaping townsfolk by ascending the church-tower of Market Drayton and letting himself down on to the stone spout a few feet from the top. We see, too, a lover of pranks and a leader in mischief, but we see him that only as a boy. There was all too little gaiety about the life at Fort St. George. It was a great pity for him that there was not. His youth ended far too soon.

The time had come when the father had to decide what to do with this boy of his. He was fourteen and obviously not suited for one of the learned professions. If the alleged remark of the father when he heard of his first success be true, that "the booby seems to have some sense in him after all," Richard Clive could not have entertained much hope for him or possessed much understanding of his nature. The choice of the East India Company's foreign service was natural under the circumstances.

So he was taken out of school and sent to study book-keeping and penmanship under Mr. Sterling's tuition at Hemel Hempstead. Robert's handwriting never became a thing of beauty—at times it is almost indecipherable—but both it and his moral character were at least good enough to secure him entrance into the service of the Honourable Company of Merchants of London Trading into the East Indies, to give its full title. This happened on Wednesday, December 15, 1742, when the Directors, proceeding as usual by ballot to the choice of writers, chose eight candidates for Fort St. George ; and among them Robert Clive.

Among the others were William Smith King, John Walsh, and John Pybus, who survived the gamble with death to become Robert's oldest friends. His father and a London merchant provided the necessary security of £500 for him.[18]

Thus it came about that three months later he boarded the *Winchester* and set out on his long and eventful voyage to India.

III

The legend of his turbulence follows him to India, and again it has been embroidered in such a way as to give a false impression of him. With his superiors at Madras he gained the altogether different reputation of being " a very quiet person and no ways guilty of disturbance," which fully accords with the impression of him conveyed by his letters. The legend seems largely a result of ignorance of the conditions which he had to face. It is based on certain stories that came home about him and may well have given people there, used to quieter ways, a totally wrong impression of his conduct, an impression that the passage of time, with the improvement in manners that it brought, was bound to deepen.

As it happens, these stories, well known to everybody who has heard the name of Clive, are fairly well authenticated.[1] But apart from any question of authenticity, they bear the stamp of truth upon them.

There is, for instance, the story of the time when he was ordered to apologize for some piece of impertinence to the official in whose charge he was, and complied, but when the official invited him to dinner, he returned the answer, " No, sir, the Governor ordered me to apologize, but he did not command me to dine with you."

We see at once both the well-known obduracy of his nature and the proudness of his spirit, the spirit that made his early years

[1] They first appear in the second edition of a contemporary work, the *Biographia Britannica*. The materials for the sketch of Clive's early life given therein were supplied by the Rev. Archdeacon Clive, his cousin, and a " Mr. Burman." Who was this Mr. Burman, whose first initial was apparently not known, and did he have personal knowledge of Robert Clive ? We cannot be quite sure, but when we find that there was an Edward Burman listed among the inhabitants of Fort St. George at this period it is reasonable to assume, the name being sufficiently uncommon, that it is the same.[19] Edward Burman arrived as an uncovenanted servant in 1736 and was listed as present in 1744, the year of Clive's arrival, and in succeeding years. In 1745 he entered the Bengal shipping service. When war struck Madras he became a lieutenant of artillery, and on the restoration of Madras he received the command of the *Snow Brilliant*. The last year in which his name appears in the lists is 1758.[20]

miserable and some of his later ones scarcely more happy. When we read, also, of his two vain attempts with a pistol to take his own life, our minds jump at once to the final tragic scene and we remember that one of the foes he had to contend with was melancholia.

"It seems that fate must be reserving me for some purpose." Perhaps nothing but this strange, uncanny experience of seeing the pistol that he had twice aimed at his own head go off when the trigger was pulled a third time could have given him the utter contempt for death that he was to show again and again. He was to bear a charmed life, so charmed, in fact, that we too can scarcely escape the thought that Providence was reserving him for some purpose. The laws of chance were all against his survival. Again and again others were to be taken but he left.

In India he had joined an ill-tempered and rough-mannered community. The ill-temper was due to several causes. To climate and diet—the latter being as unsuitable to the former as the former was to Europeans—to boredom and to an intensely competitive spirit. An observer noted some years later—and no doubt the observation made in 1761 would have been true fifteen years earlier—how little politeness there was among them : " as they have no ties of blood to cement their friendship, 'tis no wonder we find them so selfish. Every man's fortune seems to depend on the death, ruin, or removal of another." [21] The selfishness was to grow with the increase of opportunities for enrichment and causes for jealousy. Even the best society of that age had only a veneer of politeness. Whilst religion for the most part was little more than a husk of observance. Every settlement had its chaplain, every settlement made attendance at divine service compulsory, but the true status of religion and the true ambitions of its servitors may best be appreciated from what one of them wrote : " I am extremely anxious to go as chaplain on the East India fleet. The stipend is small, only £40, but there are many advantages. The last brought home £3000. . . ." Nothing but the colour of their cloth distinguished them from the members of their flock. [22]

The result was that quarrels were as frequent as they were violent and apt to be bloody. The convention of the day demanded the satisfaction of personal honour in all cases where it had been insulted. This was particularly true of the military gentlemen among whom Clive was soon to be numbered. Even

though the authorities professed to frown upon duels it was
a refusal to fight when real provocation had been given that could
most surely break an officer.[23]   To suffer indignities without
attempting to avenge them was the quickest road to ignominy.
If a man did not stand up for his rights and acquit himself in a manner then considered manly, India was no place for him.   Public
schools and Indian settlements were in this respect very much
alike.   And Robert Clive, as it happened, was the very last man
among them to submit to insult, to submit to anything, indeed,
except the lawful orders of his superiors and what his own mind
told him was right and proper.   If he was turbulent it was in his
relations with his fellows and equals, not with his superiors.   No
one had a better sense of discipline and order than he.   That is
why, though he must have been in many fights, he was still able to
win the reputation of being a very quiet person—a paradox of
real significance in judging his character and tracing his road
to success.

For it was upon success that his mind was set.   His letters home
leave no doubt on that score.   He would not run into debt for
fear of incurring the Company's displeasure.   " The Company
have given strict orders to enquire whether we are persons to
whose conduct they may entrust their affairs, and have
empowered them either to degrade or turn out such persons as
don't behave consistent with their promises."   And he already
had a clear notion of the way in which advancement could be
speeded.   That is to say, by his father's influence at home.
" The world seems to be vastly debased of late, and interest carries
it entirely before merit, especially in this service, tho' I should
think myself very undeserving of any favour, were I only to build
my foundation on the strength of any favour."   Interest and
merit were to be the twin pillars of his career.   Nor, as he said,
would he let any opportunity slip " of improving myself in everything where I can have the least view of profit."

To succeed one needed some education.   At seventeen the
youth had already put his schoolmasters and the English
educational system to shame by employing his leisure during the
months of waiting on the Brazilian coast in learning Portuguese.
If he had not the mind of a scholar nor any interest in learning for
its own sake, his practical desire to learn kept pace with his
expanding ambitions.   Had he not in his first letter home asked
his father to send him books ?

So it is fitting to conclude this description of Clive's youth by taking a look at him seeking a cure for his loneliness and a means for self-improvement in the Governor's library ; for in no other respect are we more likely to find a mark distinguishing the future Lord Clive from his fellow servants at Madras. It was not a very good library as libraries went, but it contained some works, amidst the usual plethora of Greek and Latin classics and theological tomes, that must have brought joy to his heart. Plutarch's *Lives,* Baker's *Chronicle,* Ralegh's *History of the World,* Hakluyt's *Voyages,* Berrier's *Travels in Hindustan,* Herbert's *Travels in Persia.* Here was some of the right kind of food for his mind. But here also were Vauban's standard work on military science and the *Compleat Captain,* the drill and field manual of the company officer of that day. With England and France at war and the threat of that war extending to the European settlements of those nations in India, his mind may well have been already turning towards a military career. His future commander was to be astonished at his knowledge and aptitude. Need we look elsewhere for the secret of the one than the library of Fort St. George (though how inadequate those books were when compared to the list that Wolfe recommended for an officer's education !) or for the other than to his ancestor, Colonel Robert Clive of Cromwellian days ?—

> From Wem and from Wyche,
> And from Clive of the Styche,
> Good Lord, deliver us.

So the Royalists of Shropshire had amended their litany ! [24] Many of those who were to have dealings with the later Colonel Clive may have uttered the same prayer.

Chapter Two

A CHAPTER OF GENESIS

" Have the French for Friends but not for Neighbours "
EMPEROR NICEPHORUS

I

CLIVE CAME TO INDIA at a decisive turning-point in its history. The long, winding lane stretching back into the mists of many centuries, its beginnings unknown, its early course unchronicled, was about to take a sudden acute-angled turn—westwards. A turn that would quickly—according to the time span of the " changeless East "—transform a congeries of warring races, tongues, creeds, and castes of ancient civilizations into an inchoate nation, knowing one suzerain, one law, one rule, one peace, and one goal—all in a space of less than two hundred years. But at the point where this decisive turn came there was nothing but confusion. The future was invisible.

If anyone had predicted in 1744 that within a hundred years the British would be the rulers of an Indian empire such as not even the Moguls had dreamt of, he would have been laughed to scorn in every part of the world. Nor would the laughter have been the laughter of fools. The wise could have joined in it without any risk to their reputations.

Even if acute observers were already noting the circumstances that brought the conquest of India within the bounds of possibility—the same set of circumstances that have until recently been present in China—they did not have the British people in mind as the one likely to take advantage of them. They would have said rather, and quite correctly, that the British political machine was not geared for military conquest. They would have said the British people had deliberately sacrificed the benefits of a strong central government for the delights of individual liberty.

Whenever their monarchy had shown signs of becoming strong and efficient they had at once shackled it, even overthrown it. Whenever a man had appeared who could have set their feet on the

29

road to empire—Strafford, Cromwell, Marlborough—they had turned against and rejected him, refusing to reap the harvests of power and glory that each by his genius had prepared for them. Twice had England had an army that could have vanquished any in the world, and twice—such was her hatred of a standing army —it had been disbanded as soon as the urgent need for it had passed. She had had a navy, too, fit for any task of transoceanic conquest, and it had likewise been allowed to decay as soon as the need for it had passed. When England signed the Treaty of Utrecht it must have seemed to the world, as it certainly seemed to the defeated Grand Monarch of France, that she had deliberately let slip the opportunity to make herself the greatest military power in the world. All was at that moment in her grasp—the road to Paris lay open to Marlborough's victorious army—yet her rulers had thought only of peace and their own domestic affairs. Moreover, the generation that had succeeded the peace-makers had done everything to strengthen that impression. They had put a final end to the possibility of a strong monarchy by placing a foreigner on the throne and making a puppet of him, and then they had taken his inheritance and divided it up among themselves as though it were as much private property as their lands and titles. The State as such had practically ceased to exist. It had only the feeblest army and none too strong a navy. Everything of worth in it—its great offices, its powers, its patronage rights, its services— belonged either to chartered corporations or to individuals, and both were guided as much by self-interest as by a sense of duty to the nation. Could any country in the world have appeared less likely to begin a career of military expansion and conquest rivalling Rome's, far exceeding Spain's ?

True, she had acquired an empire in the west, but that was a very different kind of empire, acquired by different means— small, independent companies of colonists landing on uninhabited shores, or shores inhabited only by savages, requiring only ships and supplies and enormous endurance and courage to overcome the obstacles, largely natural, in the way of permanent settlement. There was no political power, no ancient civilization, no numer- ous population of natives to dispute their possession. Given the urge to leave their native land and venture forth in search of a new home, and the rest was a matter of their individual human qualities.

But India was another world, offering an entirely different

prospect. Thickly populated, with a highly developed civilization, warlike races, rulers ready to resist aggression, it was difficult to imagine it being conquered by any other method than the one employed by all its previous conquerors—the method of Alexander the Great, Mahmud of Ghazni, Timur, Babar ; the method of the Spaniards in Peru and Mexico, of Mussolini in Ethiopia, of the Japanese in China : deliberate military conquest.

The English in North America had a strong motive to settle and conquer. The English in India had none. India had not for them any colonizing value, as it had had for the Moguls, Afghans, and Persians and as Manchukuo has for the Japanese and Ethiopia for the Italians. It had no value at all for them but that of trade, and they had already been exploiting that trade for a hundred and fifty years without the slightest idea of ever advancing from it to conquest. They had also been engaged in trade in many other parts of the world where it was not to result in any attempt at conquest.

There was then no reason discernible to the men of the 1740's why they should have expected to see Britain shortly acquire the empire of India.

If there was any European power that might reasonably have been associated with the idea of Indian conquest it was France, with her strong, centralized monarchy, powerful fleets and armies, and imperialistic ambitions. But even Austria, despite her lack of sea power, might have seemed more likely, for she too, had the strong military and imperial traditions that seemed essential, and for a brief space, during the existence of the Ostend Company (1722 to 1731), her government had had its own commercial ambitions in the East, which it had only surrendered in the face of fierce British opposition.

It is a curious and significant fact that a suggestion of that sort was actually made to the Imperial Austrian Government by none other than an Englishman. It was made, too, in 1746, when neither of the subsequent contenders for that empire, the French and the British, had progressed beyond the first round of what was regarded by both as purely commercial rivalry. Still more interesting is the fact that the plan outlined anticipated exactly the method which the British themselves, without premeditation, without intention, and, as it were, by accident, were to adopt only nine years later.

A certain Colonel James Mill drew up in that year (1746) a

scheme for an expedition under the Imperial flag to conquer Bengal. With extraordinary accuracy he assessed the weakness of the dissolving Empire of the Moguls. It was a miracle, he said, that no European prince with maritime power had ever thought of attempting its conquest. " 1500, or at most 2000 regulars, with shipping and stores in proportion, are sufficient for this undertaking." The author of the plan was even willing to answer for the success of it with his own head. By a single stroke infinite wealth—everybody thought then and for long after that the Mogul Empire was overflowing with gold and silver—might be acquired which would counterbalance the mines of Brazil and Peru. He even anticipated the fact that the Mogul Emperor would be delighted to help in the enterprise against a rebel province. And Britain, he suggested, could be invited to join in it to anticipate France. England could at least supply the ships !

Clive was to prove that it was not even necessary to have that number of regulars, and that sepoys armed, drilled, and led by Europeans with a small core of European troops as stiffening, even of indifferent quality, were sufficient for the task.

But nobody in Europe paid attention to Colonel Mill. They were all engaged on other business, as were also the few hundred European merchants whose business India was.

The whole long seaboard of India, east and west, was dotted with their little settlements and had been for nearly two hundred years, but none of them had made any progress—and only the Portuguese and Dutch in earlier days had tried to make any—in acquiring territorial power. Due to the changes in the balance of national power in the last century, the French and English had out-distanced their rivals and now shared most of the trade between them. The Portuguese had dropped out of the competition, whilst the Dutch were more and more confining themselves to the rich Spice Islands beyond, which they had made exclusively their own. Gradually the English had founded, or acquired, and developed one small settlement after another : Surat, Madras, Bombay, Calcutta. Concessions we should call them to-day.

Madras had just celebrated its centenary when Robert Clive landed. Purchased from the local chief in 1639, it had made slow but steady progress as an *entrepôt* for trade. The Carnatic was not a rich country, not nearly as rich as Bengal ; it was not, as Dupleix found out to his cost, a fruitful field for trying out expensive imperialist schemes ; but its people were fine weavers of calico and muslin, cloths in big demand at home, and Madras was well situated for purposes of trade. A quarter of a million people had come to inhabit the Black Town, having been attracted thither by the English trade and the shelter of the English fort. Occasionally, and recently more often, the English merchants, had been made sharply aware of the insecurity of their position amidst an India dissolving into chaos. With the withdrawal of the restraint of a central government, whose power was never very effective in the southern part of the peninsula, the local princes and viceroys, potentates capricious and avaricious, had taken to paying visits to the settlements in the hope of extracting something by way of blackmail. Once, in 1702, in the days of stout-hearted Governor Thomas Pitt, Fort St. George had withstood a four-month siege at the hands of a greedy prince. It was for such purposes of legitimate defence, not against the French or other European rivals, that the fort had been built, and its defences and garrison were of a kind that could only be of use against the undisciplined, ill-armed native levies.

The French had arrived later than the English and had imitated their methods of peaceful trading rather than the more aggressive and warlike tactics of the Dutch. They had established themselves at Pondichéry a hundred miles to the south of Madras, where at first they were so weak that they were dependent on English goodwill. But as time went on they had grown stronger and their trade had expanded, so much so that jealousy had sprung up, until now their rivalry with their neighbours had reached the dangerous stage when the slightest provocation would cause open hostilities. Each settlement maintained a hawklike watch over the other's activities, and anything like a European war between their respective countries would put a severe strain on their resolve, hitherto maintained, as peaceful traders not to mix war with business.

Policy in important matters of this sort was determined by the directors of the companies in London and Paris. But when such a man as Joseph François Dupleix, who had been appointed Governor-General of all the French settlements two years before Clive landed, is made responsible for the carrying out of a policy at a distance of 12,000 miles from the source of his authority, the nature of it is likely to be determined as much by his temper as by his orders. In point of fact, the policy of M. Dupleix and the

C

policy of the French East India Company were to be seldom the same.

A great deal was to depend upon the temper and personality of this Frenchman. A vast amount of history to begin with. And most important for our present purpose—the life, career, happiness, and success of Robert Clive. For without Dupleix there would probably have been no Lord Clive. Fate might not have given him any other opportunity to distinguish himself.

Dupleix was, above all things, vain. He was also a hardworking, conscientious servant of his country striving mightily for its honour and glory ; but his vanity was the predominant part of his character. To it almost all his other qualities could in some way be related. An unquenchable vanity, it had to be administered to in multitudinous ways. Fortune, though a notoriously fickle jade, had nevertheless to subject herself to his will. Failure he could not tolerate, still less could accept as his own. Consequently he was forever to be retrieving the failures of others—his officers—but never his own ; and when those failures were reported to him, they had to be softened and disguised if they could not altogether be conjured away. He lived on an unwholesome diet of optimism and sent to daily perdition all who intervened between him and the success he craved for himself and for France. He could brook no rival near his throne, looked with jealousy and distrust upon those around him, and exacted an endless tribute of flattery. Unable to associate failure with himself, he possessed quite exceptional tenacity of purpose and an ingenious aptitude for making bricks without straw, but lacked the clear-sighted objectiveness necessary to relate his ambitious purposes to the realities of hard and generally disagreeable fact. From the unassailable heights of his egotism he misjudged both men and circumstances, for the thing that he never faced was the cold, impersonal truth about anybody or anything, least of all about himself. Things were what he wanted them to be, and for a long time, during his twelve-year reign of power, it was to seem as though they actually were. Clive, among others, was to be the means of restoring the true relation between fact and one man's vanity.

List this man's virtues and you have one of France's greatest patriots and statesmen. You have a man of whom it is said that when something remained undone he felt as if he had accomplished nothing, a man who sought his own interest all the time, yet managed all the time to entwine his self-interest around the interests of his country. List his failings, the foibles of inordinate vanity, and you have a butt for ridicule. You have a man who believed firmly in the workings of Divine Providence, but more especially when his enemies came to their appointed evil end, who loved giving advice so much that his officers quite forgot that they had minds of their own, who said he would be delighted if they would make suggestions and grieved because they never did, who loved his enemies when they interposed no difficulties to his plans and hated them with an exceeding great hate when they did, who went into a paroxysm of rage when even mere chance threw an unkind monkeywrench into an otherwise well-thought-out scheme. List, finally, his vices and you have an object for severe reprobation, for he was a callous, cynical, covetous, vindictive man who believed so wholeheartedly and with such conscientious zeal that the end justified the means that he had no scruple and was as ruthless in his own methods of obtaining that end as he was condemnatory of those employed against him.

But not even a man like Dupleix nor his employers, nor the English Governor at Madras nor his employers, could be the sole masters of their destiny, whatever it was to be, whether war or peace, victory or defeat. India was busy making its own history, quite apart from any contribution that these Europeans might make, and with their puny forts and puny resources of men the very idea that they might make any important contribution at all seemed at the time fantastic both to them and to the Indians themselves. Dupleix might have ambitious schemes in his head, but at the beginning they concerned the English alone.

Locusts are a fearful curse to the lands that have to endure their depredations, but their ravages can be no more destructive than the plague that for the next forty years made the country of the Carnatic, in common with most other parts of India, a land of desolation and famine—the plague of warring armies.

India had until recently known—the nearest it had ever come to knowing—the meaning and the value of peace and security under one rule. The Mogul Empire with its capital at Delhi had flourished for a century and a half, from the accession of the great Akbar in 1556 to the death of Aurangzeb in 1707. That empire was now no more, and with the shattering of the whole ordered life of the country which depended upon it, disaster had overtaken the land. The invasion of India by Nadir Shah, the King of Persia, in 1739, culminating as it had done in the total overthrow of the imperial army and the capture and sack of Delhi, was a knock-out blow from which the empire of the Moguls never recovered. Its dismemberment had, indeed, already begun ; and it was to proceed at such a rate that within a very few years India was to have as many separate states and principalities as the continent of Europe, and wars even more calamitous.

The Marathas were a complete plague in themselves, even without the able assistance of ex-Mogul governors struggling to establish dynasties on the ruins of imperial authority and the still more able assistance of the sons of those governors fighting over disputed rights of succession. The Marathas came from the west, from the hill country near Bombay, and they had been, until less than a hundred years before, a race of sturdy Hindu farmers, brave and self-reliant but not aggressive. Then they had undergone a strange and—for India—disastrous metamorphosis. Through the genius of one man, Sivaji, they had become a nation of warriors, the terror of their neighbours and the scourge of the Mogul power. They had come down from the hills to the plains, where another change had turned them into horsemen, twice as formidable as they were before. Now they roamed India far and wide in search of plunder—north to Delhi and the Punjab, east to the rich alluvial plain of Bengal, south to the Deccan. And like the locusts', their incursions meant death and destruction to every hope and every prayer that the toiling peasant could utter. In their own homes they had been distinguished for their kindliness and simple manly virtues. But now they were little better than free-booters bearing off the plunder of their neighbours, carrying no freedom to the peoples whose territories they visited, not even to their co-religionists, giving no organized government to take the place of the many governments they weakened and destroyed, but, instead, leaving their victims prey to every evil that follows the destruction of authority and the breakdown of law and order.

Three years before our story opened they had come to the Carnatic and ravaged it from end to end. The Moslem rulers of the land, through their own jealousies and enmities, had been defeated one by one. And wrote a Jesuit father : " When they leave,

what a sad plight we shall be in ! Famine inevitably follows on
the heels of war. The country is deserted and everything has
been destroyed. When the people return to their houses they
will find the land fallow and there will be no rice or grain. God
have pity on us ! " But God was to have no pity on this land for
many years.[25]

Trade cannot thrive if there is nobody to trade with. Dupleix
was profoundly discouraged by the condition of things he found :
all in ruins and everyone in panic for fear of another Maratha
visitation, the merchants scattered and the weavers gone, and in
addition lack of rain, portending a great rise in prices. " These
are too many scourges coming at the same time on a country
which has in itself so few resources." [26] The Marathas did not
ravage the Carnatic that year—they had gone to Bengal—but
instead had come the Mogul viceroy of the Deccan, and when he
encamped with 70,000 horsemen and a great swarm of elephants,
camels, and camp followers at Arcot, the capital, it looked " as
though the sea was rising and flooding the land." He had come
to drive out the Marathas who had ensconced themselves at
Trichinopoly and to sweep up all the wealth that their brothers
had left behind. So once more the country was ravaged and
the price of food mounted, and the Europeans were filled with
alarm and their trade declined. The weavers ceased to weave, the
farmers were idle, the ships of the European merchants sailed
half-empty, and Dupleix was in despair for lack of funds.

II

On September 16, 1744 news of the declaration of the long-
expected war with France—the war of the Austrian Succession—
reached Madras. At once the question arose, was there to be
war in India as well as in Europe ?

In the eighteenth century this question did not receive the
immediate affirmative answer that would be given to it to-day in
the twentieth. Those were almost unimaginable days, so long
before " totalitarianism " that states might be at war and some of
their citizens not ; when men were free to serve their own gods
and not compelled to worship those set up by an omnipotent
entity called the State, nor compelled to fight if they preferred to
trade. The state had in centuries past crushed its most serious
rivals to supremacy—the Church and feudalism—but there were

still interposing forces. Individual and individualistic man was the chief, ably supported by law and tradition.

Among the institutions that stoutly resisted encroachment was the chartered corporation : such a corporation, for instance, as the East India Company of England, whose charter gave it semi-sovereign powers over its own concerns. If this company considered that its interests would be better served by peace and the directors of the French company in Paris came to the same conclusion, it lay within the powers of both to arrange for a neutrality as between themselves. But if, on the other hand, one or other decided for war, being quasi-independent bodies they would have to fight largely with their own resources and could expect but little aid, and that only spasmodically, from their national governments.

Both companies were divided on the question. Those who advocated war did not do so because they had any ideas of Empire in their heads, but because they saw a chance to destroy a rival's commerce. Those who advocated peace saw that commerce-destruction was a game that two could play, and doubted whether in the double process their profits and dividends would benefit. The French company was more inclined to peace than the English because its financial position was weaker. Dupleix wanted peace because Pondichéry was quite unprepared for war, and Governor Morse at Madras wanted it for the same reason ; but neither, as the event turned out, was to have his desire gratified. For the Directors of the English company had hit upon what seemed to them a better plan than either absolute war or absolute peace. The value of sea power was something that every Englishman understood from birth. What was the use of the Royal Navy if it could not be used to destroy the commerce of the national enemy ?

On May 1, 1744, Commodore Barnett, a gallant and able officer, sailed with a squadron for Indian waters, and when he arrived there he found nothing to impede him from sweeping the seas, for Dupleix did not have a ship and the French squadron of M. La Bourdonnais was at the French Islands far away.

For the time being there was nothing that M. Dupleix could do in retaliation. He waited with mounting rage while the number of French ships taken grew and grew. With their capture went the loss of the greater part of the private fortunes of himself and his Council—and his indignation at what he termed the black treachery of the English waxed great. He sent frantic appeals to La Bourdonnais to come to his rescue.

La Bourdonnais was coming hotfooted for the fray, which he had been urging upon the French Government since long before the declaration of war. But first, he had to complete the gargantuan task of equipping a squadron capable of meeting the English on equal terms with the very limited resources of the Islands.

Meanwhile Dupleix had fears for Pondichéry itself, which was almost as defenceless as Madras. In order to overcome those fears he made use of his greatest advantage over the English, his ability to deal with Indian potentates. In this he was the inventor of a new weapon in commercial warfare—a weapon that he was to use with the utmost skill.

The credit for it was not entirely his. He had had the good luck, or wisdom, to marry a half-Indian lady of exceptional strength of character and talents for diplomacy, as that art was practised in the East. She had passed all her life in India, and though her father was French, she herself was entirely Oriental in tastes and feelings. As a mate for Dupleix she was in every way worthy, for she not only matched him in business ability but also in spirit, pride, energy, courage, and determination. That she was a woman of stamina is proved by her having had a previous husband to whom she had presented eleven children. And when in addition we find it said that she possessed beauty and a ready wit, there can be no doubt that she was a quite remarkable woman who may have been considerably the bigger half of the combination. That she was also an adept at chicanery, bribery, and corruption made her none the less useful to her husband. Altogether, she and he together made a team to which the English as yet had none to oppose.

Their solution to the present difficulty was clever and guileful as befitted a joint Indo-Gallic production. Dupleix obtained from Anwar-ud-din, the Nawab of Arcot, an order directing the two nations not to make war in his dominions and forbidding the English to attack Pondichéry. Governor Morse and Commodore Barnett agreed to respect the prohibition provided the French would do the same. Dupleix had his own ideas about that, but for the present he kept them to himself. He first had to solve the problem of sea power, which dominated the whole situation.

Dupleix knew exactly what he could and would do if only that power could for a brief space be transferred from English hands

39

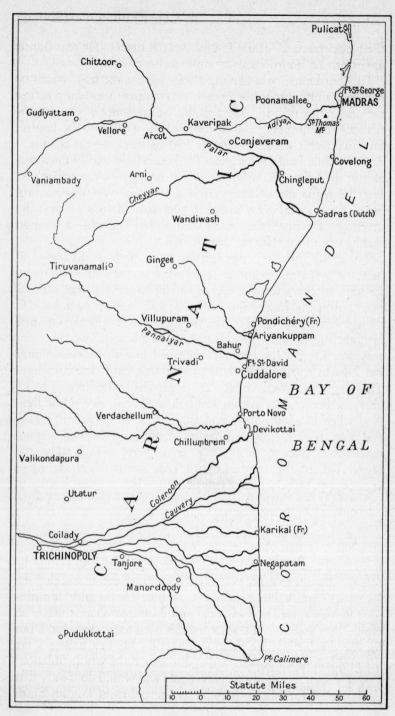

THE CARNATIC

into his own. The reports of his spies and engineers made it perfectly clear and simple. Madras was so weakly defended that it could not be held against a serious attack. Barnett had noted the fact as soon as he arrived.

It was the old story of British unpreparedness for war, largely explained in this case by the natural disinclination of a mercantile company to spend money on anything so unprofitable as armaments. A governor of Bombay had been dismissed for committing this grave indiscretion ! Of course, now that war had been declared, " steps were being taken " at Madras and there was some hope that by the time peace was signed Fort St. George would be put in order. Barnett's words have quite a modern ring : " True old English management ! The Directors copy the Court and never guard against a war till it is declared, and of course too late to be properly provided." To the Directors he wrote : " The works seem rather built by chance than design ; the bastions are placed contrary to all rules ; . . . if I was Governor, I should never sleep sound in a French war if there were 500 Europeans in Pondichéry."[27]

Dupleix bided his time. He had no money, his settlement was heavily in debt, his credit was exhausted, he had received no succour from home. There was nothing he could do until La Bourdonnais arrived except work on his own defences, which he did with a will. But in his desk he had a complete plan of attack on Madras worked out by Paradis, his chief engineer.

III

Eighteen months have passed since we left Clive suffering torments of homesickness and loneliness at Madras. After he wrote, in February 1745, the letter to his cousin in which he laid bare the wretchedness of his plight (. . . " If the state I am now in will admit of any happiness it must be when I am writing to my friends. Letters were surely first invented for the comfort of such solitary wretches as myself " . . .), silence descends upon him, as his letters for the period of nearly ten years have not been preserved to us. Consequently, in interpreting his character we shall have constantly to bear in mind that he is thirty before we begin to get anything like a complete view of him. He will then already be on the threshold of his greatest achievement, with his character fully formed. The greatest handicap, therefore, that his biographer labours under is his inability to see the various stages in his development.

Though the silence is regrettable, it none the less correctly symbolizes Robert Clive's life at this time. While great events were in the making, events that were to determine his life, he himself at first was an entire nonentity, a spectator when he was not a humble participant. And we can but imagine, each for himself, what his thoughts and emotions were.

There is but one entry about him in the official records of the year 1746. In April he was transferred from the secretary's office to the accountant's.

IV

He was within a month of his coming of age when the quiet current of the lives of himself and his companions was violently disturbed and its course permanently changed.

Dupleix had his plan ; in August 1746 he had the means for executing it. La Bourdonnais had arrived at Pondichéry with his ships and men and Peyton, the incompetent successor to the deceased Barnett in command of the English squadron, could not be counted upon to do his duty. On August 18 the French commanders gave the English at Madras the first inkling of what was in their minds. On that day the French squadron appeared before Madras and fired a number of broadsides at the *Princess Mary* lying in the roads.

Governor Morse and his councillors were still not seriously alarmed, because they assumed that Captain Peyton would be on hand immediately. What, then, was their consternation when they heard that he had taken their danger as the signal for his own departure for Bengal waters ! They began at once to remember all the things they had left undone that might have made their fort more defensible.

The day after news of the war had reached them they had selected a safe site for their new powder magazine. Now, a year later, it was still unbuilt. So, too, when they came to examine their military stores, they found how few they had. The so-called garrison of Madras consisted merely of a heterogeneous collection of Europeans and Portuguese half-castes to the number of some three hundred, each man thoroughly untrained and undisciplined. Their commander was one Peter Eckman, an ancient

Swede whose proper place was in the ranks, where he had once been, but who now bore, for the sake of appearances, the rank of first lieutenant. He had to assist him nine officers, who were like unto himself in their complete lack of qualifications. It is doubtful whether any member of this puissant garrison had ever in his life fired a musket with intent to kill. It is true that they had nearly 200 pieces of cannon, but this advantage was somewhat lessened by their ignorance of how to use them.

Governor Morse and his Council in their plight immediately bethought themselves of Anwar-ud-din's promise not to permit any hostilities in his dominions, but they forgot the biblical warning, "Put not your trust in princes." True, Anwar-ud-din responded with the desired orders to the French, but it needed more than orders and threats to make Dupleix and La Bourdonnais desist from their cherished plan. The only thing that immediately threatened to interfere with that was the fierce quarrel that had already broken out between the two men, each of whom claimed to be superior to the other.

On September 13 [1] the French armada of nine sail was sighted from the walls of Fort St. George. They made an unopposed landing with over 2000 troops some distance to the south of the fort and marched up the coast pillaging the country. Five days later their batteries began to play from the palmyra groves on the beach. For three days and nights they dropped bombs into the place, at the end of which time Governor Morse was ready to surrender. Only six persons had been killed, but the impact of gun shot had dissipated any slight appearance of order and discipline. When a bomb broke down the doors of the liquor supply the garrison ceased altogether to function. On September 20 the fort surrendered. La Bourdonnais marched his Frenchmen in, and all the English, including Clive, became prisoners.

The terms La Bourdonnais gave them might have been worse, as the outcome was to show. The town was to be held for ransom at eleven lakhs of pagodas, or £421,666, payable in three years. In addition, all the company's goods, amounting in value to another four lakhs, were to be confiscated. The additional lakh that Governor Morse and his Council collected and gave as

[1] New Style. The Gregorian calendar was not introduced into the English settlements until September 2, 1752, when eleven days were omitted. For convenience I have adhered to the new style throughout this and the following three chapters.

a personal present to the French admiral had not been without its effect in inducing him to be moderate in his demands. La Bourdonnais was, indeed, quite willing to hand the place back immediately and sail off in search of fresh and equally lucrative fields to conquer ; for he was a sailor of the Drake and Hawkins tradition, sailing the seas for private profit as well as national glory ; which was fully in accord with the practice of a time when wars had not yet become so nationalized that no private interest, except those of profiteers and armament manufacturers, could be served by them at all. But La Bourdonnais had forgotten one thing : he had reckoned without his host. He had forgotten that M. Dupleix also had an interest to be served. And M. Dupleix had no intention whatever of letting M. La Bourdonnais dispose of this rich prize on terms that suited himself only. So Clive and his fellow captives now had the pleasure of sitting by and watching their two conquerors disputing fiercely over the spoils.

They must certainly have wanted the Admiral to win the contest, because Dupleix was threatening far worse things : to make Madras into a French colony, to destroy it utterly, to give it as a peace offering to the now thoroughly incensed Nawab. It was not quite clear which of these things he intended to do if he could wrest the place out of the hands of his insufferable colleague, but it was quite certain that Dupleix, more than the rest of his countrymen, was imbued with the Roman spirit that, whatever the incidental gain to individuals, Carthage must at least be destroyed.

Back and forth for days the struggle swayed. For pieces the Admiral had his ships' captains and for pawns the men he had brought with him from France. Dupleix, directing affairs from Pondichéry, had his pieces too, his Supreme Council, but he lacked pawns—he had only the small detachment from his garrison that he had sent with the expedition. La Bourdonnais' opening move was magnanimously to seek the Council's advice. But the Council sent him not advice but orders, which he ignored. To excuse himself he said he had already given his word to the English, which as a man of honour he could not break. Dupleix retorted by refusing to acknowledge his authority and sending commissioners to divest him of command.

The scene of the comedy was now shifted to the Fort itself. Mr. Morse and his fellow prisoners being summoned were informed by Dupleix's commissioners that the terms of the surrender were cancelled. The fort was *not* to be restored to them. But the obstinate Admiral refused altogether to accept " mate " in this manner. With a nicely planned and executed *coup* he called " check " himself ! He sent the Pondichéry troops on board his ships and then had the commissioners and all Dupleix's officials seized. This turned the game very much to his favour. But now a third, uninvited, player entered it and proceeded to upset the calculations of both.

The north-east monsoon usually strikes the Coromandel Coast about October 15, and when it struck in those days no ships of wood and sail were safe against its force. The whole coast being quite devoid of good harbours, shipping had to find shelter as far away as Trincomali in Ceylon. The French Admiral, long experienced in Indian waters, knew this and was anxious to get away. It was now October 8 ; so that he had only a week to clear up affairs, complete inventories of his booty, and get it on board his ships. Then, as far as he was concerned, the English could have the place back. But, as it happened, he was not to have his week. The monsoon does not always keep to schedule.

La Bourdonnais tried desperately to get his treaty accepted by Dupleix before sailing. Letters passed quickly back and forth while Dupleix hummed and hawed and tried hard to be polite. On the night of October 13 the monsoon struck, and struck with hurricane force. When day broke not a French ship was to be seen. Four had been swallowed by the waves, four had been dismasted, and the ninth driven so far south that she could not gain the coast again. Twenty other ships belonging to different nations had either been sunk or driven on shore. And when the wind moderated, at noon of the 14th, La Bourdonnais knew that his power was broken. He could no longer oppose Dupleix. He could no longer even face the English squadron—should it once more return to its duty. So he collected together the battered remnants of his squadron, made what repairs he could, and sailed away for home, leaving behind him the 1200 good French troops he had brought with him—a most important legacy to Dupleix this, and one that was to be a big factor in producing the events that followed.

The departure of La Bourdonnais restored Dupleix's temper and happiness. It left him pretty much master of the situation, which was the only kind of position he could be happy in. And not only was he master of his own camp and master of Madras, but he had also in the last few days gone a long way towards becoming master of the Carnatic.

Anwar-ud-din had failed to act quickly enough to save Madras for the English but he had no intention of allowing Dupleix's insolent flouting of his orders to go unpunished. He had despatched his son with an army of 10,000 men and this army reached Madras a few days after the hurricane.

The French remained quietly within the fort until the Moors (for such the Europeans called them) threatened to cut off their water supply. They then came out to fight. And the manner of their fighting and still more its result were deeply significant. Except for one or two small affrays, it had been more than a generation since Europeans had faced Moors on the field of battle, and on the last occasion, in 1687, the English had been armed with pikes and their artillery had fired far too slowly to check a cavalry charge, the favourite, almost the only, form of attack of a Moorish host. By 1746, however, the Europeans were armed with muskets and bayonets and their artillery could fire from ten to fifteen shots a minute, instead of the former rate of possibly one every four minutes ; which meant that disciplined European infantry possessed the secret of repulsing cavalry. The demonstration that the French now gave of that fact was so conclusive that it removed any remaining doubt about the ability of Europeans, with their superior discipline and military science, to meet and overcome the much larger numbers of the armies of Indian princes.

Four hundred men marched out on to the plain with two field-pieces concealed within their lines. The Moors shouted with glee at the opportunity. Mounting their horses and wheeling their squadrons, they swept down upon the motionless French. Nearer and nearer they came, till only a few yards separated them. Then the French, moving as though on parade, opened their ranks. The two guns spoke, and kept on speaking much faster than the horses could gallop. Seventy Moors rolled in the dust, the rest were seized with panic and fled.

A few days later the French gave another demonstration even more convincing than the first. This time, as the attackers, they proved how helpless the native levies, armed only with matchlocks and worthless cannon and not knowing the meaning of discipline, were to withstand the steady advance and well-sustained fire of French regulars.

Dupleix now turned to the real matter in hand, the disposition of Madras. On October 30 the English captives were drawn up to hear the new dispensation of M. Dupleix read to them. They were told that the terms under which they had laid down their arms were null and void. Instead, everything they possessed was to become the property of the French Company—everything, that is, but what they stood up in and could take with them, and the jewels of their women. They were required to give their parole not to serve against the French until they had been exchanged, and those who refused were to be sent as prisoners to Pondichéry. Nothing at all was said about ransom or the return of the settlement! For it was Dupleix's intention to obliterate Madras as a rival emporium, and to that end he sought by blandishments, threats, confiscations, and bribes to entice the native merchants to come and do business at his own much more salubrious, attractive and less dangerous establishment. In this latter attempt, however, he failed. For some inscrutable reason the merchants preferred to stay where they were, " all," said the disgusted French Council, " save a few wretches neither rich nor respectable," and this notwithstanding the fact—or perhaps it was because of it !—that half their town had been demolished by their would-be protectors.

Clive was not among those who were asked for their parole and given four days in which to quit the town. According to his own account he had already quit some time before. " I made my escape the beginning of October, disguised in the habit of a Dubosh [native interpreter] and black'd, and arrived at St. David the same month "—no doubt having given Pondichéry, which he had to pass, a wide berth on the way !

Chapter Three

A TALE OF MISADVENTURE

"If a sparrow cannot fall without God's knowledge, how can an empire rise without His aid?"

BENJAMIN FRANKLIN

I

THE COUNTRY CHANGES its character as one makes one's way southward from Madras. It becomes more fertile and vegetation more abundant. Villages crowd together and broad fields of rice, corn, and maize succeed to the bareness of scrub-land broken only by patches of cultivation. After the rains everything is fresh and green as in an English garden, and the air too is fresh and clear. Clive must have appreciated the change, as well as other differences he found between the two settlements.

For the English at Cuddalore and Fort St. David had responded to these natural advantages in a way characteristic of their race. Within the ample bounds of their settlement, four miles by three, they had built themselves country houses with shady groves of coconut trees and stately avenues of the evergreen tulip tree, planted in such a manner as to make one visitor think of the elms in St. James's Park, with pleasant walks under their leafy branches and well-laid-out gardens where they were able to grow all manner of fruits, from pineapples and oranges to mangoes and pomegranates.

Time has dealt hardly with memorials of those romantic early days, but the largest and finest of these country houses still stands. It belonged to the Deputy-Governor of the Fort and was known as the Garden House. A handsome, roomy, and well-built house, it had a courtyard with additional buildings on each side of it, and behind, a large garden enclosed with a brick wall, with long avenues of trees front and back. Not India, this, but a little corner of England, and a very historic spot.

The finger of romance touches all associations with the place, even to its founding. It was purchased from the Marathas in the year 1690, the cession including not only the fort but also the adjacent towns and villages " within ye randome shott of a piece of ordnance." Mr. Hatsell, who was sent from Madras to complete the purchase, took with him the best brass gun at Madras and the most skilled gunner. On September 23, 1690, the gun was fired and the " randome shott " fell beyond Cuddalore, thus giving the English their pleasantly ample bounds. Several villages were included which are still known as *Gundu Gramam* or " cannon-ball villages."

Cuddalore, the " Black Town " where the Company had its factory and warehouse, had become quite a thriving centre of trade during these fifty years. North of the town, just a mile away across a broad river, the English had built their fort, St. David's, on rising ground facing the sea. But it was only a little fort of practically no military value except to keep out Maratha raiding parties and such occasional annoyances from the interior. The bounds of the settlement, too, were defended only by a thick aloe hedge along its four-mile length, with one or two small bastions, while around the town was merely a wall of no great height or strength. As for garrison, the place was no better supplied than Madras : 200 Europeans and 100 half-caste Portuguese called " topasses " were its full extent. Hitherto subordinate to Madras and of small account, Fort St. David now sprang into sudden prominence because upon the capture of Madras it became the seat of government of the East India Company's operations on the Coromandel Coast.

Not everyone, however, appreciated its natural advantages as a place of residence ! These, after all, were principally enjoyed by the Governor and senior merchants. As a garrison town its attractions were distinctly limited. " As damned a place as ever men were trooped in," was the opinion of one officer who came here in January 1749 with Boscawen's expeditionary force. " Black women instead of white ; with boiled rice instead of bread ; and the punch houses such cut-throats that a man need have the Indies to pay their bills ! " [28]

When Dupleix turned his attention to completing his victory by the taking of Cuddalore, he quite naturally thought that he had an extremely simple task. To take Fort St. George, which lay a hundred miles from him, had required a powerful armament and control of the sea. But little St. David lay right under his nose, a scant twelve miles away to the south. Seemingly, all that he had to do was to send a few hundred men on a day's march and the fort was his almost for the asking. And had he not a vast superiority of disciplined troops, thanks to M. La Bourdonnais and the hurricane ? The task was absurdly easy.

But Fortune had decided to play some of its queerest pranks upon these, as yet, wholly unconscious contenders for empire. All the laws of mathematical probability—even certainty—were to be broken in the story of how the French failed to complete their triumph by depriving the English of their last foothold in southern India.

II

Clive reached Fort St. David safely at the end of October with two companions, one of whom, Edmund Maskelyne, was to be a life-long friend. He found Deputy-Governor Hinde and the gentlemen there in astonishingly good heart considering the situation. They had duly given thanks to the kind Providence that had sent the storm to drive away the French fleet, " though it is the opinion of most of our officers that, had they come, we should have taken up more of their time than they had to spare." Brave words and, it would seem, soberly spoken ! Unlike their Madras colleagues these gentlemen had been using their time to good purpose. They had been stocking the fort with provisions and doing all that they could to ensure being able to make a sturdy defence. Nor did they overlook the precaution of appealing for help to the Nawab, doubly indignant now against the French because of the defeat of his son. The help from this source was to arrive most opportunely.

Clive was for the time being unemployed and unprovided for. Once more he found himself among strangers and his plight that of all refugees. The gentlemen of one settlement were under no obligation to provide for those of another. The tedium of idleness here was scarcely less than at Madras and of amusement there was an equal lack. He was not the kind of man that cared so much about amusement, however ; what he wanted was work and activity. If it had not been for the French, who thoughtfully supplied those lacks, it would certainly have gone as hard with him here as it had during his first months in Madras.

After a while the governing council decided that they could use the services of these refugees. They offered them monthly writerships until such time as they could return to their own station. But Clive and Maskelyne decided that they could serve the Company's interests better by, as Clive put it, " acting in a military sphere," though then, as he correctly added, " at a very low ebb." Such a low ebb, indeed, that " acting in a military sphere " did not mean joining the profession of arms ; for of real soldiers there were as yet none. There were merely some persons who were prepared to fight when and as required and others who disdained such humble employment. In the eyes of the latter it was not fit for a gentleman ; besides which, it took their minds off business. " Trade," Clive was to say, " is a study very foreign from an officer." [29] Few of his brother officers of that day would have agreed with him ; they would have said rather that being an officer interfered with trade.

In M. Dupleix's eyes, too, fighting was bad for trade, so he was in a hurry to conclude his business. The monsoon rains that year had failed and the country was in a bad way, with famine threatening. So he lost little time in sending to ask for the surrender of Fort St. David. Unfortunately his officers would not serve under the commander of his choice, the able Paradis, because he was an engineer and therefore not a real soldier. As a consequence the command passed to a complete incompetent.

An all-night march on December 20 brought them to the Garden House, which was, as has already been remarked, a very pleasant spot, and they were tired. There had been nothing as they passed the bounds to indicate that they would meet with any resistance ; a few scattering shot only, according to Clive, had been fired at them from the hedge. So their commander decided to rest there awhile before marching into the fort. His men stacked their arms and busied themselves preparing breakfast. And, wrote Clive sixteen years later, when telling the story of his first military adventures, " in this unsoldierlike and scattered condition were the French when the whole Moorish army were descried marching towards the plantation and the Garden House." As luck would have it, Anwar-ud-din's army had arrived the day before ! The French just had time to grab their arms and run, and they kept on running for three miles, leaving all their military stores and baggage behind them. The little garrison of the fort, with Clive shouldering a musket for the first time, went after them, but by the time they overtook them the French had recovered themselves and their breath sufficiently to form their ranks. " In short," said Clive, " the French arrived at

Pondicherry the evening of the same day greatly fatigued and frightened."

Dupleix was not perturbed. He was even glad, feeling that his officers had been properly punished for their insubordination.[30] He promptly despatched another party, this time by sea. But now it was the winds that were unkind, and such of the boats as were not driven on shore returned. This second failure led him to open negotiations with Anwar-ud-din, thinking that if he could detach him from the English the land way would be clear.

The technique that M. Dupleix, aided by his wife, employed to obtain an end of this kind was somewhat as follows. First would come a shower of flowery compliments. This would be followed by threats to lay waste the Nawab's country ; then a demonstration to show that the threat was not idle ; then a subtle suggestion that his nobles might be incited to revolt ; then a small present to show that there was no ill-will, this being accompanied by boasts of the greatness of the French nation and its obvious superiority to the despised English. Finally, when it was shown that these arguments were having their effect, a really large present of, maybe, a lakh would be made in order to clinch the bargain. Dupleix did not make the English mistake of trying to economize in his gifts. He knew that good results could not be obtained without paying pretty heavily for them. In this particular instance he had to augment his presents very considerably before he could persuade Anwar-ud-din to relent from his anger and make peace with him.[31]

Later, of course, it was to be the Europeans who were in a position to confer favours on the Moors, and then the presents were to pass the other way.

Meanwhile, Mr. Hinde and his Council were wishing wistfully for a little assistance from their countrymen and fellow servants in Bengal. They were also saving their money—what little they had—by refraining from a futile attempt to enter into a bargaining match with M. Dupleix, who had all the plunder of Madras at his command. They complained of the Nawab's "extreme lucrative disposition," and it was but small consolation to them that their presents to the country government had amounted to no more than 3000 pagodas, if they derived no benefit at all from their expenditure. They tried persuasion and argument, but Dupleix could employ stronger of both. He could point, too, to the fact that the English wanted active aid, not having the price of it, whereas all the French wanted was neutrality. Altogether, it was unequal competition. Consequently it was not long before Dupleix's mind was at rest and he was free to make another attempt on Cuddalore.

On March 13 the French came again. Dupleix had again not been able to persuade his officers to serve under Paradis, and he fumed and wept from mortification. But the force he sent was considerably larger, some two thousand men. In fact, he denuded his garrison.

Clive and his comrades, only 200 strong, marched out to meet them with three field-pieces, which they disposed along the bank of a river to dispute its crossing. They and the French spent a day cannonading each other at this safe distance and then towards evening, when the French showed signs of wanting to cut off their retreat, they retired to the fort with the loss of eight men. The French again took possession of the Garden House (delectable spot that it was to rest weary soldiers' bones !) and they were all ready next morning to march into the fort. But, wrote Clive, " we shortly after discovered something of a much more agreeable nature, which was the sight of Mr. Griffin's squadron, and as soon as the French had made the same discovery they retreated a second time to Pondicherry with great precipitation," and not, too, without some minor mishaps.

This time Dupleix was quite unable to control his feelings. With good reason he felt that the untimely arrival of the British squadron (once Peyton's but now under Commodore Griffin) was unwarranted interference of Providence in his affairs. His tactful *dubash,* Ananda Ranga Pillai, who kept an invaluable diary of all these events, consoled him with the thought that the taking of Cuddalore was only a matter of time. In April his affairs would prosper. A Brahman astrologer had said it.[32]

But the astrologer did not understand the meaning of sea power, which the English once more possessed. So long as Mr. Griffin remained off the coast not only was M. Dupleix unable to think about a fresh attack on Fort St. David, but he had to give all his attention to warding off attack on his own fortress. Mr. Griffin stayed quite a long time.

Clive had evidently made a good impression in the " military sphere." In a despatch to their employers dated May 2, 1747, the Governor in Council reported that " Mr. Robert Clive, writer in the Service, being of a martial disposition and having acted as a volunteer in our late engagements we have granted him an Ensign's commission upon his application for the same." The Directors in their reply told the Governor and Council to " be sure to encourage Ensign Clive in his martial pursuits, according to his merit : any improvement he shall make therein shall be duly regarded by us "—a promise that they were to honour handsomely.

Dupleix did not know it, though perhaps he already feared it, but his chances of taking Fort St. David were being steadily reduced. Admiral Griffin had landed 100 Europeans from Bengal and he had also loaned the garrison 500 sailors and 150 marines. These reinforcements were followed by others : 100 men from the Bombay European regiment, 150 recruits from England, and 400 sepoys from the English settlement of Telli-cherry on the Malabar Coast. Then, on New Year's Day 1748, arrived the most important reinforcement of all in the person of Stringer Lawrence. Because what use were all these men without a commander ? They were now to have a com-mander who could turn them into soldiers and, later, lead them to victory.

A big man of fifty, with a rotund face, a double chin, and a pot belly, Stringer Lawrence was anything in appearance but the *beau ideal* of a gallant soldier. But appearances are frequently mis-leading in judging character, and though his general excess of flesh would have caused him without his uniform to have been taken for a too-successful and well-fed city merchant, his career and achievements were to be sufficient to show that he did not possess the character of one. A closer study of his portraits reveals the strong chin and firm mouth of a fighter—and a fighter he was. He became, in short, the father of the Indian army, familiarly known to his men as " the Old Cock."

Whether it makes a difference, as Havelock Ellis has tried to show, what part of Great Britain a man comes from—West country, North country, Cornwall, or the Fens—it remains true that upon the Welsh border-land has been conferred the distinc-tion of producing the three men chiefly responsible for the found-ing of the British Empire in India—Robert Clive, Warren Hastings, and Stringer Lawrence.[33]

Lawrence was born in Hereford in 1698. When he came out to India he was a superannuated army captain having seen active

54

service in Spain and Flanders and during the '45 rebellion of the Young Pretender. He had participated in the two outstanding battles of Fontenoy and Culloden, and now, when the Company had been aroused to the necessity of strengthening their garrisons, they had selected him, giving him the rank of major. Actually his appointment was for the garrison at Madras, the news of its capture not having yet reached England.

Major Lawrence's services were instantly required. The garrison of Fort St. David had been considerably enlarged, but it was still completely undisciplined and unorganized. Europeans from Madras, Bengal, and Bombay were mixed with raw recruits from England, sepoys from Malabar, topasses, and peons. Almost his first duty was to deal with treachery among the Tellicherry sepoys. This he summarily stamped out with hangings and banishments. He formed the Europeans into a battalion of seven companies and the sepoys and peons into companies of their own. He also formed a company of artillery and a troop of horse. He introduced regular army drill, formulated a military code, and in a very short time created a fairly respectable little force. Clive, a willing volunteer, had someone now who could teach him the fundamentals of soldiering.

In January, a few days after Lawrence's arrival, Dupleix made his fourth attempt on Fort St. David. But, like the others, it never reached the fort nor compelled the new commander to do more than encamp his men near the Garden House. Dupleix was trying to seize the opportunity presented by Griffin's absence for a few days to make an assault in person, but he had only progressed a short distance from Pondichéry before a messenger overtook him with word that English sails had been sighted. He instantly halted his men, read the letter, sat motionless on his horse for five minutes with clenched fists, dismounted, and stamping the ground, exclaimed, " Never was anything so unlucky ! It is just the same as the last time." And, as it happened, this was the most formidable and best organized of all his expeditions.[34]

Luck was against him, but he still did not give up hoping that it would change. " God is on our side," he optimistically told Ananda. And in June he made his fifth try. Griffin was again away, as he had to be in order to make any attempt worthwhile. He had gone in futile search of a French squadron that had just appeared and landed 400 soldiers and some much-needed bullion at Pondichéry.

This time it was to be a surprise attack by night and not to be made on the fort, but, by a detour around it, on the town to the south of it. As, however, the English intelligence service was working well, the plan was known to Lawrence. The French arrived at ten o'clock at night, thinking they would escalade the south wall. As it happened, they hit upon the point where the wall was highest. This, combined with the fact that Major Lawrence was ready with a warm reception, led to their being beaten off with considerable loss. Clive took part in the affair and later on wrote an entertaining account of it for Orme. Like a patriotic Englishman, he always took considerable relish in recounting the discomfiture of the national enemy. He did not overlook the opportunity on this occasion.

Upon hearing the news Dupleix withdrew to his chamber to conceal his emotions. His last chance was gone and he knew it. A powerful English fleet under Admiral Boscawen was daily expected to arrive. When, on August 8, it did arrive it proved to be, when combined with Griffin's squadron, the largest armada that had yet appeared in Indian waters : no fewer than thirty ships, of which thirteen were of the line, having on board some 1500 troops organized in independent companies, which had been specially recruited in England and Scotland (from their jail resources !) for this service, the specific purpose of which was the taking of Pondichéry and all other French settlements in the East. For the British government was taking a more than casual interest in the outcome of this East Indian war, and had immediately responded to the Company's appeal for aid after the loss of Madras.

III

The attempt upon Pondichéry was a fiasco from beginning to end. Boscawen was in command of both sea and land operations, but it is usually only given to royal princes to shed equal lustre on their ranks of admiral and general. Ordinary commoners have no such amphibious ability. Boscawen was a sailor and an able and gallant one, as he subsequently proved in American waters, but he was no soldier and still less was he an engineer. At sight of the enemy good sailors make haste to lay their ships alongside, especially on such fortunate occasions as this when they have an overwhelming superiority of numbers. And this was what Boscawen now proposed to do. The difference between

Pondichéry and an enemy's fleet was to him less apparent than it was to Stringer Lawrence. Moreover, he allowed himself only ten days of preparation. With an untrained land force it was altogether insufficient.

Clive, looking back on the siege with the elevated view of his subsequent rich experience, saw things in a different light. In the account he sent Orme he wrote : "If there be any officers or soldiers in India remaining of those who were at the siege of Pondichéry, twelve or thirteen years' experience must have convinced them how very ignorant we were of the art of war in those days. Some of the engineers were masters of the theory without the practice, and those seemed wanting in resolution ; others there were who understood neither, yet were possessed of courage sufficient to have gone on with the undertaking if they had known how to go about it. There was scarce an officer who knew whether the engineers were acting right or wrong till it was too late in the season, and we had lost too many men, to begin an approach ; in another (*sic*) the duty of the engineer was in a great measure performed by the office of artillery and they seemed to be the only people who knew something of what they were about during this memorable siege."

In Pondichéry the French had a settlement which for size, spaciousness, layout and general air of refinement and prosperity far excelled anything the English could show. Nor was it, in the English fashion, divided into white fort and black town (thus early did English racial exclusiveness show itself in India !), but it was all one city shared in common by French trader and native merchant, giving equal protection to both. François Martin, its founder, had sought to turn an Indian village into a little Paris beyond the seas. So he had built fine palaces, houses, and shops with a true French appreciation of architecture (again so unlike the English) and laid out wide streets and *places* ; and, most important of all, he had given the town a citadel on the best approved Vauban lines. When he died, in 1706, he left Pondichéry a truly fine monument to French intelligence, energy, and taste, with no less than 50,000 inhabitants. His successors carried on the work, and Dupleix upon his appointment had at once set to work to construct new fortifications. So that when Boscawen came against Pondichéry he came against a fortress that could only be taken by regular siege tactics skilfully employed. A heavy wall pierced by five gates was protected by a deep moat and a further wall outside. Strong batteries stood guard against attack from the sea, as an additional defence on the land side there were four outlying forts, and all the country on the west side was marshy and unsuitable for siege operations.

If there was a single blunder that the besiegers did not make, history does not record it. Approaching from the south, they came upon one of the small outlying forts on the Ariyankuppam River. They did not need to attack it, as their numbers were quite large enough to take care of it if its defenders persisted in holding it. But they decided nevertheless that it had to be taken before they could proceed farther, though that could only be done by bombardment, as its works were strong. Their engineers reported, however, that there were trenches in front that must first be stormed. So a picked body of men, the cream of the army, with the only available artillery officer of experience was sent to the attack. They advanced with great spirit and courage, only to find the alleged trench to be a pile of rubbish and themselves exposed to a terrific fire from walls they could not climb. In this way 180 valuable lives were lost, including that of the gallant artillery officer upon whose knowledge everything depended. The morale of the army never recovered from this deplorable beginning.

Eleven days were now wasted in battering the fort. A night was spent building a battery to counteract a French battery across the river, but when it was finished and morning came it was found that a thick wood intervened ! No sooner had this little mistake been rectified and approach trenches at last been dug than a panic swept the occupants of the trenches upon the appearance of a French troop of horse and—crowning blunder !—they allowed Major Lawrence, their best remaining officer, to be captured. Then, when they were no nearer than before to taking the fort, a chance shot caused the explosion of the French gunpowder and with it the destruction of the whole guard of a hundred men ; by this means they were able to occupy an abandoned fort.

Time was rapidly passing and the monsoon approaching. Yet for some unfathomable reason Boscawen and his men thought that they ought to put the captured fort in a state of defence. This took five more days—and they were still three miles from Pondichéry ! At last, " with great caution and circumspection,"

Clive tells us, they moved forward—only to choose the one worst spot of all to make their assault, one, again to use Clive's words, "fraught with every disadvantage which could attend a siege !"

In the first place it was to the westward of the town, where the ground was softest and only waiting for the monsoon rains to be turned into a quagmire. And in the second, it was the farthest away from the ships, which consequently could render the besiegers the least assistance. Supplies for the army were on board the ships, and not only had they to come a distance of seven miles, but, being compelled to pass under the noses of the French, they had to be escorted every day by 500 or 1000 men, whose services might have been much better employed in the actual siege operations. And even when so escorted they were often set upon by the French and taken. Well might the pious Ananda give God the credit for making the English select such a position !

Having chosen their position it took the English engineers still more days to bring their heavy guns into play. They opened ground too far back, and when, after much arduous labour, they got within 850 yards, they thought they were within 500 yards ; so they erected their batteries at a distance too great to do any damage to the French defences. In fact, so far were these from being destroyed that the defenders increased their fire every day, while the English fire steadily diminished. " To have seen a plan of this siege," commented Clive, " an experienced officer would have thought the besiegers were the besieged, so much were we beset by the enemy's batteries without the walls of the town."

Meanwhile it had begun to rain, the trenches were filling with water, and the sentries were taking alarm at the slightest excuse. And all the time, too, Dupleix and his wife daily walked the ramparts encouraging their men, discovering the weak spots in the defences, and showing an intrepidity of conduct that was equally praiseworthy in each.

One day the garrison made a sortie at the point where Ensign Clive and his platoon were posted in the front line. First one platoon fled when its captain fell. Then another. And only Clive's platoon of thirty men remained. The French grenadiers approached under cover within ten yards and fired on them steadily for four minutes, but the platoon held its ground and finally drove them back. This was Robert Clive's first out-standing piece of gallantry.

But the sortie was important for another reason : it cost Dupleix the loss of his best, his only good, officer. Paradis was shot through the head and killed. A random shot had disposed of the one man who might have proved a match for Lawrence and Clive in their subsequent exploits.

As a last resort the English ships joined in the attack, but they did not come close enough to make their fire effective, and now the monsoon had burst in earnest and sickness at once became rife in the water-logged camp. The besiegers had shot their bolt. On October 17 the Admiral raised the siege and withdrew his shattered forces to St. David's. Casualties amounted to nearly a third of their number, chiefly from sickness. The French losses by comparison were trivial.

Two months later news was received of the signing of peace preliminaries in Europe, and in May (1749) of a general peace. So the first round in the rivalry of French and English in India ended with the honours fairly even. What the war had lost to the English the peace restored. Madras was handed back to them in exchange for Louisburg in North America—an exchange which suited neither Dupleix nor the American colonists. But for the time being Clive and most of the English remained at Fort St. David, which continued to be the seat of government.

IV

Clive's introduction to military life could not have been any easier than his previous introductions first to public school life and then to life at Madras. He always had been what Americans call a two-fisted man. But now he had to overcome the usual military contempt for civilians at the same time as he contended with the appallingly bad discipline that existed at that time. It is difficult for us to conceive of a military service in as miserable a condition as the Company's was prior to the arrival of Stringer Lawrence : totally lacking in *esprit de corps,* discipline and morale, inferior in every way to the civilian service, without an officer worthy of the name, and a rank and file drawn from the dregs of Europe. So ill-considered was it that the officers were drawn from the ranks, received no promotion and very poor pay. A drunken lot they were, with Ensign Hyde Parker a fair repre-

sentative. One day Clive happened to meet Parker rolling drunk
through the streets of Cuddalore arm-in-arm with a sergeant, and
was invited by him to roll with them. He returned an indignant
refusal. That he should have given up the superior dignity and
advantages of his civilian status to join such riff-raff speaks volumes
for his character and the desperate thirst for action that possessed
him.[35]

Now it was that his power to command men, his rare ability
to compel them to yield to his will, made itself felt. Now, too,
he displayed that meticulous sense of justice, that insistence upon
his rights, that inflexibility of temper which made up the strongest
part of his character.

Two of Burman's stories illustrate these qualities to perfection.
There is the one of the duel with the card-sharp. It is a well-
known scene. A group of officers are playing cards in the fort
one evening and among them Ensign Clive. All the money is
going to one player, a noted gambler and duellist. A feeling of
tenseness creeps into the air. Suddenly the heavy silence is
broken by Clive leaping to his feet and accusing the winner:
" You have cheated, sir, and I am damned if I shall pay you."
The inevitable challenge follows and pistols are produced. Clive
misses his shot, whereupon his antagonist walks up to him, puts
his pistol to his head and demands that he ask for his life. Clive
does so. The other, not content, demands that he retract the
charge and pay the money.

" And what if I refuse ? "

" Then I fire."

" Fire and be damned ! I said you cheated and I say so still,
nor will I ever pay you."

And the other, calling him a madman, flings the pistol away.

It's a grand story and the sequel to it is no less impressive. The
story naturally went the rounds of the fort and Clive was urged
to make the matter public. This he refused to do or to say a
word against his opponent. " He has given me my life, and
though I am resolved on never paying money which was unfairly
won or again associating with him, I shall never do him an
injury."

During the siege of Pondichéry there was a very bold man who
dared to call him a coward behind his back. It happened when
Clive left his men to get supplies of ammunition. When he was
told about it upon his return it was all that his companions could

do to prevent him from dealing with the offender on the spot. The matter was reported and a court of enquiry was held. Its verdict absolved Clive entirely from blame and his accuser was ordered to beg his pardon before the assembled troops. But for Clive, a stickler for justice, this was not enough. The other had not only offered him a deadly insult but had also struck him, and for that affront he still lacked personal satisfaction. When upon seeking it he found the man craven with fear, he contented himself with contemptuously waving his cane over his head, and the next day the other resigned his commission. Clive's conduct fulfilled every requirement of the case according to the code of the day.

Another similar episode is fully recorded in the consultations of the Madras Council. Charles Floyer succeeded Mr. Morse as Governor in 1747 and being a cheerful, convivial person more addicted to the gaming table than to business, he had allowed discipline to become so relaxed as to cause the Company in three years to dismiss him. The Fordyce case affords evidence of these conditions.[36]

It happened at Fort St. David in February 1749, a few months after the suspension of hostilities. Mr. Fordyce was the chaplain. Though he was by courtesy and profession a reverend gentleman, he was also a gentleman who apparently made it a practice to call all other gentlemen whom he did not like scoundrels and cowards. According to Clive and others who gave evidence before the Governor and Council, his insolence on several occasions had exceeded all bounds of tolerance and he was reckoned generally a thoroughly obnoxious and detestable person, whom nothing but respect for his cloth had hitherto protected. There had been many victims of his spite, but none of them had had the courage of Clive, who thought Mr. Fordyce ought to be dealt with in the ordinary secular manner. Having heard that the clergyman had employed the same kind of language about him, he met him one day in Cuddalore and proceeded to give him a severe caning. When Mr. Fordyce complained, the Governor summoned both parties to come before the Council for an examination into the affair. Mr. Fordyce declined to recognize the jurisdiction of the Council, declaring that " no part of the laws of England can justify Mr. Clive or any other person in assaulting a clerk, much less a clergyman." The Council thought differently, and when Mr. Fordyce refused to answer any questions and insolently walked out of the room they immediately dismissed him from the service.   They sent the following report to the Court of Directors :

"A complaint having been brought before us by Mr. Francis Fordyce for an assault that was made on him by Mr. Robert Clive, which it appearing that Mr. Fordyce had given great provocation for such proceeding, by having frequently scandalized his character in a most insufferable manner, and being further acquainted that in making use of many unbecoming reflections on the President and all the members of the Board, in consequence of this, his aggressions and disrespect, together with the many instances we have had of his insolent and meddling disposition, we came to a resolution of suspending him your Honours' service, and besides the reasons already given for our so doing, we might still add that he was in general remarked to be extremely negligent and remiss in the several duties of his functions, particularly in the burial of the soldiers and seamen, which part of his office he scarce ever attended, notwithstanding he had been twice or thrice rebuked by the President for not, and which neglect had at length began to create great discontent in our military. We therefore presume that upon a due consideration of all these circumstances, your Honours will concur with us in the measures we have taken herein. In which dependence we shall only add, as it is not to be doubted but Mr. Fordyce will set forth his own story to your Honours, and lest the same should be to Mr. Clive's prejudice, we think it not improper to assure you that he is generally esteemed a very quiet person, and no ways guilty of disturbances."

Thus it was that Stringer Lawrence found ready to hand the right man to act as his lieutenant in fashioning into an army the most unpromising material that had ever been given to a commander. One of the several explanations required for Dupleix's ultimate failure is provided by the presence of these two men in the British ranks.

Chapter Four

PEACE BUT STILL WAR

*" He alone succeeds whose destiny it is and whose hand is marked with
the line of victory"* ANANDA RANGA PILLAI

I

CLIVE WAS NOW to be part of an historical process of immense
importance. The process that was to transform traders and
adventurers into soldiers, rulers, administrators, empire-builders
—a process that was to be seen not only in India, but wherever
the expanding mercantile power of the British took root.

With the signing of the treaty of Aix-la-Chapelle on April 30,
1748, England and France became officially at peace. Their
armies and navies returned home and were largely disbanded.
But actually the peace between them had no more reality than it
was to have in our own time between the nations and political
systems of Europe. Intervention in the affairs of another people
was as practical and serviceable a method of pursuing international
rivalries then as now. It seemed just as expedient to take advantage of a civil war to support a side and back it to win, and there
were just as valuable concessions to be gained as the price of that
assistance. Thus after the French had for half a century been content to share the trade of India with the English, Dupleix, who had
now become definitely aggressive in his views, saw the way in
which that trade could be monopolized to the sole benefit of his
country. And the English in self-defence were forced to resort
to the same interventionist policy.

Like our modern interventionists, too, they did not fight in
India under their own national flags, being mutually anxious to
preserve the fiction of " peace," and when either broke the convention by holding its captured opponents as prisoners-of-war they
were righteously indignant and fulminated about a breach of
international law. But the outcome of the war was in like manner to depend upon the number of " volunteers " that they were
able to put in the field and the efficiency of their leadership.

64

The advantage of numbers was generally to lie with the side backed by the French, but the English were to supply the better " technicians," and it was the " technicians " like Lawrence and Clive who finally were to bring victory to Muhammad Ali's " rebel " cause.

The analogy must not, however, be carried any further. These eighteenth-century interventionists were not fighting for a principle or seeking to impose any system of government of their own upon the land over which they fought, nor were they, at the beginning, seeking an extension of empire, in terms, that is, other than of trade. They were, too, much more motivated by their own private interests than are our own super-nationalistic patriots and bond-slaves of the state. Their acquisitive instincts were still alive and active and functioning in a normal manner. Theirs was, indeed, by far the more complex problem : they had somehow to correlate three distinct sets of interests, their own, their employers', and their country's. As the days of simple peaceful trading passed this became more and more difficult.

High-ranking officers of the army and navy quarrelling over the distribution of prize-money, junior officers resigning *en masse* because of dissatisfaction with their allowances, the ranks mutinying because of insufficient material rewards of their service, officials from the Governors downwards accepting presents and *douceurs* upon all possible occasions and making handsome profits upon all government business—these things were the rule, not the exception. For private business and the service of the state were not put into different compartments, one labelled " this shall be for gain " and the other " this shall be solely for the glory of the State." The second like the first was only worth while in their eyes if profitable to the individuals concerned as well as to the nation.

The agents of the English and French Companies devoted part of their time to the employers' interests and part to their own, and they were paid by their employers only on a part-time basis. If discipline was good and times normal the employers restricted their agents' methods of private money-making to legitimate trading. If discipline was lax the agents followed their acquisitive instinct wherever it led them. War was a powerful loosener of discipline and a prodigious manufacturer of new opportunities. Wars in India, as Orme observed, always made immense private fortunes. There were then lucrative contracts of all kinds to be

E

portioned out among the servants according to degrees of seniority, favour, and merit. If the seniors tried to combine public duty with private profit the juniors had less cause to be conscientious. More often they had to be shown the profit before they would do their duty.

It follows that when these agents saw a chance of vastly increasing their profits by extending their operations to other business than trading they eagerly took it. When, that is, they saw the gainful possibilities of mixing in native politics, making kings, hiring out troops, farming revenues, they did not allow considerations of public policy to stop them from seizing them. Public policy was a secondary consideration, when it was a consideration at all.

And the time was to come, and that very soon, when they were to find these additional operations more profitable than the first. Their interest in their original line of business was then progressively to decline, and as land revenues displaced piece-goods in their balance sheets, so they became tax-gatherers instead of traders, and, at last, administrators of an empire. Only, unfortunately for the French, by that time the British had prevailed in the private rivalry between them and were left masters of the field.

So the British Empire in India came into being !

Yet the really remarkable fact about this evolution of British traders into imperial public servants was the swiftness with which it came. Thirty or forty years is not a long time in which to effect such a profound transformation in the point of view, manner of thought, and conduct of a whole set of men. " The self-restraint and conscious rectitude of a neo-Puritanism, ' undemonstrative, gentlemanlike, and reasonable,' had to be superimposed on the curious, voracious, acquisitive, utterly egotistic, and a-moral energy of the eighteenth century, before the Englishman could change from a rover into a ruler. The eighteenth century was the childhood of Imperial Britain."[37] Even to this day the change has never yet been fully explained, but without it there would be no empire to-day.

Clive was to occupy a prominent place in this transition. He was, in fact, to embody its earlier stages.

II

The first opportunity that the English had to enlarge their operations in this way came immediately upon the cessation of hostilities with the French. They then found themselves in possession of a large body of unemployed troops, with a commander smarting under his defeat at Pondichéry.

Just south of Cuddalore lies the rich country of Tanjore. Like every other province of India at this time, it was being contended for by rival claimants. In Tanjore the rivals were Hindu, offshoots of the Maratha power. That they were blood-brothers too was only in the normal course of things. Almost all the dynastic strife of this unhappy period was fratricidal. The fact that one of the brothers, the one who held the throne, had actively aided the French at Pondichéry gave Floyer and Boscawen sufficient excuse to regard him as a usurper and to respond to the request of the other for English aid. The price of assistance was to be the fort of Devikottai at the mouth of the Coleroon river, in addition to the expenses of the campaign. Devikottai was believed to have a harbour, besides being the centre of a prosperous manufacturing district. It was, therefore, a tempting bait for these easily tempted gentlemen.

On March 1, 1749, Clive was promoted lieutenant. A month later he set out on the first frontier expedition of the English in India, Captain Cope in command. The distance they had to go was only thirty miles, but it was the first time the English had ventured so far from their settlements, and their ignorance and inexperience betrayed them at every turn. Their pretender, like all pretenders, promised that the country would rise as one man to place him on the throne. It did not so rise. Instead, with each mile of their advance the enemy gathered in ever larger numbers on their flanks and rear, alarming them exceedingly. A cyclone struck them and tore their tents to ribbons. (An appalling storm, it destroyed no less than forty vessels on the coast, among them three of Boscawen's men-of-war, lying in the roads, including his flagship.) And the farther they went the more woody the country became, and every bush seemed to conceal an enemy.

Orders reached them to attempt the fort of Devikottai, even if they could attempt nothing else. They hurried on through the woods, " frightened and harassed "—Clive is again our authority

—"most of the way." They hoped when they got to the fort to find the ships of the fleet waiting with supplies and reinforcements. But though the ships were there, not four miles away, Captain Cope and his men were so bewildered by their strange situation and so entirely ignorant of the country that they did not know where to look for them. They possessed nothing but field-pieces—four of them—with which to bombard the fort, and the briefest trial at once proved their ineffectiveness. Clive wanted to use them to batter down the gates, but Cope condemned the idea as being too risky. By now, too, the scanty provisions they had carried with them were exhausted. So they were forced to pack up and march back the way they had come, accompanied by the enemy who fired on them constantly from both flanks. Their haste in crossing a nullah under fire with the tide in caused some four hundred of their coolies to be drowned and they lost most of their baggage. They got back to Fort St. David next day much fatigued and thoroughly scared.[38]

The episode is important only as further proof of the military weakness and incompetence of the British in India at this date. It required the combined efforts of the fleet and garrison to redeem this failure against an insignificant Indian fort. Devikottai was taken in the ensuing operation, but the only man who can be said to have enhanced his reputation by it was Robert Clive.

As leader of the storming party he had his first real chance to show his quality as a soldier. The attack nearly cost him his life when the men behind him fled, but his own intrepid conduct shone out all the more clearly in consequence. The eyes of Lawrence were upon him as he strode fearlessly into the breach under heavy fire, and again as he valiantly rallied his men for another, and this time successful, assault.

He won his spurs at Devikottai. He not only made a secure place for himself in Lawrence's favour but earned his entire confidence. "This young man's early genius," wrote Lawrence afterwards in his account of the war, "surprised and engaged my attention as well before as at the siege of Devikottai, where he behaved in courage and judgment much beyond what could be expected from his years, and his success afterwards confirmed what I had said to many people concerning him."

A genuine friendship grew up between them. Clive became his commander's right-hand man in matters of business. When in August Lawrence went to Pondichéry to receive Fort St. George back from the French he took Clive with him as his quartermaster.

At last the doorway to success stood invitingly open before Clive. Inevitably now, the material rewards of favour would follow.

III

Upon the return of peace the East India Company lost no time in wielding its favourite economy axe upon wasteful military expenditures. One stroke of it chopped off the useful troop of cavalry, another put a stop to the much-needed refortifying of the forts, a third revoked Lawrence's military code, even though it was the very foundation of an efficient garrison. Evidently the Directors at home believed Dupleix's fit of aggressive madness to be over and they could happily and safely return to the peaceful trading of former days. Boscawen's services being no longer needed, he departed for home, leaving behind him 500 of his jail-birds to form a useful though entirely inadequate, addition to Lawrence's command.

Under these circumstances it is not surprising that army life ceased to have attractions for Clive. What allurement could routine garrison existence, with its miserable pay and much inferior status, have for anyone, least of all Robert Clive? Having by his partnership with Orme amassed a little capital, he had no difficulty in deciding to return to civil employ with the greater freedom and opportunity it gave for lucrative enterprise. His friend Maskelyne was less fortunate ; lacking even Clive's moderate means, he had no choice but to remain in the military branch of the service.

With the resignation of his commission the winds of fortune turned definitely in Clive's favour.

His upward path to be easy had to be paved with gold. Now it was that the favour of his Commander brought him to the first important milestone. He was appointed steward for the settlement.

In that capacity he was responsible for the provisioning of the settlement and the garrison, and, in the event of war, he became the logical person to take charge of the commissariat of the troops in the field. There was no more lucrative post in the service. He took up his new duties on December 1, 1749, and at once began to accumulate wealth.

Periods of activity, however, were always for him to be followed by illness and nervous collapse. The cycle seems first to have manifested itself now. The illness that overtook him shortly after his retirement from the army was described as a fever of the nervous kind, accompanied by a hard swelling at the pit of his stomach. His old enemy melancholia also assailed him, necessitating the constant presence of an attendant. When he was convalescent he took advantage of the cold season in Bengal to make a voyage to the English settlement at Fort William, Calcutta. And in this way he made his first acquaintance with the scene of his greatest labours and greatest triumphs.

In 1750 that scene differed little from what he was already used to. A bigger fort, but scarcely any more formidable, a larger settlement, many more ships and sailing craft, a more profitable trade, but, for the rest, the same kind of life inside the settlement and the same dirty and evil-smelling black town outside ; the same few garden houses for wealthy merchants and the same lack of facilities for exercise and recreation ; the same sacrifice of moral and physical welfare for the sake of gain. And here—to make matters worse—instead of a level plain with its dry, healthy, even if extremely warm air, there was only a swamp so infested with malaria and other noxious fevers as to give the place a well-earned reputation of being a graveyard for Europeans worse than Madras and scarcely any better than Bombay.

Clive had once desired transfer to Calcutta. It is not recorded whether he still desired it after his visit.

IV

The political history of southern India at this time is an arid desert, with scarcely ever an oasis where the human spirit can find refreshment and not a landmark except those that mark the scenes of violent death. It is a story punctuated on its every page by wars, treacheries, intrigues, cruelties, murders and the whole foul catalogue of human iniquity. Told in full in all its complexity of sordid detail, it makes history an unprofitable bore. Reduced to simple essentials, it presents a situation full of potential drama.

In the centre of the stage while this drama is being played, and dominating it, we observe first the dynamic, spider-like figure of the French governor, Dupleix, weaving all the while with infinite resource and pertinacity his intricate web of intrigue and alliance by which he plans ultimately to make his countrymen the dominant power in the country. Somewhat to the side and, at first, completely overshadowed by their European rivals, we next observe the English, slow-moving, gravely hesitant, sincerely reluctant at first to embroil themselves in the dangerous confusion, desirous of obeying their employers, who have strictly charged them to have as little as possible to do with the native powers—to lend them no money, to give them no larger presents than is absolutely necessary, and to place in them no trust.[39]

These are the real principals in the drama. But in the background, the dark and murky background streaked with blood, thinking themselves the principals are the respective Moorish contenders for each of two thrones, the overlord's throne of the Deccan at Hyderabad, hitherto held in the firm grip of the Mogul's viceregent Nizam-ul-mulk, and the lesser tributary throne of the Carnatic, with its capital at Arcot. All of them puppets, virtually, in the ever more powerful hands of the Europeans. And lurking in the wings, but making repeated appearances upon the stage, like ravenous wolves eager to share in the feast, we see the Marathas. For wherever there was trouble, breakdown of government, with the likelihood of plunder or of a good sale for their arms, there were the Marathas too.

It was the death of the Nizam in 1748—more disastrous for this part of India than the downfall of Delhi—followed by the French-contrived slaying of Anwar-ud-din the following year, that had released all these beasts of prey. Disputed successions were ever the curse of India. The law of the jungle prevailed when a ruler died. And dynastic war beginning in the suzerain's dominions led inevitably to dynastic war also in the vassal province. With the claims of the contesting heirs almost equally good under Moslem law, each could rally large numbers of supporters. Consequently, with the balance of forces evenly drawn, alliance of one side with the foreigners from across the seas with their disciplined troops, now no longer employed in their own warfare, was quite sufficient to turn the scale.

Dupleix, swept on by the tide of his ambition, was not slow to seize the opportunity. Allying himself with Chanda Sahib and Muzaffar Jang, confederate contenders for the two thrones, the one for the Carnatic and the other for the Deccan respectively, he opened what was to prove a new era in the history of India, the era of Western domination. The overthrow in battle of Anwar-ud-din in August 1749, when the French troops bore the brunt of the fighting, was the first link in a long chain.

Between this date and August 1751 these allies were to carry all before them. Such setbacks as they received were soon retrieved by Dupleix's indomitable purpose and fertility of resource. And each fresh success enabled Dupleix to extract what favours he wanted from each of his candidates. In October 1749 Governor Floyer had to report home the regrettable news that " in spite of the peace affairs are more embroiled than even during the war, owing to the artifices of Dupleix, who so hates the English as to be unable to refrain from underhand acts of hostility."[40]

French territory began to grow alarmingly, particularly, the English noted gloomily, in the vicinity of Madras and Cuddalore. Around St. David's the white flags planted to mark French territory actually became visible from the ramparts of the fort. The threat that this represented to English trade, the threat of strangulation, soon became real and menacing. In sheer self-defence the slow-moving English were compelled to retaliate in kind. In a muddled, ineffectual sort of way they allied themselves with the other combination of contenders, Muhammad Ali in the Carnatic and Nazir Jang in the Deccan. Then the game of seeing who, French or English, could first bankrupt their company—or, possibly, win for it in the end a veritable empire of trade—was on.

Needless to say, trade suffered. Hordes of armed men, marching and counter-marching, greater hordes of camp followers and riff-raff, and even greater hordes of bullocks desolated the land. The weaver fled to the seaports, the peasants deserted their fields. The whole province was given over to war and destruction.

The culmination of the French success came when they triumphantly escorted Salabut Jang (Muzaffar Jang had been killed, but there was no difficulty in finding another claimant to take his place in the French schemes) to Hyderabad and placed him on the throne of the Deccan, buttressed invincibly by 500 Europeans and 1800 Sepoys led by the ablest French general, the Marquis de Bussy. De Bussy had previously taken the " impregnable " fortress of Gingee, making Chanda Sahib also master of all the Carnatic except the town of Trichinopoly, where the other nawab, Muhammad Ali, still maintained his feeble court, supported by such weak and ineffective aid as the English had so far given him.

Thus when the year 1751 opened English prestige was at its lowest point. It seemed as though it would be only a matter of months before M. Dupleix would be the acknowledged and undisputed master of a dominion the size of France with 30,000,000 inhabitants. His European troops were twice as numerous as those of his English antagonists—1800 to 800—and he had far more than twice the resource and adroitness. The one serious, and in the event disastrous, mistake he had made was in dividing his forces and sending Bussy, his best general, away to distant Hyderabad. Grasping at all southern India, even at all India, he risked the loss of that which was actually and by right his. But the risk must have seemed to him at the time well worth the taking.

Despite these spectacular results, however, Dupleix was far from satisfied. His appeals to his officers—d'Auteuil, Brenier, Law—to show a little enterprise, to fight or, if not willing to do anything quite so bold as that, at least to do *something*, became in time quite heart-rending—and also quite useless. There was not one of them who was not more concerned with the rewards of the service than with the service itself. Campaigning with the sole or even the chief object of defeating the enemy was scarcely their idea of an Indian career, nor was the morale of the troops themselves any better. India was a land that could demoralize Europeans quicker than any country on earth. Their very success won so easily was their undoing. It debauched them.

So for a year the English had been apprehensive spectators of Dupleix's grandiose schemings, wondering what the next move would be of a man who doubled his stakes with every turn of the wheel, who never allowed possible failure to enter into his calculations, who was always sanguine, always underestimating his enemies, and always believing himself on the verge of final success.

But in September 1750 a change had taken place in the English ranks, little attention though Dupleix paid to it. The incompetent, pleasure-loving Floyer had been displaced by a " cold, austere and silent man," a strict man, who " is always upstairs," always, that is, in his office attending to business, a man of the genuine " strong, silent " type, imperturbable, deliberate, long-headed, and not likely to be dazzled or intimidated by Dupleix's sensational but—as a clear-sighted man could see—largely super-ficial triumphs. Thomas Saunders became Governor of Fort St. David. And this is the man of whom Orme wrote : " Had I anything on earth to expect or anything to fear, he is the man on earth I should dread as an enemy." [41]

Among the men under him, too, was Robert Clive, even though Clive at the moment may not have been thinking of possible military glory to be won at French expense for the reason that he was busy making money. He and Orme in partnership had but recently despatched to Calcutta a cargo of merchandise that they had bought by borrowing 1000 rupees from Captain Cope, to be paid upon return of the ship. And in December he was writing from Madras : " I am chin-deep in merchandise, having been employed ever since my arrival in getting upon freight two sloops and a ship, one I despatched for Fort St. David three days ago with our adventure, which I don't doubt will turn out well." Clive's great moment of emergence was, however, fast approaching.

No startling success attended Governor Saunders's first moves. Indeed, the prospect became immediately even more discourag-ing. For Lawrence threw up his command in disgust. He seems to have misled the Governor and Council into thinking that the Company had granted him a more liberal salary than in fact they had. When they removed Floyer the Directors also ordered that the Major's pay should be reduced to the original stipulation. Lawrence resented the order so much that he sailed for home to have it put right. This left Saunders with only Captain Cope and a Swiss officer named de Gingens, entirely inadequate substitutes for " the Old Cock."

In January 1751 Governor Saunders and his Council took the momentous decision to support Muhammad Ali by every means in their power. The Governor foresaw a long war and asked the Company for a force large enough to curb the French. A detachment was sent to Trichinopoly under Captain Cope and shortly afterwards another small force under Captain Gingens was sent to interpose between the allied army of Chanda Sahib and the French and Trichinopoly. But the campaign that ensued was entirely inglorious, serving only to make the contrast with what was to follow all the more dazzling. When it ended in August, with Gingens, in Saunders's caustic words, " still conquering, still retreating," it left the English cooped up with Muhammad Ali in Trichinopoly, incapable of making any kind of move that showed either intelligence or vigour.[42]

Meanwhile, it had become a busy time for Commissary Clive. Now that the army had taken the field his post was no sinecure. He had to find provisions in a desolated land, as well as oxen to draw the supply train and the guns. And he had to deal tactfully, patiently, firmly with the mixed human elements that composed his department, the native merchants, agents, drivers, and sepoys of different castes. In this way he came to know the people of the country, and it was by this experience that he was to perfect his mastery of the art of leading Indian troops and inspiring them to give him the best that was in them. An aspiring young man as he was, his commissaryship was proving a great piece of luck. He was given half a rupee per man per day and as he only expended four fanams—about two-thirds of the amount—it was a very advantageous contract. Actually he made five rupees a month on each European soldier, and when he ceased to be commissary he found himself richer by £40,000.[43]

Yet as he watched the hopeless incompetence of Captain Gingens and the wretchedly poor behaviour of the English troops —on occasions as he accompanied the army vainly trying to stay their flight—he must have felt an itch to get back into the fray himself. Where all were amateurs in soldiery, he was an amateur who knew by instinct what should be done and how to do it. Mere money-making, attractive though undoubtedly it was to him, did not satisfy his ambition—and besides, could he not fight and make money at the same time ? He could be both commissary and company officer. What would suit him better ? It was the right combination for his career.

On July 22, his request to be restored to the army being granted, he was given the brevet rank of captain.

Three months before this, Ananda Ranga Pillai, the fervent supporter of the French and even more fervent admirer of Dupleix, his master, had complacently recorded in his diary : " Just as even a worm will raise its head and dance when it sees the Cobra dancing, so the English, their hearts burning with jealousy of the French, have themselves attempted to conquer their enemies and get possession of territory. But who can get what he wants by the mere force of desire ? He alone succeeds whose destiny it is and whose hand is marked with the line of victory." [44]

Ananda Ranga Pillai had spoken truly. Robert Clive's hand was marked with the line of victory. Success was his destiny.

In August—in the same despatch that he reported the decision of his government to make a diversion towards Arcot—Governor Saunders also saw a great light and announced it to his employers : " The weakness of the Moors is now known, and 'tis certain any European nation resolved to war on them with a tolerable force may overrun the whole country."[45] The grasping of this fact made the end of Moslem rule in India only a matter of time and circumstance. But for the present the two likeliest heirs to that dominion were intent only on their own contest, which was about to enter a decisive phase.

Chapter Five

ARCOT

" Success is the child of Audacity "
BENJAMIN DISRAELI

I

ARCOT HAS NEVER been listed as a decisive military event.   It has rather been ranked as a gloriously heroic feat of arms, of the same order as Sir Richard Grenville's fight of " one against fifty-three " or the charge of the Light Brigade—something immortal, to be remembered when everything else is forgotten. Arcot and Plassey! The descendant of Macaulay's super-intelligent school-boy (how decadent he is to-day !) *does* know about them, if he knows not a single other fact about the hero of these occasions.   It is only surprising, and a pity, that a Coleridge or a Tennyson, or Macaulay himself, has not perpetuated their fame in verse in a fittingly heroic manner.   Clive and Horatius would then have been comrades in epic as in spirit, holders of bridge and breach, victors over overwhelming odds.   To Clive has been denied this last apotheosis, but it has been about all that fame has denied him.   Denied the verse, he has had his recompense in prose.   Macaulay might have turned him into a lay ; he chose instead to put him into an essay.   The result, if less memorable, has been scarcely less effective.

But the truly remarkable thing about Arcot is that neither Robert Orme nor Thomas Macaulay was the first to think of celebrating this heroic feat.   The mullahs of India, we are told, were the first.   We can but regret that what they wrote, assuming that they carried out their intention, has not been preserved to us.   It would be much more significant of the true importance of the defence of Arcot than what comes to us through the pages of the two English historians.   For Arcot was more important in its effect on the Indians than on the English or French.   It was a psychological triumph fully as much as it was a military one, and as such its effects were more lasting and decisive.

77

The sending of an expedition to Arcot was for Muhammad Ali, its proposer, a means of replenishing his exhausted military chest. For Mr. Saunders, its sponsor, it could have seemed only a forlorn hope of saving a nearly hopeless situation. For Robert Clive, its youthful executor, it was a heaven-sent opportunity to distinguish himself. All three must have been surprised by its far-reaching results. The one owed his throne to it, the second his chance to frustrate Dupleix's designs, and the third, most fortunate of all, became a National Hero.

Saunders, when he decided to adopt Muhammad Ali's suggestion, found that he had no one to send but a young man of twenty-six, the most junior captain in the service, who had hitherto held no independent command. All his other officers were with the hopeless Gingens cowering under the shelter of Trichinopoly's great rock, waiting for help of which there was none to send them. But Saunders remembered that this young man had caught the eye of Lawrence and had behaved well upon all occasions. He was well thought of, too, by Mr. Pigot, one of the Council. He was quite evidently a resourceful young man, ardent for service, devoid of fear, and a born leader—just the man for a forlorn hope. So that when Clive volunteered his services to lead the proposed expedition Saunders readily accepted them.[1]

On Monday, August 19, he received orders to proceed by boat to Fort St. George with such Europeans and sepoys as could be spared, there to be reinforced by such men as the gentlemen there could spare, and then to march straight to Arcot.

The plan was based on the sound strategical idea of making a diversion that would relieve pressure on Trichinopoly. Yet there was nothing to buttress it but hope. Arcot was a large fortified city and well garrisoned. The total number of men that the two forts between them could furnish for its capture was only 200 Europeans and 600 sepoys, and of officers to command them only eight, six of whom had never before been in action and of those six four were civilian volunteers, who, like their leader, had embraced the military profession only because of the emer-

---

[1] In marked contrast to Orme's version of the expedition's inception is the following taken from an anonymous contemporary work entitled, *A Complete History of the War in India from the year* 1749 *to the taking of Pondichèry in* 1761, and published in 1761: "Now hearing at St. David's that it was resolved to make a diversion in the province of Arcot, by sending a fresh detachment, in order to divide the enemies' forces he (Clive) offered his services as a volunteer without pay to command the troops destined for this expedition."

gency.   Of discipline they knew little or nothing.   For artillery they had only three small field-pieces.   In fact, of the requisites of a military force they had only one—the right spirit ; but that, as the event was to show, was all-sufficient.   Clive was to take Arcot without firing a shot or having a shot fired at him !

It was a foolish man who said that the age of miracles is past ! History is made up half of miracles and half of " economic consequences " of this war and that peace.   Certainly the history of the British in India is a mixture of that kind : the mediæval chroniclers and Karl Marx.

On September 6 he set out on his march.   He had sixty-four miles to go across the burning plain.   Before him lay long stretches of level ground, studded with low, kopje-like granite hills, intersected by rivers whose beds in the dry season are mere stretches of sand.   It was the dry season now, though it was nearing its end.   The heat was stifling.   The dust hung in clouds about them as they marched.

They marched fast.   In three days they covered the forty miles to Conjeveram.   They learned here of the strength of the garrison.   Somewhat daunted by this, Clive sent back for two eighteen-pounders.   It is a little difficult to understand why, if such weapons were available, he had not brought them with him, but perhaps it was because he was depending primarily upon speed and surprise.   At any rate, he did not wait for them, but pressed on.

On the fifth day the miracle began to happen.   A terrific storm of thunder, lightning, and rain hit them.   Now, apparently, the faithful followers of Allah would have paid heed to this obvious warning from on high and would at least have sought shelter. But the Englishmen, oblivious of what was expected of them, kept on marching, though the dust turned to deep mud at their feet and they were drenched to the skin.   Nor did they pause until they had arrived ten miles from Arcot, when they camped for the night.

News of this demoniacal conduct sped to the city and the panic-stricken garrison decided that all resistance was useless.   They evacuated the town that night, and next morning at ten o'clock, September 12, Clive and his band marched in and took possession. The inhabitants gave them nothing more unpleasant than ugly looks. One wonders who were more astonished, they or their new garrison !

Twice in his life Clive had the rare experience of entering the capitals of rich kingdoms as a conqueror, and the two experiences were similar in many ways. Money was one of his principal objectives, both as a private individual and as an officer of the Company, and in each instance money presents in place of opposition were what was offered to him.

It was scarcely the most elevating influence for a young soldier in his first command thus to be sent on a money-grubbing expedition. It was also unfair to subject anyone so young as he to the temptation of being, at least for one splendid moment, absolute master of a rich and populous city ; unfair, that is, if you expected him to show a complete disregard of the chances thrust upon him. The giving and receiving of presents, so consecrated a custom of India, was not something that a young man austerely thrusts away from him. Yet its dangers were already evident enough, particularly to a clear-sighted man like Saunders. The Governor, who was himself a man of exceptional integrity, could see the tremendous harm it was doing to the French, who had caught the disease of accepting presents as badly as any native of India.

So when Clive, reporting his success, reported also with rather callow enthusiasm the warm reception given him by the native merchants and bankers of Arcot and their desire to make him a present, Saunders replied, " 'Tis nothing extraordinary when you consider that these people were entirely in your power. If the merchants have a mind to make you a present, I have nothing to say to the contrary ; but take care there is no compulsion, and what particularly deserves your regard is to keep a watchful eye over your people that they are not guilty of oppression."[46]

Saunders was too intelligent not to know that presents mixed with business were to be regarded with suspicion in all countries, at all times, under all circumstances. Usually fathered by fear and mothered by expectancy, their birth was doubtfully legitimate, to say the least.

Mr. Saunders could scarcely have had much hope of Clive seizing Arcot, otherwise he would surely have given him explicit orders of what to do after he was in possession. As it was, Clive was in considerable doubt. He was not fully sensible of the immense political value of his own exploit, and he indicated his intention of either retiring to Trimidi, even to Madras, or dividing his force and occupying several forts in the neighbourhood of

Arcot. The Governor had to counsel him : " Let me advise you not to grasp at too many things at once . . . would it not be better to keep your force entire ? " [47]   And Pigot reinforced this suggestion with a friendly note of advice :

" Dear Clive,
          " To receive intelligence at any time of our troops' success gives me infinite satisfaction, but there is an unexpressible addition to that pleasure when I hear of any advantage they gain under your conduct.   I very heartily congratulate you on your Nabobship as I do also the gentlemen with you on the several dignities I presume you have bestowed on them, particularly the Duan, for I make no doubt that's my friend Pybus. . . .
          "In regard to what you write the Governor of making Trimidi your sanctuary in case of an attack, instead of Arcot, though he had not mentioned it to you, I believe he thinks if the latter is tenable you should by no means quit. . . .   There is another thing that (tho' I don't mind money myself) your expedition will make you a much better figure in history if it pays itself than otherwise.   Take care of that and collect some of the rents before you return, for the Company's expenses are very great and the Nabob will never be able to reimburse them unless he is successful." [48]

As Clive still appeared in doubt two weeks later Saunders wrote him more imperatively : " The possession of Arcot is deemed of the utmost consequence.   It does not appear by your letters to Mr. Prince [1] whether you intend for Madras.   'Tis my opinion that you should keep in motion in the Arcot districts, as your being at Madras will carry an air of retreat and possibly damp those spirits that your taking possession of Arcot has raised."   Foreseeing the enemy's next move—for Captain Cope had reported from Trichinopoly the dismay that the news had caused in the allied camp of the enemy—he warned him to lose no time in securing provisions for a siege.[49]

The directing hand is visible in all these communications, though largely invisible in Orme's account.   The youthful ardour, bold spirit, and ready ability of Clive gave the expedition its chance of success, but the shrewd brain of the governor

---

[1] Deputy-governor of Fort St. George.

F   81

did the planning and directing. It was proof of Saunders's sound commonsense that he left his youthful officer, too far away to be minutely directed, so large a measure of discretion. The Arcot expedition reveals Mr. Saunders as a worthy antagonist of the great Dupleix.

Clive may be excused for thinking Arcot indefensible. So by all military standards it was, considering the size of his force. A glance told him that the city itself was indefensible against any kind of enemy, as it was nearly five miles in circumference. There was still the citadel, however. This was a fort, unquestionably, as it had a wall, ramparts, bastions, a parapet, and a moat, but the wall was in many places tumbled down, the parapet afforded little or no cover, the bastions were too poorly planned to be of much use and the moat was in some places dry and in others easily fordable. Even a veteran commander of veteran troops might have been appalled at the prospect of having to defend it.

But perhaps that is the very truth of the situation and the explanation of everything. A veteran commander *would* have been appalled, so appalled that he would have felt it madness to attempt to defend the place with such a force as Clive's, and by all the laws of military science he would have been right. It required a reckless young man who was not a soldier by profession to fail to see it. Inexperienced youth with its spurs waiting to be won was willing to take the chance that an older, more experienced man would have rejected. And Saunders, too, may have realized that in that rashness, which is the fault, or virtue, of inexperienced youth, lay the one chance of success.

So Clive had his orders. And meanwhile he had not been idle. Idleness and inactivity were the things most foreign to his nature. It was out of his intensely active, restless, daring nature that he was able to produce the key to success in this peculiar kind of warfare, so unlike what the text-books dealt with in Europe.

It may even be said that his very ignorance of the military art as taught and practised in Europe was his greatest advantage. His natural aptitude was not, except for the elements of drill that Lawrence had taught him, fettered by rules and regulations laid down for the conduct of regular operations. Wolfe, his great contemporary, maintained that " next to valour, the best qualities in a military man are vigilance and caution." And Wolfe, of course, was right. But Clive, who knew nothing of regular warfare, was never cautious and sometimes not even vigilant. That he succeeded despite his disregard of these elementary rules was due partly to what he himself called " his usual good fortune," which never failed him, partly to his extraordinary resourcefulness, which also never failed to extricate him from tight situations, but most of all to the extremely poor quality of the opposing leadership and troops. For in reviewing his military career as a whole one fact that will not escape us is the supine way in which his opponents repeatedly played into his hands. Caution in these circumstances was almost a wasted virtue ; as employed by an officer like Gingens it was a very definite vice. Rather, the reverse was true—reckless boldness and courage paid as nothing else could possibly do.

A great deal of nonsense has been written about Clive's military genius. He has even been compared to the great captains of history. There seems not to be the smallest ground for such a comparison. What he might have become had he adopted the army as his profession and applied himself to it, as Wolfe did, is a matter for speculation. The natural aptitude was plainly there. But it is grossly extravagant to put his actual achievements on the same plane as those of Napoleon or Marlborough. Not once did he fight against good troops, not once against even a second-rate commander. And how can his campaigns with armies of a few hundred men over a few square miles of territory, and in the course each time of a few days, be compared to the vast operations of great armies over whole countries and continents and in the course of months and years ? The absurdity of the comparison is too patent to require examination. And Clive himself was to admit his own limitations, which must have been only too clear to himself, when he shied away from the chance of commanding in the field against regular French troops.

The one real requisite for military success at this moment on the plains of the Carnatic was the ability of dynamic, daring personal leadership. It was all that counted with the miscellaneous hirelings and riff-raff that composed the European forces of both sides and it was all that counted even more with the impressionable sepoys.

That leadership Clive supplied. Instead of calling him a master of war, let us rather, then, call him an ideal company commander, giving him in that capacity ungrudging praise. The way he disciplined and inspired his men, the way he led them on swift night attacks and sallies, rallied them when they were breaking, and infused in them a spirit that they had previously totally lacked, were all, indeed, above praise.

His example, too, was contagious. Dalton said of the early English failures, "We were all young soldiers, at that time little experienced in the country method of making war." [50] But once Clive had discovered the right method, others, like Dalton himself, were quick to imitate him, and they became as gallant a band of young soldiers as ever did battle for their country.

II

So now at Arcot. The first rule with raw troops is to give them confidence. This Clive did by twice sallying forth in search of the enemy and engaging them in brief skirmishes. And on each occasion his men behaved well. Following instructions, he then began to prepare for a siege by repairing the defences of the fort, constructing new works, and collecting provisions. While he was busy at this the enemy, reinforced by 5000 men and emboldened by his seeming inactivity, advanced and encamped within three miles of the city with the declared intention of beginning the siege. But Clive knew exactly how to deal with such an enemy.

That night, taking with him three platoons and the sepoys, he stole out of the fort with the intention of raiding their camp. The discipline of his men was already so good that they maintained dead silence in the ranks and reached the camp unobserved. There a few volleys sufficed to create pandemonium. Then, having achieved their object without the loss of a man, they returned to the city, there to enjoy a few more days of quiet possession before the enemy's numbers again increasing, they began to be hemmed in on all sides. [51]

On the 27th Clive learned of the approach of the two eighteen-pounders from Madras, escorted only by a few sepoys. As he knew that the enemy were planning to intercept them, he despatched the bulk of the garrison under Lieutenant Bulkeley to meet them, retaining only a few men besides the sick to guard the fort. Four days later the enemy, becoming alert to the situation, entered the city to attack them.

The situation, with its result, was typical of Clive's military experiences. For the enemy, instead of attacking simultaneously from all sides, which could not have failed of success, chose to attack only one section of the wall at a time and, to oblige him further, each time they advanced they made enough noise to give ample warning of their approach ! Consequently, he was able to keep his little party together, and by moving it quickly from one threatened point to the next to beat off the feeble assaults. Was this luck, one wonders, or acute understanding of the enemy's psychology and correct estimate of their military abilities ?

In the morning the garrison returned with the eighteen-pounders safely in tow, and Clive went on preparing for the inevitable siege.

He had not long to wait. Dupleix had at first treated the *coup* as of no importance, but when he realized how seriously Clive's occupation of the capital was interfering with the collection of Chanda Sahib's revenues he became frantic and hurriedly despatched 200 French soldiers from Pondichéry to join the 4000 men that Chanda Sahib detached from his own army at Trichinopoly. The allied force entered the city on the night of October 4, and with its arrival the famous siege began.

Once again Clive demonstrated his lack of regard for the ordinary axioms of war and his equally keen perception of the way in which success could be attained in the unique circumstances of this Indian warfare, where numbers counted for much less than morale. By the rules he should not have made a sally, as he did, because he could not afford to lose a man nor expect to gain any military advantage. The enemy were not in the open, where musketry and gunfire could be effective. Rather, it was Clive's own men who were exposed and the enemy safely ensconced in the buildings that crowded close to the walls of the fort, and in addition the enemy now had French gunners, who knew how to shoot. The result of a fruitless effort was that he had fifteen of his Europeans, including an officer, killed, and another officer and sixteen men wounded. And he himself, standing in the hottest of the fire, had one of his luckiest escapes from death. One of his officers saw a man taking aim at Clive from a window and pulled him to one side, receiving the shot through his own body.

Yet there can scarcely be any doubt that his men gained in courage and confidence from the fearless example of their captain and the enemy acquired a new respect for foes whom they had hitherto only despised ; and both feelings were to be worth a great deal to Clive during the remainder of the siege.

While more reinforcements reached the enemy next day, Clive now had no more than 120 Europeans and 200 sepoys still fit for duty, and only four officers. He was completely invested, his water-supply was cut, and he had only such provisions as he had been able to collect. His supplies of ammunition, too, were running short. While every day saw the defects of the fort becoming more painfully felt. The enemy, with their great numbers, were able to keep up a constant galling fire from the houses that surrounded, and even in places commanded, the walls. The sight of a head peeping over the top instantly brought forth a volley from a range of only thirty yards. Three sergeants in succession were killed at Clive's side as he made his tours of inspection around the mile-long circuit that he had to defend. Fortunately the enemy had at first no battering guns or it would have gone still harder with the hard-pressed defenders.

By October 18 even this handicap of the besiegers was removed. The first shot of the newly arrived cannon dismounted one of the eighteen-pounders ; another put it out of action altogether. As the enemy's guns played upon the parapet the tottering walls soon began to crumble. Then the other eighteen-pounder, poorly aimed in the absence of the disabled artillery officer, was dismounted and a breach began to appear. Clive and his men worked desperately erecting new defences inside. All his ingenuity was brought into use in thinking of ways in which the breach could be held. And all the while, from every vantage point, a hot fire poured down on the dwindling numbers of his men.

Meanwhile Governor Saunders was straining every nerve to send him reinforcements. His austere and somewhat chilly reserve was rapidly thawing under the warmth of his young subordinate's unexpected success and gallant spirit. His orders lost some of their tartness and he showed an enthusiastic readiness to give all the help he could ; which was, however, very little. One hundred and thirty Europeans and fifty sepoys were all that he could find. " In case of accident we have not a single man to send out." [52] Now, too, the rains were impeding movement.

How long could Clive hold out ? There is some discrepancy in the accounts of the amount of provisions he had collected. Saunders, writing to the Company after the siege, said that he had no more than a month's provisions, but according to the Council's actual Consultations, Clive reported that he had enough for three months.[53]   Yet it is strange, if he really had so much, that there should have been as much talk of fear of starvation.   Why did the anonymous sergeant who has left a diary of the siege tell how, when relief came, " Providence disappointed our fears and relieved us from the dread necessity of starving or submitting to the terms of merciless barbarians," and how " we fully and un-molested enjoyed the fruits of the earth so long denied us ? " [54]

The truth probably is that the provisions Clive had collected and that would keep in a hot climate consisted largely of grain, and European soldiers, needing more varied and substantial fare, grew sickly with such a diet, which, while enough to support life, was not sufficient to sustain their strength.   But there cannot be any truth in the famous story, first told by Malcolm, of how the sepoys voluntarily limited themselves to rice-water so that the Europeans might have what little grain was left, and there seems no good reason for trying to rescue it from the pile of discarded myth to which it has since been consigned. Whatever the trials Clive and his men endured in this fifty-day siege, overwhelming fatigue and growing sickness, actual starvation was not one.

Nearer and nearer the enemy came.   By November 4 they had battered another hole in the weak wall and Clive could do little to stop them.   The breach widened.   Now it was forty yards wide.   The garrison toiled unceasingly building new defences. Anxious eyes scanned the bare plain for the promised relief.   A spy brought word that it had been turned back.   The only prospect of help came from Morari Rao, a Maratha chief who was hovering with 6000 horsemen thirty miles away, wondering (though he had been paid to help Muhammad Ali !) to which side to sell his sword.   Convinced at last that the English could fight—no Indian until then had thought they could—he sent back the messenger that had brought Clive's appeal for aid with word that he was coming as fast as he could.

The same news reached Raza Sahib, commanding the besieging army.   A messenger with a flag of truce approached the fort and gained admittance to Clive's presence.   Would Captain Clive accept honourable terms for the garrison and a large present for himself ?   If not, the fort would be stormed immediately and every man put to the sword.   Clive returned an Englishman's answer and sat down calmly to write Saunders that he was under

87

no apprehension whatever, " unless they should make a breach of one-half the fort."

News now arrived of the near approach of both Morari Rao and of the reinforced relief detachment from Madras. Raza Sahib had had his two large breaches for some days, but he had, through his new fear of their defenders, been reluctant to use them. Now he had no choice.

At two in the morning of November 24 Clive had word that the enemy were preparing to storm. As his preparations were already made, he lay down to sleep ordering that he should be awakened at the first alarm.

It came just before daybreak. It happened to be a Moslem feast-day, when the souls of all who fell in battle against the infidel went straight to Paradise. Aroused to frenzy by this and other even more potent aids to valour, the Moorish host moved valiantly to the assault. Hundreds bore ladders to escalade the walls. Elephants with battering rams bound to their heads were driven against the gates. Two great masses advanced against the breaches.

The attempts to escalade were easily frustrated. The gates, too, withstood the shock, and the elephants, maddened by the English musket-balls, turned around and charged through the advancing host, trampling down all who stood in their way and flinging everything into disorder. At one breach where the moat was deep the rafts bearing the enemy were sunk by well-aimed gun shot. Only at the other was the danger acute. There, the moat being fordable, wave after wave of the enemy waded across. But each one as it came through the breach was met by the concentrated fire of the defenders. Musketry, hand grenades, and grapeshot, from guns aimed by Clive's own hand, ploughed into the dense masses. Line after line went down. More and more took their places, till at last not even the mad courage of fanaticism could stand the slaughter.

The assault was triumphantly repulsed at every point. Two hundred and forty men—all that were still fit for duty—had defeated an army of ten thousand.

For one more day the besiegers continued their fire. Then suddenly it died away. All was over, and the enemy were streaming away across the plain in the greatest confusion, leaving behind most of their guns and ammunition. A few hours later the relieving force from Madras, under Captain Kilpatrick, marched in. A mere handful of men, they could not possibly have made their way through the town with every street barricaded and every house filled with the enemy.

So it ended, the first conspicuous success that the English had won in these years of miniature warfare against the French.

III

Never has a statesman been worse served by the instruments of his plans than was Dupleix at this crisis in his fortunes. His agonized moans and groans as the reports reached him of one wretched performance after another excite genuine sympathy. He, who had the honour and glory of the French nation deeply at heart and was spending himself in the effort to uphold the one and extend the other, now had to sit by in his splendid palace at Pondichéry and watch in helpless rage his great design being little by little torn to shreds. And why? All because he had not an officer worthy of the name of Frenchman. That these mishaps, too, should occur against such a contemptible foe as the English—. " riff-raff knowing only how to flee in every direction even before native troops "—was more galling for him than words could express. Objurgations flung at the heads of his officers relieved his feelings, but did not win him battles.[55]

The action at Arni was a case in point. Arcot was a blow to French plans but not an actual defeat for French troops; for reasons best known to themselves the French had taken no part in the final assault. But it was their bad behaviour at the second affair that gave Clive his first important success in the open field. There was nothing remarkable about this little victory, won a month later over the same army as he had repulsed at Arcot; nothing except the serenity of his confidence and the contrasting irresolution of the enemy in the face of it.

Reinforcements from Pondichéry had reached Raza Sahib, but they availed him nothing. Clive had been handicapped in his efforts to clear the country around Arcot by the disinclination of Morari Rao's Marathas to go anywhere where the hope of plunder did not beckon. Only when they heard that the French reinforcements were convoying a large amount of treasure did they fall in with Clive's wishes and advance with him to the attack.

They came up with the enemy on the march, and Clive at once revealed a veteran's ability for skilful disposition of his men. He had rising ground with soft paddy fields in front of him, in which the enemy's cannon-balls buried themselves without doing execution, a village with a wet trench on his right flank, and a palmyra grove on his left. He was prepared for a real scrap; but it never came to one. The poor behaviour of the French so discouraged their native allies that the whole army retreated in confusion even before the battle was fairly joined. Following the retreat, 600 of their sepoys, disgusted by the cowardice of those to whom they looked for leadership, deserted to the English.

Clive followed up this success with an attack on the great pagoda of Conjeveram, which the French had occupied to intercept communications between Arcot and Madras. Upon the refusal of the garrison to surrender, he brought up his siege guns. After two days' bombardment the French quietly evacuated the fort in the night.

Yet once again during those two days Death had passed Robert Clive by. Bulkeley, the companion in most of his soldiering adventures from the day when they escaped from Madras, was taken at his side shot through the head, and he, the child of fortune, was left unscathed.

Leaving a garrison in Arcot he now returned to Madras and thence to Fort St. David.

The importance of Arcot may now be seen. Because of its moral effect it was the turning-point in Clive's life. For in Indian warfare the battle was already half gained if one had previously established a reputation for bravery and good fortune, and a long continuance of success was certain to lead to such a reputation for invincibility that opposition was likely to dissolve before one by the mere terror of one's name.

It was prestige of this kind that Clive now possessed. Nothing in all these months and years of desultory fighting had so captured the imagination of the Indians. Saunders verified the fact when he wrote to tell him that the mullahs were writing a history of the wars of Arcot " wherein you will be delivered down to the future ages." [56] He had stamped himself upon their superstitious minds as the most favoured of fortune's children, the invincible in war. Hence the desertion to him of 600 of the French sepoys after Arni. Men who were by nature unwarlike now became, when led by Clive and other British officers like him, very nearly the equals in valour of the English. Arcot, therefore, made everything else in his life possible.

Chapter Six

KAVERIPAK AND TRICHINOPOLY

"I am well assured that fortune is bent in your favour"
MUHAMMAD ALI TO CLIVE

I

KAVERIPAK IS CLIVE'S MASTERPIECE as a commander in the field. He is seen at his best—a swift-moving, daring, and resourceful soldier, able to turn certain defeat into victory.

He had all of the French enthusiasm—nothing of which was evinced by them in these Carnatic campaigns !—for the attack. Speed of decision, speed of movement characterized everything he did. Forethought was not one of his qualities. He met occasions as they arose, relying on his astonishing resourcefulness to carry him through. He was a veritable Houdini in his ability to wriggle out of tight places.

It was now February and Clive was at Fort St. David, busy preparing a relief force and convoy to take to beleaguered Trichinopoly, when news arrived that Dupleix had copied the English strategy and put a force in the field to create a diversion in the Arcot district. Not only was the small English garrison which Clive had left in the capital threatened, but English territory had been invaded and villas of the Madras merchants at the foot of St. Thomas's Mount plundered and burnt. Raza Sahib, whom Clive had defeated at Arcot, was in command of the raiders. The despatch of Clive to Trichinopoly had to be postponed, and Saunders ordered him to proceed at once to Madras and deal with the situation.

Within a few days Clive had taken command at Madras and was in the field. The enemy in considerably larger force held a strong position seventeen miles to the south-west of the settlement. Urgent messages arrived from Captain Gingens asking him to come to Trichinopoly as quickly as he could. He planned to make short work of Raza Sahib and then march rapidly south.

Clive received intelligence that the enemy's entrenched camp was not as strong in the rear as in front, and accordingly he moved to attack it from behind. The enemy, thrown into a panic by this move, hurriedly deserted their position, although they out-numbered him by two to one. Twelve hours after occupying their camp Clive heard that they were at Conjeveram, twenty miles away, and evidently on their way to Arcot. He made a forced march to Conjeveram, received the surrender at the first summons of its small sepoy garrison, and then, after only a short halt, hurried on towards Arcot. On the way he heard that the enemy had entered the capital, skirmished with the garrison, and disappeared as suddenly as they had come. What direction they had taken he did not know, but he pushed on towards Arcot with undiminished speed.

Night was now falling, his men had marched forty-five miles in two days, and they were utterly fatigued as they approached the village of Kaveripak, nine miles from Arcot.

Suddenly, without any warning, the darkness ahead of them was split by the fire of guns only 250 yards from his advance guard. Having no cavalry to act as scouts, he had marched into a trap. It was a situation that would have tested the fibre of any commander—darkness, worn-out men, surprise, a superior enemy in a strong position. The enemy had nine guns to his six, a body of 2500 native cavalry, 2000 sepoys to his 1300, and 400 Europeans to his 380.

Surveying the situation with all speed, he found that the French infantry and artillery were drawn up behind a breastwork on the edge of a mango-grove to the right of his advance, with their sepoys and cavalry forming their centre and right flank on the open plain. His men were entirely exposed and dropping fast. But, happily, to the left of his advance, running parallel to the road he found a deep watercourse which was dry, it being the dry season. Hurriedly he threw his men into it, leaving his guns in the road to check the French fire and sending his baggage under guard to the rear. Then followed a weird and exciting battle under the ghostly light of the bright Indian moon.

The enemy attempted to advance down the watercourse and at the same time spread out over the plain with the inten-tion of taking him in flank. To check them Clive brought two of his field pieces over from the road. Meanwhile, his gunners were suffering severely from the superior fire of the French battery. Long minutes were passing and every advantage lay with the enemy. Unless he could find some way to attack the grove he knew he was beaten. A frontal attack was clearly out of the question.

It was six o'clock when they first encountered the enemy and it was now ten. How long could he sustain the unequal fight ?

There was just one chance, which was that the French might not be guarding their left flank and rear. As quickly as the idea came to him he sent off a sergeant and some trusty sepoys to find out. In a short time they returned with a report that the position was entirely uncovered and unguarded. Joyfully, then, he ordered half his force to undertake the enterprise with the sergeant as guide, accompanying them part of the way himself. But when he returned he found that the rest of his men had given way under pressure and were leaving the watercourse in full retreat. Rallying them with difficulty, he led them back and then waited in the utmost suspense for word from his detachment.

It was past eleven before it came : they had surprised and routed the French infantry and taken all their cannon. One volley poured into the backs of the unsuspecting Frenchmen at a distance of fifty yards had won the battle ! The French fled, leaving behind their guns and baggage, fifty prisoners, and more than sixty dead besides a great many sepoys.

The battle was fought on February 22, and a few days later Clive was marching south on his way back to Cuddalore. Passing by the French bounds, he destroyed a village and large *choultry*, or rest-house for travellers, that Dupleix had erected to commemorate the dastardly murder of Nazir Jang which had so furthered his plans for French domination, calling it Dupleix-Fateabad, the town of Dupleix's victory. And on March 11 Clive was once more at Fort St. David busying himself with preparations for the relief of Trichinopoly.

II

The situation at Trichinopoly urgently demanded his presence. Here the main forces on both sides were gathered and here, therefore, the war would be decided. Clive's swift dashes into the northern section of the country had been extremely effective not only in diverting part of the enemy's strength from around the walls of the great southern fortress but also in destroying, as he had done at Kaveripak, the only available

French troops that Dupleix had to send to reinforce Law's army. But Gingens and Cope were still faced by a superior allied army and their supplies were running short. The advantage in the war lay with Dupleix as long as this situation remained, and if Trichinopoly fell and the English army surrendered it is difficult to see what could have stopped the triumph of his plans.

The situation at Trichinopoly was one of stalemate. " The city of the Three-headed Demon," which lies at the foot and under the shadow of a great rock over 200 feet high, was an immensely strong fortress girt with high walls and a deep, wide moat. If the English commander was incompetent, so also was the French. If Gingens thought only of clinging to the protecting walls of his fortress, Law contented himself with bombarding the walls from a safe distance and cutting off supplies. Though Dupleix deluged his officer with appeals for vigorous action, all he got in reply were assurances that Trichinopoly was about to fall ; all he needed was just a little more time.

Dupleix had reason to be impatient ; he realized that he had cause to fear the young Englishman who had already twice dramatically upset his calculations and was now, as he knew, about to go to Trichinopoly. The balance of native forces, too, was now turning against him. The French reputation for invincibility had been sadly shaken by the recent events, the news of which, spreading far and wide, was bringing unexpected succour to the hitherto despised cause of Muhammad Ali. Not only had Morari Rao's Marathas transferred their alliance to him—or, rather, more specifically to Clive—but Haidar Ali had come down from the hill country of Mysore with a large body of men and the King of Tanjore had also sent a contingent. Thus the numbers opposing Chanda Sahib's host outside Trichinopoly were steadily growing.

No wonder the great Frenchman fumed and wept as day after day passed without visible sign of progress ! He must have known that his own fate depended upon the taking of this city. For he had not only the English, whom he affected to despise so heartily, to reckon with but the Directors of his Company as well. His war was not only undeclared but also unauthorized, and nothing could possibly justify it in the eyes of the authorities at home but success. So far it had been productive of nothing but expense and supported only by promises. It is a bold man who attempts to convince a trading company that war is its best policy. Dupleix was now expected to show results in terms of francs. What, then, if he could only display failure ?

It was now the middle of March. Supplies had been collected and everything was in readiness for Clive to set forth with his convoy. What command did Mr. Saunders expect that he would hold when he reached the army ? Not the chief command, surely. That would have been impossible for a junior captain. Even to have suggested it would have caused a mutiny among his superiors. But without an important command what could he have effected ? Probably nothing.

Happily the question was to need no answer. Just as Clive was about to march, the *Durrington*, outward bound from England, anchored in the roads, and from its decks stepped the round, familiar figure of Stringer Lawrence, whom the Directors had sent back with his pay restored and his rank raised to that of Commander-in-Chief of all the Company's forces in the East.

Within forty-eight hours Lawrence had taken the command and the march was begun. 400 Europeans, 1100 sepoys, with 8 field pieces, made up the force. The sepoys were not like the sepoys hitherto seen in these parts, troops of extremely doubtful quality. These were the heroes of Arcot, Arni, and Kaveripak, disciplined and inspired by Clive himself, and that they entertained no small opinion of their own prowess they were shortly to show.

The march was uneventful until they neared the besieged city. Twelve miles from it, at the fort of Coilady, directly on the route they were taking, was a vital spot where, if anywhere, an intelligent enemy would try to bar their way. The fort stood directly between the rivers Coleroon and Cauvery, which then diverged and made their own separate ways to the sea. Trichinopoly stood on their southern bank, so that a force approaching from Cuddalore had to cross the Cauvery in order to reach it. Would their passage be opposed in strength, as it should be ?

The incapacity of the opposing command was never more in evidence than now. Law could easily have sent half his army to Coilady and safely dared the unenterprising Gingens to attack him. Instead, however, of heeding Dupleix's frantic orders he sent only a small detachment, and the ability of Lawrence and Clive to get safely past it was never in doubt.[57]

As soon as they came within range of fire from the fort Lawrence stationed Clive and the guns to cover an oblique movement to the left. When this was successfully accomplished Clive rejoined him without further hindrance. After crossing the river they camped for the night.

Before dawn on the following day they were joined by a party from the garrison. But soon after they had resumed their march a member of Gingens's staff rode up with news that the French had taken up a position blocking their path. Once more they swung off the road to the left to make a detour.

As the sun came up the heat became almost insupportable, this being one of the hottest places in southern India. At noon a halt was taken for refreshment. While the men were resting the scouts came in with word that the enemy were advancing in force and the Maratha cavalry had already been put to flight. As Captain Dalton had now joined them with another body of men from the garrison, they had little need to worry about the enemy's superior numbers.

A quick reconnoitre showed Clive a large *choultry* not far in front of the advancing French. It was the key to the situation and with speed it could be seized. Lawrence at once agreed. Clive with nine guns and the grenadiers made a rush for it. The enemy opened on them as they came, but Clive reached the position first and brought his guns into action.

All advantages of position were now with the English. The French stood exposed on the open plain. They had twenty-two guns to the English nine, and for half an hour they stood their ground. The cannonade was the hottest that had yet been seen in India. At length the French wavered, and finally retreated, leaving Lawrence and Clive free to finish their march to the city.

III

Scenes of bitter strife must have taken place in the English officer's mess after the arrival of the relieving force. Some of Gingens's officers were intensely jealous of Clive, fortune's darling as they considered him, and Lawrence's marked liking for him, amounting to affection, could not have diminished their feeling. It must have been then that this group presented the Commander-in-Chief with the following (undated) letter :

" Sir,—We most heartily congratulate you as well as ourselves upon your safe return to India ; and we think ourselves happy to serve again under a commander so justly entitled to

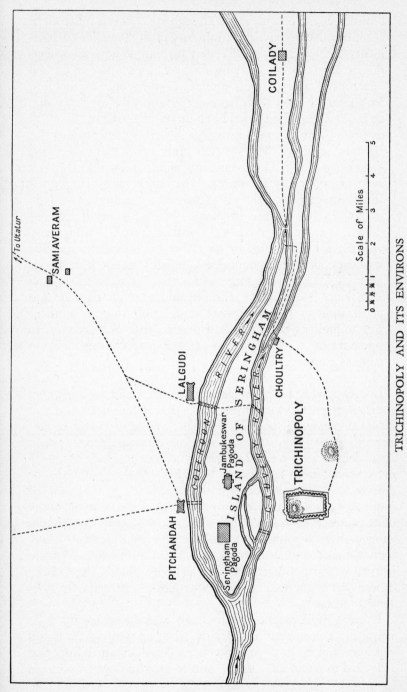

COILADY

To Utatur

SAMIAVERAM

Scale of Miles

0 ¼ ½ ¾ 1   2   3   4   5

LALGUDI

COTROON RIVER

ISLAND OF SERINGHAM

CAUVERY RIVER

CHOULTRY

TRICHINOPOLY

Jambukeswar
Pagoda

PITCHANDAH

Seringham
Pagoda

TRICHINOPOLY AND ITS ENVIRONS

G

97

our respect and confidence. Though we claim no other merit as officers than to have done our duty in all the various departments of the military service, and are sensible how subordination is necessary for carrying on operations with success and unanimity ; we cannot dissemble our surprise and discontent to see a man who, till lately has emerged from the obscurity of a counting house into the field of honour, preferred by favour to an honourable command, to which several of us had a prior right by seniority, and we may truly say a knowledge and experience acquired in divers Campaigns, before his name was even mentioned as an officer. His unbecoming haughtiness and want of regard for our opinion in measures carried on without even intimating his designs, but to his friends and confidents, is a contempt we will not submit to. We hope you will make him sensible of his illiberal deportment, and that whatever idea the honourable Company might have of his great exploits, there is none of us but were capable to conquer a province which the enemy abandoned with disgrace and pusillanimity. Lest the service should suffer by our divisions and animosities, we think it consistent with prudence not to sign our names. We hope this gentleman's preferment will not serve as a precedent, etc." [58]

Lawrence very properly ignored the letter and took his own course in respect to the subject of it. But in his own account of these campaigns he·stated his emphatic opinion : " The expedition (to Arcot) was attended with uncommon success, which some people were pleased to term fortunate and lucky ; but in my opinion, from the knowledge I have of the gentleman, he deserved and might expect from his conduct everything as it fell out. A man of an undaunted resolution, of a cool temper, and of a presence of mind which never left him in the greatest danger—born a soldier, for without military education of any sort or much conversing with any of the profession, from his judgment and good sense he led an army like an experienced officer and brave soldier, with a prudence that certainly warranted success."

Nothing did Lawrence greater credit than the generosity of his praise for a man who had already when he wrote these words outshone him in the popular favour. To call the small force that Clive led to Arcot an " army " was to give him even more than

98

his meed. But history records few instances of as kindly and generous treatment of a subordinate as Lawrence showed to Clive, and it is as well for Clive's reputation that he was to show himself appreciative of it.

The officers' letter throws, incidentally, a flood of light upon what Clive had to contend with in his upward course, and it is more than likely that the unkindness of the military gentlemen at this time permanently embittered his feelings towards their profession.

The immediate occasion for this letter, the "honourable command" referred to therein, was the choice of Clive to command the division that was sent across the river to cut Law's communications with Pondichéry.

Law had himself facilitated this daring move by withdrawing, after he had been thoroughly frightened by a night attack on his camp two days after Lawrence's arrival, within the safety of the island of Seringham, between the two rivers directly to the north of the city. By surrendering his positions to the east he made it possible for the English to divide their forces in this way, at the same time maintaining communication between them, and by shutting himself up on Seringham he was plainly courting disaster. As soon as his communications were cut he would become the besieged instead of the besieger.

It is uncertain whose plan it was, Lawrence's or Clive's.[1] It was extraordinarily risky, as it depended entirely for its success upon utter lack of enterprise on the part of Law, who from his central position could fall in overwhelming force upon either of the divisions before the other could come to its assistance, and upon the character of the officer chosen for the detached command. One feels safe in saying that if Clive had not been available Lawrence would never have adopted the plan. He correctly judged that Clive alone possessed the necessary qualities.

Yet, as the officers' letter shows, the choice was most unpopular. In fact, the deciding factor that gave Clive his opportunity appears not to have been Lawrence's choice of him, but the flat refusal of the Indian troops to serve under anyone but Clive !

[1] Professor Dodwell (*Dupleix and Clive*) writes: "The proposal came from the bold spirit of Clive and there were not wanting officers who exaggerated Law's capacity and predicted nothing but failure from the scheme." He gives as his authority for this statement what Dalton wrote Clive on May 15 (see below, p. 105). It seems more likely, however, that Dalton was referring not to this earlier plan but to the later one by which he himself was sent to deal with d'Auteuil, which is known definitely to have been suggested by Clive.

To such an extent already had he impressed his personality upon them.

On the night of April 15 he set out, taking with him 400 of the best Europeans, 1200 of his own victorious sepoys, and 4000 native horse. He crossed the rivers seven miles below Seringham and in the morning was safely established in the village of Samiaveram, nine miles to the north. There he immediately began to throw up earthworks, with the intention of settling down for a long stay. Two days later the enemy made a weak attempt to dislodge him, but were easily repulsed. Lawrence came over to visit him and they agreed that his next move should be to storm the fortified post of Lalgudi on the north bank of the Coleroon as a preliminary to attacking the more important fort of Pitchanda, which commanded the river-crossing opposite the great pagoda of Seringham. Lalgudi was important to Law because he had stored here most of his provisions. Despite this fact it was garrisoned by only a small party of sepoys, and Clive carried it without difficulty three days later.

Meanwhile, Dupleix had been exerting himself to the utmost. He had scarcely any troops left at Pondichéry, but what he had he sent. He also had no better officer—or was it no better relative?—to send with them than the ancient d'Auteuil. Law's suicidal retirement to Seringham had reduced him to a state of almost speechless rage and he intended to reinstate d'Auteuil in the chief command. "I am sure," he scathingly wrote Law, "that this arrangement will give pleasure to your wife, who longs for the moment when she can hold you in her arms." [59] But how was d'Auteuil to reach the army he was to command with Clive now blocking the way?

On the 25th Clive heard that d'Auteuil had reached Utatur, fifteen miles from Samiaveram, and was marching in a westerly direction around his position. D'Auteuil's actual force was inconsiderable, but it was convoying a large sum of money and much-needed supplies. It was, therefore, vital to the whole campaign that Clive intercept this convoy. But how to do so safely was a problem that caused him much natural perplexity. Lawrence had already reported that the enemy on the island were showing signs of activity. An intercepted despatch explained the reason. Law had awakened sufficiently from his state of lethargy to wish also to effect this vital junction with d'Auteuil. Clive's force was too small both to hold Law at bay, should he take it into his head to attack and to go after d'Auteuil ; and he had no time to consult Lawrence. Having to act quickly and on his own initiative, he chose the same kind of audacious course as he had adopted at Arcot.

The great pagodas on the island of Seringham made excellent watchtowers for M. Law. There was not a movement that the English on the plains could make in the daytime that the French did not spot. So Clive waited until nightfall before setting out on a forced march to find M. d'Auteuil, leaving only a squad to guard his camp.

After covering fourteen miles he learned that M. d'Auteuil had had warning of his coming and hastily retired to Utatur. There was nothing for him to do now but to turn back, as a surprise attack upon d'Auteuil was impossible. Quickly retracing his steps he returned to Samiaveram shortly before dawn, his men ready to drop with fatigue after an all-night march of twenty-eight miles. Then followed the most extraordinary incident of the campaign.

There were two pagodas in the village. In the larger one were quartered all the Europeans and most of the sepoys. In the lesser one there was only a small party of sepoys who served as a bodyguard to Clive, who slept in an adjacent *choultry*. Between them ran the main road from Trichinopoly to Pondichéry, upon which had been erected a battery.

As ill-luck would have it, the enemy had by treachery learned of Clive's intended march and had sent a party of 80 Europeans and 500 sepoys to take possession of his deserted camp. An hour after Clive's weary men had flung themselves down to snatch a little sleep this party approached the camp, entirely unaware as yet that its owners had already returned to it. As another piece of ill-luck, forty of the party were English deserters with an English officer at their head.

So it happened that when this officer was challenged by the sepoy sentries he replied promptly that he was sent by Major Lawrence with a party to reinforce Clive. Upon the other deserters confirming the quite likely story the sepoy officer of the watch not only omitted to ask for the password but had the whole party conducted to Clive's headquarters. When they came to the small pagoda they were challenged again, and this time they returned the challenge with a volley into both pagoda and *choultry*. Two musket-balls shattered a box at the foot of Clive's bed and another killed the servant sleeping at his side, but these narrow escapes he did not discover until it was all over.

A scene of utter confusion followed. In the eerie half-light of dawn it was hard to distinguish friend from foe and even harder to grasp exactly what had happened. Clive, roused from a deep sleep, rushed out in his shirt. At once he ran across the road to where he found his Europeans hastily seizing their arms. It did not occur to him that the enemy could actually have got into the middle of the camp without an alarm being given. As he advanced at the double with his quickly assembled party, he thought that the men he saw in front of him were his own sepoys and attributed their strange firing to unsteady nerves, which was not an uncommon occurrence. And not even when he was stabbed in two places by a sepoy officer whom he was upbraiding for his conduct did the truth yet dawn on him. That unhappy moment only came when he chased the sepoy officer over to the little pagoda and found himself surrounded by six Frenchmen !

Even then his amazing presence of mind did not fail him. He loudly called upon them all to surrender.

"Take a look out," he cried, "and you will find yourselves surrounded." If they did not surrender immediately, he told them, they would have no quarter.

Now when Clive issued an order it was only a fool or a very bold man who thought of refusal ! There was something about his manner that boded so ill as not to permit much demur. People obeyed him first and stopped to think about it afterwards. So it was with these Frenchmen. They could scarcely accept his invitation quick enough ! Three of them rushed into the pagoda to tell their comrades the good news that their lives would be saved, and the other three put themselves at once in his hands.

Clive now turned around to deal with the sepoys, realizing at last who they were. But he found that they had seized the convenient moment to disappear.

It was not yet light and all was still ignorance and confusion. The three prisoners whom Clive had just taken, together with some others, were placed in charge of a sergeant's party. The sergeant carefully escorted them to the large pagoda, where he was about to hand them over to the French, who were in possession, and the French were so surprised at this unexpected courtesy on the part of the national enemy that they made no attempt to detain the equally surprised sergeant, who thereupon returned in haste and reported to Clive that the pagoda was full of Frenchmen !

But this truth had now dawned on Clive himself and he was already making his dispositions to attack, though for all that he yet knew the whole of Law's army might be upon him.

The attempt to storm the narrow entrance proved costly, but when an attempt to sally forth had proved equally costly to the enemy, Clive boldly went to the gate to summon the officer in command to surrender on pain of no quarter.

Weak with loss of blood, he had to be supported on the arms of two of his men. As he drew himself up to make the summons, the Englishman who led the deserters, knowing what fate was in store for him if his party surrendered, quickly aimed his musket and fired. The two men upon whose support Clive had been leaning were both shot through the body and killed, though he himself was untouched.

Without further argument the French surrendered, and the party of English deserters passed into the hands of their countrymen to await their fate. Upon receipt of orders from Lawrence two days later, they were all hanged. The unfortunate sepoys who had eluded Clive in the camp were overtaken by the Maratha horse before they could get back to their own camp and disposed of with similar ruthlessness.

So ended as astonishing a series of hair's-breadth escapes in a single hour as history can produce. And so incredible did it read in the pages of Orme that one of Clive's enemies, George Johnstone, referred to it as another one of " Orme's miracles of Lord Clive " ! [60] For its veracity we are entirely dependent upon Clive himself. Yet we know him to have been that kind of man and to have enjoyed that kind of luck. The story leaves one with the strange feeling that perhaps destiny really did intend India to be British and not French and that it was preserving Clive's life to that end.

Lawrence wrote : " I rejoice at your success, as your wounds are not dangerous, and if they spoil the beauty of your face they raise your fame in having served your country when you got them." [61] Clive's portraits do not show that the wounds left any scars.

IV

It was now the end of April and the rains of the south-west monsoon in the mountains above them were swelling the rivers, so that it was no longer an easy matter for one division of the army to come to the assistance of the other. Clive thought that Lawrence should transfer still more of the army to his side so that he might have nothing to fear from a concerted move against him by both French commanders. Lawrence disagreed. He pointed out that his own division was already weaker than Clive's and to weaken himself still further would only improve Law's chances of making a sudden break through his line to the sea. " I need not sum up more particulars, as your own judgment will best point out to you what may be done, but shall conclude with assuring you that it's my opinion you are more than a match, considering the situation you are in, for all their force weakened and dispirited as they are." [62]

The following day the fort of Coilady surrendered, and now Law was completely invested and began to suffer acutely from want of provisions and the desertion of his native allies. Clive crossed the river to consult with Lawrence about the next stage in the operations. D'Auteuil's continued presence at Utatur was preventing him from besieging the fortified pagoda at Pitchandah. Nor did he want to try again his previous expedient. Lawrence finally adopted his subordinate's view and despatched Captain Dalton with a small force to deal with d'Auteuil.

On the night of May 9 Dalton's company crossed the rivers and marched all day across the plain towards Utatur. Law from his watch-towers saw the column and, judging it to be part of Clive's force, at once crossed the Coleroon with his whole army with the intention of taking him in the rear. Clive on hearing of it advanced to meet him.

Law was so disconcerted by the appearance of Clive's whole force where he had only expected a rear-guard that he halted and took up a strong position along the river-bank. His numbers were too great for Clive himself to attack, and all day the two armies faced each other. In the night the French recrossed the river. It was practically Law's last chance. Once again he had allowed himself to be overcome by timidity and entire lack of confidence in himself and his men.

Meanwhile, Dalton, with a vigour and resource worthy of Clive himself, had come upon d'Auteuil near Utatur and by fooling him into thinking that he was in the presence of Clive's whole force had put him to flight.

Dalton wrote to Clive : " I give you joy, my dear friend, on the success of your scheme, which I think must be utter ruin to the enemy's army. As everybody almost disapproved of it, you have all the honour."   His admiration of Clive was genuine : when he received Lawrence's order to join Clive, he gladly agreed to serve under him as a volunteer, his seniority of rank preventing him from doing so officially.

At last the British were ready to close in on their doomed foe. Pitchanda was cut off from Law's main body by the rising of the Coleroon and this gave Clive his chance to take it.   Accordingly, he took post on the banks of the river and erected batteries for the breaching of the pagoda.

From where he stood on a high mound he could look over into the enemy's camp on the island.   Thousands of tents were spread out to view.   The multitude of camp followers, of elephants, camels, horse, and oxen, that accompanied every Indian host occupied every square yard of the cramped area.   Princes and nobles had their harems, soldiers and servants their wives and families, shop-keepers had opened their bazaars : it was a veritable canvas city, going about its routine ways as though no such thing as war existed !

The sight of all this under his very nose and within easy gun-shot was too great a temptation.   Bringing up his guns he opened fire.   It was a cruel act, but the effect was all that any artillery officer could have wished.   It was as though an earth-quake and tornado had simultaneously struck the canvas city. Piercing yells and cries and the bellowings of frightened and wounded beasts rent the air, and in a moment all was hideous confusion.   The canvas city began to disappear, like snow in May, as tents were torn down and dragged away, and the whole vast assemblage of men, women, children, and animals surged terror-stricken across the island to get out of range of the shot.   Then the guns of Trichinopoly joined in from across the Cauvery. The frenzied mass was caught between two fires, and not until it had fled away down the island beyond the pagoda of Jam-bukeswar did it get beyond reach of the death-dealing monsters. But the canvas city never resumed its former size and air of busy prosperity. The proof that Chanda Sahib's cause was failing had been too appallingly positive !

Clive's battery was now completed, and on the following morning the work of reducing the post began. A few hours' bombardment was enough to effect a breach. But the enemy, too discouraged to await the assault, surrendered at once.

Thus Law and Chanda Sahib were shut up on the island, and it only remained to compel their surrender. With their whole camp exposed to fire and their provisions nearly exhausted, that was merely a matter of time.

Defections from their ranks became increasingly numerous. First, most of Chanda Sahib's nobles and chief officers went in a body to him to hand in their resignations from his service. They received from the English safe-conduct through their lines. Soon 2000 of his horse and 1500 of his foot deserted. Then all the independent chiefs and their followers left. So that by May 29 the whole canvas city had vanished, and only Chanda Sahib, with a few thousand faithful adherents, and the luckless French themselves were left. To escape the English fire they had sought refuge in the two pagodas.

Lawrence now crossed to the island and encamped to the east of the pagodas, hemming the French in more closely with an entrenchment stretched across it.

Still Law did nothing. It was as though he had fallen into a complete stupor. He might still have made a bold dash for freedom : he was urged to it by Chanda Sahib, whose very life hung upon escape. But he refused to move, obsessed by the notion that d'Auteuil would come to his relief and that together they could hold the pagodas until reinforcements arrived from France.

Even this tenuous hope was soon taken from him. D'Auteuil, under the unmerciful proddings of Dupleix, had recovered enough of his scattered courage to venture forth again. Clive upon learning this immediately set out to meet him. Having, because of the intolerable heat of the day, marched at night, in the morning he reached Utatur. He remained in the fort there all that day and the following night in the hope that d'Auteuil would venture near enough to be waylaid. But d'Auteuil sensed the danger, and having arrived within seven miles of where Clive was waiting for him, he turned back ; he was badly outnumbered and on a hopeless errand. Clive sent the Maratha cavalry after him to harass his retreat and give time for the main body to come up. When d'Auteuil reached the walls of Valikonda he was compelled to turn and draw up his small force for action.

Now again Clive's sepoys showed the effect of his inspired leadership. Outmarching the Europeans, they were in the van of the column as it came up, and no sooner did they come within cannon-shot of the enemy than—to use Orme's words—" they ran precipitately to attack them, without regarding any order. They received the fire of the enemy's cannon and musketry, which killed many of them, but did not check the rest from rushing on to the push of bayonet."

After a brief encounter, d'Auteuil retired within the walls of the town. But the walls were weak and he wanted to retire farther. Vainly he asked permission of the Indian governor to enter the fort. The delay while he forced his way in was fatal ; Clive was already at the gate of the town. In fact, he was through it before the last of the French had got into the fort. There was obviously no resisting him, and d'Auteuil surrendered.

This was on June 9, and the same day Clive heard from Lawrence that the battering guns were expected in camp on the morrow and then all would be in readiness for the final assault on Law's position. " Dear Clive, make haste here." Clive made haste and was back in camp the same night.

Law still seemed quite unaware of his impending fate ! He even, when it was quite too late, showed something of a fighter's spirit by a defiant reply to a summons to surrender at discretion, declaring he would defend himself to the last unless permitted to evacuate under arms. Lawrence curtly rejected the proposal.

That night Chanda Sahib took a desperate course in an attempt to escape. He surrendered to the leader of the Tanjore contingent. Solemn vows were given that he should not be betrayed. But vows meant nothing under circumstances like these. Bitter enemies having him in their grasp, two days later his head was struck off.

Law surrendered on June 14. By this victory, which was as complete as the manner of its gaining was brilliant, thirty-five commissioned officers, 725 European rank and file, and 2000 sepoys became prisoners of war. Ananda Ranga Pillai sorrowfully recorded in his diary that when the news reached Pondichéry Dupleix was so overwhelmed that he could neither go to mass nor eat his dinner.[64]

Chapter Seven

THE DOWNFALL OF DUPLEIX

"Are all thy conquests, glories, triumphs, spoils, shrunk to this little measure?"

SHAKESPEARE: *Julius Caesar*

I

THERE WAS a little clearing up of French garrisons to be done before the English could rest on their muskets. Muhammad Ali had to be put in possession of the rest of the country to the north, where French power, greatly weakened by Clive's two incursions, was not yet broken. But troubles with the Nawab and his allies the Mysoreans and Marathas, both of whom had claims upon Trichinopoly, delayed matters, and it was not until June 28 that Lawrence, accompanied by Clive, again set forth, leaving the city in charge of a strong garrison under Captain Dalton.

Madras had now once more become the seat of government of the East India Company's settlements in the Carnatic. It had been left in a deplorable condition by the French and the fort had had to be completely rebuilt, but the English noted with pardonable pride that the native merchants had come flocking back to their ruined homes " as gladly as if each had received a fortune," Madras was a better *entrepôt* for trade than Cuddalore, as it possessed larger warehouses and the ships could anchor nearer the shore.

Saunders and his Council were installed in Fort St. George when Lawrence and Clive came there to rest. The health of both men had suffered by the strenuous campaign in the scorching heat. After receiving the surrender of the garrison of Trivadi on July 7 they left the army and retired to recuperate.

Without Lawrence and Clive the war resumed the appearance it had worn before their startling entrance. Nor did it need more than a certain measure of success, like the defeat of the unfortunate Major Kinneer, fresh from England, to revive Dupleix's drooping spirits. The resiliency of the French governor was almost

incredible. By adding a batch of fresh recruits from France—
sorry specimens of manhood only half of whom were fit for
service—to the few veterans still left him he even managed to
put another army in the field. He could then for a brief space
take further hope from the fact that, while opposed to Gingens,
this army, commanded by his nephew de Kirjean, managed to
maintain a fair appearance of possible future success.

But not for long ! Its doom, like Law's, was sealed when
Lawrence resumed command of the English. With one smashing blow at Bahur Lawrence destroyed this new army as completely as he had the former at Trichinopoly, leaving Dupleix
once more bereft of means to carry on the war. The battle was
noteworthy for being the only occasion in the war when bayonets
actually crossed in hand-to-hand combat.[65]

There was still officially peace between England and France,
a fiction that both sides tried hard to maintain. When Dupleix
captured boats conveying English troops down the coast, Lawrence apparently saw nothing incongruous in the protest he made
to Dupleix, in which he described the peace that Dupleix had
violated as " sacred here, as well as in Europe, though we were
allies in different causes." Dupleix, however, made the apt retort,
" But why, if it is so sacred to you, do you hold all my men that
you captured at Seringham as prisoners of war ? " [66]

It was now Clive's turn to re-enter the field. It is amusing to
read of the utter contempt that Dupleix feigned for this young
man ! Judging from his letters and Ananda's diary, one would
think that Clive had scarcely even appeared above the French
governor's mental horizon, being described only as an arrogant
fellow given to much boasting, a coward, too, who had remained hidden behind a tree during the whole of one engagement.[67] Yet it may be noted that when Dupleix thought
he had a chance to capture him he did not let the opportunity
slip ! [1]

The task that Mr. Saunders gave to Clive was to take the two
strong and well-garrisoned forts of Chingleput and Covelong
that lay to the southward of Madras menacing the security of
the English settlement. Despite the apparent formidableness
of the task, he was given only 200 raw recruits of the worst

---

[1] Dupleix's chief reason for seizing the English boats passing down the coast to
Cuddalore was a false report of Clive being aboard ! [68] It appears that Saunders
had sent Clive warning of Dupleix's intention only the day before.[69]

quality, fresh from England—fresh, that is, from its jails and slums
—and 500 equally raw and untrained sepoys.

His first parade of this magnificent army must have been a
sight not to be forgotten. With what feelings of bitter scorn and
grim amusement at his own expense did he survey the men that
he was supposed to lead to victory and glory ? It was a sight to
arouse painful emotions in the breast of any commander, and to
an officer of Clive's stamp it must have been to the last degree
repellent. The slouching, stunted, twisted bodies of England's
wrecks—physical, mental, and moral ! Faces marked by vice,
drunkenness, brutality, crime, misery, grinding poverty !
Natures untouched by discipline, *esprit de corps*, experience of
war, or anything that makes the brute man a soldier. His army !
And with them the sepoys, hastily armed, drilled, and put into
uniform ! Undoubtedly as specimens of human kind they were
a far more agreeable sight, but how could he help thinking regret-
fully of his own dark-skinned veterans who had just given the
French such a severe trouncing down south ? It must have been
with tightened lips and strong misgivings that he put himself at
their head on September 15 and began his march.

The next day he reached some rising ground two miles from
Covelong fort and camped for the night. Before daybreak he
sent forward half of his men to take possession of a garden
situated a quarter of a mile from the fort, and he himself followed
with the rest two hours later. Upon approaching the garden he
was met by his men running for their lives ! The garrison had
just sallied forth, and the fall of the detachment's commanding
officer had been the signal for flight. The expedition nearly
came to an end then and there, as it was only with the greatest
difficulty and the use of violence that Clive was able to rally the
fugitives. He drove the enemy back into the fort, reoccupied
the garden, and on the following day summoned the fort to
surrender. Upon a blunt refusal being returned, he proceeded to
erect a battery of two 24-pounders at a distance of 300 yards.

This took three days, and before it was finished Clive learned
that a detachment from Chingleput had arrived within four miles
of him. But the French, fortunately for him, were labouring
under the same handicaps as he : no sooner did they see the party
that he despatched to meet them approaching than they retired
with great precipitation.

Meanwhile the besiegers had suffered various misadventures.

It was all that Clive could do to prevent his men from deserting their posts at the least alarm. As usual, his chief resource was to expose himself constantly wherever the enemy's fire was hottest. He had placed a strong guard on a rock a hundred yards to the left of the battery, and one unlucky shot hit the rock and with the splinters it made struck down fourteen men—with the result that it was some time before any of the survivors would again expose themselves. But three days under the command of Robert Clive were worth a month under any ordinary commander. He possessed the secret of making soldiers out of any material in the least possible time.

The battery was duly finished, and when it was ready for action it was found that the garrison had lost heart and was quite willing to surrender. Clive took possession of the fort in the afternoon.

The following morning one of his officers happened to go for a stroll and saw not a mile away the Chingleput detachment again approaching. Unaware that the fort had already fallen, they were marching determinedly to its relief! He brought the news on the run and Clive quickly led his men out of the fort and concealed them. The French marched straight into the ambush, and one volley at close range was enough to cause the surrender of the whole party.

Deprived in this way of its commandant and thirty Europeans, the garrison of Chingleput lost heart. Clive marched at once to its attack. The fort was so strong that his assault could with a little resolution have been easily repulsed, but he had no sooner breached the walls than the garrison offered to yield.

On October 9 it was recorded in the Consultations of the Madras Council that " Captain Clive complained of want of health, and desired to return—which, as he had executed his plan, was granted." He had fought—as it happened—his last campaign in the Carnatic, and it had been, wrote Saunders to Lawrence, a glorious one. He had driven one more nail into the coffin of French hopes and ambitions. Muhammad Ali had been placed in possession of practically all his dominions. The rainy season was now on. Surely the New Year would see the final quietus given to Dupleix's schemes.

II

But it was not to be so at all ! If Dupleix was beaten he was the very last person in the world to know it or to acknowledge it, or even allow his enemies to think it. (" The French," wrote Captain Dalton, " will never be quiet, tho' we often thrash 'em heartily." [70]) Indeed, he was proclaiming to all and sundry that victory was just around the corner with more confidence than ever. He discounted every defeat and magnified every small success into a triumph. It was his fond conviction that it could only be a matter of time before the English Company would confess its inability to support such a war, and that it would then disavow its agents' meddlesome conduct and recall them, on moral grounds if on no other. He himself had no words strong enough to describe what he thought about the behaviour of Saunders, Lawrence, Clive and Co. Their support of a rebel against the lawful ruler of the land, their perjury, inhumanity, cowardice, duplicity, and general contempt for morality and honour, and above all—their most heinous offence—their retaining of all French troops captured as prisoners of war ! Every despatch home, every letter in his acrimonious correspondence with Saunders was filled with howls of indignation and dire threats of what an aroused French nation would do to these perfidious Englishmen and all their settlements.[71]

Saunders was not the man to be moved from his purpose by any lightning flashes and growls of thunder from Pondichéry. Like a mariner who has lashed his helm, he held serenely to his course confident of his employers' approval and his own ability to weather the storm. Yet even he must have marvelled at his rival's pertinacity. It must at times have seemed to him, and to other observers, that the more this man Dupleix was beaten the more invincible he became. And, indeed, it was almost so. Nothing could beat him—nothing, that is, but the order of recall from his own government.

What Dupleix lost on the field of battle he regained in the arena of diplomacy. In this game he was playing with the English, wits could be made to count for as much as weapons. When, as now, he had nothing to offer but promises, none could make a promise sound more alluring ; when, as also now, he had no money, none was more skilful in obtaining it. Chanda Sahib's death would to anybody else have seemed an unmitigated disaster.

Not so to Dupleix. To him it was even convenient. Chanda Sahib had not given entire satisfaction. He had shown himself no soldier and he had grown less and less amenable to dictation. As a financial milch cow he had also proved disappointing. Dupleix had, in fact, been planning to dispossess Chanda Sahib and take the nawabship of the Carnatic upon himself! He had, indeed, already arranged the transfer with Bussy. For if Bussy's position as the real ruler of the Hyderabad court had no other advantages, it had one that was positive and clear, if rather illusionary : Bussy could put at Dupleix's disposal the name and authority of the Mogul Viceroy of the Deccan, the constitutional superior of all territorial kings, princes, and nawabs. It is true that it was somewhat like being given a millionaire's power of attorney at the moment when the millionaire has ceased to be a millionaire and his bank account stands empty ! But for what Bussy's position was worth, Dupleix made full use of it in his usual wily manner.

Dupleix's methods and reasoning are important for us because of their subsequent influence upon Clive and his adoption of them. The symbols of power had some value, even though the power itself might be lacking.

The mind of the average Indian still—and for some time to come—regarded the Mogul name and authority with awe and, when backed with possible force, even with trepidation, and paid it lip-service, while evading on all possible occasions the performance of actual obligations like the payment of tribute. Dupleix, it is true, attached undue importance to the symbols—Clive was to attach considerably less—but unquestionably the appointment that Bussy had obtained for him as Mogul Viceroy for all the country south of the River Kistna had its very definite value in his dealings with the Indian princes and potentates of this area. It is scarcely surprising that it should not have helped him in his dealings with the English. Saunders certainly was not to be duped by such a barefaced pretence.

One tangible fruit of the appointment and a signal triumph for Dupleix's diplomacy was the detachment of the King of Mysore from Muhammad Ali's side. The way had been prepared for it by Muhammad Ali's wholly insincere promise of Trichinopoly as the reward for Mysorean aid. When the cession was not forthcoming after Law's capitulation Dupleix with his usual cleverness took the promise upon himself as supreme lord of all this territory

H

and told the Mysoreans that if they paid well for it they could have French aid in capturing the city. The Mysoreans accepted the bait and Trichinopoly once more became a besieged city, with Captain Dalton, whom Lawrence had left in command of the garrison, upholding Muhammad Ali's cause.

It was a simpler matter to buy off the Marathas. They wanted nothing but solid cash. The promise of a lakh and a quarter of rupees a month—and Dupleix was actually still trying to convince the Company's Directors that the war was costing them nothing !—brought them over to the French side.

The problem of finding a new nawab to take the place of Chanda Sahib was not so easily or satisfactorily solved. For a time Dupleix flirted with the idea of standing forth himself as nawab, but this for somewhat obvious practical reasons he deemed inadvisable. All he wanted from a nawab was obedience to his wishes—and money ; and for Nawab Dupleix to exert himself constantly to find money for Governor-General Dupleix seemed an unwise multiplication of responsibility ! So he looked around for some wealthy nobleman who might be induced to accept the office as his deputy. He found one who had done his full share of murdering unwanted princes and heirs, and for a time all seemed well. The new Nawab, Murtaza Ali, did what was expected of him—visited Pondichéry and contributed five lakhs to the French treasury—but then he saw through Dupleix's scheme a little too clearly and ceased to be of any further use.

Dupleix did nothing by halves. All that he did ministered to two things, both very dear to him—French power and his own vanity. With the recklessness of a gambler he even threw his own great wealth into the tilting scales. But power and conceit were rapacious, insatiable deities. They exacted the utmost farthing from him and then turned and rent him. He died a ruined man in poverty and distress. So now—the last thing he would have thought of doing would have been to allow his august position as Mogul Viceroy to be a mere matter of empty form. Besides, he was too good an Indian politician to think that the Indians would be impressed with a legal document without its embodiment in a person whom they could see and fear. So, when Salabut Jang's messenger arrived with the Viceregal Commission, Dupleix pretended that the messenger was none other than an ambassador from the Great Mogul himself and had him received with all the honour and ceremony due to such a personage. Mounting an elephant, he went forth with music and dancing girls to escort him in, and having received his commission he seated himself upon the viceregal *musnud* and held his Durbar, every inch the Oriental potentate. To make the comedy complete in every particular, he had his officers as well as the Pondichery natives advance, salaam, and make the conventional presents. Was it any wonder that in moments like these he appeared to the watchful, impressionable, childish Indian world a far more wonderful and powerful being than any of the English ; than Governor Saunders, for instance, with his chilly reserve, prosaic matter-of-factness, and quiet absorption in his work ?

The Indians love and are unduly impressed by pomp and parade ; they like to see their ruler and not merely feel the weight of his impersonal authority. An absent power, like a Company with headquarters in Paris or London, had no appeal for them. Dupleix and his clever Oriental wife knew this and they played on the Indians' susceptibilities in a way that the English had not as yet dreamed of doing. Dupleix had long ceased to think of himself in terms of trade and commerce. He was at heart a viceroy, Mogul or French it made no difference. And that is why he was about to lose his post, because if there was one thing the *Compagnie des Indes Orientales* was determined upon it was to remain a trading corporation and not to be led off by the ambitions, vanities, and wild-eyed schemings of one man into an adventure that could cause nothing but unending trouble with their English rivals and seemed to have no possible end but their own bankruptcy.

Dupleix, too; had not been honest with them ; he had never explained the real scope and purpose of his policy. He had tried to hoodwink them into thinking, as he thought himself at the time, that the troubles with the English would soon blow over and peaceful trading be re-established. He failed to see that nothing short of extermination of the English settlements would make the accomplishment of his great scheme possible. It was a war to the death that he had declared against them, as the English saw quite clearly. If he had been honest and explained that he wanted to give France an empire, and explained also, as Clive was to be careful to do, how it could be made profitable and a sound business undertaking, there might have been a different story to tell. The French were not apt to overlook an opportunity of that kind. The lesson of these mistakes, however, was not to be lost upon Clive.

Meanwhile the English, in their slow manner, were making their own important discovery. They were coming to realize that there was another way besides Dupleix's—an improvement on his—in which to gain power over the natives of India. It was the way that Clive had found for them.

The Indians might be dazzled by the vision of power incarnate that Dupleix tried to give them, but they—or at least the Hindu section of them—were even more impressed by something quite different, not Mogul or Moorish or transitory, like political power and personal vanity, but of themselves, inherent and permanent—superiority of caste.

One of two things was necessary to dominate the Hindu race, brute force or superior caste (not religious, necessarily, but personal and social). The Moslems coming down from the north had employed the first and with their superior virility and brutality had conquered. The Brahmans owed their unchallenged authority over their co-religionists to their highest caste. And now the British were to owe their own domination of India not to one but to both of these possessions.

In their first manifestation to the Indian world as peaceful, undistinguished traders they had made no impression and had certainly been given no superior caste. In their second, as soldiers of valour led by a Clive, they were recognized not only to have caste but a very high caste. In fact, in the eyes of the lower castes, who hated the Brahmans, the English became the highest caste of all, the one to which they willingly gave their loyalty and for whose service they were willing even to give their lives. The Brahmans were distinguished by their lighter skins, so—as it happened—were these new lords from the northern isles. A coincidence of course, but none the less important in its consequences. That much remarked and abused, but also none the less useful, superiority of manner of the English helped a great deal too. It marked them out as real Brahmans, in fact as super-Brahmans. The British won India because they out-Brahmaned the Brahmans in the use of caste and out-Moslemed the Moslems in the efficient (not ruthless) use of force. The French, lacking that superb aloofness of manner that betokened such an obvious racial superiority, could scarcely hope to compete !

India's rulers and nobles were, at this decisive juncture of its history, a decadent race of men. If they had been otherwise the intruders from the west would never have passed the bounds of their small settlements. India was ripe for a revolution. But however strong a hold legitimacy had on the Indian mind, the power necessary to effect this revolution could not be conferred by *parawanna* and *sanad*. That was what made Dupleix's diplomatic triumphs so hollow. The power had to come from below and outside. That is to say, it had to come as a result of a strong outside force working on and through the Indian masses. Not a strong outside force alone, be it noted. There was to be nothing remotely resembling the Italian conquest of Ethiopia and very little that resembled the Spanish conquest of Mexico.

National pride needs to be restrained in dealing with India (if, indeed, there is cause for pride in any domination of one people by another). The part that the Indians themselves played in the revolution (for that describes the process better than conquest) that overthrew their former rulers and substituted the British gives the event its uniqueness in history. And the failure to grasp this essential fact is what has caused so much foreign misapprehension about the origin and nature of British rule in India.

Not a conquest but rather a curious kind of partnership—a partnership in the beginning and still a partnership to-day ; a partnership that took the government out of the hands of the Moguls and their Moslem hierarchy, and, to a lesser extent, out of the hands also of the Brahmans, and gave it at first largely to the British, then increasingly, and now almost wholly, to the Indians themselves, regardless of race, creed, or caste. That, in a sentence, is the history of India since 1750.

It indicates clearly what was the real nature of Clive's achievement. Call him if you will the British Cortes, but the comparison has little value. Call him the precursor of Lawrence of Arabia and you have a more apt analogy, but still quite inadequate. As actual personalities Clive and T. E. Lawrence had practically nothing in common, though as influences over their respective Asiatic races it would be difficult to say which was the greater. Their methods were entirely different. Clive had little knowledge of the native tongues. He adopted neither native dress nor native ways of living. He did not try to assimilate his ideas, manners, and speech to those of the people he was leading. He did no more than exercise care " to entwine his laurels round the opinions and prejudices of the natives "—in other words, to show ordinary tact in his dealings with them. The contrast of method is a measure of the difference between the Hindu and Arab races.

Clive's method was the one that succeeded best in India. He was the first of the sahibs, of the long line of great white chiefs whom the Indians accepted as lords and masters and also, frequently, as friends. It was part of his exceptional talent that he knew as though by instinct the secret of Indian rule. He applied it in the Carnatic as a soldier. Later, in Bengal, he was to apply it as a statesman and administrator.

So far as actual policy was concerned he did, of course, profit greatly from the lessons and examples of Dupleix and Bussy. For practically everything Clive was to do in Bengal the French had supplied precedents. Particularly is this true in the matter of obtaining territorial and economic concessions, together with large presents and pensions. The system and methods by which the English constructed an empire in the north had been evolved and put into practice by the French in the south.[1] [72]

National pride has garbled much of this history. The exploits of this gallant band of Englishmen—a mere hundred or two— who " conquered " India have been sung and sung many times. That they overcame the French by superior valour—the natural possession of the British race !—has been commonly assumed. That the so-called " British " troops were not strictly British at all but made up in large numbers of recruits from all parts of Europe besides—Swiss mainly, but also Dutch, Germans, and Swedes—has often been conveniently overlooked. Their com- manders did not overlook it at the time : British and French alike called their men " Europeans." And the frequency and the ease with which they deserted to the rival company were a matter of constant complaint from both sides, revealing how homo- geneously heterogeneous were the two contending parties and what little part patriotism or nationality played in their martial feats. Dupleix never ceased bewailing the fact that nothing but " rabble " was sent to him from France. Saunders was in the

[1] " From the first Bussy (at Hyderabad) had understood how to manage Indian princes, showing due deference and doing nothing without permission. His manners gave no hint of his power ; he never seemed to despise the weak or the vanquished. In his hand was armed force ; but he always thought that gentleness was better than the laurel of victory. As he himself said, he was more of a states- man than a soldier ; he was a born diplomatist. But his resolutions were firm, his action bold. When a decision had to be taken, Bussy saw straight to the heart of things and carried his purpose into effect, though without brutality or offence." [73] Most of this can be applied equally well to Clive.

same plight. Wherein, then, did the superiority of the British reside ? It lay partly in the professional superiority of men like Lawrence and Clive, and later Forde and Coote, as soldiers. It lay also in the possession of superior sea power, able at every critical moment to command the sea. But it also lay in that new quality of leadership that Clive introduced.

Thus it was that, given an equality of European " rabble," the English were still superior to the French because of their sepoys. Having fired their imagination at Arcot, Clive had gone on feeding those fires ever since. He had, in fact, become Sabut Jang, " Daring in War " (a title that Muhammad Ali had given him), the man in whose favour fortune was bent. To the super-stitious Indian mind it was enough. This man was sent to lead them, and led by him and other English officers, fired by his genius and example, they themselves became invincible. It was Sabut Jang who was giving the English the victory !

III

Clive left India in March 1753. For a year and a half after that the plain of Trichinopoly continued to be the battlefield of French and English and their Indian allies. Lawrence won several notable victories ; he also suffered some reverses. The balance lay definitely in his favour, but the larger number of recruits that Dupleix received from France compared to those that reached Saunders constantly evened the scales.

On August 1, 1754, the *Duc de Bourgogne* anchored in the Pondichéry roads and from it landed M. Godeheu. Dupleix came down from his palace to meet him and Godeheu handed him the King's warrant of dismissal. Dupleix read it with perfect composure, bowed, and said, " Monsieur, my only thought is to obey the King and submit to all." The following day M. Godeheu was proclaimed Governor-General of the French nation in India.

But Dupleix could not forget that he was still a Mogul Viceroy. Clothing himself in Moorish dress and surrounding himself with all the pomp of his high rank he went to dine with M. Godeheu.

The day Godeheu arrived he notified Saunders that he had come to make peace. The following month Admiral Watson with a large English squadron reached Madras and landed an entire regiment of Royal troops. On September 29 articles for a suspension of hostilities were signed. And on the following day M. and Mme. Dupleix embarked for France.

With them went the French hopes for an Indian empire. Bussy was still at Hyderabad, the French still held their gains in the Carnatic, much warfare was still to come, fortunes were still to fluctuate, Madras was again to be besieged—not, in fact, for fifty years were the French hopes to be completely extinguished ; but from this point on the British were to hold the upper hand with all the advantages of position and resources.

Chapter Eight

SPRINGTIME

" . . . in the very May-morn of his youth,
  Ripe for exploits and mighty enterprises "
                              SHAKESPEARE : *Henry V*

I

IN JUNE OF THE YEAR 1752, when Lawrence and Clive were still occupied with M. Law in the vicinity of Trichinopoly, an event had befallen at Madras that had excited the gentlemen there more than anything that had happened since they had been taken prisoners by the French. War had its excitements, but it had, after all, become part of their routine daily existence, whereas *this* event—it was nothing less than epochal ! What sight could young exiles wish for more than that of some free and unattached members of the opposite sex from their own country ! The only European women seen there hitherto had been the few who had come out with their husbands. But now in June eleven had arrived together ! [74]

No wonder that their coming had been heralded by letters from home ! No wonder, too, that Clive's friends should have hastened to tell him of it while he was yet campaigning ! " There are eleven ladies coming out, viz. Mrs. Keene and Mrs. Edwards, two young ladies to Mrs. Ackell, Miss Eliot and Miss Austin, Miss Ross, a Scotch lady, and a prodigious fine girl it's said, and Miss Maskelyne your friend's sister. The others I have not heard the names of, but however I would advise you to guard your heart well against them, when you think of the time of seeing us, as I don't doubt but after such a campaign as you have just had, these beauties will have a wonderful effect upon you."

There could be little doubt either about the wonderful effect that Clive would have upon these ladies ! He was a very different young man from the wretched, penniless youth of a few years before. He was no longer thinking of suicide, no longer without friends, no longer shy and diffident. He was now an acclaimed hero with such fame and wealth as few men have acquired in a life-time, and with many who were happy to call themselves his friends. Of all the gentlemen of the settlement he was easily the greatest catch.

There was no secret about why these ladies had come so far at such hazard to their lives and at the price of so much physical discomfort. It was neither for any love of the sea nor for need of a change of climate. They had come, quite simply and openly, in search of husbands, of richer husbands than they could expect to find at home. And out there in India, where the demand so far exceeded the supply, they had a more than excellent chance of finding what they sought.

"And Miss Maskelyne your friend's sister "—she had come too. Was Robert Clive excited by the news ? Was this the reason why he obtained leave of absence from the army in the following month and repaired to Madras ? There is a romantic tradition that he had seen and been fascinated by the miniature of a young woman in his friend's room and asked who she was and that upon being told he urged Maskelyne to invite her out. Edmund had invited her out, but was under the impression until her actual arrival that she was not coming. He had expressed the hope that her decision did not proceed " from some more agreeable views at home, as otherwise I can't but blame you for it ; matches in this country generally proving so vastly superior to what are made in Europe " ; and he had supported his advice " by the most solid reasons he could urge." Was Robert Clive the chief of these reasons—or, perhaps, all of them ?

Dupleix in his youth had once asked his brother to send out some girl whom he might marry : " No European women," he wrote from Chandernagore, " come here to us, except those not wanted at Pondichéry." Charming thought that the great Dupleix once had only the left-overs from whom to choose his women friends ! [75]

If tradition does not lie, Clive was more discriminating in the way he made his choice, and he was also to take his time making up his mind.

On their first Sunday in the fort these eleven fortunate ladies would find themselves met at the church door by a crowd of gentlemen, young and old, eager to hand them from their palanquins. They would also find upon every day in the week that they had afforded the gentlemen a splendid excuse for displaying

" the vain and ostentatious pomp of India." The gentlemen loved gay clothes, so now they arrayed themselves as peacocks. The gentlemen loved entertaining and feasting on a lavish scale, so now they endangered their health and emptied their pockets, more even than was usual with them. All in an attempt to convince these fair ones, with their complexions still unspoilt by the cruel Indian sun, that they had not come to a place of complete barbarity !

And now at last Clive had obtained his sick leave and was in their midst.

Dalton from his lonely post at Trichinopoly wondered why he did not hear from him. He wanted to know all about " the new-arrived angels " :

> " What can be the meaning I can never have the pleasure of a line from you ; you now & then favoured me with one when you had infinity of business on your hands & now you neglect me when you have no employ than gallivanting the ladies and jovially entertaining your friends. I hear that you keep one of the best houses in Madras—not in the least resembling our Bandipolem economy—however recollect at a leisure hour that you have a friend at Trichinopoly to whom the news of your health and welfare will always give infinite satisfaction & I'm sure you will write me." [76]

What was Clive doing ? Lawrence had once thanked him for his punctual correspondence—but he did so no longer. Repington told him that " from one of the best correspondents you are grown as lazy as can be."

Then rumours began to fly that explained much. His friends were congratulating him on his latest successes at Covelong and Chingleput. Lawrence had written, " I believe you know that no one can wish you more success than myself," and then when he heard of the success—" One and twenty guns and a dram extraordinary with three cheers ! " [77] But Dalton had added, more to the immediate point : " the swarthy world here had spread a report that you were on the point of committing matrimony, but Maskelyne has undeceived me in that particular. Pray, when do you think of going to Europe ? " [78]

Evidently Clive was taking his time. There was his health to consider. It did not improve, which, perhaps, under the circumstances, was not surprising ; Lawrence expressed concern at the continuance of his "fits." Clive had made up his mind to go home and was making his preparations.

The tone of Lawrence's letter breathed the warmest affection : " As I'm perswaded however distant we are from each other our friendship is unalterable I shall be always anxious for your well doing and the oftener I hear from you the more real satisfaction it will give to, dear Clive, your affectionate friend, S. Lawrence." [79]

The veteran would have liked nothing better than to be going home with his young friend, especially as his relations with Mr. Saunders were becoming more and more strained, but he knew that duty held him to his post.

Plans for returning home had to be made well in advance. The first enquiry was about sea captains. As Clive said, " 6 or 7 months agreeably spent depends upon the captain." He offered to pay 500 rupees for himself and servant. The next enquiry was about ways and means of transporting home one's fortune. As there were no banking facilities this was always a puzzle. Clive had 120,000 rupees awaiting transmission home if he could obtain a draft on the Company's funds. When he sailed he converted part of his wealth into diamonds, but left most of it in the hands of his attorneys, Messrs. Walsh, Vansittart and Maskelyne, and his agent, Mr. Levi Moses. The safety of all fortunes so left behind was apt to be precarious. [80]

There are deplorable gaps in Clive's life. We know nothing of his courtship of seventeen-year-old Margaret Maskelyne. We know for actual truth that she was a refined, beautiful, and cultured girl who was to be much loved by an ever-widening circle of friends. She came from an old Wiltshire family with fine traditions, several members of which had East Indian connections. Two of her aunts had married servants of the Company, one of them in the same church as she and Robert were to be married in. Her father was a clerk to the Duke of Newcastle in the Secretary of State's office. Two of her brothers became Fellows of Trinity College, Cambridge, and one of them, Nevil, went further and became Astronomer Royal and Fellow of the Royal Society. The third was Edmund, who remained Robert's closest friend through life.

It was a fitting moment in his life for Clive to get married, for this was his springtime, his moment of greatest happiness, while his success was still unmarred by any clouds. He was about to go home having completely shattered all the gloomy prognostications that his family had been making about his fate. " The booby has some sense in him after all "—what triumphant retort must have been on Bob's lips if he knew that his father had uttered such a remark ? Not only had he sense, but he was going to show the world how truly indebted a father could become to a son. Were there not mortgages on the old estate at Styche that were waiting to be lifted ? How pleasant for him to be the one who could lift them !

They were married on Sunday morning, February 18, 1753, in the little church within the walls of Fort St. George. The ceremony was performed by a Danish Protestant missionary, the Rev. John Philip Fabricius. And the happy bridegroom donated to Mr. Fabricius' mission " so great and undeserved a present whereby you have made us amazed and ashamed."

It is typical of him in this moment of his happiness. He had also shared his good fortune in the matter of his commissaryship with some of his friends.

The wedding made the utmost stir in the little colony, and the couple were showered with congratulations. His bachelor friends envied him sincerely :

" This is much better in my opinion than going home on Cook and I don't doubt that a series of health, long life and content will attend this prudent step, which you know my dear friend are the only things to be coveted. Add to this you have generously obliged a man who loves you, made a little family happy and are a gainer into the bargain. That every good may attend you whose heart is so much inclined to do good is and shall be the constant prayer of

James Repington.
" Palk adds a p.s. of good wishes." [81]

His old commander was more pleased than any of them. Clive had expressed his great indebtedness to him—" For God's sake why do you mention obligation to me, I never thought you under any, and the proof you have given me that I was not deceived in my opinion from the beginning affords me much satisfaction. May you have health to enjoy the future your merit has gained." [82]

A month after they were married, on March 23, 1753, they sailed for home on board the *Bombay Castle*, accompanied by Robert Orme, who decided to sail with them at the last moment.

II

It would be misleading to imply that nothing but the best of feeling for him prevailed throughout the settlement. The voices we have heard are the voices of his friends, whose letters were duly preserved by Orme. There were other voices, though we only know of them indirectly and have no real idea of what they were saying.

" I am not surprised," wrote Lawrence, " that envy has made a scratch at you. 'Tis no more than what you ought to expect after so much deserved good fortune, if you consider the world we live in which abounds with snarlers. However let them snarl on since they can't bite. You are right in making it a subject of mirth." [83]

Without a doubt one cause of the snarling was the extraordinary good luck that had brought him a fortune at the age of twenty-seven. £40,000 was a lot of money, several times greater than it would be to-day. The Governor and Council had already realized that the terms of the contract they had given him were far too generous and had consulted Lawrence about a change of system. But though his profits had been enormous they do not appear to have been irregular according to the ethics of that day, nor more excessive than those being made out of government contracts at home.

His friends rejoiced in his good luck, as some of them had every reason to do. " You have deserved your money, Clive," wrote Repington, " and every honest Englishman will think so ; besides I could prove that no man unless a soldier beloved by the country people and either in command himself or highly in favour with the commander can ever make half so much of the employ as you have done on the same terms."

There seems no reason for doubting the truth of this assertion. In his own eyes and in the eyes of his friends he always " deserved " his money. But the jealousy and enmity his good luck aroused was the inevitable price he had to pay for being so highly favoured. The real trouble was to come when he was in command himself and was favoured even more highly.

Mr. Saunders, too, seems to have become a little cool towards him and lacking in that enthusiasm over his success that he expected. When Clive handed in his resignation all he received in return was a formal acknowledgment.

Clive was annoyed. He wrote to Lawrence : " I think in justice to the military I cannot leave this coast without leaving a paper behind me representing the little notice taken of people of our profession. I hope the world will not accuse me of vanity or be of opinion that I think too highly of my own successes as I seldom or ever opened my lips upon the subject. All that I ever expected was a letter of thanks and that I am informed is usual upon such occasions."

He had another cause for annoyance. The Governor had sent for him and informed him that Muhammad Ali had made him a present of 40,000 rupees. But that was the last he heard of it before sailing, and he asked Lawrence to stand his friend in the matter. In view of Mr. Saunders's views about presents it would not be surprising if the Governor was reluctant to press the Nawab to make good his promise.

Chapter Nine

ENGLAND

" You will hear little news from England but of robberies "
HORACE WALPOLE

I

MILITARY GLORY of the kind that Clive had given it was something that the English nation in 1753 was not used to. Sporadic successes like Dettingen had been all it had known for a generation and more, ever since, in fact, the time of Marlborough, whom only the older generation could remember. Therefore the adulation that awaited Clive, while excessive, was understandable. The news of Arcot and Trichinopoly burst upon a nation that was not only extremely bored with itself but in a state of almost constant disgust with its rulers. It had no heroes. It had not even a public figure whom it could admire and respect. No patriotic sentiment attached to a court that was more Hanoverian than British in its interest and outlook. For a brief space, ten years before, the nation had tried to make a hero of the young Duke of Cumberland, three years Clive's senior, but close experience of his too-Germanic love of thoroughness in suppressing the '45 rebellion had changed that feeble love into hate and earned its object the nickname of " Billy the Butcher." Since that date the country had remained in a state of unrelieved gloom. The late war had not been glorious ; not even at sea, where the nation was accustomed to success, except upon one great occasion when Anson had met and destroyed a French fleet of nine ships of the line and eight Indiamen. (His victory, gained off Cape Finisterre in 1747, had more than anything else saved Fort St. David from suffering a like fate to Madras at Dupleix's hands.)

The political life of the country stagnated. A corrupt and subservient ministry was chiefly engaged in obtaining subsidies from an equally corrupt and subservient Parliament, and in order to pay for them sacrificing the country's armed forces. The Prime Minister, Henry Pelham, was a colourless, pedestrian

128

politician with not an achievement of note or worth to his name. His brother, the Duke of Newcastle, was adept only in the black arts of borough-mongering and corruption. And William Pitt—the Great Commoner to be—so far from having done anything as yet to justify his future reputation, had recently squandered whatever popularity he possessed by toadying to the Pelhams. The sessions of Parliament were humdrum in the extreme. When the public became excited, not having anything better to become excited over, it was concerning such matters as the reform of the calendar (which was quite enough to excite the gin-besotted mob—gin being the latest plague of London—to clamour for their " eleven lost days ") ; Lord Hardwicke's Marriage Act abolishing " Fleet marriages " ; and the naturalization of Jews. All these being admirable measures of reform, they excited the violent hostility characteristic of the period, and the last especially so. Outbursts of anti-semitism are rare in England, but when we read that the popular slogan of the day was " No Jews : Christianity and the Constitution," and that " a man of dark complexion is scarce safe in the streets," it brings to mind current happenings in another country.

All of which helps to explain the exaggerated praise that was bestowed on Clive's achievements. His father had not been slow about exploiting the news to his own and his son's advantage. Forsaking the moss-covered and mortgage-bound walls of Styche he had transported his large family to London, where he had taken a large and expensive house in St. Swithin's Lane. From this convenient vantage-point he bustled about town making the acquaintance of everybody in any way connected with India. One day he dined with ex-Governor Floyer, another he waited upon Directors of the Company, and every day kept his ear well down to the ground. Never has father basked more comfortably in the reflected glory of a son or set himself more determinedly to further a son's interests. That he was also piling up debts for himself at a rapid rate must have worried him not at all. Did he not have a dutiful son who had acquired a fortune ?

He was, indeed, most anxious that his son should make all the hay possible while the sun still shone, and therefore advised him not to be in too much of a hurry to return home. But the son did not receive the letter, as he was already on the way. Nor did he receive his mother's, in which, true to maternal instinct, she told him that she waited only to welcome him as soon as possible.

I

The son did not disappoint the father's expectations. October 14 saw the *Pelham*, to which he, Margaret, and Orme had transferred at the Cape, come to anchor in the Thames after a propitious voyage. And Robert arrived, saw, and gave—gave, indeed, a much larger part of his fortune than he could comfortably afford. From now on his family had few worries, except those caused by Richard Clive's own follies and mistakes, and even from these the son could rescue it. The mortgages which lay so heavily on the family estate began one by one to be lifted.

Clive took a house in Queen's Square near St. James's Park. The difference in location marked a discernible difference in outlook between father and son. The father still looked towards the City and India House. The son at once cast his eyes westwards, towards the world of fashion, wealth and power that had grown up under the shadow of the halls of Westminster and the Court of St. James. It was a true instinct that made him do so, besides a natural desire to share in the superior delights that this world had to offer to a young man in his happy position. The centre of gravity of Britain's connection with India had already begun to move westwards, from the city of merchants to Westminster, the city of politicians. Clive was to keep abreast of the change. He was, indeed, to be the chief factor in causing it, both by his achievements and by his set purpose.

The directors in Leadenhall Street had already written to Mr. Saunders expressing " the great regard they had for the merit of Captain Clive, to whose courage and conduct the late turn in our affairs has been mainly due." They had, also, according to his father, toasted him at a public banquet as " General Clive." And now when he went to pay his respects they received him with unusual graciousness. They were not accustomed to their servants performing feats of arms and they were quite dazzled. If, for the moment, they overlooked Lawrence—glaringly, so it would seem—it was, after all, only natural. He was not a Company man, but a professional soldier. So it was easy for Clive to establish a quite novel influence over them.

What kind of impression he made on others of his countrymen, and particularly on the officers of the army, is another matter. It comes as no surprise to find his enemies in later years asserting that he made none at all : " they envied him for his good luck but could not admire him for his knowledge of the military art " ; and quoting Charles Townshend as saying :

" The fellow was right to transplant himself, he could not thrive in his native soil." For one can well imagine that he experienced more difficulty in conquering the world of fashion and affairs than he had the less sophisticated Court of Directors. With his ungraceful manner and possibly ungracious manners London society was not likely to take him to its cold and critical heart.

The Company voted to present him with a sword set with diamonds to the value of £500. At the end of May the sword was presented to Clive at a special meeting of the Court. By Clive's insistence there was to be a sword also for Lawrence of £700 value. Clive wrote to his friend :

" Dear Major,—I could not let any more ships sail for India without writing. I have taken the Opportunity of Mr. Orme's return to make him the Bearer.

" I deliver'd Your Letters safe to the Secretary, & your two Runts in good Health to My Lady Delves she returns you many thanks & is vastly pleas'd with them, at the same time wishes for the Sake of the Breed they had not been both of the Female kind. You know her Ladyship is a Quicksighted woman in these Cases.

" It is natural to imagine that many Questions would be ask'd about the Indies and especially of the Dispute between You and Mr. Sanders, I gave my Opinion with sincerity & I must do many of the Directors, especially the principal, justice to say that they spoke highly in Your favour at the same time that they express'd their Concern least something prejudicial [result] to their Affairs through your Disagreement. I assured them to the Contrary & that your Zeal for the Publick would not suffer Animosities to interfere with their Interest.

" I must refer you to Orme who is a Master of the Subject for an Acct of what is carrying on in England, I·sincerely wish Peace may be the thing at last, the Directors have and are still, [illegible in original] all ways and Means to make everything as agreable to You as possible, they have always express'd the highest Sense of Your Services and Mine & as I am inform'd are going to make You a Present of a Sword set with Diomonds of L700 Value & me another of L500.

" I give You Joy of the Mutiny & Desertion Bill which will be most certainly past, & made perpetual it is the best thing that has happen'd for the Company these many years, our Goven'ors will now be no longer afraid of the Consequences of signing a Death Warrant when it [is] for the Publick Good.

" The Compy have made me some advantagious Offers in a Civil Way. I am sorry my Health will not permit me to accept them however I hope the next Year the same Opportunity will offer again & that I shall have the Pleasure of seeing You and my Friends a second time in India—Mr. Pigot who is appointed Mr. Saunders' Successor I am sure will make India more agreable to You than it has hitherto been & I have/enjoy great Pleasure in the thoughts of spending a few more Years there in Harmony & Peace my best Wishes attend Messrs. Paulk Rippington & all my Brother Officers &

    " I am Dear Major

        " Your Affect Friend & hum l Serv

                " ROBERT CLIVE."

This letter is a good example of Clive's flagrant disregard for such elegances as spelling, grammar, and punctuation. Not until he attained to the services of a secretary did his letters acquire any grace or reveal any power of self-expression.

Meanwhile Clive had been busy in other directions. His health had continued troublesome. He had written his brother-in-law Edmund on March 3, " Your sister will be brought to bed in two or three days, & then I shall make a trip to Bath for the recovery of my health." It was characteristic of him through life to rate the state of his own health as of equal importance with the birth and death of his children !—even the birth now of his firstborn. And it was also characteristic of him that no domestic concerns ever prevented him from taking full advantage of every opportunity to make influential friends.

For, indeed, his ascent of the ladder of success was made with a clear head and a sure purpose. He had a good sense of the relation of things—wealth, interest, fame, influential friends, publicity, opportunity—and knew that not by one of them alone would his ambitions be gained ; all were needed to supplement his abilities.

His return home may have been necessary for reasons of health, but it was also well judged. By staying in India he might have won fresh laurels, but laurels, after all, like medals and diplomas, are valueless in themselves. It was correct strategy for him to come home to convert them into the gold of promotion while their exchange value was high, and it was not long before he realized the wisdom of his act.

The ease with which his friend Orme obtained preferment pointed the way for himself. " I find *by experience*," wrote Clive to a friend, " that a man is not the farther from preferment by paying a visit to his native country." [1] He blamed it on his health that he himself was not able to accept the offers that had been made him. On the other hand, it is possible that the offers had not been tempting enough. In an undated and almost illegible letter to Walsh he said, " Want of ambition etc. hath never been charged to me," adding significantly : " If I could have got the Govt. of Madras I do assure you I would have set out the last year from death's door." [84] And we may accept the assurance. His health might frequently be bad, but it was not yet bad enough to interfere seriously with his career. Mind was master over body, and his recoveries were rapid whenever the call to action sounded. Not until the gloomy last chapter of his life did his mind succumb and lose its mastery.

So now, much as he valued his interest with the Court of Directors, he cultivated the favour of politicians with even greater assiduity. If such worthies as Henry Fox and the Earl of Sandwich proffered their friendship, who was he to rebuff them ? It was not for an aspiring young man to be too particular. Not even in respect to a man like Sandwich, of whom it has been said : " Nothing substantially impaired him in the estimation of his countrymen, because no possible revelation could make them think worse of him than they thought already."

> Too infamous to have a friend ;
> Too bad for bad men to commend,
> Or good to name. . . .

Not all who showed him favour were as disreputable as these two. Among others were Lord Hardwicke, the Lord Chancellor, the Archbishop of Canterbury, Lord Holdernesse, Lord Barrington, and Mr. Murray, shortly to become, as Lord Mansfield, the Lord Chief Justice.

---

[1] Clive was aware that Orme's appointment would " be disagreable to every one under him. It is very natural, yet you will allow that Dear Self gets the better of every other consideration. Make this case your own—would not you and every one else gladly have ascended the ladder by the like means ? "

II

Clive was in one respect unfortunate in being born at the time he was. Though it gave scope for achievement, it did not give equal scope for the development of high moral character. First there had been his schooling and then there had been India, and whatever may have been his school influences, it certainly cannot be said that the India of the 1740's and 50's was designed for the moral improvement of youth. The picture it presented was composed largely of greed and no thrift, vulgar display and little culture, luxury and low social standards, self-seeking and few opportunities for disinterested public service, incessant strife and few inconvenient scruples, much cruelty and little moral sensitiveness, bloodshed and comparative indifference, too much leisure and too little chance for an elevated use of it. And now, to top these influences, he was subjected for eighteen months to close contact with the upper crust of English society during the worst period in its history, a period famous for the low tone of its public life.

Such paradoxes as paragons in politics, which have occurred at other times, were distinctly not in evidence in the age of the robber baron brought back to life in a new incarnation. If there were men in politics who stood for anything higher than self-enrichment, they were careful for the most part to withhold the fact from their fellows. Morals were something to be practised, if practised at all—which was only occasionally—in the privacy of the home ; to parade them in public was the height of bad taste and the surest road to the political wilderness. Men made fortunes out of politics with as much ease and readiness as they were to make them out of the public domain and natural resources of the United States of America in the following century, and with as few contemporary stigmas. The last failing that could be attributed to the English nobility was any sort of squeamishness in such matters. In fact, never was a set of men more generous at the public expense than the small set of aristocratic gentlemen who ruled England in the 1740's, 50's, and 60's. They were nearly as prodigal in their benefactions to their friends and hangers-on as they were to themselves.

Politics was in every way a much simpler profession than it has since become. The only important qualification to enter it was birth, and the higher the birth the fewer the requisite brains—

which was why the Prime Minister was usually a duke or at least a marquis. Men who tried to enter it on the strength of brains alone could never hope to overcome that original handicap, no matter how hard they might try. Given birth, nothing more was required of the members than dexterity in dividing the loaves and fishes of the State among a rapacious and clamorous multitude. If you had birth but had unfortunately ruined your fortune, the profession gave you the easiest and readiest means of repairing your mistake at practically no expense of time or labour.

It was a robber age in a double sense. The return of peace in 1748 had relieved the country's statesmen of the necessity of supporting a large army and navy out of public funds that could be put to much better use. Out of the disbandment of the fighting forces had come a crime wave. The men who had lately been defending their country continued, for want of any better means of support, to live illicitly at the expense of their countrymen. They were, indeed, making the streets quite as unsafe for them as they had previously made the seas unsafe for the French. The Foxes of that age had their holes in the public treasury, but the sons of ordinary sinful man had nowhere to lay their miserable heads but in the noose of the public gallows. It was a matter of constant lament how ineffective was the bloody remedy of the penal laws. It was also a matter of constant lament by the Foxes how hard they had to strive to fill their wants. "There is no living in this country," declared Horace Walpole, "under twenty thousand a year—not that that suffices; but it entitles one to ask a pension for two or three lives." When Walpole wrote to a friend, "You will hear little news from England but of robberies," he was, of course, referring to the unprivileged members of society, not to himself and his exalted friends. Only an impious age like the present would dare to make such an offensive identification of terms.

There was, of course, a distinction between the two sets of robbers. The one robbed for bread. The other elevated the practice of robbery into an occupation worthy of their rank, one to which wealthy but always avaricious gentlemen could devote their lives and their ambitions. It has been said of Henry Fox that "intent upon heaping up a colossal fortune, he tamely consented to abandon everything which makes ambition honourable and self-seeking respectable." When war came again the members of one set, if their life had in the meantime been spared to them by a grateful country, would return to the job of defending that country and expanding its empire, while the members of the other would joyfully seize the opportunity to make fortunes that would make their earlier achievements beggarly by comparison.

Clive being a soldier as well as the heir of Styche Hall knew both sets, and if he hobnobbed with one and sought its favour, it is at least within the bounds of possibility that he recognized, though perhaps as a gentleman never admitting the knowledge even to himself, that the other conferred more real and lasting benefits on their country. It is possible, too, that he was aware of the fact that the British Empire was won by the blood and sweat of men who were left to starve when their services happened not to be required. For if Clive was not born a soldier, happily for himself and for England he was not born an aristocrat either, but only the son of a poor country squire, and happily for himself and for England he became a soldier with something of a soldier's sense of duty and of honour. And though, in the eyes of severe critics, he was to dishonour himself as a soldier, his dishonour was to be a thing of shining whiteness compared to what passed for honour among most of those who had been born to higher things—born, that is, to wealth, power, and privilege. The chief difference between men like Fox and Sandwich and Robert Clive was not in the abundance of the things they possessed or the way in which they used the wealth, of which all three acquired far more than their rightful share, but a difference between infamy and true fame. For while *they* diminished the national wealth by consuming it themselves, *he* was enormously to increase it.

III

Not the least, therefore, of Clive's achievements was the way in which he managed to resist the worst effects of the many varied demoralizing influences to which all his life he was to be subjected. Just for a short time now it was to look as though the English aristocratic influence might be about to secure him as a victim. "If I had a son," declared one member of Parliament, "I would say to him, 'Get into Parliament. Make tiresome speeches. Do not accept the first offer ; but wait till you can make great provision for yourself and your family ; and then call yourself an independent country gentleman.'" These were undoubtedly

Clive's own ultimate ambitions. And his father may well have given him this same advice. Or if not his father, the Earl of Sandwich. Clive at least seems to have listened to advice not unlike it. And if he looked into the possibilities that Parliament held he must soon have found that it was not always necessary to make " tiresome speeches " (in the plural) or to refuse the first offer. One speech, if sufficiently tiresome, was sometimes enough. For his one speech, so tiresomely brilliant that he was ever afterwards known as " Single-Speech," a man named Hamilton had been rewarded with the Chancellorship of the Irish Exchequer, no mean plum ; in fact, every sentence of that speech had become worth to him a quarter's salary. An alluring prospect, surely, to one whose fortune, fair as it was, was by no means adequate to support himself and his two families—his parents' and his own—in the style to which he wanted them to become accustomed !

In the general election of April 1754, which followed upon the death of the Prime Minister, Henry Pelham, and the succession to power of his brother the Duke of Newcastle, Clive allowed the Earl of Sandwich to become his patron and to put him forward as a candidate for the pocket-borough of St. Michael in Cornwall.

Happily for him and his country the Duke of Newcastle had other ideas about the representation of this borough. He put up an opposing candidate. Clive and the other Sandwich candidate were returned victorious in the poll with thirty votes against twenty-five for the Newcastleites, but eighteenth-century Prime Ministers had ways of getting around such difficulties as this. As soon as Parliament met, petitions were lodged against the new members. Now to buy a seat in Parliament was expensive enough, but to fight a contested election was to take a straight road to ruin, and Clive was soon well started on it. There were intrigues within intrigues, moves within moves, in this game of aristocratic politics ; what at first seemed merely a minor affair of rival politicians engaged in borough-mongering developed into a hot contest between Newcastle and Fox, Clive's other and more influential ally, for control of the House of Commons.

All through the winter of the following year the factions wrestled and manœuvred—and Clive's fortune dwindled. Members talked about the merits of the case, but voted in the customary way according to partisan interest. At last, on

March 12, the Committee that had been appointed to decide the case decided that Robert Clive was duly elected a burgess. Twelve days later the House itself decided that he was not ! The inconspicuous Tories had realized that they held the balance of power between the two contending Whig factions and, overjoyed at this rare opportunity to make their presence felt, had voted solidly for Newcastle against Fox.

It may or may not have been a narrow escape for Clive. It is difficult somehow to see him succumbing at this early stage of his career to the distressing fate that threatened him. For the moment it must have tickled his fancy and his ego to think of himself as a member of this exalted body, but he certainly was hunting bigger game than this. Parliament for him could have been but a means, not an end, and not a means, surely, just to inglorious and wealthy oblivion.

" My seat in Parliament," he wrote to Walsh, " hath caused me infinite trouble and is likely to cause me much more, and till that be decided India must not be thought of. This perhaps may appear strange to you, but there are connections concerning that affair which cannot be set aside, the reasons are too long to trouble you with."

Whatever those " connections " were, he did set them aside. Before the contest was decided he had already taken a step that effectually debarred him from taking his seat even should it be awarded to him. It came as a great surprise to Lord Sandwich one day to learn that his protégé was to receive a Lieutenant-Colonel's Commission from the king, and he lost no time in writing to acquaint him of the fact that the instant the king signed the commission his seat would be vacant ! But his indignant protest did not make Clive change his mind. The breath of Indian ambition was once more in his nostrils and it was overpoweringly strong.

We need not enquire too minutely how he obtained such rapid promotion. It could not have been by merit alone, however great we may judge that merit to have been. " Of the ' two golden rules ' which governed the services, ' interest and seniority,' the former was infinitely the more important."[85] He had no seniority, but by dint of his father's, his own, and the Directors' efforts he did have interest.

Chapter Ten

DUAL CAPACITY

" Want of ambition, etc., hath never been charged to me "
CLIVE

I

CLIVE LEFT ENGLAND in a great hurry. The day after the House of Commons expelled him he signed his agreement to re-enter the Company's service. Five days later he was actually setting out from London. His commission from the Crown, not yet signed, had to be sent after him along the road. He and Margaret boarded the *Stretham* on April 5 and sailed eighteen days later.

If Robert's affairs required only a day to settle, what of Margaret's ? Little Edward, her first-born, was just a year old, and her second child, another boy, had been born to her only a few weeks before. She had to leave both of them behind. The baby was ailing, and the first news she received upon reaching Bombay was that he was dead.

All her married life she was to know what it meant to be the wife of " the conqueror of India." First this experience when she accompanied her husband, then the different one, when he went out again, of having to stay behind because of another pregnancy, and then, after being separated from him for three years and losing her child, the experience of having to care for a returned husband sick both in body and mind. If we chart their married life and reckon the periods during which it may have been normal, the result can more accurately be stated in months than in years. If Clive was not a hypochondriac, he was never free from worry about his health. His rushing off to Bath immediately after her first delivery was a typical incident. During the last seven years of his life when they were at last together this major concern became a routine part of their existence. And when he was not preoccupied with the state of his health he was preoccupied with affairs of state. Even now when

139

she sacrificed her little family to stay by his side the sacrifice was in vain for much of the time. She could not accompany him to fight the pirates of Gheria nor to recapture Calcutta. When he left for Bengal she had to remain at Madras and wait for him to send for her.

It would be merely employing conventional terms to speak of such a marriage as being "happy." But Margaret Clive did her duty with a rare devotedness and loyalty. There is not a hint that she ever regretted her choice, not a suggestion that she did not do everything that a wife could do for a husband; and in addition she maintained a happy life of her own filled with friends who loved her, and left behind her when she died, many years after her husband, a fragrant memory of wit, charm, and goodness.

II

There was talk of war on every side as they left, and preparations were going on apace in the dockyards and munition factories of England and France. Braddock had sailed for America at Christmas. The French were preparing an expedition of their own. The same month as the Clives sailed for India Boscawen also sailed with a fleet to intercept the French on their way to America, and George II departed for Hanover, the part of his dominions that he valued the most. All over Europe men were making ready for war. And England, while she would have to wait three years for her Pitt to take the helm and steer her to victory, was beginning to awake from the long sleep of apathy and inertia to which Walpole had lulled her and gird herself again for imperial endeavour.

Clive had, in common with all other Englishmen in India, become the sworn enemy of the French. The responsibility for producing this enmity lay principally with Dupleix. His breach of faith at Madras and his firm resolve to expel the English from India were bitter memories. The days when the officers of the contending armies exchanged pleasant courtesies before the walls of Trichinopoly and tried to do each other as little harm as possible were past. The imperceptibly advancing shadow of State control over the East India Company was also having its effect in giving all the Company's activities an increased political tinge. No longer was it conceivable that the Company might remain neutral when the State was at war.

Clive's mission, therefore, was a mission of war, a mission to destroy French power. For whereas Dupleix was gone, Bussy remained. French power had been broken in the Carnatic, but was growing steadily at Hyderabad. The services that Bussy had rendered to the Nizam in his wars with the Marathas had been rewarded with huge grants of territory along the eastern coast. With Masulipatam and the Northern Sircars the French were masters of 450 miles of seacoast stretching all the way from the river Kistna to Orissa on the border of Bengal.

Clive told the Court of Directors that " so long as there was one Frenchman in arms in the Deccan or in India, there could be no peace. For his own part he desired nothing better than to dispute the mastery of the Deccan with M. Bussy." To ministers and the Court he had outlined a scheme of operations : to attack the French not from Madras but from Bombay, which was much nearer, and to do so in alliance with the Marathas, whose territory stretched from the coast opposite Bombay to the Nizam's border.

The Company had appointed him senior of Council at Fort St. George and Governor of Fort St. David, but when ministers approved Clive's plan and gave him a royal commission, it was agreed that he should land at Bombay and carry out his expedition before proceeding to the Carnatic. He was not to be in command, however. The Duke of Cumberland had interfered and insisted that the command should go to a court favourite, Colonel Scott, who had been sent out the previous year. It was the Directors' hope, as it must have been Clive's, that something would happen to Colonel Scott before he arrived.

On April 23 the *Stretham* sailed in company with other ships bearing the expedition. The voyage was uneventful. At the end of October the *Stretham* and her companions came to anchor in Bombay harbour, alongside Vice-Admiral Charles Watson's squadron, which had come out the previous year with His Majesty's 39th Foot Regiment under the command of Colonel Adlercron, this being the first appearance of Royal troops in India.

Clive's hopes were at once dashed. He found the Bombay gentlemen not in the least inclined towards war. In fact, all their talk was of peace. Mr. Saunders and M. Godeheu had in the previous December concluded a truce for the Carnatic, and Mr. Bourchier and his Council first wanted to know whether it would be confirmed at home and extended into a general peace for India before undertaking any military operation against the French nation. They were especially averse to any operation that would involve them with the Marathas if there was a chance of the whole business suddenly being called off; for good relations with their immediate neighbours were more important to them than the expulsion of Bussy.

So the expedition was called off—or at least postponed until further word from England; which was all the more disappointing to Clive because, as it happened, Colonel Scott *had* died while he was on his way out, and he would consequently have been in command of the expedition himself.

He and Admiral Watson were thus left kicking their heels in Bombay. The invitation, therefore, that came to them from the Bombay gentlemen was all the more welcome. The Bombay gentlemen wanted to know if they would care to undertake a matter of private business for them and the Company.

What was the business? Well, there was a nest of pirates down the Coast that had bothered them for years. The Company's marine force had the previous year destroyed one of their nests, but this other one at Gheria was quite a stronghold. Talaji Angria was the pirate chief. His boats infested the west coast of India and frequently captured vessels belonging to the Company. Mr. Watson and Mr. Clive would be doing the Company a real service if they put an end to this nuisance, and, of course, there might be a rich haul of prize-money for the lucky conquerors.

The invitation thus put was naturally attractive to both officers, and they accepted it with alacrity. They had a little preliminary difficulty settling the division between them of the prospective prize-money, as Watson, who was a stickler for the rights of the senior service and the claims of superior rank, denied Clive's claim to share equally with Rear-Admiral Pocock, the second in command; but they managed to reach a compromise. Clive was impressed with the importance of loyal co-operation between the services and was doing his best to preserve harmony. "It has been my good fortune hitherto to agree with all parties, and I am sure it will be so during this expedition."

This matter of co-operation was, indeed, of the utmost importance. More military operations have been ruined by jealousy than by the enemy. The quarrel between Dupleix and Labourdonnais was soon to be repeated in India by Lally and Bussy and in Canada by Vaudreuil and Montcalm. The personal jealousies and antipathies of her commanders may almost be said to have cost France her empire. The English managed to avoid these extremes, and the relations that Clive and Watson established now, while not perfect, were notable for their excellence. Serious occasions for difference were to arise, but they were to be overcome in a way that did equal credit to both men.

The expedition sailed on February 7 and arrived off Gheria four days later. There the operation proved as easy and profitable as any commanders could have wished. In fact, the chief problem of Watson and Clive was to prevent the Marathas, who assisted on shore, from being beforehand in looting the nest of its rich stores of honey ! The Maratha leaders tried all their cunning to get into the fort first. They wanted the Admiral to postpone his attack until they had arranged for the pirates' surrender. When the pirates refused to surrender Watson took his squadron in among the rocks and poured broadside after broadside into the fort, silencing its ineffective fire within a few hours. While this was going on Clive landed his men and prudently interposed them between the fort and the Marathas, so that when the pirates were ready to capitulate he should have the honour and profit of entering the place ; and when the fort was taken the mortified Marathas were still warned off at the point of the musket.

With a loss of only twenty men the expedition collected booty worth £150,000, which was divided up in accordance with the arrangement made at the previous council-of-war. The East India Company, not having been directly represented at the council, got none of it !

Clive was now impatient to proceed to Madras. The squadron was leaving for there in four days, so Clive obtained permission to go with it, there being no immediate prospect of any expedition against Bussy. He had had, too, a quarrel with Mr. Bourchier over a court-martial, which increased his eagerness to be on his way. Accordingly, he sailed with Watson on April 27, reaching Madras on May 25.

There he greeted old friends : Pigot, who was now Governor, Lawrence, who had also been promoted to Lieut.-Colonel, but who was now in poor health (it was a marvel that he had survived at all), and Orme ; he took his seat as senior member of Council, and heard about the treaty with the French. He found that it was likely to prove nothing more than a truce, as Mr. Pigot was bickering warmly with M. Duval de Leyrit, the new Governor of Pondichéry, over certain districts that each claimed, and he himself knew how near the two countries were to war in Europe. The Council eagerly discussed again the prospect of ousting M. Bussy from Hyderabad.

Clive's new post, however, was not at Madras but at Fort St. David, and June 22 found him there ready to take up his duties as its governor.

III

Let us consider this elevation to the governorship of a fort whither only ten years before, when still a " writer," Clive had come as a refugee from Madras. He was now in his thirty-first year, and it was not yet fourteen years since he had been admitted into the Company's service. Such promotion was rapid. Mr. Pigot was thirty-six and had spent eighteen years in the service when he became Governor of Madras the preceding year. Yet Clive, so far from being satisfied with his rapid promotion, had aspired to be Governor of Madras himself ! Had aspired, that is, to the highest post in the service before he was thirty !

He had not got it, but he had got a very fine consolation prize. As Governor of Fort St. David he was first in line to succeed Mr. Pigot.

Certainly both he and Orme could congratulate themselves on their wisdom in going home as they had done. Early plums of promotion have to be plucked ; to wait on seniority is the way of fools. Nor had it been difficult for them to gain what they wanted. It was no great feat to convince the Court of Directors that Clive was a military expert worthy to rank equal with Stringer Lawrence. The good city fathers could scarcely tell one end of a musket from the other ! That is why Orme's last-minute decision to return home with him must have proven singularly fortunate. He could leave Orme to do the talking while remaining himself a picture of the modest hero. But of course Orme was pushing his own interests as well. They were, in fact, rivals for the Governorship. And it was that rivalry that now made Orme not a wholly loyal friend.

If he had been, how could he have included Clive's name among those about whom he was now writing his confidential, and none too complimentary, reports to the Chairman of the

Company ? How could he write to Mr. Payne, as he was to do when Clive in Bengal refused to heed the orders for his return ; " The prevalence of Clive's genius is, by what I have observed of it, to be fighting; that he is not averse to advantages is certain, and if both these prospects have united I am no longer surprised that he has lost his reason on this occasion " ? [86] The characterization may have been true, but it was not the act of a friend.

What, one wonders, did the gentlemen who had stayed behind at their posts think when the new Deputy-Governor and Lieut.-Colonel arrived ?

The situation was nicely calculated to irritate a good many people. It gave Clive a rank equal to Lawrence's, though a year junior. Lawrence's name was already greatly revered in the army, and as he continued his faithful, arduous service against the mounting handicap of years and ill-health, so did the respect and admiration for him grow. And so also did the apparent discrepancy between the honour and fame that came to him and that which followed, as though drawn by a magnet, his former subordinate. The ill-feeling so created may not have been justified, but it was none the less a potent factor in determining the kind of atmosphere that increasingly surrounded Clive on his upward path.

A little of it already seems to have been present. When Orme reached Madras he found two letters waiting for him from Captain Henry Speke of the *Kent*, Admiral Watson's flagship, which had just called there. They shed further curious light on Orme's loyalty to his friend. In the first the Captain wrote : " I have heard a great deal about the Hero (who will lose his election) which I will show you when we meet to make you laugh. I think you need not entertain any fear of his rivalship. His reputation dwindles very fast." And in the second, " Will there be no envy attending the Hero who saved the Capitol ? Will his folly be deemed Humour and his Ribaldry wit ? " [87]

If this is at all a fair specimen of the sort of opinion entertained of Clive *before* his arrival with his two appointments, what must it have become *after* ?

We are in considerable doubt about Clive's general standing and reputation at this time. The evidence is all too slender and none of it conclusive. He may equally well have been the popular hero of the Company's service or the unpopular favourite of the Directors. There is absolutely nothing that enables us to

K

establish either possibility. Lawrence had defended him earlier against the jealousy of unsuccessful rivals, but we cannot be certain that he did not change his sentiments later. If he continued to write him affectionate letters, they have not survived. And even if his liking for Clive continued undiminished it would prove nothing of itself, as the love that he bore Clive was the love of a father for a son and may have been entirely without discernment. We know too that Lawrence was vain and susceptible to flattery. The testimony of Clive's enemies must, of course, be even more suspect. They would have us believe the worst about the way in which he gained his promotion and the impression it created in the minds of his associates.

There is one man that might have told us the truth. That is Thomas Saunders. It is most unfortunate that none of his private letters has survived, because he seems to have been the kind of man that has exceptionally keen insight into human character. His known characteristics, a man of few words, cold, unenthusiastic, unresponsive, of complete integrity, austere in his sense of duty as in his relations with his subordinates, clear-sighted and full of common sense, suggest great penetration into the hearts of men and situations. One would give a lot to know what such a man really thought of Clive. Yet the clues to his thought are very faint, even if they do point one way. His attitude about the present offered Clive at Arcot and his apparent reluctance to proceed in the matter of Muhammad Ali's present suggest that he saw in Clive an over-eagerness to make money by what he considered illicit means. With his strong sense of duty he may also not have approved of Clive's haste in returning home in 1753. His acceptance of his resignation had been distinctly chilly. In January of that year he had mentioned in council that he had offered Clive " A Major's brevet to a glorious purpose would his health have permitted him to accept it." What would Saunders have said if he had known that later Clive had written from England, " If I could have got the Government of Madras I do assure you I would have set out the last year from death's door ? " Might not he have said, " Here is a man who was too ill for service in India as a mere major (though not too ill to gallivant with the ladies and get married !), yet would have left his death-bed to have taken *my* place as governor ? " Perhaps Saunders did know of this discrepancy in Clive's conduct, but his cryptic comment on Clive's dual appointment tells us nothing of how he felt : " It is said Captain Clive is gone abroad both in a military and civil capacity. The former is particularly his genius and what he may again reassume or by your orders. One of the superior Council should be with the Deputy-Governor at Fort St. David. . . ." [88]—nothing, that is, except that Clive needed guidance in the matter of civil business, a fact that need arouse no surprise.

We are thus left in the tantalizing state of complete uncertainty. Nevertheless, if we take a long view forwards and then one backwards we can see that we have reached a kind of watershed in Clive's life. The streams that we have been following have flowed in one direction : towards fame honourably and worthily gained in the service of the Company. As Lawrence said, he had deserved his good fortune and success ; as Repington said, he had earned his money. But now the streams begin to diverge and flow in different directions. They are broader streams as national affairs mingle with them, and the farther Clive advances along them the more turbid they become. They carry him to greater power and importance, but they take him away from the old safe reaches of the Company's service and his popularity among his old associates suffers as a result. He no longer needs Saunders and Lawrence to help him along the new way. Soon he will not need even the Directors. If he needs anybody it will be peers of the realm and prominent politicians. With their aid he can go almost as far as he wants, but he will have to pay the price. His old associates cannot be altogether blamed if they see him as an ambitious young man who is using the Company's service as a means to advance his own personal and separate interests.

They would, of course, be unjust if they denied his sense of duty which blends insensibly with soaring ambition. There will be moments when he is an Englishman working for the aggrandizement of his country in the true Machiavellian tradition, other moments when he will appear as a self-seeking adventurer turning success to his own advantage ; but for the rest of the time he appears as a man performing his duty to his employers with zeal and ability. For Clive was a far more complex character than he has generally been regarded.

Dupleix had given this ambitious young man his first opportunity—with this result : Deputy-Governor and Lieutenant-Colonel. Siraj-ud-daula, Nawab of Bengal, was now to give him his second—with results far more startling.

Chapter Eleven

THE BENGAL EXPEDITION : (1) CALCUTTA

"I go with great forces and great authority"

CLIVE

I

THE BENGAL EXPEDITION was Clive's introduction into a bigger, harder world than he had yet known. It gave him the supreme test of all his abilities. And it is from that December day of 1756 when he landed in Bengal that we really begin to gain a clear light on his character and the working of his mind.[89]

All his latent powers, latent traits of character were about to be called into play. It was his first genuinely independent command, when he not only had to decide tactical problems of warfare but the infinitely more difficult problems of political strategy. As military tactician he had to cope with entirely new geographical conditions. The physical difference between the Carnatic and Gangetic delta country of Bengal is as great as that between the western plains of the United States and the bayous of Louisiana. In the Carnatic he had been able to make his swift, thrilling dashes across the country, covering sometimes twenty miles in a day, with only hard ground under his feet, not even troubled by the rivers he had to cross, because in the dry season of campaigning they were either dry or easily forded. But now he was to find the physical conditions the chief of his enemies. How well was he to meet them ?

Furthermore, in the Carnatic he had acted under orders. If there had been conflict of authority between Saunders and Lawrence, representing the civil and military powers, it had scarcely concerned him as the subordinate of both. Now he was to be one of the principals in a conflict of authority of much greater complexity and extreme delicacy. He had to deal on the one hand with the royal authority vested in Admiral Watson, who was supreme over the King's ships, officers, and men, and on the other with the local civil authority of the Governor and

Council of Fort William.   He had to contend with the inevitable rivalries and jealousies of two distinct services, the King's and the Company's, and of two independent governments, Madras and Calcutta, each regardful of its own needs, dignity, and interests.

Some of the decisions he had to make were to be of the utmost difficulty—whether to make war or peace with the Nawab of Bengal, whether to make war or peace with the French, whether to obey orders from Madras and return with his forces or stay in Bengal.   He had to think not merely in terms of the local interests of Madras or Calcutta but of the interests of the East India Company as a whole.   Hitherto each settlement had managed its own affairs under direct orders from home.   Now for the first time the representative of one of them was placed in a position where he could in large measure control the destinies of all. Upon his decisions now would depend whether the course that the English merchants had hitherto followed in India was to change or remain the same.

The man who undertook these onerous responsibilities went in apparent complete unawareness of what was in store for him. He was in high spirits, as he must have been when he set out over the plains for Arcot.   For him it was merely another grand and unlooked-for opportunity to win fame and fortune. " This expedition," he wrote his father, " if attended with success may enable me to do great things.   It is by far the greatest of my undertakings.   I go with great forces and great authority."   He hoped by means of it, also, to recoup some personal financial losses.

He was still a youth when he left Madras filled with youthful ardour and ambitions, eager for adventure, and free of cares.   A great change was swiftly to overtake him.

In the middle of August 1756 when Clive was at Fort St. David attending to his governorship and the gentlemen at Madras were discussing ways and means of expelling Bussy from the secure place he had made for himself at the Nizam's Court at Hyderabad, with all the power and territory it had given the French in the Deccan, an urgent summons came to Clive to go to Madras.   Word had just reached there that Calcutta had been taken by the Nawab of Bengal, Siraj-ud-daula.

II

" The Europeans," said the old Nawab of Bengal, Aliverdi Khan, " are like a hive of bees, of whose honey you may reap the benefit but if you disturb their hive they will sting you to death."

Aliverdi Khan was wise among rulers of his generation. He feared the European merchants who had settled with such an air of permanence in his dominions, and he was cautious in his dealings with them. During his long reign he had left them in peace, though never at liberty to do as they pleased. Mutual respect and fear as well as a sense of sound business interest had held both in equal restraint. As he approached his death-bed he became increasingly apprehensive, however. Wise and able ruler as he was, he had made a mistake he could not now undo. He had raised up an heir who was utterly unfit to succeed him.

That heir, Siraj-ud-daula, his grandson, had all the vices of all the spoiled favourites of history. Although scarcely out of his teens, early and prolonged debauchery had disordered his nerves and intellect, rendering him a despicable creature hated by all his future subjects.

Aliverdi Khan saw only too clearly what would happen as soon as he was in the grave. He predicted that the Hatmen (Europeans) would possess themselves of all the shores of India. But he was powerless now to avert the doom. Siraj-ud-daula had thoroughly prepared the way to the throne by murdering all possible rivals.

Clive and Watson were on their way from Bombay when Aliverdi Khan died. The succession of his grandson took place quietly. But the very first act of his government was to pick a quarrel with the English, exactly as the old man had feared.

This was easy enough. The English merchants had long been irked by the restrictions and exactions imposed upon them. From time to time they had even discussed using force against their tyrannical ruler.[90] And they stood so little in awe now of Siraj-ud-daula that they were daring to shelter a Hindu merchant whom he wished to plunder and insolently refusing to give him up. They were equally indiscreet about the fortifications they were building against the menace of a French war. When the Nawab, whose mind was already inflamed with suspicion against them on account of recent happenings in the Deccan, misinterpreted these signs of activity and sent orders for them to desist and destroy the new works they had constructed, they tactlessly replied that they must be prepared to defend themselves against their rivals.   Under the circumstances the Nawab could scarcely be blamed for accepting the implication and being incensed by it : that what had happened in the Carnatic might happen in his dominions and that the Europeans were not relying on his power to protect them.   The French at Chandernagore, similarly engaged, received the same orders, but had the presence of mind blandly to deny the charge, thus escaping the wrath that was already on its way down the river.

If Siraj-ud-daula was apprehensive he was also avaricious.   The reports he had of the wealth stored away in the vaults of Fort William were absurdly exaggerated, but no less effective.   Under an Oriental despotism wise men conceal their wealth as carefully as under a Western dictatorship they do their opinions.   The English did not do so, and Calcutta seemed to the Nawab a fine town to plunder.

If the English merchants were not unready for a quarrel they were quite unprepared for an attack.   In Fort William they had an indefensible fort, in Roger Drake an incompetent governor. Their garrison was as weak as the fort, having been starved to supply the needs of Madras, and its commander as incompetent as the Governor ;   whilst of military stores there were practically none.   Madras in 1746 and Calcutta in 1756 were, in fact, on a par in the matter of defence.

The only cause of surprise, then, was the speed with which the punishment for insolence and tactlessness came.   On July 14 there was entered on the Consultations of Council at Fort St. George the receipt of letters from Fort William reporting trouble with the country government and asking for reinforcements. On August 3 there came the news of the loss of Kasimbazar and a request for more reinforcements.   Fourteen days later there arrived word that Calcutta itself had been captured.

It had taken Siraj-ud-daula only three weeks to accomplish the seizure of the English settlements !   The English factory at Kasimbazar surrendered on June 4.   Although between that town and Calcutta lay 160 miles of trackless country and it was the hottest season of the year, the Nawab's great army, with a cumbrous train of artillery drawn by oxen and elephants, had covered the distance in eleven days.   And having reached the city on June 16 he had captured it on the 20th.

True, the defenders laboured under every kind of handicap, but they might have held out longer if the cowardly Governor and Commander and a large part of the garrison had not fled, taking all the ships with them. After that ultimate act of betrayal the remnants of the garrison could only prolong the resistance a day. Their surrender had then been followed by that famous horror of the Black Hole, when only twenty-three people out of 146 survived their night of hideous incarceration in the small prison hole of the fort. An accidental tragedy, no doubt, and the fault of his officers, but it was Siraj-ud-daula's responsibility none the less and fully accorded with his sadistic nature.

This was, of course, his supreme blunder. The hive of bees that was capable of stinging a disturber to death had been most violently disturbed, and was now moved to take a speedy and effective revenge. " Every breast here," wrote Clive to the Court of Directors, " seems filled with grief, horror, and resentment." As surely as the Mahdi aroused England to conquer the Sudan, so now did the Nawab arouse the gentlemen at Madras when the news flew there on swift wings.

The prospect for a successful attempt to retrieve the disaster was promising. Pigot, like Saunders, was a public-spirited Governor, quick and bold in decision and action, and he was well supported by Lawrence and Orme. At the first report of trouble they had got busy with relief measures, despatching Major Kilpatrick with 200 men. When they realized the full extent of the disaster they decided to make the utmost efforts to retrieve it, giving up entirely their plans against Bussy. They called Admiral Watson into their consultations and sent Clive his summons.

Clive came at once. Arriving at Madras on August 24, he immediately offered his services for the expedition.

His good fortune was never more in evidence than now. He was not first choice for the command. Far from it. Mr. Pigot would have taken it himself if he had had any military experience. Colonel Lawrence would have had it if health had permitted him. Colonel Adlercron of the 39th would have had it if he had not made the most extravagant and absurd claims for himself as a King's officer and showed a complete disregard for the Company's rights and interests. It was only when all three senior officers had been eliminated that the Council paid heed to Orme's advice and offered the command to Clive.

The difficult question of what authority to vest in him was next answered in an equally fortunate way. Normally he would have been under the orders of the Fort William government, but the recent catastrophe had utterly discredited it, and, besides, Madras wished to retain the right to recall the expedition in case of need, war with France being obviously imminent. It was at first agreed to send two deputies from Madras with the expedition, then a member of the Calcutta Council arrived and protested so loudly that the plan was dropped. Finally, under the vigorous proddings of Clive and Orme, it was agreed that the leader should be responsible for his military conduct solely to the Madras Council ; which meant that except for having to consult with and explain himself to the Bengal Council, he had independent powers and was free to use his own judgment upon all occasions. For it was impossible for anyone to define exactly where military authority began and ended.

It was a surprising and momentous decision. Surprising because it was unprecedented in the Company's service to place the military above the civil branch of the service. Momentous because of the extraordinary use that Clive was to make of his powers. The Bengal gentlemen naturally were very much annoyed at the decision and the Directors extremely wroth. But it explains so much in the history of these events that the letter in which the Directors expressed their anger was dated August 3, 1757, a whole year after the powers were granted, when their consequences had already followed. " Had we not," they wrote, " the highest opinion of Colonel Clive's prudence and modera- tion, there would be no end to the disagreeable reflections we might make of so extraordinary a precedent."

From now on events in India were to pass more and more out of the control of the Directors at home, and it was from that cause primarily that the British Empire in India came into being. In the same way as Dupleix had pursued a policy contrary to the desires of his employers, so Clive was to do now, but with one all-important difference, that Clive was able to make his policy appear profitable to his employers, which Dupleix could never do.

There were more delays before the expedition sailed. The third problem that had to be settled was the size and composition of the force. Should Madras on the eve of war be practically denuded of its garrison ? Yet a small force might not be adequate for the purpose. The wise decision was taken to accept the first risk with the understanding that the expedition would be recalled in case of need. But at once Colonel Adlercron interfered to prevent it being given full effect. The Royal Artillery had already embarked when this Royalist gentleman interposed his veto on their sailing without him. " Surely, gentlemen, you are not so unreasonable as to expect that I will send part of His Majesty's train or regiment and leave to *you* the nomination of the person who shall command them."

The objection was insuperable. These were the days when Colonels practically owned their regiments and the King's service lorded it over the Company's. Adlercron, although he had been sent to serve his nation in the East, rendered his allegiance only to " the King, my master " and none to the Company. So the Royal Artillery had to be disembarked and some of the Company's substituted.[1] By the time this was done, the favourable season for sailing was passed and the expedition had to encounter the full force of the north-east monsoon.

It is easy now to see why Clive should have been in high spirits. Things could scarcely have worked out better for him. He was avid of authority and he had received it in astonishing measure. He liked to lead men of spirit and he had them in good number : " A fine body of Europeans full of spirit and resentment for the insults and barbarities inflicted on so many British subjects." He had his orders and they seemed clear enough : he was to retake Calcutta, re-establish the Company's affairs, obtain reparation for its losses, if necessary make war on the Nawab, and, if news of war with the French should come, take their settlement at Chandernagore, and then return to Madras.

Siraj-ud-daula had been apprised by Mr. Pigot of the meaning and purpose of the expedition in beautiful Oriental language, flattering to Clive's ego :

" The great commander of the King of England's ships has not slept in peace since this news, and is come down with many ships ; and I have sent a great Sardar, who will govern after me, by name Colonel Clive, with troops and land forces. Full satisfaction and restitution must be made for the losses we have sustained. You are wise : consider whether it is better to engage in a war that will never end, or to do what is just and right in the sight of God ; a great name is obtained by justice as well as by valour. You have heard that we have

[1] See Appendix A.

fought and always been victorious in these parts. The Nawab of this province writes you how much we have assisted in his affairs, and always acted in support of the orders of the King of Delhi. Salabut Jang asked our assistance, but we determined to obtain satisfaction in Bengal. Mr. Clive will explain all things to you. What can I say more ? "

Only two fears, in fact, worried Clive ; that of being recalled before he had completed his mission and that of being checked in his progress by the terrain over which he would have to advance, knowing as he did that it was impassable for a train of artillery. Both fears were justified. News of the declaration of war with France reached Madras within a month of his sailing.

III

The expedition sailed on October 16. It consisted of Admiral Watson's squadron of four ships : the *Kent*, of 64 guns, bearing the Admiral's flag and with Clive aboard ; the *Cumberland*, 70 guns, bearing the flag of Rear-Admiral Pocock, second in command ; the *Salisbury*, 50 guns ; the *Bridgewater*, 20 guns ; and the East Indiamen *Walpole* and *Marlborough*, together with several smaller craft. The land force consisted of 596 Europeans (34 officers, 562 other ranks) and 940 sepoys, together with three companies of the 39th Foot, whom Adlercron had been unable to prevent from serving as marines on board His Majesty's ships. One of the companies was commanded by Captain Eyre Coote, for whom thus began a distinguished career of twenty-five years in India.

It was impossible for the ships to take the direct route in the teeth of the howling gales that now swept down the Bay of Bengal. They had to strike across the Bay to the coast of Burma and then beat back to Balasore roads. And for the first twelve days they were driven steadily south even as far as Ceylon. As they were victualled and watered for only six weeks, their anxieties were doubled. By November 10 the squadron was put on two-thirds allowance, five days later this was reduced to half and scurvy began to appear. Before the squadron regained the Indian coast the *Salisbury* had sprung a leak and the *Marlborough* had dropped out of sight. The *Cumberland* went aground off Point Palmyras and had to be left behind. It was December 5 before the rest of the ships anchored in Balasore roads, where Watson took on board a pilot for the extremely dangerous crossing of the unchartered shoals at the mouth of the Hugli. They were all by this time in great distress for lack of water and fresh provisions, and sepoys were dying for want of rice.

While they were waiting for a tide to carry them across, Messrs. Watts and Becher came on board the *Kent* as deputies

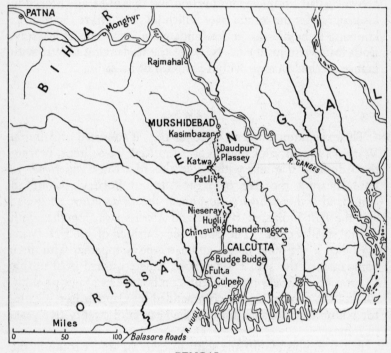

BENGAL

from the Bengal Council and told Watson and Clive of the sore plight of the refugees.

They told of how Governor Drake and his companions, having escaped from the doomed city, had taken refuge at Fulta, a little village near the mouth of the Hugli, where they had been waiting six months for the help from Madras; of how, having escaped from Siraj-ud-daula's hands, they had fallen into the no less deadly clutches of malaria-infected swamps, Fulta being one of the most desolate, unhealthy, God-forsaken places in the world, and this the most unhealthy season of the year ; of how the refugees had mostly lived on board the ships, " which were so crowded that all lay promiscuously on the decks without shelter from the rains of the season and for some time without a change of raiment " ; of how quarrels and recriminations had broken out among them, the younger men blaming their superiors and their superiors each other ; and how Governor Drake was so discredited that he could not get his authority recognized. They also told how they were denied provisions by the Mogul officials and were nearly starving ; how Kilpatrick had arrived with his 200 men, but now, such was the mortality and sickness, he had only thirty left fit for duty ; and how the whole body of refugees could muster no more than 100 effectives all told.

The following day, the dangerous crossing having been made safely, the *Kent* with the *Tyger* and *Walpole* came to anchor off the desolate village of Fulta and the members of the expedition surveyed a land " so low that not a mole-hill is to be seen ; full of woods and thickets, the haunt of tigers." The *Bridgewater* and *Salisbury* arrived ten days later, but brought with them the unwelcome news that the *Cumberland* and *Marlborough* had been forced to put back to Madras. Those two ships carried nearly half the entire force. So already Clive's high hopes were being dashed. His forces were now anything but " great."

The joy of the miserable survivors ashore, however, was naturally immense. Governor Drake hastened to make Watson and Clive members of the special committee of the Council that had been appointed to conduct the Company's affairs in Bengal. But neither man had any intention of relinquishing his separate authority. On the day of arrival Clive exercised that authority to open negotiations with the Nawab and Manichund, whom Siraj-ud-daula had appointed Governor of Calcutta.

The Nawab had returned to his capital boasting of his victories. From exaggerated fear of the Europeans he had, with his dis-ordered mind, passed to an equally exaggerated confidence in himself and contempt for them. He thought there were not more than 10,000 of them in all Europe. How, then, could they return against him in force ? He had not bothered to expel the fugitives, as he flattered himself they would soon come crawling to him to ask for pardon. Thinking of himself as a favourite child of fortune, he had summarily disposed of a rival to his throne, gone gleefully to count the gold in his treasury, and allowed his people to spit upon any European found in the streets of his cities.

Clive abruptly dissipated these fantastic dreams. With a slash of his pen he cut through the objections of Manichund to the tone of severity employed in the letter he had composed to the Nawab. He had threatened war. Manichund wanted him humbly to beseech favour. Said Clive : " We are come to demand satisfaction for the injuries done us by the Nawab, not to entreat his favour, and with a force which we think sufficient to vindicate our claim."

The Nawab's reply was to assemble his army and give orders for the English advance to be opposed.

Meanwhile, the men had been landed and had celebrated Christmas by falling speedy victims to the malignant swamp. Clive himself was suffering from a feverish cold. It was most necessary for them to press on as quickly as possible to healthier country.

So two days after Christmas the advance began. The first objective was the fort of Budge-Budge, which lay on the river bank. A council-of-war overrode Clive's wishes, deciding that the Company's troops should march overland while the ships should follow the winding course of the river and bombard the fort. Clive with the land force was to cut off the enemy's retreat.

Now Clive and his men were to suffer hardships " not to be described." All his fears about the country were at once realized. The effort to drag even two field-pieces over swampy ground intersected by innumerable deep streams and through miles of thick jungle nearly broke them down. They marched from four in the afternoon until eight the following morning, sixteen hours of prolonged torture. As the country was uninhabited they could gain no intelligence of the enemy.

In order to carry out their purpose they made for a village a mile and a half north of the fort. Upon arriving there Clive sent a detachment forward towards the fort and posted the rest of his men in the village and a cleared hollow nearby to await developments.

It is at this point in his account that Orme suddenly becomes critical of Clive's conduct. He has passed now from Volume I to Volume II of his history, which was, as we have seen,[1] written

[1] See p. 7.

under very different circumstances and with very different feelings towards his one-time friend and hero. It is this difference which may account for the following passage :

" The troops being excessively fatigued, were permitted to quit their arms, in order to get rest ; every man laid himself down where he thought best, some in the village, others in the hollow ; and from a security which no superiority or appearances in war could justify, the common precaution of stationing sentinels was neglected. In a few minutes they were all asleep." [91]

None of this, nor Orme's circumstantial account of what followed, appears in Clive's military journal, a fact that cannot, however, be considered conclusive or even good evidence that Orme's story was fabricated. Nor can the judgment be accepted that Clive was incapable of such laxity. He was noted more for his courage than his caution. He may, of course, have posted sentries, and the sentries after their exertions may have fallen asleep along with the rest.

Following Orme's account then, we read that while Clive and his men were thus asleep they were suddenly attacked by Manichund with 2000 horse and foot. A scene of utter confusion followed during which the field-pieces, deserted by their gunners, were for a few minutes in the enemy's hands. As soon as Clive had managed to rally his men and form them in rank, the attack was speedily beaten off, but, added Orme, had the enemy at once employed his cavalry as well as his foot, " it is not improbable that the war would have been concluded on the very first trial of hostilities." By the time the horsemen appeared on the scene the English panic was over.

Although his casualties numbered only eighteen, the experience shook Clive's confidence, and for the first time he confessed to a sense of discouragement. Orme says that as a result of it most of the English officers gained a much higher opinion of the troops of Bengal than they deserved, a fact that would help to account for Clive's behaviour before Plassey.

It was late afternoon when this skirmish ended, and meanwhile the ships had been bombarding the fort, whose fire had gradually slackened and died. Eyre Coote was put ashore with 400 sailors and was about to storm the place that same evening when Clive, coming on board the flagship, got the attack put off until

159

the morning, when he and his men would be rested. However, neither he and his men nor Coote and his were to be necessary. A drunken sailor strayed away from the landing party, entered the fort, found it practically deserted, captured a battery single-handed and, when his comrades had heeded his shouts and come to his aid, proceeded to capture the fort itself, much to the disgust of Coote, who felt himself cheated of the glory ! [1]

All this time a storm had been gathering in the heavily charged atmosphere of the expedition. Clive's relations with the King's officers were most unhappy. It is easy to see why. His holding of a royal commission technically made him one of them and senior to all of them except the Admiral. But it was much easier for him to obtain the commission than to get its validity recognized by his brother-officers. Undoubtedly they treated him as an outsider who had pushed his way into their service by favour and influence. Undoubtedly they resented his superior rank. Why, they must have asked each other, should this man, who is merely a successful amateur, be senior to us, who have served for long terms as officers in the regular army or the Royal Navy ? [2] Among these officers was Captain Speke, the Admiral's flag-captain, who had gibed at Clive to Orme.

Clive, for his part, bitterly resented the way in which he and the Company's troops were being discriminated against and his claim to command all the land forces, King's men as well as Company's, denied. That appalling march across country had been forced upon him by a council-of-war. He had vainly asked to be transported on the ships and landed at the place which he finally reached only after his sixteen hours' march. Transport on the ships was reserved for Captain Coote and the King's men, who were then, according to the plan arranged by Coote with the Admiral, to have the honour of taking the fort. This seemed to Clive most unfair, and he could fairly blame his unhappy experience at the hands of Manichund upon the jealousy of the King's officers.

[1] When the sailor Strahan, thinking himself the hero of the occasion, was brought before the Admiral next morning to be reprimanded for his grave breach of discipline, he presented a picture of acute bewilderment. Twirling his cap and scratching his head, he replied to the charge, " Why, to be sure, Sir, it was I who took the fort, but I hope there was no harm in it." Watson dismissed him with a severe rebuke and threat of future punishment. " If I am flogged for this here action," the puzzled man was heard to mutter, " I'll never take another fort by myself as long as I live, by God ! " He probably never realized that he had committed the unpardonable offence of making his commanders look foolish !

[2] Coote, a captain, had served for twelve years.

Clive exerted his authority after the capture of Budge-Budge. Only the sepoys were compelled to march to Calcutta, and Clive with the Company's Europeans remained on board the ships. But the storm that was threatening burst as soon as Calcutta was reached and occupied, with practically no resistance, on January 2.

Admiral Watson sent Captain Coote with his company to take possession of Fort William in the name of His Majesty, giving him orders not to quit his post or deliver up his command until he received further orders from him. Coote interpreted the order literally. When a party of sepoys tried to enter the fort they were ignominiously thrown out. When Clive shortly afterwards arrived and demanded entrance Coote showed him his commission and informed him that none of the Company's officers or men could be admitted.

Clive was flung into a fit of rage by this contempt for his rank and, daring the sentries to try to stop him, entered the fort, told Coote that the Admiral had no right to appoint an inferior officer to this command, and threatened him with instant arrest if he did not obey his orders. Coote gave in, but asked that the Admiral be informed of what had taken place.

Watson at once sent Captain Speke ashore to enquire by what authority Clive had assumed command of the fort. Clive replied, " By the authority of His Majesty's Commission, as being lieutenant-colonel and commander-in-chief of the land forces." Hot words followed between Clive and Speke and both men lost their tempers. Speke returned to the flagship to consult the Admiral. When he came back to the fort he brought a letter from Watson in which the Admiral wrote :

" Sir,—After what I have said to Major Kilpatrick, I am extremely surprised to find you have not withdrawn the Company's troops, which puts me under a necessity of acquainting you, if you still persist in continuing in the fort, you will force me to take such methods as will be as disagreeable to me as they possibly can be to you. I hope that, after you have prudently considered this affair, you'll not drive me to the extremities I should be sorry to be urged to, for the plea you make of being commanding officer of the land forces gives you not the least authority to enter a place (forcibly) conquered by me and garrisoned by troops under my immediate command."

Speke informed Clive bluntly that if he did not leave the fort he would be fired out.

" I cannot answer for the consequences," Clive replied, " but I will not abandon the fort." He offered to leave only if assurances were given him that he would command there.

Once more Speke returned to the flagship. After more discussion he wrote Clive that the Admiral had commanded him

" to tell you that, as neither in this affair nor any other he ever meant you any dishonour, he is disposed to give you any reasonable proofs of it ; but as by forcing the guards placed in the fort by his orders you have offered him a personal affront, and through him to his Majesty's authority, the duty he owes to himself as an officer trusted with the care of his Majesty's honour in supporting that of his Forces will not admit of his promising anything till you have first, by withdrawing the troops under your command, acknowledged the insult you have so unadvisedly offered. That done, if you will give yourself the trouble to step aboard, I dare promise you, you will receive clear proofs how very unwilling Mr. Watson is to disagree with a man for whom he has always had an esteem."

Clive refused to do any of these things. He was as stubborn and intractable now as he had been on those occasions in his early days in the service. It was Mr. Watson, showing remarkable control of temper, who had to yield the point at issue. Tactfully he sent Captain Latham of the *Tyger* instead of Speke to settle the dispute. Latham managed to calm Clive down, and it was soon agreed between them that the Admiral should solve the difficulty by coming ashore himself and commanding in person. This Watson did the following day, when Clive delivered the keys of the fort to him and the Admiral turned them over to Governor Drake and his Council. As a final affirmation of their restored harmony and common purpose they issued a joint declaration of war against the Nawab in the name of the King and the East India Company.

Yet if Clive's relations with his fellow-officers were disagreeable, they were scarcely any more pleasant with the men whom they had all come to save. He was not one to hide his feelings, and his feelings for Mr. Drake and his Councillors were those of unmitigated contempt, not only for their behaviour in running away from Calcutta, but now when they were being restored to their settlement. " The loss of property and the means of recovering it," he remarked to Mr. Pigot, " seem to be the only objects which take up the attention of the Bengal gentlemen." Of course, they had immediately voiced their dissatisfaction at his authority, and he had congratulated Mr. Pigot upon having taken such a prudent step :

" I would have you guard against everything these gentlemen can say ; for believe me, they are bad subjects and rotten at heart and will stick at nothing to prejudice you and the gentlemen of the Committee ; indeed, how should they do otherwise, when they have not spared one another ? I shall only add, their conduct at Calcutta finds no excuse, even among themselves ; and that the riches of Peru and Mexico should not induce me to dwell among them."

This feeling of disgust had now taken complete possession of him. " Between friends," he wrote Pigot from Calcutta, " I cannot help regretting that ever I undertook this expedition." Could anything mark a greater change of feeling from the one expressed to his father on the eve of sailing ?

Perhaps the Bengal gentlemen thought they could best get rid of Clive, now that Fort William was once more in their possession, by increasing his disgust to a point where he would gladly throw up the service. If so, they had seriously mistaken their man. They wrote him a rude letter, bluntly ordering him to surrender his independent powers and place himself henceforth unreservedly under their orders.

His response was immediate and very much to the point :

" What I have had the honour to represent to the Board I now take an opportunity of repeating in writing, that I do not intend to make use of my power for acting separately from you without you reduce me to the necessity of so doing, but as far as concerns the means of executing those powers, you will excuse me, Gentlemen."

Not having known him very long the gentlemen, perhaps, had not yet realized the absurdity of their demand. Clive's mind was moving, as it had always moved, in a precisely opposite direction : more power, not less, was what he wanted.

" The hour is great ; and the honourable gentlemen, I must say, are small." Clive must have voiced Carlyle's sentiment on this occasion.

IV

The hour was great. The critical hour of the expedition had, in fact, struck. Siraj-ud-daula was approaching with a vast army. England, it was now generally known, was at war with France, and Clive expected that the French at Chandernagore would unite their forces with the Nawab's as he marched by their settlement. Fort William was in such a sadly ruinous state, the Moslems having torn down part of the curtain to make room for a mosque, that it was barely tenable. Clive could expect no more reinforcements from Madras. In fact, any day might bring him the order to send back part of his forces to guard Madras against the expected arrival of a French armament. Yet even after the arrival of the missing *Marlborough* with the field artillery and stores on board, Clive had only 705 European effectives, with 144 sick.

While Watson with the ships went up the river to destroy the Nawab's grain stores at Hugli, Clive busied himself at Calcutta repairing the fort and raising a body of Bengal sepoys. His thoughts at this critical juncture were directed much more towards making peace with the Nawab than war. His own personal disgust with the whole business made him eager to clean everything up and get back to Madras, whose Governor he still hoped soon to become and where he wanted to strike again at his old foes. To await the Nawab's coming he posted his little army in an entrenched camp a mile north of the town and half a mile from the river bank. In view of his danger he succeeded in inducing Admiral Watson to part with the King's troops and place them temporarily under his orders—a loan recallable upon demand, though Clive privately had other views.

In this situation he wrote his father :

" We are encamped with our little army ; and the Nabob is at the head of forty thousand men to give us battle. I am in hopes everything will be concluded to the Company's advantage, though not in so glorious a manner as I could wish. For more particulars I must refer you to Mr. Mabbot.

" It is not possible to describe the distresses of the inhabitants of this once opulent and great town. It must be many years before it is restored to its former grandeur. It is computed the private losses amount to upwards of two millions of sterling.

" I enjoy my health better than could be expected, and think my nervous complaint decreases. Mrs. Clive was very well when I last heard from her, which was the fourth of last month.

" Colonel Lawrence is Governor of St. David's during my absence. I believe it would be no difficult matter to get appointed from home Governor of this place ; but it would be neither agreeable to me nor to my advantage. I heartily wish in these perilous and uncertain times all my money was in England ; for I do not think it safe here ; no one knows what the event of war may be in these parts. My loss by the capture of Calcutta is not less than £2,500 ; so that hitherto I am money out of pocket by my second trip to India. I hope the end may crown all."

If Clive's mind had not been so much centred on peace he might not have missed the very favourable opportunity that occurred to strike a powerful, and possibly decisive, blow at Siraj-ud-daula when the Nawab's army made its appearance on February 3. To reach Calcutta the enemy had to pass within sight of the British camp. They also had to cross a bridge over an extensive salt-water lake. Clive could have held the bridge with his guns while he flung the rest of his force against the open flank of the enemy's unwieldy mass. But according to Orme he despaired of victory over the Nawab, even though the French had committed the supreme blunder of asking for a neutrality agreement ihstead of sending their 300 Europeans and train of field artillery to join Siraj-ud-daula.

Instead of attacking or even impeding the enemy's march, Clive wrote proposing peace, and all day long the host of 18,000 horsemen, an incomputable number of foot, with 40 cannon and 50 elephants, defiled past the British camp. Only towards evening, when they had passed, did Clive leave his position to find out where they had camped. He found them sprawled out all over the ground to the east of the city, whilst the Nawab himself with his bodyguard had actually crossed the Maratha ditch, which formed the boundary of the city, and encamped in Omichand's garden. Clive's men were greeted with cannon fire, and when night fell he returned to his camp.

That night and the following day Siraj-ud-daula amused Clive with peace negotiations while he prepared to storm the city. But when Clive's envoys, Watts and Scrafton, returned from the

Nawab's headquarters not only empty-handed but fully convinced of the Nawab's hostile intentions and in fear of their lives every moment they were in his camp, Clive was forced to the conclusion that he had to take some strong action to incline the Nawab towards peace. He was forced to this conclusion even more strongly by what had happened in the English camp. All the natives upon whom the English depended for supplies had taken fright and fled, nor were they likely to return as long as the Nawab remained in the vicinity. For Clive to have remained longer in his camp under the double threat of starvation and an assault upon Calcutta was to court utter disaster.

Yet having missed his opportunity, he found himself without any good plan of action. He made up his mind too late in the evening to attempt a night attack. The next best course was an attack at dawn. Remembering his success outside Arcot and knowing that there was never any order or vigilance in these Mogul armies, that the camp followers in thousands and all the camp-equipage lay mixed up with the fighting men, he must have felt reasonably hopeful of at least creating so much disturbance and instilling so much fear that Siraj-ud-daula would sue for peace. Yet there was no doubt of the risk he was taking. At dawn the camp would be stirring and the cover of darkness would be removed.

Acting with decision, he went at once on board the flagship and obtained from the Admiral the loan of a detachment of sailors to draw the guns and carry the ammunition. By 1 a.m. the sailors were on shore. An hour later the troops were under arms. At four they marched.

A division of sepoys headed the column, then came the King's and Company's grenadiers led by Eyre Coote, then the European battalion with Clive at their head, followed by the artillery, sailor-drawn, with the rest of the sepoys bringing up the rear. They numbered 470 Europeans, 800 sepoys, 600 sailors, and 70 artillerymen with six field-pieces and one howitzer.

Clive's plan was to penetrate a section of the enemy's camp where it sprawled eastwards of the city and then to proceed westwards by a high causeway across the swamps that bounded Calcutta to the Maratha ditch and from there, heading back northwards, to the Nawab's headquarters in Omichand's garden, which lay just inside the ditch. Orme says the plan was defective :

" The troops ought to have assembled at Perring's redoubt, which is not half a mile from Omichand's garden, to which they might have marched from the redoubt, in a spacious road, capable of admitting twelve or fifteen men abreast, on the left exposed indeed to the annoyance of matchlocks, from some enclosures, where, however, cavalry could not act ; but their right would have been defended by the rampart of the Morattoe ditch, contiguous to which the road lies ; and their only danger would have been in front, from onsets of cavalry, and the discharge of what pieces of cannon the enemy had got near the garden."

Clive may have formed his plan hastily and overlooked this alternative route, but it is equally possible that he deliberately aimed more at the centre of the enemy's camp in order to produce the maximum effect.

At 6 a.m., as dawn was breaking, the column approached the enemy's camp and were received by the fire of the pickets. Here occurred the first mishap. A rocket struck a sepoy's cartouchebox, exploded it, the explosion spread to his companions, and a platoon of fifty men were blown up. This threw the advance guard into such confusion that Coote had to halt and rally it.

The sun was now up, but instead of the darkness being dispelled it grew thicker as a dense fog, common at this time of year, arose from the swampy ground and obscured visibility beyond two or three yards. The guides lost their way and bore off too far to the left, taking them straight towards the middle of the enemy's camp. In this situation the fog proved a fortunate mischance, as it concealed them from the enemy and their massed squadrons of horse.

Suddenly out of the fog came the thunder of hoofs. A large body of horsemen blundered upon them and were within almost a bayonet's length before they were seen. It was the Nawab's own bodyguard, that had been stationed outside the ditch. A moment's weakness now and nothing could save Clive from disaster. But with perfect calmness his men halted and delivered their fire. Most of the saddles were emptied, and the few horsemen that were left disappeared into the darkness as suddenly and swiftly as they came. The fog, however, persisted. Nothing could be seen but the flashes of the guns as the artillery, firing blind, strove to clear the path of their advance to the right and left. They had come a mile, and now the steep sides of the causeway loomed up before them. Up its banks went the sepoys and, facing right, began to advance along it. But the artillery behind were still firing, unaware of the change of front, and to escape from it the sepoys were compelled to jump into the ditch on the other side of the causeway. Clive promptly ordered the whole line to follow. But so much confusion resulted that the

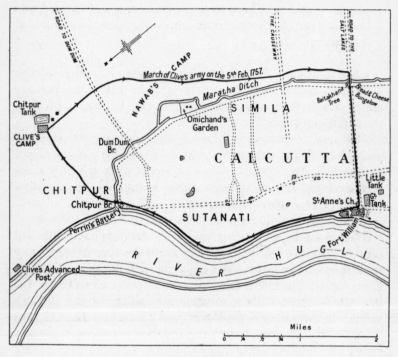

CALCUTTA
Clives' attack on Siraj-ud-Daula's Camp, February 5th. 1757

whole column of march had to be reformed before it could proceed.

The Moorish army was ready for them now, and like a great beast slowly awakening from its torpor was preparing to strike. Straight ahead of Clive's men on the causeway was a barricade. They were just about to storm it when two heavy guns opened on them from a bastion beside the ditch at point-blank range. Canister shot tore great gaps in the close ranks. Twenty men fell. A second discharge and more fell. All hope of using the causeway had quickly to be abandoned. They had to turn left again, scramble across the ditch, and make their way as best they could through boggy rice-fields, southwards, towards a road a full mile and a quarter distant which ran parallel to the causeway.

It was now nine o'clcock and the sun was rapidly dispelling the mist. Soon the air would be clear and the enemy would be presented with a splendid target in this small, straggling body of men marching across the open country under their very noses. On every side appeared masses of horsemen, hovering, waiting for a chance to dash into the thinning ranks. More and more guns came into action. Now Clive was rallying his men, trying to be everywhere at once. Now he had his aide-de-camp and secretary killed at his side. Now he was throwing out platoons to right and left to ward off the threatening squadrons. Now he was directing the sailors where to place the guns. Each small rice-field was fenced off with an embankment and over each embankment and through each muddy field the guns had to be hauled by the sweating, cursing sailors, bitterly resentful at being used as coolies. Two guns had to be abandoned.

Slowly the march continued. It was ten o'clock before they reached the road where they turned west towards the city and safety. Coming to the Maratha ditch, they found the enemy drawn up in strength to bar their way. But nothing could stop Clive's men now, the shelter of the city beckoned them on. A few point-blank volleys from the leading platoons and the way was clear. Clive and his tired men crossed the ditch into safety.

The plan to turn right and move along the ditch to the Nawab's quarters was now out of the question. To have done so would have exposed them to an enfilade fire along its entire length, and this, tired and somewhat demoralized as they were, they were in no condition to meet. So they marched on towards Fort William, which they reached shortly after eleven, and after halting there the rest of the day, they returned to their camp in the evening.

It had not been a happy experience. According to Orme: " the troops, officers as well as common men, dispirited by the loss which had been sustained and the risks to which they had been exposed, as they thought, to very little purpose, blamed

their commander, and called the attempt rash and ill-concerted."
The losses had, indeed, been heavy, considering the smallness of
their numbers : 39 Europeans and 18 sepoys killed, 82 Europeans
and 55 sepoys wounded ; about one-tenth of their total strength.
The attack, too, by Clive's own admission had failed in its main
object owing to the fog. He confessed to his father that it was
the warmest service he had yet engaged in.

Yet if a tactical failure, morally it could not have succeeded
better. "The boldness of design and vigour of execution,"
Clive correctly stated, "terrified the Nawab, who the following
day moved out into the open plain and expressed his readiness to
negotiate."

At this point there is an extraordinary gap in practically all the
accounts of Clive's life. This is perhaps partly explained by the
fact that he now committed what seems in the light of all the
circumstances to have been a palpable blunder ! The blunder
lay in not following up his success with another smashing blow
at the Nawab's retreating, panic-stricken army. By his failure
to do so he threw away the chief fruits of his expensive but intelligently planned attack on the Nawab's camp. Instead, he allowed
his anxiety for peace to gain the better of his military judgment
and the Nawab to outwit him.

For it was quite true, as Clive said, that Siraj-ud-daula was
terrified and only too anxious to remove himself from close
proximity to these dangerous Europeans, but it was not so
certain that he was genuinely ready to make peace. He had not
been decisively beaten, and it would not have needed any
profound knowledge of psychology to guess that the effect of his
panic was likely to wear off with every mile that he put between
himself and them.

There was only one hope, as the English saw it, of their once
again enjoying peace and security in this country, and that was
to rid the Nawab of the false notion that they could safely be
treated with contempt. And now when he had made the initial
blunder of leaving his capital, where he was safely out of reach,
and coming down to Calcutta, instead of conducting war at a
distance, which would have made matters extremely difficult for
them, he had given Clive the supreme opportunity to demonstrate his mistake in a way that would have left a lasting impression. One lesson was not enough, especially one that was so
inconclusive.

Admiral Watson realized all this and strongly urged Clive to attack. He wrote the following night :

"I am now fully convinced the Nabob's letter was only to amuse us, in order to cover his retreat and gain time till he is reinforced, which may be attended with very fatal consequences. For my own part, I was of opinion that attacking his rear when he was marching off, and forcing him to abandon his cannon, was a most necessary piece of service to bring him to an accommodation ; for till he is well thrashed, don't, sir, flatter yourself he will be inclined to peace. Let us therefore not be overreached by his politics but make use of our arms, which are more to be depended upon, and I dare say will be much more prevalent than any treaties or negotiations."

Why did not Clive adopt this excellent advice ? Why had he permitted the Nawab to pass in full retreat before him without so much as firing a gun ? The answer seems to dispose of Clive's claims to be considered as a master of war. Instead of acting he called a council-of-war ! And true to the nature of all councils-of-war, this one unanimously voted against an attack. Clive accepted its decision.

In his own mind he may have felt that this was a wise decision. His force had been badly mauled ; it was fatigued and apparently discouraged—and the Nawab had already signified his readiness to make peace. Orme suggests in his account that Clive never properly estimated the enemy's military strength, vastly over-rating it, and this seems a probable explanation of his conduct now and, later, on the eve of Plassey. His decision to attack the camp must have been made in desperation, so that he was satisfied to have attained his immediate object.

The possible consequences of Clive's failure to act have been entirely lost sight of because of their obliteration by Plassey. But to see things in this way is entirely to miss the essentials of the situation. That situation demanded a speedy and lasting peace with the Nawab so that the expedition would be free to return to Madras. The inability of the expedition to return because of the unreality of the peace with the Nawab jeopardized the safety of Madras. And if Clive had soundly trounced Siraj-ud-daula at Calcutta he might never have had to embark on his tortuous and unworthy conspiracy with Mir Jafar and his highly perilous march to the capital.

Clive replied to the Nawab's overtures by offering him terms of peace. Two days passed without further word from him. And already it had become a question whether Watson was not right and peace farther away than ever. Peremptorily Clive wrote again, demanding immediate acceptance of his terms on pain of renewed war. Siraj-ud-daula might be foolish, but he could at times, like all Orientals, be shrewd. Did he now think that if he signed a treaty of peace the English would send away their ships and men? Or was it the memory of his late terror that still operated upon it?

He returned the treaty signed the following morning. By its terms he agreed to restore to the Company all its factories and privileges and all the plunder that he had taken and to grant it the liberties of fortifying Calcutta as it pleased and of coining its own rupees.

A few days later he agreed further to enter into an offensive and defensive alliance with the Company.

What was not stipulated, however, and what caused much heart-burning among the sufferers, was that he should compensate individuals for their losses, though some of them had been ruined in the sack of Calcutta.

Chapter Twelve

THE BENGAL EXPEDITION :
(2) CHANDERNAGORE

" The whole history of our connection with India shows that for a native prince to apprehend danger is to precipate it by his own conduct. He is more often ruined by his fears than by anything else."

J. W. KAYE, *Life of Sir John Malcolm*

I

CLIVE NOW, AS ALWAYS after his big successes, surrendered himself to the luxury of self-gratulation. Only a few days before he had been regretting that ever he had come upon this expedition, and now—" this expedition is attended with nothing but reputation." A few days before he had been fearful of effecting nothing against the Nawab, and now—" I expect to return very shortly to the Coast, as all is over here " ; a firm peace had, he said, been effected. In fact, he wrote to tell his employers that he was returning.

It is clear that his nature was unstable : that he was subject to moods of mental depression when he exaggerated his difficulties and saw everything in a pessimistic light, and then to moods of high exuberance when he made light of everything and entirely overestimated the value of his accomplishment.

Being an egotist, too, it was characteristic of him to relate all success to himself. The impression his reports of the expedition give is that he was responsible for its success. The part that the fleet had played is scarcely mentioned. It is true that he was to admit that Mr. Watson had " done everything that could be expected from a brave and gallant man and had been greatly instrumental towards settling the affairs of this province." But the very tone of the tribute is indicative of his attitude. It is condescending. It is the tone of a superior officer. One would not imagine from it that it had been Mr. Watson and not Mr. Clive who had actually been in command of the expedition and directed most of its operations.

The truth is that his was not the kind of nature that thrived on barren soil and in harsh conditions. As a sensitive plant needs rich soil and no frost, so he needed success and no failure. He needed richness of fortune, richness of power and reputation. If the realization of success acted like wine upon him, sending his hopes, his spirits, his ambitions soaring, so did the thought of possible failure unnerve him. That, with any other kind of blow to his pride, was what disturbed him the most. His energy and zeal were boundless, but his patience and command of temper were slight, and of equanimity, except in moments of physical danger, he had little or none.

So it was quite characteristic of him now to allow his expectations to over-leap his actual achievement. To the impartial eye it might seem that he had done no more than might have been expected of him, justified his somewhat rapid promotion and the trust that had been imposed in him. But no ! not in his own eyes. He makes now a breath-taking revelation. Though not yet thirty-two he dares to think of himself as Governor-General of all the Company's possessions in the East ! Yes, and he at once despatches letters heralding his success to those friends in high places whose favour he was assiduously cultivating while in England. No feelings of delicacy restrain him—only a common sense that counsels discretion. To his father he writes :

" As this success has probably saved the Company, this is a proper time to push my interest. I have written to my Lord Chancellor, the Archbishop, Mr. Fox, and my Lord Barrington, Secretary at War, to desire their interest. I have likewise wrote to Messrs. Mabbot, Drake, and Payne. I am desirous of being appointed Governor-General of India if such an appointment should be necessary. I have opened myself a little to Mr. Mabbot ; however, I would have you manage this affair with great prudence and discretion and not mention the word Governor-General without you find it hinted at by other hands. Consult Mr. Belchier and don't make the contents of this letter known to anyone else but the Judge and Mr. King. Consult them."

He enclosed the letters to Great Men for his father's perusal and delivery, begging him not to be too sanguine in his expectations or expressions. (He knew only too well how much his father needed to be restrained in that way.) The letters were practically identical. The closing words of the one to the Lord Chancellor sufficiently reveal their purpose : " As your Lordship heretofore honoured me with your favour and protection, I flatter myself with the hopes of a continuance of it, and that if your Lordship thinks me deserving, your Lordship will recommend me to the Court of Directors."

Few men have pursued their ambition as resolutely and clearsightedly as did Clive. Few men have been more prompt to link personal advancement with the performance of public services or more quick to note whether the appreciation received equalled in amount their estimate of what was deserved. That he made something of a study of the roads that lead to success is suggested by what Mr. King, his attorney, wrote him after Gheria : " Colonel Clive was again in all the newspapers. I believe you have made a maxim of what I have somewhere read that ' a man who has got himself a great name should every now and then strike some *coup d'éclat* to keep up the admiration of the people.' " One feels that Clive would have appreciated and utilized to the full all the means for publicity that are available to modern celebrities.

Nor did he fail at this time in tact or to show proper respect to the Court of Directors, that Court which he was so soon to treat with insolence and contumely. The time was not quite ripe when he could afford to dispense with its favour and stand upon his own proud and sufficient feet. Nothing, for instance, had aroused more contempt in him than the despicable conduct of Governor Roger Drake, junior ; yet in his letters to the Court he virtually exculpated him from blame. And, perhaps, we need not seek further for the explanation of such leniency, so contrary to the severity he had employed in his letter to Mr. Pigot, than the fact that Roger Drake, senior, the Governor's uncle, was a member of the Court.[1] The Court was Clive's ladder, as he well knew. When with its support he had climbed to the top he might, if he wanted, kick it away, but not before.

Clive had made a peace that was not popular with most of his countrymen at Calcutta, but it was well calculated to please his employers. The Bengalers might feel that he had been too hasty and had not obtained good enough terms. They might par-

---

[1] He wrote to William Mabbot (January 31, 1757), asking him to assure Mr. Drake "of my gratitude and respect; assure him at the same time, that if his nephew has erred I believe it is in judgment not principle."

ticularly resent his failure to obtain them reparation for their heavy and in many cases ruinous losses. But to his employers he stated his reasons with a cogency that must fully have confirmed the confidence that they had placed in him :

"If I had consulted the interest and reputation of a soldier, the conclusion of this Peace might easily have been suspended. I know, at the same time, there are many who think I have been too precipitate in the conclusion of it ; but surely those who are of this opinion never knew that the delay of a day or two might have ruined the Company's affairs, by the junction of the French with the Nabob, which was on the point of being carried into execution. They never considered the situation of affairs on the Coast, and the positive orders sent me by the Gentlemen there, to return with the major part of the forces at all events ; they never considered that, with a war upon the Coast and in the province of Bengal at the same time, a trading company could not subsist without a great assistance from the Government ; and last of all, they never considered that a long war, attended through the whole course of it with success and many great actions, ended at last with the expense of fifty lacs of rupees to the Company."

Clive was not a soldier save by accident, and that for as long as soldiering suited the purposes of his career. He was a politician who was now in process of transforming himself into a statesman capable of taking a broad view of a complex situation. He showed here a sure ability to speak the kind of language that would appeal to a Company of merchants. Later he was to show equal adroitness when he addressed himself to ministers of the Crown. Never at any time was his outlook limited or conditioned by the needs and interests of the profession he had ostensibly embraced. And in that fact lies a partial explanation of the bitter hatred that developed towards him in the members of that profession, who felt that he had made use of the honourable profession of arms for his own ends and then betrayed them in the interests of a Company whom he had also betrayed.

Fantastic as was his expectation of being appointed Governor-General now or in the near future—and even his best friends implored him not to breathe a word of it to anyone for fear of the hurt it would do him—he was not far wrong in assessing his own qualifications for the post, should it have been in contemplation, if only because of his extraordinary ability to deal with new situations as they arose and to keep pace with a course of events that was now becoming bewilderingly rapid. His experience had been such that he had already outgrown the particularist sentiment that hitherto governed all the settlements. He had served at Madras, Bombay, and now at Calcutta, so that he knew, perhaps better than any of the Company's servants, the needs, situation, characteristics, and weaknesses of all three. Above all, he had two inestimable advantages over his colleagues at Calcutta. The first was that he had watched from the beginning the work-ings of Dupleix's and Bussy's policy in the Deccan. He knew, therefore, much about Indian statecraft ; far more than they, who knew nothing—nothing, that is, until it had felled them with a blow from which they were still recovering ! The second was that he had revisited England, where he had not only acquainted himself fully with the views of the Company but had obtained their special favour and confidence. Thus it is not surprising that his dominance in the mixed councils of Calcutta should gradually now become more and more marked. The Admiral, the Colonel, and the Governor formed at first a triumvirate, just as three Consuls were to form a triumvirate to rule France, but in each case the soldier emerged as the sole ruler, and in each case it was because he had the necessary will-power and determination and the support of his constituents.

What Clive did not possess as a statesman was any remarkable foresight or clearness of purpose. He did not at this moment command the course of events in Bengal. He was commanded by it. Whatever he became later, he was at this stage of his career an opportunist and his policy a series of brilliant improviza-tions. He was not deliberately trying to do what Dupleix had far more deliberately done in the Carnatic. Otherwise he would scarcely have proclaimed so confidently that " all is over here." He was, indeed, in the throes of imitating Dupleix, but he was not yet aware of it. He was far too conscious of his immediate difficulties—something that Dupleix never was—to have any big views of policy or long-range plans. The conquest of Bengal was improvised, it was not premeditated. It was a most extra-ordinarily lucky accident, falling to the lot of a most extra-ordinarily lucky man. It was, indeed, merely the by-product of an attempt to rediscover a stable political foundation for the

M

resumption of trade. When peaceful means failed to produce that foundation, war was resorted to—and suddenly much to their own surprise, the English were to find that they had conquered the country !

II

Though they had patched up a peace with Siraj-ud-daula, Watson and Clive still had the French to deal with. An attack upon Chandernagore had been part of their plans from the expedition's inception, and now in order to clear the way for their return to Madras it became the next item on their programme. But there was one big difficulty in the way : the Nawab's attitude. For he was, after all, still ruler of his dominions. His defeat at Calcutta had sobered him and terminated his short-lived dream of invincibility, but he had not yet been reduced to the helpless condition of his Moslem brother-princes of the south. The maintenance of internal peace is a most cherished part of the prerogative of sovereignty ; and in his occasional moments of acting and feeling like a great and mighty prince the thougth that these pestiferous Europeans were planning to introduce their private enmities into his dominions filled Siraj-ud-daula with a natural and justifiable rage. Unfortunately for him, those moments were but rare and always short-lived. However, even he could see that it had become more vital than ever before for him to enforce the ancient neutrality of the Ganges. The English with their ships and men and able leaders were threatening to become over-powerful and he needed the French to act as a counter-weight. By a policy of playing one rival off against the other, while not letting them come to blows and keeping the balance of power in his own hands, he could preserve his authority intact. The destinies of Bengal and probably of India itself hung on his ability to follow this obvious and not too difficult policy.

The French, for their part, had had their chance against their rivals and had failed to take it. They could have accepted the Nawab's offer of an alliance, joining with him in the attack on Calcutta. The news of the declaration of war in Europe following hot upon the arrival of the English expedition had filled them with acute anxiety. They were at a complete disadvantage and knew they could not withstand an English attack, most of their military strength having been drained to supply the needs of Bussy in the Deccan. For that reason they chose to trust their fate to a continuance of the neutrality that they and the English had always observed in Bengal. They made a proposition to that effect immediately upon the expedition's arrival, but Clive and Watson had taken no decision pending a settlement with the Nawab. After the conclusion of the peace the negotiations still hung fire, but now it was because the minds of Watson and Clive were set upon obtaining the Nawab's permission to make war.

The month following was entirely taken up with manœuvres, intrigues, and negotiations revolving around this vital question. Watson and Clive did not want to embroil themselves again with the Nawab, which would be the certain consequence of attacking the French without his permission. Fear of a combination against them of the Nawab and French in alliance governed their actions. Even though there were only a few hundred French soldiers in Bengal, the addition of these with a few well-served field-pieces to the Nawab's army and of their commanders to his counsels, so much in need of a little wisdom, would produce a combination far too strong for their puny forces. From the start their hope of success had lain in keeping their adversaries apart to be dealt with separately.

But Clive was in a dilemma. He now had his orders from Madras to return. If he obeyed them without having first destroyed French power, all the fruits of his expedition were likely to be lost as soon as he and Watson had taken their departure. He suspected Siraj-ud-daula of having formed that very design. But he saw clearly enough the consequences of ignoring the Nawab. "If you attack Chandernagore," he warned the Committee, " you cannot stop there ; you must go further. Having established yourself by force, and not by the consent of the Nawab, he by force will endeavour to drive you out again." Obviously all efforts had to be centred on gaining that permission.

For this purpose diplomatic relations had to be established with the Nawab's durbar. Clive was already too well versed in politics as practised in the Moorish courts of India to imagine that he could gain his ends by the simple means of correspondence. Nor, as he must have realized, would an English agent unaided carry sufficient weight or possess sufficient *savoir faire* to make the Nawab do something that was so directly contrary to his interests and so repugnant to his wishes. Craft, chicanery, bribery, these would be necessary, and Clive was not the man to hesitate about employing them. He was ready to compete with Moslem rulers on their own ground, opposing corruption with corruption, duplicity with duplicity. So he employed not one but two agents, an Englishman and an Indian. The first had the best talents that could be found among the Company's servants for diplomatic work, practically none of whom had acquaintance with the court or even any knowledge of native languages, customs, or politics. William Watts had the advantage of having been the factor at Kasimbazar in close proximity to the capital. The other was the already notorious Omichand (Aminchand).

Clive could scarcely have been ignorant of Omichand's character. If he had not had time to gain that knowledge for himself, the inhabitants of Calcutta were only too able and ready to give it to him ; they had known Omichand quite intimately for a long time. He had settled among them some forty years before from his Punjabi home and had acquired for himself much rich honey. from their bee-hive. With shrewdness born of greed he had attached himself to their service, but not, as they discovered in the recent troubles, entirely wholeheartedly and faithfully to their interests. When the Nawab marched upon their city they discovered Omichand in treacherous intercourse with his spies and promptly arrested and imprisoned him. When Siraj-ud-daula released him he repaid the favour by transferring his allegiance to him. His record at this point is not clear. The English victims of the Nawab's carelessness in the matter of their incarceration may have been quite unjust in laying all the blame for their suffering upon Omichand, but the point is that they did lay it on him, conceiving that desire to revenge himself for the indignity he had suffered at their hands made him instigate Siraj-ud-daula's cruelties. Accordingly, as soon as the English repossessed themselves of the city they ordered his house and all his possessions to be seized and sequestered, with the full approval of its inhabitants, both white-skinned and dark.

But Omichand, who was persistent and far-seeing, did not consider that this ended his connection with the English. That connection had been very profitable, and as soon as he perceived that fortune might after all bestow her favour upon his old masters he sought an opportunity to adjust his own position accordingly. Besides, Siraj-ud-daula had been foolish ; he had yielded to the temptation of the merchant's wealth, removing a large amount of treasure from his house, and was very ready with excuses for not returning it. The wily Sikh found his opportunity when he accompanied his master's army to Calcutta and, having witnessed the Nawab's discomfiture, remained behind to participate in the peace negotiations. These he engineered in the English favour, and he then felt it opportune to write to Clive. In his letter he praised God for restoring Calcutta to his former masters. God, he said, had answered his prayer, and he hoped now that he himself would be restored to favour. Clive heard this prayer and invited him to come to see him, with the result that Omichand was taken back into employment.

No doubt his suave, imperturbable manner was equal to any test, even to that of imposing upon Clive and Siraj-ud-daula alike. How far Clive trusted him does not appear. We are told that when Omichand accompanied Mr. Watts to the capital his " conduct in the late negotiations had effaced the impressions of former imputations, insomuch that Mr. Watts was permitted to consult and employ him without reserve." Very likely there was no one else with Omichand's influence that Clive could find to act as intermediary. Having decided to embark on a highly ticklish business his only chance of success lay in placing someone with Omichand's peculiar qualifications and inside knowledge at Watts's elbow to advise him, as well as to handle those subtle financial transactions that no Englishman could have handled himself. But the result from Omichand's point of view was highly advantageous. He had placed himself—or rather Clive had placed him—where he could hunt with the hounds and run with the hare to his heart's content, and to the great benefit of his bank account. No hampering considerations of race or religion or the welfare of his country impeded him in the pursuit of his own quarry. For like many gentlemen of great wealth, he was wholly intent on increasing it.

Omichand of the smooth tongue and the deceitful heart now became the diplomatic mentor of Robert Clive, teaching him the way in which power could be obtained in a country like Bengal, where the strong ruled the weak and where all its men of importance at this moment, Moslem lords and Brahman officials alike, could be counted among the weak. Clive was a ready learner. In fact, it is doubtful whether he needed much instruction. The desire and ability to subject men to his will was part of his very nature.

III

At the end of the second week of February (1757) Watts and Omichand set out for Murshidebad. On their way up they stopped at Hugli for a meeting with Nuncomar (Nandakumar), *phousdar*, or military governor, of the district.

Nuncomar was a fair enough villain himself, as all who have read the life and tribulations of Warren Hastings will recall. In fact, the palm for villainy should probably be awarded to the Brahman rather than to the Sikh, as the deceits and treacheries that the merchant practised for greed seem almost venial compared to the forgeries and plots which the other, a politician, practised to satisfy his ravenous hunger for power.

At this meeting Nuncomar showed himself in his true colours immediately. He was quite ready to betray the Nawab. He told Omichand that the Nawab was offering the French assistance against an English attack. For the sum of Rs. 12,000 he would prevent that assistance from reaching the French. This was a good beginning, and Watts made haste to report it to Clive. "If you approve of giving this present, all that you have to say to the bearer of this letter is *Golaub que Foul*, or 'a rose flower.'"

One need not suppose that Clive hesitated about speaking the word. *Golaub que Foul*, the rose flower, became the symbol of a new, but happily short-lived, chapter in Anglo-Indian relations.

When Watts and Omichand arrived at court they sought to lay all Siraj-ud-daula's fears of English intentions at rest. It was their job to soothe him with agreeable ideas of English virtue at the same time as they stirred him up against the French. So they proceeded to tell him that it was never the English who were the aggressors and never the English who broke faith; always, they said, it was those damned French. And it was the French now who treacherously threatened the peace and quiet of his Excellency's realm.

Look at the menace of Bussy's army in the Nizam's country! What a simple thing it would be for M. de Bussy to transfer it to Bengal! In fact, it was rumoured (the rumour being manufactured by Clive!) that Bussy was on his way—and Watts and Omichand well knew how alarmed the Nawab was at the report. Whereas the English—they were paragons of honour and integrity! For forty years he, Omichand, had lived under the English protection and not once had he known them to break their word, to the truth of which he took his oath by touching a Brahman's foot : "if a lie could be proved in England upon any one, they would be spit upon and never trusted."

The Nawab's sensitive soul may have been pleased by this glimpse of human nature so much nobler than any he had yet encountered but he was not convinced. Not, at least, to the extent of staking his kingdom on its existence. His own secret service must have told him, too, that Bussy was not coming after all. On February 20 he wrote letters to Watson and Clive absolutely forbidding any attack upon the French on pain of his coming to their assistance with his utmost force.

For once Siraj-ud-daula was firm in defence of his kingdom. His reply seemed to hold out no hope of a change of mind. Reluctantly, therefore, Clive turned towards the solution of his difficulty that the French were still holding out to him. The matter had to be settled quickly, as the season for departing ships was fast ending. The return of the south-west monsoon in March would compel him to stay where he was until September. So now a favourable answer was returned to the French proposal. Deputies came from Chandernagore and negotiations proceeded without a hitch. A treaty was agreed upon and copies of it were exchanged for signature. One copy was sent to Admiral Watson, who had taken no part in the negotiations, but whose signature on behalf of His Majesty's government was necessary.

Watson refused, however, to sign it. His objections were logical and considered in the abstract sound, though they did not take sufficiently into account the necessities of the situation. He enquired, first, whether the French deputies had the power to conclude a treaty of neutrality that would be binding on all the representatives of the French nation, both royal and Company's.

No, they were forced to confess, they had not : it would need to be ratified by their superiors at Pondichéry.

But that, the Admiral pointed out, would mean a delay of several weeks, and meanwhile all the advantages of neutrality would lie with the French. Suppose the treaty were not ratified, suppose a French fleet arrived, suppose Bussy came with his army, then the English would have lost their present favourable opportunity to take Chandernagore.

Clive felt, so long as they were forbidden by the Nawab to attack, that they had no option but to sign the treaty. Watson was obdurate on both points. To attack Chandernagore now, he said, would be a breach of faith not to be contemplated until the Nawab himself broke faith. This made Clive indignant. Had not he and the members of the Committee already pledged their word ? Had not they given assurances to the Nawab that they would respect the neutrality, and had not he guaranteed it ? What would he and all the world now think when they found it refused ? " That we are men without principles or that we are men of a trifling disposition."

Besides, what was he, Clive, to do now ? The refusal of the neutrality would certainly increase the chances of the Nawab and the French combining against them, and if they did so, he could by no means be sanguine of success. Mr. Watson, he said, had done everything that could be expected of a brave and gallant man and had contributed greatly towards the success of the expedition thus far, but future operations against the Nawab would depend chiefly upon the land forces, and their own officers must be the best judges of what they could effect. So if Mr. Watson continued obdurate the responsibility for any resulting misfortune to the Company's affairs must rest with him. He himself would leave all the forces he could spare for the defence of Calcutta and return with the rest immediately to Madras in pursuance of his positive orders. And for this purpose he requested the ordering of proper conveyance.

It was this critical moment that Siraj-ud-daula selected to throw the whole game away, and with it his best chance of keeping his kingdom. A new fear had come into his life—that miserable life of his that was so controlled by fear and passion. Wisdom and judgment had long ago fled from his feeble and diseased mind, if they had at any time found lodgment there. His passions and vices were his own, but anyone and everyone could play on his fears, and for the English and French agents at his court it had become a tug-of-war to see which could play the stronger on them for their own ends.

Now it was a new fear that was tormenting him, and the English were quick to take advantage of it. Ahmad Shah, King of Afghanistan, had recently come down from his mountain passes and repeated Nadir Shah's feat of sacking Delhi. He was threatening now to proceed onwards to Bengal. Siraj-ud-daula began looking for aid against him from the people best able to supply it and who had contracted to do so.

On March 6, the day after Clive had delivered his ultimatum to Watson, letters were received from the Nawab and Watts suggesting that the Nawab was now willing to trade his permission for an attack on Chandernagore in exchange for English assistance against the Afghan.

The effect was magical : the Committee forgot about the proposed peace in their eagerness to begin the desired war. Watson and Clive replied to the Nawab separately ; the one in highly menacing terms, demanding the permission, demanding also the fulfilment of every article of the treaty of peace in ten days on pain of " kindling such flame in your country as all the water in the Ganges shall not be able to extinguish " ; the other, Clive, regretting in more diplomatic language the inability of the French to conclude the neutrality and subtly conveying the information that he was on his way to Chandernagore, where he would await a reply, " which I hope will be satisfactory," before commencing hostilities.

Thus the die was cast. By taking the road to Chandernagore the English were already on the road to Plassey. And from Plassey to Murshidebad, and Murshidebad to Lucknow, and from Lucknow to Delhi, and so on, until the road by slow stages was to lead to every part of India. The march towards an empire was begun. Clive was looking for security. But security in India, as elsewhere, was to prove a will-o'-the-wisp. In the name of security extensions of influence and dominions were constantly to be made, but each extension was to bring forth a fresh crop of menaces. Nothing but the natural frontiers of a virtual continent—the ocean and the mountains—could end that ceaseless, reluctant search. And when it ended how much real security had been gained ? Nothing but the realization of Cecil Rhodes's dream of a true Pax Britannica world-wide in extent could make an Indian Empire genuinely secure.

IV

Clive broke camp on March 8 and began a slow advance northwards. A reinforcement of 114 men had just landed from Bombay, but it was far from large enough to remove his worry over his small numbers. The long missing *Cumberland* reached the mouth of the Hugli on the 7th, too late for the detachment on board to join him, but if he had counted on its aid he must have been disappointed, because of the 300 Europeans who were aboard when the expedition sailed, only 90 very sick men were left ; the rest of them had been reclaimed by the Madras government to strengthen its garrisons.

On the 9th Clive encamped near the Danish factory at Serampore. To a demand from the French Council for an explanation of his advance he unblushingly replied : " I very sincerely declare to you that at this present time I have no intention to attack your settlement. If I should alter my mind, I shall not fail to advise you of it." Somehow he forgot this promise : when next M. Renault, the Governor, heard from him, four days later, it was to receive a summons to surrender !

However, the French were by no means unprepared for such an eventuality. They had prudently begun to overhaul the state of their defences as soon as the English recaptured Calcutta, and still more actively when news of the declaration of war reached them. And when on the following day Clive encamped two miles from the French gardens, where the Chandernagore officials had their country estates, his real intention must have been perfectly plain. At all events, the French got busy erecting batteries in the streets of the town leading from the south.

Clive's march was deliberately slow. He was waiting for that reply from the Nawab, which he hoped would be " satisfactory." On the 12th he encamped two miles to the west of Chandernagore. On the 13th the reply came. No matter what its nature might have been, it is difficult to believe that Clive and Watson would now have desisted from the intended attack. The Nawab, as it happened, saved them from having to consider such a problem, or rather it would be closer to the actual facts to say that Watts and Omichand saved them.

For Siraj-ud-daula had already repented of his peace with the English and was deeply incensed, as well he might be, with the Admiral's threatening and insulting letter, and it was therefore fortunate that Watts and Omichand were on the spot to counteract French influence and to remove the Nawab's wrong impression that Watson was responsible for the failure of the neutrality pact. They pointed out an aspect of the matter that the Nawab might otherwise have overlooked : namely, " the condescension shown by the British by accepting, and the indignity offered to him by the French in rejecting his expedient." They also did not fail to make skilful use of the Nawab's dread of the Afghans. He said he needed English assistance against this menace. Very well ; but how could he expect the English to leave their settlement undefended against an attack by their enemies ? Let the English, who always remained faithful to their promises, first deal with their treacherous foes and then they would march whithersoever the Nawab wished.

The Nawab in his miserable state of fear seems to have been somewhat impressed by this argument, though to what actual extent cannot be known. He directed that a friendly letter be written to the Admiral. And it was here that fortune dealt him one of her unkindest blows. Their object within their grasp, Watts and Omichand were taking no chances of the letter not being worded in the desired way. They bribed the Nawab's secretary "to pen this important Epistle in a proper style, so as to permit the Attack immediately, and to despatch it without delay."

The thing was done with proper Oriental enigma. After a paragraph accepting the English contention that the French were responsible for the failure of the negotiations, came this sphinx-like yet, to the waiting Englishmen, all-too-easily-solved riddle : " You have understanding and generosity : If your enemy with an upright heart claims your protection, you will give him his life, but then you must be well satisfied of his intentions ; if not, whatever you think right, that do."

We who are accustomed to a less ambiguous manner of speech might consider this a trifle inadequate for Clive's and Watson's purpose ; and so may they have done. But they were in no mood to be critical. They were, indeed, ready to grab at any kind of word from the Nawab that might be construed as a consent. For the letter arrived at another critical moment, as a council-of-war, called by the Admiral, was sitting to consider what was best to be done, and there were still some who favoured the neutrality pact. The letter, wrote Watts in his memoirs, " cut the Gordian knot and put an end to the debate."

It so happened that Watson's attitude had undergone a transformation in the last few days, and he was now as eager for the fray as Clive. What might seem to anyone not cognizant of the etiquette of a royal service a somewhat slight cause had brought about this marked change of sentiment. The Right Honourable the Lords Commissioners of the Admiralty had officially notified him of the existence of a state of war with France. Hitherto he had only known of it unofficially, which was not apparently sufficient for his strong sense of professional propriety. Now, however, that his Royal Master had informed him personally, he was ready, nay, anxious for immediate action. It had become his duty to distress the national enemy by every means in his power. He wrote to the Select Committee to this effect on March 12, and on the following day Clive summoned the Governor of Chandernagore to surrender.

Chandernagore owed as much to the vigorous, improving hand of Dupleix as did Pondichéry. Its prosperity and importance dated from his governorship, and it was, as Clive says, " a most magnificent and rich colony." It was also, unlike Calcutta, strongly fortified. Nobody could walk into Fort d'Orléans as Siraj-ud-daula had walked into Fort William and the French into Fort St. George. It was a well-constructed work 120 yards square, mounting ten guns on each side of its four bastions, besides others along the connecting curtains, and from its eastern side, facing the river, stretched a ravelin to the river bank upon which were mounted eight more guns. The other three sides were surrounded by a ditch. As was usual, buildings during peace-time had been erected close to the walls obstructing the range of fire, and M. Renault had not had time to tear them all down, but he had erected barricades with supporting batteries in the principal streets leading to the fort and he had also erected a six-gun battery on the river bank as a further protection against what he feared most of all, a bombardment by the English squadron. His preparations were far from complete, however, and his garrison was small. It numbered, all told, some 800, of whom only 230 were regular French troops, the rest being sailors, sepoys, topasses, and civilians. The Nawab had left 2000 of his troops to aid the French in case of an English attack, but these were useless and fled at the first shot.

While Watson was slowly, and with the infinite caution that such an operation required, working his ships up the river, Clive began the assault by attacking the batteries that guarded the approaches to the fort. After Eyre Coote's men had worked their way forward and gained possession of the houses adjacent to and in the rear of a battery to the north-west of the fort, so rendering the position untenable, the French abandoned all their outworks on the land side and retired within the shelter of the fort.

On the following day, the 15th, Clive occupied the abandoned area and advanced his lines to within a hundred yards of the fort. He then brought up his artillery and supplies and set about his preparations for bombing the place. The French, meanwhile, kept up a hot and well-directed fire which impeded and even threatened at times to prevent the erection of batteries. It was not until the night of the 22nd that everything was in readiness, and by then, too, Admiral Watson had brought his ships safely to anchor.

The Admiral needed flood tides to carry his large ships over the innumerable shoals and sand-banks. These he had for three days after he sailed from Calcutta on the 15th, and they brought his flagship the *Kent*, with the *Tyger* and *Salisbury*, safely to within sight of Chandernagore. But there he was stopped by the considerable obstructions that the French had placed in the passage, which was at this point very narrow. They had sunk several vessels and had thrown across two booms moored with chains. They also had moored three large ships above the fort in readiness to be used as fireships.

During the night of the 19th Watson sent the ships' boats up the river strongly manned and armed. They cut the booms, slipped silently by the fort, and cut also the cables of the three French ships, and while passing over the sunken vessels they were able to make a surmise, which proved to be correct, that the channel was not entirely blocked. A French officer is said to have betrayed the fact that the French had left a passage open for their own ships in case of need.

On the following night Watson sent an officer to make soundings to discover its exact whereabouts. He did his mission under heavy fire and came back with the welcome news that there was room for one vessel at a time to pass with safety. Watson now only needed a good tide to carry him before the fort. While he was waiting he was joined by Admiral Pocock, who upon arrival at the mouth of the river on board the *Cumberland* and hearing what was afoot, had transferred to his barge and had himself rowed up the river in order to be in time. A few hours before the attack Mr. Pocock hoisted his flag on the *Tyger*.

At daybreak on March 23 the combined land and water attack on Chandernagore was launched. The *Tyger* led the way past the sunken ships, followed by the *Kent* and *Salisbury*. Simultaneously Clive opened fire with his batteries and raked the ramparts with musketry. The French stood gallantly to their guns and greeted both their assailants with a hot and accurate fire. The ships withheld their fire until they had reached their appointed stations, the *Tyger* opposite to the north-east bastion, the *Kent* opposite the ravelin, and the *Salisbury* abreast of the south-east bastion. Unfortunately the *Kent* failed to reach her station, as the tide had begun to ebb, and before she came to anchor she had drifted backwards and finally brought up at the point where the *Salisbury* should have been. Consequently the *Salisbury* had to anchor lower down and could not get into action.

The action lasted three hours, during which time the French guns did great execution and damage to the two British ships. Most of the officers of the *Kent* were killed or wounded. One shot exploded some cartridges and started a fire which caused a panic among the crew. The *Tyger* suffered nearly as severely and Admiral Pocock himself was among the wounded. But each successive heavy broadside told still more severely on the French. Their guns were one by one dismounted, their parapet crumbled, and their men were struck down. Clive was waiting for the moment to storm, but before it came the French, seeing that further resistance was impossible, surrendered.

In after days, when all these happenings became the source of retrospective bitterness against Clive and the Company, it was claimed on behalf of His Majesty's forces that it was they on board the ships, and not the Company's forces on land, that had taken Chandernagore—a claim that cannot be disputed. Clive lost hardly a man, whereas the casualties on board the ships numbered over 130.

Chapter Thirteen

THE GAME

" To deceive a deceiver is no deceit "
ULPIAN FULWELL

I

THERE IS ONLY ONE safe and prudent way in which to regard the intricate intrigues, plotting, and barefaced duplicity that absorbed all Clive's attention after the taking of Chandernagore, and that is the way he regarded them—as a game : " The nice and important game that was to be played with the late Nabob." For a game, not being governed by the ordinary ethical code, but having its own rules, which may, as in the case of poker, demand of its players the utmost deceitfulness, is exempted from the kind of moral judgment passed upon the conduct of human relations in general. By accepting that view, the historian of Clive saves himself a great deal of worry and difficulty, for there is no surer way for a biographer or historian to get into trouble than by attempting to apply moral judgments. When, too, it is recognized that Clive's opponent was playing the same game as he, that it was the game being played simultaneously by all the statesmen of Europe, who had their Casanovas and Cagliostros to act the parts of Omichand and Nuncomar, and that there never was any need for him to try to justify it to his contemporaries, the only justification required being success, we can with an easy mind forget about ethics and settle down to watch the skill of the players.[1]

The rules of Clive's and Siraj-ud-daula's game called for the writing of innumerable letters. The letters seldom expressed the real sentiments of the writer. They were merely part of the palaver of diplomacy, and the flattering tones generally employed

---

[1] Compare Orme with John Payne, Nov. 17, 1757, *re* some dubious negotiations with Muhammad Ali : " I know not whether such double dealing may square with the politics of Europe but in Asia nothing but dissimulation will do." [92]

deceived no one, though they must have added much, certainly, to Clive's amused enjoyment.

The day, for instance, upon which Clive appeared before Chandernagore he received the agreeable assurance from the Nawab that he was very impatient to have the pleasure of seeing him and " our friendship shall never cease, but be always increasing." Interpreted, this meant, " I am counting on you to help me against the dreadful Afghans." And four days later, when the Nawab's apprehensions were temporarily set at rest by reassuring news from the Afghan camp, he wrote : " I look on this blessing as the effect of my friendship with you. I therefore write that you need not give yourself the trouble of coming. I have great pleasure in your friendship. Since on a single letter of mine you were ready to come to my assistance, I make no doubt that whenever I shall desire you to come and assist me, you will be ready to join me."

It followed that since the Nawab no longer needed English assistance he was no longer willing to pay the English price of assistance, so he repented of the implied consent to the attack on Chandernagore almost as soon as he gave it. The news that Chandernagore was actually being attacked consequently disturbed him greatly, and he ordered Nuncomar at once to send assistance to the French. According to the rules of the game this move could be, and was at once, checked by Clive by the simple expedient of a fresh bribe to Nuncomar. When Siraj-ud-daula went further and ordered up a division of his army under Rai Durlab, Clive sent Rai Durlab a polite but unmistakable warning to keep his hands off :

" I hear you are arrived within twenty miles of Hughly. Whether you come as a friend or an enemy I know not. If as the latter, say so at once, and I will send some people out to fight you immediately. If as the former, I beg you will stay where you are, for we can conquer the enemies we have to deal with here if they were ten times stronger."

The similarity of Clive's game to poker will now be fully apparent.

It was also part of the game to pretend complete obtuseness as to the other's true sentiments. This was a department of it in which Clive especially shone. With what boyishly malicious glee he must have penned this announcement to the Nawab of the surrender of Fort d'Orléans ! Not content with ascribing his success " to the blessing of the Almighty and the influence of your favour," he added :

" As I am persuaded you will be pleased at my success, therefore I thought proper and necessary to send you the particulars of this victory. My heart is earnest in your interest, and shall be always ready with my own life and that of my whole army to drive away your enemies. I hope that by your Excellency's favour all our enemies in your country will fall into our hands."

The Nawab was furious at the news, but strict observance of the rules was one of his more agreeable characteristics. So he wrote :

" The particulars of your victory, which I had long been impatient to hear, gave me inexpressible pleasure. I thank God that your enemies so easily fell into your hands, and that their great place is fallen into your hands. You have no longer any uneasiness on their account. It has pleased God to make you and all your friends happy in this great victory."

How important a part of the game this epistolary exchange was may be gathered from the fact that Clive is said to have received from the Nawab no fewer than ten letters in one day, all in different tones, like the notes of a scale—because the rules did not compel you to be always friendly and cordial if you knew how to be politely insolent and threatening. And you might even change your key and introduce a dissonant chord of decided hostility. But whatever the note struck by the Nawab, Clive was equal to the appropriate response. He answered the letters " punctually with all the calmness and complacence imaginable."

Nor, of course, did your actions have to tally in any way with your words. This was one of the rules that Siraj-ud-daula understood better—but only a little better—than Clive. Clive understood perfectly well the diplomatic value of a *fait accompli*, and such the prompt capture of Chandernagore certainly was. He knew also the value of keeping up a bold and intimidating front. After the fall of Chandernagore, when Watson returned with the squadron to Calcutta, Clive made his camp a mile to the northward of the town, intending by this small advance " to strike some awe into the Nabob and facilitate our business at the Durbar."

N

That business now, as he explained to Watts, was to persuade the Nawab " to abandon the French to us." To this end the somewhat ingenuous argument was to be employed that " what we have done is best both for him and for us." Compare what the French had done in the Deccan with what the English had done ! Whereas the French had made themselves masters of the country and extracted whole provinces from Salabut Jang, " the man that we support is immensely indebted to us." Siraj-ud-daula had to be made to realize that " our sole view is to stop the ambitious progress of the French, to effect which he must enter into a strict alliance with us," against them and all their evil designs, and that henceforth the English for their part would act only as merchants.

It was naturally a little difficult to make Siraj-ud-daula believe this, even though the safety of his throne depended—as it did—upon his believing it. Having regularly done the wrong thing so far, it was to be expected of him to do the same now. He had attacked the English in their weakness, believing that weakness to be helplessness. When he found out that mistake, he had failed to do the obvious thing and unite with the French to restore the balance of power. And now, when face to face with the victorious English, he again refused to adopt the only wise course left open to him, which was to take the English at their word and rely on their promises. For the truth was that they really *did* want peace with him, even if they were inclined to interpret rather liberally in their favour the terms of it.

It was axiomatic with Clive that French and English could not exist side by side as political rivals in India. The surrender of Chandernagore had not terminated the French menace. Bussy was still at large, rumoured to be somewhere not far from the borders of Bengal, with a force of disciplined troops. The French also still possessed a factory at Kasimbazar close to the court of Murshidebad and its head, M. Law, was a recognized power in the Nawab's counsels. The garrison of this factory, moreover, had now been increased by fugitives from Chandernagore. Accordingly, on March 29, Clive demanded that the Nawab deliver up to him the persons and effects of the French at Kasimbazar.

At once the battle at court between French and British diplomacy for control over the fickle Nawab was resumed with unabated fury. Both sides resorted to bribery as the only means to effect anything. If information was needed, the Nawab's head spy was the man to be bribed. Omichand's help and experience were invaluable to the English in these transactions.

Yet it was several weeks before the English agents, with the help of the longer purse, finally succeeded. And in the meantime the Nawab was writing imploringly to " the Distinguished of the Empire, the Sword of Riches, the Victorious in War, Monsieur Bussie Bahadur " to come quickly to his aid : " What can I write of the perfidy of the English ? "

He twisted and turned backwards and forwards in his attempt to evade Clive's inexorable demand. Now he took the line that the French surrender must be voluntary, and then he tried to shift the burden of decision on to the Mogul Emperor. It was useless. Clive's demand was firmly based on the terms of the treaty that Siraj-ud-daula himself had signed, and he was able solemnly to call upon him to comply with its terms in all particulars.

At last the Nawab, driven to the wall, ordered the French to leave the country ; but this, as Watts warned Clive, was probably only a stratagem to gain time. Anger, resentment, fear—that haunting fear that never left him—played on the wretched man in turn. Now he ordered Watts to be expelled from the Durbar. He was heard to mutter, " I will destroy them and their nation," and he even ordered Mir Jafar, his army commander, to march. Next day he countermanded the order to Mir Jafar and recalled the British agent and presented him with a dress of honour.

Such fear ! He even feared that the English warships with their terrible guns would sail all the way up the river and bombard Murshidebad—a feat that would, surely, have equalled the proposed use of the Bronx river to defeat Washington's army !

Admiral Watson, for his part, conspicuously failed to play the game. He had, indeed, a most complete contempt for it, the same contempt that many busy men have for any kind of game. He was an honest sailor—by God !—and a sailor's job was to fight, not diddle, his country's enemies, and more especially the French. From the beginning his letters to the Nawab had been quite lamentable in their total disregard of the niceties of style and the conventions of the game. That threat to kindle such a flame in his country as all the water in the Ganges should not be able to extinguish—what a breach of etiquette ! Obviously it was the voice of a man who could not tell the difference between an

" informative " and a " business double ! " And now, when he was told that the Nawab was engaged on some hocus-pocus business with the French, he wrote him in the same blunt and indiscreet terms : " I have already told you, and I now repeat it again, that while a Frenchman remains in this kingdom I will never cease pursuing him " ; and he demanded leave for the English troops to march north and do the ejecting of M. Law's party themselves.

It is apt to be embarrassing to have such men as Watson around, even as partners, when there is monkey-business afoot, and there was plenty of such business afoot now. For Clive was no longer finding the game amusing. It was becoming, in fact, as all games are apt to become, deadly serious.

He had excused himself to Pigot and the gentlemen at Madras for his failure to return by pointing to the taking of Chandernagore as a worthwhile object : " of more consequence to the Company, in my opinion, than the taking of Pondichéry itself." Unavoidably now, on account of the season, he would have to wait until August, and that time could be profitably spent by cleaning up what was left of French influence on the root and branch principle. But the Nawab's defiant attitude was threatening to upset this plan. The time had, in fact, come for a showdown, and he made it plain to the Nawab that thoughts of war were in his head. By this time he had come to know Siraj-uddaula's nature very thoroughly. He correctly guessed that his defiant attitude was due to the removal of fear of the Afghans that had recently been troubling him. Ahmad Shah was, as a matter of fact, on his way back to his own country.

On April 30 Clive wrote to Governor Pigot :

" The most of the articles of the peace are complied with ; yet, from the tyranny, cowardice, and suspicion of the Nabob, no dependence can be had upon him. . . . One day he tears my letters, and turns out our *vakeel*, and orders his army to march ; he next countermands it, sends for the vakeel, and begs his pardon for what he has done. Twice a week he threatens to impale Mr. Watts ; in short, he is a compound of everything that is bad, keeps company with none but his menial servants, and is universally hated and despised by the great men. . . . For my own part, I am persuaded there can be neither peace nor security while such a monster reigns."

Thus at last after four months of constant effort to restrict the purposes of his expedition to the simple one of restoring to the English their former rights, privileges, and possessions in the Nawab's dominions (with the all-important additional one of dealing with the French), Clive arrived at the momentous conclusion that what he sought was impossible without going a great deal further, even to the length of deposing the reigning prince— something that lay far outside the scope of his orders.

The conclusion was arrived at by himself alone, and from now on he was to play practically a lone hand. Nobody else on the English side was capable of forming, let alone carrying out, such a design.

II

Clive had some excuse for wanting to enter the conspiracy against Siraj-ud-daula. When the conspiracy was first heard of towards the end of April it had every appearance of being a genuine, spontaneous, *bona fide* revolt of subjects of worth and substance against an intolerable tyranny. The conspiracy party was so strong in numbers, power, and influence that its prospects must have seemed very bright and its aim easy of attainment. Indeed, the news of it could scarcely have appeared to one in Clive's difficult position in any other light but as a simple, providential, and legitimate solution to an otherwise insoluble problem. It would be asking too much to expect him to foresee the actual course that events were to take, with their moments of agonizing doubts and uncertainty, their peril, and the complexities of intrigue and deception in which they were to involve him.

A revolution had been brewing in Bengal almost from the day Siraj-ud-daula ascended the *musnud*. The madness of the man's conduct towards the Europeans had been duplicated by his behaviour towards his own subjects. "Him whom the gods wish to destroy they first make mad." He could with impunity have struck Jagat Seth, a Hindu, on the face and mortally affronted him with threats of circumcision, if he had not at the same time behaved in similar outrageous fashion to his Moslem nobles, filling them with such disgust and, what was worse, such a feeling of complete insecurity for the safety of their lives, honour, and property that, as the contemporary Indian chronicler, Ghulam

197

Husain Khan, tells us, the desire to rid themselves of this cruel, treacherous, capricious, avaricious, and insensate ruler was general among the chiefs at court and in the army, particularly among the old ministers of Aliverdi Khan and among also the principal citizens of Murshidebad, all of whom joined together to contrive some way of overthrowing him. The help of the English was felt to be necessary, and the banker Jagat Seth, who was the brains behind the movement, was delegated to make the approach to them.

The first view of the project, as it was laid before Clive in the reports from Watts at the end of April, was as clear and attractive as anything of the kind could be. The Nawab—so it was said—was about to march northwards, and as soon as he did so Mir Jafar and the other chiefs would join forces, seize him, and set up another prince. Apparently all that the English were expected to do was to lull him into a sufficient sense of security to enable them to carry out their purpose. Would Clive write and say what the English wanted in the way of money, land, and treaties in return for their assistance ?

But it was not by any means as clear and simple as that. Oriental politics never are. Nothing was more difficult for anyone, least of all the English, than to find out the exact situation and discover all that was involved in a plot of these dimensions. All kinds of rumours were reaching Clive, and he had only Watts to keep him informed. But if he did not know all, he knew enough to decide that if, as seemed certain, a revolution was pending, he wanted to be a party to it. So he was " ready for the worst "—ready, as he said, to march immediately. He could not leave camp to come to Calcutta " on any consideration "—not even to consult with the Committee.

The Committee, however, wanted very much to see him, and would not be put off so easily. They had a right to know everything he did, and they particularly wanted to know about his new plans. They did not like the way he was taking more and more upon himself without consulting them and was now corresponding directly with the Nawab and with Watts and Luke Scrafton (the latter he had recently sent to Murshidebad as his own agent). Clive urged on his own behalf that speed and secrecy required this correspondence. The English having assumed the character of conspirators had to take every precaution. Watts was insisting on the need for utmost secrecy and wanting all surnames to be put into cipher. "Talk of nothing else but merchandise," he implored Clive.

To satisfy the objectors Clive went down to Calcutta on May 1, laid the whole correspondence before the Committee, and had no trouble in obtaining its approval for his proposed support of Mir Jafar. Armed with this authority he returned to camp determined to see the business through, come what might !

The game with the Nawab now assumed a new and grimmer aspect. To give time and opportunity for the conspiracy to be properly hatched Siraj-ud-daula's nerves had to be quieted ; the illusion had to be preserved that the English were still his friends. So Clive wrote him what he called a " soothing " letter and accompanied it with an appropriate gesture " to take away all suspicion " :

> " Yesterday my army broke up their camp, more than half is gone to Calcutta, the rest remain at Chandernagore. Calcutta is become a place of such misery since your army has almost destroyed it, that there is not room for more soldiers without endangering their lives by sickness. However, farther to satisfy you, I shall order down to Calcutta all my field cannon. I expect to hear that your army has retired likewise to Muxadavad, and that you have been as expeditious in performing what you promised as I have."

Siraj-ud-daula, however, was not so gullibly minded. Not only did he keep his army at Plassey, but he carried on a correspondence with the French with a view to a joint attack upon the English.

By what might be described as the same mail Clive instructed Watts to enter upon the business with Mir Jafar at once :

> " I am ready & will engage to be at Niesaray in 12 Hours after I receive Your letter, which place is to be the rendezvous of the whole Army. The Major who commands at Calcutta has all ready to embark at a Minutes Warning & has Boats sufficient to carry Artillery Men & Stores to Niesaray. I shall march by Land & Join him there and we will then proceed to Muxadavad or the place we are to be joined at Directly.
>
> " Tell Meir Jaffeir to fear nothing, that I will join him with 5000 Men who never turn'd their Backs and that if he fails seizing him we shall be strong enough to drive him out of the

Country, assure him I will march night & day to his Assistance and stand by him as long as I have a Man left. I am in great want of Draft Bullocks, you must send some at all Events when you hear I am upon the March."

Clive was clearly in a state of high nervous excitement when he sent these orders. He was ready immediately to embark on what he knew would be the greatest adventure of his life, and he could scarcely wait for it to begin. At no time could his high-strung temperament stand the strain of waiting. Nothing, therefore, could have been more upsetting for him than what actually occurred. He had to stand ready to march at an hour's notice and yet it was to be more than a month before he actually marched, and that month was filled with nothing but nerve-racking delays and uncertainties ; such an experience for him was torture. Indeed, he nearly broke under the strain. It was not until he was at last on the field of battle—that field upon which he staked everything—that he was able again to show the coolness and collectedness which in moments of peril had never failed him.

It was now that he was to discover the mistake he had made in employing Omichand. It is hard to see how, having made this initial mistake, he could have avoided letting him into the plot, even though the man's previous record must have given some warning of what to expect of him. Omichand had a nose for plots and if he had smelled out this one, as he most assuredly would have done, his revenge for not having been made a party to it would have been speedy, effectual, and most disastrous.

His response to the news imparted to him by Watts was not, however, exactly encouraging. He did not belong to the Mir Jafar party, he did not relish the idea of Mir Jafar becoming Nawab, and his relations with the Seths were anything but friendly. But as an alert man of business he could not fail to see that a perfect opportunity had been offered to him to obtain his heart's desire, wealth beyond even the dreams of his great avarice. Armed with the knowledge he now possessed he could ask for almost anything he pleased, and the conspirators would have to give it to him if they wished to preserve their dangerous secret and with it their lives ; and he had no niggardly ideas about the value of his services or the worth of his silence, as what he demanded shows. Five per cent. of all the wealth found in Siraj-ud-daula's treasury and a quarter of his jewels !

Now, of course, none of the English had any real idea how much wealth the treasury contained, still less how much would still be there when the revolution was accomplished. As Watts had visions of £40,000,000, he had visions, too, of Omichand receiving a commission for services rendered of no less than £2,000,000 *plus* the jewels. This naturally seemed to both him and Clive absurdly exorbitant. Even at the lowest estimate Omichand's share would not have fallen far short of one million pounds. Clive had been prepared to give him a commission of 5 per cent. on all the money that would pass out of the treasury into English hands, but even this seemed to Watts altogether too generous, and he did not mention the offer to Omichand.

Omichand, however, had no objection to blackmail, and he put Watts—and Clive—into a real quandary when he threatened to betray the plot to Siraj-ud-daula if his demand were not granted. Watts knew and Clive knew and Omichand knew that if he did so every Englishman within reach, which included Watts himself, would most certainly be killed. Omichand may have been bluffing, but neither Watts nor Clive wanted to take that chance. So Watts persuaded Omichand to be content with thirty lakhs (£350,000) and inserted that figure in the proposed Articles of Agreement which he sent down to Clive for the signature of the members of the Committee.

Those thirty lakhs would have been a cheap price for Clive to have paid—though Clive himself would not have had to pay it !—for the saving of his honour and for the prevention of all the damaging publicity that has been given to his subsequent action from that day to this. But Clive did not see things in that light. He knew how strongly opposed Mir Jafar and the Seths were to. Omichand being mixed up in the business at all, and, besides, he had all of an Englishman's natural dislike for being tricked and swindled and, above all, blackmailed. He wanted to see the villain *damned* first, and damned—or at least justly and deservedly swindled in return—he was going to be if Clive knew anything about the sentiments of the Select Committee. He himself knew perfectly well what *he* wanted done.

He received Watts's communication on May 16 and took it at once to Calcutta. What followed is only too well known. The Committee agreed to all the terms except the one relating to

Omichand. They could not swallow that, any more than Clive could, and they accepted—all but Admiral Watson—the way out that Clive suggested. When he returned to the French Gardens it was with the Committee's permission to prepare two agreements, one real and the other—for Omichand's sole benefit—fictitious ; both were to be signed by the members of the Committee, but the real one omitted mention of any payment to Omichand.

He wrote : " Gentlemen,—Enclosed you will receive the real and fictitious Articles of Agreement, which you will please to sign ; the Admiral promised me to do the same by the real one, but not the fictitious one ; if he makes any scruple send it without & we will sign it for him in such manner that Omichund shall not discover it."

It came to pass as Clive had anticipated. Watson refused his signature to the fictitious treaty ; but he seems, on the weight of evidence presented before the House of Commons, to have given some sort of tacit consent at least—of a " do as you please " kind—to his name being put to it in order that the whole scheme should not be overthrown. This was accordingly done by Mr. Lushington, who was the bearer of the papers, and both treaties were thereupon despatched to Watts.

Perhaps at no moment in history has a moral scruple been displayed more inconveniently than in this famous episode. But for it there would have been no shining example of rectitude with which Clive's treatment of Omichand could be contrasted, nor would Clive have been under the disagreeable though, for him, completely shameless necessity of committing forgery. We may well believe Clive when he said that he thought it perfectly warrantable and that he would do it again a hundred times. Yet, even while we are doing all the judging and condemning that may seem right and proper for the case, we cannot withhold a certain admiration for his immoral moral courage and his frank and challenging readiness to avow the deed, even to glorying in it.

III

The sooner things were now brought to a conclusion the better. Each day's delay increased the chances of discovery, and, besides, the rains were approaching. But first a conference had somehow to be arranged with Mir Jafar, and it had to be without the

Nawab's knowledge, else his suspicions would certainly be aroused. Scrafton was to manage this while he was ostensibly on his way up to see Siraj-ud-daula. And meanwhile the game of deception had to be played to the limit against Omichand too.

"Flatter Omichund greatly," Clive told Watts ; " tell him the Admiral and Committee and self are infinitely oblig'd to him for the pains he has taken to aggrandize the Company's Affairs, and that his Name will be greater in England than it ever was in India." To give him no possible ground for suspicion Clive had deducted ten from the thirty lakhs he had demanded and substituted five per cent. of the whole sum received, " which," he cynically added, " will turn out the same thing."

Omichand, for his part, acted true to character. He never remained satisfied with a bargain if he saw a way of making a better one. Why take money only from the conspirators if a little of the information he possessed would serve also to extract money from the Nawab ? Not that he thought of revealing the whole plot, for that would defeat it, but just enough of it that could be sold with safety. Not being able to visit the palace without it being known, he took Watts into his confidence and told him that he was going to divulge a momentous secret to the Nawab, which was nothing less than an Anglo-French alliance to conquer and partition Bengal ! Whether this was the nature of his communication to Siraj-ud-daula or not—and Watts did not believe it—the fact remains, and Watts had the evidence of his own eyes to prove it, that a large sum of money was brought to Omichand that same night—no less than the sum, £40,000, which the Nawab had removed from his house in Calcutta, together with the rest of his goods and an order for the payment of an additional four lakhs.

Truly Omichand had made up his mind that whoever by the intervention of divine providence was to rule Bengal, he at any rate was to be a much richer man ! It was no doubt some satisfaction to Clive to learn that the man he was duping had obtained such solid provision for himself by other means.

Omichand's visit may or may not have had anything to do with Siraj-ud-daula's sudden distrust of Mir Jafar as well as of the English, but certainly that distrust was noticeably greater after than before, so much so that Watts began to lose his nerve. " For God's sake make haste," he wrote to Clive on the 20th ; "you are very sensible how extremely dangerous the least delay may be."

Scrafton was unable to get his private interview with Mir Jafar ;
the Nawab's guards were there to prevent it. Instead, he had to
endure two very unpleasant interviews with Siraj-ud-daula. Yet
all this while Clive and the Nawab went on exchanging their
masterpieces of insincerity almost daily, mingling threats and
warnings with professions of undying friendship. Each accused
the other of breaking the treaty and each asked the other for a
proof of sincerity.

Clive was now completing his preparations to march. He
asked and received from Watson the loan of some sailors (not
this time to be used as coolies !) ; but the admiral, with marked
aversion for the whole business, was not optimistic : " I do not
think your letters carry the most promising appearance of
success ; you cannot therefore be too cautious. . . ." But
Clive was not in the mood to be cautious.

On May 31 came a note from Scrafton : " I saw D (Mir
Jafar) this morning, his confidant sets out with the Article to-
morrow. Nothing can detain us a moment after his arrival.
B (Omichand) is along with me."

Omichand was along, but his reluctance to leave was most
evident. He would not leave without his precious money, and
when he had it he still was not satisfied. Before they reached
Kasimbazar he was discovered missing, and when he was found
it was in the treasury, where he was trying to extract still more
money. Next morning he was gone again, and this time he had
visited the camp at Plassey for a long talk with Rai Durlab. The
English suspicions of him had become so strong that they could
not get him down to Calcutta soon enough.

And still the agreement was not signed ! The terms of it were
liberal enough to the English : it confirmed all their privileges,
provided compensation for the losses that Siraj-ud-daula had
caused them, granted them the territory later known as the
twenty-four Paraganas, prohibited the building of any forts
(other than English) within twenty miles of the Hugli along its
whole course below Calcutta, and promised mutual assistance
against all enemies (with the Nawab paying for English military
aid whenever he required it). But what was of more immediate
consequence to Mir Jafar, and also to the English gentlemen
conducting the business, was the separate agreement covering the
donation of presents to those responsible for his elevation. These
were more than liberal : twelve lakhs to the Select Committee

and forty akhs to the army and navy, over and above the sums payable as reparations under the treaty—a total of £650,000.

It is, perhaps, little wonder that Mir Jafar should have wanted to consult with Rai Durlab, the State treasurer and an important member of the conspiracy before signing. This meant waiting until June 2, when Rai Durlab arrived in the city. And then Rai Durlab, not unreasonably, raised strong objections to the enormous money payments on the ground that there was but little money in the treasury. Watts, thinking that these objections were unsurmountable, wrote Clive, "Our scheme with Meir Jaffeir is upset, and there is reason to believe that Omichund's four hours' visit to Roydulub at Plassey has been the cause of it."

It is somewhat surprising that the cause of it had not been Siraj-ud-daula, who must have been under strong temptation to remove the danger by cutting off Mir Jafar's head ! Why he did not do so, unless it was that he was too much of a coward, is hard to explain.

When Clive received this gloomy message his temper, patience, and nerves gave out completely. "I will not embark in any undertaking with such a set of cowardly rascals," he cried in a fit of rage. The rains were nearly on him, and, worse than that, he found that the affair was being quite generally talked about in Calcutta ! He was certain Watts had allowed himself to be duped, and he angrily told him so.

But three days later Mir Jafar thought better of his refusal, and everything was settled—or so at least it seemed. Mr. Watts, not being able to have a meeting with Mir Jafar in any other way, had himself carried into Mir Jafar's palace in a dooly (a covered palanquin only used by Moslem women), and there in one of the apartments of the seraglio he obtained Mir Jafar's signature and his oath on the Koran to perform faithfully all that he had promised. The treaty was promptly despatched by bearer to Calcutta, and Watts told Clive to march immediately. Mir Jafar was to proclaim by beat of drum that the English were joined to them just as soon as Watts himself and his party had got themselves out of danger.

"I march Monday morning." And on Monday morning, June 12, the treaty having the day before been safely delivered to the Committee, Clive put his army in motion.

Chapter Fourteen

PLASSEY: (1) THE GAMBLER'S THROW

"Glory is a gamble and the definitions of history go to the winning side"
SEAN O'FAOLAIN

I

HISTORY HAS BEEN REMARKABLY KIND to Clive in the way in which it has presented the campaign of Plassey. The well-merited reward of great daring is the common verdict. History is always kind to conquerors. Though the difference between victory and defeat may often be as a hair's breadth, a yawning gulf divides them in the popular mind, too prone to categorical ways of thinking. Final success, however accomplished, whether merited or merely lucky, is the best protection that a man can have against a too-minute examination of the conduct that led to that success. But let him fail and the contrary at once happens ; his conduct is then subject to the severest tests that critical ingenuity can devise—his mistakes, his rashness, or his over-caution, his moments of hesitation, are probed for, and when found ruthlessly exposed.

History is concerned with events rather than with processes, but for the biographer the event, the accomplished fact is never as interesting or as important as the process by which it was achieved. The biographer has a different set of values from that of the historian. The event may be what it is, but he is concerned with the man behind it, with seeing him as a man and not merely as a maker of history. Plassey was an epochal event and Clive was its victor—thus history has it. But more interesting for the biographer is the fact that forty-eight hours before the great event the victor-to-be had decided that he dared not risk a battle !

Between February and July 1757 Clive was spoken of as "fortune's darling child." He was just that. Seldom has a man been more blessed with good fortune than Clive in bringing off his grand coup against Siraj-ud-daula. His contemporaries were

206

dazzled by his good fortune and so have his critics been, but good—or bad—fortune is not a criterion for judging either character or conduct.

II

Clive was fortunate, to begin with, in reaching Bengal at Christmas-time. The climate of Lower Bengal is very pleasant during the winter months, when the temperature averages between 50 and 70 degrees, and Europeans are able to engage in their multitudinous activities—so foreign to the Bengali nature— without discomfort or danger to their health. But the cold season is short. By April the heat is becoming oppressive, and it gets worse, with increasing humidity, until the " turkish-bath " stage is reached. In June the rains begin, which soon flood the low, alluvial plains so as to convert the Gangetic delta into a steaming hot sea strewn with many islands, a veritable archipelago through which there is little communication except by water ; and this is the season when Europeans are reduced to a miserable condition of sweaty prostration and morbid fear for their health.

For four months their whole existence partakes of this morbid tone ; it affects their general behaviour, their relations one with another, their letters home, their whole outlook on life. Intelligence and science have mitigated the severity and deadliness of this season for the successors of these eighteenth-century martyrs to the profit motive, but survival of it in those days was a matter of such profound thankfulness that the fortunate ones met together annually on October 15 to mourn the late departed, but still more to rejoice at their own preservation.

Clive was about to experience his first rainy season. " I hope you enjoy your health this hot weather," he remarked at the end of May to Admiral Watson, who was also new to the horror that was upon them. It was still hotter two weeks later, when Clive began his march ; in fact, the temperature then undoubtedly hovered around 100 degrees in the shade. The rains were beginning. It had been their near approach that had made him in such a hurry. And he had scarcely begun his campaign before they burst upon him with full tropical violence. Altogether, it was not the most propitious time of year in which to begin a campaign, and perhaps it is subject to doubt whether a prudent commander would have so opened it.

The army that was to found an empire consisted of 1022 Europeans, organized in two battalions, one led by Major Kilpatrick, the other by Captain Coote, and 2100 native infantry, sepoys from Madras and Bombay and the newly raised Bengal battalion, with ten field-pieces. A few invalids were left to garrison Calcutta, a few artillerymen manned the guns on the ramparts of Fort William. Every available man was needed in the ranks of Clive's army of adventure. If that army were destroyed, nothing but the guns of the fleet would be left to protect Calcutta from the same fate that overtook it the previous June. Bengal would again be lost and Madras would not get back the forces that it was counting upon for its own defence.

On the evening of June 12 the whole force, with the detachments that Major Kilpatrick had brought up that day from Calcutta, was gathered at Chandernagore. At daybreak on the 13th they set out. The Europeans, with all the artillery, ammunition, and stores, went in boats, which were towed up the river ; the sepoys on foot marching in column parallel to them along the state high-road that followed the right bank to Murshidebad, one of the few roads that the country possessed at this date. That night they camped at Nieseray. At three o'clock on the following day, as they approached Kalna, fifteen miles north of Hugli, they were met by Mr. Watts and his party.

For a diplomatic mission the departure of Mr. Watts and his companions from the capital had scarcely been dignified, but the acute danger of their position had prevented them from standing on ceremony. For several days before they left the conspiracy had been the talk of the town, including all manner of precise particulars about Clive's plans.

Watts obtained the Nawab's permission for himself and his two companions, Sykes and Collet, to have an afternoon's coursing. They rode out towards Kasimbazar, leaving directions at their house for supper to be prepared for them. When they had reached the open plain they dismissed their native grooms and made a dash for the safety of Clive's approaching army. After nightfall they came upon a division of the Nawab's army encamped on the plain near Daudpur and had to make a cautious circuit of it. By 1 a.m. they were back on the road, and then suddenly found themselves in the midst of a body of horse that had been stationed there to prevent the passage of Europeans. The horses neighed and kicked, but their riders fortunately slept.

The party quickly dismounted, left their horses, and made their way to the river, where they were lucky enough to find two open boats, and so were able to complete the rest of their flight by water.

On the 17th, the advance being resumed, Pattlee was reached and on the following day Major Coote was sent forward to take possession of the town and fort of Katwa, which he did after overcoming a brief resistance. On the 19th Clive joined him there. They were now 100 miles from Calcutta and forty from Murshidebad, and half-way between them and the capital on the other side of the river lay the entrenched camp of Plassey, where it was expected that the Nawab's army would be found. The moment of final decision had come.

It found the English commander singularly unprepared for it. The whole adventure was based upon Mir Jafar's active co-operation. Clive had expected that Mir Jafar would join him at Katwa with at least 10,000 men. Now that he was at Katwa there was no sign that Mir Jafar had any such intention. Every day Clive sent appeals to him to act, and Mir Jafar in his replies had been most disturbingly vague. The fog of uncertainty instead of dispersing grew thicker with every mile of the advance. Clive had no longer any means of knowing what was happening. For all that he knew the whole conspiracy might already have collapsed.

Indeed, that seemed the most likely supposition. The air of Bengal was as foul with treachery as it was heavy with vapour, and one final act of treachery against himself was to be put among the more probable possibilities. The few stray scraps of information that reached him—from Omichand among other contaminated sources—pointed strongly in that direction. What could he make of the strange fact that Mir Jafar still held his command in the Nawab's army when laid side by side first with Watts's news about the whole conspiracy being common knowledge in Murshidebad and then with the incontrovertible evidence of his own march and the unmistakable nature of his errand?

The day that Clive set out on his march he had sent Siraj-ud-daula a frank announcement of his intentions. He said he was on his way to Murshidebad to put the English disputes to arbitration before Jagat Seth, Rajah Mohunlal, Mir Jafar Khan, Rajah Rai Durlab, " and the rest of your great men "—that is to say, before the conspirators themselves ! " The rains being daily

o

increasing, and it taking a great deal of time to receive your answer, I therefore find it necessary to wait on you immediately, and if you will place confidence in me, no harm shall come from it. I represent this to you as a friend. Act as you please."

It is to be noted that Clive did not forget the rules of the game. " I represent this to you as a friend " was surely an example of finished technique !

There was really only one safe conclusion to be drawn : namely, that Mir Jafar had thought better of his agreement with the English and had reconciled himself to his prince. Otherwise it was as sure as night follows day that Siraj-ud-daula would have despatched him with Oriental and dictatorial promptness. Unless, of course, Mir Jafar had merely reconciled himself to his prince in order better to betray him later ! Who could possibly tell what was in the mind of such a man or how many treacheries he might not be harbouring there ? That some act of reconciliation had taken place was admitted by Mir Jafar himself in his letters—a matter of expediency, he told Clive, that was all.

What actually happened was that Siraj-ud-daula in the madness of his arrogance and infatuation, after dismissing Mir Jafar from his command and posting guards and spies on his palace—this was when he first came under suspicion—had thought to take more subtle and certain vengeance upon the English by detaching the traitor from their side, and so, instead of seizing him in his palace, as was naturally his first impulse when his suspicions became confirmed, he had gone to see him. In their interview they had exchanged solemn vows of loyalty and mutual support, and the Nawab had thereupon ordered his mutinous army to advance towards Plassey, Mir Jafar accompanying it.

Clive could no longer put confidence in anyone or anything. Every letter that he received had to be carefully scrutinized to make sure it was not a forgery, and having no trustworthy messengers he never knew when his own letters to Mir Jafar would be delivered into the Nawab's hands. In addition, there was the constant danger of their being intercepted.

And now, while he was vainly waiting at Katwa for Mir Jafar, the monsoon broke with its full fury. From the overcharged heavens descended torrents of rain in blinding sheets. Though this was his first experience of the formidable Bengal rains, he knew the hopeless conditions for military operations that would soon result. He knew, too, that the river would soon become unfordable. Little wonder, then, that his appeals to Mir Jafar become blunter and blunter ! That he abandons the empty verbiage of Oriental flattery and bombast and pleads like the man who has risked everything.

Little wonder, too, that his " puzzling " situation—as he in after years described it—was reflected in what he wrote to the Committee ! He assured them that until he had sufficient proof of the sincerity of Mir Jafar's intentions he would not cross the river. He would act with such caution as not to risk the loss of their forces. " Whilst we have them, we may always have it in our power to bring about a revolution, should the present not succeed." He thought he could find enough grain in and about Katwa to feed his men during the rains and could utilize the time either to bring the Nawab to terms or to obtain help from the Marathas or from the powerful Nawab of Oude. " I desire you will give me your sentiments freely how you think I should act, if Mir Jafar can give us no assistance."

This was a different Clive, surely, than the one who a few weeks before had been unwilling even to consult with the Committee ; who was ready to march at once, and who could not go to Calcutta " on any consideration " ! Now he was asking, almost imploring, their advice !

On the following day, June 20, he wrote to the Rajah of Beerbhoom asking for the aid of some horse, of which he was much in need. The Rajah was a not very powerful semi-independent chief, holding his hill-country principality on the borders of Bengal upon a military tenure from the Nawab. Between him and the English army lay more than fifty miles of rivers and swamps and almost impassable jungle, so that there was little likelihood of timely help from this source. Clive received a reply full of promises three days after Plassey, and on July 2 he received another letter, written after the news of the battle had reached the Rajah, saying that he had been on the march when he heard of the victory !

On the evening of the 20th Clive heard again from Mir Jafar. The letter came sewn up in a slipper.

" To-morrow, the day of the Eade (festival)," he wrote, " by the blessing of God I shall march. I shall have my tent fixed to the right or left of the army. I have hitherto been afraid to send you intelligence. After I am arrived in the army mutual intelligence will be easier, but here the Nabob has fixed *chokeys* (guards) on all the roads. Your letters come too open to me ; I hope that till our affairs are publicly declared you will be very careful."

To know that Mir Jafar was accompanying the Nawab in his forward move and that he would be " on the right or left of the army " was not comforting information. In fact, Clive decided that he could no longer place any dependence upon the man, and having decided that, he also made up his mind that he could not go forward.

Presumably reluctant to take the sole responsibility for such a complete change of plan, he called a council-of-war on the morning of the 21st, and proposed to it the following question : " Whether in our present situation, without assistance and on our own bottom, it would be prudent to attack the Nabob, or whether we should wait till joined by some country power." By " country power " he meant Mir Jafar or the Marathas or the Nawab of Oude or the Rajah of Beerbhoom.

In his evidence before the Committee of the House of Commons in 1773 he gave as his reason for calling the council that

" he thought it extremely hazardous to pass a river which is only fordable in one place, march 150 miles up country, and risk a battle, when if a defeat ensued not one man would have returned to tell it."

But he had already marched a hundred of those miles.

Clive gave his vote first. Major Kilpatrick and Major Grant and seven other officers supported him. But Major Coote, Captain Alexander Grant, and five others voted for an immediate attack.

According to Coote's evidence before the Parliamentary Committee, Clive informed the council-of-war that

" he found he could not depend upon Mir Jafar for anything more than standing neuter in case the army came to an action with the Nabob ; that M. Law, with a body of French, was then within three days' march of joining the Nabob, whose army, by the best intelligence he could get, was about 50,000 men ; and that he called the Council together for their opinion, whether, in those circumstances, it would be prudent to come to an immediate action with the Nabob, or fortify themselves where they were and remain till the monsoon was over and the Marathas could be brought into the Country to join us."

Coote then gave the following reasons for his own vote :

" Having hitherto met with nothing but success, which consequently had given great spirits to our men, I was of the opinion that any delay might cast a dampness ; 2dly, that the arrival of Monsieur Law would not only strengthen the Nabob's army, and add vigour to their Councils, but likewise weaken our force considerably, as the number of Frenchmen we had entered into our service after the capture of Chandernagore would undoubtedly desert to him (Law) upon every opportunity ; 3dly, our distance from Calcutta was so great, that all communications from thence would be entirely cut off, and therefore gave us no room to hope for any supplies, and consequently that we must be soon reduced to the greatest distress. For these reasons, I gave it as my opinion that we should come to an immediate action ; or, if that was thought entirely impracticable, that we should return to Calcutta ; the consequence of which must be our own disgrace and the inevitable destruction of the Company's affairs."

III

Most of Clive's biographers have yielded to the temptation to gloss over this affair of the council-of-war, just as Clive himself did his best to cover it up. It is surely not without significance that his report of the campaign to the Secret Committee of the Company omits all mention of it, and that, likewise, the " Journal of Military Proceedings on the Expedition to Muxadavad," written by a member of his personal staff (probably Maskelyne), *contains no entries at all for those two fateful days, June 20 and 21.* The full facts were only given to the public when the Committee appointed by the House of Commons to investigate the truth of these singular happenings obtained them from Clive and Coote sixteen years later.

It is not, of course, at all strange that Clive should have wished to conceal the facts : his fame, fortune, and reputation rested upon this victory for which he always claimed sole credit. It is more strange that historians and biographers, with the facts before them, have not approached the matter with greater openness of mind and greater readiness to admit that their hero on this occasion did not cut the finest of figures. They have rather dismissed the whole thing briefly as a temporary aberration, quite understandable and excusable under the circumstances. The idea that all is well that ends well is an extremely superficial and obtuse way of regarding an episode that was, in point of fact, most significant in the light it throws on Clive's character and still more important in its effect on his career.

Its significance only becomes clear when we examine his and Coote's evidence before the Committee. It is nonsense to maintain, as some of Clive's biographers have done, that Coote's view of the situation was not emphatically correct and his arguments unanswerable. In the light of the fact that Clive himself made no attempt at the time to answer them and, indeed, adopted them tacitly as his own within an hour of the ending of the council, how can this unfair attitude to Coote be maintained? Yet Clive professed afterwards nothing but scorn for those arguments, disposing of them with the remark that Coote " did not even understand the subject upon which he delivered so peremptory an opinion." He naturally, therefore, denied that Coote had had anything to do with his change of mind.

The Committee's report of Clive's evidence reads :

" Every member gave their opinion against the attack except Captains Coote and Grant. His Lordship observed, this was the only Council of War he ever held, and if he had abided by the Council it would have been the ruin of the East India Company. After about twenty-four hours of mature consideration his Lordship said he took upon himself to break through the opinion of the Council and ordered the army to cross the river. He did not recollect any memorial from Captain Coote upon that occasion, nor was he of rank sufficient at that time to have any influence upon his conduct ; and whatever he did upon that occasion he did without receiving advice from anyone."

Clive's memory was at fault to an extent that can only be described as remarkable. It was at fault about this being the only council-of-war he ever held ; it was at fault about the number of officers who voted against him ; and it was not entirely accurate about the time of his change of mind.

Coote, recalled to the witness-stand, stated that "about an hour after the Council broke up, Colonel Clive informed him unasked . . . that notwithstanding the resolution of the council-of-war, he intended to march the next morning, and accordingly gave orders for the army to hold themselves in readiness, leaving a subaltern officer's command in the Fort of Cutwa." He denied, however, the allegation that he had presented a memorial to Clive after the council-of-war.

Clive then in reply admitted that he had made a mistake about the number of officers who had voted against him, explaining that he had not consulted any of his notes since the battle. He also stated that "although he might have informed Captain Coote of his resolution to attack Siraja-Dowla notwithstanding the opinion of that council-of-war, he did imagine that he had not concluded upon the whole plan till twenty-four hours after, because the troops did not cross the river to make that attack till June 22 in the evening and the discourse between Captain Coote and him was the 21st in the morning."

There are discrepancies in Eyre Coote's list of officers at the council and that of the original record, but both show that a majority of the officers belonging to the Bengal army (as opposed to those of the Bombay and Madras contingents) voted with Coote, a not unimportant point.

The fact that emerges most clearly from this testimony is Clive's hostility towards Coote, and it is a fact of much importance, as will be seen later. The remark that Coote was not of rank "sufficient at that time to have any influence upon his conduct" was merely spiteful and directly contrary to the truth. Coote was junior in rank only to Kilpatrick and was given the local rank of Major by Clive himself on the march to Katwa, and Clive, too, at that time recognized his outstanding quality as a soldier by so often giving him the most responsible commands. He had led the advance in the battle of Calcutta, he had led the assault on Chandernagore, he had been sent on ahead to capture the fort of Katwa, in two days he was to lead the attack at Plassey, and afterwards he was to be entrusted with the command of the detachment sent to take Law's party. In none of these operations did Kilpatrick, the second in command, figure as prominently.

The fact was that Clive may be said to have owed as much of his success to Coote as Stringer Lawrence had earlier owed to Clive, but—and here a weak point in Clive's character emerges—

Clive, unlike Lawrence, did not give his subordinate the same amount of credit, or even any credit at all. To Clive had to go all the glory, even for Plassey ; indeed, more especially for Plassey, since Plassey was to be the supreme justification of his subsequent conduct. Everything he valued most—the right to his immense wealth, the high honours, the claims to special privilege, special authority, special attention, the power, fame, reputation—all alike were to rest upon that " Great Event." He was to be unable to share with anyone the credit for it, as Lawrence had shared the credit for the defeat of Dupleix with him— shared it in such a way as almost all of it, in the popular mind at least, came to Clive. It had to be solely, uniquely his.

But there were to be consequences, bitter consequences. He was laying up for himself a fearful harvest of jealousy and hatred. Coote, we are told on good authority, was on all occasions ever ready to do justice to Clive's merit,[93] but he would not have been human if he had not wanted to tell his version of the campaign of Plassey and of the events that went before it. He was to do so when he returned home the following year. And it is from that moment that we can mark the beginning of Clive's downfall : because the feeling of jealousy once engendered grew and grew and was fed by many different sources until it resulted in that attack upon Clive's honour in the House of Commons and that monument of hate, Charles Caraccioli's *Life of Lord Clive* in four huge volumes.[1] For what Clive did was to put too much weight upon a somewhat slender arch, the keystone of which was Plassey, and it was the sagging, if not actual collapse, of that arch that was to bring ruin to him. That, in short, was to be the tragedy of Clive's life—the tragedy of too much ambition built upon an insecure and insufficient foundation.

IV

The hour of deep meditation in the mango grove did not, as one would imagine from the testimony, put an end to Clive's " moment of hesitation."

A moment of hesitation ? Nay, rather the darkest, gloomiest hour of his life, an hour when he descended into hell and came up still without hope. Why should we pretend differently when his

---

[1] See Appendix C.

own letters to the Calcutta Committee and Orme's " unexpurgated " account tell the story so clearly ?

His telling Coote that he had changed his mind and decided to march the next morning was undoubtedly a blind. It could not have been anything else. As he himself said, it was another twenty-four hours before he gave the order for the advance.

What that hour of reflection must have told him was that he had to save his face with Coote. He could not let him see the true state of his mind. For while the professional soldier was obviously right, realization of that fact did not make a decision any easier, because it did not lessen at all the fear of defeat that was gripping Clive's soul. That he now had no good choice but to go on in the face of overwhelming odds must only have laid bare to him the appalling fact that he had blundered—and blundered irretrievably. But Coote would have been the last man to whom he would have made such a confession, because of the fact that Coote was a King's officer, a Regular-army man, and the jealousy between the two services was something that cut very deep.[1] Clive shared to the full the prevailing inferiority complex that afflicted the Company's officers and made them extremely sensitive to any slights upon their ability. None of the many writers who have told the story of the campaign of Plassey has made enough allowance for the shifts to which Clive's abnormally sensitive pride would have forced him on this occasion in the effort to conceal his predicament.

Certainly what Clive wrote the Committee does not tally with what he told Coote. He passed all that day in a state of anxious waiting for some encouraging word from Mir Jafar, and when it did not come he sat down at night and wrote to the Committee as follows :

" I am really at a loss how to act at the present situation of our affairs, especially should I receive a confirmation by letter of Meir Jaffeir's resolution to stand neuter. The Nabob's forces at present are not said to exceed 8,000 (?) men, but a compliance with their demands may easily encrease them. If we

---

[1] How deep may be inferred from a letter from Captain Richard Smith to General Stringer Lawrence undated (probably December 1760) : " Happy for me that my services have been separated from the Royalists ever since you left us. They look down with such disdain upon the Company's Corps that I could never have served with them with satisfaction, and at last we have convinced them that the Company's troops perform their service with vigour and regularity when their own Corps was in disorder and confusion." [94]

attack them it must be entrenched, and ourselves without any assistance. In this place a repulse must be fatal ; on the contrary success may give the greatest advantage. The Nabob's apprehensions at present are great, and perhaps he may be glad to grant us an honourable peace. The principle of fear may make him act much against his private inclination, and I believe that has been the case ever since the capture of Chandernagore. There still remains another expedient of sending an embassy either to Gazoody Khan [1] or the Marattoes to invite them in. I beg you will let me have your sentiments how I ought to act at this critical juncture."

Could anything reveal Clive's state of mind more startlingly ? Had his nerve failed him completely ? The probability is that it had. Where was that dauntless spirit, that decision, that bold assurance for which he was so famous ? For the proud and haughty Clive now to implore his colleagues at Calcutta, those colleagues whom he so despised, to send him advice, that is surely a sufficient measure of his collapse during the last few days. He had taken the sentiments of his officers, now he was appealing to mere civilians a hundred miles away. And thoughts of peace, not victory, were in his head ; thoughts of sending half-way across the continent for assistance ; thoughts of inviting the Marathas to come in—as he must have known, to rob and kill and burn and inflict nothing but havoc and destruction upon a helpless peasantry. What thoughts were these for the great Clive, the victor of Arcot, the hero of a score of battles, the darling child of fortune, the heaven-born general that Pitt was so rapturously to applaud—what thoughts were these for him, of all men, to be harbouring ?

And if he really felt that he dared not risk a fight with his present force, is not this an admission that he had blundered, blundered so badly that the thought of what he had done was torture to him, that by his recklessness he had brought his army, the sole military reliance of his countrymen in Bengal, to the very edge of destruction ? Is it any wonder that afterwards he wanted to blot out the very memory of this zero hour in his life ? And may not his almost fanatical antipathy to Eyre Coote have dated from it ? For Coote was with him and may have sensed, even if he did not actually witness, his humiliation.

[1] The Nawab of Oude.

That night when he sat alone in his tent with his agony of mind, with the monsoon rain beating a thunderous tattoo upon the canvas, and the flickering light of the candles casting weird shadows around him, when he knew that the fate of everything—the lives of the 3000 men with him, Calcutta, the Company, his own career—rested in his hands and his alone, and realized at the same time the full peril of his position, the dilemma in which he was placed—that night must have etched itself deep into the very consciousness of his being and left an impression there that nothing could ever efface. At last he was face to face with destiny itself ; the thought of what that destiny *might* be made him numb with fear.

Yet the morning came—could the night have been other than sleepless ?—bringing him no fresh word from Mir Jafar.

It was three o'clock in the afternoon when at last a messenger came with a letter. Mir Jafar now informed Clive that he was on the march from Murshidebad. He urged Clive to lose no time in falling on the Nawab before he had time to entrench his camp. " As yet you are now only designing, but it is not now proper to be indolent. When you come near I shall then be able to join you. If you could send two or three hundred good fighting men the upper road towards Cossimbuzar, the Nabob's army would of themselves retreat. Then the battle will have no difficulty. When I am arrived near the army I will send you privately all the intelligence. Let me have previous notice of the time you intend to fight."

The assurance was poor and no better than all Mir Jafar's earlier assurances ; yet it was better than the previous day's silence. With the desperation of a drowning man Clive clutched at it and made his resolve. " I shall be on the other side of the river this evening " came his reply, and he asked Mir Jafar to join him at Plassey. Having done so and, perhaps, though he was not a religious man, entrusted his soul to God, he gave orders to his army to march.

Chapter Fifteen

PLASSEY : (2) THE ACTION

"This star of England : Fortune made his sword,
By which the world's best garden he achieved"

SHAKESPEARE, *Henry V*

I

AT FIVE THAT EVENING the river was crossed. An hour later Clive scribbled a note to Mir Jafar : " Upon receiving your letter I am come to a resolution to proceed immediately to Placis. I am impatient for an answer to my letter by the trusty man."

Rain was falling continuously as the slow, fatiguing advance proceeded. It was nearly midnight when the van completed the fifteen-mile march to Plassey grove. The rear did not come up before three in the morning.

The drenched little army bivouacked for what was left of the night among the mango trees while Clive made his headquarters in Plassey House. This, the Nawab's hunting-lodge, was a solid brick house surrounded by a high wall, situated on the river-bank to the north of the grove. The sound of drums and cymbals coming from the entrenched camp a mile farther to the north acquainted them all with the fact that the Nawab's advance guard was already on the spot.

The English soldiers slept, " but few of the officers, and least of all the Commander, who was observed to pass the night in much agitation both of body and mind."[95]

Similarly so the Nawab, though with less apparent cause. In his entrenchment, enclosing a peninsula made by a wide bend in the river, he was strongly placed ; he had 34,000 infantry, 15,000 cavalry, and 53 heavy guns. Thus he had overwhelmingly all the advantages both of position and of numbers. Yet his mind was sorely troubled. Terror gripped his heart as he thought of all the treachery that might that very hour be in preparation against the morrow. He was hated—was there anyone upon whose fidelity he could rely ?

The enemy's camp was early astir, and as dawn broke over the wide plain the host of horsemen and foot came pouring out of their entrenchments. When the hot sun rolled away the mists from the rain-soaked ground, an awesome and unforgettable sight was presented to the scanty band of Englishmen and their Indian auxiliaries upon awaking from their few snatched hours of sleep : " What with the number of elephants, all covered with scarlet cloth and embroidery ; their horse, with their drawn swords glittering in the sun ; their heavy cannon drawn by vast trains of oxen ; and their standards flying, they made a most pompous and formidable appearance."

For the opening scene in the English camp on this fateful June 23, we must go direct to Orme :

" Colonel Clive not having received any further intelligence from Meer Jaffier during the night saw the morning break with increasing anxiety. At sunrise he went with another person upon the terras of the hunting-house, from whence having contemplated the enemy's array, he was surprised at their numerous, splendid, and martial appearance. His companion asked him what he thought would be the event ; to which he replied, ' We must make the best fight we can during the day and at night sling our muskets over our shoulders and march back to Calcutta.' Most of the officers were as doubtful of success as himself ; but the common soldiery, being mostly tried men who had served under Major Lawrence on the plains of Trichinopoly, maintained the blunt spirit of Englishmen, and saw nothing in the pomp or multitude of the Nawab's army either to admire or to fear."

The enemy, spreading out on the open plain, formed their line of battle in a great crescent extending from their camp to a point 800 yards east of the southernmost corner of the mango grove. They were drawn up in columns of horse and foot interspersed with batteries of guns. In front of the Nawab's camp were two tanks, surrounded by large mounds of earth. The farthest one, only two hundred yards from the British lines, was occupied by a party of fifty Frenchmen with four field-pieces. Behind them, in support, lay the pick of the Nawab's army, a division of 12,000 men under the command of his only loyal officer, Mir Murdan. The Nawab himself remained in his tent to await the fortunes of the day.

Thus confronted with overwhelming numbers, Clive made the best dispositions he could of his slender force. Realizing that his one chance lay in showing a bold front, he drew his men out of

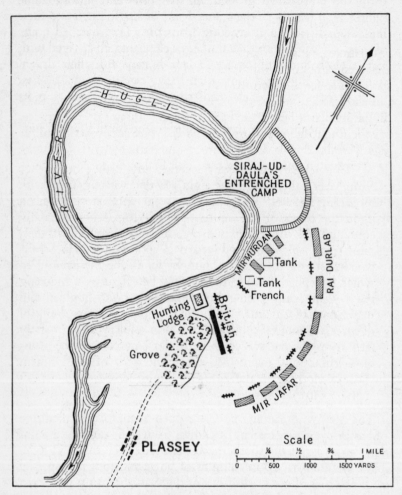

BATTLE OF PLASSEY
Position of opposing armies at 8 a.m.

the grove and disposed them in a single line facing the enemy's camp stretching from the house to a little distance·beyond the right of the grove. It was " the thin red line " of Waterloo, only thinner ! Its right was completely exposed and outflanked, and his only hope of not being attacked there and in the rear lay in the chance that Mir Jafar commanded this part of the Nawab's line and would at least remain neutral during the battle.

II

The battle of Plassey, as all the world knows, was a complete anti-climax. It is, perhaps, the greatest anti-climax in all history. Between its political importance and its military lies a discrepancy so vast as to seem ludicrous. Yet it is scarcely any larger than the one that existed between the size of Clive's fears and the depth of his despondency before the battle, and the amount of justification for them that the event itself supplied. No fiction writer in his senses would dream of committing such an elementary mistake as to crown an exciting narrative with bathos so deep.

Indeed, Clive may be pitied for the trick that fortune, all too kind, played him on this occasion. If she had given him a real chance to show his valour, if she had withheld her favour until the last tense minute of a fiercely fought day, if, in other words, she had given him a Blenheim or a Waterloo, she would have been a much kinder goddess. She would have saved him from the cruel jeers and envious thrusts of too many of his contemporaries whom she had apparently favoured less. She would have saved him from the sneer that all that he had done to earn his military reputation and high honours and great fortune was " to make timid Asiatics run."

Those sneers were to be hurled at him in a crescendo of hate as the years went by, and they were to become harder and harder to bear, as with them were joined the voices of other, more dangerous enemies, sustained by stronger emotions than envy.

Some commentators have stood in awe of this triumph that was Plassey as though it were inexplicable. But why ? If three-quarters of Siraj-ud-daula's army had not been commanded by traitors it might still have been just possible for the British to have gained the victory. Not, perhaps, if they had not had the good luck of striking down early in the encounter Mir Murdan, the one real leader that the enemy possessed. For it was in the nature of these huge, undisciplined, unorganized Mogul armies to be greatly dependent upon their commanders, who were always mounted upon elephants so as to be in full sight of all. If their commander fell, then the chances were his men would conclude all to be lost and flee. There were no veteran troops among them, only raw levies, mortally afraid of gun-fire, whose very numbers, so imposing at a distance, were a source of weakness rather than strength as they added to the danger of panic and rendered them less controllable. Even the superbly prancing horsemen, always the chief arm of a Moorish army, were not the menace they seemed. To any Asiatic force like themselves, yes ; but not to a compact, well-disciplined, highly trained body of infantry equipped with European muskets and field-pieces ; for they had little control over their horses and shared the prevailing distaste for fire. Nor were their huge-calibred guns to be feared, for they could neither manage them properly nor easily move them. Indeed, the British had almost more cause to fear the fifty Frenchmen who were posted with four field-pieces 200 yards from their line than they had to worry about the greater remaining part of this imposing host.

There were two phases to the battle. The first was an artillery duel which opened at eight o'clock as soon as the British line was formed. The French guns at the tank began it, their first shot killing one and wounding another. The enemy's heavy guns joined in shortly afterwards. As both sides presented each other with good targets most of the British casualties occurred at this time.

After half an hour, during which ten Europeans and twenty sepoys had been struck down, Clive decided that cover for his men was more important than the appearance of boldness. So he ordered them to retire within the grove and lie down behind its protecting bank of earth, at the same time keeping the guns outside to continue their fire.

This fire had been effective. It naturally was most effective against the elephants, large targets in the forefront of the enemy's line, upon which were mounted their commanders, and Mir Murdan came by his death in this way. The cannon-balls, too, bored big holes in the serried ranks behind. And now that the British were behind shelter most of the heavy-metalled shots of the enemy whizzed harmlessly over their heads into the branches of the trees.

This part of the battle lasted four hours. It was around noon when the monsoon took a hand in matters. The thunder drowned out the discharges of the guns and the rain descended in torrents. The shower lasted for nearly an hour, during which time the enemy, who did not protect their powder as the English did, stopped firing. As their horsemen, however, thought this was their opportunity, it was only the steady continuance of the British fire that prevented a massed assault on their line.

The cannonade was resumed when the rain ceased. But around three o'clock the enemy began to retire to their camp, moving off in good order, hauling their cannon along first. This was the time that Mir Jafar, who was stationed on the left of the line, chose to make his first move, but the British could not determine whether it was with friendly or hostile intent (as he had omitted to inform them of his intentions in advance, or even of his exact position in the line). Taking no chances they kept him at a distance by turning their guns in his direction.

Clive now thought the battle was over. It was his intention to wait until nightfall and then to withdraw from his uncomfortable position by making a desperate midnight dash into the enemy's camp and forcing his way through it to safety. Experience told him that therein lay his best chance of escape. Accordingly, he went into Plassey House to change his rain-soaked clothes and rest, leaving orders with Major Kilpatrick that if the enemy made any fresh move he was to be immediately notified. According to Coote, he had come from the house at twelve and called the captains together for a council-of-war, but changing his mind had returned without holding one.

While Clive was gone Kilpatrick noticed that the French had abandoned the tank where they had been well-posted all day. Quick to seize the opportunity, he advanced from the grove with two companies and a couple of field-pieces, sending back word to Clive of what he was doing. Clive, indignant that any move should be made without his orders, hastened after the party. He caught up with them just as they were reaching the tank, and nothing but a prompt apology saved Kilpatrick from being placed under arrest. Clive sent him back to the grove and assumed direct command himself.

It was the action of his subordinate that precipitated the decisive moment that brought victory. To retire back to the grove now would be disastrous. All retirements, whether "strategic" or otherwise, had to be avoided in this Asiatic warfare, in which the psychological factor played so big a part. It was, as Clive well knew, a case of venturing all or nothing, as the Indian mind interpreted all retreat in terms of fear alone. So Clive had no alternative now but to attack with his whole force. He sent back

P

orders to the grove, and Eyre Coote marched out with his division. The grenadiers were sent to get as near as they could to the enemy's entrenchments.

The battle broke out now with real but short-lived fury. The huge, unwieldy host of the Nawab tried to issue forth once more from the camp, but as they came this time they were met by a hot fire from the four field-pieces that Clive had brought up to the tank. Men and horses fell rapidly, and, as at Arcot, the elephants, maddened by the constant patter of musket-balls on their hides, soon got out of hand. The loss of four more principal officers was even more destructive of morale. When utter confusion began to appear in the enemy's ranks, Clive saw at last that victory was within his grasp. He ordered Eyre Coote to lead the assault on the camp.

The day, however, was still not lost for the Nawab if he had only possessed the least ounce of courage. But he lost it inevitably when he chose this of all moments to flee. No Moorish army had been known to stand its ground when it learnt that its leader was making his own escape. Siraj-ud-daula's first fatal step had been his failure to press an attack upon the grove. That failure had been due to the traitor Mir Jafar, who, when the terrified prince had thrown himself on his mercy and supplicated him to preserve his honour and life, had coldly replied that the day was too far spent for an attack. The second fatal step had been the retirement within the camp, and that order Siraj-ud-daula had given on the advice of Rai Durlab, the other principal conspirator in the plot against him. The news that the British were actually attacking the camp completed his ruin. He called for a swift camel and departed for his capital as fast as the camel could take him.

By five o'clock the British were in complete possession of the camp, the great host of the Nawab was in flight, and Eyre Coote was directing the pursuit. The country for miles around was strewn with baggage, stores, camp equipage, and cattle. All the heavy guns were taken. But unable to overtake the flying foe without cavalry, the pursuit halted six miles beyond the camp.

The Nawab's army, according to Clive's calculation, lost 500 men. His own losses amounted only to four killed, twenty wounded, and four missing among the Europeans, 14 killed and 36 wounded among the sepoys.[96] The six-pounders had fired 511 round shot.

III

The campaign was successful and the battle that was to decide the fate of a continent was won. But the manner of its winning still invites consideration. Was the campaign well-conceived and well-planned and its success deserved ? Or was it, as has been suggested here, a gambler's throw, an enterprise that no one trained in the profession of arms would ever have undertaken ?

There can surely not be much doubt about the answer. Clive's own behaviour immediately before and during the battle, the belief of most of his officers, and, above all, the opinion of Eyre Coote, make it clear. That Clive was in a real predicament, not a fancied one, on June 21 can scarcely be doubted. The opinion of the council-of-war, and not least of all Coote's, confirms it. When an advance is made and a battle fought merely because any other course would be certainly, not probably, disastrous, it does not suggest great foresight, great planning, or even great courage and daring. It does not, in other words, suggest all the praise that has so freely been bestowed upon Clive's conduct on this occasion.

It does not, for instance, suggest all that Sir John Malcolm, Clive's first and, perhaps, best biographer, says :

" From the period of the capture of Chandernagore till Mir Jafar was established upon the throne Clive was unaided in the great and difficult task he had undertaken. He rested solely upon his own judgment, which in almost all cases was in opposition to that of the persons with whom he was associated. Admiral Watson, though he had withdrawn himself from any participation in the enterprise, stated honestly and decidedly his doubts of its success. The Select Committee of Calcutta threw off all responsibility. Thus unaided and alone, Clive had to counteract treachery, to stimulate timidity into action, and when the period arrived, openly and boldly to confront danger. He was throughout this arduous labour supported by the conviction that the end he sought was indispensable to the interests, and indeed to the safety, of the government he served, and that the means he employed were the only ones by which it could be accomplished. With this conviction he proceeded towards his object with a caution and firmness that have seldom been equalled and never surpassed." [97]

He had this conviction unquestionably, but did he have this caution and firmness? Granted that his judgment was in opposition to that of his associates, particularly Admiral Watson, was his judgment good, was it better than theirs? Did not his conduct show, rather, that he thought he had misjudged. When actually confronted with the odds he thought they were too great. It is easy to be carried away by the greatness of his triumph, but to do so prejudices an evaluation of the man. It is curious to note that practically all criticism of Clive's conduct prior to Plassey is confined to his deception of Omichand and the business of the forgery. On that subject there is nothing more that can be said. But historians and biographers have completely overlooked that Clive's Plassey campaign was based on a calculation that no prudent commander should have accepted as sound.

The calculation was that Mir Jafar would join Clive with his whole corps not on the day of the battle but on the march up-country. And it was the last-minute realization that this reliance was fallacious that upset Clive's whole plan of action—upset, too, his matchless *sang froid*, leaving him such a pitiable object of fear and hesitation. The question may reasonably be asked, therefore, Was it excusable for him to fall into such an error, taking into account all the circumstances?

First, we may note that Clive had ample warning that little dependence could be placed on Mir Jafar. On June 3, ten days before he began his march, Watts informed him: " We can expect no more assistance than that they [*i.e.* the conspirators] will stand neuter and wait the event of a battle. If we are success-ful they will reap the benefit of it ; if otherwise they continue as they were without appearing to have been concerned with us." Than which a more accurate forecast of what was to happen could not have been made ! And even without such a warning Clive should have known from his experience how little reliance could be placed on such promises as Mir Jafar made him.

Secondly, the whole plan from its inception depended for its execution upon the *active* participation of Mir Jafar and his party. The Select Committee in their much-ridiculed but quite sensible letter written on the day of the battle in reply to Clive's appeals for advice, reminded him of that fact :

" At the same time it must be remembered when we engaged in the confederacy to change the Government in favour of Meir

Jaffeir we were informed that Roydolub, Jugget Seat, and others had likewise entered into it : we think, therefore, that we should not act of ourselves only, unless we find no assistance can be expected from them, in which case we must conclude the whole is united against us."

The time for Clive to begin his march should surely have been *after*, not *before*, Mir Jafar declared himself, and if he did not declare himself, *then he should not have marched at all*. Clive was not supposed to be *creating* a revolution, but merely taking advantage of, by assisting, one that was about to occur anyhow.

The question remains : granted that Clive gambled with the forces entrusted to his care, gambled, indeed, with the fate of Calcutta and all his colleagues, was he not practically forced to do so by his situation, by the fact of his recall to Madras and of the approach of the rainy season making military operations impossible for several months ?

Clive himself did not seem to think so when he wrote to the Committee suggesting postponing action until after the season : " Whilst we have them [the forces], we may always have it in our power to bring about a Revolution, should the present not succeed." Which indicates that he realized then that the safety of his forces was more vital than the revolution. His actions, before and afterwards, showed that he never regarded very seriously the orders from Madras. Always there was an excellent excuse why he could not send back the troops or return himself (though there is no reason to doubt the sincerity of his earlier desire to return). The troops never did go back to Madras, not even when Madras was being closely besieged.

There seems, therefore, not to have been any compelling reason why Clive in June had to " march at once " ; no reason at all except his fear that the conspiracy was about to collapse owing to too much publicity and his own impatience and reckless impetuosity. The fact was that he had set his heart on effecting this revolution and was willing to take a tremendous chance. In other words, it was a gambler's adventure, not a soldier's carefully-planned and well-considered stroke, and it is difficult to regard it in any other light.

The " revolution," in any case, probably would have suffered no harm if it had been put into cold storage for the summer. Perhaps it would even have improved with keeping, as Mir

Jafar might later have been induced to adopt a less equivocal attitude—always assuming, of course, that he was not cut off in the meantime !

IV

Did Clive sleep during the battle ? The question, interesting in itself, deserves a moment's consideration because of the wide currency given to the assertion. The story is, that when Major Kilpatrick's aide-de-camp arrived at Plassey House with the message for Clive of the enemy's retirement, he found Clive asleep. The wide currency that has been given to it is entirely due to Orme, who did not delete this statement from his published history, as he did those other two passages that seemed to reflect on Clive. But Orme did not invent the story, which was current in or before 1763.

Purely on the face of things, without reference to the evidence, it is not at all unlikely. Clive had not slept at all the previous night and very probably not the night before that. He had been under a prodigious strain for three days, and that strain was still at its height. He knew that there would be no sleep the following night with his night-attack planned, and, perhaps, if he had to retreat, none for several more nights. There had come a lull in the fighting, and he was not expecting any fresh action until nightfall. Surely, then, this might have seemed to Clive a wise moment in which to snatch a few minutes of rest before the really critical hour arrived. Like most hardened campaigners, he no doubt possessed the faculty of dropping off to sleep as and where he was. In fact, so far from there being anything shameful about the allegation, it might even be regarded as the most sensible thing that Clive could have done. Moreover, there are instances of similar behaviour in his previous career : at Arcot, when he slept on the eve of the enemy's assault, and at Budge-Budge, when he and his weary men were taken completely by surprise by Manichand—a much more serious matter.

But the evidence, what there is of it, is definitely against the story. It first crops up in 1763 in two letters (which seem no longer to be extant) addressed by William Belchier, Clive's former banker, styling himself an old proprietor, to the Proprietors of " East India Stock," which John Walsh, Clive's secretary, promptly answered with a positive denial.[98] It next appears in the " Genuine Minutes of the Select Committee " published by T. Evans in 1772, wherein is given what purports to be a *verbatim* extract from Coote's Journal ; but the words stating that Clive was asleep when Kilpatrick's messenger arrived do not occur in Orme's copy of Coote's Journal.[99]   The first Report of the Select Committee of 1772 simply records : " Sir Eyre Coote here read a description of the Battle of Plassey."   But if that description of Coote's had contained the statement, Clive would surely have challenged it, and his denial would have been recorded in the report.

The most convincing piece of evidence, however, is one that has passed practically unnoticed.   It is that of Surgeon Ives in his account of Watson's expedition published in 1773.   It is convincing because he was not, like Walsh, a member of Clive's staff, and because he gives Coote as his authority for his denial and actually quotes his words : " that the publications before mentioned " (no doubt referring to Mr. Belchier's letters) " were absolutely false, that any person might be convinced thereof by appealing to the minutes of the Committee of the House of Commons, where what was delivered by him on this examination was committed to paper." [100]

Incidentally, it may be noticed that Mr. Walsh's account of Plassey was not in the least candid : " The Commander-in-Chief, far from having any thought of making overtures of peace to Suraja Dowlet, took upon himself to cross the river, march to the enemy, and fight the Battle of Plassey contrary to the general opinion of the officers in a Council of War."

Chapter Sixteen

PLASSEY : (3) THE FRUITS OF VICTORY

" So that this great Revolution, so happily brought about seems
Compleat in every respect"

CLIVE TO THE EAST INDIA COMPANY

I

CLIVE WAS HIMSELF again. He was more than that. Success enlarged him, and Plassey was his greatest success. If before he was proud, he was now in danger of becoming arrogant ; if presumptuous, he was now doubly so because he was triumphant. He was a conqueror, a ruler, a master of men and situations, and the knowledge gave him a confidence and assurance that he had hitherto lacked.

Plassey had in the twinkling of an eye resolved everything for him—his difficult relations with the Bengal Committee, his subordination to Madras, his dependence upon Admiral Watson and the King's officers. All tiresome ties were broken. He could dispense with the Royal Navy. As for the gentlemen of the Committee, he was now their master, beyond any questioning on their part or hesitation on his.

With what contempt he must have read Mr. Drake's congratulations with the grovelling reminder that he was now in a position where he could render great favours ! He had nothing but scorn for those colleagues whose only contribution to the solution of his difficult problem of a few days before had been to instruct him to force a decisive engagement if there was any prospect of success. He received their letter three days after the battle and answered it with a gibe : " I have received your letter of the 23rd instant, the contents of which are so indefinite and contradictory that I can put no other construction on it than an intent to clear yourselves at my expense, had the expedition miscarried. It puts me in mind of the famous answer of the Delphic oracle to Pyrrhus, ' Aio te Æacide Romanos vincere posse.' "

The victory was his, to be exploited to the utmost ; and he,

232

its victor, was ready to bestride his enlarged world like a Colossus. For the moment that world was confined to Bengal. Later it was to extend to the seat of Empire itself, London.

In his dealings, too, with Mir Jafar he was now himself. For he could not help seeing the humour of the situation : he now the chief *entrepreneur* in an enterprise of which he had previously been the paid assistant, and the other merely a beneficiary of his valour ! But he was somewhat cruel in the way he expressed the sense of the situation to that beneficiary. Though that bold and gallant rebel had taken no bigger share in the battle than the narrative indicates, he received from Clive congratulations upon a victory " which is yours not mine."

Mir Jafar could not yet appreciate the full ironic flavour of the jest, for time alone would disclose its bitterness. That he was fully conscious of his, to say the least, embarrassing position he showed by his behaviour on the morning after " his " victory. It was a thoroughly apprehensive and mistrustful man who came to the English camp to meet his victorious comrade in arms. When the guard was called out to give him a royal salute, " he started as if he thought it was all over with him ; nor did his countenance brighten up till the Colonel embraced him and saluted him Subah of the province."

Swiftly now Clive moved to garner the fruits of his triumph. Having sent Mir Jafar off to make speed to the capital, he followed himself with the army. By June 25 he was encamped outside Murshidebad awaiting the propitious and safe moment for his entry.

Four days later, with a small escort of 200 Europeans and 300 sepoys, he rode through the narrow, winding ways of the populous city. The streets were packed with people curious to see this novel sight. For was it not but a year before that four representatives of this same European nation had been led like felons through these self-same streets, and that they, its inhabitants, had been told that they could safely hoot at any others that dared show themselves ?

Both Holwell and his companions and Clive and his escort were led in the same direction, towards the royal residence, but whereas the former were housed in a stable, the latter found a sumptuous palace at their disposal. And no sooner, too, had Clive installed himself in it than he obtained his first glimpse of what traditionally it meant to be a conqueror in India. For to him now came

233

Jagat Seth, the millionaire banker, and others of the great men bearing rich gifts as tokens of their submission and the purchase price of his favour.

It was Clive's proud boast, to be made repeatedly as his enemies thrust their poisoned darts into his tortured flesh, that the fabulous riches of the Indies might now have been his for the taking, with none to say him nay—and he did not take them :

"Am I not rather deserving of praise for the moderation which marked my proceedings ? Consider the situation in which the victory at Plassey had placed me. A great prince was dependent on my pleasure ; an opulent city [more opulent and populous, he declared, than London] lay at my mercy ; its richest bankers bid against each other for my smiles ; I walked through vaults which were thrown open to me alone, piled on either hand with gold and jewels ! Mr. Chairman, at this moment I stand astonished at my own moderation ! "

There is little real cause for surprise. As payment for his services Clive received from Mir Jafar the enormous sum of £234,000. What need had he, then, to accept anything from these, mere subjects of the state ? To have done so would have been to demean himself and make himself no better than a freebooter, on a level little higher than those useful allies in war, the Marathas. And Clive, with all his undoubted desire for wealth, never demeaned himself so. His pride, if nothing else, made him receive his wealth only at the hands of the greatest : from the lord and sovereign of these rich hands, the Mogul emperor, and from his vicegerent the Subah. Besides, he was no fool, and only a fool would have accepted the obvious bribes of these people.

Yet it was entirely characteristic of him to try to make a virtue of his restraint and " moderation." " If I had been disposed to grow rich by receiving presents from any other hands but those of the Nabob," he wrote to the Chairman of the Company, " surely no one had ever the like opportunity ; but there is not that man living among the daily temptations which offered who can accuse me of receiving anything of value but from the Nabob himself. I have troubled you with these particulars because among some it may be computed as a crime my being rich : if it be a crime you, Sir, are truly acquainted with the nature of it."

So Clive waived the bearers of gifts away as Cromwell did the

Crown, with the assurance that he desired nothing but their assistance in settling the government.

In the afternoon he proceeded in state to the royal palace, where Mir Jafar and all the rajahs and great men of the court were assembled. And here, finding that Mir Jafar declined of his own accord to seat himself upon the *musnud*, the seat of power, he handed him to it and gravely saluted him as Nawab, and all the courtiers thronged to congratulate Mir Jafar and pay him homage. Clive then addressed the new ruler and the assembled company, assuring them that he had only made war on Siraj-ud-daula in self-defence, and that now that a brave and good prince was on the throne the English would return to Calcutta and attend solely to commerce, which was their proper sphere and their whole aim in those parts, and leave the government wholly in their hands.

And who shall say that the promise was not made with a fair attempt at sincerity, even though it omitted the all-important proviso that nothing must be done thereafter contrary to the English will ?

But before the promise could be carried into complete effect there were several pieces of business to be attended to. Especially, the price of English assistance had to be paid. And here there came at once a clear indication that everything was not to be entirely plain sailing for the new regime. Mir Jafar and Jagat Seth, who was to be his finance minister, made the sad announcement that the contents of the treasury did not nearly come up to expectation. In fact, to put it bluntly, there was not enough treasure in it to meet both the expenses of government and the debts contracted to the English.

Clive suspected, with good reason, that he was being deceived. (Suspicion points at Omichand, who, it is said, had concocted a plan with Mir Jafar for the removal of the bulk of the treasure to the female apartments, which they knew the English would not enter.) But realizing the indelicacy of investigating the matter, he accepted the situation as gracefully as he could, and after a long but friendly argument with Jagat Seth came to a settlement much exceeding his expectations. It was agreed that the English should be paid one half of their demand immediately, two-thirds of it in money and one-third in jewels, plate, and goods, and the other half should be discharged in three annual instalments. It further satisfied him to know that Jagat Seth would take good care of

English interests and would use his powerful influence at Delhi to obtain them any *firmans* [1] that they might happen to want to assist them in their trade.

No revolutions are painless and few bloodless. Omichand and Siraj-ud-daula were the two principal sufferers in this one. The time had come when the former had to be told the painful truth about the treaties, and it proved an affecting scene. " The indignation and resentment expressed on that man's countenance bars all description," so the man who had tricked him told his questioners in the House of Commons fifteen years later. " This cannot be the treaty," the Sikh exclaimed ; " it was a red treaty I saw ! " " Yes," answered Clive, " this is a white treaty." " You see, Omichand," explained Scrafton, " the red paper is a trick ; you are to have nothing." And with that Omichand fainted and had to be carried home in a state of complete collapse.

It was naturally a hard blow to anyone so afflicted with avarice as he, but it was not possible for even him to think of himself as a ruined man. Nor did he become insane, as was once believed by those inclined to be sentimental over his bitter disappointment. His usefulness to the English was, however, largely over. On August 6 Clive wrote to the Court of Directors : " Omichund likewise had merited well while acting in concert with Mr. Watts, but I had reason to think his intriguing disposition was carrying him too far in the pursuit of his private interest, therefore recommended to him a visit of devotion to Malda. He is a person capable of rendering you great services while properly restrained, therefore not to be wholly discarded."

Nor was Omichand wholly discarded : he was still useful for supplying saltpetre under contract, and he was still able to obtain for himself extremely liberal terms. But history at least knows him no more, except to record the fact that he died at an advanced and no doubt honourable, old age in Calcutta, and, oddly, left a large legacy to the Foundling Hospital in London.

Siraj-ud-daula's fate was infinitely more painful and lurid. His swift camel had carried him safely to his palace, and the day after the battle found him there wrestling frantically, but all too vainly, with the problem of what to do. Fight another battle or surrender to the English ? His own miserly carelessness about paying his troops had contributed to their misconduct and his own overthrow. Why had he been so stupid ? Seized with this idea,

[1] Royal patents or privileges.

he began to ladle out money in handfuls—they could now have all they wanted if only they would fight for him again. But it was to no avail. Those around him advised him to surrender to Colonel Clive. He paid no heed. Traitors, all of them traitors ! Midnight found him still in the palace, but midnight also brought him word that Mir Jafar was already in the city with the English troops close at his heels.

The coward and the miser in him had been his undoing at every point in his brief reign ; they were now to destroy him utterly. If he had followed the sensible advice of his officers and surrendered to Colonel Clive he would at least have saved his life. Instead, he summoned coaches and palanquins, piled into them a quantity of gold and jewels, loaded elephants with furniture and baggage, took Lutf-unnisa, his queen, and a few attendants, and fled.

A week later he returned to his capital, a prisoner in chains ! Evil fortune pursued him to the end. He directed his flight towards M. Law and his party of Frenchmen, who were hastening from Rajmahal to join him and were only a three-hour march away when he was seized. But afraid of being intercepted on the road, he deserted his coaches and elephants and took to the river. There he might have been safe if his avarice had not caused him in his haste to remember his jewels and overlook the importance of taking food enough for the journey. After five days the famished party having disguised themselves as ordinary travellers landed on the river bank in search of food, but the dervish at whose lonely cell they happened to stop penetrated their poor disguise. Chancing to have a grievance of his own against the luckless Nawab and rejoicing at the chance to revenge himself, he immediately sent word to Mir Jafar's brother-in-law, detaining the travellers in the meantime. Mir Kasim came quickly, seized them and sent Siraj-ud-daula under a strong guard to Murshidebad.

On July 2 the miserable man, with his silks and jewels stripped from him, was led through the streets of his former capital like any common criminal and lodged in his palace to await the fate that was now inevitable. For Mir Jafar, fearful lest Clive put in a plea for clemency, at once called together his confidential advisers and decided with them that he should immediately be put to death. The horrid job was given to Miran, Mir Jafar's sadistic son, whose bloody reputation as an assassin without compunction was already well established. The deed was performed that same night ; on the following day the mangled remains of a man who had not yet attained his twenty-first year were paraded through the streets of the city. Thus was Aliverdj Khan's baleful prophecy fulfilled.

II

That same day in Murshidebad saw another parade of a different kind, and one of much greater importance to the English, more interested in gold than blood. Two hundred country boats were drawn up along the river bank and into them were piled the gold and jewels from the palace that were to go down the river to Calcutta, escorted by a strong detachment from the army.

In a long procession they started off on the strong current. When they reached the main stream their numbers were swelled to three hundred by the boats of the squadron. "With music playing, drums beating, and colours flying," they swept on down past the Dutch settlement at Chinsura and the now half-deserted French settlement at Chandernagore, exhibiting to their inhabitants, as Luke Scrafton might well say, " a scene far different from what they had beheld the year before, when the Nawab's fleet and army passed them with the captive English and all the wealth and plunder of Calcutta." Indeed, history has recorded few such complete reversals of fortune in so short a space of time. They reached Calcutta on July 6, there to be greeted with a frenzy of rejoicing by all its inhabitants.

The sums received by individuals were enormous. Clive's share of £234,000 (£160,000 of which was a private gift from Mir Jafar) was naturally the largest, but none of the others could complain. Watts received £117,000 ; Walsh, £56,250 ; Drake, £31,500 ; Scrafton, £22,500 ; each member of the Select Committee, £27,000 ; and each member of Council a lakh of rupees (£12,000). Major Kilpatrick received £33,756 as his portion of the prize money for the army in addition to his share as a member of the Committee. A subaltern's share of the prize money amounted to £3000. The sufferers in the sack of Calcutta also received the compensation that they had previously lacked.

No wonder that Clive was popular now at Calcutta ! " We talk of great things on this happy occasion and expect a world of guns to be fired and the ladies all to get footsore with dancing. I can assure you that a bumper goes to your health each day in every house from the Admiral's downwards."

But only one result could attend this overwhelming shower of gold—the demoralization of its recipients. Avarice in its crudest form quickly took possession of them. No less than 50 lakhs (£600,000) were to go to the army and navy. What a prize was this for these few hundred men ! What a grand bone of contention ! If the situation at Katwa had required the calling of a council-of-war, how much more now did this ! Clive summoned one at Murshidebad on the day the treasure was despatched, and officers attended from every corps.

It had been agreed before the expedition left Madras that there should be an equal distribution of prize-money between the army and navy, but this was forgotten now by the army in the intoxication of the moment. The navy was not on the spot to claim its half or even to share at all, and with scarcely a dissentient vote— with the important exception of Clive's—the council-of-war agreed " that the Officers and Sailors belonging to the Squadron which came with the Army on this Expedition to Muxadavad are not to receive Prize money with the Military." Nor did they want any waste of time in distributing the money : they insisted that it should be distributed immediately !

-Clive's vigorous protests were drowned out in the hungry clamour, and when he found that they would not listen to him he angrily overruled the votes and broke up the meeting. This, in the state of discipline existing then in the army, was an invitation to mutiny. A group of resentful officers sent him a protest. He retorted by having them put under arrest and sending their ringleader down to Calcutta. To those who had signed the protest he sent the following reply, which is a good specimen of his manner of dealing with malcontents :

" Gentlemen,—I have received your remonstrance and protest. Had you consulted the dictates of your own reason, those of justice, or the respect due to your commanding officer, I am persuaded such a paper, so highly injurious to your own honour as officers, could never have escaped you.

" You say you were assembled at Council to give your opinion about a matter of property. Pray, Gentlemen, how comes it that a promise of a sum of money from the Nawab, entirely negotiated by me, can be deemed a matter of property ? So very far from it, it is now in my power to return to the Nawab the money already advanced and leave it to his option, whether he will perform his promise or not. . . . You have stormed no town, and found the money there ; neither did you find it in the plains of Plassey, after the defeat of the Nawab. In short, Gentlemen, it pains me to remind you that what you are to receive is entirely owing to the care I took of your interest. Had I not interfered greatly in it, you had been left to the Company's generosity, who perhaps would have thought you sufficiently rewarded, in receiving a present of six months' pay ; in return for which, I have been treated with the greatest disrespect and ingratitude, and, what is still worse, you have flown in the face of my authority, for over-ruling an opinion, which, if passed, would have been highly injurious to your own reputation, being attended with injustice to the navy and been of the worst consequences to the cause of the nation and the Company.

" I shall, therefore, send the money down to Calcutta, give directions to the agents of both parties to have it shroffed ; and when the Nabob signifies his pleasure (on whom it solely depends) that the money be paid you, you shall then receive it, and not before.

" Your behaviour has been such, that you cannot expect I should interest myself any further in your concerns. I, there-fore, retract the promise I made the other day, of negotiating either the rest of the Nabob's promise, or the one-third which was to be received in the same manner as the rest of the public money at three yearly equal payments.

" I am, Gentlemen,
" Your most obedient, humble servant,
" Robert Clive."

Muxadavad,
" July 5, 1757."

The malcontents, sobered by this display of firmness, at once withdrew their protest and acknowledged their error with humble apologies. Clive replied : " Gentlemen,—I have ever been desirous of the love and good opinion of my officers, and have often pursued their interest in preference of my own. What passed the other day is now forgotten, and I shall always be glad of an opportunity of convincing you how much I am, Gentlemen, your most obedient, humble servant." He sent Admiral Watson a full report of what had happened with expressions of regret.

III

M. Law with his body of Frenchmen still had to be dealt with. How fortunate it had been for Clive that they had not reached Siraj-ud-daula in time for Plassey ! They were now retreating by forced marches towards Benares.

On July 6 Clive sent Coote upon the longest, the most arduous, and the most difficult expedition into the interior that the English had yet undertaken in India, and the manner in which Coote conducted it proved conclusively his fine soldierly qualities. Clive gave him 220 British troops and 500 sepoys and ordered him to overtake Law. The task was quite impossible. The Frenchman had given himself fully eleven days' start of Coote, who could not reach Rajmahal, the point from which Law had started his retreat, in less than five.

Everything was against success for Coote from the start. With the Ganges at full-flood stage, more like a sea than a river, with violent monsoon storms constantly sweeping across it and whipping up its great waters ; against the fury of wind and wave, with a strong adverse current to contend with every mile of the way, no transport but the clumsy, inadequate boats of the country, poorly manned by native boatmen and ill-conditioned ; little assistance from local officials, more disposed to be hostile than friendly ; and, finally, with troops dissatisfied because of not at once receiving their prize-money and murmuring ever more loudly at the great fatigues they were forced to undergo, Coote performed a feat of heroic endurance and determination in covering nearly 400 miles and reaching Patna, even in twenty-one days.

For several of those days he was stranded by the series of accidents that befell his fleet of boats. The culmination of his misfortunes, when his own budgerow was stove in and other boats narrowly escaped being lost and he had to land his men and all the guns and supplies and proceed on foot, was a mutiny of his Europeans, who refused to march a step farther. He then had to embark them again, while he himself pushed on with the sepoys, who, though they had had to march practically all the

Q

way and were suffering greatly from sickness and lameness, were still willing to go on. At last at Patna even the sepoys threw down their arms in weary disgust and had to be cajoled and bribed with promises of reward before they would agree to proceed a little farther. But by this time Law and his Frenchmen had escaped across the border into Oude and further pursuit was useless. The fact that they had done so full seventeen days before showed that Coote's quest had been hopeless from the beginning.

Clive, however, seems to have had no sympathy for his subordinate's difficulties and worded his letters in terms of sharp reproof. " When I sent you after M. Law I gave you positive orders to pursue him. Why then do you delay when your force is larger than his ? " There is an implication here of cowardice on Coote's part ! " I would have you follow him at all events, whether you are joined by Country people or not. . . . I rely on your not giving over the pursuit while there is a possibility of overtaking him." From a local official he received a lying and malicious report that Coote's men had been guilty of rapine and violence in his district : such a complaint, he wrote to Coote, " as had made me blush, tho' I know not how to give credit to it." Yet, apparently he did believe it for he added : " Such behaviour may give the Country people a disgust to us and be of the utmost ill consequence to the Company's affairs. I desire that henceforth you will not enter their forts nor take anything from them, not even provisions if to be bought, and that you will have as little connection with Country people as possible."

These were nothing less than insults to a soldier of Coote's quality, and are added proofs of Clive's marked dislike for him. Coote replied to Clive's reproofs with dignity and feeling :

" I assure you Sir, I have oft revolved in my Mind those Orders, but could not find any One of them could Oblige me to do Impossibilities. If you'll only take the Trouble to peruse my letters you'll find my Reasons for staying two Days at Rajamal were for want of Dandies [boatmen] & Boats : & to endeavour to repair our Shattered ones. I may venture to say, had I taken the advice of all the Officers of the Detachment, I shou'd have made a longer stay there than I did : having come Away almost in as bad a Condition as I arrived there. . . . Had you yourself known the fatigue of Body, & uneasiness of Mind I have suffer'd since I came upon this Expedition, you

would have pitied me, Instead of Condemning my Conduct :
But I thank God I have long ago learnt to bear with Resignation this & other Ills attending the Life of a soldier—I am
persuaded If you Converse with men who are Acquainted with
the Journies we have made, that you'll find none of them of
Opinion we have been Dilatory In getting half way to Patna,
at this season of the Year in Ten Days.   I assure you sir 'tis my
greatest Ambition to merit your approbation : But I fear I
have not yet been so happy, nothwithstanding my best
endeavours, as to Obtain It. . . ."

Coote must have confided his hurt feelings to Major Kilpatrick, who in reply sympathized with him in his disagreeable
command.   " All your friends and indeed everybody are well
satisfied that you have done as much as could be done on the
occasion. . . .   Let me assure you," he added, surely with some
significance, " there is not a man in India that I esteem more
worthy of the title of a friend, a soldier and a man of strict honour,
nor whose merit and conduct I am more sensible of than Major
Coote's." [101]

Coote forwarded a request of his officers for special *batta* [1] in
consideration of the exceptional expense and fatigue of this piece
of service.   The demand was to be frequently repeated by the
officers of the whole Bengal army and was to cause infinite trouble
to the Company as well as to Clive.   Nor was it wholly without
a show of justice, considering the circumstances of the time, the
rapid and devastating spread of the " get-rich-quick " spirit
following Plassey, and the examples of successful greed that the
civilian servants of the Company were about to give to their
military brethren less fortunate in their opportunities.

But Clive set his face sternly against it from the start.   The
application, he said, gave him infinite concern.

" I always thought their own Reputation and the honour of
their Country would have been incitement sufficient with them
to undergo hardships and fatigues, which could not much
exceed those which the whole Army suffer'd in their march
from Calcutta to Cassimbazar.   I am the more surprised at it,
because their allowance is beyond everything heard of in any
other Service, without mentioning the good Effects of the
Nabob's generosity."

[1] An extra allowance to officers when in the field, or on other special grounds.

IV

It was now the end of July. Clive was ready to leave Murshidebad and return to Calcutta.

At this point our story suffers a palpable let-down after the nervous tension of Plassey. It is merely in accordance with the truth that it should. To try to maintain that tension during the months that followed would be to falsify history. Clive himself suffered from a severe nervous reaction. When he had placed Mir Jafar on the throne, gathered up the fruits of victory, sent Coote to capture the last remaining Frenchmen in Bengal, there was only one desire left in him : that was to leave the country and go home.

That this should have been his desire tells more eloquently than any words he might have used both the state of his nervous system and the content of his mind as he viewed the situation created by his great victory.

Climatic conditions were almost sufficient of themselves to account for his complete lack of interest in the kingdom that he had conquered. The utter prostration that they caused Europeans during the summer months was now upon him. Everyone of these unacclimatized people must in August when the sailing season approached have thought wistfully of returning home. None of them stayed longer than was necessary to accumulate a sufficient fortune. If their sufferings during the summer months were worse than usual, if their health was breaking, they did not wait until they had accumulated all that they wanted. They went before the advent of another unhealthy season proved fatal to them.

Clive's chief inducement for staying had been suddenly taken away from him. He had his fortune, beyond his or any one's dreams. He could not at this moment have thought of increasing it.

Why, indeed, tempt his luck by staying longer ? His had been a gambler's luck, and he must have known it. All of them were gamblers, gambling against death and ill-fortune. Most of his friends had lost. Not one of them had won as he had. How long would his luck continue ? A shrewd gambler knows that he must not play his good luck too long.

He was having a recurrence of his nervous disorder. That, no doubt, was the natural reaction to the intense strain and anxiety of the preceding six months. It had happened after Arcot and Trichinopoly and had supplied him then with an excuse to go home. It may have been an excuse or it may have been a genuine cause. Only a neurologist could determine such a difficult question.

Margaret, too, had now joined him from Madras. And it must certainly have been her wish to return home as soon as possible to their infant son.

If nothing else could have made him want to take ship as soon as possible, the sudden death of Admiral Watson, following immediately on Clive's return to Calcutta, would have done so. The Admiral had sent him a note welcoming him back, and in it he had complained of not feeling quite well. A week later he was dead. Here was a case of a man who had overstayed his time. For Clive it must have been a dire warning for himself and Margaret.

He was truly shocked. He wrote the Directors :

" Mr. Watson is no more, everyone here received the melancholy news of his death with much concern ; his generosity, disinterestedness, and zeal for the service must for ever endear his memory to the Company. Unhappy Fate ! After having escaped all the risks of war to be thus untimely cut off in the midst of his successes, crowned with glory and reputation. This is but one of the many lessons given us of the instability of human nature. Concern for this good man's death hastens me to a conclusion."

The passing of the brave, able, honest, and high-minded sailor at the age of forty-three was mourned by the whole settlement, and a vast assemblage followed his body to the grave. Clive was one of the pallbearers.

Yes, Clive may well have reflected now on the instability of human life and wished himself with his wife and fortune safely in England.

Besides, he had his ambitions. Nor did they, even now when he had conquered a kingdom, lie in India. That conquest was with him more of a means to an end than an end in itself. And the end lay in England. He had stumbled upon the conquest as a means of extricating himself from a difficult and nerve-racking situation. But the reward for it could be his just the same. And that reward would surely be a peerage and the red ribbon of the Bath. Now surely he could get into Parliament and cut a real figure in English society. He could buy himself an estate and compete on level terms with the landed aristocracy. What use did he longer have for India ? What use especially for Bengal ? He hated that country. What was Calcutta but a devastated city of open drains and ditches, of fetid filth and putrefying garbage, so vile and unhealthy a spot that he dared not even bring his troops there ? He would before Plassey have gladly gone back to Madras, but now there was no occasion even for doing that.

As far as he could see he had completed the purposes of his mission. He had thought so before—he had said after his treaty of peace with Siraj-ud-daula, "All is over here " ; but now there could scarcely be any doubt about it. The cause of all the trouble was dead and a new prince, grateful to the English for his elevation, sat upon the throne. What possible cause for his staying could there be now ? He had told Mir Jafar and his nobles that for the English it was again to be " business as usual." He must have thought when he left Murshidebad that he would never revisit it, except possibly once more before he sailed to see that all was well. His great revolution seemed complete in every respect, so he wrote to the Directors.

Yet his decision could not have been made quite so easily as that. There was still the duty he owed his employers to be considered. What the precise extent of that duty was or how it was interpreted by the Company's service is a little hard to say. It certainly did not connote any large amount of self-sacrifice or a very rigid code of conduct. Yet it plainly involved staying at one's post as long as one was needed. Governor Drake had fallen far short of the required standard.

Did duty require him to stay ? He was not yet sure. He wrote the Directors : " For my own part be assured, Gentlemen, that it is solely a desire of seeing your affairs, important as they now are, firmly established, that detains me in Bengal." That was in August, and he was still planning to leave in a few months. Obviously even that brief delay was enough to fill him with a sense of having done his duty by staying. He knew that Bengal was of more consequence to the Company than all their other possessions put together. How soon could he honourably get away from it ?

Watson's death decided him to put Margaret on board ship immediately and to follow himself in January. " If I can but leave this country in peace, which I believe I shall, nothing can detain me longer." So he wrote to tell his father of his plans and to give orders for the immediate repair of Styche. It was with pride that he could announce that he was bringing cousin George home with him with some £20,000 in his pocket and Edmund, his brother-in-law, with another similar sum. He wanted to get into Parliament—"but no more struggles against the Ministry ; I chuse to be with them." To each of his sisters he was giving £2000 and would take care of his brothers in due course. "I would advise the lasses to marry as soon as possible, for they have no time to lose. There is no occasion for your following the law any more. But more of this when I have the pleasure of seeing you, which I hope will be in 12 or 14 months."

To his London banker, Mr. Belchier, he added a word of warning. He was fearful of the effect that the news of Plassey would have upon his father ! " As this good news may set my Father upon exerting himself too much and upon paying too many visits to the Duke of N——, Mr. Fox and other great men ; I desire you will endeavour to moderate his expectations, for although I intend getting into Parliament and have hopes of being taken some notice of by H.M., yet you know the merit of all actions are greatly lessened by being too much boasted of. I know my father's disposition leads this way, which proceeds from his affection for me." If only Clive had heeded his own warning, his life might have been happier. But perhaps his father was more to blame for his subsequent disappointments than Robert himself. Certainly Robert's methods would appear to have been a shade more discreet.

" What has not poor Judy's father to answer for in not suffering his daughter to come to India ! " This to Sir Edward Clive, Bart., the said Judy's father. Poor Judy had undoubtedly missed the chance of making a good match ! " I should be glad if an opportunity offers (before I can arrive in England) of bargaining for an estate of two or three thousands pounds p.a. at a distance of 60 miles from London more or less, it was not neglected."

To Orme at Madras he had already written in like vein. The thought that he was about to leave for home had raised his spirits immensely.

" Dear Orme,—Probably the News overland will reach you before this, informing you of the Great Revolution effected in the Kingdom of Bengal ; this Expedition has perfectly satisfied me as to Circumstances, I only wait to see everything firmly settled before I steer my Course for old England ; so far from being a + to your aspiring thoughts I shall be of great Assistance by my Interest which you may depend upon.

" I am possessed of Volumes of Materials for the Continuance of your History, in which will appear Fighting, tricks, chicanery, Intrigues, Politics and the Lord knows what ; in short there will be a fine Field for you to display your Genius in ; so I shall certainly call upon the Coast in my way to England. I have many particulars to Explain to you relating to the said History which must be published——

" I must now trouble you with a few comm.s concerning family Affairs—Imprimis, what you can provide must be the finest and best you get for Love or Money ; 200 Shirts, the wrist Bands work'd, some of the Ruffles work'd with a Border, other in Squares, & the rest plain ; Socks Neck Cloths & Handkerchiefs in proportion, 3 large of the finest Stockings, for the above take Walsh's Muster, several Pieces Spotted Muslin & plain 2 Yards wide for Aprons, Book Muslin Cambricks or a few Pieces of the finest Dimity and a Compleat set of Table Linnen of Fort St. David Diaper made for the Purpose—You will have 5 Months for these Matters, and tho' there may not be time to get a compleat set of Chintze Furniture for a room, Bed, Chairs etc. it may follow. Mrs. Morse is a great Connoisseur in these Affairs excuse this trouble from a Friend & believe me

" Dear Orme
" Your aff.te Hble Sert
"R. C."

In a postscript he gave directions for the settlement of various outstanding debts, besides the loaning of 10,000 rupees at 4 per cent. interest to John Pybus, for whom he professed a great regard. In his reply Orme wrote, October 22 :

" I must confess to you that my fingers itch to write your Revolution. How that may be blended or published connected with my other history is a consideration which we will discuss when we meet. I think it may be made a piece of about the extent of the Jugurthine War, or if you prefer it as

long as Daniel's History of the Reign of Philip Augustus.
We men who are dealers must be able to fashion our work in
great or in little, but in our trade, contrary to most others, the
first model is generally in large, the finished piece is generally
in miniature. Dear Clive, I laugh with you, but if you pub-
lish my trifling chat, I shall be laughed at, which I abominate.

" I wrote Mrs. Clive that I partook of your good fortunes.
At that time I knew not what they were. I knew not they
were likely to affect my future state. I meant that I received
much satisfaction from hearing of them. I knew not that I
was essentially to benefit by them. You seem to think I shall.
I shall ever esteem all expectations uncertainties but am pleased
to find you wish me well.

" Your unbounded generosity has made many completely
happy. Of these is Mr. Pybus to whom I shall pay 10,000
pagodas. . . ."

In conclusion he solicited aid for a Mr. Roberts—not just a
short-term loan but something longer. Clive replied telling him
to advance Mr. Roberts 20,000 rupees.[102]

So that was the tenor of all his thoughts. He would go,
if——

The full meaning of that *if* had not yet dawned upon him.
It is not clear that it ever fully dawned on him how completely
he had placed himself upon another plane of duty by his dealings
with Mir Jafar, that his fortune had not been acquired by such
ordinary means as enabled a man to go home with a clear conscience as soon as his desires were gratified. Ordinary commercial money-making may incur no obligations. A man makes his
money by trade or investment ; then if he wishes he retires, with
no one having the right to question his doing so. But with Clive
it was entirely different. He had not made his money in trade,
but in politics. His old chief Saunders would have been the first
to see the difference. Clive did not ; he had, like so many of his
contemporaries, a big blind-spot in money matters. Tragically
for himself he was not to see the difference until it was made
abundantly clear for him by other men imitating his method, and
even then he was never able honestly to apply the realization to
himself. He made instead a false, because an entirely minor,
distinction between money won by the sword and that made by
his successors without use of the sword.

He had incurred obligations to Mir Jafar, whom he had placed upon the throne. He had incurred obligations to his employers to see that the money owed to them by Mir Jafar was paid. Even he could see that he could not leave without definite assurance on these points. There was a special obligation laid upon him to leave the country in peace and good order. Was there an obligation also to the inhabitants of it, the millions of toiling peasants ? If there was, it was not recognized by the men of his day, and it was not recognized by Clive. But it was the other two obligations that kept him—and with him Margaret—in the country for two years after the date he had fixed for his departure. For almost as soon as his decision was taken he found that the condition for it was not fulfilled.

Chapter Seventeen

A PROBLEM IN POLITICAL MANAGEMENT

"It is difficult to contend with a Conqueror"

HORACE

I

CLIVE'S PICTURE OF A REVOLUTION "compleat in every respect" had no sooner been composed than it began to dissolve. There could be no greater delusion than to imagine that the former status of merchants could be restored by means of a military revolution. When the English had to resort to arms to enforce their rights, that status was gone for ever ; and all their strivings, all their efforts to evade the ineluctable consequences, were of no avail. They were caught now in a current that was to bear them at a rapid pace down an ever stronger, ever-widening stream of empire. Again and again they might try to stay their course by clinging to what seemed like solid land, but each time the current proved too much for them, and every time they made a mooring a fresh flood came down and swept them on. And as they went they had by rapid degrees to undergo the most complete and painful transformation that any company of merchant adventurers has ever been forced to undergo. In an age of intense conservatism no institution was more conservative in its outlook than the East India Company, or more loath to adapt itself to changed conditions. It did not at first even want to recognize that there had been any change. Long after its local representatives were thinking in terms of forts and garrisons and military resources and political alliances and the administration of lands and revenues, the Directors at home were still mainly concerned with trade, the quality and quantity of their imported goods, the price of their stock, and the size of the dividends to be declared at the next General Court.

"We cannot avoid remarking," they were to write their Bengal agents in March 1759, "that you seem so thoroughly possessed with military ideas as to forget your employers are

251

merchants, and trade their principal object, and were we to adopt your several plans for fortifying, half our capital would be buried in stone walls." Their idea of a sufficient military force for Bengal was 300 Europeans " and no more."

But Clive, even if he could not foresee the other consequences of his revolution, had been quick to realize its military requirements, and he was already writing home urging the need for supplies of men and military stores to secure the rich prize he had won, and especially for some good experienced officers to fill the places of those who had been killed or died. " There are many promising gentlemen in the King's Regiment, but the person [Colonel Adlercron] who commands them will never shine himself or suffer any under him to do it. Colonel Lawrence is grown old, and his intellects begin to fail him ; besides, he will not act." [103]

Clive organized a second battalion of regular sepoys. He immediately began also to plan for the building of a new Fort William on a better site and brought the Company's engineer, Brohier, from Madras for the purpose, and never ceased to urge upon the Select Committee the need for haste in erecting it.

Ominous signs that he had been far too optimistic in his hopes and plans appeared immediately. Just as soon as his back was turned things began to go wrong at Murshidebad. He spent a few days at the capital in September arranging for Eyre Coote's return from Patna and the quartering of his men at Kasimbazar, and consulting with Mir Jafar about the need for a joint military demonstration in Bihar to establish the Nawab's authority. He then returned to Calcutta to prepare for the demonstration, which was timed to begin at the end of October.

On October 8 Luke Scrafton, whom he had appointed Resident at the court, wrote to him, " The Nabob has quite forgot the humble Meer Jaffeir. Roydullub seldom goes near him, his son never, and his officers are more than half of them disgusted. In short, as he conducts himself at present I see little probability of his wearing his head long." So alarmed was he indeed, at the prospect of another revolution that he demanded Clive's presence. " I could not have believed him such a bad man as I find him." [104] The English were now to find that it was easier to install a new prince than to set up a satisfactory government.

The first symptoms of another evil that was going to ruin Clive's settlement had also appeared. It was no coincidence that the two should appear simultaneously, for the germs of both were inherent in the revolution itself. The English flag was already being used as a pretext for evading the Nawab's jurisdiction ; boats passing under English colours were claiming exemption from the customary tolls and duties. Even Clive's own servant used his name to extort money from Manichund, late Governor of Calcutta, and had to be punished severely by his master for the offence. Clive, however, set his face firmly against this incipient evil from its first appearance, insisting upon the removal of all English flags outside the settlement. " The reputation we have established by the force of our arms makes it necessary for the Company's advantage as well as for the benefit of the trade in general that we establish the like reputation for equity and moderation."

When Clive marshalled his men for the new expedition he found that practically his entire force had perished from sickness—or by drinking themselves to death on the proceeds of Mir Jafar's bounty !—and that most of the survivors were unfit for duty. Major Kilpatrick was one of those who had died. The detachment of King's troops could muster only twenty privates, the Madras detachment only 150 ; so that the troops left to him were composed largely of foreign deserters and " topasses." The receipt on November 2 of another urgent note from Scrafton reporting the insults he had to endure from the Nawab and the precariousness of the situation compelled him to ask Admiral Pocock, who had succeeded to Watson's command, for the loan of the King's troops. " It is but too plain that all the Company's acquisitions are in great danger."

Yet he dared not confess as much to his employers—not after all the fair hopes he had raised of an end to all trouble ! To them he reported : " The present face of affairs seems fortunately to require but little service from our arms ; political negotiations are likely to be more necessary."

The Admiral agreed to his request. But then it was found that the officers of the King's troops had had all the Indian service they wanted. With the notable exception of Major Coote and one other officer, they signed a letter to Clive expressing their disinclination to go with him. So, feeling that it was better, as he said, " for the Company to be served by those who are willing, and may be attached to their service, than by persons who seem to have lost all remembrance of what they owe to them," he relinquished their services entirely and set out from Chandernagore with only the Company's troops and the faithful sepoys.

" Sir," wrote the now thoroughly frightened Resident, " I can only say, if you don't set out, with or without troops, permit me to go to Calcutta. I can't carry that authority, that sway, which the Company's affairs require ; and will not stay on the terms I am now with the Nabob. I clearly comprehend the political disease of the Nabob's affairs, but it is you only that can apply the remedy."

And that, in fact, was the exact worth in terms of durability of Clive's vaunted revolution. It depended entirely for its success upon one man only—the man who had brought it about. Hence the explanation of why Clive did not sail for home in January 1758, as he had planned.

II

In a letter to the Directors dated December 23, 1757, Clive drew the following picture of the state of affairs in the government of Bengal six months after Plassey :

" In laying open the state of this government I am concerned to mention that the present Nabob is a prince of little capacity, and not at all blessed with the talent of gaining the love and confidence of his principal officers. His mismanagement threw the country into great confusion in the space of a few months, and might have proved of fatal consequence to himself, but for our known attachment to him. No less than three rebellions were on foot at one time ; one at Midnapore, headed by Rajah Ram ; another at Purnea, under Abdul Sing ; and a third at Patna, under Ram Narrain : all which may be very well attributed to the Nabob's own imprudence. Rajah Ram's two brothers, after being invited to Moorshedabad, were imprisoned, which was quite sufficient to deter him from surrendering himself as he intended. Meer Azuffee was appointed to the government of Purnea to the general satisfaction of the people ; but soon laid aside for Cuddum Hussein Khan, a relation (it is true) of the Nabob, but a tyrannical, rapacious fellow, and odious to the last degree to the Purneans. As for Ram Narrain, after he made his submission, and the Nabob had sworn to continue him in his government, apparent measures were taken for his overthrow."

Clive went on to tell of the mutual suspicions of the Nawab and Rai Durlab, the Prime Minister, of how Rai Durlab went in fear of his life, and how Mir Jafar "cut off" Siraj-ud-daula's brother, "a young lad and almost an idiot," on surmise of Rai Durlab's intention to make him Nawab.

Clive's analysis of the ills afflicting the Bengal state went no further than to attribute them to the defects of the new Nawab's personal character, but this was a superficial view of the situation. Actually what had happened was that the revolution and the manner in which it had been brought about and the manner in which it was now being supported had undermined the foundations of the Moslem government and destroyed the Nawab's authority.

Clive's policy was quite simple : to maintain the Company's military supremacy, to support the Nawab but retain constant control over him, and to protect the Hindu noblemen who were the principal officers of state, and through them maintain real power in the government. But this policy, while obviously suiting English interests, reckoned not with the disastrous consequences it would produce for the whole fabric of government in the state itself.

The Moslem oligarchy that had held the reins of power may be likened to the Whig oligarchy that monopolized the government of England, in that they were weak men but proud and jealous of their monopoly. Yet they now found themselves in a doubly humiliating position : first, to be controlled by a body of foreign merchants, infidels to the faith, who had just previously been humble suppliants for trading privileges ; and then, to find that the crafty, pliant Hindus were not only siding with the new masters but usurping the chief offices of state and being maintained in them by the English. The British have often been accused of exacerbating communal jealousies and divisions. In Bengal, at the beginning of their rule, they undoubtedly did so. It is, therefore, no wonder that the revolution was followed by an outburst of cruelty and violence. Moreover, to make matters worse, power was now being transmitted through the English to the meanest of the natives in their service. The fact that the Moslem nobles could lay the blame for this intolerable situation only upon themselves and their unbridled passions, divisions, and jealousies did not make it any less galling to them. Divided they had fallen, when united they could easily have withstood Clive and his small force. Those of them that had for reasons of personal ambition and hatred of Siraj-ud-daula made a connection with the English forfeited the respect of their followers.

In this way the coming of the English created divisions in the state that had not existed before. It sometimes happens that when two parties have arrived at a satisfactory understanding and *modus vivendi*, the appearance of a third party will upset everything. So it was now. Before Siraj-ud-daula's crass folly had provoked a spirit of revolt and the English had appeared on the scene to take advantage of it, Moslems and Hindus had maintained a sort of uneasy equilibrium, tacit and arbitrary, but none the less effective. Now the English had come necessarily seeking connections in the country, and immediately the harmony of Moslem and Hindu was broken. Mir Jafar had bought his throne from them, but when he realized the price that he had to pay for it, when he realized that he had forfeited the loyalty and respect of his fellow Moslems and that only the English army kept him on the throne, he naturally wanted to destroy those from whom he had made the purchase. Thus the immediate and direct result of the English incursion was the destruction of the Moslem state through feuds, rebellions, and revolutions, accompanied by a disappearance of any small remaining sense of public morality or public duty. When once the threads that held the state together were broken the English had little difficulty in taking it apart and injecting their own supremacy into the rent fabric. Then when they tried to bind it together again they were to find that they could only do so by taking the government into their own hands.

Thus Mir Jafar was one of the unhappiest princes that ever lived. His own inadequacies for the position became painfully obvious from the day of his accession. That he was weak, shifty, generally unreliable, and unable to pursue a consistent policy cannot be denied, but Clive showed a singular lack of comprehension in his estimate of his performance and of the *malaise* that was afflicting the state generally. " The wavering disposition of the Nabob and the ear he gives to evil counsellors who endeavour to inspire notions into him of our having too great an influence in the country, have occasioned me some trouble in these mediations. However, as he perceives in the end that my endeavours are entirely directed to his good and the public quiet, his jealousies are quickly effaced." So he described matters to the Court of Directors. But when as time passed the Nawab showed no sign of mending his ways and appreciating Clive's efforts in his behalf, but rather the reverse ; when he showed clearly that he wanted nothing so much as to be freed from his benefactors, Clive saw in it merely another proof of the ingratitude that was characteristic of all Moslems. It was no doubt comfortable to his ingrained sense of English superiority to be able to say, "The Moors are bound by no ties of gratitude, and every day's experience convinces us that Mussulmen will remain firm to their engagements no longer than while they are actuated by principles of fear, always ripe for a change whenever there is the smallest prospect of success." But such a view shows a complete inability to see anyone else's point of view but his own and that of his countrymen.

Clive has been credited with an extraordinary understanding of the Indian character. What he had was rather an extraordinary understanding of the worst sides of that character ; its better and more likeable sides were a closed book to him. If a police-officer were to derive his opinion of humanity entirely from his professional experiences, he would have the same low opinion of his fellow-men as Clive formed of the Bengal Moslems, because his dealings with them were also largely of a police nature. Most of his time during the remainder of his stay in India was to be spent trying to penetrate the real meaning of the Nawab's actions and to uncover his plots. Always he had to suspect that the obvious meaning was not the correct one, always to be taking precautions against treachery. That he showed uncanny skill in this detective work is not to be questioned. Others might be deceived by the cleverness of Mir Jafar's schemes, but not he. In the battle of wits between the Nawab and Clive the Nawab was always worsted, until it is not surprising that Mir Jafar came to hold the Englishman in superstitious awe as one gifted with supernatural powers, combining the courage of the lion with the wisdom of the serpent.

This was shown clearly in October 1758, when the Nawab concocted a new scheme to rid himself of Rai Durlab. He displayed to Warren Hastings, who had just taken Scrafton's place in the difficult post of Resident, a letter purporting to be written by Rai Durlab which incriminated the writer in a treasonable conspiracy. Hastings forwarded the letter to Clive. The question at once arose, was it genuine ? Hastings was inclined to believe it was. Not so Clive. He at once suspected a plot, with

R

Nuncomar at the bottom of it, for it was known that Nuncomar was scheming to get Rai Durlab's post. He argued that it was exceedingly unlikely that Rai Durlab would be so foolish as to commit to writing anything of a compromising nature (he had shown himself too cautious for that at the time of the conspiracy against Siraj-ud-daula) ; nor would he be likely to enter into an intrigue whilst he was actually, as he was at that moment, living under the very noses of the English at Calcutta. It was, also, too obvious that Nuncomar stood to benefit largely if the business of the letter were brought to a good conclusion. There was no way of getting to the exact truth, but there can be little doubt that Clive was right.

The strongest claim that Clive has to real statesmanship during this period of trying to preserve his political settlement of Bengal and make it work is that, despite everything, despite Mir Jafar's conduct and his own views of it, he never swerved an inch from his fixed line of policy. English policy in India has so often been weak and vacillating that Clive's firmness stands out in sharp and pleasant contrast. He steadily supported Rai Durlab, Ramnarayan, and the other Hindu dignatories of state, but he equally steadily supported Mir Jafar.

His method was that of the iron hand in the velvet glove. He counteracted the plots without ever outraging the Nawab's feelings or exposing him to public contempt. "In short," he instructed Hastings, "I would have you act upon all occasions so as to avoid coming to extremities, and at the same time show as much spirit and resolution as will convince the durbar that we always have it in our power to make ourselves respected." And again, with regard to the necessity of protecting Rai Durlab, "The withdrawing of our protection from a man to whom it has been once promised would entail disgrace and infamy on the English nation."

Thus, if he had no respect or sympathy for the Indian people, either as individuals or as a whole except in so far as he recognized their worth to the British as sepoy soldiers, if he made no attempt to acquire more than a smattering knowledge of their languages or to understand their point of view and their mental processes except in so far as it was necessary to preserve power over them, if he was only concerned with them as their behaviour affected British interests, if he was not interested in them as human beings but merely as producers of the wealth of which his countrymen now happily had the chance to be large partakers, the fact remains that he was now in his own person the only element of stability that the state of Bengal possessed. Though the very antithesis of T. E. Lawrence in his relations with them, yet the ascendancy, the mastery he established over them was no less strong. In fact, only once or twice in history has one man so stamped his personality upon an alien people. That it was a domination based on fear and not devoid of superstitious elements should not obscure the fact that it was also a domination by strength of character. One man's strong mind, strong will, with a single firmly grasped purpose, prevailed over their weak minds and wills, the more so because of their personal jealousies and rivalries and racial and religious divisions.

But it was a stamp, by its very nature of being personal to himself, without any lasting qualities. Remove it, and the impression it had made would fade immediately. The real testing-time would come when the control fell into the hands of Englishmen who did not possess his prestige, who did not know how to prevent things from coming to extremities, or how to make themselves respected. Clive's power was that of a dictator, and shared with all dictatorships the same fatal weakness of impermanence. The basis for the ultimate permanent solution to the situation created by Plassey had not been created, nor could it, by the very nature of the situation, be created for some time to come. When at length the time for finding it came, it had to be sought for on quite other principles. Meanwhile, it was inevitable that the intervening years would be very unhappy ones for all three elements involved, the new rulers, the old rulers, and the ruled.

III

When Clive arrived at Murshidebad at the head of his depleted forces on November 25, the troubles that had so exercised the mind of the British Resident instantly began to disappear. The rebellious Rajah of Midnapore needed only to be assured of English protection and the Nawab's pardon to make his submission. The Purnea rebels fled at his approach. And while the rift between Mir Jafar and his diwan, Rai Durlab, was of a nature that could not be healed, being complicated by doubts of Rai Durlab's complete loyalty to the new regime and the terms of settlement with the English, Clive succeeded by an admirable display of firmness and patience in bringing them together and settling their affairs for them.

Already the Nawab was in arrears in his payments on the English debt and Clive needed no one to tell him that those arrears would tend progressively to increase as Mir Jafar's dependence on the English decreased. There was, therefore, an especial need for bringing Nawab and diwan together. After much persuading Rai Durlab was induced to leave the safety of his palace and come to Rajmahal, where the army was encamped, and allow himself to be formally reconciled with Mir Jafar. This was followed by a conference (December 30) at which the Nawab and his minister entered into an agreement for the immediate payment of arrears, the assignment of the annual revenues of various districts for the payments of the balance, and the grant without further delay of the lands promised to the Company.

The guarantee of protection to Rai Durlab was shrewd politics on Clive's part, because it gave him a tight hold over him and ensured his fidelity to these arrangements. It was through this dependence of so many of the principal officers of state upon English support that Clive was able to establish his mastery—a clever application of the maxim " Divide and rule."

The way was now clear for an advance into Bihar, where the maxim could be given another application in the case of Ramnarayan, its deputy governor, whose loyalty to the new Nawab was also in question. The evidences of his hostility that Coote had supplied on his expedition to Patna had determined Clive to depose him, and he had actually sent Coote orders to that effect, but Coote had not carried them out, having been prevailed upon by Mir Jafar's friends not to do so. Clive had been displeased : " Unless you chastise some of these treacherous and turbulent dispositions," he had written Coote, " every petty rajah will dare disobedience." Now, however, both he and the Nawab had reversed their attitudes. Mir Jafar was going to Patna with the deliberate intention of deposing Ramnarayan in favour of his brother-in-law, Mir Kasim, and Clive, upon receiving assurances from Ramnarayan of fidelity to the Nawab, was equally intent upon protecting him. A battle of wits and wills was fought by Mir Jafar and Clive from the time Ramnarayan joined them on the march to Patna until Mir Jafar departed thence with his army in April. Suspicion of intended foul play was never absent from Clive's mind, and so great became his fears that he encamped on an island in the Ganges where he could be sure of not being over-whelmed by a sudden attack. It was not until the middle of February that he was able to extract from the reluctant Nawab the confirmation of Ramnarayan in his government, and even then he could not at once leave Patna, being quite sure that Mir Jafar would revoke the appointment as soon as his back was turned.

He was taken ill shortly after this and for several days was in much pain. On March 3 he wrote the Nawab :

" I am sick in body, but much more in mind, for it is with great grief of mind I observe your favour for the English decreasing daily. It is true when any report of the Mahrattas or Sujah ud Daula's coming into this country prevails, then we are thought useful, at all other times the English are thought troublesome. I know not the meaning of all this, but this I know we are the same people who obtained you the Subaship and preserved your life at Plassey, and that we are determined to support your Excellency in your present great state against all your enemies as long as we have a man left." [105]

At the beginning of May Clive and Rai Durlab returned to Murshidebad, only to find that Miran, the Nawab's evil son—a fair replica, to all seeming, of Siraj-ud-daula—had been up to all kinds of mischief in their absence. His bloodthirsty hatred of the Hindus and the English made him the natural champion of the Moslem chiefs and soldiers who wanted to wipe out the stain on their honour and recover their power. Once more, however, Clive showed his calm mastery over the Indian mind. Dynamite was ready to explode on every hand, but it did not explode. Miran may have been planning to seize the government and murder his father. Instead, when Clive appeared, he hastily muttered his apologies and dismissed his following. Clive put his troops into cantonments at Kasimbazar, near enough to the capital to overawe its turbulence, and with all the aplomb of a conqueror returned to Calcutta on May 28. Yet not for a day thereafter could he relax his vigilant watch of Mir Jafar's and Miran's activities.

On February 19 he had written informing Mr. Pigot of his intention of staying another year :

" Though there is nothing I so earnestly wish for as returning to the Coast that I may have a good plea for quitting the service

entirely, yet I have set my heart so much upon a happy conclusion of the Murshidebad Expedition that I am determined to
stay in Bengal another year if no news from England prevents
it, for there is such a connection between the Nabob, myself,
and his great men that I greatly fear my absence would throw
all into confusion and there would be an end of the remaining
part of the debt and of the fortifications. Besides, so large a
sum has been advanced by the Company to the Navy and
Army I think myself bound to see the major part of it repaid
by the Nabob. By that time 18 out of the 20 will be received.
I hope my good friend will acquit me the crime of vanity in
expressing my apprehensions of the evil consequences of my
leaving Bengal at this juncture ; these foolish people ground
their opinions and confidence on one man's abilities alone."

He added a severe note on Roger Drake, Junior, still officially
Governor of Calcutta : " I am afraid good advice is but thrown
away on such a wretch, lost to all sense of shame. Not a week
passes but at his own table he is saluted with the title of scoundrel
and rascal from the meanest of the inhabitants without showing
the least resentment. . . ." Nothing could make a man sink
lower in Clive's estimation than conduct such as that.

IV

Clive's return was most welcome to his colleagues. All their
fears of the French had returned in full force with the news they
had just received of the long-expected arrival on the coast of a
great French armament under the command of Comte de Lally,
and of the immediate capture of Cuddalore, the threat to Fort
St. David, and the indecisive engagement that Admiral Pocock
had had with the French fleet off St. David's road on April 29.
Clive's weight in the councils of Calcutta was now as great as
his mastery over the Indians, and to him alone did they look for
guidance in this new crisis. There was good reason to fear that
the French armada might be bound for Bengal. In that case,
what was there to prevent it from taking Calcutta ? So far as the
members of the Select Committee could see, and Clive among
them, there was very little. For the work on the new fort was
proceeding with maddening slowness, and complaints on this
score were to be recorded in Council Consultations for some time

to come. Clive did his utmost to speed things up, but in the middle of June, when an attack was expected any day, the Committee could think of no way to defend the town except by erecting heavily armed fascine batteries at points along the river, sinking ships and placing chains higher up to block the passage.

Happily the French did not come. Instead, they concentrated their efforts in the Carnatic. Bengal was, as Clive now knew, worth more than anything that the French could acquire in the way of an empire in the Deccan; but the French seat of government was still at Pondichéry and Bussy was still ensconced in Hyderabad, so it was natural that the French should try first to expel the English from the Carnatic before turning their attention to Bengal.[1]

Bussy at Hyderabad was in exactly the same position as Clive at Murshidebad. He had encountered the same problems and employed the same solutions, but he was having much greater difficulties in finding money to pay his troops. At first, like Clive, he had thought the wealth of the country inexhaustible, but he was now finding his venture to be at best barely self-supporting. He and his chief officers were able to make great fortunes, but there was nothing left over for the French Company.

Clive's acquisition, on the other hand, could with good management be made to yield rich profits for both servants and employers. That was one reason, and no doubt the chief one, why Clive positively refused to leave it to take any part in the war for the possession of the south. His one fear was lest the French should see the truth of the situation too and leave Madras and the devastated Carnatic alone in their unprofitableness and come to where the hunting was still good.

Such was the state of affairs when the *Hardwick* arrived from England bringing out what Clive termed "the most uncommon form of government for Bengal I believe that ever was heard of."

V

The news of Siraj-ud-daula's capture of Calcutta had been slow in reaching London—not until June 2, 1757—and though it had

---

[1] This was the French intention: after taking Fort St. David, Lally wrote to Bussy: "It is the whole of British India which it now remains for us to attack. I do not conceal from you that having taken Madras, it is my resolution to repair immediately, by land and sea, to the banks of the Ganges, where your talents and experience will be of the greatest importance to me."

naturally caused general consternation, it had happily been quickly followed (July 22) by the news of its recovery.

The Directors hushed up the disaster as much as possible and did not even enquire deeply into its circumstances, realizing that they themselves were not free from blame because of their neglect of Fort William's defences. So they did not look for scapegoats, especially as any misconduct on the part of their servants had been fully paid for by their subsequent sufferings. In appointing a new council they at first named Clive for the head of it, but upon receipt of his later reports indicating that he was about to leave everything in tranquillity in Bengal and return to Madras, they excusably assumed that this was what he had actually done and so did not name him on the fresh commission that they despatched on November 11 by the *Hardwick*. Instead, they named only those of their servants whom they concluded were still in Bengal, appointing a council of ten, with a select committee of four to transact business with the Country government, and included a plan for rotating Governors whereby the three senior members of council were to take the chair in succession, each one for four months.

Clive poured ridicule upon the plan when it reached Calcutta, and in the light of Plassey and subsequent developments it cannot but appear as absurd. But in fairness to the Directors it must be remembered, what Clive overlooked, that they were still in ignorance of what was really happening in Bengal, and his own optimistic reports of a speedy settlement upon the old mercantile footing had not been calculated to open their eyes to the need for any radical change in the system of management. True, the rotation of Governors was a distinct innovation, poor under any circumstances, but it was not as great an innovation as it might seem. The Company had never vested much authority in its presiding officers, having an inveterate dislike, natural to Englishmen and still more natural to a body of merchants, for giving wide powers to an individual. It had even disapproved of the wide powers that Madras had granted Clive. It was wedded to the idea of government by committee, and its slow and reluctant surrender of it was part of the aforesaid painful transformation of the Company from trade to government. The Company, too, was faced with the difficulty of not knowing whom to appoint as Governor in view of Clive's supposed departure and the proved incompetence of Drake and most of his colleagues.

Thus the plan was intended to be merely a stop-gap until further light was thrown on the situation.

In the same letter Mr. Payne, the Chairman, complained bitterly of the conduct of the Company's servants in appropriating all the profits of their warlike undertakings in India to themselves and leaving the Company to bear all the expenses ! [106] This had for long been the baneful rule in the French service ; hence the straits to which the French Company was reduced. And now it had happened in the loot of the Gheria pirates' nest. Clive, it must be said, showed in Bengal much greater regard for the interests of the Company and had a right to their gratitude for the treaty he had made with Mir Jafar.

If the new commission of government angered Clive, it filled his colleagues with positive dismay. They realized only too well their own inadequacy for dealing with the new situation with all its many difficulties and perplexities, so now in the present grave crisis they were unanimous in wishing to refuse the joint honours that had been so unexpectedly thrust upon them. They surmised, quite correctly, that the Directors would undoubtedly have appointed Clive if they had known the actual state of affairs. Therefore, wrote Messrs. Watts, Manningham, Becher, Collett, Mackett, and Boddam, to Clive, would he not accept their offer of being sole President till a person was appointed by the Honourable Company ?

Clive accepted with alacrity. It was in his eyes the only possible, the only conceivable solution. The post was his by right established by him a score of times in the past eighteen months, so there was no call for any show of reluctance. If he really felt any of the disinclination he expressed to Pigot, it was because of his chagrin at the Directors' act in revoking their nomination of him without explanations or apology. By this his sensitive pride had received a deep wound which rankled painfully, and there now began that hostility to the Court of Directors which as it grew was to have the gravest consequences for both him and the Company.

Chapter Eighteen

TRIPLE THREAT

" Remember, all is at stake in India, and necessity has no law "
CLIVE TO PIGOT

I

WITH THE OUTBREAK of renewed war between England and France—the great imperial war that was to determine which of the two Powers was to acquire an empire upon which the sun never sets—the fighting in India assumed an entirely different character from what it had had in the days of Dupleix and Saunders. This change has been somewhat slurred over by the champions of Clive, but it dominated the minds of the anonymous and forgotten champions of the professional soldiers who waged the new war, those champions whose pitifully inadequate efforts formed part of Charles Caraccioli's *Life of Robert, Lord Clive.*

The pigmy days of Dupleix and Saunders were gone. Regular troops, in numbers sufficient to be dignified by the name of armies, now did service for their respective countries. Great national states were grappling together, and India was of as much consequence to them both as North America. The great Pitt was in command in England and Pitt's heart was set upon India : " there where I had garnered up my heart, where our strength lay, and our happiest resources presented themselves." When the French government sent out powerful forces, Pitt countered by sending out still more powerful forces. The two East India Companies were scarcely any longer concerned in the military part of their affairs. The struggle had passed far beyond the scope of their puny strength. The national governments now supplied the ships, the officers, and the regiments.

When the squadron of Bouvet arrived at Pondichéry on September 8, 1757, it was with the Régiment de Lorraine on board, under the command of M. de Soupire, 1000 strong. When the squadron of d'Aché brought the remaining part of the expedition in the following April, it was with the Régiment de Lally on board, under the command of the Comte de Lally, also 1000 strong. With the artillery and the forces of the French Company already at Pondichéry and with Bussy at Hyderabad, the French now had over 4000 French troops in India. In the fighting that followed it is little wonder that Clive's exploits with a few score white men and a few hundred sepoys against the miscellaneous " riff-raff " that was all Dupleix had to pit against him faded into comparative insignificance—at least in the minds of those now engaged in this greater warfare.

It was now, too, that Clive made his confession of reluctance to command again in the field. On the first anniversary of Plassey he wrote Colonel Forde, the officer whom he had chosen to act as his understudy :

" I learn that Mr. Pitt and Lord Barrington have acquainted the directors, the King intends sending me out a Colonel's Commission. I am much obliged to His Majesty for the honour intended me, but I shall never make use of it, for I am not at all inclined to enter the lists with Mons. Lally. Experience, discipline, and, perhaps, bravery likewise would be all against me ; for you well know the men which come to India are the worst of their kind, and surely the best men of France are equal to the worst of England." [107]

It is a curious letter for Clive to have written, and is susceptible of various interpretations. It is curious that he should have confessed his disinclination so frankly when he could so easily and justly have said that he was fully occupied with the all-important work of consolidating British power in Bengal. It does not sound like the same man who once knocked a batch of raw recruits into shape in a few days and carried two French forts with them. It suggests a man who has laid aside his military career and is taking an opportunity to assure his chosen successor that he has no intention of taking it up again. Had Plassey cured him of his love of fighting ? Or was he merely being modest in order to pay Forde the greater compliment ? It is certainly true that from his own standpoint he would risk everything to gain nothing by pursuing a martial career further.

II

With the arrival of Lally the wars of the English and French in India took on a ruthlessness, as well as a regularity, never known before.

Lally was not cruel by nature, but his experiences in India from the day he landed drove him nearly mad with vexation. He was an Irishman, with a French mother, being one of the many of his race who preferred the service of His Most Christian Majesty to enduring the lot of his co-religionists and countrymen in Ireland, and he had many of an Irishman's endearing qualities and faults. Brave, generous, warm-hearted, and possessed of a strict sense of honour, he was also hot-tempered, arrogant, tactless, violent, and impulsive—all to a degree that rendered him quite incapable of performing the exceedingly difficult task with which he had been entrusted. So disagreeable was his command likely to be that, though he had seen considerable service and was an able officer, it is not clear whether he owed his appointment, important as it was, to his being in favour with Madame de Pompadour or to his being out of it ! Whichever it was, he hoped for the marshal's baton : he was to get, instead, the Bastille. And instead of executing his plans, he himself was in the end to be executed.

It would have needed someone with the genius of a Napoleon and the patience and long-suffering of a Washington to execute those plans. He was to expel the English from India. He was at the same time to reform the whole French system of colonial administration. Considering that the English held the command of the seas, that they held in fee, too, the treasure-house of Bengal, that their greatest war minister was at the height of his power, that they numbered among their officers one of the finest groups of commanders that they ever possessed, and that their governor at Madras, George Pigot, was no slouch, it might seem that the first mission alone was quite sufficient for any man ; that it was, in fact, as difficult as Bonaparte's when he set out to conquer the East *via* Egypt. As regards the second, the administration of Pondichéry was so honeycombed with corruption from top to bottom that its reform was a task comparable only to the one undertaken by Clive in his purging mission of 1765. For its accomplishment it needed all, and more of the powers and advantages that Clive possessed, and of which Lally possessed none.

The number of handicaps that he laboured under were prodigious. He was not a young man as young men went in India in those days : he was 58. Furthermore, he sailed for India just about a year too late. He should have sailed at the same time as Clive, as he would then have arrived in nice time to take advantage of Siraj-ud-daula's efforts to a similar end. But the French had begun one of the most critical wars in their history totally unprepared. He was wholly ignorant, too, of the country and people. This would not have mattered so much, as he shared this handicap with most of the British commanders that Pitt was sending out ; only, he was not simply ignorant, he was utterly contemptuous. He cared nothing for rules of caste and the sanctity of shrines, outraging native feelings with reckless disregard of consequences. He was as arrogant and obstinate as Dupleix, but without Dupleix's great experience, cleverness, and fortitude.

There was nothing wrong with his spirit for the war. Combining a Frenchman's with an Irishman's hatred of the English, his intentions were in harmony with his orders : he was determined to destroy the English settlements utterly, one by one, as captured. This gave the war its *à outrance* character that was reflected in Clive's views and actions and in the spirit that the war engendered.

His campaign from the day of landing resolved itself into a gallant, furious, desperate effort to make war with all the material and even moral elements of successful war lacking. All save one : he had the men, two or three times as many at first as the British. But he had no money, no transport, no system of supply, nor even the supplies themselves, no stores of munitions, no gunpowder, and no sea-power to help him to make up these deficiencies. The French admiral d'Aché fought Pocock twice, had the worst of both encounters, and was then compelled to resign the command of the sea to him and return for refitting to his base in the French Islands. So desperate, in fact, was Lally's need of money that he had to put it first among his military objectives, even to embarking on arduous campaigns with that as his sole object. He was never to get within fair measuring distance of achieving his purpose, but he made a grand showing : he forced the English to put forth their utmost efforts to withstand him, and if Pitt's reinforcements had not reached Madras in the proverbial "nick of time," they might have been really hard-pressed. He also succeeded in giving them one terrific shock.

As in previous wars, that shock came at the beginning ; the English victories were to follow. As soon as he landed, after taking one look at the administration he was supposed to reform, Lally rushed off, characteristically impulsive, to attack Fort St. David. And on June 2, 1756, Fort St. David surrendered to him after a scandalously brief and half-hearted resistance.

The news reached Calcutta the same day as the *Hardwick*, and powerfully contributed to the offer of the presidency to Clive and its acceptance by him. He was fiercely indignant when he learned the details of the surrender. Memories of 1747 and 1748 must have flooded in upon him adding strength to his anger. Then St. David's had been but a little place, miserably garrisoned and poorly fortified, and it had stood all alone on the coast. Yet it had withstood Dupleix when Dupleix was flushed with victory. But now—St. David's had recently been strongly fortified, it possessed a garrison of over 600 Europeans and 1600 sepoys, it had a strong and ably commanded British squadron within easy reach of it, and Madras still flew the British flag. Yet, and the shame of it pierced Clive to the heart, its garrison surrendered before even a breach had been made or one assault delivered. " Infamous ! " he cried, and demanded a court-martial to make the severest examples of the guilty parties. " Had there been no powder at all left but for the musketry "—lack of powder had been the chief excuse—" where was the excuse for giving up the place till a breach was made, the covered way stormed, and the ditch filled ? Had they no bayonets ? Were our enemies supplied with wings to fly into the place ? "

" May infamy and disgrace attend all those who are backward in their country's cause," he wrote to Admiral Pocock, who also had had the mortification of seeing certain victory in one of his fights slip through his fingers owing to the misconduct of three of his ships' captains. " And may the worst of punishments attend those who so shamefully gave up St. David's to the French. I cannot think of that transaction with common patience. Every reflection about it wounds me to the very soul, and the more I enquire into facts the more reason I have to lament the departed reputation of the English on the Coast of Coromandel." [108]

The defender of Arcot had a right to his contempt. All his fighting blood, a little in danger now of cooling, was aroused once more, and every report from the south only served to fire his temper and determination to resist this new onslaught of the national enemy. But not to the extent of wanting to go to meet the foe himself on those plains which were once more the battle-field of Europe in Asia. For it was now that he wrote that reveal-ing letter to Forde.

He saw at once that this was no gentlemen's war. It was a war of survival or extinction. "Remember, my good friend," he wrote to Pigot, somewhat patronizingly perhaps, "Remember, all is at stake in India, and that necessity has no law." [109] If Lally were ruthless, it was up to the English to be equally so. As lack of money was Lally's greatest weakness, any and every method must be employed to increase it, even to desolating the whole country once more. "By ruining the country you will infallibly ruin M. Lally. . . . Can't a body of Maratha or other horse be taken into pay to burn, ravage and destroy the whole country, in such manner as that no revenue can be drawn from thence ? "

As for the French in Bengal, Clive could be ruthless too. Their expulsion from the country and the complete destruction of Chandernagore was in his eyes a just reprisal for the wanton destruction of English country houses at Madras. The inhabi-tants might protest, and Clive's colleagues in council might be inclined to lenience, but not he. Chandernagore had to be destroyed. And destroyed it was, even to the Italian Capuchin missionary church—how hard its head pleaded for it to be spared !—all except the houses of a few indigent widows.[110]

III

The dreaded month of August had come around once more in Bengal, making hypochondriacs of the exiles and sending their thoughts longingly homewards.

Clive had put off his departure one year. Was he now to put it off another ? His disgust with Calcutta had not abated. Rather, it was mounting. His fastidious sense of order and discipline could not patiently abide the laxity of conduct that he saw growing there by leaps and bounds. "A kind of levelling principle reigns among all the inhabitants of this place," he complains to Mr. Payne. He has no personal interests to serve now, nor axe to grind. His own thoughts are set upon England. But he still has his duty to do, his work to finish. It will not be finished until the new fortifications are completed, the army brought up to requisite strength, the treaty fulfilled, and Mir Jafar firmly established on his throne.[III]

It made him indignant to see others preparing to do what he had a so much better right to do. There was no longer any inducement for the members of the council to stay; Mir Jafar's bounty had removed that inducement. But if all the Councillors went home together, who would be left to run the government? None but himself and untrained juniors. "If affluence of circumstances could warrant such a step I had before this been one of the many now preparing to enjoy in their native country the fruits of our success at Plassey; surely there is no one can plead stronger inducements" (November 23, 1758).

Now, as always, he was exigent of his deserts. His colleagues might, and may, have retorted that, by accepting from their hands the Governorship, he had relieved them of both the moral obligation and the inducement to a longer stay. *He* was clearly indispensable. *They* just as clearly were not. Be it so or not, they went home and he remained—for another year at least.

There can be no doubt that Clive felt that his services to the Company had put him on a totally different level from the rest of them—an inverted level of duty from the one seen by taking the view that because of the greater responsibilities incurred through his revolution, he was less able to leave. When Orme also announced his intention of going home Clive did not forbear from administering a stern reproof. It was no time, he said, to be thinking of going home, "when the service of every individual is wanted"; to do so would justly expose Orme to the censure and resentment of the Court of Directors. When the time came, a year later, when he himself announced his impending departure, he received from Warren Hastings a most earnest appeal to stay, based on well-justified forebodings of what would happen in his absence; but he paid no heed.

Meanwhile, there was no end to the ever-recurring fresh demands upon him. Vain indeed was to be the hope for a cleared desk that every executive likes to see before starting on his holiday.

In August the new business was the entertainment of the Nawab and the seizure of a good opportunity just presented to deliver a telling blow against the French.

The first was closely related to the second. Word reached Clive that Lally had summoned Bussy to join him for the siege of Madras. The withdrawal of most of their troops had weakened the French hold on the Deccan. One brigade only had been left for the defence of the Northern Circars, and trouble for the French followed immediately. A local chief made a raid on Vizagapatam, took it, hoisted the English flag, and appealed to Madras and Calcutta for support. Madras had its hands full with its own defence, but Clive was quick to see the opportunity thus presented to him.

He took a decision immediately, overruling the unanimous objections of the council, to despatch an expeditionary force to the Circar Coast. But in so doing he was undoubtedly taking a risk. He was, in fact, confronted with a ticklish situation that had to be handled with great care and diplomacy.

Lally's arrival and still more his early success against Fort St. David had naturally had a disturbing effect upon Mir Jafar and his volcanic court, where hopes began to be entertained of the French coming to free them from the English yoke. The fierce passions that seethed there could be held in check only by unwavering firmness and the most bold assurance. For that reason any indication of fear of the French might have been disastrous. When the panicky council had suggested asking the Nawab to send down a force to Hugli as a protection against a French invasion Clive had interposed with an emphatic veto. But if the Durbar had to be overawed, it also had to be tactfully conciliated, and this became all the more necessary now that the Company's armed forces were about to be reduced by half. It was imperative that a rupture with the Nawab be prevented. This was the task that Clive entrusted to Warren Hastings, the new Resident, and supremely well did Hastings acquit himself in its performance.

To this end Mir Jafar was invited to pay a state visit to Calcutta. He accepted and came. The size of his retinue indicated the scale of entertainment expected, and since every effort was made to send him away satisfied with his reception, Scrafton, the interpreter, was probably not the only one among the English who groaned under the weight of an endless chain of festivities and

S

functions. "Thank God, His Excellency is at last gone," wrote Scrafton to Hastings. "He has led me a hell of a life here by the constant attendance I have been obliged to pay to him and his wenches, for he never went twenty yards from his house but they were with him."

The visit cost the Company 79,542 rupees, but the English told themselves that the expenditure had been worth while. It was a little hard, however, to find actual proofs of the good effects. Mir Jafar, with the able assistance of Miran and Nuncomar, seemed possessed of an inexhaustible box of plots. Only a few days before the visit Scrafton and Watts had arrived at Rai Durlab's house barely in time to rescue him from a gang of cutthroats in Miran's employ, whilst after it there was the disturbing incident of the letter incriminating the same minister. There was in fact still to be scarcely a day when Hastings could relax his vigilance or lower his tone of respectful authority.

As soon as the Nawab left, Clive set about preparing the expedition. The officer he chose for it was Colonel Francis Forde. When Kilpatrick's death and Coote's return home left him without a senior officer to command the troops, Clive had invited Forde, who was Adlercron's second in command of the 39th, to resign his commission in H.M.'s service and come to Calcutta to take the command. Forde had consented and arrived in January. There had arisen a difficulty over the compensation of £5000 which he demanded for relinquishing his royal commission. The Committee had not been willing to grant him more than half this sum, and Clive rather than lose his services, recognizing his outstanding merit, had paid the difference out of his own pocket. He had even offered to pay him more, but Forde had refused.

Clive showed great wisdom and discernment in this choice, and he at once established the happiest relations with Forde. Together they reorganized into one battalion the various European detachments that had come from the other settlements, with much improved discipline as a result. So that when the expedition dropped down the river towards the end of September, Clive had every confidence in its success.

But he had some very faint-hearted gentlemen to deal with among his own colleagues. It had suddenly dawned upon them, as the men were actually embarking, that the colony was being left practically denuded of its garrison. No stores or ammunition and no more than 280 effectives—and those " the very scum of the men ! " What if the French were to come now ?

But Clive had well grasped the essential truth of the situation : the French were not in the least likely to come if they were kept sufficiently occupied on the Coast. He had, in fact, no fears about Lally and felt quite sure that he would destroy himself. Nothing less than an overwhelming superiority of forces could possibly give him the victory, and English reinforcements were known to be on their way.

The outcry served one useful purpose. It gave Clive an excellent excuse for not sending the expedition to Madras as he had promised the gentlemen there that he would. For at Madras its control would have passed out of his hands. On September 6 he had written Stringer Lawrence a letter which shows the undiminished affection he still felt for his old commander :

" My dear friend,

" I have heard with some surprise that M. Lally has set himself down before Madras, not with an intent, I believe, to besiege it in form or carry on approaches ; if he does, I think he must be either mad, or his situation desperate ; at all events, I hope it will be the means of adding fresh laurels to those already gained by my dear friend.

" Colonel Forde has orders to join you with his company of one hundred rank and file from hence. In short, we have put everything to risk here to enable you to engage Lally in the field. I hope, Mr. Bourchier will spare you some men from Bombay. I enclose you a short sketch of our strength in these parts ; and, considering how much depends upon keeping up our influence in Bengal, you will say there never was a smaller force to do it with.

" God give you success, which will be an increase of honour to yourself and of much joy to

" Dear Colonel,
" Your affectionate friend and servant,
" R. C."

On the fifteenth he wrote Pigot telling him he must not expect these forces to proceed to Madras on account of the alarm and strenuous opposition of his council.

His position was exactly the same as that of Madras when it sent him to Bengal. As he pointed out also to Pigot, Madras would derive just as much assistance from the expedition by its present destination, since it would prevent the French from concentrating their whole strength against Madras. At least in this respect the French actually did play into the British hands, by leaving a division behind to guard the Circars when they should either have made Madras their sole objective or continued to hold the Deccan in force. Bussy with part of his army had already joined Lally for the siege.

The expedition sailed on October 9 and reached Vizagapatam eleven days later. On December 6 it justified all of Clive's hopes and confidence in its commander by inflicting a total defeat upon a greatly superior French force under the Marquis de Conflans in the pitched battle of Condore. Following this, with great skill and dash, Forde stormed Masulipatam, completed the conquest of the Circars, and disposed the Nizam to a change of sides. These operations profoundly affected the issue farther south.

IV

Clive needed to have no fear of the news of Plassey not bringing him the desired appointment. Plassey took England by storm. A jubilant father wrote of his joy " beyond all possibility of expression. The whole kingdom is in transports for the glory and success their countryman has gained. Come away and let us rejoice together." How grand it was to know that the name of Clive was actually being used everywhere as a reproach and stimulant to unsuccessful generals—and of unsuccessful generals there were at that moment far too many ! What music it was in a doting father's ears to be told how Lord Ligonier had asked His Majesty whether the young Lord Dunmore might go as a volunteer to the army of the King of Prussia and, upon leave being refused, had asked if he could not join the Duke of Brunswick, only to meet with the King's scornful reply : " Pshaw ! What can he learn there ? If he wants to learn the art of war, let him go to Clive ! "

And then, to cap the triumph, had come Pitt's eulogy in the House of Commons :

" We have lost our glory, honour, and reputation everywhere but in India. There I find Watson, Pocock and Clive.

What astonishing success has been Watson's with only three ships, which had been laid up for some time on land ! He did not stay to career this and condemn that, but at once sailed into the body of the Ganges. And by his side Clive—that man not born for a desk—that heaven-born general ! He, it is true, had never learned the art of war or that skill in doing nothing which only forty years of service can bring ! Yet he was not afraid to attack a numerous army with a handful of men with a magnanimity, a resolution, a determination and an execution that would charm a King of Prussia and with a presence of mind that astonished the Indies."

Pitt's extravagant words expressed the general opinion. Yet it would have been far better for Robert Clive if they had never been spoken. They gave too good an opening for the jeers and spite of his enemies when the true story of Plassey became known : " the heaven-born general " then became the easy butt for their ridicule.

No, there never had been any danger of his services not being appreciated. His father had access to the Duke of Newcastle, the fount of favour and patronage, and some months earlier His Grace had written to the chairman of the Company to say that he was recommending Colonel Clive to the Crown for some special mark of approbation, " as I have the pleasure of knowing Mr. Clive personally and have a great regard for his father." The Duke implied by this that he wanted Clive singled out for special honour, ignoring Watson and everybody else, but this was too much even for the Directors, and Mr. Payne persuaded him to drop the idea.[112]

February had brought the news of Plassey, and in March the Directors appointed him " in consideration of his eminent and repeated services to be sole President and Governor of Fort William in case it should suit his health to remain in India."

The appointment reached Calcutta at the end of November (1758), and it clenched Clive's decision to remain on another year.

v

Clive had been long enough in India to know that storms, both monsoon and political, arose there with little warning. " 'Tis hard to say how long the calm will last," he wrote to the Court

277

at the close of the year in making a renewed plea for reinforcements. Such reinforcements as had arrived—and they were, he said, "more fit for hospital than for duty"—he had sent to Madras.[113] Then, early in the new year, a storm was seen to be brewing in the north-west.

India was full of adventurers seeking their fortunes amidst the distracted state of the country, and the latest of these now was the son of the Mogul himself, who had fled from Delhi and taken refuge with the Nawab of Oude. He had collected around him a following of some 8000 and was planning with the aid of Shuja-ud-daula to take advantage of what he deemed a propitious moment to invade Bengal and divest Mir Jafar of his kingdom, expecting, as Clive had done, to find sufficient help there to effect a revolution. At the beginning of February the threat was becoming real as the Emperor's son, known as the Shah Zada, had entered Bihar and was on his way to Patna. Mir Jafar wrote earnestly imploring Clive to take the field immediately.

Clive at once wrote to assure the Nawab of full English support. Mir Jafar, true to his nature, had thought first of buying off his enemy, but Clive would not hear of it. Ramnarayan's courage also needed buttressing by the promise of English assistance.

On February 25 Clive set forth with 450 Europeans and 2500 sepoys to meet an army which was now said to have grown to 30,000. The Shah Zada sent envoys to him demanding his allegiance. Clive wrote to the Nawab saying that they had made him offers of " provinces upon provinces, with whatever my heart could desire," but he had dismissed them with a warning " never to come near me again, for, if they did, I would take their heads for their pains."

On March 8 he reached Kasimbazar. He made a short halt in the capital, where he had a stern talk with the Nawab about all his shortcomings as a ruler. But, not the least put out by that, Mir Jafar invited him to ride with him on his elephant during the march. Now the news came that Ramnarayan had gone over to the enemy. Hearing that, Clive pushed on with so much speed that his advance-guard covered 400 miles in twenty days.

On April 4 it was within ten miles of Patna, which was on the point of falling. Ramnarayan had successfully kept the enemy at bay all this time by his crafty pretence of submission. But nothing but the arrival of Clive's letter had kept him loyal and nothing but the timely approach of Clive's army saved the city.

" God knows," he told Clive " it is on your account that I am the Nabob's servant."

The news of the English approach did, indeed, end everything. The Shah Zada and his allies quickly raised the siege and departed as fast as they could go. On April 8 Clive entered the city, leaving it at once to pursue the enemy. The 27th found him near the banks of the Karamnasa, which divides Bengal and Bihar from Hindustan. But the host of the Shah Zada had by this time completely dispersed, and the Shah Zada himself was soon left a wanderer with a handful of men and with nowhere to rest his head. He began to bombard Clive with miserable appeals for protection, which Clive had to refuse.

After subjugating the frontier chiefs who had joined in the invasion, Clive returned to Patna. July found him on his way back to Murshidebad and thence to Calcutta.

Meanwhile, the grateful Nawab of Bengal had not been entirely idle. He had apparently thought the moment opportune for an intrigue with the Marathas, no doubt regarding them, in default of the French, as a convenient counterpoise to the English. " I know not which to admire most," wrote Scrafton to Hastings, " his folly or his treachery." Hastings in order to divine the Nawab's purposes had suggested a harmless little stratagem, and Clive took the occasion to read him a lesson on the position of the English in India. " I do not think it right," he said with rare forgetfulness, " that such artifices should be put in practice by us. I would leave all trickery to the Hindoos and Mussulmen, to whom it is natural, being convinced that the reputation we have in this country is owing, among other causes, to the ingenuity [i.e. ingenuousness] and plain dealing for which we are distinguished."

Upon hearing of Clive's latest and most impressive success, Mir Jafar thought better of his intrigue and decided instead to give his too successful benefactor a real proof of his regard. In other words, we may suppose that he had decided that the time had come to pay him off, so that, if Allah willed, he should no longer be in his debt. The famous *jaghire* was the means to that end.

The matter had been under consideration ever since Plassey, when the Mogul Emperor had confirmed his action in placing Mir Jafar on the throne by sending Clive a patent conferring on him the rank of a commander of 6000 horse. The patent was, of course, useless to Clive without the customary accompanying grant of revenues to support the dignity of so great a noble of the Empire, but Clive had heard nothing about this. In January of this year he had written to the Seths to enquire about it. He suggested that as the Seths had procured him the patent they should now likewise procure him the *jaghire*. But their reply when it came only spoke vaguely of a *jaghire* somewhere in Bihar, the province then being invaded. They soon had a better idea, however. The need for propitiating Clive having become sufficiently evident, they suggested to the Nawab that he should be given as his *jaghire* the quit-rent paid by the Company for the district around Calcutta. Mir Jafar promptly adopted the excellent suggestion. He was so heavily in debt to the Company that he was sure he would never receive the rent in cash. Why not, therefore, hand it all over, rent and revenues, to these burdensome but at the same time seemingly indispensable English ?

Was there any thought in the Nawab's weak but crafty mind, one cannot help wondering, that by making Clive wealthy he would the sooner get rid of him, and by getting rid of him he might at last hope to break the English yoke ? The tears that Mir Jafar is said to have wept at Clive's departure, the lament that the soul has now departed from the body, may easily have been borrowed specially for the occasion from one of the crocodiles of the Ganges. We are told on high authority that the grant was " an indubitable proof of reconciliation, and such improvement of feeling between the Nawab and his protectors was fortunate in view of the events which were about to follow— the attempt to replace the English by a Dutch ascendancy in Bengal." [114] It was indeed fortunate, but it was also at the same time not a little curious that the Nawab should actually have been intriguing with the Dutch at the very moment he was making this supposed " indubitable proof of reconciliation ! " To a sceptical mind it seems more likely that both his actions had a direct connection with Clive's announcement that August of his impending departure.

What was really unfortunate for Mir Jafar, and upset what may have been a very cunning scheme, was that the Dutch were in too much of a hurry. If they had waited to put their schemes into effect until Clive had actually taken his departure, their chances of success would have been vastly improved.

In short, the return of Clive from his latest triumph of prestige, achieved because the fame of Arcot and Plassey and the rest of his unbroken series of successes had spread all over India, thus relieving him of the necessity of fighting, was a convenient and highly diplomatic moment for making out the order for the *jaghire*. By it Clive became wealthier to the extent of £30,000 a year.

The grant made Clive a fully endowed noble of the Mogul Empire, as Marlborough after Blenheim became a Prince of the Empire with an estate by which to maintain his dignity. It furthermore made him the feudal superior of his own masters; and that fact, if not the other, distinguishes his case from Marlborough's. He had accepted it, too, without first obtaining their permission, but so confident was he of their approval that he expected them to express pleasure at his good fortune and satisfaction at having him as their over-lord instead of the Nawab. He was to be bitterly disappointed when he found that they were not even inclined to acquiesce.

It was not a present. Certainly not. It was "the fixed emolument of the high office and title bestowed on him by the Mogul Emperor for great service rendered to the Mogul Empire." What greater service could a man render that Empire than setting up a new ruler in one of its greatest provinces and supporting him against all his enemies? It is good to know that the Emperor had the sense to realize that in Clive he possessed a most loyal and obedient servant, and to reward him as he deserved. But Clive must surely have realized that there were bound to be certain persons in England who would not appreciate these facts, nor see matters in quite the same light.

VI

Meanwhile, old Stringer Lawrence—he was now sixty-two—had fought his last fight, and a splendid fight it had been, a fitting close to a great and noble career. Promoted Major-General in February, he had handed in his resignation, broken as he was in health, the following month. But he did not do so until he had brought Madras through its greatest peril by defending it in a siege that lasted from December 14 to February 17.

Pigot and Lawrence, with two officers just arrived from England, Draper and Brereton, formed the committee of defence. For garrison they had 1700 Europeans and topasses and 2200 sepoys. For months they had been anticipating Lally's attack and had laid in plentiful supplies. Owing to the monsoon Pocock was absent from the Coast, and this had given Lally his chance. Though his deficiencies in the sinews of war were as stringent as ever, though his men were mutinous for lack of pay, and his relations with his colleagues, particularly Bussy, extremely bad, he did his utmost to take the place before the return of Pocock and the arrival of Pitt's reinforcements. Engaged thus in a race against time he could not even pause to take the important and strongly garrisoned fort of Chingleput, which lay athwart his line of communications with Pondichéry. Arcot and most of the country—except Trichinopoly—were his, but all his conquests would be vain unless he took Madras, whither the English had wisely withdrawn all their garrisons except the two at Trichinopoly and Chingleput.

For three weeks after entering the black town Lally's guns were silent for lack of ammunition. On January 2 they opened fire and maintained a steady bombardment for six weeks. After a month a breach of sorts appeared in the defences, but in the face of the undiminished fire of the garrison it was declared impracticable and was never attempted. Caillaud, the able commandant at Trichinopoly, and Yusuf Khan, a veteran sepoy officer of Clive's making and the only one in the Madras army to be entrusted with independent commands of any consequence, came up from the south and, using Chingleput as their base, skirmished successfully against the French flank, withstanding every effort to drive them away.

Lally's hopes sank lower and lower as each day passed. On February 16 they disappeared entirely when the ships bearing the expected reinforcements from England hove in sight. That night the French evacuated their trenches, and next morning they were gone. The English had suffered 468 casualties. "The constancy and perseverance of our people," said Colonel Draper, writing from the shattered remains of Madras, "deserved the highest encomiums, as we had no places of security from the enemy's shells when off duty, so that many were killed in their sleep. . . . The brave old Colonel Lawrence, the Governor, Mr. Pigto, Brereton, and myself determined from the commencement of the siege not to listen to any terms of capitulation, for the loss of this place would have drawn after it the entire loss of the country."

After Lawrence retired, not exactly a poor man but certainly not wealthy by the standards of Indian fortunes being set up at that time, Clive showed his gratitude and affection for him by settling an annuity of £500 upon him. "It gives me great pleasure," he wrote, "that I have an opportunity given me of showing my gratitude to the man to whom my reputation and, of course, my fortune is owing." There seems no reason for doubting the genuineness of Clive's act, but it was only with considerable difficulty that Lawrence could be induced to accept the gift. He lived to the age of seventy-seven, dying a few weeks after Clive.

VII

The Dutch incursion put Clive to his final test. But it was not a very severe test; rather, the kind he took more or less in his stride.

The existence of peace between countries in Europe had of late become largely a technicality for their agents in India; in any case it could be technically observed by Clive against the Dutch as easily as it had been by Dupleix against the English and by Saunders against the French: by the device of hoisting the Mogul's colours and going forth to do battle on behalf of him and his vicegerent, the Nawab. That, as Clive saw, was the convenience of the fiction that the Nawab still ruled Bengal, and for the remainder of his life he was to insist upon the wisdom of preserving that fiction. When Warren Hastings swept it away in the interests of better government, he was to incur the fierce opposition of Philip Francis, upon whom the mantle of Lord Clive, somewhat incongruously, descended. Thus it was that, when at the beginning of October seven Dutch ships appeared at the mouth of the Hugli "crammed with soldiers," Clive was at no real loss to decide what to do about them.

Warning of their coming had been received at Calcutta as early as July 22, when the English agent at Batavia advised of the despatch from that port, the headquarters of the Dutch East India Company, of an expedition bound ostensibly for Negapatam. Nor was there anything surprising in this display of Dutch hostility. It was only natural that the Dutch should have hated the results of Plassey, which put them and their Bengal trade at the mercy of the English, in the same position exactly as Dupleix had once threatened to put the English in the Carnatic;

and everything that had happened since had only served to make the Dutch more and more restive. One of the important products of Bihar was that necessary ingredient of gun-powder, saltpetre. All the Companies had competed for it, but Clive had obtained from the Nawab a monopoly of it for the English, and the cutting off of the French from this vital supply played a part in the defeat of Lally.

Thus provoked, the Dutch began to intrigue against the English, finding in Mir Jafar a ready listener to their plans ; but the one thing they overlooked was that the wily Mir Jafar was not in the least likely to help them until they had actually proved their ability to overthrow the English. And it so happened that when their ships arrived he was in Calcutta visiting his friend Clive, which made it distressingly difficult for him to render any assistance.

The Dutch made a second big mistake when they allowed their resentment at the way in which the English insisted on searching their boats and obstructing the passage of their troops to lead them into giving Clive a convenient excuse for opening hostilities. They seized a number of small English craft, made prisoners of their crews and burnt the English Company's houses at Fulta.

Clive was daily expecting word from home of the declaration of war on Holland, and he at once utilized the Dutch action to relieve his scruples. Having received ample warning of the Dutch intentions, he had already made his preparations. Forde was back from the Circars to command the garrison. The forts were manned and heavily reinforced with cannon. The troops were under arms. The Dutch were still trying to disguise their intentions, but Clive refused to be daunted. He accepted the responsibility. As the Dutch ships were slowly ascending the river, Clive ordered the three armed East Indiamen that were at that time in port at the mouth of the river to follow them up, pass them, and interpose between them and Fort William.

On November 21 the Dutch ships cast anchor within cannon-shot of the English batteries below Calcutta. That night they landed their troops on the opposite shore, to the number of 700 Europeans and 800 Malays, and then dropped down the river a short distance.

The news decided Clive to attack them immediately both by land and by water. The Commodore of the three Company's ships was ordered to demand immediate restitution of the English vessels seized and, if it was refused, to attack forthwith. Restitution was refused. On the 24th the English ships attacked, and a stern fight of two hours ended in the complete defeat of the Dutch and the surrender of every one of their ships.

It was now Colonel Forde's turn. As soon as he heard of the Dutch landing he sent to Clive for orders. His note reached Clive when he was at cards. Clive, according to the well-known story, took a pencil and wrote on a bit of Forde's letter : " Dear Forde, fight 'em immediately ; I will send an order of council to-morrow." Accordingly, Forde crossed the river to interpose between the advancing Dutch and their settlement at Chinsura. On his way through the ruins of Chandernagore he found the Chinsura garrison posted there. He made short work of it and was ready to meet the new arrivals on the morrow.

The engagement was, as Clive states, " short, bloody, and decisive." It was all over within half an hour. Put to total rout, there was nothing the Dutch could do now but make a complete submission. They disavowed all their proceedings, acknowledged themselves to be the aggressors, and agreed to pay an indemnity. When the agreement was ratified on December 5 Clive's work was practically done, and there was nothing to hinder him from putting into effect his resolve to go home.

This affair was the occasion for Clive's remark that " a public man may occasionally be called upon to act with a halter round his neck." He had, it is true, risked something by taking the responsibility of beginning hostilities against a nation with whom his country was still at peace, but it was a well-justified risk, for there was never any real doubt that his country would support him.

He had thought at the time, too, that he was risking his own private fortune, as he had recently remitted to Europe £180,000 by bills on the Dutch Company. Actually, however, his agents had already obtained the money, though they had had " the devil of a time " getting it on account of the near state of war. William Smith King wrote him on July 13 to say that his three Dutch assignations for £183,000 " were about two months ago consented to be paid by that Company after our undergoing for more than a year the utmost anxiety and trouble from their most scandalous and rascally behaviour, and from our fears that they would not pay them at all, unless compelled thereto by a suit at law in their own country or by the prevalence of your ministers here." The " knavish hands " found a further pretext for withholding £11,000, six per cent. of the money, as commission.[115]

285

Chapter Nineteen

AN IMMOVABLE BODY : LAWRENCE SULIVAN

" My experience has taught me that men who correspond over a space of 10,000 miles should watch their pens ; for ink comes to burn like caustic when it crosses the sea "   LORD DALHOUSIE

I

IN THE ANNUAL ELECTION of Directors during the spring of 1758 Lawrence Sulivan was elected Chairman of the East India Company.   The fact deserves more attention than has been paid to it. In the life of Robert Clive as in the political history of the Company during the next fifteen years the emergence of Sulivan in control of the Company was of vast importance.   The destinies of all three became inextricably interlocked.   To Clive personally it portended nothing but calamity.

Of few men of his power and importance is there less known than of Lawrence Sulivan.   He does not even appear in the *Dictionary of National Biography*, though he was during the most critical years in its history the uncrowned king of the East India Company.   Nothing is known of the personal character of this autocrat of Leadenhall Street except what can be inferred from his public conduct, and that is very little.   Historical research has passed him by—or, perhaps, seeking, has found nothing, not even a portrait or a description of him.   Yet he has by no means escaped the judgment of history.   On what would seem to be insufficient evidence he has been contemptuously dismissed as " a man without an idea in advance of the low level of his time." [116]

Surely a sweeping judgment of a man of whom so little is known, and of that little not all of it necessarily discreditable to him !   That such a man as Warren Hastings held a " great opinion " of his integrity is thought only to reflect on Hastings's judgment of men (which certainly was by no means infallible), and to add nothing at all to Sulivan's stature.

Upon close examination of his career, however, it appears that

286

Sulivan, while obviously a politician of the wire-pulling stamp—
what else he may have been does not appear—was guilty of only
one major offence, but that one great enough to cause his instant
condemnation in the court of history *nem. con.* He was Clive's
bitterest enemy.

A collision between them was inevitable from the beginning of
their connection. The men being what they were, strikingly
similar in their temperaments and dispositions, nothing could
have averted it. They both rose to the top simultaneously,
Sulivan as Chairman, Clive as Governor (and would-be
Governor-General), and both wanted to be masters in the same
concern. When to that fact is added another, that they were
upon the same path but headed in opposite directions of policy,
it will readily be seen that a collision *was* inevitable. It was to be
a clear case of an irresistible force meeting an immovable body.

Only two facts are known about Sulivan before his emergence
as Chairman, but both are suggestive. First, he was an Irishman.
Originally his name had had the prefix " O'." The second is that
he was a Bombayer. During the course of twenty years' service
as a covenanted servant at Bombay, he had risen through the
regular grades to be member of council. He had then retired
and immediately upon his return home had been elected a member of the Court of Directors. Now, at the age of forty-three,
he was its chairman.[1]

The probable effect of those two backgrounds, Ireland and
Bombay, upon his relations with Clive is not difficult to imagine.
Of the first it need only be said that the racial antipathies of the
British races is a factor not always taken sufficiently into account
in discussing personal enmities of this sort.[2] Bombay's likely
influence is much more clear. It was at that time " the Cinderella
of the English settlements, the unhealthiest, the poorest, and the
most despised." Compared to it Madras was a health resort, and
even dismal Calcutta could not show such ghastly morbid records
as Bombay annually produced. The Bombayers were subject to
consumptions, fluxes, fevers, cholera, scurvy, berbers (a kind of
paralysis), small-pox, gout, the stone, prickly heat, tetters or
worms, and other less grievous ailments. It was commonly said

[1] For those who are interested in such matters it may be added that he was
born on April 24, 1713, and had married in 1739 Elizabeth, the daughter of Richard
Owen, a free merchant and master of the ship *Bombay Merchant*. It is to be hoped
the rest of his personal history will soon come to light.[117]

[2] Coote was an Irishman too !

that two monsoons were the life of a man. Nor had its unfortunates the same opportunities for quickly acquired wealth.
Bombay was both deadly and unprofitable. It is only surprising
that the proposals that were from time to time made for its
abandonment as a trading station should not have been adopted
by unanimous vote. One's first guess is, therefore, that those
who were sent to Bombay were those with the least influence,
and it is not unreasonable to suppose that the Irishman Lawrence
O'Sulivan was among them.

Each of the three presidencies developed its own peculiar
spirit, Bombay's being quite different from that of Calcutta or
Madras. This difference became most pronounced after the
latter two settlements had embarked upon their careers of political
adventure. For life in Bombay was extremely dull and uneventful. There had been on their coast no Dupleix to stir them out of
their sluggish mercantile routine. They counted their money in
single mohurs, not in lakhs. And they remained dominated by
the spirit of pure commerce long after that spirit had been at
Calcutta and Madras contaminated, and very much diluted, by
other considerations.[118]

Sulivan was a product of this atmosphere, and he imported it
into the management of the Company's affairs ; though, in
truth, it was already there. The spirit of Bombay was also the
spirit of the Company before the phenomenon that was Dupleix
shook it out of its concentration upon its well-ordered accounts
and strict attention to business, and before the even more startling
and upsetting phenomenon that was Clive destroyed for ever the
existence of the Company as a purely commercial institution.
For as long as it could the Company tried to preserve that fiction,
and Sulivan, during the years immediately following Plassey,
was the leading exponent of that idea. Naturally, as a good man
of business should, he saw certain advantages to be gained from
the conquest of Bengal, among them being a monopoly of the
trade, particularly in saltpetre, so essential for the conduct of
war. He certainly, too wanted to see the French expelled
because of the threat they represented to that trade. But anything more—anything in the way of territorial acquisition or
political responsibility—no ! They were dangerous and a sure
source of unjustifiable expense to the Company.

This, then, is the man who became the immediate superior of
the victor of Plassey when the full flush of that staggering victory

was upon him and he was already weaving great designs of how it could be turned to still better account !

Strangely enough, the relations of the two men at first could scarcely have been more cordial. Among the many letters of congratulation that Clive received after Plassey, Sulivan's was one of the warmest. And Clive for his part was delighted to hear of Sulivan's election, as he believed firmly in the advantage of having someone at the Company's helm who had had local experience and possessed some knowledge of India. In December 1758 he wrote to his father and agents in England directing them and all his friends to use their influence in support of Sulivan, even to the extent, if necessary, of employing his funds for the purchase of India stock to increase their voting power. At the same time he communicated his views to his future foe in one of his rare, long, confiding letters.

If Clive had deliberately sought a breach with Sulivan he could not have written a letter better calculated to cause one ! What made it even more ironical still was the fact that the primary object of his writing at all was to express his " hearty and sincere congratulations on an event long most impatiently wish'd for by me," Mr. Sulivan's election. It is not at all difficult, however, to imagine Mr. Sulivan's emotions when he read such passages as these :

"The opportunities afforded me by the late Revolution have given me a just knowledge of the subject I am writing upon. Experience, not conjecture, or the report of others, has made me well acquainted with the genius of the people, and nature of the country, and I can assert with some degree of confidence, that this rich & flourishing kingdom may be totally subdued by so small a force as two thousand Europeans, and the possession thereof maintained & confirm'd by the Great Mogul upon paying the sum of 50 lakhs per annum paid by former subahs.

"The Moors, as well as Gentoos, are indolent, luxurious, ignorant, and cowardly, beyond all conception ; the country itself is full of great and navigable rivers, is very woody, enclosed by mountains with narrow passes ; in short everything conspires to render infantry formidable and cavalry (in which the chief strength of Indostan consists) a mere bugbear. The soldiers, if they deserve that name, have not the least

T

attachment to their prince, he only can expect service from them who pays them best, but it is a matter of great indifference to them whom they serve ; and I am fully persuaded that after the battle of Plassey I could have appropriated the whole country to the Company and preserved it afterwards with as much ease as Meer Jaffeir the present Subah now does, through the terror of the English arms and their influence. . . .

" I am persuaded you will believe I do not want to aggrandize the Company at the expence of all equity and justice ; long may the present Subah enjoy the advantages gained him by our arms, if he abides strictly by his treaties. But you, Sir, who have resided so long in India, are well acquainted with the nature and dispositions of these Mussulmen, gratitude they have none, bare men of very narrow conceptions, and have adopted a system of politicks more peculiar to this country than any other, viz. to attempt everything by treachery rather than force. Under these circumstances may not so weak a prince as Meer Jaffeir be easily destroyed, or influenced by others to attempt to destroying us. What is it then can enable us to secure our present acquisitions or improve upon them but such a force as leaves nothing to the power of treachery or ingratitude ? "

Clive, of course, did not know his man ! But that does not excuse the imprudence of expressing such views as these without the slightest idea of whether they would meet with approval. The truth would seem to be that Clive was by now so obsessed with his own power and importance, and so carried away by the greatness of his achievement, and his quick perception of all the possible fruits of it, that it is much to be doubted whether he even stopped to think that he might possibly encounter opposition. Was he not dangling before the nose of the Chairman the richest prize that had ever been offered to a company of merchants ? It probably did not occur to him that the Company might not want it, would, indeed, be aghast at the prospect of getting it. Men of enlarged views like Clive never can understand the reluctance of other, lesser, men to fall into step with them. Their reluctance first exasperates, then infuriates them.

Of the views themselves little need be said. They reveal the full-fledged Imperialist. They are almost Napoleonic in their vision of easy conquest, and more than Napoleonic in their obliviousness to the problems of administering and retaining an empire when conquered ; that boast of an acquaintance with " the genius of the people " being nothing less than fantastic to those who really know the people. They reveal that Clive was at heart a militarist who could conceive of no other way of governing an Indian empire but by the power of the sword, and who believed that that power was all-sufficient in itself. Nobody at that time professed the slightest regard—or if they professed it they seldom acted upon it—for the welfare or the wishes of the people themselves, so that aspect of the matter may be passed over in silence. It would be unfair to judge Clive according to enlightened humanity !

As fate would have it—and fate loves to be ironical—this letter from Clive, so naïvely confident, so free from any doubt of its reception, crossed a letter from the Court of Directors that obviously expressed the views of Mr. Sulivan. One could search the records of government and not find a greater contrast in point of view and content than there is between these two letters. Warning of what was coming was contained in an earlier letter from the Court (dated November 1, 1758), also on its way, in which complaint was made of the inattention of their Bengal servants to business :

> " From the lights at present before us there appear such flagrant instances of weak management, such gross neglects of our interest, that were the facts properly established, would oblige us to animadvert upon your conduct in the severest terms ; however, we are willing to hope that many things may be cleared up to our satisfaction and your credit." [119]

Unfortunately, subsequent advices from Calcutta did not clear these matters up ; they only made them appear worse. So Mr. Sulivan let fly with both barrels. It was, he and his brother Directors said, most extravagant and unreasonable of their servants to expend 45,000 rupees to carry a few Frenchmen (the Chandernagore officials) from Bengal to Pondichéry ; the contract for their transport was ill-arranged. To incur the heavy charge of demurrage by allowing ships of the Company to lie by the walls—even though the reason given was that they might be needed in case of attack—was showing disregard for the interests of the Company. Why were not any efforts made to suppress the smuggling about which Mr. Ralph Leycester had given information ? " If, when the consultations come it shall appear nothing further has been done tending to such discovery, we shall have reason highly to resent your conduct. And here it is proper to acquaint you that we shall expect in future the strictest regard to all our former orders for the discovery of illicit trade." And why was Omichand given so much more favourable terms for the supply of saltpetre than Mr. Pearkes ? " Your giving such a great price to Omichand and at the same time (as we are informed) tricking Mr. Pearkes in his purchases seems to us so very extraordinary and we are afraid a sinister affair very materially affecting your characters as well as the Company's interest, that we do positively direct you do fully explain the whole to us by the first opportunity." And why is the investment so poor ? If the Portuguese can send home rich cargoes from Calcutta, why not their own servants ? Extreme negligence had been shown in the affair of " the produce of the plunder and booty taken from the late Nabob " : " in fine, we expect a full, satisfactory, and explicit account of all your transactions on this head." Why, also, this extensive scheme of fortifying Kasimbazar ? What object would it serve ? Security for the subordinate factories could only be found in the influence and power of Calcutta : " Therefore, you are not to deviate from the rules laid down to you last season respecting the carrying on our affairs in Cassimbazar and other Subordinates, without the least parade of soldiers, fortifications, or even the least appearance of military strength." Why were not the inhabitants of Calcutta required to contribute part of the heavy expense involved in refortifying Calcutta, inasmuch as it would benefit them too ? Why, above all, were they distressing the Company by drawing so many short-term bills upon it ?

And so it went, a whole catalogue of complaints : " In short, in many other instances you seem to have acted like men divested of your understanding." Until it reached a magisterial conclusion worthy of the " Autocrat of India House " :

" Many of you are persons of approved characters and abilities and as such stood high in our esteem. We are therefore willing to attribute part of the chain of irregularities, omissions, and deviations from our interest pointed out in the course of this letter, to the amazing and sudden transition from uncommon distress and misery to an affluent situation. We also make allowance for conducting a Colony emerging out of confusion into some regularity and order, which must engage your attention. In fine, our inclinations strongly lead us to wish to find you faithful as well as able servants, and that the very gentle admonitions and animadversions in this letter, considering all circumstances, may excite you to a just and studious discharge of your duty. If, contrary to our expectations, your conduct should not be entirely reformed, we must then be under the indispensable necessity of doing ourselves justice." [120]

Perhaps nature had really intended Mr. Sulivan to be a school-master. At least, Clive knew when he got this letter that he had been properly and publicly spanked ! He also knew that a worse spanking was in store for him if he did not at once mend his ways. There had been extenuating circumstances, yes—trouble with the late Nabob, causing " confusion "—but now the class must get back to work ! " Business as usual " must be their only watchword.

It is a matter for speculation which letter caused its recipient the greater amount of annoyance, but it is a matter of record the precise amount Sulivan's caused Clive. In the General Letter to the Court of December 28, 1759, signed by himself and four members of Council, he gave full vent to his anger :

" Permit us to say that the diction of your letter is most unworthy of yourselves and us in whatever relation considered, either as masters to servants, or gentlemen to gentlemen. . . . Groundless informations have, without further scrutiny, borne with you the stamp of truth, though proceeding from those who had therein obviously their own purpose to serve, no matter at whose expense." They appear to have been " the only source of general reflections thrown out at random against your faithful servants of this Presidency—faithful to little purpose, if the breath of scandal, joined to private pique or private and personal attachments, have power to blow away in one hour the merits of many years' services, and deprive them of that rank and those benefits which are justly a spur to their integrity and applications. . . .

" The little attention shown to these considerations in the indiscriminate favours heaped on some individuals, and undeserved censures on others, will, we apprehend, lessen that spirit of zeal so very essential to the well-being of your affairs, and consquently, in the end, if continued, prove the destruction of them. Private views may, it is much to be feared, take the lead here, from examples at home, and no gentlemen hold your service longer, nor exert themselves further in it, than their own exigencies require. This being the real state of your service, it becomes strictly our duty to represent it in the strongest light."

The language that the Court had used to its Council was the kind that it had frequently used in the past ; it had used it, for instance, towards Governor Floyer of Madras ; it was the language of masters speaking to their servants. The language that the Bengal Council had now used to the Court, on the other hand, was of a kind that had never been used before ; it was the language of a servant who was preparing to dispute the mastery of the Company with its masters. It could not fail to have the gravest consequences.

II

Other causes of quarrel were scarcely necessary, but it happened that there were at least two others equally serious. Two days after Clive had penned that first provocative letter to Sulivan, expounding his expansive views, he had written in similarly unguarded manner to Pitt setting forth the same design in much the same words, but with one very important difference. Writing as he was now to the chief minister of State, he suggested that it should not be the Company that should acquire the sovereignty of " these rich kingdoms," Bengal, Bihar, and Orissa, but rather the English nation. " So large a sovereignty may possibly be an object too extensive for a mercantile Company ; and it is to be feared they are not of themselves able, without the Nation's assistance, to maintain so wide a dominion ; I have therefore presumed, Sir, to represent this matter to you, and submit it to your consideration, whether the execution of a design, that may hereafter be still carried to greater lengths, be worthy of the Government's taking it in hand." And he went on to dangle before the ministerial nose the same rich prize of " an income yearly of upwards of two millions sterling, with the possession of three provinces abounding in the most valuable productions of nature and art . . . an acquisition which under the management of so able and disinterested a minister " (" as yourself " implied) " would prove a source of immense wealth to the kingdom, and might in time be appropriated in part as a fund towards diminishing the heavy load of debt under which we at present labour," with other monopolistic trade advantages over European competitors thrown in for good measure.

Horace Walpole tells a story which illustrates how tempting was the bait that Clive dangled before the nose of the war minister wrestling with problems of finance. According to Walpole, Richard Clive used to carry proposals from his son to the minister, and on one occasion made an offer that if Pitt would send Clive some ships and men his son in return would send back enough treasure to pay the national debt (which then stood at nearly £100,000,000). " ' That is asking too much,' said Pitt ; ' fifty millions would suffice.' ' Lord, sir,' replied the old man, ' consider—if your administration lasts, the national debt will soon be 200 million.' "

It was not his father, however, who was the bearer of this indiscreet letter to Pitt. It was John Walsh, his secretary, who carried it home with him from India together with the one for Mr. Sulivan. Did Clive realize that by making the same proposal to Crown and Company he was certainly making trouble for himself and for everybody concerned ?

It has been customary to bestow great praise on this letter to Pitt. It has been said that " the mind which at that time could travel to such a far-reaching change was worthy of a great statesman." [121] It is difficult, however, to see why a scheme which contemplated little more than putting two million pounds' worth of the wealth of India annually into the national treasury instead of into the Company's should be so highly regarded. It was undoubtedly a clever manœuvre on Clive's part, designed to place him prominently on the national political map. But it seems ridiculous to hail it as anticipating the great transfer of sovereignty that came a hundred years later—a transfer, happily, that was not to be based upon financial considerations.

Another point has not always been given the importance it deserves. Clive was not a statesman free to express his mind as he pleased ; he was a covenanted servant of the East India Company, and as such he was not free to make presents of its future property, or what it certainly would think was its property, to anybody, not even to the Crown of England. The letter he wrote to Pitt was a most improper letter, and, because of the fact that they had jealously to guard their rights from encroachment by the Crown, a virtual betrayal of his employers. It was, besides, most imprudent. He might have known that a copy of it would reach Sulivan. Sulivan may not have had, " like Clive, the genius of a great administrator," and he may have been " incapable of framing an opinion on the wise policy suggested by Clive," but few men are capable of so much disinterestedness as to be willing to surrender an income of £2,000,000 for no other reason than the alleged incapacity of himself and his constituents to administer it—especially when the allegation of incapacity comes from one of those constituents' own covenanted servants !

In this connection it is worth noting now that the far-sighted Pitt, so far from welcoming the suggestion and endorsing its wisdom, pointed out at once to Walsh the major objection that the acquisition of so much wealth by the Crown would only increase its patronage and endanger the national liberties. There was, in fact, fully as much objection at that time to the Crown receiving the prize as the Company, and it would have been far better if there had been no talk of giving it to either. Yet if Clive had waited until he had retired from the service, he would at least have been within his rights to have made the suggestion.

The third cause of quarrel concerned Eyre Coote. The same despatch from the Court of March 23, 1759, that had so aroused Clive's ire on other grounds had also contained the exceedingly unwelcome annulment of Colonel Forde's appointment to the Bengal command and the announcement that Coote, now promoted to Colonel, had been given the command-in-chief of all the Company's forces in India, in place of Stringer Lawrence who was retiring. Coote being a King's officer and Forde now a Company's, Clive saw in Forde's supersession discrimination against the Company's officers. In a sense, of course, it was discrimination—Coote had been junior to Forde in Adlercron's regiment—but the Court based the appointment upon " the great advantages and benefit that must arise to us by connecting the King's and our own forces under one commander." With the irreconcilable jealousies existing between the two services and with the King's arrogating to itself the rights of the superior, it is obvious that, if there was to be unified command, it could only take place under a King's officer.[1] But Clive felt that the Company had "surrendered" to the intolerable pretensions of the Royal service, which refused to recognize that the commissions of the Company gave any valid rank ; he remembered also the Adlercron episode. His own solution to the problem was that the Governors of the three Presidencies should each be vested with the rank of Major-General and given the supreme command within his own sphere. Undoubtedly, however, his chief objection to the Company's appointment was his personal dislike for Coote and his special liking for Forde.

Of the intensity of his dislike for Coote he now gave plentiful evidence. In condoling with Forde he expressed his contempt of "those leaden-headed Directors" and "that fellow Coote," adding, "however we have taken care he shall not come to Bengal" :

> "I can easily conceive such rank and honour bestowed (I think I may say without flattery) to one so much your inferior in every respect must give you much concern. I assure you it has affected me greatly and is one of my principal motives for wanting to push home with the utmost expedition on the *Royal George*. I flatter myself the request I have to make will not be denied me, which is that you will stay in Bengal all next year, provided Coote remains on the Coast. If within that time I do not get you a Colonel or a Lieut.-Colonel's commission and an appointment of Commander-in-Chief of all the forces in India I will from that instant decline all further transactions with Directors and East India affairs." [122]

To Henry Vansittart, member of Council at Madras and soon to be his chosen successor in the government of Bengal, he wrote (August 20) :

> "The news from the Coast this year has been very important and interesting. The defence of Madras will do much honour to our arms in India, and greatly heighten our reputation as soldiers in these parts. I would gladly have given some of my

---

[1] The same consideration compelled the appointment of Foch to the Supreme Command of the Allies in 1918.

riches to have shared some of your reputation.[1]   I know it has been a conceived opinion among the old soldiers in England that our exploits in India have been much of the same nature as those of Fernando de Cortes, but your foiling such a man as Mons. Lally and two of the oldest regiments of France will induce another way of thinking and add a fresh lustre to all our former victories.   Neither do I think Colonel Forde's successes fall short of those of Madras.   His victory over the Marquis de Conflans was but one of the many we have gained over our enemies in the like circumstances, but his taking by storm such a place as Metchlepetam with a garrison superior to the force which attacked it, is I think one of those extraordinary actions which we seldom hear of in these modern times and must gain him great honour, when it comes to be known at home."

He criticized Madras for not sending Forde money and sea transport and for trying to get Forde to send his army to Madras instead of letting him divert French forces from there, as he so successfully did.   "For I can never be persuaded that the addition of 200 infantry would either have lost or gained us a battle over Mr. Lally, but the withdrawing them from Deccan would certainly have rendered fruitless all that has been done."

All of this shows Clive favourably in the light of military expert and strategist.   But then came this passage, which makes extraordinary reading in the light of what was so soon to happen :

"I am preparing for you many papers and accounts which may give you some insight into the affairs of this province and of our great consequence at this juncture in Indostan.   As I have fixed upon you for this government it is necessary you should know how glorious a government it may prove to yourself and the Company.   I hope to God my interest may not fail me in England.   I tremble when I think of the fatal consequences of such a mercenary man as Coote commanding here.   If you have any regard for your future government for God's sake keep him on the Coast.   There he can only get a little drubbing, but here he may ruin the Company's affairs for ever." [123]

---

[1] Compare this with what he wrote Forde (p. 267).

Then this to Governor Pigot :

" If you expect any assistance or supplies from hence or think Bengal of any importance to the Company, for God's sake keep Coote with you, take but the man and you shall have the 1000 men into the bargain."

Why did Clive object so vehemently, so frenziedly to Coote ? In one breath he says it was because he was " mercenary " and in the next because he was a bad soldier who was bound to be beaten. Whatever the reason, it is quite obvious that he believed the fate of India depended upon keeping Coote away from Bengal.

III

No figure of Anglo-Indian history aroused more conflict of judgment among his contemporaries than Eyre Coote. He was hated and loved with equal ardour. Judged by the comments of men like Warren Hastings and Josias Du Pré, governor of Madras, he was the bane of their existence as members of council, and they, like Clive, could not wish him far enough away. They could not abide his petulance and quarrelsomeness, his conceit and obstinacy. He was a man who had to have his own way or he made the lives of everyone around him miserable, particularly those of civilian colleagues who made claims to a voice in military matters. But when he could have his own way, when he was commander-in-chief in the field, then he was an entirely different man, then he was without a peer, " the nearest imaginable approach to perfection as a soldier."

The tribute just quoted was that of a soldier to a soldier. For it was soldiers who loved Coote and only civilian colleagues, compelled to deal with him around the council board, who expressed such hearty dislike of him. The eulogist is Colonel Mark Wilks, who wore the mantle of Orme as military historian of India. Wilks served under Coote in his later campaigns and was, therefore, better qualified to estimate Coote's abilities than Orme was to estimate Clive's.

" Nature," he wrote, " had given to Colonel Coote all that nature can confer in the formation of a soldier ; and the regular study of every branch of his profession, and experience in most of them, had formed an accomplished officer. A bodily frame of unusual vigour and activity, and mental energy always awake, were restrained from excessive action by a patience and temper which never allowed the spirit of enterprise to outmarch the dictates of prudence. Daring valour and cool reflection strove for the mastery in the composition of this great man. The conception and execution of his designs equally commanded the confidence of his officers ; and a master at once of human nature and of the science of war, his rigid discipline was tempered with an unaffected kindness and consideration for the wants and even the prejudices of the European soldiers and rendered him the idol of the native."

The tribute was fair and just. Lawrence, Clive, Forde, and Coote were four able soldiers, but the greatest of the four, judged purely as a soldier, was Coote. He fought more and harder battles than any of the other three, and won them all. Both a sound strategist and a brilliant tactician, he had the additional gift of inspiring his men with complete confidence in him and in themselves. No matter how great the odds they faced and no matter what the situation, he remained serene, resolute, fearless. He won the hearts of his men most especially by his generous appreciation of their conduct and gallantry and by never failing to refer to them in his despatches in a way that few generals have done. He was accused of being "mercenary"—though the charge looks not a little strange coming from Clive—and undoubtedly he was insistent about being given large allowances, but he was a soldier first and last, his heart was in his work and with his men, and he thoroughly earned by his sterling services the handsome allowances that he received.

After the battle of Wandewash he issued a general order stating that, as it seemed unlikely that the army would derive any pecuniary advantage from its great successes and as he felt that the substantial gain he had met with since his arrival in India was owing to the gallant behaviour of the officers and men he had the honour to command, he proposed to hand over for equal division throughout the army all the money presents which, according to the custom of the country, had been paid or promised to him as commander, this being "the only acknowledgment he could at present make the army for the services they had done their country." [124] Was it any wonder that Coote was the idol of his men ? By the sepoys, we are told, he was

revered as more than human.   And the concrete historical result
of Coote's appointment as commander-in-chief in India was that
he first completed the work of Lawrence, Clive, and Forde by
totally expelling the French in a series of brilliant strokes, and
then, at a later date, saved the nascent empire from the greatest
military menace that had threatened it since the days of Dupleix—
the devouring onslaught of Haidar Ali, the savage warrior-king
of Mysore.

Coote was also magnanimous, as he showed by his conduct
before the siege of Pondichéry, when superseded, according to
stupid orders from home, by Major Monson, his second in
command.   Monson, by the orders, was not to exercise the
command until Coote had left for Bengal.   "But the spirit of
Coote would not permit him to make any advantage of this
indulgence ; and had he been less a man of sense and temper, had
he been more governed by that boyish sensibility to injury
which among vulgar people passes for honour, this imprudent
step of the Company would have been attended with the most
serious consequences."   Coote was to take his regiment with him,
but to have done so would have meant no siege, so he "consented
that his regiment should remain, to encircle the brows of another
with laurels which belonged to his own."   Monson, happily,
was wounded, thus compelling the command to return to
Coote in time for him to complete his unbroken succession of
victories.[125]

This, then, was the man that Clive stigmatized as mercenary,
declared a menace to the security of Bengal, and hated with such
apparently fanatical hatred that he was ready to go to any lengths
to obtain his removal.

If Clive had been a civilian, his feeling for Coote would have
been thoroughly understandable.   But as a soldier himself, as a
sympathiser of Lawrence in his tussles with Thomas Saunders,
as one who has been generously praised by his biographers for his
rare ability to discern talent,[1] his feeling is incomprehensible
unless we search further for an explanation of it.   And the nature
of that possible explanation has already been suggested.   It dates
back to Plassey.

---

[1] Sir George Forrest glosses the matter over by saying : " Clive had then had no
opportunity of discovering that Eyre Coote was a consummate master of the art of
war " ; but the truth, of course, is that he had had *every* opportunity.   If *he* had not
had the opportunity, who had ?   He had discerned Forde's talent when Forde had
done practically nothing to reveal it.[126]

Coote left Bengal for home at the close of 1757. He was the first of the heroes of Plassey to appear in England, he was also the senior King's officer during the campaign, and it was natural, therefore, that he should have been received with enthusiasm. He must have been pressed to tell and retell the story of the great victory, and obviously his account must have differed materially from that of Clive. Probably not until now had the people at home heard anything about the council-of-war. We are told that the belief arose that it was Eyre Coote and not Clive to whom the credit must be given for the victory and that the belief remained current until it was " shattered " by Eyre Coote's own evidence before the Committee of the House of Commons.[1] [127] There is no need, however, to assume that Coote attempted deliberately to disparage Clive or steal his laurels ; a simple statement of the actual facts would have been quite enough to modify people's ideas of the battle, and that modification, reflecting back on Clive, would be quite enough to account for his fierce hatred of Coote.

Coote's return to England in 1758 had been as helpful to his ambitions as Clive's own similar return in 1754. He had considerable charm of manner, in which he had a great advantage over Clive, and he knew how to make himself liked. Pitt, who had a sure eye for good men, spotted him at once. Coote also attached himself closely to Lawrence Sulivan. So when a regiment was raised for service in India, he was given its command. In January 1759 he was gazetted Colonel of the 84th and at the same time appointed by the Court of Directors to the Bengal command, with the option of remaining in Madras if he considered it necessary. On October 27 Coote landed at Madras and took charge of the operations against Lally. Three months were all that he needed to justify fully the confidence of Pitt and Sulivan in him. The battle of Wandewash, which ended with the complete defeat of the French, was fought on January 22, 1760.

As the *Royal George*, bearing Colonel and Mrs. Clive on their homeward voyage, was coming out of the river Hugli a month later, " it was met with an express, despatched from the Coast of Coromandel, with advice that Colonel Coote, having attacked the French in their intrenchments, the latter were totally defeated

---

[1] Actually, as we have seen, Coote's evidence " shattered " nothing except any illusions still remaining about Clive's part in that victory.

with the loss of their cannon and baggage, general Lally wounded, and M. de Bussy and Col. Murphy taken prisoners." Nor did Coote stop there : he followed it up by laying siege to and taking Pondichéry, thus completing the destruction of French power in India.

One wonders what were Clive's thoughts as he read this despatch. The man who could "only get a little drubbing there" had triumphed, and he—was he going home to more success, to receive the honours that he felt he had earned, or had the tide of fortune begun to turn at last against him ?

Chapter Twenty

THE LEGACY OF CONQUEST

"Conquests are easily made in this country, but not easily turned into money"
                                                     HENRY VANSITTART

I

CLIVE HAD BEEN EXCEEDINGLY LUCKY in the times of his comings and goings. He arrived in England in 1754 just when the nation was wanting a popular hero. He arrived back in India just in time to lead the Bengal expedition. And now he was departing again just in time to escape the unpleasant consequences of his own revolution.

He had feared a reversal of fortune before he could get away. It had not come. The tide of his success had swept on and on. Indeed, it seemed as though all the national enemies were in league for the greater glory of Robert Clive, presenting him with the very opportunities he needed, and at precisely the right moment. In 1759 he needed another resounding victory to supply him with a good curtain for his exit from the Indian scene. The Dutch had kindly provided it, timing it exactly right and making it sufficiently exciting without being too dangerous ; in other words, perfect for the purpose of showing off Clive's extraordinary histrionic abilities to best advantage. It had not given him agonizing days of worry and anxiety, nor presented him with complex problems to solve. He had won undying fame simply by breaking off a game of cards for two minutes and scribbling "Dear Forde, fight 'em immediately." For him nothing could have been easier. It was a made-to-order situation. The victory bore the authentic stamp of his name ; it had just enough of the glamour of Arcot and Plassey to serve its purpose for publicity. What if his enemies should say scornfully that it was just another of his easy victories—like Gheria and Plassey ? No one would listen to them ; their mouths were incessantly full of sour grapes.

Now there was no more glory to be won in India. None at

all. And none for some years to come. Upon the day that Pondichéry surrendered all glory departed from the Indian scene.

Orme discovered this when he was writing his history. He went happily forward until he reached this point : "Colonel Coote embarked on the 13th of March, leaving his regiment to follow ; and with him our narrative returns to the affairs of Bengal." It did not return. It stopped right there. And why it stopped is clear. Orme "had lived amongst heroes in an Age of Iron, and had told their story in language which did honour both to himself and them ; it was not fitting that he should describe how lesser men thought that in the misery of the country they had found an Age of Gold." [128]

They may have been lesser men, these successors to Saunders, Pigot, Lawrence, Clive, Forde, and Coote. One assumes that they were. Yet it is so much easier to win reputation when one is fighting a successful war against the national enemy, with no thoughts to trouble one but the making of one's military plans and the circumvention of the enemy's, than afterwards when facing the consequences of victory. Peace, we are told, has its victories no less renowned than war—but the historians take a long time to discover them. All too often peace is where the glory ends and the headaches begin. It is much easier to be a hero in face of foreign menace than domestic trouble. Dictators know it. Clive must have known it. He had an extraordinary instinct in such matters. The aftermath of Plassey, the French war, and the Dutch incursion was bound to be anti-climactic in every way. Clive had many good and sufficient reasons for leaving at that moment. It may have been and probably was just luck that they should all have worked together at this moment to his advantage. He was an extraordinarily lucky man, and his luck still held when he boarded his ship on February 21, 1760, and said good-bye to Calcutta and India, for, as he thought, the last time.

The sense of impending calamity had fallen upon everybody as soon as he announced his intention. He might believe the Directors incapable of managing their own affairs, he might feel that he could render the Company more service in England than by staying, but that was but poor comfort to the men whom he was leaving to shift for themselves. Not without excellent cause they felt themselves unequal to the task that lay ahead of them. Even Mir Jafar, much as he had chafed at Clive's control, seems to have awakened to the evil prospect that stretched before him,

U

to the realization that he was surrounded by enemies and was now being left without anyone upon whom he could rely to maintain him upon his uneasy throne. Hated by his Moslem nobles, threatened once more by the Shah Zada in alliance with the Nawab of Oude, conspired against by his own son, his sole dependence was upon the English, and by the English he meant Clive, the only Englishman he knew intimately, respected, and trusted. He had no other friends among them and he felt not unreasonably that he was being left in the lurch. He asked Warren Hastings to try to persuade Clive to postpone his departure. And Hastings, who discerned the signs of the times as clearly as anyone, joined his own representations :

" With great concern I learnt that your resolution is fixed to return this season to Europe. The disinterested regard, which, without fearing the imputation of flattery, I may declare you have ever shown for the Company's welfare convinces me that you would not have determined upon this step, were it in the least inconsistent with that principle. Yet permit me, Sir, to lay before you such consequences as, from my little experience of the Durbar affairs, I apprehend may attend your absence.

" I am, and always have been, of opinion, that the nabob is, both by interest and inclination, heartily attached to the English ; but I think it as certain that the people about him, especially his Muttaseddies, and the Seits, who are evidently great sufferers by the large acquisitions of power which the English have obtained in this Government, would gladly use every possible means to alienate his affections from us. At present, the personal obligations which he confessedly lies under to you are sufficient to intimidate them from any open attempts against us ; but as your absence will encourage these people to throw off the mask, and the Nabob is but of an irresolute and unsettled temper, I don't think it possible that he can hold out against the united influence of so many evil councillors, as will be perpetually instilling into his mind the necessity of reducing the English power. As there is nobody to succeed you with the same influence, and other advantages which you possess, nothing but a large military force will secure our privileges from being encroached upon as soon as you quit the country." [129]

To these and other like appeals, Clive, having taken his resolve, replied only with reassuring words. He declared he had every confidence in Major Caillaud, whom he had placed in command of the army. He assured both Mir Jafar and Ramnarayan that Caillaud would protect them. And so, after paying one more visit to Murshidebad to introduce Caillaud to the Nawab and concert measures for dealing with the Shah Zada, he sailed.

II

The man least to be envied in this whole story is the man who succeeded Clive. Nobody who succeeds a Clive in any walk of life is to be envied. But Henry Vansittart's job was certain to be not merely thankless but personally disastrous. It was his misfortune to find the dice loaded against him at every throw of the game. Even if he had been a genius it is hard to see how he could have succeeded.

Not the least of Vansittart's misfortunes is the utter dependence of his reputation upon Clive's. That is the penalty he paid for undoing Clive's work. And with Clive's reputation reposing upon such a sure foundation of approved authority it is easy to see why Vansittart has been doomed to everlasting disrepute. The more one acclaims Clive the more one must disparage Vansittart. Even to admit the possibility that Vansittart was confronted from the start with a hopeless task at once brings the merit of Clive's achievement into question.

There was, indeed, no way for him to gain reputation. If he had continued Clive's policies and succeeded in maintaining everything as he had found it, the fact would have redounded more to Clive's credit as the initiator of them than to his. If he changed them he did so at his peril because in Clive's hands they had seemed wise and the acme of statesmanship. And if he failed and tried to lay the blame for his failure on Clive, no one would listen to him. The glamour of Clive's name was too great, the evidence of his success too strong, the power of his personality too dominant. Clive had the ear of the public at home. If it came to a test of whose voice would prevail in the court of public opinion, there could be no doubt that it would be Clive's ; and in the high appellate court of history the likelihood was that it would still be Clive's. Truly Vansittart was one of History's unfortunates. For History is little better able than the *vox populi* to discriminate between times when fame and reputation are easily won and the times when they cannot be won at all.

Vansittart had gained a big reputation as a member of the Madras Council. On this point Clive, Sulivan, Saunders, and Pigot were all in hearty accord. " The merit of Vansittart," wrote Clive in that happy, confiding letter of his to Sulivan, " shines with so peculiar and bright a lustre as must make his services coveted by every well-wisher to the Company." That was praise enough, and many echoed it ; in all the heat of faction that followed there were many who remained deeply attached to " Mr. Van.," stoutly championing him against his detractors.

But Clive had not helped his chosen successor when he induced four members of council to sign that indignant letter of protest to the Court of Directors, since it brought forth an immediate order from Sulivan for their dismissal and that of two others ; thus depriving Vansittart, inexperienced in Bengal affairs, of the help, at a critical moment, of the men best able to advise him and, worse than that, depriving him of his support in the council. For, as so many other senior servants had gone home following the Plassey shower of gold, Vansittart found at Calcutta none to compose his council but raw, rapacious juniors still in their twenties, with the one important exception of Warren Hastings. Nor had he over them any constitutional authority in virtue of his office. The prestige and the lead in affairs were his, being President, but all decisions were the decisions of the council, in which he had only one vote. The responsibility was largely his, the power theirs. This, combined with the resentment of the Bengalers at the preference shown to a Madras man, gravely handicapped him from the start and practically foredoomed him to failure despite his best efforts.

When a man is in such a predicament as Vansittart was, it is only fair to let him present his case. Vansittart's, however, has not received much attention. Upon his retirement he published a three-volume record of his administration, which contained little more than documents and showed dignified restraint and commendable freedom from reflections upon others, particularly upon the man who had preceded him and selected him for the post. Inevitably, however, it was liable to criticism, as are all such publications, being *ex parte*, and it was open to any of his opponents to reply suitably in kind. But the reply came, typically enough, not from one of these opponents but from a henchman of Clive ; the reason being that Vansittart had, in defending himself, trodden rather badly on Clive's toes by implying that all was not quite perfect in the system of government he inherited.   The temerity of Luke Scrafton, who had attained the dignity of the Court of Directors, where he sat more or less as Clive's representative, in publishing his *Observations on Mr. Vansittart's Narrative*, was remarkable.   Vansittart had been very careful not to throw aspersions on Clive, for whom he still professed regard, and it would have been much wiser for the Clive party to have maintained a discreet silence.   As it was, Vansittart came out into the open with a *Letter to the Proprietors* in which he recited the facts of the situation that had confronted him on assuming office, facts that might otherwise not have been suspected.   It is this second document rather than the first that is Vansittart's real *apologia*. [130]

In considering Clive's achievement it is usually only the political and military aspects of it that we are asked to regard. We are shown the speed and sureness with which he scattered the forces of every enemy, the firmness and adroitness with which he dealt with Mir Jafar, the cleverness with which he divided Moslem and Hindu, the undeviating support he accorded to Rai Durlab and Ramnarayan, and the consummate ease with which he maintained control over them all.   In contrast we are shown the lamentable failure of his successor in these same respects. And we are asked to draw the self-evident conclusion that his success and Vansittart's failure is full proof of Clive's worth as a practical statesman.   However, it is not to these aspects of his policy that Vansittart would draw our especial attention, but rather to the one that is usually ignored in any glittering picture of conquest—are not all pictures of conquest glittering at first sight ?—that is, the financial aspect.

It should be a truism, if it is not already, that it is easier to conquer than to make a conquest pay.   Finance is the Achilles-heel of most conquests—only it is frequently not the conqueror himself who suffers the penalty for that weakness, but the men who wear the armour after him.   The conqueror is apt to see only the gains of conquest.   He is apt to be bad at figures and unable to tot up accurately the bill of costs.   When he presents a balance sheet it is sure to look attractive with every entry in black ink.   But his successors are sometimes compelled to revise it in red.   This seems to have been Vansittart's experience. He claimed to have found a completely bankrupt exchequer.

Clive made certain substantial gains for the Company. These were, first, the crore of rupees, £1,250,000, that Mir Jafar paid by way of reparations ; second, the yield of the ceded districts, amounting, after payment of rent—the £30,000 that now came to Clive as his *jaghire*—to £70,000 ; and thirdly, the lakh of rupees, £12,500, that the Nawab paid monthly for the services of the Company's army when required. Clive had boasted a great deal of these immense acquisitions. But, as Vansittart showed in his analysis, the first sum had not sufficed even to cover the three items of additional expense incurred after Plassey ; namely, Forde's expedition, the new fort at Calcutta, and the general increased expenses of government.

In an optimistic moment after Plassey Clive had exuberantly told the Company that Bengal would need no supplies of money from home for three years. The Directors, very pleased, had taken him at his word. But even before he left he was in such dire straits for money that he had been forced to borrow upon high interest and draw bills upon the Company, for doing which he had brought down upon his head that stinging censure from Sulivan. The Company having insufficient funds at home to meet the bills had been humiliatingly forced to ask the bill-holders for a delay of payment.

That was not the whole story, however. For not only was the new revenue inadequate to cover these new items of expense, but the one lakh for the army was insufficient to pay for *that* expense. Consider, said Vansittart :

"Before the capture of Calcutta two hundred or two hundred and fifty soldiers composed the whole force of Bengal, without sepoys, without artillery and camp equipage, without field allowances, without fortifications, and an innumerable train of incidental articles. Now let the Directors' account be taken of the force which Colonel Clive left in Bengal ; the number of men will be found to have increased forty-fold, and the other concurrent expenses in a much greater proportion, a fortification fit to command an empire succeeded to the old fort or factory at Calcutta ; and an alliance was made with the Nabob of the provinces by which the company became his protectors, and the sole defenders of the country, instead of being a factory of merchants trading under his permission and good pleasure."

And what was there, asked Vansittart, to pay for all this? Nothing but £70,000 a year and a lakh of rupees a month, "which would not make good the extraordinary camp-charges."

Here was a financial crisis of first magnitude. "It was," Vansittart remarked dryly, "Colonel Clive's good fortune to leave India before the Company's treasure was totally exhausted." Nor was Bengal alone affected. The Company used to keep all the settlements regularly supplied with bullion for their purchases and expenses. Since receiving Clive's assurances that Bengal could supply the needs of Madras and Bombay as well, it had sent none ! Vansittart had left Madras at the moment when the siege of Pondichéry was about to be begun, but without money, of which Madras had none, it could not be carried through. Thus the final triumph of the English over the French depended upon Vansittart solving the difficulty.

He solved it by means of his ill-famed revolution, the dragging down of Mir Jafar from the throne and the setting up of Mir Kasim.

III

The story of Vansittart's administration is a story of disillusionment, the slow and painful awakening of the English to the realities of their new situation. His policy was a beautiful illusion in itself, the illusion that they could retain the gains of Plassey without the attendant ills, the advantages without the expenses and the responsibilities, the power without the government.

The story has more than academic historical interest. At first sight it would seem impossible to draw a comparison, still less a parallel, between the nature of the British adventure in India in the eighteenth century and the Japanese adventure in China in the twentieth, their points of difference being too great. But they do bear a close resemblance in their aims—political, military, and economic supremacy over native government and foreign rival alike—and some clear resemblance in their methods—the driving or freezing out of their rivals and the setting up of puppet governments in the conquered areas.

But it is the main difference between the two adventures that may prove in the end to be most instructive, as well as decisive in preventing a repetition of history. The British enterprise was not a national one, like the Japanese, backed by all the national resources, but one of a semi-private trading company that, despite its affiliation with the state, still had to pay its way and produce annual profits. And that, though it might not seem so, was all to the advantage of Great Britain. It reduced the attendant risks to the State, it eliminated the very real danger of national bankruptcy, it kept the whole enterprise rigidly within the bounds of the strictly practical, it compelled a strict attention to ways and means. Hard-headed men of business ran it, instead of wild-eyed imperialists and military commanders inflated with a sense of their own invincibility and utterly unable to think in terms of political and economic realities. If they had not been running it, the military commanders would shortly have had their way and marched on Delhi and from there have made war on every military power in the country, landing the Company in the bankruptcy to which, despite surface appearances, it was already heading after Plassey. The slow, piecemeal advance of the British, consolidating their gains as they went, keeping their eyes anxiously fixed on their balance-sheets (which, as it was, were seldom very good), was all that enabled them to carry the adventure to a successful conclusion. And if the adventure had failed, it could have failed without disaster to the whole state ; a trading company would have wound up its affairs as the French Company had done, the shareholders would have taken their losses, and the nation itself would have gone on with its more prosperous affairs at home and in other parts of the world. But the adventure did not fail, though it came very near doing so. When it was finally a proved success, but not before, the State intervened and took over the enterprise as its own, making the Sovereign of England the Sovereign also of India.

None of these things are true of Japan's adventure, nor of Italy's in Ethiopia. And when they are pondered it will be seen that the drawbacks of the totalitarian State are nowhere more clearly seen than in this comparison.

Thus we see that the English in India had in 1760 reached the stage when the real difficulties of conquest begin. Clive had set up a puppet government in Bengal, but he had underestimated the expense of controlling it and had not acquired sufficient funds to meet the increased costs. He had, too, made a poor choice of a ruler, Mir Jafar having conclusively proved his incompetence. " I do not think Colonel Clive could have supported him twelve months longer if he had stayed " was Vansittart's verdict. There is reason to think it was correct.

A prince that could not govern, could not defend his realm from any sort of enemy, even from the miserable Shah Zada, manage his finances, keep his army from mutinying, meet his obligations to the Company, and could not even be depended upon to keep faith with the power that made and maintained him—what use was he to anyone ? Vansittart saw nothing sacrosanct in the arrangement. Mir Jafar had only too completely relieved the English of their obligations to him. Even Clive had contemplated the desirability of deposing him at some future date when the English were ready to assume the government. Why, asked Vansittart, sacrifice the existence of the Company for such a man ?   It was not, after all, as though there were nobody to put in his place; Miran, his evil son, had come to a fittingly violent end, slain by a bolt of lightning in his tent ; but Mir Jafar had a son-in-law, Mir Kasim, a far abler man, who had won the respect of Warren Hastings, presumably, as Resident at the durbar, the best judge in such matters.

There were two advantages to be gained, as Vansittart saw it, from making a change of rulers. First, it would more nearly carry out what Vansittart correctly judged to be the Company's policy, namely, to have as little to do as possible with matters of government. Secondly, it would enable him to solve the financial difficulties. It was fine to have a puppet Nawab, but not at all fine if you had to interfere all the time in his affairs and do half his job for him. Clive had correctly interpreted the Company's wishes when he had made that promise to the assembled notables at the court that " for our parts we shall not any ways interfere in the affairs of government, but leave that wholly to the Nabob and attend solely to commerce, which is our proper sphere and our whole aim in these parts."   He must have soon become convinced that it was impracticable, but he had not convinced the Company of the fact, and Vansittart in adopting a policy of non-intervention was only carrying out orders, Mr. Sulivan's in particular.

When the policy failed, Clive, seemingly wise in his discernment before the event and still wiser afterwards, was to say in so many words, " I told you so."   But it seems unfair to Vansittart to condemn him on this ground alone. His failure really served only to emphasize the essential inutility to the Company of Clive's settlement, except as a half-way house along a road that the Company most decidedly did not as yet wish to take : the road to empire. Clive had been working at cross-purposes with the Company. Should the Company be blamed for wishing still to follow its own purposes and not to take Clive's road ? Hardly. To our modern age, no longer enamoured of the spectacle of empire, with a far keener consciousness of all the material evil and moral injustice involved in the conquest and rule of one race by another, and the small gain to either, the earnest desire of Law-rence Sulivan and Henry Vansittart to rescue the Company from too deep involvement in Indian politics and confine it to its proper sphere, makes them seem more sympathetic, even wiser, figures than Robert Clive.

It is quite another question whether it was blind folly on the part of Sulivan and Vansittart to think that it was still possible for the Company to draw back and take that other road. In the light of events it has seemed folly to most historians. There has been a school of thought to whom the gradual extension of British power over the whole of India had already become, even at this early date, Britain's " manifest destiny," so inexorable in its compulsion that those who resisted it were untrue to their responsibilities and guilty almost of criminal shortsightedness. But to-day we have accustomed ourselves to the view that an imperial power can, if it will, put a limit to its own advance, can even surrender ground already won, with wisdom as well as honour and without disaster. We have seen it done in Egypt and Irak. Who will say to-day that it could not have been done in India if men's minds had been so inclined ? The reluctance to go forward was there in those early days, but it was not reinforced by a firm and intelligent resolve to resist the many forces that sought constantly to draw the Company in deeper and deeper. The control over policy from London was unavoidably too loose for such a will as Sulivan's to make itself felt. The pace of the forward advance was set always by the men in India, naturally inclined for the most part in that direction, and the Directors at home could provide little more than an ineffectual brake.

It was, therefore, the men under him who were at least partly responsible for Vansittart's failure. If they had been willing to cooperate loyally with him, restrain their eagerness for exploiting the wide avenues to wealth and power laid open by Plassey, avenues which led directly and inevitably to conflict with the Nawab, he might have succeeded. But they were not willing to give him that cooperation and he had no control over them. He lacked Clive's masterful personality, and even Clive, given no more authority than Vansittart had, might have failed. The evil about which Vansittart complained so bitterly, the participation of the Company's servants in the inland trade of the country free of duty, was already in evidence before Clive left. If Vansittart had been armed with the authority that was later vested in Clive's Select Committee, when the evil had already been done and the foundations of the Bengal state destroyed, there might have been a different and happier story. As it is, he was in a minority of two on that subject, his sole supporter being Warren Hastings.

We have to set alongside this picture of avaricious men another of an able, ambitious prince, for such Mir Kasim was, scheming to free himself from the control of these unwanted Europeans, interpreting every display of moderation and con-ciliatoriness on their Governor's part as a sign of weakness, and capitalizing every concession to his own advantage. It is one of the unanswered questions of history how far Mir Kasim's ambitions would have carried him if in the resulting collision he had not been met head-on by the turbulent English. Would he have been content with re-establishing Aliverdi Khan's authority, or would he have acted like Siraj-ud-daula and practically forced the English to make war upon him if they were to retain even such privileges as they had always enjoyed ? [131]

In Clive's opinion, and in the opinion of all who saw things as he did, Vansittart's policy of non-intervention was from start to finish a colossal blunder and, in the lengths to which he carried it, something even worse, a gross breach of good faith which inflicted a deplorable stain on English honour. But the truth seems rather that Vansittart carried his policy through with a logicality and sincerity that could almost appear praiseworthy if it had not been attended with such disastrous results. A policy of non-intervention that did not include withdrawing English interference in the Nawab's relations with his ministers would have been a sham unworthy of the term policy.

The core of Clive's system had been his extension of British protection to Rai Durlab and Ramnarayan, the two chief

Hindu ministers of state, conditional upon their loyalty. But no man can serve two masters, and what Vansittart saw when he arrived was two men being maintained in office against the will and interests of their lawful sovereign, using the British protection they enjoyed to serve chiefly their own interests. They were charged by Mir Kasim with embezzling his revenues and being a standing invitation to all his zemindars to do likewise, and as ruler he demanded the right to remove them. The first charge was probably true, but not proven. Of the truth of the second there can be no possible doubt. How could any government maintain its authority over its subjects in the face of such a glaring invasion of its most elementary rights? That, at least, was how Vansittart regarded the matter, and the Directors, too, who gave him their support in the change of policy.

Naturally the opposition from those who had imbibed Clive's views and believed that his policy should be adhered to was fierce and loud, and equally naturally Clive's earlier promise to the notables at Murshidebad was forgotten and his later promises to Ramnarayan and Rai Durlab, so at variance with it, were remembered and hurled in Vansittart's face. Not all of those, however, who cry, " Honour, honour " the loudest love it the most. Those who shouted against Vansittart the loudest upon this occasion were those who, for good and sufficient reasons, were wedded to Clive's system. Among them, for instance, were the army commanders, Caillaud, Coote, and Carnac. It was most natural that they should have opposed the new policy and objected strenuously to acting, actually as well as ostensibly, under the Nawab's orders in fulfilling the duty of defending his dominions. This was merely another one of the many difficulties that stood in the way of a policy of partial withdrawal and helped later to make it appear totally misguided. Officers who had learned by Clive's example and success to adopt an attitude of contempt for the potentate who was their lawful sovereign, and believed as he did in the supreme efficacy of military force, now so completely in their hands, may be forgiven for their sense of indignation at seeing one by one the checks that Clive had placed upon the Nawab's power removed and themselves reduced to a subordinate position. It was, in their eyes, a reversal of the natural order of things. Needless to say, therefore, in their personal relations with the Nawab they did nothing to cement the better feelings that Vansittart was striving so hard to create.

Mir Kasim, as soon as he was allowed to do so, removed Ram-narayan from office, imprisoned him, and later, when the rupture with the English came, put him to death, as well as the Seths, other former tools of the English ; and the blame for their deaths has been laid at Vansittart's door.   How far it deserves to be his must be left a matter of opinion.   Needless to say, the with-drawal of English protection from where it had once been pledged involved a serious loss of prestige that weakened the whole English position in Bengal.   It is the price paid for the attainment of any kind of power in Asia that retreat is always difficult and hazardous.

"When the Colonel leaves India," Luke Scrafton had prophesied as early as September 1758, " my life on it, if we have anything of a force, we shall not be long without a second rupture with the government."   He was right, and he was right because he knew that the English would never voluntarily relinquish the position that their military power had won them, no matter what Sulivan or Vansittart might wish or do.

" If we have anything of a force "—Clive had seen to that ! The English now had an army of some 10,000 men, and when at last Mir Kasim, goaded beyond endurance by the refusal of the English to heed either him or their own governor, had recourse to the arbitrament of war to enforce his rights and realize his ambitions, it was the army that promptly took matters into its own hands and put a final end to any nonsense of independence.

IV

Vansittart himself insisted that his revolution was primarily a financial measure.   He deposed Mir Jafar, he said, because he could expect no aid from him in extricating the Company from its embarrassments.   There was only one solution, and that was to obtain for the Company a grant of more lands.   Mir Jafar could not be expected to make such a grant, whereas Mir Kasim was only too ready to make it as the price of his own elevation. Mir Kasim surrendered lands worth £625,000 a year.   These were the three districts of Burdwan, Chittagong, and Midnapore. Not only that, but he was a capable administrator and prompt in his payments.   Thus in no time at all the financial crisis was ended, two and a half lakhs were promptly despatched to Madras for the siege of Pondichéry, and Vansittart received the heartfelt

317

thanks of his employers. In view of this fact we have less reason still to wonder why Lawrence Sulivan held no great opinion of Clive's services to the Company and a very high opinion of Vansittart's.

The matter of Mir Jafar's financial mismanagement should not, however, in fairness to all parties be left there. In touching on this topic Vansittart, it is much to be feared, came closer home to Clive than was good for his peace of mind. Clive had every reason in the world why he should not have wished the question to be discussed at all or the facts laid bare, because sooner or later he must have realized how deeply implicated he was in the Nawab's chronic indisposition, or inability, to pay his debts to the Company. The very moment one begins enquiring into the matter one is brought up against Clive's private transactions, which cast such a doubtful light upon his conduct of public affairs.

The main facts have been stated, but there are some considerations that cannot be overlooked in forming a correct estimate. Clive was ever ready to challenge comparison of his virtue with that of others, but not always so ready to put the full facts before those who were asked to judge. No one knew better than he how to make out the best possible case for himself and ignore inconvenient facts that spoiled his picture of himself. Of nothing is this more true than of the way he later defended himself in the matter of the acceptance of presents.

There was as yet no reason for him to offer any formal defence at all. The Company's regulations did not prohibit the acceptance of presents ; giving them was a custom of the country, and the donations obeyed the laws of ordinary business in the matter of size. Clive, given the biggest opportunity ever vouchsafed to a European in India to make a scoop, had taken all that Mir Jafar had offered him, rejoicing at the unexpected size of his haul. Singularly lacking in judgment and foresight in such matters, he probably had no doubts about the wisdom of his action ; its undoubted legality was all that seemed to matter. Nor had he seen any need for informing his employers of the precise details of a transaction that had been a private one between himself and Mir Jafar and did not concern them. Of course, he could not conceal the fact that he and the other gentlemen involved had benefited very considerably from the new Nawab's generosity, nor did he want to ; he felt that it should be an occasion for general rejoicing at their good fortune ; but he did not state the amount. He had written John Payne, the Chairman of the Company : " Exclusive of which treaty, or any agreement whatever, the Nabob of his own free will for the services rendered him made me a present much beyond my expectations, part of which I bestowed on those immediately about me and one or two of the principal officers : I never made the least secret of this affair but always thought the world ought to be acquainted with the Nabob's gratitude."

The Directors, not knowing as yet any reason why they should not rejoice with him, had sent him their congratulations. In all innocence they had written : " We do not intend to break in upon any sums of money which have been given by the Nabob to particular persons by way of free gift or gratuity for their services." Thus Clive was ever after able to flourish before a censorious world the official approval of his employers. But how little the Court knew of the transaction that was putting £600,000 into private pockets may be seen from their expressing the wistful hope that there would be a surplus left over from the indemnification of individual sufferers so that the Company could pay off some of its own losses ! [1]

How little the Company knew ! How little anyone, unacquainted with the character of the people Clive was dealing with, knew ! The situation was designed by nature for misunderstandings. Even the wily but childish Mir Jafar may well have misunderstood. Misunderstood, for instance, the true status of the great and prepotent Colonel Clive. Orientals are more accustomed to dealing with flesh-and-blood persons than with absent corporations belonging to another continent. And if, as it is said, Mir Jafar got confused about the relative importance of the gentlemen visible and gentlemen invisible and thought the former more to be feared and the more important creditors, it is scarcely to be wondered at ; especially as Clive's delineation of the character of a servant left something to be desired in the way of convincingness. But the Asiatic debtor's mind goes further than merely making shrewd distinctions between creditors, a habit not confined to the East. Mir Jafar hoped or believed—it is impossible to decide which—that in making such handsome donations to the visible powers he was

[1] It is interesting to note that the native inhabitants of Calcutta received approximately half their losses, the Armenians their bare principal, and the English their full principal plus 20 per cent. interest. The Company retained a small surplus, and the indignant English inhabitants sued them for it ! [132]

purchasing immunity from his obligations to the invisible ; in other words, he designed the donations as " private bribes to defeat public ends, in Oriental politics an engine seldom worked in vain." Clive may not have encouraged him in this delusion, but it cannot be said that he did much to remove it. Mir Jafar's thoughts may, therefore, be imagined when he discovered gradually that this time the engine was being worked in vain !

They were gloomy thoughts ; he must have felt that these Feringis were not playing the game ; but he was at first far from despairing. It was only after long and painful experience, and wasting a fearful lot of good money, that he and his successors and brother-princes learned how impossible it was to bribe an Englishman ! What gave him reason to hope now was the sight of the visible embodiments of power helping themselves first to his payments. His disillusionment did not come until it was the Company's turn to be paid. He must still have remained a little incredulous, not knowing the English very well as yet. Perhaps he believed that he had not been sufficiently generous to his friend Colonel Clive and so bethought himself of that promised *jaghire*. It would be a natural instinct with him when confronted with a disagreeable situation to try to buy himself out of it. And then, having taken out that piece of insurance, he tried yet another time-honoured dodge.

When Clive appeared before the House of Commons' Committee he was asked some questions which showed that his questioners were quite ready themselves to be deceived if it helped their case against him. He was asked whether at the time of the grant of the *jaghire* he knew that Mir Jafar was surrounded by his troops mutinous for lack of pay. Yes, he replied, he certainly knew ; the arrears of pay amounted to three or four millions sterling. It was, he lightly added, the custom of the country never to pay the army more than a quarter of what was due until absolutely necessary. Asked whether at the same time the Nawab's jewels, goods, and furniture were not being publicly sold and his lands mortgaged in order to obtain money to pay the Company, he again answered, yes. But he was apparently given no opportunity to elucidate the matter further and explain for the benefit of these ignoramuses of Parliament that appearances of poverty in the East, as sometimes in the West, are deceptive. We can imagine the defiant contempt with which he faced his accusers at this moment. [133]

The ease and rapidity with which Mir Kasim paid off the balance to the Company as well as to his army exposed Mir Jafar's trick rather too clearly. But, perhaps, one result of Clive's acceptance of the *jaghire* under these circumstances was that nothing but his deposition could convince Mir Jafar's sluggish mind that he could not ignore the Company's claims as safely as he could his own lawful sovereign's, the Mogul Emperor's. No one understood the devious workings of his mind as Clive did, or was more ready to forgive and overlook his failings, but no one, too, took greater personal advantage of his weaknesses. Mir Jafar might be excused if, upon finding himself at Calcutta, a pensioned-off prince, he had felt a bewildered sense of grievance as one who had in some way, not exactly clear to himself, been defrauded by the man who had put him upon his throne. Yet apparently he entertained no such sentiment, not at least against Clive, for whom he felt a curiously deep regard. He no doubt laid the blame for all his troubles on those invisible gentlemen in London who did not understand Indian ways of doing business and imposed upon him and their servants alike.

Clive was later to defend the *jaghire* transaction by saying that the Company would not have had more by his having taken less. But this, as we can now see, was a superficial view of the case. He might have seen at the time that the £30,000 that now went into his pocket, while it never would have reached Mir Jafar's on account of his indebtedness, could with much greater propriety have been credited to the Company's account, and if that had been done it might have saved Mir Jafar his throne. But, as we have noted, there was a distinct blind-spot in Clive's mind on money matters, as, indeed, there was on all matters requiring refinement of reasoning and judgment. If it had not been there he would scarcely have impressed upon Mir Jafar, during his last visit to the durbar, so seriously the need for economy, and " with an optimism which his strong common sense seldom permitted, he seems to have supposed that he had succeeded." [134] Clive's common sense was not at all proof against that kind of optimism, nor did he apparently see anything incongruous in his recommendation.

The reader has now before him all the main facts of the situation that confronted Vansittart when he reached Calcutta on July 27, 1760, and can judge for himself how far Vansittart was

X

justified in upsetting Clive's settlement, cleaning the slate, and changing his policy. " The present system is rotten to the core," wrote Major Caillaud flatly to the Council only two days after Clive left, and it is difficult to withhold agreement. Vansittart's only biographer has written : " Owing chiefly to his quarrel with Clive, Vansittart has been unjustly treated by writers on Indian history. His conduct in Bengal was farsighted and his dealings with the subadar were distinguished by statesmanlike moderation." [135] That judgment seems, upon reflection, somewhat fairer than another passed upon him : that his whole policy from beginning to end was nothing but an " appalling blunder."

Clive on his return to India in 1765 pursued the quarrel thus begun. He discovered and gave information to the Company that Vansittart had accepted five lakhs from Mir Kasim, corruptly so Clive implied. History, however, has completely acquitted Vansittart of self-interested motives in elevating Mir Kasim to the throne, or in any other of his dealings with him. Mir Kasim had wanted to make the usual donations at the time of his accession, and Vansittart had not only refused them, but also had vehemently opposed the subsequent action of his Council in demanding their payment. Presents were received by members of council, notably by Holwell, but Vansittart himself refused to take anything until Mir Kasim had paid off all arrears and brought his finances into good order. Then, and not till then, did he accept the five lakhs. He refused another five lakhs from Mir Jafar, once more restored to his throne, upon the eve of sailing. He declared that he had made it his principle that " no private interest of mine should ever come in competition with the demands of the Company and the public." " I really think," he added, " that his Lordship might have spared his reproaches upon this score." [136]

Chapter Twenty-one

MEMBER FOR SHREWSBURY

"If less had been said I should have been less ambitious and consequently less unhappy"
CLIVE

I

IF CLIVE CAUGHT THE OUTGOING TIDE of glory in India he missed the incoming when he returned to England. His instinct in wanting to return home after Plassey had been right. The moment would have been as favourable to his ambitions as had been that of his previous return. The news of Plassey had followed a long series of shameful disasters—Minorca, defeats in Germany, the occupation of Ostend and Nieuport by the French, the convention of Kloster-Zeven, the failures at Rochefort and Louisburg. Nothing but Watson's and Clive's successes had redeemed the record of war from dismal, utter failure. No wonder that Pitt, concerned for his own position as war minister, had tried to make the public forget the disasters by pæans of praise for Watson and Clive !

But by mid-summer 1760 the whole picture had changed. The *annus mirabilis* had intervened. First Louisburg, then Minden, Quiberon Bay, Quebec. Again and again London had blazed with bonfires. The grand climax had come with the way in which the news of victory at Quebec had followed hot upon the report of failure. England was now as sated with victory as before she had been sickened by defeat. The inevitable result was the eclipsing of Clive's fame and reputation.

Could England be content that she still had her Clive when she had lost her Wolfe ? Could Watson's and Clive's operations be compared for difficulty to Saunders's and Wolfe's ? Or the conquest of Bengal with the conquest of Canada ? What glory gained on the Hugli was comparable to that imperishably gained on the St. Lawrence ? Any man who cared to do so could make the contrast, needing none to make it for him. Quebec was glory untarnished, an epic of heroism, devotion, and military

323

skill. And England knew—as she was to know again after Trafalgar—that in Wolfe she had lost one of her greatest sons and noblest heroes. The whole nation mourned when his body was brought back for burial. An ecstatic mixture of joy and sorrow filled its heart as the funeral procession passed slowly along the streets of London. How could it any longer make a hero of Clive when it now knew what true heroism was ? One does not need concrete evidence of the profound effect that this contrast must have had on the popular opinion of Clive. If his standing with the public now underwent a sudden change for the worse, so that for the rest of his life he was to contend with mounting enmity, encountering again and again " ingratitude " when he expected to find the reverse, we surely need not look elsewhere for an explanation. How could a nation that had known a Wolfe ever feel that it " owed " to a Clive anything more than it had already given him or that he had taken for himself ? Because a man who takes for himself deprives gratitude of most of its strength and all of its pleasure.

The contrast between Clive and Wolfe seems to us, in fact, to supply the key to a full understanding of Clive's life, character, and subsequent trials, giving us the best kind of yardstick to judge him both as a man and a soldier.

They were exact contemporaries. For while Wolfe was two years younger, his military career began four years earlier and closed the same year. (For all practical purposes we can regard Clive's military career as terminating with the defeat of the Dutch.) And the points of similarity between them were as marked as the ways in which they differed. As soldiers they may be bracketed equal in their youthful ardour, natural aptitude for war, their originality (Clive with his sepoys and Wolfe with his Light Infantry), their resourcefulness and quick grasp of situations, physical courage, and spirit of do-or-die. They both fretted under inaction, both were equally keen for promotion and impatient with the incompetence and laxity of the day. In natural ability and spirit, then, they were rivals far surpassing their brother officers. Clive's commentary on the fiasco against Pondichéry may be compared for acuteness of judgment with Wolfe's on the similar fiasco against Rochefort.

Wolfe, however, had at the age of fifteen chosen the army as his profession, made it the whole of his ambition, and striven to the utmost to perfect his proficiency. He embodied the professional spirit at its best. Nothing of this was true of Clive. Wolfe, too, was essentially a modest man ; zeal, his spirit of selfless devotion to his calling, spurred him on in his eager pursuit of promotion and opportunity. Having no money and very little family interest, he had to depend upon merit and force of character to gain him what practically everybody else gained much more easily by favouritism and purchase. He cared nothing about material gains ; at twenty-eight he was not " master of £50," yet worried only because poverty hampered him in his career. Thus true greatness of soul went hand-in-hand in Wolfe with brilliance of talent. He was a thinker as well as a fighter, sometimes even a dreamer and a philosopher, with insight into and a wide outlook upon life, and his letters reveal a genuine, lovable, clean-cut personality, full of depth, colour, and warm human qualities. And again, none of this is true of Clive. Wolfe's ardour had a genuinely beautiful and inspiring purity that made Clive's by comparison seem largely self-seeking.

We repeat that a country that had once known a Wolfe as England came to know him in glorious death could never regard a Clive as highly as it had once done. The memory of the lost hero would always interpose between it and its appreciation of the services of the living, and as it watched the subsequent behaviour of the victor of Plassey, so different from what would have been that of the victor of the Plains of Abraham, it could not help but experience a revulsion of feeling against him.

Clive missed his tide, and that tide was now to run continuously against him. The honours that he gained were not given to him freely by a grateful nation ; they had to be acquired by dint of his own unceasing efforts ; he had to become a power in politics in order to obtain them at all.

II

His voyage was rapid and uneventful. He and Margaret landed at Portsmouth on July 9, and a day or two later were once more reunited around the family hearth in Swithin's Lane. He was most graciously received at Court, where he hastened to pay his respects. The other seat of power, now made semi-regal by his successes, was equally cordial. It still had no reason to be otherwise, since the offending letter from the Bengal Council, which carried in addition the notification to the Company of his *jaghire*, was slower in reaching England than the man responsible for it.

The letter did not arrive until September 23, which was the day before the regular quarterly meeting of the General Court at which it was proposed to vote the thanks of the Company to Vice-Admiral Pocock, Colonel Stringer Lawrence, and Colonel Robert Clive for " their many eminent and signal services to the Company." How Mr. Sulivan received it we do not know, but we can imagine his angry feelings. However, no single voice was heard to oppose the resolution, and the marked favour that Clive had always received from the Court of Directors continued apparently undiminished for a little time longer. The Court ordered busts of all three officers to be made and placed in the House. The fact that he had signed the letter was something to be tactfully overlooked, even excused. " We have reason to believe "—so they wrote in their general Bengal letter of March 13, 1761—" he is sorry that he signed the letter, for we must remark that not one of the heavy charges in our letter of the 23d March 1759 stood against him, their foundation was prior to his being connected with our Bengal affairs, consequently he is excluded from any share in those scandalous and outrageous replies to such charges."

The *jaghire* was too substantial an item to be treated quite so lightly. Not once, not twice, but *every year* £30,000 of the Company's cash had now to be paid over, not as formerly to the recognized lord of their lands, the lord of all Bengal, but to one of their own former servants. It would take some time for the full realization of such an unprecedented and extraordinary situation to penetrate home, but when it did so the effect was bound to be cumulative. Each year's payment would serve as a fresh irritant. Yet what the Directors could do about it, other than accept the situation as gracefully as they could, was something that must have worried them considerably. They were not prepared to return a quick answer.

It was natural that the nation at large should have exaggerated the amount of wealth the victor of Plassey brought home. They had known nothing quite like it since the days of Marlborough. The chronicler of the day estimated that he was worth £1,200,000 in cash, bills, and jewels, not to mention his lady's casket of jewels, which was estimated at £20,000 at the very least : " So that he may with propriety be said to be the richest subject in the three kingdoms." [137] Clive was not quite that. Fortunes as large as his were uncommon, but not unknown. The Earl of Bath left one of £1,200,000. But Clive's seemed the largest because of the way he spent it and because India was regarded as an Eldorado.

For now began, with the coming of the first and the greatest, the age of the nabobs, which was to give such plentiful material for the pens of all the wits in town for many a long day and to cause such heart-burning and genuine perturbation among more serious thinkers in the kingdom. The full flowering of that age was yet a little while in the future, but Horace Walpole, its principal recorder, fired the opening gun of his bombardment when, with a humour more American than English, he declared that the cost of living rose immediately with the coming of this Crœsus " all over estates and diamonds. . . . If a beggar asks charity, he says, ' Friend, I have no small brilliants about me.' "

Whatever the public at large may have thought of him, in his father's house all was perfect happiness and contentment. " May Heaven preserve you safe to old England," the old man had written, " where not only your friends and relations, but strangers who never saw you, will congratulate you for the glorious actions you have done your country. With what joy shall I embrace you ! Oh, may I live to see that day ! Your mother and sisters are sitting with me round the fire, drinking to your health and safe voyage." And well he might rejoice ! For he had more cause than anyone else to be grateful to his son. Because of his positive genius for making a mess of his affairs nothing but Robert's success and filial generosity had saved the family from ruin.

It appears that Richard Clive had, as a tax collector, become responsible to the state for a sum of something like £10,000, representing Shropshire land-tax that had been collected but not paid in. Father and son had had dealings for some years with William Belchier, banker, government financier, dealer in pocket boroughs, and member for Southwark. In the severe financial crisis of 1759 Belchier had underwritten a government loan of eight million pounds to the extent of £250,000. He had then gone bankrupt, and apparently Richard Clive's £10,000 had been in his hands at the time.[138]

So from William Smith King, his agent, came to Robert this urgent appeal for help :

"Dear Clive, permit me as a friend jealous for your honour and the happiness of all who belong to you, to entreat you to deliver your father from this oppression, I do not mean by only ordering this debt to be paid, the amount of which I am ignorant of, perhaps, ten thousand pounds, but of which Mr. Clive has assured me, he would himself let you know the full extent. I say I do not entreat for the payment only of this debt, for I am sure you will not hesitate in discharging it, but that which I am particularly solicitous for is that it may be done in such a manner as may save a Father from the confusion he must undergo if in the discharging the debt you should in the least testify your being offended at his having so imprudently involved himself. Your elevation is such both from your merit and fortune that it is not sufficient for you to do a generous action, without its being accompanied with that peculiar grace that great men dispense their favours with. Pardon me the liberty I have taken in making this request, which does not arise from a doubt of the nobleness of your disposition, but from a love of your fame, and a promise I have made to your father, to use the influence of the friendship you honour me with that this business may be determined without at all injuring him in that filial affection you have so largely testified to him ; of which I daresay he is truly sensible, and never unmindful of all those great benefits that he and his family have, and will derive from the prosperity your merit has been attended with." [139]

The appeal closed with a hint that Clive should hurry up with the payment, otherwise the Crown might attach his Styche estate to satisfy his father's debt ! And without a doubt Clive had hurried up and with all the gracefulness desired of him. His brother-in-law and cousin, Sir Edward Clive, Bart., the judge of circuit, no doubt had this and other instances of his filial piety in mind when he congratulated him on making his family "happy." "Assisting a parent must be the most agreeable sensation to good hearts."

Clive's generosity has been warmly praised, and it was indeed the most agreeable part of his character. His income was in the region of £45,000, and he is estimated to have spent at least £50,000 in gifts and annuities, and probably a good deal more. He showered his largesse upon all for whom he felt regard, his sisters and his cousins and his aunts, besides his brother-in-law Maskelyne, his old commander Lawrence, and countless others. He seems to have had a particular abhorrence for his female relatives remaining in the unhappy state of singleness, and, believing rightly in the power of money to correct all such ills, he had oiled the machinery of matrimony to such good purpose that courtiers for his sisters' hands sprang up like fairy princes. The eldest had married Sir James Markham, Bart., soon after his first return to India, and when he got home he found that three more of them had taken the same judicious step. Only poor Sally, his cousin, still languished in singleness of state, comforted, indeed, by the fame that the Colonel had brought to the name of Clive, but regretting that she was not one of his sisters. Her famous cousin had promised to bring her home an Oriental prince and a bushel of diamonds, but she vowed that she would be quite satisfied with Captain Clack !

This must have been the one supreme moment of happiness in his life. He was barely thirty-five, yet all his ambitions had been gratified, his deepest desires satisfied. He had undergone all the risks and perils of Indian service, fearful as they were, and he had emerged far from unscathed, but yet with sufficient health, vigour, and youth to give him a prospect of enjoying life in new-found ease and comfort for many years to come. It is much to be doubted whether his ideas extended at first far beyond this. India had not by any means passed beyond his horizon, but assuredly he must have wanted to enjoy himself for a space before plunging again into the turmoil of politics.

Unhappily his brief hour was all too short. Before he had even begun to taste these new-found joys ill-health overcame him. It does not appear to have been the fault of the Indian climate, though his health had been indifferent before he left Calcutta, so much as of that highly nervous temperament of his, which made him an easy victim to periodical nervous breakdowns as soon as the need for action passed, complicated this time by gout.

He was ill for over a year, so ill, he said, that "for twelve months it was difficult to pronounce whether I was to live or die. In so dreadful a situation I could not think much of India, or indeed of anything else but death," but in this he exaggerated. He was not so ill that he could not attend to the business of getting himself and his family elected to Parliament.

III

Clive's mind had, as we have seen, been set upon getting into Parliament. It was the first object of any ambitious man of that time. "You must first make a figure there if you would make a figure in your country," Lord Chesterfield advised his son. But Clive had learnt something from his previous unhappy experience. He would now be with the government, not against it ; he would work with those who could make his path to honours and influence smooth ; he would capitalize the assiduous efforts his father had been making to cultivate the Duke of Newcastle, the dispenser of crown patronage and fount of honours.[140]

Shropshire was the obvious choice for a field of operations, both by reason of the family connection of long standing and his Grace's special political connection with that county, maintained through the local magnate and Lord Lieutenant, the Earl of Powis. This nobleman was the leader of the Shropshire members, at least eight of them forming a solid group behind him. As their leader he was also their political broker, soliciting and negotiating for them favours and places from government, which meant from the Duke, arranging election affairs, and deciding how the group was to vote. The arrangement was beneficial for all concerned, as the support of these eight votes meant much to his Grace, who as manager of the government machine was ready to grant many favours in exchange for it. One of the most consummate politicians of the day and a born negotiator, Lord Powis had obtained his own earldom from Newcastle not many years before by not too delicately suggesting the unfavourable impression that disappointment would create among his friends !—a suggestion that seldom failed to work with Newcastle. Obviously, therefore, it would be sound policy on Clive's part to attach himself firmly to this group, the only kind of party that existed at that time.

Although his father had done most of the spade-work for him with both Duke and Earl, it was by no means a foregone con-clusion that the next election, which was pending, would see him returned as member for a Shropshire borough. There were five boroughs and only one of them could be bought. The other four were, despite Lord Powis's influence, "singularly free from an over-towering aristocratic territorial influence." Some dozen local families competed for the right to represent them, but the

Clives were not as yet one of them. However, the military successes of the son and the diplomatic efforts of the father had put them in a favourable position. When in June 1759 Robert's name was put forward as a candidate to succeed the sitting member for Shrewsbury, Mr. More, the father's recommendation was known to have the backing of Newcastle and Powis.

But a very powerful opponent soon afterwards appeared in the field in the person of the Earl of Bath, who had large estates in the county and wanted the seat for his own son, Lord Pulteney. " Mr. Clive," said the Earl, " is a very worthy man, as well as a very dangerous antagonist, but yet I must support my son. . . ." And being an overbearing man he was extremely irate when he found how little the Corporation were disposed to heed his wishes. The mayor wrote to tell him that " the Colonel being of a family of great antiquity and merit amongst us and having so remarkably distinguished himself in the service of his country, was agreed by all to be a proper candidate." The Earl wrathfully accused the town of allowing Lord Powis to dispose of it as he pleased, and appealed to the Duke of Newcastle, scornfully calling Clive a nabob. This placed his Grace in the uncomfortable position, to which, however, he must by now from long experience have become accustomed, of being caught between two powerful lords both wanting the same thing. He tried in vain to appease Bath and arrange a compromise, but no compromise was to be found.

Matters were in this shape when Clive returned home. His personal appearance on the scene put an end to all doubts. Young Pulteney found at once that he had no chance and withdrew, his father sourly observing that " it was in vain to contend with the power of the Corporation and the wealth of the Indies." Tories and Whigs combined in support of Clive, and at the general election in April 1761 he was returned unopposed. The House of Commons was certainly the gainer, as Lord Pulteney is described as " a young man burdened with difficult parents, an unhappy youth, little character, and no merit."

Meanwhile Richard Clive had been active in his own behalf. His enlistment under the banner of Lord Powis enabled him, too, to appear in the new Parliament as member for Montgomery. As John Walsh, with the help of the Colonel and Newcastle, also obtained a seat at Worcester, Clive found himself the possessor of

three votes, which at once made him a powerful member of the
" Powis gang."

He might have had even more votes. Remembering that he
brought his cousin George home with £20,000, and had sent his
brother-in-law Edmund ahead of him with Walsh the year before
worth £10,000 or £11,000, we need feel no surprise at finding
both gentlemen candidates at Penryn in Cornwall, with Clive
putting up £2000, which was the current price of seats, for each
of them.   The Clive connection with Cornwall had arisen from
Sir Edward Clive, first cousin to Richard, being member for St.
Michael, which Robert had contested in 1754, and the friendship
of Lord Hardwicke a prominent landowner in the county.   But
here, as at Shrewsbury, he was fighting powerful interests, none
less than the Earl of Bute, the new King's favourite, and though
the attempt that was made to get Clive to withdraw his candidates
failed (" Mr. Clive is Lord Powis's election bull-dog ; and the
master can certainly call him off ") George and Mun were beaten
at the poll, and Robert had to look elsewhere for seats for them.

This opportunity was to come two years later.   Bishop's
Castle, one of the five Shropshire boroughs, was of the pocket
variety, belonging automatically to the largest land-owner of
the district, who was at this time Mr. Walter Waring.   But his
grip on it was not strong and Clive determined to take it from
him.   He began operations by buying a large estate, Walcot.
In September 1763 one of the sitting members conveniently died,
making a by-election necessary.   Clive seized the chance,
nominated cousin George, and tried to persuade Mr. Waring,
who wanted the seat for himself, to withdraw.   Though he did
not want the expense of a contested election, he was, as he wrote
Newcastle, determined to win : " Your Grace I am persuaded
knows enough of me to be convinced that I will spend the utmost
farthing sooner than give up my interest in this borough, which
I have great pretensions to from my late purchase."   When Mr.
Waring proved unamenable, being backed by the government
to which his Grace no longer belonged, Clive was forced to
apply corruption in a thorough-going manner : " I have just
now received advice that £500 have been offered for ten of our
voters, but to very little purpose, nothing can hurt us provided
the returning officer be steady, which I have reason to think he
will be, the only thing which gives me uneasiness is that I have
not yet got his son discharged, although Colonel Reynolds has

made a promise to General Mostyn. I wish your Grace would press this matter to the Duke of Devonshire and Lord Rockingham." Mr. Waring was foolish to decline Clive's offer of £1000 for the expenses already incurred in return for his withdrawal, for if the election depended upon getting the returning officer's son discharged from the army, surely Clive with the combined assistance of three great noblemen must have succeeded in arranging such a simple matter ! At any rate, when the poll was declared on November 24 cousin George was duly elected by 80 votes to 53.

Four years later Clive was to make doubly sure of Bishop's Castle by buying Mr. Waring's estates for £30,500. He was then able in the general election of 1768 to secure both its seats without opposition, brother William being returned along with cousin George to bring the Clive representation in the House of Commons up to the respectable total of seven (including Sir Edward Clive and Henry Strachey, Clive's secretary). As George Pigot also sat for a Shropshire borough, it may be said that Shropshire did its duty nobly in seeing that India was properly represented in the Imperial Parliament !

Mr. Namier has disposed of the idea that there was anything special to distinguish the Parliament of 1761 from its predecessors : it was " remarkably normal." That is to say, there was no change in the character of the House of Commons, no widespread corruption, no more than a slight rise in the price of seats, and no influx of nabobs or profiteers. Horace Walpole merely discovered a mare's nest when he gave vent to his oft-quoted description of that election. Whereas he had a snobbish dislike for all new wealth like Clive's and affected to see the *nouveaux riches* corrupting the pristine purity of English politics, the whole history of English political development had been one, and continued to be one, of a steady infiltration of new men into Parliament, filling up the ranks of the landed nobility and gentry.

Clive's methods of getting himself and his connections into Parliament had, also, been " remarkably normal," and his behaviour when there was the same. That is to say, now that he had an " interest "—that word of omnipotent power—he wanted to use it to obtain favours for himself and his friends. And, first, there was the matter of a peerage for himself.

There was some uncertainty at first regarding to whom Clive would attach himself. His own personal leanings were towards Pitt ; naturally, in view of Pitt's record as a war minister, the hearty support he had rendered to the Company, his eulogy of Clive, and the not entirely unsympathetic reply he had made to Clive's overtures through Walsh. The two men had long talks during the weeks preceding Clive's illness, but by the time Clive had recovered sufficiently to take an active part in politics a great change had come over the English political scene.

There was a new king, and like most new and especially youthful sovereigns, George III did not wish to employ the same set of ministers as his grandfather. He had his own favourite Bute, and it soon became clear that the old firm of Pitt and Newcastle was about to be dissolved by the playing off of one partner against the other. Both were doomed to go, but Pitt went first because his war policy clashed with George III's and Bute's desire for peace. When the King at his first meeting with the Privy Council stigmatized Pitt's great imperial venture as " a bloody and expensive war " it became clear that the war minister's days of power were numbered. His resignation came within twelve months. On October 5, 1761, he handed over the seals of office and power passed into the hands of men who cared not for national glory, too expensive as it was for their liking and too remote from their personal interests.

Any hope that Clive may have had of carrying out his extensive scheme for turning his conquests into a national possession went with Pitt. India, instead of being the preoccupation of the one serious statesman in the kingdom, was now to become the plaything of politicians manœuvering for personal advantage and petty objectives. Clive also was to suffer personally : the victor of Plassey and the conqueror of a kingdom in the eyes of Pitt, he was to be nothing more than a powerful politician, the owner of votes, in the eyes of the new ministers.

He adjusted himself quickly to the changed circumstances. The split between Pitt and Newcastle having become complete by the general election, Sandwich saw that a favourable moment had come to secure Clive for the Newcastle interest, " as he is dissatisfied with the person to whom he seem'd most inclined to attach himself, which I did not fail to make the proper advantages of." To weight the scales in favour of Clive's well-known desire for a peerage there was the important fact that he would carry at least two members besides himself, " and will never have anything to ask beyond the present favour." In this latter statement Sandwich was being somewhat optimistic.

Sandwich was successful in his efforts both with Clive and Newcastle. Clive wrote him from Bath, May 3 :

" I am more obliged than words can express for the part your Lordship has taken on my behalf, any notice taken of me, as the reward of my successes (rather than merits) cannot but be very acceptable, I should have been sav'd from much anxiety, if when so many others were thought of, I had not been forgotten, not that I pretend to plead any other merit than the notice which was taken of me by the Duke of Newcastle and the public. If less had been said, I should have been less ambitious and consequently less unhappy."

He was promised the red ribbon of the Bath, and during the summer negotiations went on about the peerage, which was solicited for him by Lord Powis and the Duke of Devonshire.

The fact that it *had* to be solicited by powerful noblemen, that even the great Clive needed patrons to obtain what would to-day be considered the ordinary reward for his services, tells the whole story of English political life in that age. It is nothing less than a wonder that England achieved a great empire at that time, and mere ordinary retribution that she was now about to lose one : she was governing her empire by means of an exclusive social club whose chief occupation had nothing to do with government.

It was a bitter disappointment to Clive when he found that he only rated an Irish peerage, the gift of which had nothing at all to do with his services, but everything to do with Newcastle's desire to separate him from Pitt. He blamed it on his illness. " If health had not deserted me," he wrote his friend Carnac, " in all probability I had been an English peer instead of an Irish one, with the promise of a red riband. I know I could have bought the title (which is usual), but that I was above, and the honours I have obtained are free and voluntary. My wishes may hereafter be accomplished." But there again he miscalculated the realities of English politics. At a time when honours came as the reward of steady support of the government his friends were about to be ejected from office. Nevertheless, he dutifully thanked Newcastle as " its first cause and principal promoter," duly appeared at the meeting of Parliament in November to vote for Newcastle, and in December duly kissed the royal hand as Baron Clive of Plassey, County Clare, in the kingdom of Ireland.

Bitter irony attaches to this title. He, who must have wanted to be known as Clive of Styche in the county of Salop, had had to buy himself an Irish estate and rename it for the victory that only in his own mind was being celebrated. He never visited the estate. He remained at Styche the following summer, where he invited Orme to come to write his history and repair his health. The thought that his great victory was reduced to the level of a miserable Irish village must have been almost more than his pride and ambition could bear.

And now Newcastle's turn for dismissal had come. The age of " the Whigs in clover " had ended with a vengeance ! Lord Powis was doing his duty by his followers by harassing the Duke with requests on behalf of Clive and Walsh, the latter " a very sensible man, and not unworthy of your attention . . . who has your Grace's service very much at heart," and three days before the Duke left the Treasury he importuned him to help Edmund Maskelyne to a Commissionership of Taxes. Almost for the first time Newcastle had to plead inability. That was in May 1762. Now Bute was in power and employing Henry Fox to form a Court party to sustain him there and force the peace treaty that was being negotiated with France through the House.

Approaches were made to Clive with the tempting bait of more honours. Was he to desert Newcastle and Powis, who had been stripped even of their Lord Lieutenancies, and accept the bribe to go over to their ministry, as many prudent men were doing ? He had one friend in it, George Grenville, the Secretary of State. He wrote to Carnac in India that he had decided to stand aloof :

' Now that we are to have peace abroad, war is commencing at home amongst ourselves. There is to be a most violent contest at the meeting of Parliament, whether Bute or Newcastle is to govern this kingdom ; and the times are so critical that every member has an opportunity of fixing a price upon his services. I still continue to be one of those unfashionable kind of people who think very highly of independency, and to bless my stars, indulgent fortune has enabled me to act according to my conscience. Being very lately asked by authority, if I had any honours to ask from my sovereign, my answer was, that I thought it dishonourable to take advantage of the times ; but that when these parliamentary disputes were at an end, if his Majesty should then approve of my conduct by rewarding it, I should think myself highly honoured in receiving any marks of the royal favour."

The reply did him credit, but it was not the sort of reply that was expected or tolerated in those days when such independency was a luxury usually possible only for country squires who asked for nothing and had nothing to lose. Clive, as we shall soon see, was not quite as free as he thought to act according to his conscience.

The terms of the peace with France was the question that was agitating all minds. For the government it was to be a crucial test of strength. For Pitt it was to be the last chance to make his voice effective in national policy before the war that he had waged with so much success was ended. The forces of the opposition were united on this issue. But alas for Pitt's hopes ! Opposition to the government upon principle was almost unknown at that time. The scramble for honours, places, commissions, pensions, and preferments was too great. Ministers automatically had a majority as soon as they entered office. And with Fox wielding the whip they were as secure upon this occasion as upon any other. Only a few of the members were deeply concerned about the terms of peace. The fact that the terms were more favourable to France than the nation had a right to expect after the spate of victories and conquests influenced but few votes. Clive, however, was one of those few. He wanted a Carthaginian peace—at least so far as India was concerned.

The last stages of the struggle with the French in India had, as we have seen, been decidedly Carthaginian. The French paid severely for the orders they had given Lally, thus proving how double-edged a weapon ruthlessness in war can be. When Pondichéry surrendered to Coote on January 16, 1761, after a long and most gallantly sustained resistance, the English proceeded at once to its demolition. Dupleix's magnificent palace, fit home for the founder of an empire, was destroyed, the fortifications were blown up, even the houses of the inhabitants were pulled down and their materials carted away. The Punic war of English and French was over. It was just a little more than fifteen years since Dupleix had begun it by taking Madras. Few of history's dramas possess the completeness and perfection of

Y

form and design of this one : a clear-cut theme, a pregnant situation, a succession of vivid and arresting characters, a plot as filled with suspense and changing fortunes as any fiction writer could desire, a combination of comedy, farce, melodrama, and tragedy all rolled into one glorious whole, mounting here to the heights of heroism and sinking there to the depths of cowardice. And the final climax was worthy of the whole, the last-ditch resistance of the famished grenadiers of France when all hope of relief was gone. Even the elements co-operated to preserve the perfection of form : in the prologue there had been a cyclone that had destroyed La Bourdonnais's fleet, in the epilogue there was another that destroyed Admiral Stevens's fleet. The struggle had swayed back and forth just enough to keep the final outcome in doubt, but throughout it all the steady, unrelenting force of sea-power had been visible as the decisive factor that rendered all the efforts of the French on land unavailing. When that last storm came there was no French squadron in Indian waters to take advantage of the opportunity. The French surrendered sixteen days later.

And now the peace. Was it to be a peace according to Pitt's and Clive's ideas, or according to Bute's and Sulivan's ? Was it to be a peace of imperialism with the French excluded from India, or a peace of commerce with the French restored to their settlements ? Both Clive and Sulivan tried to influence the opposing statesmen.

Sulivan wrote to Pitt seven days after the news of Pondichéry's surrender reached London. He tried to demonstrate that the French had been " the authors of their own ruin " inasmuch as they had not rested satisfied with remaining a Mercantile Body, and that the English should heed the lesson and remain just that. M. Dupleix had avowed the false doctrine that no trading in the Deccan was profitable without the possession of countries and their revenues. Mr. Sulivan with his seventeenth-century ideas—and perhaps twentieth-century too—would have none of that doctrine : " If I could not clearly confute his reasoning I should wish our trade in India at an end." In Bengal the English had " a solid, extensive, and valuable commerce," which they should maintain intact as a monopoly. Let the French, therefore, be restored to their settlements in the south, but let them be excluded from Bengal.

Clive agreed with his rival on one point, that the French should be absolutely excluded from Bengal, but his satisfaction with the results of the war was much greater than Sulivan's. In a memorandum to Bute he rejoiced wholeheartedly that " we have accomplished for ourselves and against the French exactly everything that the French intended to accomplish for themselves and against us," and he wanted no concessions that would endanger that achievement in the slightest degree. If concessions had to be made, if the French had to be re-admitted to India, it should only be under the strictest conditions, preventing any chance of their making more trouble.

Neither got his way, but Bute, inclined to concessions, listened more to Sulivan than to Clive. In the peace treaty all her settlements as of the date 1749 were restored to France on condition that no fortifications or garrisons be maintained in Bengal and Muhammad Ali be recognized as the lawful Nawab of the Carnatic and Salabut Jang as lawful Subah of the Deccan. This latter was a particularly sore point with Clive, as he felt that the French should be given no voice in recognizing the titles of Indian princes for fear of giving them a pretext to interfere again in politics.

Clive voted with Pitt and the Newcastleites against the Government in the divisions on the Peace Preliminaries, December 9 and 10. The Government had large majorities, it was exultant, and it did not hesitate to punish those holding office from the Crown who had dared to vote against it. In the " massacre of the Pelhamite innocents " all the Newcastle placemen—and they were many—lost their places ; cries of anger and lamentation arose on every side ; the cruelty and barbarity of the act was unheard of ; his Grace the Duke of Newcastle was almost beside himself. But Clive having accepted nothing from the Crown except his title—and they could not take that away from him— had nothing to fear.

Or had he ? He may have been even now a little apprehensive. He may have realized that the disfavour of government might prove inconvenient even for him. For a contest between him and Sulivan for control of the East India Company was impending and in that struggle he would require all the assistance he could get.

IV

A sardonic grin must have appeared on Lawrence Sulivan's face when he heard about the Barony of Plassey. He must have thought there was such a thing as poetic justice. To think that the great Colonel Clive, after all his boasting and parade of achievement, had had to be content with a title taken not from his own country but from his, Sulivan's, despised land ! There had been something spurious about the victory of Plassey and it was only fitting that the title should be spurious too ; the one belonging of right to Providence, the other, unknown to cartographers, disguising a village better known to its own inhabitants as Ballykilty ! Yes, Mr. Sulivan may well have felt considerable malicious satisfaction.

As full details of Clive's transactions and proceedings trickled home Sulivan's autocratic spleen was thoroughly aroused. There had been that impudent attempt to prevent Coote from taking up his command in Bengal. Sulivan had already punished the signers of the Bengal letter by ordering their instant dismissal and return home.[141] He now wrote to Coote :

" The Behaviour of the then Bengall gentlemen to you being similar to their Treatment to their Masters, it puts an End to all reasoning, still your detention at Madrass verifies that reflection of Pope upon human Foresight ' Whatever is, is best,' & how much are we indebted to Providence, for this Disobedience to our orders. Your Country & your friend share the honour of your masterly & prosperous Conduct. General Lawrence has perused your Journal, he publickly applauds your Dispositions, and declares they were striking Proofs of great military abilities. Mr. Pitt, who you know was a Soldier by Profession, has done you high Honour in publishing his Sentiments, & with him you are a Tip-top favourite. The East India Company have a grateful sense of your Services ; Praises of such weight & Dignity must administer infinite Satisfaction to a good mind & I know you will enjoy them." [142] And again he wrote :

"Our People at Madrass we find are hot-headed, but they are able, generous and open—I can smother their Rebukes, but the ungrateful Wretches, late of Bengall, have hurt my Temper. Pray keep up a friendly correspondence with General Lawrence, he is great & good. I adore him for his distinguished & noble spirit—As I conclude you are now at Bengal, be well with Vansittart, I beg ; from his Character he is high in my Esteem, & from his virtue & abilitys I expect that lawless Settlement of Calcutta, will be reformed to Decency & Order—our military Expenses are amazingly large even beyond what we can possibly support for any time. Pray manifest your Regard to the Company in cutting off every [un]necessary charge, & do not let us be loaded with that cruel Article of Batta, when it can be avoided."

The first indications of a rift in the Company's ranks now appear. Clive characteristically was taking his own course, cutting a big figure in the world of politics, but the farther he went the farther behind he left his old associates. The references of Sulivan to Stringer Lawrence are significant ; it was about this time that in writing to Pitt he described Lawrence as " the greatest military officer that ever was in Asia." [143] There is no evidence that Clive kept up his old friendship with the General, other than giving him the annuity which, quite understandably, the old soldier was very reluctant to accept. Clive was to have his party; but Sulivan was to have his too, and not a few of Clive's former colleagues preferred to follow Sulivan.

The *jaghire* was what gave Sulivan most perplexity. He has been blamed for not immediately taking action against it. But Sulivan was too good a politician to precipitate an open breach with so dangerous an antagonist. He had his own position to consider and wanted to maintain a show of friendship with Lord Clive. " Need I say that it mortifies me when I cannot oblige you ? " he even wrote him on one occasion. Yet he had made one attempt to reach an amicable understanding. He and the Secret Committee of the Court decided to ask Clive if he would consent to surrender the *jaghire* to the Company after a certain length of time. But Clive was ill and could not see them. Writing in February 1762, he said he had heard nothing more of the proposal since. A certain grimness in his tone suggests that Mr. Sulivan would have received little satisfaction. [144] Yet at the same time Sulivan must have realized that in the *jaghire* he possessed security for his Lordship's good behaviour.

Clive's letters show that this last fact was only too true. He himself recognized that his hands were tied, that he had given the

341

Company a hostage. For his style of living made the *jaghire* a financial necessity to him. He was spending his money at a rare pace. He had already run through £60,000 and was warning his friends not to think of returning home without ample fortunes. They would need all the lakhs they could get to compete with him ! He had taken the royal and fashionable road to Bath in search of health, he had returned to the magnificence of Berkeley Square, he had spent big sums on the restoration of Styche, he had helped his family, he had bought Walcot, he had assisted his connections to get into Parliament, he now had to maintain the dignity of a peerage. Never could a man less afford to endanger the principal source of his income ! But he had to pay a price for such security. He had boasted of what he would do on behalf of his friends. He would obtain the reinstatement of the dismissed Councillors, he would obtain the army command for Forde. He would obtain these things or he would from that instant decline all further dealings with Directors and Indian affairs.

He obtained none of them. His voice was scarcely raised at all to get them. Instead, he wrote to Peter Amyatt, one of his chief friends and also one of Vansittart's chief opponents :

" Although I have such an interest at Court and in Parliament that I should not be afraid of an attack from the whole Court of Directors united, yet all my friends advise me I should do nothing to exasperate them, if they are silent as to my *jaghire*. Indeed, it is an object of such importance that I should be inexcusable if I did not make every other consideration give way to it ; and this is one of the reasons why I cannot join openly with the Bengal gentlemen in their resentment. It depends upon you, my friend, to make me a free man, by getting this grant confirmed from Delhi, and getting such acknowledgment from under the hands of the old Nabob, and the present Nabob, as may enable me to put all our enemies at defiance—In this I am sure you will be assisted by Vansittart."

He wrote similarly to his old friend Pybus at Madras :

" The Court of Directors seem to be much in the same situation as when you left England. Sulivan is the reigning director, and he follows the same plan of keeping everyone out of the direction who is endowed with more knowledge or would be likely to have more weight and influence than himself. This kind of political behaviour has exasperated most of the gentlemen who are lately come from India, particularly those from Bengal. They are surprised I do not join in their resentments ; and I should think it very surprising if I did, considering I have such an immense stake in India. My future power, my future grandeur, all depend upon receipt of the *jaghire* money. I should be a madman to set at defiance those who at present show no inclination to hurt me. I have so far fallen into their way of thinking as to preside at a general meeting of a club of East Indians once a fortnight ; and this has all the effect I could wish of keeping Sulivan in awe, and of convincing him that, though I do not mean to hurt him, I can do such a thing if he attempts to hurt me. Indeed, I am so strongly supported by the Government and by Parliament that I should not be afraid of an attack from the whole body united ; but there is no necessity of wantonly exciting them to attempts against my interests." [145]

These, surely, were the saddest letters that Clive ever wrote, and the most revealing. The complete frankness with which he lays bare the considerations that were preventing him from honouring his promises, nay, rather his obligations to his friends, shows no sensitiveness in regard to his position. Those friends had every cause to say that he was letting them down, that he had mortgaged his honour for that wretched *jaghire*. Those signers of that letter who had been so severely punished—surely they would not have signed it if they had not been assured by Clive of his protection ? The preservation of his *jaghire* had, indeed, become a supreme consideration that was to dictate most of his future actions. For its sake the proud and haughty Clive was ready to stoop.

Sulivan's term of office expired in April 1762 and he was not eligible for re-election for a year. In November of that year, a month before his vote on the Peace Preliminaries, Clive wrote to Vansittart :

"There is a terrible storm brewing against the next election. Sulivan, who is out of the direction this year, is strongly opposed by Rous and his party, and by part, if not all, of the East Indians (particularily the Bengalees), and matters are carried to such lengths, that either Sulivan or Rous must give way. . . . I must acknowledge that in my heart I am a well

343

wisher for the cause of Rous, although, considering the great stake I have in India, it is probable I shall remain neuter. Sulivan might have attached me to his interest if he had pleased, but he could never forgive the Bengal letter, and never has reposed that confidence in me which my services to the East India Company entitled me to. The consequence has been that we have all along behaved to one another like shy cocks, at times outwardly expressing great regard and friendship for one another."

Clive did not remain neuter. The prospect of Sulivan resuming the chairmanship was too unpleasant. On surveying the situation he must have come to the same conclusion that he had come to in Calcutta in April 1757, that offence is sometimes the best defence. "For my own part I am persuaded there can be neither peace nor security while such a monster reigns." Sulivan had taken Siraj-ud-daula's place in his mind.

Clive, we are told, would have been quite ready to make a Pitt-Newcastle arrangement with Sulivan. Who can doubt it? He would have liked nothing better than to have been accepted as the Company's master-mind and statesman. But if he seriously thought that Sulivan would admit to his own inferiority in that sphere and make way for him, he was making a great mistake. Sulivan would have laughed at such a notion. He needed no assistance, he would have said, from his Lordship, whose services while in employment, no matter how distinguished, gave him no right to think that just because of them he could step straight into the Chairman's shoes.

Nor does the common idea that Sulivan actually was unequal to his responsibility seem justified. The belief in his mismanagement of the Company's affairs has sprung directly from Clive, who industriously propagated it for election purposes. The facts indicate, to the contrary, that Sulivan was maintaining the Company's traditional policies ably and intelligently and in so doing was serving the best interests of its shareholders. He had set as the limits of English policy in Bengal the security of their present possessions and privileges, the preservation of peace, maintenance of the Nawab, and prevention of border raids. He was giving steady support to Vansittart, while not entirely happy about the latter's deposition of Mir Jafar, and evincing a commendable desire to be just both to the Nawab and to the Company's servants. When the crisis came he was the first to see the necessity of strengthening the Governor's hands by giving him the power to override his council.[1]

The truth simply was that there was no room in the Company for both Clive and Sulivan.

[1] Clive's case against Sulivan is hardly improved by his condemnation of that very necessary measure, which would have seemed altogether right and proper if he had been in Vansittart's place at the time. Clive was, moreover, to demand insistently that power for himself as soon as he was re-appointed Governor.

Chapter Twenty-two

THE BATTLE OF INDIA HOUSE

"A combination of ungrateful Directors"

CLIVE

I

THE STRUGGLE BETWEEN CLIVE AND SULIVAN for control of the East India Company was not merely a clash between two powerful, ambitious, mutually antagonistic personalities, each playing for his own hand, with nothing more at stake than the personal victory or defeat of either. It was a conflict between land and trade. Each man was representative of his class, and the classes as well as the men were clashing. The very existence of the East India Company as a mercantile concern was at stake. Land, with Clive as its champion, was attempting to take over India from trade, with Sulivan as its champion. It was, therefore, a conflict of the greatest importance for both Britain and India.

For in order that empire should take the place of trade it was first necessary that the landed classes should displace the mercantile in control of the Company. This process was now about to begin. The defeat of Sulivan paved the way for the Regulating Act. We have reached, in fact, the great divide in the history of Britain's relations with India. If we look backwards we see the land of trade dominated by a few high peaks—Sir Thomas Roe, Sir Josiah Child, Gerald Aungier, Thomas Pitt, Job Charnock. But before us lies the land of empire, with the towering peak of Warren Hastings dominating the whole immediate horizon. Projecting from the ridge of the water-shed are the twin peaks of Sulivan and Clive, sharing the same area of time, but each on opposite sides of the divide and representing mutually repugnant, contrary forces.

There was no such gap in England between land and trade as there was on the continent of Europe, yet there was a clear line of division. To be a gentleman in England was not a matter of heredity, nor did it require that one's hands had not been soiled

346

by trade. " Trade," said Defoe, " is so far here from being in-consistent with a gentleman, that in short trade in England makes gentlemen, and has peopled this nation with gentlemen." The line of division is clearly implied : in order to become a gentle-man you had to give up trade and become a landowner. And the paradoxical thing was that, although trade was recognized to be the great concern of the nation, none but gentlemen had any real weight in the government of the country. Land ruled, though it was trade that controlled the national destinies. The cities of Westminster and London were in close liaison, Pitt the statesman was in constant touch with Sulivan the merchant, yet they remained separate spheres, and each jealously guarded its sphere as a preserve for its own class.

The merchants as a class were as distrustful of the gentry as a class as the gentry were regardful of their own superior status. At its formation the East India Company had passed a resolution " not to employ any gentlemen in any place of charge," and had requested to be " allowed to sort their business with men of their own quality, lest the suspicion of the employment of gentlemen being taken hold upon by the generality, do drive a great number of the adventurers to withdraw their contributions." " There was suspicion of aristocratic disinterestedness and ability alike ; and, although members of the nobility adventured capital in the Company, the influx from what used to be considered the higher classes did not become considerable until Wellesley's time." [146]

This prejudice, dating from the Company's foundation, had continued. It did not operate against younger sons of the country gentry, because, not owning lands and having no prospect of inheriting any, they were not classed as members of the aristocracy. Nor for the same reason did the younger sons lose caste by being in trade or entering the professions. There was nothing else the poor fellows could do ! Yet they seldom became true members of the class to which they allied them-selves. Their ambition was usually to make enough money to become gentlemen in their own right. The merchants and bankers of the city for their own part held aloof from such pseudo-traders and were careful to retain control of their own affairs. They might have parliamentary ambitions, but their real power was of a more substantial kind : they loaned the government money. The last thing they wanted to see was any of their employees who had ambitions of becoming gentlemen, let alone noblemen, coming home, mixing in their affairs, and telling them how to run their business. It had never happened, it had been a practical impossibility, and there would have been no danger of its happening now if the Company had remained a purely trading enterprise. But war and politics were matters that gentlemen understood better than merchants ; at least, these were their natural spheres. And Clive certainly felt he knew infinitely more about them than Sulivan, and there were not a few gentlemen among the shareholders who agreed with him.

The bulwarks of the Company had been seriously weakened by recent events. The French war had diminished its independence by rendering it dependent upon the Crown for military and naval assistance. The claim that this had given the Crown upon the Company had been voiced in Parliament ; it had also led to heated discussions as to which had contributed most to the British success, the Crown's forces or the Company's. Clive's suggestion to Pitt had not fallen on entirely unfertile ground. It had started an idea working. And it was easy to predict that if the Company did acquire the revenues, the payers of land tax in Parliament would have something to say about it. [147]

Yet the merchants and bankers represented by Sulivan were still in a strong position. They had their charter and it still had twenty years to run. Pitt had looked into the matter whether the Company's acquisitions belonged to them or to the Crown, and the Judges had said they belonged to the former. Pitt had himself obtained for the Company the right to all the plunder obtained from the Moors and the right to cede, restore, or dispose of conquered territories. So long as the Company did not become an actual territorial power it was safe for awhile, except from the danger of someone working to capture it from within. And its constitution made that difficult, though, as Clive was to show, not impossible.

There were two courts. The Court of Proprietors elected the Court of Directors, composed of twenty-four members, adjusted the annual dividend rate, and enacted laws and regulations. But the Court of Proprietors did not include all the shareholders, but only such as possessed £500 of stock ; nor was the Court of Directors open to any Proprietor, but only such as possessed £2000 of stock. Thus control was effectually preserved in the hands of an oligarchy of the moneyed interests of the City. And hitherto all the business had been transacted very quietly, with a minimum of debate and public attention. If the aristocracy attended the quarterly meetings, it was as shareholders with an interest in the dividend rate, not as potential directors. In what way do the annual meetings of big companies differ to-day? Clive was the first nobleman to attempt to scale these walls.

The Company's fate—and Sulivan's—had really been settled on the battlefield of Plassey. The failure of Vansittart's attempt at non-intervention was at this moment sealing it. Very soon now they would have to accept the fact that supreme power in one Indian kingdom (actually in two, the Carnatic being the other one) was theirs. And it is difficult to see what Sulivan, even if he had won his personal fight, could have done to break the chain of circumstances that linked the Company to its fate. By preventing Clive from acquiring the *dewani* of Bengal, that final fatal step, he could certainly have postponed the day when the landed lords and squires of Parliament would intervene. But it seems unlikely that he could have done the one thing that could have definitely changed the course of events, that is, given back to Bengal the government that Clive had shattered. Sulivan was trying to put back the clock; in maintaining his belief that trade was more to be desired than empire, he was fighting a losing cause. Clive made empire seem attractive to his own class, and it was a short step from that to the exercise of parliamentary authority followed by the assumption of real responsibility. By his activities at home, as much as by his military and political successes in India, he is fully entitled to be regarded as the founder of the British Empire in India.

II

So Clive when he set out to dethrone Sulivan was attempting something very similar to what he had accomplished against Siraj-ud-daula—a revolution. His strategy and tactics too were strikingly similar. He was turning defence into offence, as he had so often done as a soldier. His enemy was in overwhelming strength, so he had to bore from within. Faction within the Company gave him his chance. He would use Mr. Rous as he had used Mir Jafar. He would create a small disciplined army of voters of his own, throw it into the election on the side of Mr. Rous, and emerge from the battle the real victor, once more a king-maker, the power behind Mr. Rous's throne. If he

349

failed . . . but Clive was ever a gambler; all his life he had played for high stakes, and he had never yet lost. It was no greater gamble than the one of June 1757. His *jaghire* might be at stake, but far more had been at stake then.

He had the materials of a small force already collected in the discontented ex-servants of the Company, particularly the Bengalers, who had been wanting him to take their part. But he needed far more. His soldier's eye enabled him to see how he could get them. He saw the weak spot in the enemy's position. His own chief strength lay in his wealth. He could use it now with great effect.

The Company's constitution, so well designed for oligarchical control, had a defect of the kind that lawyers make their practice by discovering. In a twisted sort of way, one man, one vote was a principle of that constitution. That is to say, no proprietor had more than one vote whether he possessed the requisite £500 of stock or ten times that amount, but there was nothing to prevent him from creating more "proprietors" by temporarily transferring to them his surplus holdings in £500 lots, and this could be legally done by collusion between the parties at election time quite as easily as if it had involved a genuine transfer of property. The practice was called vote-splitting, and when the election was over the partitioned stock was, if the parties were honest—and there was often the rub !—transferred back to its original owner. No doubt the discovery of this simple loophole for corruption dates far back in the Company's history, and no doubt Sulivan and all the Company's politicians had consistently made use of it in their annual campaigns; but they were now to encounter a man who could and did turn a small hole into a gap so wide that nothing could stay the flood. The agitation to have it closed arose after the world had seen the spectacular use to which Clive had put it.

Clive made deadly use of it. He bought up £100,000 of stock, all presumably that he could, for it was not easy to obtain, the total stock of the Company amounting only to £3,200,000. He then proceeded to create for himself 200 votes, and these became the prætorian guard of the army that he led on to the field as the ally of Mr. Rous. Two hundred among opposing factions numbering in all some 5000 or 6000 *might* turn the day.

"Splitting" on such a large scale involved a great deal of staff work. It required an elaborate organization operated by syndicates of bankers and jobbers. Clive created his organization. As staff he had his brother Richard, his ever-useful former secretary, now his principal agent, John Walsh, and Luke Scrafton. He also utilized the services of two banking firms, Cliffe, Walpole and Clarke, and the Goslings, into whose partnership cousin George, M.P., was shortly introduced.[148]

The election was held every year between March 25 and April 25. As it approached Clive felt confidence in his strength. His parliamentary connections were proving valuable. Newcastle and Rockingham were daily bringing him fresh adherents. The quarterly meeting of the General Court gave him by a show of hands a comfortable majority. " Our cause gains ground daily," he wrote Vansittart on March 19 ; " I should think we shall be stronger at the election than we were at the General Court. However, this time only can show, and I do not choose to be very sanguine, our opponents being very active."

He knew exactly to what use he would put his victory. He was a candidate for the direction, but he would not accept the chairmanship. That was for Mr. Rous. " I have neither application, knowledge, nor time to undertake so laborious an employ ; I shall confine myself to the political and military operations." The confession completes the parallel with 1757. He never did have the application, knowledge, or time for any kind of administrative drudgery. He might acquire an empire, but someone else would have to administer it. And the first use to which he would put his power was likewise typical. He promised Vansittart he would send out " a very large military force." Mr. Rous's role as " Mir Jafar " would no doubt extend to providing ways and means of paying for it ! Here, fully revealed, is the pattern of Clive's mind and career. He was not the builder or financier of empire, but *par excellence* its acquirer.

His opponents were, as he said, very active. They had, indeed, been in a frenzy of activity. Clive's enlistment of Newcastle's aid was, perhaps, a blunder. Newcastle wrote Clive to express his pleasure at seeing " that by this list we have so great a majority, which the Duke of Newcastle hopes will increase . . . nothing has been or shall be wanting on his part." [149] It was at an open invitation to the Government to throw in its strength on the opposite side. Sulivan was too good a politician himself to miss such a chance. His political connections at the moment were on the government side with Lord Shelburne, a follower of

Bute, his chief backer.   The Government had not forgiven Clive
for his votes against it.   So before election day Fox stepped
forward and dispensed Government funds—as paymaster he
always had large sums in his keeping—as freely as Clive had used
his own.   The balance of bought votes was tilted back against
him.   And Sulivan and his list of candidates carried the day.
Lord Clive was 81 lower than the lowest in Sulivan's list and the
highest in Clive's list was 20 below the lowest in Sulivan's.

"Lord Clive," reported Mr. West to his Grace, "must have
been strangely misled in his calculations."   "We have been
cheated out of the election by the clerks of the India House" was
the cry of the defeated party, but crafty Mr. Sulivan knew better.

III

It was the first real defeat of his career.   So strange an
experience was it that he was quite unable to see the justice of his
being made to pay any penalty for it, still less the penalty of the
loss of his *jaghire*.   And this inability has been most loyally
shared by his champions, to whom the subsequent action of
Sulivan has been attributed to the meanest spite and the basest
ingratitude.

Immediately after the election the re-Sulivanized Court
ordered Governor Vansittart to pay no more rent to Lord Clive's
attorneys and to credit the sums to the Company's account
instead.   "His Lordship's pretensions to the said Jagueer will be
settled here."

Clive replied by instructing Carnac and Amyatt—in view of the
circumstances he relieved Vansittart of the embarrassing position
of acting for him and the Company at the same time—to bring an
immediate action against the Governor and Council should they
obey the orders of the Court, and by writing the Governor and
Council forbidding them to comply with the orders at their peril.
This he termed "an act of necessity in order to save my
undoubted property from the worst of enemies—a combination
of ungrateful Directors."

Base ingratitude !   That was to be the war-cry.   Attacks upon
him had been appearing in the public press.   If he had triumphed
he could have ignored them.   "Conscious to myself that every
part of my conduct in the great share I had in the management of
the Company's affairs would bear the most rigid scrutiny, and

the more known be the more approved, I held them in too much contempt to merit any answer." But now he had to condescend to answer them, or such part of them as he considered worthy of a reply.

First as to the late contest and his part in it :

"As to myself, I can with truth affirm that the principal motive that induced me to offer myself a candidate for the India Direction, was the interest of the East India Company ; and my reasons for espousing the cause of Mr. Rous arose from a conviction of his integrity. Contrary to my expectations, my opponents, the very men who had concurred in giving me the most public testimonies of their sense of my services, were men that opposed my coming into the Direction. Better versed in such business than myself, they prevailed in this dispute, and every species of calumny was made use of that malice could invent. . . ."

One of the charges against him was that he had withheld information from the Direction regarding his presents from Mir Jafar. Eloquently now he defended his candour in this matter— yet unaccountably, forgot here, as before, to state their amount ! (About the *jaghire* there had been, of course, and could be, no secrecy.) The Nawab, he said, had offered him a fortune ; he had earned it, and its acceptance was not contrary to the interests of the Company.

"What injustice was this to the Company ? They could expect no more than what was stipulated in the treaty. Or what injunction was I under to refuse a present from him who had the power to make me one as the reward of honourable services ? I know of none. I had surely myself a particular claim, by having devoted myself to the Company's military service and neglected all commercial advantages. What reason, then, can be given or what pretence could the Company have to expect that I, after having risked my life so often in their service, should deny myself the only honourable opportunity that ever offered of acquiring a fortune, without prejudice to them, who, it is evident, would not have had more for my having less. When the Company had acquired a million and a half sterling and a revenue of near £100,000 per annum from the success of their forces under my command ;

when ample restoration had been made to those whose fortunes suffered by the calamity of Calcutta ; and when individuals had, in consequence of that success, acquired large estates ; what would the world have said had I come home and rested upon the generosity of the Court of Directors ? "

He also professed especial satisfaction that he was made lord of the Company's lands, " because the Company was thereby freed from all dependence on the Government." (The Company did not share his satisfaction. It provoked too acutely the question, should a servant be the lord of his master ? The rest of his defence provoked the question, can a man serve two masters ?) He went on to survey the whole course of events in India—managing to dispose of the defeat of the French without mentioning Eyre Coote!—and wound up with an appeal to the Court of Directors to declare " whether they think without the battle of Plassey, and its consequences, the East India Company would have been at this time existing."[150]

Mir Jafar, it will be remembered, had been ungrateful for what Clive had done for him. The English nation had been ungrateful. The Directors now were similarly ungrateful. Verily, Clive must have felt, it was an ungrateful world! Only his family and dependants had given him that splendid feeling of coming nearer to the gods that men get when they bestow prosperity upon their fellow-creatures. " What would the world have said, had I come home and rested upon the generosity of the present Court of Directors ? " The world would probably have agreed with his own opinion of such folly. Had not Stringer Lawrence received from them only a beggarly pension of £500, a sum so paltry in Clive's eyes as to be unworthy of notice ? His own deserts being so infinitely greater and not being of a trusting nature, he had taken no chances, but had attended to the matter of his reward himself. And now these base Directors were trying to deprive him of it ! Had such injustice and ingratitude ever been known ?

It was a desperately serious matter for him, and he moved heaven and earth to regain possession of his property. That is to say, he moved law and politics. It was an easy matter for him to obtain legal opinion in his favour. The Directors based their case on a ridiculously inadequate technicality—that the grant had not been confirmed by the Great Mogul, and that, therefore, the

Mogul might hold the Company to account. Quoth the lawyers : if the Nawab of Bengal had not of himself the power or right to make the grant to Clive, neither had he then to make the grant to the Company ; both employer and employee held by the same title and to impeach the one was to impeach the other—which was perfect logic. Armed with these opinions from the law officers of the Crown, Clive filed a bill against the Company in Chancery. But the mills of the law ground slowly ; it was probable that Chancery would find it necessary to send a fact-finding commission out to Bengal, and Clive was in a hurry. So he appealed to the personal powers to intervene more directly in his behalf. It was, after all, for this kind of emergency that one formed political friendships.

Clive's were most comprehensive : he was careful not to put all his eggs of friendship in one basket. So his Whig friends heard from him, Lord Hardwicke, Lord Powis, the Dukes of Newcastle and Devonshire. Mr. Pitt heard from him. And so did their opponent George Grenville, the King's new minister.

As Mr. Grenville relieved Bute at the head of the Government immediately after Clive's defeat, it was natural that Clive should have hoped more from his efforts than from all the other's. But the political situation was distinctly uncertain during the summer of that year. Negotiations were going on behind the scenes with Newcastle and Pitt, and for one moment it appeared likely that all of Clive's political connections were about to form a government together. A Pitt-Newcastle-Grenville Administration would surely have ended all his troubles ! But the hope died, and by the autumn, when the Bedford group joined the government instead, Clive found himself compelled to choose between pinning his hopes on ministers and continuing his support of his old associates in opposition. It is not surprising to discover that he chose the former.

The essential thing was that Mr. Grenville should act as mediator between him and the Court of Directors. Mr. Sulivan had been prepared to offer him a compromise two years earlier. It was a compromise that he now wanted with an anxiety that was becoming painful. On November 7 he sent Grenville the terms on which he was ready to surrender the *jaghire* to the Company : that he or his heirs should receive the amount of it annually for ten or twelve years. " If these conditions are fulfilled, I do promise you, Sir, that I never will give any opposition to the present, or any other Court of Directors, and never will interfere in any of their affairs directly or indirectly"—a statement which is considerably at variance with the way he represented his interference in Company affairs to the public.[151] A week later he called on Lord Powis, who was still acting as broker for "the Shropshire gang," said that he was supporting the government against Wilkes, whose *North Britain No.* 45 had raised such a pother all that summer, would like a stop put to the contest at Bishop's Castle, would also like an English peerage, and in exchange would promise the government steady support.[152] But it appears from what he wrote Grenville that the *jaghire* would be quite sufficient exchange :

"Discountenanced and hated by the party I have abandoned as much as I was before respected and esteemed, if I should, through the obstinate injustice of the Directors (notwithstanding your powerful mediation) be disappointed I must confess to you, Sir, that I have so much sensibility inherent in my nature, that my mind will be too much affected to recover so severe a shock for some time ; but be the event what it will, I have taken my part, and you may be assured that my poor services, such as they are, shall be dedicated for the rest of my days to the King, and my obligations to you always acknowledged, whether in or out of power."

Independence had been nice, but it was no longer practical politics for him. He declared his willingness to give up the point respecting his heirs, but he indicated that if the Directors refused his offer altogether he was quite prepared to campaign against them once more.[153]

Nothing had been settled when the quarterly General Court met on December 21 : "All that I could learn was a determined resolution in the Court of Directors to distress me as much as possible." The Court had obtained a favourable opinion for their case from Edward Thurlow, a rising K.C. In his distress Clive was contemplating seeking redress from Parliament. He consulted Pitt, who advised against it.[154]

When the Court of Directors unanimously rejected his offer, he must have come nearer to despair than at any time since his unhappy youth. The whole magnificent position he had built up for himself with such pains collapsed at once without the money to sustain it. Loss of honour and power, ridicule, even bankruptcy loomed before him. His high-tensioned nervous system quivered under the shock. What if his suit, too, were to fail ?

But salvation even then was on its way. Clive's good fortune had not entirely deserted him. India once more came to his rescue.

IV

The news that the *Lapwing* brought on February 4, of the outbreak of war with Mir Kasim, climaxed the succession of alarming reports that had recently been received from Bengal. The disputes of Vansittart and his council had already focused attention. They represented a definite cleavage of opinion in India, and that cleavage was duplicated at home. Sulivan, agreeing with Vansittart's policy, had laid all his emphasis on supporting the Governor's authority and had already chastized insubordination by ordering the dismissal of Amyatt, Ellis, and Carnac.

Clive was in a more difficult position. Both sides having originally been equally his friends, he had not wished at first to take a definite part against either. But Vansittart's and Hastings's folly now appeared to him much more glaring than the undeniable misconduct of Amyatt, Ellis, and their faction. He did not approve of the Council's insistence on carrying on the inland trade free of duty, but he most emphatically disapproved of Vansittart's policy of non-intervention. So his attitude to both sides was determined accordingly : the hard pedal against Vansittart and Hastings, the soft pedal against the rest of the Council. Whatever he might think of the latter, all the world soon came to recognize in him a pronounced enemy of the former. And, as usual with him, he could place no restraint on his feelings. Even such a trifle as Vansittart adopting, as though it were his own, his idea of sending home an elephant for presentation to his Majesty was enough to draw from him a taunting reply.

The news that Amyatt had been murdered at the head of a British mission to the Court, that Ellis had failed to gain possession of the city of Patna, and that the very existence of the Company in Bengal was once more at stake flung the nervous shareholders of the Company into a panic and caused a break in the stocks. Horror followed quick upon fear when they heard of the slaughter in cold blood of 170 prisoners at Patna. The logic of the situation

357

seemed to call once more for Clive to go and perform the same feat as he had performed in 1757.

A special General Court was called on February 27 to consider the situation. At another special Court two weeks later it was resolved to request Clive to accept the presidency of Bengal and the command of the Company's forces there.

Clive with his own victory now within his grasp seized the chance to make sure of it by making it the price of his services. " If the Court of Directors," he replied, " were as well disposed towards him as he was towards them, he should have no objection to the service ; but till he found such a disposition, he desired to be excused from coming to any resolution."

It was a suggestion to the Company to dismiss its Directors. The Directors saw the danger and tried to forestall it by unanimously assuring him of their cheerful concurrence in the resolution and their desire to put it into full effect. But Clive was not to be diverted so easily. The next election was almost due and he was determined on Sulivan's overthrow. He returned a curt non-committal reply, and when the next General Court asked him if he would accept their offer he replied that he would give his answer after the election.

The Directors then tried the manœuvre of getting the offer annulled. A motion to that effect was heatedly debated, but finally rejected. Clive, confident now of victory, came out into the open and said that he could not accept the service if the Deputy Chairman, Mr. Sulivan, remained in the lead of the Direction. He asked that he be allowed to give his final decision in a few days. Sulivan professed a desire for a reconciliation and the Court urged this course on Clive. On March 28 he sent to the Court the following letter :

" Gentlemen,—It was agreed at the last General Court of Proprietors, that I should have a few days to consider and determine concerning the terms upon which I would accept of the request of the preceding Court of Proprietors, to take upon me the direction of their affairs in Bengal.

" Although I thought I had sufficiently explained myself on that head at the time the Proposal was made, yet, as there seemed to be a disposition in many gentlemen of the Court for whom I have the highest respect, that a reconciliation should take place between Mr. Sulivan and me, so that this gentleman might still conduct the affairs at home, and that I might never-theless venture, without fear of my reputation, abroad, I thought the respect which was due to those Proprietors, the duty I owe to myself, and the regard I shall ever feel for the interest of the Company, all called upon me, in the strongest manner, once more to revolve in my mind the possibility of such an union, consistent with the services I would endeavour to render the Company, and consistent with that attention which is due to my own honour.

" This I have endeavoured to do in the coolest and most dispassionate manner, after laying aside every prejudice, and judging only from the constant experience of things.

" Upon the whole, I still continue to be of opinion, that, in case the Proprietors think it for their advantage that Mr. Sulivan should remain at the head of the Direction (or, as he pleased to term it himself, should continue him in the lead of their affairs), I cannot accept their service : but in case the Proprietors should not think it necessary to continue Mr. Sulivan in such authority I am willing and ready to accept their service, even supposing the next advices should pronounce their affairs in Bengal to be in as desperate a condition as ever they were in the time of Suraja Dowla.

" Should a Direction be settled with whom I can possibly co-operate, everything will be easily adjusted, since I have no interested views in going abroad.

" At the same time, I never desired, or even wished, to name a Direction, as some industriously spread abroad ; I only object to one man having the lead in the Company's affairs, in whom I have so often and publicly declared I never can place any confidence, and who, in my opinion, has acted, and does continue to act upon principles diametrically opposite to the true interest of the East India Company.

" I have the honour to be, with great respect, gentlemen, your most obedient humble servant,

" CLIVE.

" Berkeley Square,
   " March 28th, 1764." [155]

The letter speaks eloquently of Clive's renewed sense of power. The hour of victory over Sulivan was at last about to strike.

The election campaign was now in full swing. Sulivan no

longer had the powerful assistance of ministers to help him ward off the furious assault of his enemy. His opponents, the party of Rous, represented him now as the prime cause of the present discontents and distresses of the Company. They built their campaign around his autocratic methods and his enmity to Clive. They not only capitalized Clive's prestige to the utmost, but they set forth his personal grievances as compelling reasons why Sulivan should be deposed if the Company was to be saved. And with the Proprietors in their panicky state of mind calling for Clive, the argument was most effective. Yet it was just as well that they did not know that Clive had actually proposed airing the Company's affairs in Parliament—the one thing the Company did not want—even to suggesting the need for an enquiry ! If Sulivan had known *that*, he could have saved the election.[156]

As it was, he was only beaten by the narrowest possible margin. When the result was declared on April 12 there was found to be a tie with twelve places on the Court to each party. But on the following day the General Court broke the tie by awarding the all-important chairs to Mr. Rous and his follower Mr. Boulton.

Sulivan was beaten. But it was in no real sense a victory for Clive. He had been the stick with which the beating had been administered and he might now go to India with some feeling of assurance. But the question still had to be settled—on whose terms, his or the Company's ? It was extremely mortifying to him to find that the new Court of Directors was little more amenable to his wishes than the old. He found himself, indeed, involved in one of the hardest pieces of bargaining of his life, and the most disagreeable.

Unfortunately the records do not give us the whole story. But they give enough to enable us to follow the main thread. A contest developed between two evenly matched desires, the desire to have Clive go to India and the desire not to give him back his *jaghire*.

At first matters seem to have proceeded smoothly, with the main issue kept in the background. Two weeks after the election Clive wrote the Court a letter stating the views on public policy that he had already discussed with them. He stressed the divergence between his ideas and Vansittart's, so wide that " either the one or the other must have been totally wrong," and indicated his intention of ending the Nawab's independence. In order to stop further disputes with the government he urged the absolute prohibition of the trade in salt, beetle, and tobacco. To restore discipline in the service restrictions must be placed on the junior servants' trading privileges, so that fortunes could not be acquired too quickly, and he declared his intention not to engage in trade himself. Sulivan's nomination of Mr. Spencer of the Bombay Council to succeed Vansittart should be cancelled as certain to cause the same dissatisfaction as Vansittart's appointment had caused and lead to resignations. Then, in order to bait the hook, he emphasized that he could have no interested views in going abroad :

"I do not mean to reflect on those who thought proper to reward and distinguish Mr. Vansittart so remarkably by adding to the usual allowances of the Governor two and a half per cent. upon the Company's territorial possessions, which made the whole of his appointments more than £20,000 a year. I shall only say, I think such appointments too great a burthen on the Company's estate ; and leave it to you, gentlemen, to make me whatever allowance you may think consistent with my station."

Then, and not till then, did he bring up the matter of his *jaghire*. There would, he pointed out, be a very great impropriety in his going abroad in the Company's service while a lawsuit was pending between them, so he made his proposal that he should be allowed to enjoy it for ten years, provided he lived so long, and that on his arrival in India he should use his utmost endeavours with the Nawab to secure the reversion of it to the Company. He suggested, but without insisting upon it, that it might be continued to his heirs for five years. This was substantially the compromise that Mr. Grenville had tried in vain to negotiate with the previous Court of Directors.[157]

It was a clever letter and showed his ability to adapt his tone to the needs of the case. The gravity of the matter that had to be settled forced him to discard any hint of arrogance and employ all the finesse of which he was capable. The suggestion that the Company would save money by appointing him was shrewd. But the result was disappointing. The Directors summoned him and on April 30 swore him in as Governor and Commander-in-Chief of Fort William. They do not appear, however, to have accepted his proposal regarding his *jaghire*, or, at least, that was something that still had to be confirmed by the Proprietors. And apparently it was still so much in doubt that Clive again needed the advice and assistance of Mr. Grenville.

His alliance with the King's chief minister had just brought him the promised Order of the Bath, but only after Mr. Grenville had dared the shrill anger of the Duke of Bedford, who had wanted the vacancy for Colonel Drapier. Clive was invested with the red riband on April 25.[158]

There was to be a meeting of the General Court a week later, and the day before it Mr. Jenkinson reported to the minister that he had solicited such of their friends who were proprietors of the Company "in the manner you have desired, and I have acquainted Lord Clive of the directions you have given in this respect. I have tried to see his Lordship, that I might mention to him the advice you give him, that he should take no definitive step but in concert with his friends. I have not yet been able to see him, and I think it more prudent not to write it, lest it should be supposed to imply more than was intended."[159] News had just come of a military set-back in India. "Lord Clive's friends think that this event makes Lord Clive's presence more necessary in India." Clearly Clive was not yet out of his troubles.[160]

Now it was that Sulivan was able to take the first instalment of his revenge ! When the Court met, Clive discovered, to his intense disgust, that it required a stronger inducement before it would yield, and apparently it was Sulivan who suggested the nature of it. Clive was compelled to offer a resolution that new covenants should be entered into by all the Company's servants, civil and military, binding them not to receive gifts, presents, or rewards in India over the amount of Rs. 4000 without the Company's permission. When the resolution was accepted, only then and not before was another passed granting him his *jaghire* on the terms he had proposed.

That Sulivan had a hand in this transaction might be guessed from the situation itself. But Clive himself supplies the corroborative evidence in a recently discovered letter. Writing to Mr. Spencer on May 20 in an effort to soften the blow of his removal, he said that the new covenants had been brought about *at Mr. Sulivan's instigation.*[161]

The statement is most important. For see what a neat revenge Sulivan had taken ! What a price he had compelled Clive to pay for his victory—almost the price of his own honour ! He had compelled him to be the one who with his own hand and seemingly by his own volition would cut down the very ladder by which he had mounted to his eminence of wealth and power, cut it down not for himself only but for all who wished to follow in his footsteps, and that meant for everyone in the service ! Could he have been forced into a more humiliating, embarrassing, or odious position ?

That he should have accepted it at all is evidence enough of the straits to which he was reduced. There was apparently no sacrifice he was not prepared to make. Having to go back to India, to Bengal, which he detested so much, would have been sacrifice enough. He had not a single desire to see the country again, it never having been to him more than a means to an end. All his plans, all his hopes, all his interests, all his sources of happiness were now centred in England. He would have to leave behind his wife, who was expecting another child, and his family. He would have to subject himself again to the perils of the Bengal climate and the risks of the sea. He would have to wear himself out in a hateful job that promised to be much more distasteful and onerous than it had been before—a job that no one would think of taking if it were not for the inducement of financial gain. He must have cried out with bitter anguish that he had *finished* with Bengal and wanted nothing more than to be left alone to enjoy his hard-earned rewards. God knows he did not want to make any more money ; he merely wanted to be suffered to keep what he had !

At that moment he must have hated the Company, Directors, shareholders, servants, all, with the bitterest hate of which he was capable.

Or was he not quite so sensitive to the invidiousness of his position ? Did he hate the going more than the terms of it ? There may be a document hidden away somewhere in family archives that gives the answer, but if so it has not been given to the world. We can only judge by his behaviour, and that affords no certain clue. He was to wrap the real springs of action in masses of words that bear little or no relation to these deep realities. He was to lay down such a smoke-screen of accusation and self-vindication as to conceal entirely the one vital issue that divided him from the whole body of Company's servants. He was to wrap himself in a cloak of disinterestedness and virtue and

363

to cling so desperately to its protecting folds that none could thereafter quite succeed in stripping it away from him. He was to do all that he could, though perhaps not quite enough, to turn the accusing finger away from him, and not only away from him but at others. He was, in other words, to act as a desperate man who needed to use all his wits to prevent the truth from being known. And in order to prevent it from being known, he had to render such fresh and striking services to the Company and the nation as would silence the tongues of his enemies, or at least make their accusations of no avail. He had, as he put it, to redeem his honour and vindicate his reputation from the aspersions that were being so freely cast upon it.

And, after all, were not his honour and fortune doubly at stake ? Not only because of what an ungrateful Company was compelling him to do, but because if the Company lost its hold on Bengal and its possessions there—and it was the fear of that that had caused the clamour for his appointment—his *jaghire* would be gone too, whether the Company gave it back to him or not. His title would be meaningless, a mockery of delusory achievement. The very foundations of his grandeur would be destroyed. And he would be left a butt for ridicule and a target for every gibe of his enemies, for every charge or slander that malice could bring against him. Baron Clive of Plassey in the Kingdom of Ireland—a very barren barony Sulivan would sneer ! For Sulivan was already telling the world that it was all the fault of Clive that the Company's affairs were so desperate. Look, he was saying, what happens when a trading company makes the blunder of acquiring territory ! There is no end to the wars it has to fight and the armies it has to maintain and the calamities that come upon it. The unprofitableness of Plassey was one lie that Clive had to scotch, if he did nothing else. Another was that he was incapable of disinterested public service. He made it a point when he reached India to ram both of them down the throats of his enemies.

The Directors' attitude in these negotiations and the outcome of them must have been entirely cynical and wholly concerned with their own interests as employers. They had become increasingly aware of how hurtful to those interests was the practice of receiving presents now that so much of their revenues came from the Nawab's treasury. They had come to realize through Vansittart's revelations that the situation was that of two persons, themselves and their servants, drawing from the same well, and a well that experience had already shown was not inexhaustible. They were no doubt delighted that Clive had offered to go and put a stop to this practice ; that he was really offering to immolate himself on their altar could not have worried them in the least. Perhaps they would have been afraid to make such a vigorous ruling of their own accord. There was the difficulty of enforcement to be considered, and it was bound to be great. They had already sent out one order that was certain to arouse vehement opposition ; that had been Sulivan's prohibition of inland trading, despatched four days after the *Lapwing's* arrival. Clive's offer must have seemed to them a fair exchange for the guaranty of the *jaghire*. It would surely result in big savings to the treasury. It was proof enough, and they must have wanted proof, that he really meant to devote himself to their interests ; and it was exactly that kind of a Governor that they wanted in Bengal. Even Vansittart had not been above suspicion of self-seeking. But here was Lord Clive ready to bind himself to surrender all the usual advantages of the Governor's position, ready to propose and enforce the most unpopular measures ! Fair enough, they must have said, let him go—and let him have his *jaghire*.

But did they realize exactly what kind of a situation was being created by their excellent bargain ? Did they realize that they were not only appointing a former employee, whose record could only prove a handicap to him in disciplinary action against their servants, but at the same time practically ensuring by the orders they were giving him that there would be a revolt against their authority ? That he would have to act as a strike-breaker ? Clive knew what the simultaneous prohibition of the inland trading privileges and the presents would mean to the service. It meant the reduction of it from affluence to poverty. Fortunes had been acquired by means of them, yet without them there was very little. The official salary and allowances of a councillor amounted only to £300, and the cost of living had gone up so tremendously in Bengal that he could no longer maintain himself on less than £3000. His old resource, the trading by sea, had ceased to be profitable. The free merchants, of whom there had been a big influx, had appropriated it, having the advantages of being free from the cares of public business and able to travel and reside where they pleased. The obvious and only fair solution to the problem, the payment of proper and adequate salaries, was something that the Company still refused to entertain.

To make matters even worse, the Directors were also giving Clive orders to cut off the special allowance, double *batta*, that the army officers had enjoyed since Plassey, thus ensuring trouble with the military as well as with the civil service. The Directors were, in fact, in a ruthless economical mood, brought on by the clamour of their shareholders for increased dividends, the reports of Governor Vansittart of great laxity in the service and a general disregard of orders and of the Company's interest, and by the spectacle of their servants returning home with fortunes. The expectations born of Plassey had not been realized ; expenses were steadily mounting ; and a feeling of bitter resentment had taken possession of the Directors' minds. If they stopped to think at all, they must have told themselves that they were no longer concerned with trying to be fair to their servants, but only with enforcing their rights and establishing strict control. Any idea of tempering severity with sympathy born of understanding and with justice was entirely absent. If there was trouble, they must have told themselves that Lord Clive was just the man to deal with it—a strong governor was needed ; he was that. They may well have felt quite pleased with themselves.

That the Proprietors, many of whom had belonged to the service or had relations in it, did not feel too happy about the situation thus created, they quickly showed. They had another General Court two weeks later and passed a resolution recommending that the orders against the inland trade be relaxed or at least reconsidered. The Directors refused. When Clive sailed he carried with him orders that modified the former ones only to the extent of instructing him to frame a suitable plan for carrying on the trade and transmit it home for approval. The intention was that until approval had been given the prohibition should remain in force.

But the modification gave Clive a loop-hole of escape out of the dilemma into which he had got himself. He could form such a plan and not wait until it was approved before putting it into effect. He must have known at once that he could not attempt to enforce both orders without ruinous consequences. The one against presents was the one that he would enforce. Very wisely, however, he said as little as possible about any of his intentions before leaving. He was a man who kept his own counsel, acted according to the dictates of his own mind, and had the utmost confidence in his ability to make people see the light of his reasoning and the wisdom of his measures. If he had decided to depart from the strict line of his commission, it was not likely that he gave anybody an inkling of his intention. There was, for instance, that matter of the acquisition of the *Dewani*. It must surely have been in his mind before he left England. As the Company had passed unfavourable comments on it—at least Sulivan had—when last proposed, it is not surprising that Clive kept mum on the subject until he was well out of reach.

There was eagerness to hasten Clive on his way, but there was still the matter of his powers to be settled. And here the first evil result of his bargain was seen. To be consistent he should not have asked for extraordinary powers for himself, having previously condemned the grant of them to Vansittart as illegal. But, of course, as so many politicians have found out to their cost, the whole situation had changed since then, and consistency was now out of the question. Having undertaken the most unpopular commission that could have been devised, he might as well have stayed at home as have gone with no more than the Governor's ordinary authority. Yet with incredible stupidity the Directors refused the request !

It was an occasion for another letter to the always helpful and sympathetic Grenville :

" The great troubles of body and anxiety of mind which I have experienced for these three months past, must convince every impartial person how much I have sacrificed for the good of the East India Company ; indeed, the inclinations which you were pleased to testify for my going abroad had more weight with me than the persuasions of all my other friends put together ; at last, when all difficulties seem to have been surmounted, and I had prevailed upon myself to undertake a voyage much against my own inclination and the interest of my family, and under restrictions very disagreeable in many respects, the Directors, from timidity and want of capacity, refuse to give me those powers which they have already given and sent to Mr. Vansittart, and without which it would be entirely out of my power to render the Company the least service and would at the same time cover me with shame and disgrace among the Natives and Europeans, who by this time are acquainted with the extent of those powers given to another.

" Whatever proofs I may have shown of my disinterestedness, in giving way upon every point where that question has been agitated I cannot recede an inch where my own honour and reputation are at stake, and I am determined never to appear in India with less authority (when I ought, if possible, to have much more) than my predecessor Mr. Vansittart.

" As far as concerns myself I am very happy in the reflection of disengaging myself from a service which from the opposition which has been given, must at all events make it very disagreeable." [162]

The difficulty was overcome by a compromise that gave him as much power as though it had been granted to him alone. He was allowed to nominate a Select Committee of four to act with him as President. On May 25 it was resolved that " in order to restore peace and tranquillity in Bengal, full powers be given to our president and governor Lord Clive, Mr. Sumner, General Carnac, Messrs. Verelst and Sykes, to pursue whatever means they judge most proper to obtain the same ; but that, when it can be done conveniently, they are to consult the Council at large. However, when those desirable objects are obtained, the said extraordinary powers are immediately to cease."

The wording of the commission suggests that the sin of the Directors was not cynicism or ruthlessness, but the most amazing muddle-headedness ; either that or the rankest dishonesty. Could they have imagined that the Committee would require its special powers only for the restoration of " peace and tranquillity," if by those words they meant, what nine out of ten persons would mean by them, the ending of war and restoration of peace ? Or were they deliberately concealing the true purpose of his mission so that the odium of his measures would fall entirely upon him ? If so, why did not Clive object to such unfair tactics ? He was to declare later, " Upon my arrival in Bengal I found the powers given so loosely and Jesuitically worded that they were immediately contested by the Council.

I was determined, however, to put the most extensive construction upon them, because I was determined to do my duty to my country." But he knew of the wording before he left. So either he expected to find the country still at war, in which case everything would be simple, or he did not want to reveal too much of his purpose.

The Company was shy of granting wide discretionary powers, even when there was obvious need for them. The grant of such powers to Vansittart had certainly hurt Sulivan. As it was, the grant to Clive's committee was bitterly attacked. It could scarcely have been otherwise. Two prominent proprietors, George Johnstone and George Dempster, signed a memorial of protest to the Court, inveighing against the supersession of the senior servants as bound to provoke dissension, revealing deep suspicion of this change of policy, and predicting only too accurately the consequences that would flow from it.

Altogether, it was not a happy beginning for Clive's second administration. Everything augured ill for it, and it was to augur even worse by the time he reached Calcutta. The shadow of the *jaghire* already lay across it, poisoning in advance the atmosphere of reform. The news of all these proceedings was transmitted to Bengal, reaching there ahead of him, and at once suspicion was engendered, animosity aroused, so that he was promptly to find himself with no weapon in his hand but the ugly ones of coercion and intimidation.

2 A

Chapter Twenty-three

TIME AND TIDE

"We did not now fight our battles with a handful of men as at Plassey"
LUKE SCRAFTON

I

CLIVE EMBARKED on June 4. His party included Messrs. Sumner and Sykes, Colonels Richard Smith and Sir Robert Barker, who were proceeding to brigade commands in Bengal, and the members of his personal staff. These were Edmund Maskelyne, his brother-in-law, who was going as his aide-de-camp, Henry Strachey, his private secretary, who had been recommended to him by Mr. Grenville, and Dr. Ingham, his personal physician. From the shore he sent a few parting lines to his wife, which deserve remembrance, being almost the only genuine love-letter of his that we possess :

"My dearest wife,—God only knows how much I have suffer'd in my Separation from the best of women, however the necessity of the thing and your good Sense will I am persuaded operate in the same Manner upon You as it has upon me, let us look forward towards the happy day of our Meeting which I think cannot be farther distant than two Years, the Education of our children will be pleasing Amusement & the busy Scene in which I shall be employ'd without embarking in any more military Undertakings will greatly shorten our time of Absence.

"We shall be on board the *Kent* in two or three Hours & sail immediately the wind being fair. You may be assur'd of hearing from me by the first opportunity which I believe will be from the Cape. Adieu.

"Yr. Affect.
"CLIVE."

Margaret's concern for his welfare and especially for his health stands out clearly now on every page of her correspondence with him and with Edmund and Strachey. She sent Strachey detailed

370

instructions on a number of matters. Foremost, he was to remember to write her " how my Lord does while at Portsmouth and ever after when opportunity offers." Then he was to show kindness to various humble people on board the ship, including four musicians who had been especially hired to enliven the long, tedious hours of the voyage.

The voyage was noteworthy in several respects. One was, as on his first voyage, its duration. The fair wind that enabled the *Kent* to put out of Portsmouth and skirt the coasts of France and Spain once more outstayed its welcome and carried them steadily westwards. The result, when combined with the fact that the *Kent* was an exceptionally slow sailer, was that they reached Rio de Janeiro at the time when they should have been at the Cape of Good Hope, and even beyond it.

Another was that it afforded a proof of how great a leveller of rank, privilege, and authority the sea was in those days of sail. It was able to deflate a man's ego better than any other force in the world. It deflated Napoleon's—no wonder he hated it so ! It could not be commanded, it had no respect for persons, it reduced emperors—and Clives—to the status of helpless passengers and elevated common men to high authority. Not so to-day, when suites of rooms are palaces of exclusiveness and luxury, and ocean liners run on schedule ! The man who was about to dictate to India had to bow to his master, the sea. He had to bow to the unfavourable winds and the poor sailing. He had to accept with philosophic calm the fact that the captain was a young man new to his job, who had made such insufficient provision for his distinguished passengers that for six weeks they were reduced to a diet of pork and pease pudding ! He had to accept the fact that the hired musicians deserted the ship at Rio and could not be recovered ! He had even to undergo the supreme torture of a disagreeable fellow-passenger, accept with grace and resignation the necessity of living ten months at extremely close quarters with such a person, and make the best of the fact that she was a woman whom he had to respect because she was none other than Mrs. Sumner, the wife of his second in committee !

She was of an easily recognizable type, without which no ship's company can be considered complete She insisted on keeping all the windows and doors constantly open, so that all of them, including his Lordship, caught colds (until, as he tells us, he put his foot down and ended the nuisance), and on playing the same two humdrum tunes on the harpsichord (which was in his Lordship's quarters) for four hours every day, "without the least variation or improvement," notwithstanding the utmost efforts of his Lordship's music-master to instruct her. The presence of this lady, "of a most diabolical disposition, ignorant, ill-tempered, and selfish to the highest degree, who seemed possessed of every disagreeable quality which ever belonged to the Female Sex without being mistress of one virtue (charity excepted) to throw into the opposite scale," spoiled the whole voyage and made Clive really glad that his wife had stayed at home so that she would not have to undergo the same ordeal. The prospect of continuing with her from the Cape nearly made them all, except presumably the good lady's husband, change ship at that port.

Rio de Janeiro was reached on October 7. In its harbour were found ships which had left England a month after the *Kent*, had spent sixteen days at ports along the way, and had yet arrived there a month before ! They bore for Clive a letter from his wife and the latest news from India. This news gave him the first indication that the main purpose of his mission might already have been accomplished. How he received such tidings we do not know. Writing to his wife he naturally dwelt on the pleasant aspect, that it would speed his return to her :

> "Never entertain the least Doubt of our meeting again & that soon, the latest Advices give us reason to think that everything will be settled in India before we can arrive there, & if that should be the Case nothing shall induce me to stay in Bengal beyond the Year 1765."

The very month that found him compelled to take a longer look at the natural beauties of the Brazilian capital than he would have wished—for it was the end of November before they left— saw a decisive military event in India. The settlement that he was on his way to accomplish was proceeding at a pace that no one six months earlier could have believed possible.

II

In searching for the explanation of the progressive decline in Clive's reputation among his own countrymen that set in after Plassey we must look chiefly to what other men did, for all reputations are relative. One of the main weaknesses of much biography is that by avoiding such comparisons and keeping the spotlight always upon its subject, it distorts the picture. This weakness has been most glaringly exemplified in the case of Clive. We have already seen the necessity for considering the services and achievements of Stringer Lawrence, Admiral Watson, Colonel Forde, and Eyre Coote. We do not consider it in any way an irrelevancy to have introduced a comparison of Clive and Wolfe. And now it is even more pertinent for our purpose to speak of Major Adams and Hector Munro.

In our account of Plassey we stressed the extent to which Clive's whole position in the world was to be dependent upon that supreme event, and we have since seen how he made it the justification for his *jaghire* and all his claims upon the Company and the nation's gratitude. He was *Clive of Plassey* because Plassey had made him what he now was. But what would be his position if another officer of practically no reputation virtually repeated his feat, and if yet another, also of practically no reputation, performed an even greater one? Surely the consequences for him would be serious, especially if in addition he were to give a number of men strong motives for attacking him. So long as the world was convinced that Plassey was as represented, a supreme and unique event, its victor could hold his enemies in contempt; but what if the world's view of it changed? Yet that is exactly what now happened. Obviously, therefore, any biography that failed to put these events in their proper light would go utterly astray in its interpretation of the remainder of Clive's life.

Biographers of Clive have not been the only guilty parties in slurring the achievement of Major Thomas Adams. There are even some historians who omit all mention of his name! One can only imagine that this neglect must be due to the feeling that victories like his over the Nawab of Bengal had already ceased to be noteworthy, that the trick was of such a kind as could only be performed effectively once. The first time a feat of genius; the second time so commonplace as not even to merit a mention! Yet it is a fact, impossible to controvert, that Major Adams's performance was in many ways more notable and meritorious than Clive's.

We fear that history has not been quite fair to Major Adams. Nor was his own fate any kinder: unknown before his campaign began (he was one of Coote's officers in the 84th), he did not even have the good fortune of surviving it. Thus he was doubly doomed to oblivion.

The events of June 1763, when Amyatt and Hay were murdered and Ellis and all the English at Patna seized, threw the English back to the position they had occupied before Plassey. The gains of that battle were lost and Bengal had to be conquered afresh. The news reached Calcutta on July 4, where it found the dissensions in the Council at their height. But with the spirit of true Englishmen, Mr. Vansittart and the gentlemen there composed their differences, declared war upon the Nawab, and ordered the commander of their garrison, Major Adams, to march.

The road that he took was the same as Clive's—the road to Murshidebad. The season too was the same, with this difference, that the rains had already burst in their full violence before Adams began his march. True, his army was considerably larger than Clive's : to wit, 1100 Europeans, 4000 sepoys, and a small body of native cavalry. But to counteract that advantage he had to contend with a more redoubtable foe. Not only had Mir Kasim taken care to discipline his army in European style and arm it with European muskets (with which he had been thoughtfully supplied by his unsuspecting enemies), but he had in addition enlisted a number of Europeans, India being full of adventurers from the West, as well as a still larger number of sepoys who had deserted from the English ; and he also possessed twenty good field-pieces of genuine European make. Emphatically, therefore, the army that Adams had to meet in the field was an *army*, not a mere rabble such as Siraj-ud-daula had brought on to the field of Plassey, and it numbered some 20,000 men. Had Mir Kasim, indeed, as one observer noted, " been as good a general as he was a consummate politician, we should have had by this time little reason to boast of our sway in this country." [163] That was a fair statement of the situation, for Mir Kasim was a far abler man than Siraj-ud-daula, and there were no such divisions in the Moslem ranks, no such conspirators as there had been in 1757. Mir Kasim had, besides, shown excellent judgment in moving his capital to the more inaccessible Monghyr. There was only one thing that he lacked ; though lacking it, he lacked the one thing that might have given him success. He lacked the courage to meet his enemy on the field of battle at the head of his troops ; yet even in that respect he was little inferior to Siraj-ud-daula.

Adams advanced swiftly and fought three actions against small detachments of the enemy before reaching Murshidebad. One at Katwa, one near Plassey, and the last just outside the capital, and in none of them did he encounter much resistance. Occupying Murshidebad on July 24, he proclaimed Mir Jafar restored to his throne. He then moved to meet Mir Kasim's main army along the road to Rajmahal. He came upon it at Gheria on August 2 and overcame it, but only after a stubborn fight with the loss of 320 men. The enemy made another stand in a strongly entrenched position farther up the river, and in the storming of that the English lost another 100 men.

Adams pushed steadily forward, Mir Kasim retreating before him to Patna. At Patna Mir Kasim committed his dreadful act of vengeance upon the hot-headed Ellis and the 170 captured Europeans. But shortly afterwards Adams appeared before the city, breached its walls, and carried it by storm. Mir Kasim, still not daring to face the victorious English, escaped across the border into Oude, there to league himself with its ruler, Shuja-ud-daula, in an attempt to regain his throne. Thus Adams stood triumphant on the banks of the Karamnassa, waiting for further orders. But before they came his brief day of glory was over. His health broke down, he had to throw up the command and retire to Calcutta. And there he died shortly afterwards.

His contemporaries, if not posterity, were quick to note the excellence of his work. " No campaign," said the *Annual Register* of 1764, " had ever been conducted with more ability ; no plan better laid or more systematically followed ; no operations more rapid. In less than four months Major Adams completed for the first time of any European, the entire conquest of the kingdom of Bengal. He fought in that time four capital actions with the enemy ; forced the strongest intrenchments ; took two considerably fortified places, near 500 pieces of cannon, and prevailed over the most provoked, resolute, cautious, and subtile enemy we ever had in India." The implications of that eulogy in its bearing on Clive's reputation should not be missed. The Report of the House of Commons' Select Committee in 1772 confirmed this opinion. Its Third Report describes it as " a campaign commenced and prosecuted under the inconceivable hardships and difficulties which inevitably attend being in the field during the violence of the wet season in Bengal." Finally, the latest authority on the period, Professor Dodwell, more dis-

cerning than most of his predecessors, writes of Major Adams
"having achieved as brilliantly successful a campaign as the
English ever fought in India." [164]

Adams on the banks of the Karamnassa had stood where Clive
had stood after driving the Shah Zada out of Bihar, but now it
was as though Fate were jealous of the laurels that Clive had
gathered with so much ease. Having deprived him of one
unique title to distinction, she proceeded to dim the lustre of
Plassey even further by supplying the world with a far greater
military event. In August of the following year Hector Munro,
a King's officer of the 89th, relieved Clive's friend John Carnac
of the command. Munro found the army in the improper
posture of inactive defence against the invasion of the allied
princes from Oude and in that state of open mutiny that was
never far absent in this period. He stamped out the mutiny with
vigorous measures and then boldly led the army into Oude. On
October 23 he met the confederate host of Emperor, Vizier, and
Nawab on the battlefield of Buxar : 857 Europeans, 5297 sepoys,
and 918 native cavalry, with 20 field-pieces, opposed the most
formidable Indian army yet encountered, including as it did
numerous battalions of disciplined sepoys, field-pieces worked by
European renegades and deserters, powerful batteries of heavy
artillery, and 5000 fierce Afghan horsemen from the victorious
army of Ahmad Shah which had three years before taken Delhi
and smashed the Maratha power on the fatal field of Panipat : an
army in all numbering between 40,000 and 60,000.

The battle raged from eight in the morning until late afternoon
and was fiercely contested at every point, as is borne out by the
heavy British loss of 847 men. But it ended in the complete
rout of the enemy, who left some 2000 dead on the field and
lost several thousand more in their frantic efforts to ford a river.
The Nawab Vizier of Oude fled into the Rohilla country,
opening up the whole of his dominions to British conquest ; the
Emperor, Shah Alam (previously known to these pages as the
Shah Zada, the Mogul heir), submitted and put himself under
English protection ; while Mir Kasim, stripped of wealth and
power, became a fugitive from avenging justice and disappeared
into complete obscurity. Thus Buxar ranks with Plassey as a
decisive event and far above it as a military achievement.

It was not so regarded by everybody, however. The spirit of
faction had by now gained such complete possession of many

men's minds as to warp every view they expressed on Indian affairs. The dispute of the Clive and Vansittart parties extended to the relative merits as victories of Plassey and Buxar. Scrafton in his *Observations* upon Vansittart's narrative referred disparagingly to the military achievements of the latter's government, scornfully remarking that " we did not now fight our battles with a handful of men, as at Plassey." Vansittart replied :

" To what end does the Director labour to exaggerate the merit of the battle of Plassey, and depreciate that of Buxar ? Does he mean to add anything to Lord Clive's military reputation ? The Director knows that the battle of Plassey was the least of his Lordship's military achievements ; and that an abler pen than his or mine [obviously referring to Orme] has been employed to transmit to posterity an account of very many actions on the Coast of Coromandel that do great honour to his character ? Does the Director mean then to detract from the merit of Colonel Munro ? " [165]

Military experts will agree with the Governor that the " handful of men " argument can be overworked. It is not the sole criterion for judging the merit of a battle gained. What Scrafton should have emphasized rather was that Plassey was the necessary precursor to the greater triumph, proving to the English how little importance they need attach to the numerical odds against them.

Faction now had another equally baneful result. It extended to the matter of appointments and dismissals. Carnac had not distinguished himself in his previous tenure of the command, when he had shown a marked lack of enterprise. It was singularly unfortunate that his selection by Clive as a member of his Select Committee should have coincided with Munro's brilliant conduct, for it meant that he superseded Munro in the command ; and such a change following a great victory could have none but a bad effect on the discipline and morale of the service.

But the superior abilities of Munro were needed no longer. The British arms swept triumphantly on against the weakest of opposition. Now the Ganges was crossed and Benares reached. Now the fortress of Chunar was taken and the great city of Allahabad occupied. Now Carnac marched through Oude, visited the ancient capital Fyzabad, placed the attendant Emperor in possession of the country, and then recrossed the Ganges to oppose Shuja-ud-daula, who had reappeared in the field allied to the Rohillas and Marathas. On May 3, the day Clive landed at Calcutta, Carnac was on his way to Korah. Three weeks later he crossed the Jumna at Kalpi, drove the Marathas back towards Gwalior, and received the submission of Shuja-ud-daula.

The English were on the road to Delhi. For a long time leading minds among the English and French had cherished the ambition of some day marching thither and replacing the Emperor upon his throne. Was it because of sentiment that they had this ambition ? It was in part, and also because they wished to receive the benefits of his favour, prestige, and the remnants of his authority, and greatly exaggerated the value of those benefits. This had been Dupleix's and Bussy's dream, and now it was Vansittart's, Coote's, Munro's, and Carnac's. Nor was it beyond realization. There was no interposing enemy. Buxar and Paniput, the Afghan victory, had between them practically opened the gates of the city to the all-conquering British. For Ahmad Shah, having so nearly achieved his object of seizing the empire of Hindustan for himself, had had his ambition thwarted by a mutiny of his army and had had to return home. The answer lay with Clive, and with Clive alone. It was one of the few matters left for him to settle when he arrived.

III

Not even the affairs of Bengal and relations with the Nawab were left to be settled ! Vansittart had somewhat cruelly trotted old Mir Jafar out from his comfortable, warm stable in Calcutta and forced him, wearily now, to drag the broken-down coach of Indian government once more along the English road. And then, having stayed long enough to know that all danger was passed, he had, with Warren Hastings, gone home. That was in November. Their ship and Clive's would have passed each other near to the Indian Coast if it had not been for that luckless visit to Rio. Mr. Spencer had in accordance with Sulivan's orders come from Bombay and assumed the presidency.

If Clive had made an ordinarily fast passage he would have reached Calcutta before the death of Mir Jafar on February 5. Instead of that, he reached the Cape on New Year's day, left it ten days later, and then was becalmed for days at a time in the vast expanse of the Indian Ocean. Sighting an English sail had enabled him to hear of the battle of Buxar. But it was April 10, when at last the *Kent* reached Madras, before he learned of Mir Jafar's death. And he still did not know the use that the Spencer council had made of that event. It was the very opportunity that he himself wanted in order to put into effect his own plans for Bengal.

What those plans were, now that he knew that all the preliminary work was done and military supremacy re-established, he outlined to Rous in a letter from Madras :

" We have at last arrived at that critical Conjuncture which I have long foreseen. I mean that Conjuncture which renders it necessary for us to determine, whether we can or shall take the whole to ourselves, Meer Jaffeir is dead, and his natural Son is a minor, but I know not whether he is yet declared Successor ; Suja Dowla is beat out of his Dominions ; We are in possession of them, and it is scarcely an Hyperbole to say that the whole Mogul Empire is in our hands. The Inhabitants of the Country, we know by long Experience, have no Attachment to any Nabob whatever, their Troops are neither disciplined, nor commanded, nor paid as ours are. Can it then be doubted that a large Army of Europeans would effectively preserve to us the Sovereignty, as I may call it, not only by keeping in Awe the Ambition of any Country Prince, but by rendering us so truly formidable, that no French, Dutch or other Enemy could ever dare to molest us ? "

Clive did not, however, draw from these premises—not all of them were actual facts [1]—the conclusion we might expect. Far from it. He knew how little the Company relished the thought of conquest ; to know that the whole Mogul Empire was in their hands would give them the reverse of pleasure. So he hastened to set their minds at rest about his intentions on that point. As far as Bengal was concerned, " we must indeed become the Nabobs ourselves in fact, if not in name, perhaps totally so without disguise." But for the rest, he expressed strong disapproval of all·that had been going on, of the steady advance towards Delhi and the extending conquests. " I mean absolutely to bound our possessions, assistance and conquests to Bengal, never shall the going to Delhi be a plan adopted, if possible to be avoided, by me, and you may depend upon my

[1] Especially not the one stating that the inhabitants of the country had " no attachment to any Nabob whatever " !

putting a stop to it." He would not, he declared, have gone a step farther than what was necessary " to preserve and pursue our commercial advantages."

This sudden moderation on his part is remarkable. It is almost as though he were taking a leaf out of Mr. Sulivan's book. And this is probably precisely what he was doing. His fight with Sulivan was not over, and he must have known that Sulivan more nearly represented the sentiments of the Company than he himself did. " Commercial Advantages " was the platform upon which Sulivan stood. There were more elections ahead, and Clive to hold his ground must seem to be sharing that platform with his enemy.

But having planted that seed firmly in the mind of Mr. Rous, in his next words he neatly, though vaguely, removed it, because his actual intentions were really quite different : " But since our Views are extended and since Commerce alone is not now the whole of the Company's Support, we must go forward, to retract is impossible." And there for the moment he left the matter, and perhaps wisely, for what he meant by " going forward " was something that the Company had disapproved each time, so far, that it had been suggested.

It was none other than to accept the Emperor's repeated offer of the *dewani* of Bengal, that offer which Clive had dangled before the noses of both Pitt and Sulivan, and which would mean that the English would have the spending of £2,000,000, not all of which by any means would be needed for the expenses of government. In fact, Clive reckoned that the annual net gain to the Company would be 122 lakhs, or £1,650,000. The recent English victories had removed the objections to acceptance that Clive himself had previously considered valid, namely, the lack of power. The English now had power in plenty to exercise the time-honoured right of conquest to take tribute.

The *Kent* after a brief call at Madras sailed on. But Mr. Spencer and his Council had not waited for its long-delayed arrival to proclaim the successor to Mir Jafar and arrange terms with him. Such things could not wait, however much Lord Clive might upon arrival think differently.

Mir Jafar's death enabled the English, as Clive saw, to gain all power in the state for themselves. They had complete control of the situation, and they could now, if they had wished, have appropriated the entire kingdom. They had a choice of heirs, an eighteen-year-old son, who was a complete degenerate interested only in dancing girls, and a six-year-old grandson. With either they could make what terms they pleased. Spencer chose the son, Najm-ud-daula, and, exactly as Clive proposed doing, made him sign a treaty that put an end to any pretensions of ruling his own country. His army was reduced to a size only large enough to support his dignity, maintain internal peace, and collect the revenues. His application to the Emperor for the *sanads* that would confer on him a legal title to his throne was to be made only through the Governor and Council. And, worst humiliation of all, he was no longer free to appoint his own ministers. In a word, he was made a mere puppet. As his deputy and chief minister he was given a Moslem nobleman, Mohammed Reza Khan, the best available man for the job, but one whom he cordially feared and disliked. Vainly he asked for his own favourite, who was none other than the ever-green intriguer, the arch-troublemaker of the state, the double-dyed traitor and conspirator, Nuncomar. Spencer at first entrusted to Nuncomar and Rai Durlab together the collection of the revenues, but upon evidence of fresh treasons coming to light he acted with commendable promptness and ordered Nuncomar's dismissal and removal to Calcutta. Thus Najm-ud-daula was left with no hope at all, except the faint one that Lord Clive would upon his arrival make arrangements more to his taste.

Vansittart had previously disposed of conquered Oude. After his defeat at Buxar Shah Alam had made attractive proposals to the Governor, which he had accepted. The choice lay between giving the country to the defeated Emperor or to the defeated Nawab. Vansittart gave it to the Emperor, taking for the Company the district of Benares. Clive was to reverse the decision. But it made little difference : the battle of Buxar had shaken the state of Oude to its foundations, and whether the English wished it or not they could not now restore what they had overthrown. Under any ruler Oude's dependence upon the Company was assured, with all the disadvantages as well as advantages that entailed.

No one could object with any justice to these measures taken by themselves, but Spencer and his council had stored up immense trouble for themselves by their deliberate contempt for the Company's orders against receipt of presents. They had received the Covenants on January 24 and at once pigeon-holed them. Nor is this in the least surprising since they knew that the Covenants were merely the result of Sulivan's and Clive's private quarrel. They saw no reason for taking them seriously and fully expected that Clive when he arrived would have an order countermanding them in his pocket, as they could not really believe that he or any Governor would deliberately deprive himself and his friends of this source of income. Why, they asked, should the Council lay themselves under restraints unknown to any of their predecessors? At any rate, if Clive personally was responsible for the order, it was clearly his job to enforce it. So now that the customary opportunity for presents had come with the accession of a new Nawab, they seized it joyfully, and the sum of £139,357 passed into the pockets of the councillors.

To complete the background of Clive's assumption of office, the Council had tactlessly taken upon itself to secure from the Nawab the reversion of Clive's *jaghire* to the Company upon expiration of the term agreed upon with him. They might very well have left this little matter to Clive, having settled everything else.

In Clive's letter to Rous appears a highly significant passage, which reveals that what was to be the dominant line of thought and action after he reached his destination was fully developed well in advance :

"See what an Augean Stable there is to be cleaned. The Confusion we behold, what does it arise from ? Rapacity and Luxury ; the unreasonable desire of many to acquire in an Instant, what only a few can, or ought to possess. Every Man would be rich without the Merits of long Service and from this incessant Competition undoubtedly springs that Disorder to which we must apply a Remedy, or be undone, for it is not only malignant but contageous. The new Covenants (tho' I do not entirely approve of their present Shape) will make a beginning. Many of the Civil Servants will probably resign their Employments. The Court of Directors must supply the Settlement with young men more moderate, or less eager in their pursuit of Wealth, and we may perhaps be reduced to the necessity of drawing some Senior Servants from the other Settlements. It must be your Care and I trust you will do all in your Power to send out proper Gentlemen. Affairs seem to be coming to such a Pass that in a little time there will hardly be any body at the Council Board above the Rank or Age of a Writer. In short, the Evils, Civil and Military are enormous, but they *shall* be rooted out. Whatever Odium may be thrown upon me by the malice or Disappointment of Individuals I am resolved to act for the Advantage of the Company in every Respect. I have not here time to inform you of my whole Plan of Reformation, but the Motives upon which I have found it, being no other than the public Good, you may safely exert yourself in its Support, if it should stand in need of your Assistance, which I hardly think it can, tho' Faction should be still raging. I propose no Advantage to myself—I am determined to return to England without having acquired one Farthing addition to my Fortune. Surely then I cannot possibly design anything but public Good."

It is easy to see that Clive's accustomed good fortune had deserted him completely. He was no longer lucky in the times of his comings and goings. His victory over Sulivan had been gained when men were in a state of panic, thinking their affairs desperate and clutching at him as the one hope of saving them. How far otherwise was the actual situation ! Thus the background to his second administration contrasted strongly with that of his first, and the contrast was not at all in his favour. In 1756 he had come in very truth as a deliverer, the man that the hour urgently demanded. But now deliverance had already come, the settlement had saved itself by its own efforts, and it was neither expecting nor wanting the kind of special emergency first-aid service that Clive was best qualified to give. What could he give in place of it ? The answer lies in the first mention of the Augean stable. If he could do nothing for the settlers, he still could do much for the Directors ; he still could cleanse the stable he had discovered. And because whatever he did was bound to focus attention, the result has been that the much-publicized stable has bulked larger in the history books than the military exploits of Adams and Munro. Yet for Clive personally it would have been much better if, upon finding that his services in a military capacity were no longer required, he had foregone his unpopular civil appointment and, instead, taken ship straight back to England. Because however successful he might be in his work of reform, the consequences could not be other than disastrous to him.

Chapter Twenty-four

THE DICTATOR

"Those great and glorious advantages which they (the Company) are so
justly entitled to"   CLIVE

I

No DOUBT on the morning of May 3 the European inhabitants
of Calcutta were going through the motions of work as usual,
but a general torpor had descended upon them some weeks before
with the advent of the hot season. This was now at its height
and the intolerable heat had already sapped their energies and
frayed their tempers. It was the season when savage passions
were apt to be unloosed and deeds of violence committed.
Normally relief would be had in inactivity lasting for three or
four months. But this year, unhappily for all concerned, it was
to be very different. For on that morning the *Kent* at last landed
its passengers at Fort William.

The effect was like that of turning on a powerful dynamo.
Lord Clive's batteries of energy had been completely recharged in
England. The long voyage, the news that he had received at
Madras, and the various fresh items he learned immediately upon
landing made his temper anything but good. He could not have
received a warm welcome. He must speedily have realized how
little his arrival was desired and how angry the gentlemen of
council were at their supersession. Both he and they, in fact,
were in a mood for a quarrel and everything was set for a violent
explosion.

He lost not a moment in getting to work. He must have gone
straight from the ship to his office in Government House. For
before seeking repose that evening he had already written to tell
General Carnac that he had found the government in a more
distracted state, "if possible," than he had reason to expect.
When a man's mind is made up well in advance it is easy for him
to reach quick conclusions. For that reason it was natural that
Clive should decide that the measures taken by Mr. Spencer's

384

government in respect to the Nawab were " at best precipitate " ;
they should have waited until his arrival. " But I am determined not to be embarrassed by the errors of others, if in my
power to remedy them. At least, I will struggle hard that the
disinterested purposes of my voyage prove not ineffectual." It
was, indeed, to be a hard struggle.

When he had spent a day reading over the consultations of
council, he was armed with the information he needed for the
meeting of council, which he called for the following day.

He began its proceedings ominously enough by announcing that
the Committee was determined to make use of the powers vested
in it to their utmost extent, the condition of the country and
the very being of the Company making such a step necessary.
And instantly contention was in the air.

Councillor Leycester leaped to his feet and began to argue
about the meaning and extent of those powers.

Clive cut him short. He would not, he said, suffer any one to
discuss the matter. The powers were what they, the Committee,
deemed them to be ; they were the sole and only judges. The
councillors were at liberty to enter upon the face of the consultations any minute they thought proper, but nothing more.

Mr. Johnstone tried another line of attack, suggesting that the
Company's orders regarding the Committee's powers should be
read in their full context.

" Did he dare," Clive asked him, " to dispute our authority ? "

Mr. Johnstone hastily denied having such an intention.
" Upon which there was an appearance of very long and pale
countenances, and not one of the Council uttered another
syllable."

" To-morrow," wrote Clive grimly to Carnac after the meeting, " we sit in committee, when I make no doubt of discovering
such a scene as will be shocking to human nature." He now
knew about the presents : the recipients were " so shameless as
to own it publicly." " Hence," jumping a little quickly to conclusions,

" we can account for the motive of paying so little respect to
me and the Committee ; and in short, everything of benefit to
themselves they have in this hasty manner concluded, leaving
to the Committee the getting the covenants signed, which they
say is of such consequence that they cannot think of settling

2 B

anything final about them until Lord Clive's arrival. Alas !
how is the English name sunk ! I could not avoid paying the
tribute of a few tears to the departed and lost fame of the
British nation (irrecoverably so, I fear). However, as I do
declare, by that Great Being who is the searcher of all hearts,
and to whom we must be accountable, if there must be an
hereafter, that I am come out with a mind superior to all
corruption, and that I am determined to destroy these great
and growing evils or perish in the attempt."

With this exordium and in this spirit Clive began his second
administration of Bengal.

To his Committee on Friday he declared his purposes :

"A very few days are elapsed since our arrival ; and yet if we
consider what has already come to our knowledge, we cannot
hesitate a moment upon the necessity of assuming the power
that is in us of conducting, as a Select Committee, the affairs
both civil and military of this settlement. What do we hear
of, what do we see, but anarchy, confusion, and, what is worse,
an almost general corruption ? Happy, I am sure, you would
have been, as well as myself, had the late conduct of affairs been
so irreproachable as to have permitted them still to continue in
the hands of the governor and council."

The Committee replied by promising unanimity and support.

On Monday the council were summoned again. And when
they appeared it was to find the neglected covenants thrust before
them to sign on pain of suspension from the service. " After
many idle and evasive arguments " they signed.

As soon as the Nawab, Najm-ud-daula, heard of Clive's arrival
he signified his intention of coming to Calcutta. He was, he
said, longing to see his Lordship. What he really meant, however, was that he was longing to get rid of Mohammed Reza
Khan. Mohammed Reza Khan also wanted to come, to frustrate
the design. And Clive, for his part, wanted to see the Nawab
and his minister in order to obtain the facts about the presents.
So the visit was quickly arranged.

When the party from the Court arrived, towards the end of the
month, the Committee at once set itself up as a board of enquiry
with a willing ear turned towards possible accusations. Clive
himself had no doubt about the guilt of the late President and the
members of his council, but he had to have evidence to send home.

That he would receive such evidence was scarcely in doubt. Under circumstances like these, evidence, plenty and to spare, is always forthcoming in India, where it is the very human desire of a people long accustomed to despotic rule to stand in well with whomsoever wields supreme power. Mohammed Reza Khan, in great fear as he was, wished to curry favour with the new rulers whilst the Nawab, for his part, wished to hurt the minister who had paid out the donations. So it was not surprising that the Nawab should have handed Clive a letter in which he accused Mohammed Reza Khan of distributing the twenty lakhs as bribes to the council to maintain him in office, nor that Mohammed Reza Khan omitted to dispute the charge. Clive professed himself perfectly satisfied and sent home a full account of the shameful transaction.

The council were not prepared, however, tamely to accept their dishonour though they did not choose the ground of their defence very wisely. Mr. Johnstone desired that the question "whether the acceptance of all presents is improper" should be put to each member of the Board in turn. Naturally the accused voted one way and Clive and his Committee the other. Mr. Johnstone maintained that where they were not the price of unworthy services and no trust was betrayed for them, their acceptance was in no way improper, and in the present instance, as being previous to the execution of the deeds of covenants, as warrantable as in time past by any who had received them. And he naturally concluded by bringing up the matter of Clive's *jaghire* and throwing it in his face.

Clive, no doubt fully prepared for this, made a vehement reply expatiating upon the great services he had rendered the Nawab for which the *jaghire* was a fitting reward :

"Let the impartial world determine, whether those who have succeeded me with inferior pretensions, and even in inferior stations, have conducted themselves with equal propriety or moderation. It is unnecessary for me to dwell upon the subject of my own conduct, having long ago published every particular relating to it, and having long ago had the satisfaction of seeing it approved by my employers. If all Mr. Johnstone's transactions will bear the test as well as mine, he will no doubt receive as honourable testimonials of public approbation as I did."

Argument upon any point was utterly futile. The councillors realized they were merely banging their heads against a stone wall. " Clive is really our king," wrote one of their friends ; " his word is law, and as in your time he laughs at contradictions." [166]

Their whole point of view was, of course, entirely different from Clive's. They and he were talking about quite different things when they spoke of " peace and tranquillity." In their eyes Mr. Spencer had already restored that desirable condition. So far from his appointment having caused dissension, they claimed that he had reconciled all quarrels and was beloved and respected by them all. Which was probably true, because any governor who did not interfere too much in their pursuit of fortunes could naturally win their affection ! Even Vansittart, after having given up the vain struggle against the inland trade upon the outbreak of war with Mir Kasim, was now " adored." Their rage against Clive personally blinded them from seeing the weakness of their position, that unanimity in pursuit of their own interests was *not* the kind of tranquillity that Clive felt he had been sent to restore.

They attributed, moreover, his conduct to the basest motives : his desire to revenge himself on Sulivan, his mortification at finding " nothing left for the exercise of his genius " and at being " excluded from that merit which otherwise would have centred entirely in him," his need for finding fresh scope for his abounding energies and for discovering some pretext for assuming the powers conditionally given him, without which, they said, with his masterful nature he could not be happy a day. They were furious with the Company for having, as they thought, cravenly capitulated to him and so made them the victims of the ambition, spite, and uncontrollable disposition of one man. Finally, they believed that in order to give an appearance of virtue and integrity to his own actions and obtain the merit that his soul hankered after, he had deliberately chosen to throw reproach upon the council. [167]

No definite verdict can be rendered on this obscure and complex matter of motives. All these motives were probably present in some degree in Clive's conscious and, still more, subconscious mind. He was, as we have seen, in a tumult of conflicting desires and emotions. Desire to render genuine public service wrestled with his own urgent need to gain public applause.

He was a man tormented by the way in which fate had played him false, and all his behaviour was that of a man driven by some great compulsion along a road not of his own choosing. In the next chapter we shall examine more minutely into his conduct in order to see how it compared with his professions. Meanwhile, we shall only quote the comment of the historian James Mill as seeming to approximate more nearly to the truth than the per-fervid words of these furious men :

> " The impartial judge will probably find, that the interest of the Committee to make out the appearance of a strong neces-sity for investing themselves with extraordinary powers, after the original cause for them had ceased to exist, had *some* influence on their delineations." [168]

All this time Clive had been longing to leave Calcutta and join Carnac in Oude in order to carry through his plans for a political settlement for which conditions were now ripe. On May 26 Shuja-ud-daula, having seen his last hope of reconquering his dominions fade out when the Marathas were driven back, crossed the Ganges and surrendered to Carnac at Allahabad. Here the victors and the vanquished now waited impatiently for Clive's coming. Accordingly on June 25, after the rains had begun, Clive set out on the long six-hundred-mile journey up the river which took him to cooler, drier, and healthier country.

He was still, however, to be pursued by the heat of faction. Now it was Mr. Sumner who provoked his anger. He had left his second member of the Committee with instructions to put into effect an order for the reduction in size of the council by omitting the chiefs of subordinate factories. The reform was salutary, being directed towards strengthening the council as an executive disciplinary body, but it caused more indignation. Sumner was not made of the same stuff as Clive ; when he discovered that the order contravened other recent orders of the Company, he bowed to the storm and held the matter over. Such weakness flung Clive into a fit of rage. He soundly berated Sumner, appealed to the other members of his Committee for support, and made it abundantly clear that he bitterly regretted ever having named Sumner as his successor.[1]

How, he wrote Sumner, could he ever have allowed himself

---

[1] Clive, writing to Margaret, described Sumner as " a most despicable wretch, mean, avaricious, rapacious, tyrannical, selfish and timid." [169]

to be influenced by the arguments of the self-interested Councillors, " who by their conduct have exposed themselves to such a severe criticism that I imagine few of them will escape dismission from the service ? " He did not care what the Company's instructions were :

> " in my opinion who had the nomination of the Committee, and ought to be a judge with what powers and upon what terms I accepted the Government, we are empowered to pursue the means we think proper, and to set aside, or suspend putting in execution, any order we may think detrimental to the Company, the signing of the Covenants excepted."

The exception is significant, but the positive declaration that he was not bound by any orders is even more so. Vested with vague powers, he was acting as a dictator would and making his own interpretation of the Company's interest his sole rule of conduct. It was by the same authority that he had instructed Sumner also to prepare a plan for the prohibited inland trade in salt, betel-nut, and tobacco.

He was a fanatic now in the cause of good government. Was his fury partly that of a man with a bad conscience ? To friends at home he railed against the man who was failing to support him in " the great work of reformation."

> " If I am supported from home I will reform the settlement. If not I shall return to my family and friends well pleased with being relieved from such a burthen that I would not even Mr. Sulivan loaded with. If he knew what I suffer both in constitution and mind he would . . ." [170]

The rest of the passage is unfortunately illegible. How did he think Mr. Sulivan would feel ? Did he think Sulivan would be sorry that he had made him pay this heavy price for the confirmation of his *jaghire* ?

He suspected Mr. Sumner of scheming to go over to the side of the council as soon as his back was turned, even of trying to disgust him so that he would hasten his departure. But he positively declared that nothing would make him go until he knew that his measures had been approved.

The reports of the council's behaviour grew worse the farther up-country he went. At last at Allahabad he burst out to Sykes :

"The behaviour of the council has convinced me they are children and fools as well as knaves, and I am not at all surprised that they have demeaned themselves in the manner you represent, for we may now with great propriety let the sense of humanity give way to justice. For my own part I am determined as one to show them no more mercy. Indeed, it now becomes necessary as well for our vindication as for the advantage of the Company to make an example of them and represent them in the proper colours to the Court of Directors."

II

For the moment, however, his mind was fixed on the much more important objects of his journey, and above all on consummating the acquisition for the Company of the revenues of Bengal.

Little needed to be done at Murshidebad except to make it still clearer that the Nawab was now nothing but a pensioner of the Company and his ministers practically its servants. Clive distrusted Mohammed Reza Khan and to curtail his power he associated with him in the administration his old friend Rai Durlab and the two Seths (sons of the bankers murdered by Mir Kasim). He found the young Nawab sunk in that state of complete profligacy that facilitated, nay, rather rendered necessary his total exclusion from rulership. So his palace was now made into a pleasant asylum where he could indulge his taste for dissipation to his heart's content, unhindered by any hard need for economy, since Clive to aid him in his search for happiness gave him an allowance of 53 lakhs (£600,000) just for the expenses of himself and his household. The manner in which Najm-ud-daula expressed his gratitude for this treatment is famous : "Thank God ! I shall now have as many dancing girls as I please."

When these words were spoken the last ripple passed over the spot where once had been the proud principality of Bengal, off-shoot of the great Mogul Empire, with its Nawabs and its *durbar*, Moslem lords and wealthy Hindu bankers, magnificence and poverty, turbulence and folly. From now on the English were responsible before God, if not in the eyes of the world, and still less at first in their own eyes, for the welfare of the twenty to thirty millions of people that inhabited this great region, larger than most of the countries of Europe.

It was a terrific responsibility—awful, unwanted, undreamt of, incurred thoughtlessly by men looking only for secure " commercial advantages " and unable, as they believed, to find them except by means of military force and political power.   Is it any wonder that at first every kind of fiction was employed to conceal from their own unwilling eyes and the hostile eyes of their European rivals the fact that it *had* been incurred at all ?   They not only did not want it, but they were totally unprepared for it.   There was not a single man in the Company's ranks, director or servant, with the mentality, the training, the ability, or the knowledge needed for the task of setting up in an Asiatic country a new government, let alone administering it to the peace and satisfaction of the people.

There was just one man so gifted, Warren Hastings, a young man of thirty-three, but he was no longer in the service.   He might never re-enter the service.   He had gone home with Vansittart, having allied himself so whole-heartedly with his discredited chief that it was doubtful whether he would ever be employed again ;   not, at least, as long as Clive controlled the Company.

The man who had brought these things to pass was not likely to have been unduly troubled by such thoughts.   For to Clive the fictions were the all-important consideration beyond which he never really saw.   He, the man of action, the acquirer of empire in terms of wealth, now went on his imperious, restless way leaving the first of his fictions, the ruler of Bengal, to sink silently in a brief while into an unlamented early grave.   What engaged his mind now was the disposal of provinces and revenues, the disposition of his army, and the demarcation of frontiers—not the welfare of the hundreds of little villages that dotted the banks of the mighty river up whose strong current he was being laboriously borne.   When on August 1 he reached Benares he completed the second stage of his journey.

At this point, if we were writing of another age and another man, we might pause to describe the historical antiquities and religious and cultural associations of that great centre of Hinduism and of the regions of Hindustan that lay beyond with their memorials of ancient civilizations and living faiths.   But to do so here would be an irrelevancy and an anachronism.   Such things could have left but a slight impression on the mind of Clive, not prepared by knowledge or inclination to receive them or to let them play any part in his mental processes.

A contemporary critic described this lack of curiosity, not by any means confined to Clive, in scathing terms :

" A near acquaintance with Indostan manifests the precarious credit that is due to travellers who take a slight survey of distant countries. And, indeed, we have received very little information in regard to the few fragments of learning in that empire from the civil and military servants of the Company, who seemed to have never been diverted from a sordid pursuit after riches, by liberal inquiry into the state of arts and sciences of a people who though sunk into voluptuousness and effeminacy, still preserve latent sparks of useful knowledge. If our modern conquerors of the East returned home like the Roman generals loaded with the spoils of the vanquished, they cannot boast like them of having been tutored by Mars and Minerva." [171]

Clive, whose mind was invincibly utilitarian, had no time to waste on such matters. At Benares he met the Nawab-Vizier of Oude, who had come to meet him, and at once announced to him his intention of revoking Vansittart's arrangement and restoring to him all his former dominions, except the districts of Allahabad and Korah, on payment of an indemnity of 50 lakhs. Shuja-ud-daula was naturally pleased and expressed appropriate gratitude. "Such an instance of generosity in a victorious enemy," reported Clive to his Committee, "exceeded his most sanguine expectations, and we doubt not will be the best foundation of that union and amity which we so earnestly wish to secure."

Generous the act may have been, though at the expense of Shah Alam, to whom the territory had been previously promised ; expedient it certainly was, if the common verdicts regarding the relative fitness for rule of Shuja-ud-daula and the Emperor may be believed, for the latter appears to have been as far below the average of Indian rulers as the former was above it. The only other alternative, to take the country into British hands, would have been considered right and proper in the following century, but in 1765 it was not even an alternative.

Accompanied by Shuja-ud-daula Clive then proceeded to Allahabad, where the Emperor was waiting to be told his fate. Clive gave him as his imperial demesne the two reserved districts of Korah and Allahabad, providing a revenue of 28 lakhs, with a promise of British protection. Shali Alam, however, being an

Emperor was not so easily satisfied. He put forward all manner of demands which Clive, being the representative of the conquering power, brushed lightly aside. Shah Alam, though he was an Emperor, had to realise that he was as dependent upon English bounty as any beggar in his dominions. Then, when he had duly expressed his gratitude, Clive made a deal with him : in exchange for the *dewani* of Bengal, Bihar, and Orissa the Company would pay him an annual tribute of 26 lakhs from the revenues.

And now there was real joy in the Emperor's heart, and astonishment as well, since the imperial treasury had received none of its lawful tribute from the viceroys of Bengal for longer than he cared to remember. Indeed, it is probable that he would have been willing to grant the *dewani*, which he had previously twice pressed upon the English, without any *quid pro quo*, so little expectant was he of any favours.

The deal that was to bring the Company so much weal and woe was quickly made. On August 12 the Emperor issued the royal *firman* and mounted his throne, once more the sovereign lord of lands, once more the recipient of tribute from faithful subjects.

What matter that the " throne " was an ordinary armchair hastily dressed with a rug for the august occasion ? What matter that it stood on an English dining-table and the dining-table stood in Clive's tent ? Or that the throne the poor man really wanted to sit on was the throne of his ancestors in Delhi, the throne of Akbar made of gold, encrusted with jewels, and invested with power, honour, and dignity ? What *did* matter was that the occupant of this " throne " could still issue imperial decrees supposedly compelling all subjects to obedience. Clive's purpose was served when the English position in Bengal was legalized, as it now was, with the Company as *dewan* being made part of the constitutional framework of the empire. Now, too, he could obtain the confirmation of his *jaghire* and its reversion to the Company, as Spencer had already obtained it from Najm-ud-daula.

What matter, too, if the Emperor wished for British troops to escort him to Delhi and maintain him upon his propless throne ? That idea, like the one of making him ruler of Oude, Clive had already scornfully cast aside as rash and devoid of utility to the Company. Had not the benefits of the imperial sanction already been obtained, and if more were desired could they not be obtained with greater ease at Allahabad than at Delhi ?

There can be no denying that Clive's reasoning was based on hard reality without a trace of the sentimentality and false belief in the importance of the Mogul Empire that bemused most of his contemporaries. He recognized a ghost when he saw one and knew exactly how much value to attach to him, and how little. The second fiction, that the Company derived its status in Bengal from the sovereign of all India, was now superimposed upon the first, and with that Clive rested content.[1]

The treaty of Allahabad, signed by the Nawab-Vizier and Clive on August 16, was designed to solve the Company's defence problem by setting up a friendly buffer state on its vulnerable north-west frontier and permitting the British garrisons to be withdrawn within the boundaries of Bihar. Expansion being no part of Clive's plan, Bulwant Singh's zemindary [2] of Benares was handed back to Shuja-ud-daula with a guarantee of British protection.

The treaty was, in fact, the first attempt to solve a problem whose final solution was a frontier that stretched from ocean to ocean and from Cape Comorin to the great Himalayas, with always a big question mark to the north-west. The attempt to find the " right " frontier in that direction was to produce half the political and military history of British India for the next hundred and fifty years ; the British moved on from one line to a stronger one beyond, and even when they reached the end of the plains and faced the great mountain fastnesses of Afghanistan they still for a long time were not satisfied, because of passes like the Khyber that had for centuries afforded access to invading armies ; but bitter experience was to prove to them that they could go no farther. In 1765, where Clive stopped, there was no natural frontier at all, not even a river, and that was why some of the hopes born of his treaty were delusory. The first natural line of defence of Bengal was the Ganges, which embraced both Oude and Bengal. The Nawab-Vizier was too weak, as some observers saw at 'the time, to defend that line unaided. Clive

---

[1] The British respect for legal forms is nowhere better seen than in the words of Edmund Burke : " This is the great act of the constitutional entrance of the Company into the body politic of India. It gave to the settlement of Bengal a fixed constitutional form, with a legal title, acknowledged and recognized now for the first time by all the natural powers of the country, because it arose from the charter of the undoubted sovereign."

[2] A zemindary was very similar to a feudal fief.

had promised assistance, but he could not have anticipated how much would be required or he would have made provision for the additional expense that this would entail to the Company. This was one of the features of the treaty that Warren Hastings had to correct eight years later, when even that short space of time had revealed its glaring weaknesses.

The sad and sombre story of British relations with Oude, bound to Bengal by the closest ties of geography and mutual dependence, began with the signing of this treaty. The buffer state was to prove no buffer, but an endless source of vexation, scandal, and ignominy to successive Governors-General for a hundred years.

Nor was the other part of Clive's arrangement with the Emperor destined to a better end. Within that same eight years Shah Alam was to despair of ever obtaining his heart's desire from the hands of his British protectors and was to throw himself into the arms of the only other power capable of helping him, the Marathas, allowing himself to be conducted to Delhi by them, the victim of a far harder bargain than the one Clive had made with him : the ruler of lands at Allahabad, he was to be nothing but a captive, a pensioner like Najm-ud-daula, at Delhi.

Clive elaborated his views about British policy in a letter to the Company two years after his retirement : " An idea is adopted that if we let the King go from us we shall lose our influence in Indostan. I, on the contrary, have ever been of opinion that our connection with him ought to be shaken off as soon as it honourably can, and that the farther he removes from us the better. Our tribute of twenty-six lack paid to him will always secure tranquility in Bengal." He condemned the current notion that it would be good policy to reduce the Mogul Empire to obedience to the Emperor : " M. Bussy, indeed, entertained that project when the French were in possession of the five Circars, and directed the politics of the Deccan ; but a more wild, extravagant, and inconsistent, as well as disadvantageous plan, never was conceived. Our safety depends upon the disunion of the natives. To reduce all the independent nabobs to allegiance would be to render the King not only formidable but destructive to ourselves." He realized, too, that Oude could never be a menace to the Company and saw no sense in a hostile attitude towards Shuja-ud-daula, believing as he did that the British-led sepoys made the Company invincible against any native power.[172]

396

III

Deciding and acting with his accustomed speed, Clive spent less than two weeks at Allahabad, and by August 21 he was already on his way back to Calcutta. By that time he had also put into effect his scheme, formed while in England, for the reorganization of the army.

He formed the troops into three brigades of equal strength and composition. Each consisted of one regiment of European infantry, seven battalions of sepoys, one squadron of native cavalry and one company of artillery. The first brigade, under Sir Robert Fletcher, was stationed at Monghyr ; the second, under Richard Smith, at Allahabad ; and the third, under Sir Robert Barker, at Patna. Clive understood better than anyone else how to obtain a native army of maximum efficiency. The necessity of discipline was his cardinal principle, being noteworthy at a time when the tendency was all the other way. A flock of new officers had recently come out to bring the commissioned ranks of the units up to the strength that he required. Of those who were posted to sepoy battalions he required a sound knowledge of the native tongue and close study of native customs and habits, and he refused to permit transfers to the European battalions, his object being to build up a strong *esprit de corps* in the Bengal native army.

As his boat sped down the swollen river he wrote to his wife :

" I have received many letters from the dearest of wifes & best of parents who is seldom out of my thoughts one day together notwithstanding the great & important concerns of the Company which take up the whole of my time, indeed I am very much alter'd of late for I am always at the Pen nor can I avoid it consistent with my duty to my Employers. It must afford you a particular pleasure to hear that I enjoy my health better than in England and that action as formerly agrees better with me than indolence and laziness. I have been 700 miles up the country in the Midil of the rainy season, his Majesty the Great Mogul & the Prime Vizier & myself have been very great together. Matters are settled to the mutual satisfaction of all parties, by a firm and I hope lasting peace, so that tranquility is once more restored to these much ravaged & desolated Provinces. It would amaze you (as Harry

397

expresses himself) to hear what diamonds rubies and gold mohurs have been offer'd to Lady Clive because she has not sign'd covenants. However I have refused anything & have supported my dignity & kept up my integrity in the midil of ten thousand temptations. This will not however prevent my sending my wife some valuable presents which I cannot avoid receiving being Nagarene,[1] & presented in a public manner, it will indeed rest with the Directors whether I shall pay for them as I am determined to receive nothing not even of the most trifling nature without giving them the particulars."

The presents he sent her included a box of jewels worth 42,000 Arcot rupees, eleven bundles of muslins and shawls, two boxes of attar of roses, and two horses.

He was in a hurry now to despatch home to the Company " the most important advices they ever received."

" And if what I have already done & propose doth not convince the Proprietors of the disinterestedness as well as integrity of my principles & of my resolution to exert my abilities to the utmost in defence of their property, which has been very much sported with of late by men of as bad hearts as heads, I shall disdain in future throwing away one thought more on so ungrateful a society."

He declared that he was as happy as a man at such a distance from his wife and family could be and he had the testimony of a good conscience to support him in the most arduous task that ever was undertaken.

" Indeed I suffer no anxiety of mind but what arises on my wife's account and from the reflection of what she must suffer from so long & cruel a separation. However I am persuaded your good sense will suggest to you our separation was unavoidable, & that the duty you ow'd to a growing & increasing family was much superior to that of attending your husband, rest satisfied in the reflection of whatever *is, is right* & there is the greatest probability we shall meet again tho' not so soon as I expected when we parted from one another in Berkeley Square."

He had informed the Directors that no consideration on earth would induce him to stay beyond the following year, and he

[1] *Nuzzerana*, ceremonial presents.

expected to be home by April 1767. No cost or pains were to be spared in making Walcot, his new house, what he wished it to be against the time of his arrival. As for the house in Berkeley Square, he had noticed that the furniture was all worn out, so

"I would have the Grand Flight of Rooms furnished in the richest and most elegant manner, a man of great taste & judgment should be consulted & if any additional rooms can be built without spoiling or darkening the others you have my consent for erecting them, I do empower you to make the House at Berkeley Square as fine & convenient as you please immediately. What can I say more."

Clive was, indeed, more exultant over what he had done than over any event since Plassey, and for a reason that particularly concerned him personally. The personal motive comes out very clearly in what he wrote to Orme. "Fortune," he says, " seems determined to accompany me to the last ; every object, every sanguine wish, is upon the point of being completely fulfilled, and I am arrived at the pinnacle of all I covet, by affirming the Company shall, in spite of all envy, malice, faction and resentment, acknowledge they are become the most opulent Company in the world by the battle of Plassey ; and Sir Hannibal Hotpot [? Sulivan] shall acknowledge the same." In other words, he believed that he had delivered the *coup de grace* to Mr. Sulivan. The acquisition of the revenues was the crown to his own achievement, the fulfilment of Plassey—a *golden* crown that he had now placed upon the corporate head of the Company while the laurel wreath of a conqueror still rested upon his own brows. Sulivan had been opposed to receiving it as he had been opposed to all his work, but Clive knew that Sulivan would now be undone, the stocks would go soaring, dividends would have to be increased, and it would be *he* and no one else that the shareholders would have to thank for the boon.

No one in Bengal shared his exultation, and for reasons that were only too clear. There was no genuine merit in the achievement. Vansittart could have had the *dewani* if he had wanted it or had cared nothing about contravening the Company's orders. It was any governor's for the asking. There was, besides, the material consideration of wise policy. And here there was plenty of room for difference of opinion, not merely as to how it would affect the Company's position at home but still more

399

how it would affect the people of Bengal and the Company's problem of government.

Yet even on this last subject Clive managed to maintain a tone of complete optimism. He claimed that he had found the one certain cure for the ills that had been distressing the Company, particularly the evil of repeated revolutions, the motive for which he had now removed. The servants had been laying hands upon everything they did not deem the Company's property, but now that all the property, that is to say, all the revenues of the country, belonged to the Company, the practice was effectually stopped. But this was only one of the manifold blessings that would flow from his arrangement. It was the essence of it that the Company were not to collect the revenues nor take any part in administration ; they were merely to sit at the seat of custom and receive the revenues from the hands of the finance ministers of the state. They were to be in the splendid position of possessing all power and all the benefits of power without any of the disagreeable and arduous responsibilities. That was its chief virtue, Clive would have them know :

" All cause of contention with the government is now removed ; security to the property, freedom to the trade, and protection to the persons of the native inhabitants are insured. Funds for the provision of your investments, for the maintenance of your troops, and for the necessities of war, are established. Influence to command respect is acquired ; and we may, in our present circumstances, be regarded as the spring which, concealed under the shadow of the Nabob's name, secretly gives motion to this vast machine of government, without offering violence to the original constitution. The increase of our own and diminution of his power are effected without encroachment on his prerogative. The Nabob holds in his hands, as he always did, the whole civil administration, the distribution of justice, the disposal of offices, and all those sovereign rights which constitute the essence of his dignity, and form the most convenient barrier between us and the jealousy of the other European settlements."

Anybody who could work such a miracle as this would be justly entitled to be known as the greatest statesman the world has ever known. He would, in fact, be nothing less than a magician. But Clive was not that, for there was scarcely one word of truth in his picture. True, all cause of contention with the government was now removed, but that was because the government was merely a name and a shadow, a mask—and masks cannot contend. So far from the native inhabitants being insured anything, nothing was insured to them except their ruin. As for the ample funds that were established, nothing could certainly be easier than for a Governor to make a brilliant showing of revenue for a year or two by seeing that maximum demands were made on the tax-payers—and leave to his successor a ruined land unable even to supply the ordinary needs of government. If it were true that the English were the "spring of the government," it was also true that concealed and secret springs do not work well either in India or elsewhere. If too the Nawab still held in his hands all his old prerogatives, it was also true that he no longer had the slightest inducement for using them, and to speak as though he not only possessed them but would exercise them was merely to make a cruel mock of his position as well as completely to misrepresent the facts. For actually what had been done was to give the farmers of the revenue and the tax collectors an unrivalled opportunity to plunder the country free from all fear of government interference, and to leave the peasantry without any kind of protection.

The consequence was to be this : " It must give pain to an Englishman to have reason to think that since the accession of the Company to the Dewani the condition of the people of this country has been worse than it was before ; and yet I am afraid the fact is undoubted." The words are those of the British Resident at Murshidebad and they are to be found in an official report written less than four years later. This official went on to state a number of reasons why " this fine country, which flourished under the most despotic and arbitrary government, is verging towards its ruin while the English have really so great a share in the administration. . . ." But the causes were really only one : that the English having devoured the Nawab's private treasure had now passed on to the public revenues, and there was no one any longer to stop either them or the native officials who willingly joined in the work of spoliation.[173]

Clive has not lacked apologists. Some of them have successfully closed their eyes to the glaring discrepancy between his own beautiful illusions and the harsh realities. Others, too honest to blink the facts, have comforted themselves with the reflection

2 C

that he could have done no other than what he did because of the unpreparedness of the Company's servants to assume the responsibilities of administration. This would be a valid excuse if it could be shown that he himself was aware of the imperfections of his system and regarded it merely as a makeshift until the service was prepared, but this cannot be done. Not only is the quoted passage typical of his attitude, but to his dying day he so far refused to see the need for a radical change in his system that he felt a strong grievance against Hastings because he upset it.

Quite a different kind of apology is needed. As we see it, his mind was centred not on India and the effect of his measures on its welfare—an effect that he was quite unable to estimate—but on England and the effect of his measures on Company politics and his own position. Now, even more than during his first administration, that was what possessed his mind. He was thinking not of the people of Bengal nor of the future of the country, but of his own glory and interests. He wanted *éclat* above everything else. In particular he was thinking of Sulivan. He was—to use a good slang expression—" putting something over " on his great enemy. Even if he had had the mind of an administrator, which he certainly did not possess, he was in far too great a hurry to use it now. He may have believed what he wrote about the perfection of his system, though to think that is almost to under-rate his intelligence. Much more likely is it that he knew that he must at any cost persuade public opinion at home into thinking that he, and he alone, had been able to find the ideal solution of the Company's problems. In any case, he probably acted first, just as he had been planning to act, and did what thinking was necessary to justify the act afterwards when he was preparing his despatches. A man who was as concerned as he was with his own personal problems cannot be blamed for using every situation as a means to solving them. It just happened in this case to be India's misfortune that the solution of his problems clashed with her needs. India would have to wait for them to be attended to until a man was sent whose mind and ambition were truly centred on that task. That man was Warren Hastings.

Clive's opponents in India have been severely condemned for their behaviour in resisting his measures, but one of them at least, Richard Barwell, foresaw the consequences of his boasted act and did not hesitate to state them. His hands may not have been clean, his pen may have been dipped in gall, but he was to prove in association with Hastings that he was a far better administrator and possessed a deeper understanding of the problems and needs of Bengal than the man whom he so bitterly denounced.[174]

IV

Clive was back in Calcutta on September 6. If he expected a triumphant reception, he was sorely disappointed. The rancour of his opponents had daily increased, and all Clive's parade of achievement served only to increase their disgust. Clive returned prepared, as he had said, to show them no more mercy. So now occurred the vulgarest of all his brawls with the council.

The first appearance of General Carnac as member of the Committee was what chiefly gave rise to it. His membership of the Committee was something that the councillors could not, and with very good reason, tolerate. Johnstone had already thrown up the service. Now Grey, Leycester, and Burdett were to follow his example. The Committee having assumed the right of arresting native servants of British subjects, had begun to exercise it in the effort to build up its case against the accused councillors. Grey and Leycester taunted Clive and Carnac with attempting to set up a military despotism. Carnac lost his temper and threatened to use military force against them if necessary. Leycester by breaking the rule of secrecy and repeating the threat outside the Council Board was guilty of an offence for which the Committee suspended him. Then Grey too was dismissed when he hurled in Clive's face the Omichand affair ; his parting shot at Clive being : " Your language is more calculated for the meridian of Billingsgate or Grub Street than for the records of the Honourable Board." Finally, Burdett wrote a minute accusing Clive of persecuting all who differed from him in opinion, and suffered the same fate.

The council had thus lost four of its members. The punishment was effectual, its independent spirit being so thoroughly crushed that it became a subservient body during the remainder of his lordship's stay.

Activity had returned to Calcutta with the cool weather. Ships were arriving from England and outgoing letters and cargoes were being prepared for despatch. To Clive came a large packet of news of home affairs.

Walsh wrote him about Company politics. Sulivan, he

reported, writing in February before the election, was making a push with his usual thoroughness, being an adept campaigner, but things were not going well with him ; Lord Shelburne, the late *primum mobile* of his cause, seemed now quite inactive.

" Our friend Neville (Maskelyne) has happily got possession of the observatory at Greenwich, my friend Stuart of Athens, who is lately made the King's Sergeant Painter in the room of Hogarth, has just sent me a medal commemorating the Battle of Plassis which I now forward to you, with his letter which explains it. When the medal is made publick I will get one done for you in gold and send it to you ; for you are not virtuosi enough in India to venerate brass. Stuart is one of your warmest advocates and has shewn no little zeal in getting your statue properly executed by Schumaker and properly placed in the India House, in which he has succeeded ; and I can assure you that it is by far the most pleasing and interesting figure of the three : Pocock's is in the middle, and yours on the right hand, in an advanced and speaking attitude." [175]

A later letter from Walsh told of how :

" the poor split votes have been most violently attacked. Lists of their names have been printed, terrifying paper sent to each of them, particular persons deputed to wait upon and preach to them, the public papers filled with admonitions to them as coming from clergymen, ballads made upon them. In short every electioneering art has been tried upon them." [176]

Henry, his brother, reported on his constituencies. He said that his interest at Shrewsbury and Bishop's Castle were both being well maintained, with some expenditure of money. Lady Clive's residence at Walcot and employment of the burgesses were helping a great deal at the latter. All his family, Henry said, were well, Ned (his eldest son) was at Eton under a new headmaster, but his father had gone blind in one eye and was breaking very fast, whilst several of his aunts were dead ; big alterations were under way at Walcot.

Clive was, however, not at all happy about Company affairs. He was very disappointed in Mr. Rous, who " tho' a very honest man, is the most unfit of all men living to preside and govern a Court of Directors. I am now convinced a man of lighter principles with more abilities and a certain degree of resolution will manage both private and public concerns to more advantage than Mr. Rous." A change of attitude which may almost certainly be ascribed to Mr. Rous's annoyingly rigid attitude in respect to the inland trade.[177]

But at last came the news of Mr. Sulivan's entire overthrow, and welcome news it was. He wrote Margaret, "I feel no other satisfaction on that account than for the Company. Had that man been strong enough to have continued the opposition he would have destroyed one of the grandest prospects that ever fell to the lot of a trading Company."

For Clive the year ended with a short lull in the storm that had raged from the day of his landing. It was to break out again in the New Year, when the younger members of the services were to express their feelings. But for a few weeks he was busy with routine affairs of government, putting into effect his changes in the system of government and watching the operations of the newly-formed Society of Trade.[1] He was always busy ; the furious pace of his activity never halted. But what little of a private life he enjoyed—and he did not enjoy it very much away from his wife and family—was now, when he spent six consecutive months in Calcutta. We have a vivid picture of it and of him in the loneliness of his Indian proconsulship, taken from a contemporary account that bears on the face of it the likeness of authenticity, even though it appears in that hodge-podge of fact and libel, the work of Carraccioli : [2]

"The very furniture of Government House, the tapestries and carpets, the magnificent plate, the sumptuous equipages, were the envy of the settlement, and his frequent sumptuous costly entertainments their delight. His hospitality was ample, but in his private life his mode of living was not more lavish than what was customary in a wealthy and luxurious community. Dinner, according to the custom of the time, was served at 2 p.m., and a few select friends of his Select Committee, or some other senior servants of the Company, dined with him. His table was served with delicacy and profusion and all the most exquisite wines of Europe were at the discretion of his guests. If he were in good humour, he would encourage a free circulation of the bottle, and by intervals stimulate mirth and jollity ; but he soon relapsed

---

[1] See below, p. 420.
[2] For a discussion of this work see Appendix C.

into his natural pensive mood, and was after silent for a considerable time. His conversation was not lively, but rational and solid. As he seldom drank freely enough to be seen without disguise, he was impenetrable, except to a few confidants to whom he entrusted the execution of his schemes and designs. It was not often that his guests were allowed a greater latitude of freedom, as he was always stately and commonly reserved. After dinner he took sometimes a little repose, as it is customary in this torrid region. Towards the evening he resorted to some gardens with a few companions, and after supper either played at cards, of which he was fond in a select company, or retired with some favourite woman. It cannot be said that he enjoyed life, he only varied these fashionable amusements, which gave him no real pleasure or satisfaction. Since he had been obliged by his rank in life to converse with ministers and statesmen, he had applied himself to politics, and in reading books that might give him some useful knowledge of the English Constitution. He was not an orator, but he spoke with propriety and judgment. His style, as may be seen in his letters, was neither elevated nor contemptible. He was perfectly acquainted with the genius of the Asiatics, and nobody knows better how to take advantage of their apprehensions and pusillanimity." [178]

Chapter Twenty-five

HOW AUGEAN WAS THE STABLE?

"History can scarce furnish an instance of any subject who hath had such opportunity of acquiring an immense fortune" CLIVE

I

IT IS A FAIR QUESTION. Clive made the disgraceful conditions he found the justification for all his high-handed measures. But any attempt to answer it poses another question : how far superior in virtue were he and his colleagues of the Select Committee to the rest of the Company's servants ? And that is equally a fair question, because so far was this from being a case of Satan reproving and correcting Satan in the legitimate interests of discipline and efficiency, of poacher turned gamekeeper for reasons not of morals but of expediency, that we find Clive loudly and incessantly proclaiming the fact that he was not as these other men were, that he was infinitely more virtuous, that he was, indeed, entirely disinterested in his Herculean labours for the public good. In fact, it was not Hercules at all who had come to cleanse this Augean stable. It was Galahad. It was more even than Galahad. It was Jove himself, armed with omnipotence and omniscience, able to feel and express godlike indignation and to hurl down the thunderbolts of wrath upon all who earned his disfavour, even by so much as raising a finger or a frown against him. And a quite unusual eloquence was given to him to enable him to play his triple role and give it utmost dramatic effect.

"Two paths," he wrote the Directors,

"were evidently open to me : the one smooth, and strewed with abundance of rich advantages that might easily be picked up ; the other untrodden, and every step opposed with obstacles. I might have taken charge of the government upon the same footing on which I found it ; that is, I might have enjoyed the name of Governor, and have suffered the honour, importance, and dignity of the post, to continue in their state of annihilation ; I might have contented myself, as others had before me, with being a cypher, or, what is little better, the first among sixteen equals ; and I might have allowed this passive conduct to be attended with the usual *douceur* of sharing largely with the rest of the gentlemen in all government and disposal of all places in the revenues of this opulent kingdom ; by which means I might soon have acquired an immense addition to my fortune, notwithstanding the obligations in the new covenants ; for the man who can so easily get over the bar of conscience as to receive presents after the execution of them, will not scruple to make use of any evasions that may protect him from the consequence. The settlement in general would have thus been my friends, and only natives of the country my enemies. . . .

" An honourable alternative, however, lay before me : I had the power within my breast to fulfil the duty of my station, by remaining incorruptible in the midst of numberless temptations artfully thrown in my way ; by exposing my character to every attack which malice or resentment are so apt to invent against any man who attempts reformation ; and by encountering, of course, the odium of the settlement. I hesitated not a moment which choice to make ; I took upon my shoulders a burden which required resolution, perseverance, and constitution to support. Having chose my part, I was determined to exert myself in the attempt, happy in the reflection that the honour of the nation, and the very being of the Company, would be maintained by the success ; and conscious that if I failed my integrity and good intentions, at least, must remain unimpeached." [179]

To his colleagues on the Committee he was equally explicit about the purity of his motives and the clearness of his conscience :

" Let me but have health sufficient to go through with the reformation we intend, and I shall die with satisfaction and in peace."

" I can go through everything with pleasure so long as I can with truth and without vanity apply to myself these beautiful lines of Horace : *Justum et tenacem propositi virum.*"

" Our disinterested conduct must be admired and applauded by all virtuous and good men ; and if there be men base enough to disapprove of what we are about, we may all retire to live happy and upon the testimony of a good conscience."

It would be possible to fill up a volume with quotations from his letters answering the two questions we have posed resoundingly in his favour, but these are enough. The questions themselves remain to be answered in the light of such facts as emerge clearly from the fearful welter of charge and counter-charge, slander and counter-slander, that poured from the pens of both parties and turned for a long space the East India Company into a babel of angry, warring tongues.

The matter of the presents that Spencer's council received from the new Nawab has been considered. We find we are forced for lack of reliable evidence to acquit the Council of the charge of corruption. That leaves them guilty, legally at least, only of a breach of orders in having left their covenants unsigned.[180]

Clive, however, declared that what he found was a general corruption. When he appeared seven years later before the House of Commons' Committee he was asked upon what facts he grounded his expression of "cleaning the Augean stable." In his answers he had difficulty in being precise. He spoke at first vaguely of what he had read in Vansittart's narrative, which had just reached England, and of the accounts of people he met at Madras. When the Committee asked him to be more specific, he recited the complaints about the monopoly of the inland trade and the freedom from the duties on salt ; but he gave no concrete instances. And here it was that the Committee scored a point against him and his colleagues. Having so testified and having particularly referred to the refusal of the council to accept Vansittart's treaty with Mir Kasim, by which they would have had to pay a duty of 9 per cent. on salt, he was asked where Carnac and Verelst, whom he had recommended as the most upright men upon earth, had stood on the matter, and he had weakly to admit that they had been among those who had upheld the right to trade duty free and voted against the treaty ! [181]

The Committee questioned him no more about the Augean stable. They may have felt that his testimony, combined with the way in which he himself had organized the salt trade as a monopoly in the hands of the Company's servants, had sufficiently disposed of the Augean stable as a serious charge.

There is, of course, no question at all that discipline in the service was exceedingly relaxed and that fortunes were being made with scandalous ease and gross hurt to the inhabitants of Bengal, principally by means of the inland trade. But whether Clive was correct in his assertion in one of his letters that he knew of fortunes of £100,000 obtained within the space of two years and of "individuals very young in the service returning home this year with a million and a half" is another matter. William Bolts, an unfriendly critic it is true, but the weightiest in his documentary mode of attack, declared that he could not find one fact to corroborate that statement. "On the contrary, we find that no fortunes were ever obtained in Bengal by Europeans of such immensity, or with such rapidity, as those of his lordship and the gentlemen who were coadjutors in politics during his two administrations in 1757 and 1765." Bolts's charge is as difficult to refute (except as it related to Clive himself during his second administration) as Clive's to prove. Certainly there is no reason for believing that the rate of fortune-making declined markedly during Clive's administration, except among the junior members of the service.[182]

In that exception did, indeed, lie the real root of the matter. For if we probe into the workings of Clive's mind we shall find that what he objected most strenuously to was not the size of the fortunes, nor even the mode of their making, though he did object to that too, but the rank of many of those who were making them. He was offended by the utter lack of regard for proper subordination and order that was being universally shown. For the whole service, irrespective of rank and seniority, had with one accord joined in the race for riches. Lack of discipline had always revolted him. He had always been a stickler for the prerogatives of superior rank. And he now felt very strongly that in this matter of fortune-hunting the juniors should wait their turn. To the seniors alone should go the chance of making comfortable, and more than comfortable, the days of their retirement.

It was a perfectly natural feeling. After all, he had been twenty-five before he began to make any money himself, and he must have remembered very vividly those early days of poverty. Not all self-made men wish that youth, other, that is, than their own offspring, should enjoy advantages denied to themselves. Besides, his youth had been spent in peril and hardship and his path had been strewn with rough places, whereas these pampered youths in Bengal had to do nothing but shake the pagoda tree for rupees to come down into their lap as thick as leaves on an autumn day. *He* had been commissary of the English forces in time of war. *They* could languidly leave all the dirty work of swindling the natives to their native agents, the *banyans*, who were devilishly skilled in all such business. But, if with their maturity had come a sense of responsibility, if not for the natives, for that would have been too much to expect, but at least for the interests of their employers, those interests which even the best of them, even Clive, had sometimes forgotten, or put in second place, they might still have been forgiven. That, however, was too seldom the case. Far too many of them, having satisfied their hunger while still in their twenties, were going home. The whole rate of retirement had been enormously speeded up since Plassey, and there were no longer any older, experienced men left to fill the places in Council. This was a real evil, and Clive had the true interests of the Company at heart in trying to put a stop to it.

He was, of course, fighting human nature, and a condition that had naturally—after Plassey—inevitably arisen. Life was just as precarious in Bengal as before, and it was asking a lot to expect these young men to wait as long as Clive wished them to wait before having their chance. They must have said to themselves that the chances of living as long as that were against them. He was wanting to introduce law and order and regularity of conduct into a frontier community that was more like a gold-mining camp than a settled colony, although in all such communities the only law commonly accepted and observed is that of each man for himself and the devil take both the hindmost and the native. Eighteenth-century views of property supported him, however. The nabob in England was an anachronism thrown forward in time from a century like our own that is quite used to regarding all wealth with equal respect, even with veneration, no matter how acquired—or the age and circumstances of the acquirer. Clive differed from the aristocrats of England in this, that whereas they hated and despised all nabobs, Clive being a nabob himself wanted no more than to slow up the production of them.

An evil of this kind should, if it is to be conquered at all, be attacked from both ends, from the top as well as from the bottom, by example as well as by precept. And here, indeed, was the real weakness of Clive's and the Select Committe's position. For despite all their protestations they cannot be said to have set the best possible example. They did not set it, for instance, in the matter of luxury and extravagance of living, vices that had grown rampant in a congenial climate, going hand in hand with rapacity and greed. Not that these vices were by any means a new thing. Years before this the Directors had read sermons to their Governors about the need of combating them. They had then suggested that the best way of going about it was for the Governor to set an example of frugal and unostentatious living. Such advice would have lost none of its point, though it might not have gained anything in effectiveness, if it had been repeated now in reply to the vehement diatribes of their present Governor. Clive's only claim, in fact, to being a good exemplar to youth was that he had been a soldier, serving the Company and the nation in a distinguished way, and so, in a manner, earned his vast wealth, besides showing some moderation and self-restraint. That he had thereby established a right to express disgust at the unbridled way in which these younger gentlemen gave rein to their purely selfish appetites cannot be denied.

But the point of our enquiry is not whether Clive had a right to some feeling of lofty superiority, but whether he was sufficiently superior to them, his hands sufficiently clean, to have a right to be their judge in so sweeping a manner. Granting that whatever he had done in the past, having gone over the mill, is no longer relevant to the point in question, there remains the question whether he was such a completely reformed character that he could point a just finger of scorn and censure at those who were now servants of the Company as he had once been. Did he administer impartial justice to all? Did he keep his vow against self-enrichment in both spirit and letter? Did he provide no loophole through which his enemies could attack his integrity and sincerity? Or was it all just a pose that cannot stand the test of being subjected to facts?

It goes almost without saying that he got not the slightest credit for virtue from his enemies. Some men make enemies in a way that leaves those enemies still moved with a desire to be fair. If Clive had made enemies earlier, they had for the most part been of this milder sort. Eyre Coote, for instance, has not left on record any kind of rejoinder. But with these men in 1765-6 it was entirely different. They did not hesitate to describe his administration as " the triumph of ambition, hypocrisy, and fraud."[183] They scoffed at all his virtuous claims. They had no scruples whatever about how they slandered him. The book of Caraccioli is filled with their scurrilities, some of them so filthy and ridiculous as to defeat entirely their purpose and rob their case of much of its strength. It is easy to see that Clive had brought upon himself the same fate that overtook Thomas Wentworth when he became the Earl of Strafford and the King's chief minister. " You are going to leave us, I see," his old friend and comrade in politics, John Pym, remarked to the new peer. " But," he added, " we will never leave you while your head is on your shoulders." These new enemies were similarly to harry Lord Clive into an early grave.

Many of the facts now to be stated only came to light seven years later at the Parliamentary investigation, but they are no less pertinent to our enquiry. Rumours of them must have been flying around in the close, heated atmosphere of Bengal, and it was largely because of the fact that Clive and his committee did most of their work in secrecy by their own arbitrary will that so much of the furor arose. Suspicions grow like weeds in such a soil as Clive was cultivating.

Let us first examine the cases of Munro and Carnac for evidence of partiality.[184] Munro as the victor of Buxar may be considered, by the standard of the times and one established by Clive himself, as worthy of a very considerable reward for his services both from the Company and from the Emperor ; from the latter, even though he had been defeated in that battle, because it brought him, temporarily, the reward of the Nawab-Vizier's dominions. At least, it is arguable that if Clive had rendered services to the Emperor deserving a rich *jaghire*, so also had Munro. But it did not work out that way, and for the following reasons.

The Emperor recognized his obligation and offered Munro a *jaghire* in Bengal worth £12,500. Munro, not being, like Clive, Governor as well as Commander-in-Chief, could not accept it by his own authority, and Governor Spencer was of the opinion that as the Company was at that very moment proceeding against Lord Clive's *jaghire*, Munro had better surrender his own to the Nawab and rely upon the Company's generosity for compensation. Munro complied. Said Mir Jafar to him, with a smile : " This is a piece of generosity I am little accustomed to, but if I live you shall not be the loser," and he offered him a present of two lakhs, being the equivalent of two years' yield of the *jaghire*. A few days later the old Nawab died, but his heir said he would

413

honour the promise, and in that expectation Munro went home.
Spencer passed the matter on to Clive, who dismissed the matter
by saying that he would see to it after the Nawab's debts were
paid. Seven years later, when the House of Commons was
enquiring into just such matters as these, it was discovered that
Munro had not yet received the two lakhs nor a reward of any
kind from the Company. An all too familiar bitterness crept
into Munro's voice as he told of this treatment :

" I am very happy, from his Lordship's eminent services to
this country and the Company, that he has a more responsible
fund for the payment of his *jaghire* ; at the same time I cannot
help regretting that his Lordship did not think my two years'
rent deserved a better fund than the Nabob's outstanding
debts. Let my small services be rewarded as they may, let
individuals think of them as they please, I hope facts will come
out, before this Committee is at an end, to show them and the
world that this country has been served, that this East India
Company has been saved, by more than one or two men ;
many brave and gallant men have done honour to their King,
have done service to their country, and have saved the East
Company ; and some of them have lost their lives in the
cause."

It is the old refrain that runs through the whole of this story,
from Stringer Lawrence to Hector Munro, that one man had
somehow managed to monopolize both the fame and the profit
of British military achievement in India.

Munro was asked whether he thought it would have been
proper for Lord Clive to have ordered the Nawab to pay the
money. He replied, " Had I been in his Lordship's situation, and
he in mine, I certainly would have ordered the Nabob to pay it."

" Did you ever hear that Lord Clive ordered the Nabob to
pay such a thing to any man living ? "

" No."

He stated that he had accepted one present of Rs.80,000 from
Bulwant Singh, Rajah of Benares. That was all. He had
refused over £300,000. His applications to the Court of
Directors for the two lakhs had been made in vain.

At this point Sir George Colebrook, the Company's Chairman,
interposed by informing the Committee that orders had just been
issued for the payment to Munro of the two lakhs.

The complement to this story is the case of Carnac, Munro's successor in the command. The Emperor and Bulwant Singh showed a fine diplomatic impartiality of regard for the English commanders : they offered Carnac the same presents of two lakhs and 80,000 rupees respectively. But meanwhile the Company's orders against presents had arrived, followed by the arrival of Clive himself and the issuance of the covenants for signature. Would Carnac under these circumstances be more fortunate in his treatment than Munro ? Would he be more fortunate than, for instance, the wretched councillors ?

There could have been little doubt in the mind of anyone who knew Clive that he *would* be more fortunate. Clive was inclined to be arbitrary in such matters. He was to show now that he did not regard the prohibition of presents as an *absolute* rule to be administered impartially to all servants alike, but rather as a convenient means of bestowing or withholding favour. According to the new regulations presents could still be accepted with permission, and the channel by which such permission could be obtained was himself. When we find him saying regarding his benefit fund for the army, " I shall not hesitate to exclude any whom I may think undeserving in any respect soever," we need feel no surprise that his attitude regarding presents was a similar reflection of personal pleasure or displeasure. Hence the special sense of grievance and resentment that the councillors felt. Of course, Clive's attitude was typical of an age in which favour and interest were all-important. This may explain why it was that when Colonel Champion signed his covenant he said he did so with cheerfulness, as they appeared to be but matter of form ! Any officer in Clive's good books might have reason to think the same.

Carnac, for instance, received the covenants for the army in July and immediately passed them out to his officers, but sent his own back to have the date changed because it anteceded the receipt of his present from Bulwant Singh. That was all right, because it was the Council's fault that the covenants had not been issued earlier. But now the Emperor's present came along and he had to obtain permission before accepting it. One of his brigadiers, Sir Robert Fletcher, had actually accepted a lakh from the Emperor without permission, and for doing so he was severely reprimanded by Clive, who reminded him of the terms of the covenants, of the Emperor's dire poverty, and of the fact that his superior officer had received nothing. Fletcher was not one of Clive's favourites, but even so he received gentler treatment than the unlucky councillors, no doubt because he was a military man.[185]

Clive endorsed Carnac's application with hearty approval. "We trust," he wrote to the Company, "you will rejoice that an opportunity should at last offer of placing General Carnac in a state of independence at the eve of a long and faithful service." To make doubly sure that the Company *would* rejoice he instructed his ever-useful agent Walsh to see that the matter was pushed through against any opposition : "The Directors must be the most ungrateful of men if they do not by the return ship or the first conveyance order him this money, with a due encomium upon his services, disinterestedness, and modesty." Clive's use of these words, particularly "disinterestedness," seems to have been peculiar to himself and his friends ! The Company was capable of equal favouritism, as it had shown in the past in its treatment of Clive himself. Favouritism and nepotism were, indeed, the curses of the service. Clive had been wroth only when its favour had gone to men like Coote instead of to Forde. But now the Company showed very clearly that it did not welcome this request. They sent neither the order nor the encomium. They preferred to take the matter under consideration, and then forget about it, with the result that the General kept both of his presents, £35,000. Perhaps, therefore, Clive's enemies can be forgiven a good part of their scepticism of his professions of superior virtue and the even-handedness of his justice !

In this connection the matter of his legacy needs to be examined.[186] The way in which it came about is as pertinent to our enquiry as the actual facts about it. Bearing in mind the suspicion in which Clive was held, it need excite no surprise that when in April 1766 he suddenly revealed the fact that Mir Jafar, who had died sixteen months previous, had left him a legacy of five lakhs, the general response of the settlement was a snort of incredulity. How could they be expected to believe that it was a *bona fide* legacy and not a disguised present, when they had only Clive's word for it and all transactions with the durbar were handled by the Governor alone ?

Clive, however, testified to the House of Commons'

Committee, and brought witnesses to support him, that he had first heard of the legacy immediately upon his arrival, but had then declined it because of his vow. When he changed his mind and applied to the Nawab's mother for payment it was with the intention of devoting the money to charitable purposes as a pension fund for the army. He was at the moment engaged in the unpopular task of cutting off the army's *batta* and wanted to do something that would help remove the sting and odium of that measure.[1] So he posed the question to the council: Is a legacy a present? It was somewhat of a moot question, but the council had no difficulty in agreeing with him that it was not; perhaps by the reasoning that any exception to an unpopular rule is better than none at all. It is impossible, however, not to wonder a little whether Clive would have been quite so positive if the legacy had been left to Vansittart, say, instead of to himself!

Clive, deeming five lakhs insufficient for his purpose, next applied to the new Nawab for three additional, and the Nawab, though he might well have felt that the provision of pensions for the Company's invalided officers was the Company's affair, not his, complied, thus raising the fund to £100,000. But difficulties were encountered with the Court of Directors. They could not have relished what looked to them like exceptions to their covenants, and they held that this case, in which their consent had not been obtained, was a breach of the spirit of them. Clive maintained that, though he had been appointed Governor, he was at sea at the time the legacy was left to him and had received none of the emoluments of his office, so that he was free to receive the legacy without their consent. The matter was referred to the Attorney-General, Fletcher Norton, who rendered an opinion in favour of Clive. So that at last, on April 6, 1770, Clive's wishes were carried into effect, with the Court of Directors acting as trustees of the fund.

His generosity has been termed " magnificent," and the cause was certainly worthy. But it would have been still more magnificent if he had taken the money out of his own ample fortunes instead of out of those of the puppet Nawab, particularly at such a moment, when all gifts from native princes were under suspicion. Charitable giving of the sort that distinguishes our present age was not particularly in vogue then, and therefore it

[1] See next chapter.

need arouse no surprise that this was Clive's only public bene-
faction.

That Clive missed no opportunity to do himself and his
friends a good turn while sticking within the limits of his covenant
and, not quite so closely, of his vow, may be seen from another
small transaction. For his vow not to enrich himself by his
third voyage to India should not be taken too literally. It is one
of the advantages of being rich and important that there are so
many ways of becoming richer, ways that involve no infraction
of any law or vow and, best of all, no glare of publicity. For
those with inside knowledge there is, for example, the way of the
stock market.

By an extraordinary coincidence, at the same time that Clive
discovered the Augean stable—" nothing but anarchy, confusion,
and, what is worse, an almost general corruption "—he also discovered that the Company's affairs were in an exceptionally
flourishing condition, so flourishing in fact that it was an excellent
time to buy stock. Naturally he did not want the second piece
of news broadcast over town, for that would have spoilt his
market. So he put his letter to Mr. Rous from Madras into
cipher. The last paragraph of that letter read : " As I have
written to Mr. Walsh on this subject and thought proper to use
the same precaution as I have to you, I must beg you to furnish
him with the key and likewise with a copy of this letter." The
letter to Walsh ran as follows :

> " I have desired Mr. Rous to furnish you with a copy of my
> letter to him of this day's date, likewise with the cipher, that
> you may be enabled to understand what follows : ' The
> contents are of such great importance that I would not have
> them transpire. Whatever money I may have in the public
> Funds, or anywhere else, and *as much as can be borrowed* in my
> name, I desire may be, without loss of a minute, invested in
> East India stock. You will speak to my attorneys on this
> point. Let them know I am anxious to have my money so
> disposed of ; and press them to hasten the affair as much as
> possible.' " [187]

The House of Commons' investigating committee got wind of
this letter, for the secret had to be shared with a few ; neither Mr.
Rous nor Mr. Walsh could get their letters deciphered without
the aid of the Company's secretary. And the Committee showed

a somewhat embarrassing curiosity about it. They wanted to know why Clive considered the moment so opportune for investing in India stock, especially as the general tenor of his other letters suggested the very reverse ; suggested, indeed, that he had arrived barely in time to save the Company. They put it to him that the order to Walsh was connected with his decision to take over the revenues of Bengal. This he denied, though he supplied them with no other explanation.

Walsh received the letter on March 30, 1766. He hurried around to India House to get it deciphered and see Clive's letter to Mr. Rous. Knowledge of the matter was confined to the inner circle of the Directorate functioning as a Secret Committee. In this way it was kept from Mr. Sulivan. Rous then went to see Clive's five attorneys, and the buying of stock began. Walsh passed the good word around also among his friends. But they were only just in time. The two letters had been nearly a year on their way and they arrived only three weeks ahead of the public advices of the acquisition of the *dewani*, which at once began a boom in the stock. In that time Clive's attorneys had managed to buy £12,000 of shares at $165\frac{1}{4}$. The stock soared to 175. The following day they bought £13,000 more, and on May 9 £5,000 at 179, after which the stock rose to 190. Later it went much higher, before finally crashing when expectations of prosperity were not realized, but long before then Clive had wisely sold out and invested in land.

It will be seen that he made well over £3,000 on the transaction, his friends at home profiting in like manner. He had in addition bought all the stock he could from his fellow passengers on board ship and at Madras and Calcutta. When he actually consummated the *dewani* deal with the Emperor in August he repeated his order to his agents. He told them he was remitting home £80,000 in gold, being two and a half years' yield of his *jaghire* with interest, and they were to use it to purchase stock. If they failed to carry out this order it was no doubt because the owners of stock were no longer willing to sell and the profitable moment to buy had passed.[1]

---

[1] The attempt of some of Clive's biographers to make us believe that Clive was only buying the stock for election purposes is too childish to require refuting. Clive did no vote-splitting after he left England, and in any case he left all such matters in the hands of his agents. In his second letter on September 27, 1765, he specifically mentioned " the present flourishing condition of the Company's affairs " as his reason.

The same help that Clive extended to his friends at home he extended to his friends and colleagues in India. He was ready to help Carnac to keep his present from the Emperor. He was ready to join with the members of his Committee immediately upon landing in a private partnership for trading in the prohibited article of salt. They each invested £12,500, took a quarter share, made Verelst their manager, and at the end of nine months realized a nice profit, with interest, of 45 per cent. Clive did not take his profits for himself, for that would have been counter to his vow. We shall see presently what he did with them.

In September he carried out the plan for the inland trade that he had formed on board ship. To do this he had to ignore, as we have seen, the orders that he carried from the Directors for prohibiting the Company's servants from engaging in it ; but this, as we have also seen, he had good reason for doing. Instead of throwing the trade in salt, betel-nut, and tobacco open to the natives of Bengal he made it a monopoly for the benefit primarily of the Company's servants and secondarily of the Company. Salt, the chief article, had in earlier days been a government monopoly, farmed out periodically to the highest bidder or the Nawab's favourite, and in later days of British rule it was to become one again and remain one. So Clive had a case for opposing his views to the Company's, besides the need for finding some new way to remunerate its servants in lieu of adequate salaries. But the expedient had the great objection that, in the form he adopted, it was almost indistinguishable from the old private trading that had wrought such terrible evil in the land and against which the Directors had so sternly set their face. Clive was regulating a practice that had previously been unregulated. That in itself was a merit ; but that in their eyes was the only difference ; and when they received his request that they bless the scheme and confirm it, they absolutely and indignantly refused. It seemed to them merely a brazen flouting of their orders, and while they blessed every other part of his work they were to curse this. If Clive had actually made salt a government monopoly under the Company instead of placing it in the hands directly of the Company's servants, he might have made it more acceptable.

He organized all the servants, both military and civil, into a trading company with shares allotted proportionate to the rank of everybody from the Governor and Commander-in-Chief downwards, excluding writers and officers below the rank of majors, chaplains and surgeons. To the Governor were given five shares, to colonels and members of Council two, whilst to the Company was reserved a duty of 35 per cent., which was calculated to yield it £120,000. This company then sold the salt to the native retailers and the free merchants and their agents. Some attempt, not too successful, was made to give the native merchants a fair share of the trade and to prevent the consumer from being overcharged. But all the abuses inherent in a monopoly were still present.

The following year, in order to try to meet the Company's objections, Clive went to considerable pains to correct the defects in the plan that the first year's operations had revealed. He fixed the retail price, excluded Europeans and their agents from the trade, gave the native merchants liberty to transport the salt without exactions, and raised the Company's duty to 50 per cent. But so far as hoping to convince the Directors that they should now change their mind, it was all in vain. The Directors reiterated their orders even more strongly, going so far as to pronounce Clive and his colleagues guilty of breach of covenant. Nevertheless, Clive refused to give up his pet scheme. Only on the eve of sailing home did he reluctantly admit that the Directors appeared adamant, and even then he promised that he would do his utmost to prevail upon them. So the Council went ahead again in September 1767 and renewed the contracts of the Society of Trade for a third year. Only in the following September were its affairs at last wound up. By that time Clive's unanswerable arguments that the Company must make some provision for its servants had produced their due effect, and instead of the salt monopoly they were allowed a $2\frac{1}{2}$ per cent. commission on the net revenues of the state. The light of reason had dawned slowly on the mercantile minds of the city, but it had at last dawned. The beginning of the creation of a genuinely professional service, no longer dependent upon private trade, presents, or other irregular perquisites, may be dated from this change.

The senior servants made handsome additions to their income by the Society of Trade, intended, as we have seen, to compensate them for the cutting-off of presents. Colonels and members of Council benefited by £7000 a year, whilst the Governor's five shares were reckoned to bring him in £17,500.

Following to the end the somewhat intricate course of Clive's expedients for ensuring that neither he nor his friends would be out of pocket by their sojourn in India, we find that in September 1766 he came to the conclusion that the Governor at least, if as yet nobody else, should be debarred from private trading entirely, and he arranged for him to take instead a commission of $1\frac{1}{8}$ per cent. upon the *dewani* revenues. As this was equivalent to a salary of between £30,000 and £35,000, clearly no great deprivation was involved in the reform. Nonetheless, it was salutary on general principles and a step in the right direction.

It was quite typical of Clive's grand mode of doing things to invest the change with the utmost solemnity and to adopt the most ostentatious way of giving effect to it. A hundred and fifty of the chief officials and inhabitants of Calcutta had to go in procession to the Mayor's Court, the highest court of justice in the settlement, to witness him execute a deed. There he publicly and solemnly swore that in consideration of this percentage and of his salary, allowances and " commission upon the mint, coral and upon freight goods, and 10 per cent. interest or premium upon any sum or sums of money I shall or may hereafter lend, advance, or place out at interest as before-mentioned," he would relinquish all other emoluments or advantages, would not lend money at more than 10 per cent., would not trade, would not break his covenant by accepting any presents or rewards, either on his own behalf or on behalf of his friends, and would not receive any fees from the disposal of offices ; and the penalty for a breach of the oath was set at £150,000, which also was written into the deed.

That to most of the assembled company the occasion seemed like a solemn farce is not surprising. But that was largely because they did not, and never had, taken seriously his vow not to enrich himself a farthing by his station. They had seen his salt transactions, and now they saw him, on the eve of departure, exchanging them for an assured £30,000. What, then, they thought, became of his vow ?

But in this they did him an injustice. He had been prepared for such incredulity and from the day that he sailed from England he had kept careful accounts. By not enriching himself he had meant that he would not return home any richer, and not that he would not take enough to cover all expenses while in India.

Nor had his undertaking not to trade meant more than that he would not trade for his own profit. Hence the salt enterprise with his colleagues of the Committee, which netted each of them in the region of £5000. When winding up his affairs in Bengal he sold his interest in the Society of Trade for £32,000, not wanting to wait to receive his share until the books were made up, which might not be for several years ; but he paid back £20,000 of this, all but his first year's profits, when he exchanged the Governor's trading privilege for the commission on the revenues. Apparently, by arrangement with his successor, he took this commission for a whole year in lieu of his salt dividend on the second year's trading, although he actually gave up his office within four months of executing the deed.

Adding together his salary of £6000, his allowances, his profits on trade, his commission on the revenues, what he received in the way of *nuzzerana* (which amounted to over two lakhs), and other perquisites, we find that his gross receipts from the day he sailed until his return were, in round figures, £80,000. The accounts he presented to Parliament showed, however, that he was actually out of pocket £5,816. How, then, did he manage to spend nearly £86,000 in three years ? A list of his expenditures supplies the answer.

His voyage to India (not including the £3,000 paid by the Company)	73,489	rupees.
Sundry	99,629	,,
Table expenses	97,642	,,
Clothing and linen	16,987	,,
Wages to secretaries, assistants, and stewards	19,722	,,
Feeding five elephants	941	,,
Losses on remittance of *jaghire*	8,375	,,
Plate given to Dutch governors	2,177	,,
" For the fortune with which his Lordship was pleased to reward his faithful servant, Edward Philpot, Esq."	14,928	,,
	333,890	,,

Equalling £37,563.

And then, by a later account kept in pounds sterling :

Further charges of salaries, table expenses, and wearing apparel . .	£2,795	(excluding
Sundry	£1,846	shillings
For other fortunes given to : ·		and pence)
Henry Strachey	£15,942	
Edmund Maskelyne . . .	£13,050	
Samuel Ingham	£9,162	
Edward Philpot	£2,196	
Messrs. Wynne, Archdekin, Coxe, and Ducarell	£3,402	
	—————	
	£48,393	

Making a grand total of £85,956

What Clive meant by not enriching himself one farthing is now clear. Whatever he did not spend on his own expenses he gave to the members of his staff. The three gentlemen who accompanied him out went home with him wealthy men : Edmund, £25,000 the richer ; Strachey, £18,000 ; and Dr. Ingham, £16,000. Philpot, his servant, came away with £3,000. From this and previous evidences it is clear that Clive took good care of the men who served him. From the figures it is clear, also, that he was a lavish spender on himself. He may not have been any richer, but he did not stint himself. And, furthermore, all this time he was receiving and remitting home the income from his *jaghire*, £25,000 to £30,000 a year.

We come to the end of our enquiry. And, perhaps, if we try to rid our minds of modern notions of conduct proper to the governor of a great state and the head of great imperial services, bound by rigid rules and ethical standards, and see Clive as sharing the extreme individualism characteristic of his day, which gave to most men in public life the appearance of political adventurers, living and succeeding by their wits more than by their talents, compelled to be specious rather than sincere, clever rather than scrupulous, opportunists rather than men of principle ; if, that is, we weigh his words in the same scale as we should the words of politicians when engaged in the heat and fury of battle, we shall arrive at a fairer estimate than if we take them literally.

The Augean stable was not as Augean as, for obvious reasons, he wished his constituents to believe. Nor was his own administration so much better or his purposes so disinterested as he for the same reasons wished them to believe. His campaign of propaganda was clever, but it only partially succeeded ; it was to have much greater success with posterity than with his contemporaries, better acquainted as they were with the motives that gave rise to it and the realities upon which it rested. The Court of Directors naturally gave Clive's campaign its blessing. They wrote to him on May 17, 1766 :

> "We have the strongest sense of the deplorable state to which our affairs were on the point of being reduced, from the corruption and rapacity of our servants, and the universal depravity of manners throughout the settlement ; we agree entirely with your Lordship that the train our affairs were in would in a very few months have brought us to a most dangerous situation."

But in course of time they were to find out how delusory were the promises of improvement held out. They were also to discover that what Clive and they had together thrown was a boomerang that came back and struck them both with fearful effect as soon as these matters came up for discussion in Parliament. For it gave the national politicians the most plausible excuse for saying that if matters were as bad as *that*, it was high time for Parliament to interfere. The politicians of the Company were then hung in the same noose that they had slipped around the necks of their servants. And when the storm of abuse and recrimination reached its height, Clive was to find himself caught between two fires, the fire of the personal enemies he had made in India, not to mention Sulivan, and the fire of the righteously indignant members of Parliament.

If Clive really wished to " sell " himself to the service and the public as a model of disinterested and public-spirited virtue he should have employed, in modern style, a public relations counsel—as some of our best-known millionaire philanthropists have done—who would have saved him from some of the mistakes he made. But the job could not have been done overnight. The best that can be said of what Clive accomplished

425

by his own unaided efforts was that he did succeed in rising above the low level of his age. His approach to the problem of reform, his own qualifications for the task and his methods were all equally faulty, but in the face of all his handicaps he made a gallant showing. We can admire his energy and courage, bull-headed though the latter was. We can even admire his magnificent blindness to the weakness of his position. And when we come to watch him suppressing mutiny in the army our admiration can be ungrudging and unstinted.

Chapter Twenty-six

MUTINY

" For my own part, I must see the soldiers' bayonets levelled at my throat
before I can be induced to give way "   CLIVE

I

IN THE MULTIPLICITY OF SITUATIONS that strung together form the
thread of a man's life there inevitably occur some, if he be anything of a man, that coincide exactly with the strongest part of
his nature, enabling him to act with maximum efficiency and
maximum success. It is then that we can truly speak of him being
" master of a situation." They may be few and far between or,
with a few favoured ones of history, like Augustus and Napoleon,
they may follow each other in a dazzling succession that leaves us
amazed.

In Clive's life there were four such supreme occasions : Arcot,
the domination of Bengal, the routing of the Dutch, and the
Mutiny of 1766. The personal qualities that these situations
demanded for perfection of conduct coincided exactly with those
that he possessed : courage, resolution, bold assurance. Each
was essentially a simple situation, offering only two alternative
courses : stand fast or yield. On more complex occasions, such
as those during the Bengal expedition and the Plassey campaign,
when other alternatives were open to him, he showed no such
mastery. Thus the anecdote of his youthful encounter with a
gambler revealed an essential part of his character, which was
underlined even more strongly by his conflict with Admiral
Watson over the command of Fort William.

It is the operation of a natural law of human society that
every armed conflict of nations is accompanied by a sub-conflict
of civil and military powers within the state. Nor were the wars
of the English in India an exception. There were evidences of
that lesser conflict from the earliest days, when Saunders and
Lawrence disputed over the conduct of operations and the promo-

427

tion of officers. It was seen again when Aldercron claimed for himself the entire military authority on the coast, a claim repeated by his successors. It was seen still more in Bengal when Carnac opposed Vansittart's policy. It was seen in another form in 1757 when the whole body of officers in the Carnatic endeavoured to coerce the governing council to allow them bigger allowances, and again in 1762 when Madras tried to make retrenchments in its military expenditure and once more the officers revolted. On three separate planes, in the ranks, among the officers, and in the higher command, the spirit of insubordination was active during these years. And when Clive came back to India it was still unsettled whether the civil power would prove strong enough to curb the army and re-impose its lost authority.

This is clearly seen in what he wrote Verelst from up-country, where his mind naturally turned to such matters :

"I appeal to yourself whether the commanding officers, whoever they were, since my departure from India until my second arrival in this quarter, have not by their conduct endeavoured to impress upon the minds of the princes of the country that the power was rather in the commander-in-chief of the army than in the Governor and Council. Indeed, a few months more of Mr. Spencer's government would have made them lords paramount."

Warren Hastings when he became governor seven years later made exactly the same observation, and one of his first reforms was to restore authority once more to where it rightly belonged.

The fact that Clive was not and never had been a professional soldier becomes of first importance now. He had shown great shrewdness in never divesting himself of his civilian status as he had been able thereby to have the best of both worlds : he was the only man in the Company's service equally eligible for the posts of civilian governor and military commander-in-chief ; for the Directors would never have appointed any purely military man as the former. He had always taken pains to impress upon his employers the fact that he believed thoroughly in the supremacy of the civil power, so that he should not be suspected of allowing any perverted sense of loyalty to his adopted service to prevent him from doing his duty to the Company. Only two months after his greatest victory he had written them : " I have the liberty of an Englishman so strongly implanted in my nature that I would have the civil all in all, in all times and in all places (cases of immediate danger excepted)."

Clive had used his double status to great advantage during his first administration, but it was of even greater service now. In fact, it was almost enough of itself to justify the Company's appointment of him. What he had written to Verelst was a reflection upon his own colleague and friend General Carnac. No one but Clive, one feels sure, could at this moment have re-established the Governor's authority so easily and smoothly. His complete ascendancy over Carnac was never in doubt for one moment, whereas the lack of that ascendancy had been one of Vansittart's greatest handicaps. And his relations, too, with the brigade commanders were in striking contrast to those with the members of council.

For one thing, two of them, Barker and Smith, had been his own selection and had made the voyage with him ; and for another, they were Company's, not King's officers. With the third, Fletcher, matters were somewhat different. He was not one of Clive's choices as Clive would never have chosen such a rank bad officer for any command. He owed his appointment to Sulivan, whose chief failing as a statesman was in allowing personal and political considerations to govern him in the matter of appointments ; he was as likely to pick a Fletcher as a Coote.[1] Sir Robert Fletcher was representative of all that was worst in the service, the soldier-of-fortune type who gained promotion by intrigue and was always on the scent of spoils. Clive disliked him intensely and was to have the satisfaction of getting him court-martialled and cashiered.

His relations with Smith and Barker, able and experienced officers, may be seen from two letters he wrote them. The letter to Smith was in answer to his complaint that Clive did not give him his full confidence. They had been on cordial terms on shipboard. Why then, asked Smith, the change in Clive's attitude ? Clive ignored one such inquiry, but on receiving a second he gave him a frank, straight-from-the-shoulder reply. He instanced several occasions when Smith had offended him by the assumption of a superior tone :

[1] But surely if Sulivan's patronage of Fletcher was deplorable, he more than redeemed himself in the case of Warren Hastings !

" These, Sir, among many other reasons, have occasioned my acting with reserve towards you. Indeed, in the whole course of so long a voyage, I could observe a mind too actuated by ambition : such a tendency in Colonel Smith, to govern and command those who ought to govern and command him, that I could not be unreserved, without giving up that authority which I am determined to support ; and although I do, and always have allowed you many virtues, so long as you continue to give so much general offence by that kind of behaviour, so long will you be exposed to mortification and disappointment."

For Barker he had a particularly high regard, and when Barker made an improper request for a share in the revenue administration of Bihar Clive showed a rare gentleness and tact in refusing it :

" I must confess the receipt of your letter of the 2d. Feb. has given me infinite concern, because I feel for you as I should for myself, and there is no officer in this part of the world for whom I entertain so strong and true regard, or whom I am so very desirous of serving. I am sure, if it depended upon me, you should, upon Carnac's departure, succeed to his rank and station ; so well acquainted am I with your merits as a soldier, your moderation and temper as a man. Your being hurt, therefore, at not having an appointment which is not in my power to obtain for you, cannot but hurt me. I am convinced that, great as my interest is, were I to propose your being joined with Mr. Middleton in directing the collection of the revenues of the Behar province, I could not carry that point. Consider, Barker, how very separate and distinct the services are ; consider how very jealous the Directors are of military men ; and how very attentive they will be to every action of mine whom they look upon in a military more than in a civil light. Recollect that they would not even allow Coote to have a seat at the Board to give his advice except upon military matters only. I say further that were I to take such an unprecedented step, I doubt whether it would not add such weight of argument to those counsellors and malcontents, who are gone home with a full design to exclaim against arbitrary and military power, that the Company might be induced to disapprove of everything I have done for them, from an apprehension that I meant to accomplish every measure, by the subversion of civil liberty.

Persuaded I am, that the joining with Middleton a man of your steadiness, moderation, and discretion, would be of singular advantage to the Company : notwithstanding which, I dare not attempt to do it."

The letter clearly proves how essential it had been to Clive to preserve his civilian status. His foresight in such a matter is testimony to the consistent skill he had shown in planning and managing his career.

So much for the highest plane of conflict between the civil and military powers ; Clive had won there by combining both in his own person. But it was a test on the second plane that was now impending in Bengal : the officers of the army *versus* the government over the matter of double *batta*.

This extra allowance had first been granted the English officers by Mir Jafar out of his personal bounty following a precedent established by Muhammad Ali in the Carnatic. The Company had been quite agreeable to it as long as the Nawab bore the expense, but when by Vansittart's arrangement with Mir Kasim lands were assigned to defray the military expenses the Directors saw the matter in quite a different light : they were then, as they saw it, paying out money that would otherwise be going to the shareholders. And was not the double *batta* exceptional and contrary to the Company's practice ? It was. So the Company at once wanted to put a stop to it.

This had not been easy, however ; in fact, it had so far proved impossible. Their orders arrived on the eve of the war with Mir Kasim, an obviously unpropitious moment for enforcing so unpopular a measure. For the merest hint of it was sufficient to evoke a growl from the army, which could not see the justice of it being made to suffer in order that the pockets of the shareholders might benefit. And as the army remained continuously in the field until Clive's arrival it was reasonable for Spencer as well as Vansittart to defer enforcing it ; his was, after all, merely a stop-gap government. Thus the enforcement fell to Clive's lot, and he carried with him renewed orders to that effect. But it meant meeting head-on the challenge of an army that had developed a strong *esprit de corps*, had come to know its strength and indispensability, and had grown used to overawing the weak civilians of the council.

Clive planned all his moves with the utmost cleverness. He

must have known, as we have seen, what he would be up against even before he left England. To have attempted at once to carry out that triple commission to suppress presents, inland trade, and *batta* would have been disastrous. Not even he could have withstood the resulting revolt. So he had first attacked the matter of presents, which scarcely affected anybody outside the council and the higher command, while being careful not to be too scrupulous, as we have seen, about how the prohibition was observed by the latter. Then he proceeded by means of the acquisition of the revenues and the dispossession of the Nawab to remove the chief objection against the Company's servants' participation in the trade in salt, betel-nut, and tobacco. Having done that he organized the Society of Trade, which put that trade on a regular basis as a monopoly to benefit the senior servants, and thereby he was able to satisfy them and ensure their support, or at least acquiescence, in his measures against the junior servants. Before decreeing, too, the end of double *batta* he had been careful to make peace with the Nawab of Oude, settle all outstanding political matters, and put into effect his reorganization of the army. It was not until his return to Calcutta in September that he had issued notification that the privilege would cease on January 1, 1766.

But before the outbreak in the army he had first to meet and crush a civilian revolt.

II

The spirit of revolt against his " tyranny " had been gaining ground ever since his arrival. It came to a head early in the New Year. The civil revolt was precipitated by one crowning act of authority that spread the blaze of indignation from the members of council to the juniors in the service. The suspension of three members of Council and suicide of a fourth left vacancies at the Board which Clive, in defiance of the views he had expressed in England when he had denounced the practice of importing servants like Spencer from the other Presidencies, proposed to fill by bringing four men from Madras.[188]

He had already foreseen the need of such drastic action. In September he had looked around for suitable candidates for promotion and found none, or at least, " in the whole list of your junior merchants there are not more than three or four gentlemen whom we could possibly recommend to higher stations at present." [1] The homeward flight of the senior servants that season had reached such alarming proportions that only writers were left to discharge the duties of such important posts as the Secretary, the Accountant, Storekeeper, and Paymaster to the Army. In these circumstances Clive felt justified in ignoring the orders of the Directors. Seniority, he said, should no longer be the rule of the service. " You are now become the sovereigns of a rich and potent kingdom ; your success is beheld with jealousy by the other European nations in India, and your interests are so extended, so complicated, and so connected with those of the several surrounding powers, as to form a nice and difficult system of politics." To commit into the hands of rash, inexperienced young men the conduct of such a system was manifestly unsound. He exhorted the Directors thenceforth to allow no consideration but that of merit to influence them in their selections.

Naturally the whole service rose up in arms at the affront to their self-respect implied in this act of supersession, and their youthfulness only made their heads the hotter. To express their feelings they adopted a typically youthful method. They sent Clive to Coventry ! All visits to him were forbidden. All invitations from him and members of the Committee were refused. The new-comers from Madras were to be treated with neglect and contempt. Every member of their association who broke these rules was to be treated similarly. And a remonstrance to the Court of Directors was drawn up and signed.

But the servants were mere children in the hands of Clive, and he had not the slightest difficulty in quelling such a puerile revolt. Their ringleader was dismissed from the service ; whilst the rest of them were effectively dealt with in ways that directly affected their pockets, a possession more dear to them than honour ; for it was a simple matter to refuse them *dastaks* and so prevent them from trading. Others were removed from lucrative jobs or forced by threats into recantation. In short, said Barwell rue-

[1] Vansittart stoutly controverted the need for Clive's action and strongly condemned Clive's attempt to impeach the integrity and capacity of the whole body of Bengal servants : " During my residence in Bengal I had no reason to complain of the want of diligence, capacity, or integrity in the servants in general. There were a great number among the servants in Bengal as well qualified in every respect to fill the vacant seats in Council. . . . I take the part of no Company servant against whom the Court of Directors have any cause of complaint ; but surely it is not a crime to speak to the characters of a whole body of Gentlemen who are accused without a fault and punished without a hearing." [189]

fully, " every servant that had ventured to express detestation of the administration was marked and immediately stripped of all to their bare pay." So, " lo ! the spirited Bengallers appeared in a body one morning at the table of their lord and master " and humbly begged forgiveness ; and then only a few sparks of British spirit, lamented Barwell, remained. The Company's servants were reduced to a " slavish dependence " upon government :

> " The subjugating maxims that were adopted have been attended with extraordinary success, for there is not at this present time a civilian that sits at the Council Board, or any servant below that rank, who dares so much as hint his disapprobation of any measure, without being prepared to encounter suspension the consequence of such temerity." [190]

So much for the civilians. But the revolt of the military gentlemen still had to be faced. The effect of the order against *batta* was to place the Bengal army on the same footing as the Madras service, where the order had been enforced some years before. But in the eyes of the junior officers, who were not allowed to share in the profits of the Society of Trade, it created a real grievance, since a greatly inflated style of living had become general in Bengal with the prices of everything used by Europeans rising to fantastic levels, and until these could be reduced the allowance of a subaltern, as Clive himself admitted, would scarce " maintain him in the station of a gentleman." But orders were orders, and Clive would not listen to the murmurings and complaints that began to reach him. He was doing everything he could to redress the grievance by devising means for the officers to live cheaper.

March 20 found Clive at his country house at Dum Dum, five miles from Calcutta, resting before going up-country once more to escape the bad season and to put the finishing touches to his work of settlement. The country was in perfect tranquillity, he wrote his wife, and nothing remained to be done but some more negotiations with the princes of the country. Maskelyne, Strachey, Ingham, and Carnac would accompany him. They would be gone five or six months and would then return in time to receive an answer from home to Clive's despatches and to prepare for their homeward journey. They planned to return to England overland. " I have made enquiry of numbers who have travelled overland, who all agree that the journey is perfectly safe, very entertaining and very agreeable, and not attended with the least fatigue, if we leave Bassarah [Bussora] by the end of January or beginning of February, which I shall endeavour to accomplish by leaving Bengal early in the month of December."

Not a word about what was in store for him ! Of that he had no warning yet, though he was aware of the general feeling in the army.

The party left Calcutta a few days later. At Murshidebad Clive conferred with Sykes, the Resident, on revenue matters. He also saw the begum, Mir Jafar's widow, and asked her for the legacy that he had previously declined. On April 19 he received the first hint that something serious might be stirring. The Committee forwarded him a remonstrance from Sir Robert Barker's Third Brigade against the abolition of *batta*. It was signed by nine captains, twelve lieutenants, and twenty ensigns. Clive had the remonstrance sent to Barker with a note that the Council could take no notice of any petition that did not come through regular channels. He then proceeded with the work of settling the revenue demands for the coming year, sitting in state with the Nawab on the day of the Punia, when all the zemindars of the provinces assembled to make their annual contracts with the government.

The day before this state function, however, the existence of a conspiracy in the army was revealed to him. He received a letter from Fletcher stating his suspicions that the officers of the whole army intended to resign their commissions as from May 1, merely serving through the coming month as volunteers. From Barker he heard the same story.[191]

It was true. A conspiracy had been hatched in Fletcher's brigade at Monghyr and had spread to the other two brigades. The officers had formed an association binding themselves by oath to secrecy and to preserve, at the hazard of their own lives, the lives of any one of their number who might be condemned to death by court-martial. They knew that they were not legally debarred from resigning their commissions at will and they hoped by taking advantage of this privilege to escape the charge and the consequences of mutiny. Each officer bound himself separately by a bond of £500 not to accept his commission again until double *batta* was restored. Nor was this all. The association was in league with malcontent civilians, and £16,000 was raised

435

by subscription in Calcutta to aid them in their cause and indemnify those who might be cashiered.

The situation was rendered serious in the extreme by the fact that the Marathas were in motion and threatening an invasion of Bengal. Nothing, indeed, but Clive's resolution and the fact that the conspiracy came to light a little before it was fully hatched —the date originally set was June 1—saved the day for the Company.

Clive did not hesitate a moment. He at once sent by special messenger a letter to the council informing them of the critical state of affairs and desiring them to write immediately to Madras to ask for reinforcements of officers and cadets. When the conspirators heard of this they wrote to try to dissuade the Madras officers from coming, but Clive met this move by promptly ordering the stoppage of all private letters between Calcutta and Madras. Forty-two officers were sent up from Madras.

The situation was too serious for worry about the niceties of the law. An individual officer might be entitled to resign his commission as and when he pleased, but for all to resign together as a body admitted of only one construction : it was plain mutiny. Clive wrote to the three brigadiers ordering them to arrest and hold for general court-martial any officer whose conduct seemed to come under this head. "The ringleaders of this affair must suffer the severest punishment that martial law can inflict, else there is an end of discipline in the army and of authority in the East India Company over all their servants."

On May 4 he received the notification from Fletcher that forty officers of his command had handed in their commissions. They declared their willingness to serve as volunteers without pay until the fifteenth of the month, so that the Company's affairs would not suffer.

For it apparently did not enter their unthinking heads that Clive would stand fast. How could he ? How could he dare risk the existence of the Company ? How could Bengal be defended by an army without officers ? The officers pinned their hopes on the threatening motions of the Marathas close to Allahabad, where Smith's brigade lay. They were not, at least the majority were not, disloyal Englishmen ; they were not intending to betray their trust to the Marathas ; they merely thought they held all the aces in the pack and that Clive, like a good card-player, would throw in his hand at once ! The British trades unions had thought the same in 1926 ; they never dreamed that the nation could or would resist them successfully when they called their General Strike. It was a plain hold-up.

But how little they knew their man ! Any other man would have yielded from an obvious lack of alternative—or, as Barwell put it, " Prudence would in all probability have induced others to temporize till the risk of enforcing their resolutions had been lessened. You who know Clive's temper will not be surprised at his chusing to hazard all on the turn of dye rather than his royal will and pleasure should be contravened." Yet even Clive had to admit the possibility that he might have to yield, though only in the last resort. " For my own part," he wrote, " I must see the soldiers' bayonets levelled at my throat before I can be induced to give way; and then, not so much for the preservation of my own life, as the temporary salvation of the Company ; temporary only it can be, for I shall think Bengal in the utmost danger, when we are reduced to the necessity of submitting the civil power to the mercy of men who have gone lengths that will frighten and astonish all England." How bereft he was of aid in the emergency was shown by his appeal to the free merchants for volunteers to act as officers. Only two responded.

One thing alone was to save him. That was the fact that the officers, for the most part still sound at heart in their sense of duty and allegiance to the Company and mindful of their careers, were bluffing ; few of them were prepared to go the lengths that were necessary in order to overcome Clive's resolution. Clive won by calling their bluff.

He left Murshidebad and proceeded by forced marches towards Monghyr. On the way he intercepted a letter from Colonel Smith to the Committee reporting the Marathas' advance. Clive sent him orders to hold his ground and not make terms with his officers unless forced to do so by an actual invasion. He sent ahead of him four trustworthy officers from his staff to attempt to bring the Monghyr officers to reason.

They arrived to find the situation practically out of control. Clive's orders were that every officer who had resigned should be sent down to Calcutta. But the European rank-and-file too were on the verge of mutiny, so that everything depended on the loyalty of the sepoys. Fortunately the sepoys remained loyal. When mutiny came the Europeans found themselves confronted by the sepoy battalions led by Clive's officers with loaded muskets

437

and fixed bayonets. This turned the scale. The men went quietly back to their barracks. (Let the reader pause for a moment to ponder the significance of this phenomenon—an empire being saved for its conquerors by the subject people themselves ! It tells half the story of the " conquest.")

Rifts now began to appear in the officers' ranks. Many had joined the association from fear and not by choice. When Clive arrived on the 15th the worst danger was passed. He ordered a parade of the whole brigade and addressed it, speaking as a British soldier to British soldiers. He explained the facts about the double *batta*, declared the officers guilty of mutiny for which they would be severely punished, told the men about the fund he had founded to prove his friendship for the army and kindly thought for their interests, and then appealed to them to act as sober, right-thinking men, and remain true to their duty. He next addressed the sepoys, praising them for their loyalty. He distributed rewards to their native officers and ordered double pay for the men for the months of May and June. And he was rewarded by the acclamations of the whole brigade, which, practically officerless as it was, retired from the parade ground in perfect order.

The officers who had been expelled from the fort lay encamped a short distance from Monghyr in a complete quandary what to do. Their bluff had failed. Clive ordered them peremptorily to leave at once for Calcutta and sent a detachment of sepoys to enforce the order. Beaten and broken men now, they started in small parties down the river, leaving behind them not only their careers but in many cases their entire fortunes.

The next day Clive proceeded on to Patna. Here he found the situation less serious. Fletcher had been implicated in the conspiracy and had played a double role. He had heard about it in January, had said nothing, had even apparently encouraged it on the flimsy excuse that he wanted to win the officers' confidence and so know what was afoot. Barker, on the other hand, had shown the utmost firmness. When his officers presented their commissions he had prevailed upon a number of them to postpone action. Those who had insisted upon immediate acceptance he had sent at once on their way to Calcutta. Clive's arrival sufficed to make the rest retract.

The real danger-point was Smith's brigade, which lay part at Allahabad and part at Serajepur, a hundred miles beyond the city, where they were posted observing the near approach of the Marathas. Despite the fact that resignation for them was scarcely distinguishable from desertion in the face of the enemy, the officers had expressed their determination to resign, some at once, some on June 1. The Colonel expressed his sense of shame and indignation at their conduct, but to no avail. The officers at Allahabad were so openly mutinous that a battalion of sepoys had to be sent from Serajepur to deal with them. The sepoys covered the distance in fifty-four hours and upon their arrival the garrison commander put every officer under arrest on pain of being shot by the sepoys. The officers wavered, then quietly submitted when they heard of the failure of their comrades at Monghyr and Patna. Their leaders were sent down as prisoners to Patna, doubly humiliated because their escorts were sepoys.

The mutiny was completely broken. Many of the officers who went away went with tears in their eyes, pleading for a chance to reinstate themselves. At last they had awakened to their situation. But Clive was relentless in dealing out strict justice. Letters poured in upon him, apologetic and intercessory. The prayers of most of the junior officers he was willing to heed, feeling that they had been misled. These he pardoned. But those who had resigned their commissions in the face of the enemy—" no consideration on earth shall induce me to restore one of them to the service." They and the other ringleaders were tried by court-martial at Patna and sentenced to be cashiered. The only reason they were not shot as Clive wished was a doubt in the minds of the council whether their crime warranted the supreme penalty ; there was, after all, that question about the strict illegality of their conduct. Sir Robert Fletcher, too, was tried by court-martial for his dubious behaviour and being found guilty was cashiered.

The officers Clive chose to make examples of were treated with merciless severity. Having been ordered down to Calcutta without being given time to arrange their affairs, they were there placed under close arrest, their appeal to the civil courts being shut off. When they resisted, guards of sepoys were posted upon their houses to starve them into submission ; their deportation was then ordered ; and when they refused to go they were carried by force on board the ship. Strict orders were given to the captain that they should not be allowed ashore at any port of call for fear of their escape. The reinstated officers for their part were compelled to sign a three-year agreement, breach of which by similar conduct would expose them to the penalty of death. [192]

Fury reigned for a moment at Calcutta when the news of Clive's proceedings up-country reached there, followed by the arrival of the broken officers. The fetid air of the place reeked with sedition and violent talk. One of the cashiered officers was accused of threatening to assassinate Clive. Civilians were implicated and dismissed.

But Clive himself was quite unmoved. His disgust and disdain for all that happened since his arrival in the country had mounted to heights too great for words.

III

He returned to Calcutta on July 30 to face and survive the final ordeal of those dismal, dangerous weeks following the rainy season. For a month he hid himself away with Strachey, Maskelyne, and Dr. Ingham in faithful attendance, counting the days until his departure. In September he emerged to lay before the council his plan for the Society of Trade's operations for another year. He must have felt surprised that he was still alive ! Not only that, but he had actually, so he wrote his wife, enjoyed a better state of health and been freer from pain than at any time since his attack at Madras in 1752. He attributed the fact partly to his discovery of the value of that simple precaution of protecting the abdomen from chills.

Compelled to give up the idea of travelling overland because of having to postpone his departure until the end of January, he had instead taken his passage on the *Britannia*, Captain Rous, hoping now to see Berkeley Square in July 1767, accompanied by Mun, Strachey, and Dr. Ingham " who are tolerable well, tho' always complaining. . . . All my other followers, you know, are dead." He had already sent home an abundance of muslins and other fine things and he would bring with him many shawls and one of the finest pearl necklaces ever seen, worth not less than £2,000 ; " this is the only valuable present I have ever receiv'd, which was given me by the Vizier Sujah Dowlah."

He had been thinking all the year about where he would live in the country. Styche did not satisfy him. Margaret had reported that she liked Walcot, but he feared it would prove too damp for him. He thought one of the drier counties, Berkshire or Hampshire, would be better, besides being on the road to Bath, where he would need to go to take the waters. He had, in fact, already written to his agents telling them not to miss an opportunity to buy an estate there of from £1000 to £2000 per annum, especially if there was a good house, park, and gardens belonging to it.

" I was determin'd to make this a most agreeable and welcome letter and I think it cannot be otherwise for it contains nothing but good news."

But it was expecting too much that he would not pay the penalty he had always paid for his periods of furious activity. The army crisis had laid him under a terrific strain, coming as it did at the height of the hot weather. On May 21 he had written Verelst that he had not had three hours' sleep any day or night since he left Motijhil two weeks before. Yet nothing wore him down more than his correspondence, it being large in volume and he so meticulous in the speed and regularity of his replies. More and more indeed he had to rely upon Strachey to write his letters. Bravely now he bore up under the thought that it would all be over soon. But already he had overtaxed his strength. In October his nervous system collapsed completely. Flood after flood of hysterical weeping assailed him ; his mind passed under a cloud ; and for two months he could not put hand to paper. He had to be removed from Calcutta and kept in seclusion during the whole of November.

His life, according to Dr. Ingham, who had attended him in England, was not in danger, and by the beginning of December he was beginning to rally. There could be no thought, however, of his continuing another year in India.

An urgent request had just arrived from the Directors for him to stay. It was couched in most gratifying terms ; all of his measures, except the Society of Trade, were heartily approved, the promise of reward was held out to him, and he was asked to remain in order to consolidate and make permanent the great work of reformation he had accomplished :

" These services, my Lord, deserve more than verbal acknowledgments ; and we have no doubt that the proprietors will concur with us in opinion, that some solid and permanent retribution, adequate to your great merits, should crown your Lordship's labours and success."

Once more he had triumphed. The Directors' words could mean nothing less than an extension of the *jaghire* for another term of years. He asked for nothing more. Such a reward would mean truly that he had succeeded, that his sacrifices had not been in vain. He must have felt like a free man again, free at last to enjoy his fortune in peace. Accordingly he wrote informing the Court that his state of health rendered it impossible for him to remain. Why should he needlessly sacrifice his life when all the objects of his mission had been accomplished ?

On January 1 he was able again to write to Margaret :

" It gives me great satisfaction that I can inform my dearest wife of my recovery from a nervous attack which I thought I could not survive, it being so much beyond what I suffered even in England. Indeed I am persuaded nothing but opium could have saved me, the spasms being so strong that I was obliged to take 10 grains in 24 hours. Altho' I have been tolerably well for this year past until lately yet I could perceive the bile, which was the occasion of my last sickness, began to show itself last February. This has been increasing ever since. As this is a disorder peculiar to this country and cannot be cured but by change of climate and colder weather, I am determined to take my passage upon the *Britannia* without delay notwithstanding the earnest solicitations of the Court of Directors to continue another year. In short, everyone who understands the nature of my disorder assures me the return of the hot weather might prove fatal, or at best I should be rendered quite incapable of business with such a disease hanging over me, and that I should be subject to relapses every time I caught cold and the bile got into my blood. . . . I have received all your letters per *Mercury* and am much concerned at the loss of our youngest daughter. We should both of us have felt the loss still more if we had not three still left to comfort us." [193]

IV

He attended his last meeting of Council on January 16. He had arranged for the regime of the Committee to be continued under Verelst's chairmanship, so he now proceeded to read to them his parting advice :

" We are sensible that since the acquisition of the dewanny the power formerly belonging to the Soubah of these provinces is totally in fact vested in the East India Company. Nothing remains to him but the name and shadow of authority. This name, however, this shadow, it is indispensably necessary we should seem to venerate. Every mark of distinction and respect must be shewn him, and he himself encouraged to shew his resentment upon the least want of respect from other nations."

He particularly impressed upon them the necessity of assuming no part of the executive power and of maintaining that rigid control over the services that he had been at such pains to establish. They were, therefore, not to employ the Company's servants as collectors or in any administrative capacity ; at the same time he warned them against demanding more revenue than the country could bear. He was most insistent about the necessity of making vigorous examples of the disobedient :

" upon this point I rest the wellfare of the Company. The servants are now brought to a proper sense of their duty ; if you slacken the reins of government, affairs will soon revert to their former channels ; anarchy and corruption will again prevail, and, elate with a new victory, be too headstrong for any future efforts of government. . . .

" We have had the happiness to see our labours crowned with success. I leave the country in peace ; I leave the military and civil departments under discipline and subordination ; it is incumbent upon you to keep them so. You have power ; you have abilities ; you have integrity : let it not be said that you are deficient in resolution. I repeat that you must not fail to exact the most implicit obedience to your orders. Dismiss or suspend from the service any man who shall dare to dispute your authority. If you deviate from the principles upon which we have hitherto acted, and upon which you are conscious you ought to proceed, or if you do not continue to make a proper use of that power with which you are invested, I shall hold myself acquitted, as I do now protest against the consequences."

Thus did the man who had more of the qualities of a dictator than, perhaps, any man in modern English history, lay down his office. For prolonged unceasing activity, for the fury of its

443

tempo, and for the white heat of passion that had been generated from the first day almost to the last, there are few parallels in history to this second administration of Clive. There had been something demoniacal in the way he had flung himself into his task and kept going until his collapse. He had allowed himself no time for rest or reflection. He had allotted himself just eighteen months in which to reform and purge the services, establish a political system, and lay the foundation of empire. And however imperfect his work necessarily was, it would be unjust to deny that he had accomplished much of worth. The purge of the services had been salutary, though not, it must be admitted, particularly effective. He had begun the lengthy process of transforming traders into administrators. He had compelled the Company to see the wisdom and necessity of establishing reasonable rates of pay. He had re-asserted authority, checked, even if he did not reverse, the trend towards anarchy that Plassey had begun, and cleared the ground for a real and permanent system. The fact that the building which would have to be erected on that ground was quite different from the one he visualized does not impair the usefulness of his work.

But one would miss an essential part of his mind and nature if one did not realize how much more than this he thought he had done. Optimism and complacency, vain glory and self-praise had always been among his worst faults. And they were never more glaringly in evidence than now when he appeared to think that nothing more would be required of his successors than to adhere faithfully to his system and his principles, that no evil would come to Bengal if only his policies were maintained. In his final report to the Company his self-satisfaction reached its apogee :

"The licentious spirit of opposition and extravagance so justly complained of in your civil servants is now essentially subdued, the gentlemen are reduced to act, and likewise to think, reasonably. Perfect harmony now reigns throughout the settlement ; and all childish resentments are at an end. Nothing remains to be apprehended, but what may result from the extreme youth of the majority of your servants. . . . It is upon the best founded confidence I assert, the East India Company was never so truly secure as at the present against military ambition and encroachment. Never before have discipline, good order and subordination been so fully confirmed ; and I am persuaded that a relaxation of your orders at home and a new degeneracy of your governor and Council abroad, are the only probable, I might almost say, possible evils that can shake the prosperity of your affairs in Bengal."

The only comment needed on that last sentence is supplied by the actual history of Bengal during the next six years, when all the evil forces of man and nature were to combine as never before to afflict the unhappy land. It was to be as though God himself had decided to punish such rash boasting with all the power of His might. There is a particular Indian nemesis for talk about " no possible evils "—and that is *famine !*

On January 29 Lord Clive, accompanied by General Carnac and the members of his personal staff, embarked on board the *Britannia.* His colleagues had presented him with a farewell address that was a pæan of praise and adulation, but Barwell possibly more nearly voiced the sentiments of the European community as a whole when he said that the announcement of Lord Clive's departure " brought joy to the whole settlement." [1]

[1] Ingratitude was ever Clive's lot. Even " the father of Indian geography," James Rennell, Surveyor-General of Bengal, for whose talent and keenness Clive had found so much occupation, found nothing more to say about him after his departure than that he did not honour his promises and was by no means the generous man. " Perhaps," he wrote to a friend, " I may one day or other put him in mind of his promise [which was that he should not suffer by the reduction in the officers' allowances], but that must be when I am independent : for had I told him unwelcome truths when he was Governor of Bengal and as absolute as ever Henry the Eighth was, I should in all probability have been sent home to England, as some others have been for defending their liberties." [194]

Chapter Twenty-seven

CÆSAR INFELIX

"The Emperor is what he is; we cannot change his character. It is because of that character that he has no friends, that he has so many enemies, and, indeed, that we are at St. Helena"

GENERAL BERTRAND ("*Napoleon—The Last Phase*," *by Lord Rosebery*)

I

FEW OF THE GREAT FIGURES OF HISTORY have found themselves in a more unbearable position than Clive after his final return home at the age of forty-one. His life, up to that point a vigorous, swiftly-moving, pulsating drama, became all tragedy—a tragedy of circumstance and a tragedy of character. He had still more than seven years to live, the years of a normal man's greatest activity and achievement. Sir Robert Walpole was a comparatively obscure man until his fortieth year. Chatham accomplished nothing worthy of his great name until he was forty-six. Cromwell did not even begin his real career until he was forty-three. But Clive's career was already over; for him life, for all that it was really worth to him, was ended; he had spent his vital force; his power of achievement was gone.

To say of him that he was "still a young man" would be entirely false. For he had none of the marks of youth left upon him. Not only was he broken in health, but even more pitiful was the fact that he was less equipped mentally and morally to play a continued useful part than many a man who reaches the normal retiring age of sixty-five or seventy. Not only had he made too many drafts on his store of nervous energy but also on the large funds of good-will that men had deposited to his account. He was, in a word, bankrupt. He had no spiritual resources wherewith to meet changed circumstances. He was not made of the stuff that could meet adversity with fortitude of mind and serenity of soul. Life does not spare men like him; he was marked out in advance to be a victim of its hard laws.

446

To find a parallel one has to go to Napoleon at St. Helena. Two tragedies of ὕβρις, of overweening ambition, of power fettered and dethroned, of tremendous energies wasting away in inaction, of powerful minds revolving impotently around the circle of their own ideas, incapable any longer of objective thought, consumed by the consciousness of their wrongs, and only flashing vigorously into play when touched most nearly. But with this difference—that Clive's St. Helena was more nearly a prison of his own making, more clearly the inevitable consequence of his own life ; he had run his course, no foreign enemies sentenced him, but his own countrymen, who no longer had use for him. It cannot be said that fortune at the end played him false, that there was any violent break in the pattern of his life. The end was as its beginning—gloomy, solitary, one against the world ; and if at the end the world reasserted its supremacy, no injustice was involved. A natural law was fulfilled.

II

He returned to a situation well calculated to vex his soul, both on public grounds and private—and not his soul alone but everyone else's. To a land already sufficiently distracted by its quarrel with the American colonists and the petty factions and dishonesties of its politicians had now been added a further burden, the nuisance of the almost insoluble problem of India. And if there were some besides his personal enemies who were inclined to lay the blame for it largely at his door, the feeling can be well understood, and no amount of protesting on his part could entirely sever the connection. If the whole country did not rise up to curse him for thus adding to its troubles, it was because there was no national conscience strong enough to resist the lure of wealth, power, and glory with which he had invested not only himself but his services to the State. It sufficed that he had presented his countrymen with an empire. As they accepted the gift they had to accept the troubles that went with it. No amount of wrangling about who was responsible for them could change these two essential facts.

The fateful opening of Pandora's box was on that day in April 1766, when the news of the acquisition of the revenues of Bengal reached London. At once all the wicked winged creatures with

447

stings in their tails got busy infecting the minds of men with cupidity, envy, and every meanest vice. Promptly the quiet courts of India House were turned into a casino for gambling, producing a wild and dizzy rise in the Company's stock. Inevitably at the next General Court on June 18, after the momentous despatches had been read with acclamation, a motion was made to increase the dividend from 6 to 8 per cent. Immediately the Directors' troubles began.

The state of the Company's finances, still suffering from the expenses of prolonged military operations which had plunged it heavily in debt, did not justify any increase of dividend. Wisely the Directors wanted to apply the new revenues to debt reduction ; and for the moment their voice prevailed. In the past it always had prevailed, but that day of unquestioned authority was gone ; Clive's all too simple act, substituting easy wealth for the slow returns of commerce, had cut at the very root of their authority and transferred the real power to the shareholders.

At the next meeting of the Company, in September, the proposal was brought forward again with redoubled clamour, and this time the proposed increase was to 10 per cent. One ominous sign of demoralization after another appeared. The clamour was led by Sulivan, himself demoralized by defeat and desperate enough to use any means, demagoguery or intrigue with ministers, to reinstate himself in power ; but still worse was the appearance of Clive's friends among Sulivan's followers—truly an unholy alliance this !—" thinking that to delay the fruits was to doubt the reality of his success." Yet they were only following Clive's lead, as he himself favoured an increase, despite the fact that Scrafton had urged him not to. But perhaps worst of all the omens was the way in which the shadow of Parliament now spread itself over the proceedings. Ministers had just sent a warning to the Chairs, Rous and Dudley, that the Company's affairs would come before Parliament at the approaching session. When this alarming news was conveyed to the assembled shareholders a dead silence fell upon them, and then with one accord " lords, lacquies, and merchants ran with equal haste to the alley. Stock fell 30 per cent., while the terror and anxiety in every countenance afforded a truly ridiculous and comic scene." The politicians, it was said, wanted to treat the Company as King John had treated the Jews. Yet before the meeting adjourned the shareholders had nevertheless overborne the opposition of the

Directors to the increased dividend. Thus the grand toboggan-slide of the Company into bankruptcy had begun ! [195]

The shareholders' fears of the intentions of Parliament were justified. Here, too, the acquisition of so much easy wealth was doing its evil work in exciting cupidity. The consequences might have been a little different if the nation's one statesman had been fit for business. Pitt's tragedy was to be shared by three continents. On July 10 he had left Bath to obey the King's summons to form a government. The whole nation was looking to him to solve the imperial problem left in a state of suspense by the repeal of the Stamp Act. And now India had joined America on his waiting-list of questions. It was he who informed the Directors of what was in store for the Company. Everywhere now there was speculation about the new Earl of Chatham's intentions. The faithful Walsh, diligent as ever in his master's interests, visited Bath to obtain the statesman's views. Chatham indicated clearly to him that while he admired Clive personally no less, he was not at all happy about his latest proceedings. The new acquisitions were too vast ; the Company had gone far beyond what he had contemplated when he had obtained for it the right to retain its conquests ; and the matter must of necessity come before Parliament. Clive had made a mistake in failing to win over Chatham to his views in advance, and the great man was displeased. But how to allocate the new revenues yet remained a puzzling question. For Chatham still believed that to hand them over to the Crown, as Clive had once suggested, would be to make an end to liberty. " English kings would become Moguls, rich, splendid, weak ; gold would be fatally substituted in the place of trade, industry, liberty, and virtue." [196]

Clive's failure to heed the warning uttered seven years before now compelled a facing of the question. Chatham never made his views clear and he was too sick a man ever to evolve a comprehensive scheme of Indian government, but it appears that he was in favour of a sharing of the revenues between the State and the Company, with the larger share going to the State and the Company not being allowed even to regard its share as private property but as " in trust for the public purposes of India and the extension of trade ; never in any case to be portioned out it dividends to the extinction of the spirit of trade." In these last words he laid a sure finger on the root of the evil that Clive had caused ; in plain terms, Clive had debauched the Company.

Chatham was concerned lest he should also debauch the nation. Before deciding on a measure, however, he wanted to obtain the unfettered judgment of Parliament, and to that end he allowed a private member, Alderman Beckford, to introduce a motion calling for papers preliminary to an investigation. No wonder that stocks fell when reports of what was in the minister's mind reached Leadenhall Street !

But before the matter came before the House, before he had even explained his purposes to the Cabinet, Chatham collapsed, his mind passed behind a cloud, and his colleagues were set free to pursue their own petty, interested views. There was none now to crush the Rockingham Whigs when, through the eloquent mouthpiece of Burke, they pleaded the sacred rights of property and the sanctity of charters. Nor was there anyone to stop the irresponsible Townshend, the Chancellor of the Exchequer, from transforming the whole question into a simple one of a deal with the Company for the relief of the Treasury. Sulivan was to have his chance now to show his talents as a bargainer ; having always maintained close connections with ministers, he proceeded to use them to try to obtain an extension of the Company's privileges, including the territorial revenues and a 14 per cent. dividend, in exchange for a payment to the State. The upshot was that there was no real enquiry (though Warren Hastings, Vansittart, and a few others were examined by the House in March 1767), no reform of abuses, no provision made for the government of the conquered provinces. A bill was passed that merely confirmed an agreement with the Directors whereby the Company bound itself to pay £400,000 a year for two years and restrict the size of the dividend in return for confirmation of its right to the revenues.

Meanwhile, the repercussions from Clive's measures against the council had been increasingly manifest in the Company's Courts. The dismissed councillors had arrived home breathing vengeance. At the September Court Wedderburn reported to Grenville that Lord Clive's dispatches were coming under consideration : " I find he has not omitted writing to every quarter from whence he could expect assistance ; but the popular opinion is not at present in his favour." The anti-Clive party, in fact, continued to grow in strength. Bad publicity was given to the Company when the Directors began legal action against the ex-councillors for recovery of the presents. The accused men were wealthy, and

Johnstone in particular had powerful political friends. His brother George, generally known as Governor Johnstone because he had once been Governor of West Florida, was an influential member of both the Court of Proprietors and Parliament, as also was another brother, William, who had married into the wealthy family of the Earl of Bath and taken the family name of Pulteney. Together the Johnstones threatened to attack the conduct of Clive if the prosecutions were not withdrawn. The Directors, however, stood firm, and a fierce contest in the coming election was in prospect when the March Court was held.[197]

At that Court Walsh committed his worst indiscretion. Without consulting Directors he made a motion :

" That it is the opinion of this Court, that the important services rendered to the Company by Lord Clive, merit a grateful acknowledgment and return ; and that a grant to his Lordship and his personal representatives, of an additional term in the *jaghire* of ten years, commencing from the determination of his Lordship's present right therein, would be a proper acknowledgment and return for such important services."

In other words, Walsh was coolly asking the Company to vote away £300,000 as a reward for services that not everyone saw in the same glowing light ! Not surprisingly, therefore, the proposal released a storm of protest. What had Lord Clive done that he was to be so favoured ? Had he not been fully rewarded already by the previous grant of his *jaghire* ? Had he not declared then that he expected no further reward ? Wherein lay the special merit and difficulty of his acquisition of the *dewani* ? Why had the Directors concealed from the public the advantageous treaty with the Nawab that Mr. Spencer and his Council had made before his Lordship arrived ? Was it so that the public should imagine that it owed everything to Lord Clive ? Why this glaring partiality ?

" Fellow Proprietors, it is your business not to be led away by the cry of a faction. Every means has been used to depreciate and undervalue every gentleman who has done you service, in order to exalt one favourite minion, and to heap praise and wealth upon his head : he has not been wanting in art to accomplish this ; he has even dared to attack the characters of every single man employed in your service in

451

Bengal, in order to induce you to believe that he alone is fit to be trusted and proper to be rewarded. He has put himself in possession of all power, both in India and at home, and in order to support himself in that power, he now endeavours by means of split votes, to grant away to himself another £300,000 of your property. . . ." [198]

Walsh's resolution was carried, but only by 25 votes.

The election the following month was equally close. Rous won, though the Johnstone group split £125,000 of stock against him. But at the May Court he was soundly beaten on two vital issues : the increase in the dividend to 12½ per cent. and the withdrawal of the prosecution of the ex-Councillors. The second defeat was nothing less than a blow in the face for Clive. The stock soared again to 263, the Court petitioned against the Bill pending in Parliament, Parliament replied promptly by passing it. The deterioration of the Company was now proceeding at a rapid pace.

Such was the situation that Clive found when he landed at Portsmouth on July 14.

III

At first everything promised well for him. The disgust he felt when he heard of the recent happenings at India House was counterbalanced by the flattering audience he had with the King and Queen. He presented His Majesty with a diamond equal, it was said, to the famous Pitt stone, and George expressed the hope that he would endeavour to restore the affairs of the Company at home to the good order into which he had brought them abroad. No prospect could have given him keener pleasure. " Let me tell you in secret," he wrote Verelst, " that I have the King's command to lay before him my ideas of the Company's affairs both at home and abroad, with a promise of his countenance and protection in everything I might attempt for the good of the nation and the Company." The danger was that with this august assurance to support his pride he might fall into the mistake of thinking he could snub or dictate to Ministers and Directors as he chose.

Nor was this danger lessened by the flattering attention shown him by Mr. Grenville, who was quick to resume his old connection with him. The near approach of another general election with the prospect of an even stronger representation of the Clive interest in the new Parliament naturally made Lord Clive an object of solicitation to party leaders no less than before, and Clive the more readily gave his allegiance to Grenville because he deluded himself with the idea that Grenville was about to return to office. But not only did Grenville, whose short term of office will always be associated with the passage of the disastrous Stamp Act, express a flattering desire for his Lordship's approval of his conduct and for his sentiments on affairs of state, inviting him to visit him at Wotton on his way to the country and deputing Mr. Whately, one of his former ministers, to wait upon him for an exchange of views, but he also told him, as Clive proudly related to Verelst, that " it was the duty of the Court of Directors to let no steps whatever be taken, either at home or abroad, without my advice ; and assured me that either in ministry or out of it, he would preach that doctrine in the House of Commons." This was strong wine for Clive, who needed no such stimulants to assume a commanding air.

The fair promise died within a month of his arrival. Nothing did more to kill it than a return of his old malady, partly nervous, partly due to a deranged liver, complicated now by gallstones, which caused him excruciating pain only relieved by the use of laudanum in increasing quantities. The attack compelled him to leave town and take the road to Bath, paying the promised visit to Mr. Grenville on the way. Before long, contemporaries were likening his case to Chatham's : " his whole system of nerves destroyed ; sometimes dying, sometimes tolerably well, sometimes crying, at all times incapable of business." [199] It might have been fortunate for him if he *had* been entirely incapacitated from business for a while and had devoted himself to the recovery of his health, because nothing brought him more vexation or did him more hurt than his spasmodic and ill-judged excursions into public affairs, attended as they were by an ill humour that the state of his health could only have made worse.

Everything, indeed, conspired to place him at a disadvantage in dealing with the world. His qualities were of a kind that needed to be displayed in action against foreign enemies to seem good ; when brought into play against his own countrymen, and particularly against those in charge of affairs, they could only appear as defects. If it was meet for Colonel Clive, for the Governor of Bengal, to be imperious in his dealings with Emperor or Nawab, it was not so meet for a private citizen no longer holding any official position to be so with Ministers or Directors. His control of temper should now, for his own good, have become stronger, not weaker, nor so weak as to be indistinguishable from mere peevishness, pathetic in its futility, destructive to moral fibre, and disastrous in its effect on other men. He was about to experience the difficulty common to all men who have occupied posts of great power and importance, the difficulty of adjusting himself to the fact that while he could still advise and his advice might be genuinely welcomed, even solicited, he could no longer dictate, and that however wise his own views might be, it did not necessarily follow that they would be adopted, or that he had any right—whatever Mr. Grenville might think—to expect them to be adopted. He had been a king-maker both in India and in England, but in neither country had the kings obeyed him implicitly, and generally when they had obeyed it had been reluctantly and out of necessity. Now he was confronted with the necessity of evolving a new role for himself. Should he take an active part in Indian affairs as the foremost proprietor of the Company? Or should he confine himself to weighty utterances, as befitted an elder statesman, from his seat in the House of Commons? His temperament greatly lessened his chances of reaching a happy solution to such a problem.

He clearly started out with the assumption that he could make his influence felt at India House. The spectacle that the Company afforded disgusted him beyond measure. He had given it an empire, made it the richest company on the face of the earth, yet all its time was being consumed in wrangles over the size of the dividend. He had rescued its affairs by restoring order in India, and now all the good that he had done was being undone by the dropping of the prosecutions of the dismissed Councillors. Here, then, was his opportunity to render real service. He could be entirely aloof from these contests; they meant nothing to him any more. Now that he had his *jaghire* extended—the September Court unanimously confirmed the grant—he had nothing more to ask of the Company. For the first time, perhaps, in his life he could be truly disinterested and could apply himself with singleness of mind to the needs of the empire he had acquired. And surely none knew more about those needs than he?

Yet the irony of the situation was that the Directors were no longer willing to listen to him. The Court was still largely

composed of the men whom he had helped into office in 1764 ;
Sulivan was not among them. Yet their whole attitude had
undergone a change. They no longer acted like friends. A
lukewarmness had crept into their relations with him, even into
the way they had supported the proposal for the extension of his
jaghire. They seemed embarrassed when they saw him, as
though they wished to drop their connection with him. Even
their congratulations upon his safe return and expressions of
gratitude had not rung true. They seemed anxious only to
minimize the value of his great achievement, to conceal from the
public the true amount of the new revenues. Why ? He could
not understand. It seemed to him the basest ingratitude. He
naturally wanted his achievements to be known of all men. Had
he not earned the plaudits that they would surely bring ? Had
not that been one of the chief reasons why he had gone back to
India ? To redeem his honour, vindicate his reputation, buttress
his fame by winning more laurels. Why else had he made such
sacrifices ?

There was so much that he did not see or understand. He
never was able to put himself in the position of other men, see
himself as other men saw him. If the Directors' lack of
enthusiasm was galling and, considering their past relations, not
a little ungrateful, there were abundant reasons for it. After all,
they were practical men of affairs whose concern was not with
the past but with the present, with problems great and pressing
enough to exclude other considerations. They were, at the
moment, the most harassed body of men in the country. If they
were not proclaiming from the housetops the great works that
Lord Clive had done, it was because of the acute embarrassment
that some of those works had caused them. If they were trying
to conceal the facts about the revenues, it was in order to save the
Company from its rapacious shareholders. If they did not take
a firm stand against the Johnstoneites, it was because of the great
strength of that faction, of the threat it represented to their control.
He had incurred the undying enmity of this party ; it was mere
ordinary prudence on their part not to want to share more of it
than they could help. And if some of them thought that
£300,000 was a more than adequate reward for eighteen months
of service and that he could count himself extremely fortunate to
have got it with so little trouble, their attitude was not unreasonable, nor did it necessarily betoken any lack of friendly regard for

him. What more, they must have asked themselves, could his lordship expect of them? They and Clive were, indeed, at complete cross-purposes, and their continued intercourse with him served only to increase the distance between them.

The fact was that the Directors could not serve the interests of Lord Clive and the Company at the same time. They were choosing to serve their own and the Company's.

Ugly rumours began to fly around that Clive had expressed to Mr. Whately a very unfavourable opinion of some of the Directors, including Mr. Rous himself and his old chief Thomas Saunders, and a wish to purge the Court and take the lead himself. Luke Scrafton, now a Director himself, wrote as became a friend to allay Clive's resentment :

" The authority is so good that I suppose it a very impertinent misrepresentation of something that may have dropped from your Lordship in an unreserved conversation, for I would not wish you really to entertain such a design, for whatever defects they may have certainly the present Directors have the merit of having very steadily supported your Lordship while abroad & are entirely disposed to pay the utmost attention to your advice at home. Nor can a variance take place between them & your Lordship without fatal consequences to the Company' affairs by innovations in the system abroad if thro' our divisions the opposite party should come in with all their views and claims & by fatal effects at home from the keeping up that contention of party which is now almost subdued by our great superiority & the servants abroad are become submissive from the appearance of the power continuing in the same hands & with it a pursuit of those spirited measures which have brought them to a proper sense of their duty. If your Lordship conceives any resentment on the conduct of the Directors respecting the *jaghire* you will act from misrepresentation. One or two were cold on the subject by believing themselves the objects of your resentment in consequence of Whately's story, but the general sense was, ' We cannot as Directors recommend so large a grant, the fate the question met with before proves that many thought it too much, but we will give our votes for it.' To conclude, my Lord, I really think it for your own honour & for the interest of the Company to support the present set."

The letter crossed one from Clive of the same date (October 2) in which he denied any idea of becoming a Director : " The being a Director may be an object to the Directors, but not to Lord Clive." He made his contempt for some of them all too plain, however : " in short there are a few individuals whom I never looked upon as my friends or friends of the Company. Such cannot expect any countenance from me."

His reply to Scrafton was couched in the same haughty, ungracious tone :

" I received your letter and return you many thanks for your congratulations about the *jaghire*. However, you will scarce believe me when I tell you that I was, before it was confirmed, and am at this time, very indifferent about it. My wish was to have it brought to a conclusion at any rate ; for I could not avoid observing all parties at work to suspend coming to a conclusion ; and many were at greater pains, from rank infernal jealousy and envy, to conceal and lessen my services, in order to lessen my influence : but I thank God, I am now an independent man, what I was determined to be at all events.

" I cannot but take notice of one paragraph of your letter ; *that the Directors thought the grant too large, and therefore would not recommend it :* I am therefore the more obliged to the Proprietors, who were all of a different way of thinking.

" I am obliged to you for your advice about my conduct towards the Directors, because I am persuaded you mean me well ; but know, Scrafton, I have a judgment of my own, which has seldom failed me, in cases of much greater consequence than what you recommend. As to the support which, you say, was given to my government, when abroad, by the Directors, they could not have done otherwise, without suffering in their reputation, and perhaps quitting the Direction. In return let me ask, whose interest contributed to make them Directors, and keep them so ? My conduct wanted no support, it supported itself, because it was disinterested, and tended to nothing but the public good. From the beginning it put all mankind at defiance, as it does at this hour : and had the Court of Directors thought fit to make my conduct more public than they have done, all impartial and disinterested men must have done me justice. However, that remains for myself to make known, when convenient and proper.

" After having said this much, I must tell you (though by your writing you seem to give credit to the report), that what Whately is said to have told Wedderburn is absolutely false, as is everything else said to have been communicated by Mr. Grenville to Mr. Wedderburn ; and I can attribute these mean suspicions of the Directors to nothing but envy and jealousy. However, as I have often said before, and say now, there is nothing the Directors can do shall make me lose sight of the Company's true interest. Upon principle, I would always stand by the East India Company : I am now further bound by the ties of true gratitude. This is the ground upon which I now stand, and upon which I will risk my reputation. No little, partial consideration shall ever bias me."

Scrafton obviously had a thankless task in trying to mediate between a man in this savage mood and the governing body of the Company, and it was not made easier by the fact that Clive was at the same time pressing his own ideas upon the Directors and expecting immediate acceptance of them. In particular, there was his cherished Society of Trade and his scheme for the reorganization of the army.

Scrafton had gently to disillusion him : " I only know the pains I take to keep things right, but unless you come to town and support me I cannot maintain the proper system." A few days later he reported some success with the military plan, as it was receiving support from General Lawrence, but he could do no more than try to smooth ruffled feelings over the still rejected salt monopoly. And with ill success, because we find him expressing renewed sorrow at the direction his Lordship's mind was taking and urging him again to come to town, where the Directors would confer with him as they were doing with Lawrence, and " you would have weight to carry anything you please. What is wanted is a free discussion, without which men without the necessary local knowledge cannot comprehend nor be convinced."

There was nothing Clive wanted to do more than to come to town. He made an effort. He was actually on his way when an acute attack seized him at Birmingham and forced him immediately to return to Walcot. From there, at the end of October, he moved on to Styche. Neither place suited him, and November found him back at Bath. The Directors had sent him a courteous invitation to meet with them on the second of that month, which he had to decline.

His gloom deepened, and with it his jaundiced view of the Company. He went so far now as to describe Scrafton's well-meaning efforts as mean and sneaking. And he brought those efforts to an abrupt end by informing Scrafton that unless he were applied to formally and more attention paid to his advice, he would decline giving any advice at all. Fear, not inclination, he sneered, was all that would make the Directors pay attention to him. "No one," he wrote to a friend in India, "can entertain a worse opinion of many of them than I do."

But he was roused to one more effort when he heard that the Directors intended throwing open the salt trade and retaining only a small duty for the Company. He had passionate convictions of the crass stupidity of this course, which seemed to him the height of quixoticism. The trade, he pointed out, had always been a government monopoly, and even if the Company did not think fit to allow their servants to have the benefit of it—though why it should not, he could not imagine—it should at least retain it for itself. By the proposed course it would be throwing away, for no reason at all, £300,000 per annum and retaining only a tenth of that amount.

The Directors, however, had become inoculated with rigid free-trade principles, soon to be canonized by the publication of Adam Smith's work *The Wealth of Nations*. In their reply they declared it

> "a duty the Company owe to the natives of the country to protect them in their natural right to an open trade in the commodities made and consumed in the country and to limit the trade of the Europeans within the phirmaund [firman] bounds ; this and the conciliating the affections of the natives (which they esteem the best security of the revenues) by reduction of the price of this material necessary of life, have been the chief objects of their attention in the regulations they have formed."

It is unnecessary to discuss further the merits of the opposing views, except to add that Clive's were formed from local knowledge and the Directors' were not. In practice it was soon found that terminating the government monopoly of salt did not restore the trade to the natives, nor lower the price. It rather led to fresh abuses and to an illicit and oppressive monopoly in the hands of local officials ; therefore, one of the first measures that Hastings took was to restore the monopoly to the Company. Hastings had himself once ardently advocated throwing the trade open, but was forced to recognize the impracticability of that counsel of perfection.

One concession only did the Directors make to Clive's strong representations. They now at last took the important step of increasing salaries by appropriating $2\frac{1}{2}$ per cent. of the revenues to that purpose. It was quite beyond Clive's comprehension why they should substitute this plan for his, thereby depriving the Company of a material part of its revenue and absolutely unnecessarily. But he had to give up trying to make the Directors see reason : they were wedded to their prejudices and their ignorance.

He turned his attention instead to national politics. Preparations were under way for next year's election, when he expected his following to come in seven strong. He was still hoping for an English peerage, but the time was not ripe for applying for one, since Chatham's illness had so weakened and disorganized the government that changes were imminent. Mr. Grenville kept Clive regularly informed about developments at Westminster, expressing the hope that he would be able to attend the session after the holidays, when the Company's affairs would come before the House.

The hope was vain. His condition was so far from improving that he had one relapse after another. Frequently, as at Calcutta, he could not write. At last, at Christmas time, he yielded to the insistent advice of his physicians and decided to spend the winter in the south of France. The best that he could send Grenville was a wish for his (Grenville's) speedy return to office.

So in January he and Margaret, accompanied by the family party of Government House, Mun, Strachey, and Ingham, journeyed to Paris. At Fontainebleau he is said to have met the Marquis de Bussy and exchanged frank views with him about the British success in India and the prospects of the French renewing their bid for empire. Bussy considered the French prospects bright : " Believe, my lord, we have not given up India, our claims lie dormant at present, and we shall lay claim, when we can assert them, with the sword."

From Paris the party travelled on slowly south to Montpelier, stopping at Orleans, Avignon, and Lyons on the way. Clive took the opportunity to make lavish purchases : the rich products of French looms, silks, gold and silver tissues, Gobelin tapestries, and velvets ; furniture, porcelain from St. Cloud, French and Italian pictures. For he now had no fewer than four residences to consider and furnish to his taste, and was soon to acquire a fifth. To Styche and Berkeley Square he had first added Walcot (largely, as we have seen, for election purposes in the borough of Bishop's Castle), and just recently he had bought Lord Chatham's house in Bath with all its furnishings. He had already re-modelled Styche, employing the fashionable architect of the day, Sir William Chambers, the designer of Somerset House, to give him a house in the correct period style. Yet fears that he had expressed in India that the air of neither Styche nor Walcot would suit him had proved well-founded, and upon his return to England he was to buy a third estate, the late Duke of Newcastle's, at Claremont in Surrey.

His friends had not expected to see him come back alive. Yet his health improved rapidly and soon he was able to discontinue the use of opium and turn his thoughts homewards. After having drunk freely of the waters of Spa during the spring and early summer, he pronounced himself cured and began the return journey, refusing the advice of Dr. Ingham to spend another winter abroad. September found him back at Walcot. And at last, at the end of that month, he was able to accept an invitation from India House " to dine on a turtle with the Gentlemen in the Direction, at the King's Arms in Cornhill on Wednesday next the 5th of October, at half-past three o'clock in the afternoon."

He was back in London and able once more to turn his attention to public affairs. From Montpelier he had written :

"It is certain that both the Directors and Parliament are superlatively ignorant of our affairs abroad, notwithstanding the great lights received in the late enquiries ; yet still they remain in the dark, and comprehend nothing about it. If my constitution would have admitted of my attending Parliament and General Courts, I am vain enough to think my knowledge and influence would have set things to rights."

He would not be silent. If he was not well enough to speak, he would write.

IV

He returned to find a new government in power and a new Parliament. The incompetent, pleasure-loving Duke of Grafton had succeeded the incapacitated Chatham as chief minister. Parliament had been dissolved in March. Both Chatham and Shelburne resigned from the government shortly after Clive's return ; they were the only two statesmen that had shown intelligent interest in Indian matters.

The new Parliament was a true gathering together of the nabobs. No fewer than twenty-one of the men prominently connected in one way or another with Indian affairs were members ; for now it was that the influx of men with fortunes from the East had made itself felt in strong competition with the local magnates and squirearchy.

The list makes interesting reading :

Henry Vansittart	member for	Reading
William Drake	,,	Agmondesham
George Johnstone	,,	Cockermouth
Lawrence Sulivan	,,	Ashburton
Francis Sykes	,,	Shaftesbury
Robert Palk	,,	Wareham
General John Carnac	,,	Leominster
General Eyre Coote	,,	Leicester Town
Robert Lord Clive	,,	Shrewsbury
George Lord Pigot	,,	Bridgenorth
George Clive	,,	Bishop's Castle
William Clive	,,	,, ,,
Thomas Rumbold	,,	Shoreham
Sir George Colebrooke	,,	Arundel
Sir Robert Fletcher	,,	Cricklade
John Walsh	,,	Worcester City
H. B. Boulton	,,	,, ,,
Henry Strachey	,,	Pontefract
Richard Clive	,,	Montgomery Town
Major Hector Munro	,,	Inverness
George Dempster	,,	Forfar

Here was the setting for a grand climax to our Indian drama. Only a few of the chief protagonists in the scenes recently enacted are missing.

But Indian affairs had for the moment slipped into the background. Domestic issues fully occupied the stage. The country was more distracted, nearer revolution, than at any time for half a century. The thunder of the cause of " Wilkes and Liberty " was reverberating in every town and county. Wilkes had been elected for Middlesex, imprisoned, expelled from the House ; now he was to be re-elected, re-expelled, re-elected, re-expelled, re-elected, and finally declared ineligible. Mobs howled in the streets, great personages were attacked, petitions poured in from everywhere, the King and his ministers were assailed, derided, lampooned. America and India were for the moment almost forgotten in the general excitement. Wilkes and the mysterious " Junius " were vastly more interesting objects of popular attention than the Baron of Plassey who had been abroad for nearly a year. The climax to his personal drama was to be postponed for three years.

His return brought him face to face again with his old problem : how could he best make his influence felt in Indian affairs ? Was he or was he not to take part in the rough-and-tumble of Company affairs ? He attended the General Court at the end of September, but at once found his temper suffering from the strain. Nowhere was he more out of place now than in Leadenhall Street, the whole atmosphere of which sickened him. Yet his mind remained as active as ever, and, perhaps, never before had he so wanted to act a genuine statesman's part. India was the only question that interested him. The great questions of the day that were agitating the minds of everybody else, questions involving great constitutional principles and essential rights and liberties of the subject, seem to have meant nothing to him ; it is doubtful whether he formed any decided opinion upon them, for he was a man lacking in ideas or convictions outside the narrow field of his interest. He passed the time flitting restlessly back and forth between his several residences, seeking ever diversion and scope for his energies, trying to conserve his impaired health, ready still to jump into action whenever some new matter affecting India arose.

He appealed to Grenville for advice, and Grenville wrote him a tactful letter advising him to stay away from the next Court and reserve his fire for Parliament. " Keep yourself," Grenville advised, " in the honourable state of a public man, only contributing your advice and assistance when asked to preserve to this country that great empire which you had so great a share in acquiring." But how could he maintain this iron self-control and aloofness when Sir Robert Fletcher published a pamphlet animadverting on his court-martial, when Stringer Lawrence and Caillaud (a specially bitter pill this !) recommended an annulment of the sentence passed upon Fletcher, when a motion was made to re-admit Fletcher to the Company's service, and when the Court of Directors sent him back to a Madras command ! This was rubbing salt into Clive's wounds with a vengeance. His friends had to entreat him not to give vent to his feelings.

How little able he was to influence affairs was shown early in the New Year. The 1767 agreement between ministers and the Company expired in February. Clive had been opposed to it and was opposed now to its renewal. At the January Court he did his utmost to get it vetoed. In vain. Ministers and Directors were united against him. The agreement was renewed for another year.

Words of perception came from his pen and lips :

" Our wide and extended possessions are become too great for the Mother country, or for our abilities, to manage. America is making great strides towards independency ; so is Ireland. The East Indies also, I think, cannot remain long to us, if our present constitution be not altered. A Direction for a year only, and that time entirely taken up in securing Directors for the year to come, cannot long maintain that authority which is requisite for the managing and governing such extensive, populous, rich, and powerful kingdoms as the East India Company are at present possessed of. So far are our Ministers from thinking of some plan for securing this great and national object, that they think of nothing but the present moment, and of squeezing from the Company every shilling they have to spare, and even more than they can well spare, consistent with their present circumstances."

Every word of the indictment was true. He could not have found a worse moment in which to present his country with a new empire ! Busily engaged as it was in losing the one already possessed, what hope was there that it would retain the new one ? It had sprung unnaturally from a marriage by proxy (Clive being the proxy), and neither of its parents as yet recognized either the state of wedlock or the offspring ! No infant empire was ever in worse plight.

Parliament discussed the agreement after a fashion. But there was no real opposition to it except from Clive, who spoke long and earnestly, but all to no purpose. Burke, not yet re-incarnated as a great statesman for Indian as well as American affairs, appeared as the Company's foremost advocate and defended the annual election of Directors on the somewhat specious ground that " men continually watched by their constituents are worked into vigour."

After the futile debate was over Clive wrote to Sir Robert Barker : " To tell you the truth, after the next general election, I find myself very much disposed to withdraw myself from all public concerns whatever. My own happiness and that of my family is the only object I have in view, and that can only be obtained by retirement from the bustle and noise of a busy, debauched, and half-ruined nation." (Even now apparently he did not realize that he had at least done his share in debauching it.) We have to remind ourselves that it is a " young man " of forty-three who is speaking !

The next two months saw the beginning of a new order of things for India, the dawn of better things. But it was a very faint dawn, so faint that it could only be recognized as such in the retrospect of time, and Clive could scarcely be blamed for mistaking it for the dusk of approaching night. Especially as it came attended, ushered in, in fact, by the sinister figure of his great enemy Sulivan ! No one at the time could have attached special importance to the sailing again for India of Warren Hastings, especially as he was not on his way to Bengal, where the fate of the Empire would be decided, but to Madras. Clive had reluctantly concurred in his re-admission to the service, swallowing his dislike for Hastings's connection with Vansittart ; and apparently he had enough influence to have got the appointment vetoed if he had wished ; but as long as Hastings was not going to Calcutta, he acquiesced.

But the appointment of Hastings portended the worst of all calamities—the return of Sulivan to power.

Sulivan had never for one moment relinquished his efforts during his five years in the wilderness. A consummate politician, he had allied himself with the Johnstoneites, with the dividend party, and with ministers. He had taken advantage of all the disputes, the divisions within the Court of Directors as well as among the shareholders. And now he was once more in the ascendancy.

"Mr. Sulivan still entertains hopes of being a Director, and Mr. Vansittart of being Governor of Bengal," wrote Clive on February 10, adding, inevitably : "to which ambitious views I shall give every opposition in my power. For, if I could admit, which is far from the case, that both are every way qualified for the station they are aspiring at, yet I know their connections to be such, that they must attempt the overthrow of that system which has been attended with so much advantage to the nation and the Company." That system was his own, the so-called Dual Government of Bengal. It was that, not his *jaghire*, which now had to be defended against his arch-enemy.

He expected Sulivan to fail. He was wrong. In the April election Sulivan was returned to power. The vote-splitting reached higher proportions than at any previous election. Clive promptly gave up the Company for lost.[200]

And lost it practically was, though not because of the election result. Sulivan inherited a much worse situation than the one he had left when he had been ejected from office. The Company's revenues were declining and their expenses growing. Bengal was wracked by a thousand internal evils, ranging all the way from the grossest maladministration and misconduct on the part of the supposedly reformed servants to a deficiency of currency. Madras had plunged into a disastrous and wickedly unnecessary war with Haidar Ali, the powerful usurper of the kingdom of Mysore ; the Bengal treasury was being drained to meet the expenses of this war, which was quite beyond the slender resources of Madras ; and the Company at home was being forced to borrow to meet its obligations to the State. So bad had conditions in Bengal in fact become that Verelst, the heir to Clive's system, was forced to describe it as "a declining and exhausted country." Directors had only too thoroughly absorbed the cardinal principle of that system, that there must be no interference in administration, and had sent repeated and peremptory orders to that effect. But even Verelst had come to have doubts about its wisdom ; an honest man, he could not be altogether blind to its consequences.

Thus Bengal and the Company were far more nearly on the verge of ruin than when Clive had been sent out to save them.

Nor did Bengal any longer enjoy alone the unenviable distinction of being in need of a complete overhauling. Conditions at Madras had of late years become just as bad. But who this time was to be sent to save them ? Sulivan turned, naturally, to Henry Vansittart, wishing, as he had wished in 1764, to give him supreme authority, and this time not merely as Governor but as Governor-General. But Clive was able to get the appointment vetoed.

Sulivan now showed that he was not entirely devoid of statesmanlike qualities, nor so rancorous that he could not compromise with his old enemy for the good of the Company. His conduct out of office had been deplorable, but he was the kind of man who only shows to advantage while holding power. It was to him, as his friends said, the *summum bonum*. So now he joined the names of Luke Scrafton and Colonel Forde to that of Vansittart and proposed that the three should be sent out as a plenipotentiary commission. The inclusion of two of Clive's special friends secured acceptance, and the Commissioners sailed in November on board the frigate *Aurora*.

The measure gave general satisfaction. Hastings, for one, termed it the wisest plan the Company had ever thought of. Nobody, however, envied the Commissioners. Clive grimly observed that " if they can find the happy expedient of doing strict justice to the Company, and of giving satisfaction to the civil, military, and free merchants, they will have found out an art that I was not master of during my last residence in India." Surely for him an unusual admission ! [201]

But alas for all the high hopes raised ! After the *Aurora* left the Cape in December, nothing more was ever heard of her or her passengers.

The forces of nature seemed resolved to destroy this empire in its infancy. A land disaster followed swiftly on the heels of the sea tragedy. One of the worst famines in recorded history devastated Bengal in that fatal year 1769, wiping out an unknown number of people (officially reckoned at ten millions, or a third of the population), depopulating hundreds of villages, and throwing vast tracts of land back to jungle. Twenty years later the effects of it were still visible even to the untutored eyes of strangers. Thus had nature intervened to complete the work of destruction that man had begun.[202]

The disaster played havoc with the already strained finances of

the Company. Nothing could now keep the Company out of
bankruptcy, and bankruptcy meant that the Company would
have to throw itself on the doubtful mercy of Parliament. And
worse than that ! When the reports of the disaster reached home
they were jubilantly seized upon by the Company's enemies, to
be grotesquely and wickedly distorted by them into crowning
proofs of the villainy of the Company's servants, long talked about
by Lord Clive and by all concerned in the Company's management, and now at last nakedly revealed to the horrified gaze of
the world. For the English agents, it was said, though without
any semblance of truth, had cornered the grain !

Panic once more seized the shareholders. The stock went
into a long decline that swept away many fortunes. Among the
notable sufferers were Edmund Burke and his friends, and Sulivan
with his partners, the ill-fated Vansittart, and Palk. Sulivan
became so deeply involved in debt that he had to ask Palk's
good offices with his creditors. By 1772, when bottom was
reached, he owed Palk £10,000, Vansittart's estate £7000, whilst
various gentlemen owed him £9000. [203]

v

Each year as it passed had increased the solitariness of Clive's
position, his alienation from former colleagues. He had once
been the pride of the Madras service. Even as recently as 1768
his old friend Pybus had written to Palk, the retiring Governor
of Madras, urging him to go hand-in-hand with Clive and
Vansittart and between them take over the whole management
of the Company at home. But the rift between Clive and
Vansittart had grown steadily wider, and it was that more than
anything else which caused former colleagues to drop away from
Clive and ally themselves with his opponents. They deeply
resented what they considered his desertion of his former friend.
Palk was Vansittart's brother-in-law, and naturally he joined the
Sulivan party. We read, too, that Stringer Lawrence was a
constant visitor at Palk's country-seat. [204]

Orme was another who became estranged from the man whom
he had previously worshipped. When Clive returned home the
historian was still trying to swallow his disappointment at the
lukewarm reception given to the first volume of his work. He
was engaged upon the second, but was making slow progress

with it owing to his growing dislike for the story he had to tell.
He wrote to his friend Colonel Richard Smith (November
1767) advising him against an early return home, warning him that

" the Parliament in less than two years will ring with declama-
tion against the Plunderers of the East. How fair, how great
it will then be not to see your name in the list. I do assure you
Old Lawrence has a reputation in England which may be
envied (with all its fortunes) by the name of Clive. It is these
cursed presents which stop my History. Why should I be
doomed to commemorate the ignominy of my countrymen,
and without giving the money story, that has accompanied
every event since the first of April, 1757, I shall not relate all
the springs of action, that is, I shall be a Jesuitical Historian,
two terms which Voltaire says are incompatible, for no Jesuit
could ever tell a true tale, much less write a true history." [205]

All who have traversed this ground have felt as he did. It is, in
truth, a melancholy story.

The following year Orme declared that Clive was hostile to
him. There is a suggestion that Scrafton as well as he might join
the party against Clive.[206] By 1769 he is stating definitely
that he himself had joined that party and would henceforth have
nothing to do with his old friend, whose face he had not seen for a
twelvemonth.[207]

How few friends were left to Clive outside the ranks of his
family and personal connections ! He still corresponded with
some of his old colleagues in Bengal. Verelst, we are told,
thought him " the greatest man that ever existed, consequently
all his systems infallible." But death was now to rob Clive of
the one whose support and help had meant everything to him at
the most critical juncture of his life. In November of the following year (1770) George Grenville died.

It was a severe loss, especially coming as it did just before the
time when he would need all the support he could get at Westminster. And he felt it deeply. " Mr. Grenville's death, though
long expected, could not but affect me very severely. Gratitude
first bound me to him : a more intimate connection afterwards
gave me an opportunity of admiring his abilities and respecting
his worth and integrity."

There was now only one man of weight in the House he could
count upon to defend him. That was Alexander Wedderburn,

the able, if unprincipled, Scottish barrister who had been one of Grenville's strongest adherents. In May of the previous year Clive had, as it happened, bound Wedderburn to him by the strongest tie of gratitude by providing him with a seat in Parliament when Wedderburn had been forced to vacate his own on account of his defence of the electors of Middlesex in the assertion of their right to be represented by John Wilkes. In order to do this Clive had to displace his own brother William at Bishop's Castle. When Lord North formed his government Wedderburn joined it as Solicitor-General. He was then to be a true friend in need for Clive, not only using his influence in the Cabinet on his behalf, but becoming his advocate—almost his only advocate—from his seat in the House of Commons.

In the following year, 1771, Clive's father also died.

Two years had thus passed, and Clive remained sunk in forced retirement. Occasionally he would pick up a pen and in a private letter give vent to a Cassandra-like utterance as he watched the approaching dissolution of the British Empire. Its western and eastern branches were alike falling into anarchy and confusion, with no hope of saving them. He had lost the desire to make the attempt, he had lost the power to render the Company any service. "The disposition to ease and retirement gains ground upon me daily." After the death of Grenville he professed complete indifference to the world in general. He had lost his taste for politics with the passing of his one political friend, and felt no inclination to attach himself elsewhere. All his old physical enemies, as well as human—who never left him alone—were assailing him once more ; melancholia weighed down his spirits, already heavy-laden with the boredom of inactivity and useless existence. If he was building himself, like Dives, still bigger barns, if, as Horace Walpole jeered, he was throwing his money away by paying preposterous prices for indifferent antiques, it could not have been from any real satisfaction derived from these extravagances. [208]   Indeed, from the advice he gave to a young kinsman in India it may be deduced that he realized only too well that he had purchased his wealth at too heavy a cost : " The best and soundest advice I can give you is to return to England rather with a moderate competency, while you have youth and constitution to enjoy it, than by staying longer, lose that youth, and sacrifice that constitution, which no riches can possibly compensate for." Yet now that he had neither youth nor constitution nor influence, the spending of his money was the only diversion left to him. Palaces are, after all, symbols of power, and he desperately needed the symbols now that the power itself was gone. In that respect his plight was not very different from that of the Mogul Emperor, who had just succeeded in getting himself escorted back to his palace at Delhi.

Yet he was still Lord Clive, the owner of a great name, the possessor of a powerful mind, the leader of one of the strongest personal followings in the House of Commons. The world of politics was not likely to ignore him completely. Prime Ministers wanted votes at least as much as they wanted counsel. And they would want the latter when at last they were forced by the actual bankruptcy of the Company to give serious attention to India.

Lord North, the new Prime Minister, made overtures to Clive in May through Lord Rochford, his Secretary of State. Lord Rochford, he was told, wanted to have a talk with him. But Clive expressed only the mildest interest in the suggestion. He had turned all his Indian materials and ideas over to Strachey, who would require another eighteen months at least before he could produce a scheme. He would not be in London before the end of July and then only for a few days. He was hoping to winter in Italy.

Meanwhile Sulivan had been wrestling with the Company's complex problems. His efforts to stave off bankruptcy at home were to fail completely, but he was introducing a significant change of policy abroad. Already in June 1769 orders had been issued to Bengal for the appointment of Councils of Revenue at Murshidebad and Patna. The Company under Sulivan's guidance was moving, as Clive had anticipated, towards a complete change in his system. By slow and faltering steps it began to assume the responsibilities that he had declined for it. Dimly it perceived that actual governing, the redress of grievances, and the inspection of administration, could no longer be shirked. Sulivan, who had once been the great opponent of territorial power, was now the man who led the way towards the actual establishment of British government upon the ruins of the Mogul empire. He had resisted the pressure of facts while there was any hope of retaining the Company's commercial character. Now there was no longer any hope, now the continued attempt to have the best of both worlds was proving the surest road to ruin ; and he, a realist if ever there was one, was taking the only way out.

The miserable disputes in England obscured the eyes of his countrymen at home to what he was doing. They could only see the desperate, pitiful shifts to which he was driven in his last-ditch dealings with shareholders and Parliament, his last vain efforts to save the Company. The next two years were to be sensational in England; with Clive damning everybody, ministers, Directors, servants, shareholders alike, for the mismanagement of India; with the Directors damning their servants, with the Proprietors damning the Directors, with members of Parliament damning all three indiscriminately, and with Clive's enemies bringing to a head their own private feud with him. Yet during these years the Court of Directors managed to send to Bengal a series of despatches of epoch-making importance! It has often been remarked that the Company had become a Janus-faced monstrosity. So it was, and there could scarcely be a greater contrast than between the face it showed to England and the one it now showed to India.

True, a certain lack of knowledge of the actual facts of the situation was displayed in these despatches. They attached more importance to investigating and punishing the misconduct of officials—Sulivan had always been strong on disciplinary measures!—than to the working out of reforms. But both weaknesses could be corrected by the men on the spot. The point is that at last there was awareness of the evils, there was intelligence about the way to correct them, and there was a will. And who were the men on the spot? Or rather, who was the man? One who was more thinker than man of action, a true administrator, devoted to his work and gifted with warm human sympathy and a kindly tolerant spirit—Warren Hastings.

Sulivan had not been so busy with sordid intrigues that he had not recognized Hastings's outstanding talents. In April 1771 he quietly transferred him from Madras and sent him to succeed the inadequate Cartier as Governor of Bengal. And during the months of crisis that followed, when we might almost expect to find that Directors had no time at all for consideration of difficult matters of Indian government, he continued to give him steady support and much wise counsel (mixed with much that was unwise!). If Lawrence Sulivan deserves no other word of praise for what he did during his career as dictator of Leadenhall Street, he deserves it for this: that he upheld Hastings during the critical first two years of his administration, those years when the real foundations were being laid of decent government in Bengal, and thereby materially aided in getting him appointed the first Governor-General, an appointment that Lord North would not have made without the sanction of the Company's chairman. For without that appointment all Clive's prognostications of ruin would surely have been realized.

More than that. On August 28, 1771, the Court of Directors despatched the most important order that had yet been sent to India : the order for the Governor and Council of Calcutta to remove Mohammed Reza Khan and take into their own hands the government of Bengal.

" It is, therefore, our determination to stand forth as Dewan and by the agency of the Company's servants to take upon ourselves the entire care and management of the revenues. In confidence of your abilities to plan and execute this important work, we hereby authorize and require you to divest Mohammed Reza Cawn, and every person employed or in conjunction with him, or acting under his influence, of any further charge or direction in the business of collections ; and we trust that in the office of Dewan you will adopt such regulations and pursue such measures as shall at once ensure to us every possible advantage and free the ryots from the oppressions of the zemindars and petty tyrants under which they may have been suffered to remain from the interested views of those whose influence and authority should have been exerted for their relief and protection."

It meant the complete undoing of Clive's system. But it meant, too, the salvation of Bengal. It alone made possible Hastings's great work of reform and reconstruction. Sulivan and Hastings were almost alone in seeing that the troubles in India were not due only, or even chiefly, to men and their misconduct, but to the want of a proper system. Clive, on the other hand, having set up his system, blamed everything on the men who ran it. It was natural that he should, but it meant that he was not now qualified to legislate wisely for the needs of India. This was not the least tragedy of his closing years, that he was utterly out of sympathy with the only policy that could save his own achievement.

His only intervention in the Company's affairs during this period came when all hope had been given up for the lost *Aurora*

473

and her passengers and the question was being considered whom to send in their place. The general opinion was that there must be an over-riding authority in India over the Governors and councils of the local settlements. Clive believed that that authority must not be vested in servants of the Company, but in "men who stood high in public character and reputation." Accordingly, when his opinion was asked, he recommended his friend Wedderburn, Mr. Cornwall (afterwards Speaker of the House of Commons), and Sir Jeffrey Amherst, an able soldier, suggesting that to them should be added Hastings as Governor and one of the present council of Bengal. The proposal foreshadowed the composition of the Supreme Council appointed by the Regulating Act. The Directors, however, demurred and Amherst declined. Clive then proposed another Select Committee like his own. When this also failed of acceptance, the whole matter was held in abeyance, so that Hastings was left alone for a while as Governor, inheriting the instructions given to the Commissioners, but with none of their powers. Clive sent him a letter of congratulation and advice, which was an ironical commentary on their respective situations, viewpoints and ideas, so different in all respects.[209]

Chapter Twenty-eight

THE FINAL RECKONING

"Take my fortune, but save my honour"

CLIVE

I

INDIA WOULD NO LONGER PERMIT of being put off from session to session. As George III had at last got a ministry to his liking, there was not the slightest excuse for the neglect of such pressing business. If anybody could have found an excuse, surely Lord North would have found it, so easy-going was he, so good-natured, "so fatally unwilling to disoblige." The Indian question was full of trouble for everybody; it was the kind of question that politicians instinctively wish to shun. Lord North was to make a great success of botching it, but his first impulse at least was sound. At the end of October 1771, shortly before the meeting of Parliament, he sent the call for help that Clive ever since his return home had been waiting for. The personal letter of the Prime Minister was almost beseeching in tone. Wedder-burn supplemented it by telling him that ministers were so ready to defer to his superior knowledge that they would pursue any plan he suggested.

This was almost too good to be true; indeed, it was too good. But Clive responded to the appeal with alacrity. He left Bath at once and came to town. His first talk with North was success-ful; more talks followed, and an exchange of letters; Wedder-burn acted as the assiduous go-between; and for the moment everything looked promising for Clive's becoming the govern-ment's chief adviser on Indian affairs. Then Sulivan made trouble. It was only natural that he should. For some years he had been a personal friend of the minister, and considered himself by virtue of his office the proper person to advise the government. So once more the personal rivalry of these two men, which had been dormant while Clive's influence was in eclipse, was renewed, with the battleground transferred from Leadenhall

Street to Westminster. Sulivan was determined, if the Company's affairs had to come before Parliament, to make his own views prevail. Clive being the obstacle in the way, he directed his efforts towards nullifying his influence with ministers and in the House. To this end he had many means ready to hand. A word of encouragement to Clive's personal enemies was all that was necessary to release a flood of virulent abuse in the public press. Gloves were off in this fight, and no limit was placed to the foulness of the stories that were circulated. The materials that later formed Caraccioli's so-called *Life of Robert, Lord Clive* [1] came in useful now. The heaven-born general was held up to derision. Even worse. He was represented to the public as a murderer, a tyrant, an extortioner, a monster of cruelty, an adulterer, the worst character of that or any age.

There was nothing particularly novel about this extreme mode of attack. It had been employed fairly consistently for a century and more. It was in full flower under the Stuarts, when it had been used very effectively against Strafford, and was still not extinct at the end of the century, when Edmund Burke used it against Warren Hastings. It was deplorable, but Burke was an honourable man, and so may have been some of those who employed it against Clive.

Early in the new year Sulivan took a personal hand in the campaign. Anticipating the meeting of Parliament by a fortnight, he had the Secretary of the Company send Clive some papers containing a series of charges, anonymous in origin, appertaining to his second administration, and ask for his observations upon them. Clive disdained making any observations. The whole of his conduct, he said, was upon the public records of the Company.

When Parliament met on January 21, the debate on the King's speech made it evident that the Company's affairs were not to be neglected. Sulivan was busy preparing a bill that he intended introducing aimed at tightening up the control of the Company over its servants and improving the administration of justice. The Directors made a last-minute attempt to conciliate Clive in the hope of preventing him from opposing the bill. It failed. Thus when Sulivan rose on March 30 to ask for leave to bring in his bill, it was certain that the debate would turn as much on the conduct of Lord Clive as on the motion. And so it proved.

[1] See Appendix C.

Clive was the last man to sit silent under attack. Almost before the debate was fairly under way he was on his feet and launched into a long speech defending himself against those anonymous, and quite untrue, charges that the Company had sent him. It was a supremely able speech, "one of the most finished pieces of eloquence," declared Chatham, who was in the Peers' gallery, "he had ever heard in the House of Commons." He first told, with all the force of language of which he was capable, the story of his second administration, employing the same words and arguments as he had used in India. He then made direct connection between his cleansing of the Augean stable and the scurrilities of the press and the recent charges. He disposed of those charges quickly and convincingly. His defence was in every way admirable and conclusive. And had he sat down when he had completed it, he might have closed the mouths of his enemies. But the temptation to expound his views on the causes of the present troubles and to retaliate on everyone who had vexed him during the past five years was too strong. As he had done so often in his career, he turned defence into offence and proceeded to arraign the conduct of everybody connected with the management of Indian affairs since his return home, not sparing even ministers. Four causes, he told the House, had brought the Company to the brink of ruin : " A relaxation of government in my successors ; great neglect on the part of Administration ; notorious misconduct on the part of the Directors ; and the violent and outrageous proceedings of General Courts, in which I include contested elections." Furthermore, he enlarged upon each with characteristic vigour as though he wanted to see his hearers, many of whom though not named were included in the indictment, squirm in their seats before him.

It was a foolhardy act. Never had his want of tact, his disdain for conciliating opinion, his contempt for other men's views, interests, and sensibilities been displayed more glaringly. At the moment when his enemies were thirsting for his blood he threw away the support of the House.

Yet there may have been policy as well as temper in his outburst. If he was deliberately trying to kill Sulivan's bill, nothing was better calculated to do so, since it made it a foregone conclusion that the House would demand an enquiry before proceeding with it. An enquiry was the last thing Sulivan wanted, yet it is difficult to believe that Clive wanted one either. Both men were, indeed, caught in the snare of their own enmity ; neither, for different reasons, wanted an investigation, yet each by his conduct towards the other made an investigation inevitable and necessary. The public needs of the Company and the private feud between Clive and his enemies were so tangled together that it was impossible to separate them. Every time that Clive now opened his mouth to speak on India his enemies jumped into it !

So it was that when, two weeks later, Sulivan laid his bill on the table of the House and it had received its second reading, Colonel Burgoyne, an independent member, moved for the appointment of a Select Committee of enquiry. How, he pertinently asked, could members vote on a bill without first examining the state of the country to which it referred ? He disclaimed all partial views, disowned any hostility to the Company or its servants. After a long debate, in which Burke offered strenuous opposition, the motion was carried without division and a committee of thirty-one members was chosen by ballot.

It was a representative body, including as it did Clive himself and his friends Strachey and Wedderburn, his avowed enemies George Johnstone and William Pulteney, and a number of gentlemen like Charles James Fox, General Conway, Sir William Meredith, and its chairman Burgoyne, some of whose minds may still have been tolerably open.

It got to work at once and presented its first report on May 24. In less than six weeks it had surveyed all the chief events in Bengal from the capture of Calcutta by Siraj-ud-daula to the victory of Buxar, heard the evidence of numerous witnesses, including Clive, Coote, Munro, and Walsh, who were members of the House, and compiled a bulky document filling several hundreds of pages. It continued its work during the summer recess.

It was in the course of his examination before the Committee that Clive made the famous remark : " Mr. Chairman, at this moment I stand astonished at my own moderation ! " He had just confessed the amounts he had received from Mir Jafar—until now the world had not known them—at the same time vigorously denying that he had in any way acted contrary to honour or duty. " Am I not rather deserving of praise for the moderation which marked my proceedings ? Consider the situation in which the victory of Plassey had placed me. A great prince was dependent on my pleasure ; an opulent city lay at my mercy ; its richest bankers bid against each other for my smiles ; I walked through vaults which were thrown open to me alone, piled on either hand with gold and jewels ! " It was the thought of these rejected opportunities that made him astonished at himself.

The Committee has been roundly condemned by some for departing so far from the purpose of its appointment as to make these matters the subject of its enquiry. We can readily grant that it acted most indelicately in enquiring into transactions that Clive considered purely private matters between himself and Mir Jafar, yet its members would scarcely have been human if they had not shown some slight curiosity about how he got his wealth. And how much poorer our historical literature would be without Clive's classic remark ! It is odd that anyone in a country that boasts of a free Parliament and a free press should ever have objected to the process of enquiry that made these facts and the facts of the Omichand business known. One wonders a little what is the use of Parliamentary investigations if they are to spare the feelings of the individual. For it can scarcely be claimed that the matters themselves did not merit public attention or that they were not germane to the subject under review. The British public had a right to be informed.

The Prime Minister's attitude in this matter was, as usual, ambiguous and undefined. His habitual reluctance to disoblige people increased in direct ratio with their possession of votes and influence, and therefore it was on full display now with Lord Clive. He tried to be neutral, allowing his colleagues to go which way they pleased. It was a little awkward that Clive expected his active support, and he must have welcomed the opportunity that occurred during the recess to oblige him without committing himself to his defence.

Clive's appetite for honours had never been satisfied. Nothing less than an English peerage could satisfy it. In June he had been duly installed by the King as a Knight of the Bath in a ceremony of much pomp, though the pleasure of the occasion may have been a little spoiled for him by the fact that he had to share it with, among others, Sir Eyre Coote ! However, in September the Earl of Powis died and made vacant the Lord Lieutenancy of Shropshire. Clive at once aspired to it, but was uncertain how to proceed, knowing no more about the Prime Minister's attitude towards him than Lord North knew himself. His friends advised him to go straight to the throne, but that would have been to court the minister's real anger. The helpful Wedderburn, however, once more came to the rescue and whispered the suggestion in Lord North's ear. As it fell on a mind prepared to receive it, Clive was able on October 9 to kiss the royal hand as one of the acknowledged territorial magnates of England. An English peerage being but a short step from this, he would no doubt have received it if he had lived longer. A few months later he obtained the same office for Montgomeryshire.

That summer the Company failed. The Directors concealed its condition from the shareholders up to the last possible moment. They even allowed the General Courts to go on steadily voting dividends, which had risen to the statutory limit of $12\frac{1}{2}$ per cent. Sulivan was not one of the chairs that year ; the Court had become an increasingly fluctuating body with the chairs changing hands at each election. When things at last became so desperate that the demands of creditors could not be met, recourse was had to the Bank of England and £400,000 borrowed. But it was far from sufficient. When the Bank refused to increase the loan, the truth at last came out. The Directors applied to the Government for £1,500,000, listing liabilities amounting to £2,247,200 and assets only to £954,200. The stock quickly dropped from 219 to 160. Most of its holders were caught, as the Directors had given out false information, though they themselves had taken the precaution of previously unloading.[210]

An indignant cry for vengeance went up. Lord North replied to the application with the ominous statement that he could give no aid without the sanction of Parliament. Parliament was called early to deal with the petition. It was in a dangerous mood, as many of its members had lost considerable sums of money in the panic. So before any heed was paid to the Directors' demands a fresh enquiry was called for, and a Secret Committee was appointed to investigate the causes of the collapse.

The work of investigation by both Committees went on through the winter with recriminations of all kinds flying thick through the air. The Directors, caught between their shareholders, creditors, and Parliament, threw the blame on the management of their servants abroad ; shareholders and ex-servants lustily threw it back again. It was a game that all could play.

The curious product of so much enquiry and emotional disturbance that at length emerged was Lord North's Regulating

Act, which became law that session. Much obscurity surrounds its authorship. Even Francis Sykes, prominent Proprietor and close friend of Clive as he was, confessed he did not know who had been chiefly consulted. " It must have been," he said, " some person who was very ignorant of the Company's concerns, both at home and abroad." Even Sulivan could have done much better ![211]

Clive had made his contribution, and it was no fault of his that the act was so bad. He had written Strachey in November : " Lord North, when I saw him, seemed industriously to avoid entering upon the subject of Indian affairs ; and I do verily believe, from sheer indolence of temper, he wishes to leave everything to Providence and the Directors ; and that he means nothing more by the meeting of Parliament than to enable the Company to find money to discharge the demands that are at present made upon them." But he added : " I will not patiently stand by and see a great empire, acquired by great abilities, perseverance, and resolution, lost by ignorance and indolence. If Administration should think proper to see our affairs abroad in the same light as I do, 'tis well. If not, I shall have done my duty." Strachey helped him to prepare the memorandum that he sent to North. [212]

Comparison of the memorandum and the Act of Parliament indicates that North took the former as a basis and then, with the greatest possible skill, altered it so as to destroy all its virtue. He could not have done a better job of emasculation. Clive wanted the government of India vested in the hands of a strengthened and purified Court of Directors at home, freed from its old baneful dependence on the shareholders and made much more responsible to the Crown. Abroad he wanted a Governor-General and Council with full and extensive powers limited only by the superior authority of the home government. Instead, North made only some small immaterial changes in the Company's constitution, none of which did anything to improve the efficiency of the Court of Directors, and while he set up a Supreme Government in India he carelessly and fatally left its authority vague. Moreover, though Clive termed the idea of introducing English law into India absurd and impracticable and suggested only a strengthening and extending of the existing system of justice, the minister displayed his superior knowledge and wisdom by setting up an English Supreme Court of Justice manned by English barristers to administer English law. The resulting instrument of government came near to destroying the empire that it was intended to save.

II

The final scene of this Parliamentary drama was a repetition of the preceding ones. It opened on May 3, 1773. Once again the motion before the House, this time a motion moved by the Prime Minister himself, was for leave to bring in a bill to regulate the government of India. Once again Clive turned the attention of the House upon himself and made the debate personal.

The Select Committee's reports, which had been appearing one after another, had aspersed his character, attacked his reputation ; he could not let them go unchallenged. So he craved, as he also taxed, the patience of the House while he vindicated himself. And once again his vindication of himself led him into recriminations upon everybody connected with the Company's management.

One of his hearers wrote :

" Lord Clive's speech was certainly a very able one, but it was not calculated to conciliate matters. He laid about him on all sides : he reprehended the Court of Directors, past and present, the Court of Proprietors, the citizens of London, the country gentlemen of England, the servants of the Company abroad, the Secret and Select Committees, the Opposition, the minister and ministry. He paid a compliment to the King. He declared he would support Government where he could do it honourably. He offended the opposition without gaining the Minister." [213]

He reserved the sharpest of his shafts for Sulivan. Towards the end of a speech that lasted for more than two hours came these words :

" My situation, Sir, has not been an easy one for these twelve months past ; and though my conscience never could accuse me, yet I felt for my friends, who were involved in the same censure as myself. Sir, not a stone has been left unturned, where the least probability could arise of discovering something of a criminal nature against me. The two committees, Sir, seem to have bent the whole of their enquiries to the conduct of their humble servant the baron of Plassey ; and I have been examined by the Select Committee more like a sheep-stealer than a member of this House. I am sure, Sir, if I had any sore places about me, they would have been found ; they have probed to the bottom ; no lenient plasters have been applied to heal ; no, sir, they were all of the blister kind prepared with Spanish flies and other provocatives. The public records have been ransacked for proofs against me ; and the late deputy chairman of the India Company, a worthy member of the House, has been so very assiduous in my affairs that really, Sir, it appears that he has entirely neglected his own. As the heads upon Temple Bar have tumbled down, and as there appears no probability of their being replaced, for Jacobitism seems at an end—at least there has been great alteration in men's sentiments within these ten years ; I would propose, Sir, that my head, by way of pre-eminence, should be put upon the middle pole ; and his Majesty having given me these honours, it is proper they should be supported : what think you then of my having the late chairman and deputy-chairman on each side ? "

It was magnificent in its way, the superb, scornful defiance of a lion at bay—but it was not prudent. It brought down the House, it convulsed it with laughter for the space of ten minutes ; but the one man who did not laugh, who sat glowering with rage, still had it in his power to retaliate.

Retaliation was swift in coming. Ministers conferred, showing their hostile intent by excluding the Solicitor-General from the meeting. Thurlow, the Attorney-General, who had represented the Company in its suit against the *jaghire*, proposed the confiscation of all the gifts and grants received by the Company's servants to the relief of the Company, justifying it on the ground that whatever was obtained by the military forces of the country belonged to the state. There was some objection, but not enough, and Lord North, influenced by the King, who had suddenly, in his strange, irrational way, turned against Clive, was inclined to acquiesce. [214]

A week after Clive's speech the attack was launched. Burgoyne conducted it, basing it upon the reports of his committee, which, he said, revealed crimes that shocked human nature. But the true nature of his object only came into view at the close, when he moved three resolutions. They were a

483

preliminary : they did not ask for actual restitution of the sums received, they merely declared the state's right to them. They were carried without a division.

One acute and modern-minded observer noted a glaring inconsistency in the debate. For whereas all the English transactions in India for the past sixteen years were treated without distinction as a disgrace to the nation, there was not the least suggestion that the disgrace should be removed by restoring to the injured people of India the territories and revenues that had been so unjustly acquired.[214]

On May 19 Burgoyne got down to business and turned from general principles to an open attack on Clive. He ended by proposing a resolution :

" That the right honourable Lord Clive, Baron of Plassey, in the Kingdom of Ireland, in consequence of the powers vested in him in India, had illegally acquired the sum of £234,000 to the dishonour and detriment of the state."

Clive spoke again. And this time he was strictly on the defensive and on his guard. He must by now have realized the seriousness of his situation. Gone were the intemperate gibes and taunts and scathing indictments, and in their place came a reasoned defence of his conduct, an impressive statement of his services, an eloquent plea for sympathy and justice.

We need not follow him over the old ground. No one who has read these pages can fail to see that in matters touching his own honour and the service of the state he could make out a well-nigh impregnable case. No fair-minded man, if he judge the matter in the light of that day, could possibly agree with his accusers that his deposition of Siraj-ud-daula was a shocking and disgraceful act, or that his acceptance of huge rewards from Mir Jafar merited the supreme penalty of confiscation. And when he pleaded that if the resolution were carried he would be a bankrupt with nothing left to him but his patrimony of £500 a year—" but upon this I am content to live, and perhaps I shall find more real content of mind and happiness therein than in the trembling affluence of an unsettled fortune "—he made the strongest possible plea to the sense of justice and fair play of the House of Commons. He made the resolution appear the monstrous thing it was. All his words now were well chosen and telling : " I have one request to make to the House, that when they come to decide upon my honour, they will not forget their own " ; and those with which he concluded another short speech when the debate was resumed on the 21st : " Take my fortune, but save my honour."

With those last ringing words he left the House. A dramatic, well-timed withdrawal, far more effective than if he had stayed to conduct his defence in person. His defence was safe, much safer, in the hands of Wedderburn.

In his absence his enemies pressed the attack. Burgoyne presented a new motion, the first part of which stated again the sums that Clive had received from Mir Jafar, and the second carried the argument a step further—" that in so doing the said Robert Lord Clive abused the powers with which he was entrusted, to the evil example of the servants of the public." At once an amendment was moved to separate the two parts. It was accepted. Then another amendment was moved to weaken the force of the resolution by omitting the clause stating that he had obtained these sums " through the influence of the powers with which he was intrusted, as a member of the select committee and commander-in-chief of the British forces."

The debate now reached its climax. More and more members were rallying to Clive's side. The Government following was divided. Lord North went with the Attorney-General in opposing the amendment, but his influence was more than offset by the opposition, most of whom supported it.

The amendment was carried by a large majority. The vote was decisive in Clive's favour. There was nothing objectionable then in the main question, which was merely a statement of fact, and it was accordingly put and carried. Then as dawn began to lighten the windows of the Chamber after an all-night session, Burgoyne put the second part of his original motion. It was rejected without a division. Triumphantly Wedderburn rose again to drive his victory home. He moved that " Robert Lord Clive did, at the same time, render great and meritorious services to this country." The resolution was carried without a division. The attack on Lord Clive was over.

III

Looking back on the attack from the vantage point of to-day, we can see that it deserved to fail, that it had to fail if justice were to be done. There were no specific grounds for a criminal prosecution of Lord Clive. That was the all-important point. There were no specific charges that could be brought home to him as an individual. His enemies industriously sought such charges, they brought quite a few more than are mentioned in this book. And the reason they are not mentioned here is that they are not worth attention. Clive disposed of them so easily and convincingly that they only served to strengthen his position and expose the vindictiveness of his accusers. Indeed, on *specific* grounds he was in a considerably stronger position than Warren Hastings, against whom a much more formidable case was to be constructed fifteen years later. That is one reason why Hastings was impeached and Clive was not.

Another reason was that the temper of the House was in Clive's favour, whereas it was not to be in Hastings's. Clive was not made an issue between government and opposition. There were no leaders of a powerful party, no Burke, Fox, or Sheridan, to put him in the forefront of their programme of action ; and therefore the House was under no such temptation to do wrong, as it was, for instance, when Wilkes was the object of attack. " The House accordingly acted with the good sense and good feeling which may always be expected from an assembly of English gentlemen, not blinded by faction."[215] Clive could rely upon its justice. The result was a triumph of equity and moderation, a real victory for the good sense of the House of Commons.

Even the Committee of Enquiry, the weapon of his enemies, was not glaringly unjust. The fervent defenders of Clive have tried to persuade us that it was nothing better than a packed body of men animated with a desire to dig up incriminating evidence against him. It does not appear to have been that. True, its members questioned him closely, probed deeply into his actions, revealed suspicions of his motives ; but that, after all, was what they were appointed to do. If they had done otherwise they would have failed in their duty. Nor need we assume that because he figured prominently in all their lines of enquiry and came under investigation more often than other participants, it was because their only object was to incriminate him. Can we have *Hamlet* without the Prince of Denmark ? Clive was the Hamlet of the whole subject under review. . Where else could he have been in the picture that was thrown on the screen but in the forefront ? Where else would he, until now, have wished to be ? When he said that he was examined like a sheep-stealer, all he suggests to us is that he hated to be examined at all.   All his life he had hated anything that seemed to cast doubt on his integrity and the absolute purity of his motives and actions.   He expected men to take his word for them.

Actually, if he could have swallowed his inordinate pride and seen himself and things in general as other men saw them, he might well have welcomed the investigation.   It did very little more than lay bare facts, and innocent men usually depend upon facts to acquit them.   And as it happened it *was* the facts that acquitted him.   His enemies must have been bitterly disappointed at the paucity of damaging evidence the Committee turned up.   After all the shocking things they had been saying about him, of what value were the trifles that the report revealed ? Opinion was bound to react in his favour.   It may even be said that the much maligned Committee saved his honour by drawing practically all the poison out of the barbs of his enemies.   He should have been properly grateful, as historians, too, should be grateful for the results ; as one of them has said, the reports of the Committee of 1772 and 1773 are " a valuable storehouse of facts for the history of the East India Company."[216]   Parliament performed one of its most valuable functions in uncovering them.   Should it have been concerned that some of the disclosures happened to be disagreeable to Lord Clive ?

What has upset subsequent opinion is the moral character that the attack assumed.   It is easy to perceive that there was scarcely a man among his judges fit to render judgment on that ground. But let us be careful before we convict them of hypocrisy and damn them in consequence.   The indignation expressed was wholesome and honourable, even if it had no right to clothe itself in righteousness.   It was of a part with all the moral indignation that has so often brought the charge of hypocrisy upon the British nation ; for it is so easy to see the glaring discrepancy between profession and behaviour.   Yet it has only been by means of its capacity to feel *post facto* moral indignation that the British people has advanced, as we believe it has, to higher levels of conduct.   If the conduct of their countrymen in India in Clive's and Hastings's day had not aroused indignation at home, *no matter how hypocritical some of it was,* there never would have been anything approaching decent government in India.

Rather, then, than emphasize the hypocrisy and doubtful motives of such an assailant of Clive as Burgoyne, we can be grateful, even proud, that there were Englishmen even in that age who had sufficient regard for the national honour to evince something more than cynical, callous indifference to the means by which the national power had been extended and cold-blooded acceptance of the material benefits the extension brought. Suspect their motives and their sincerity as we may, they were expressing honourable sentiments and laying foundations for a nobler conception of government. They were, in fact, helping to save the British from the fate that overtook the Spaniards in Peru and Mexico.

If this can be said for the Burgoynes, what can be said for the Johnstones and for Sulivan? There is something rather pitiful about their failure. They had waited so long for their revenge. They bore so many heavy grudges against Lord Clive. For all these years he had been riding roughshod in pursuit of his ambition, caring little about the feelings or reputations he hurt along the way, doing nothing to allay the jealousies he aroused, intent always and only upon his goal, which some may see as the public good and the aggrandizement of the nation and others as personal advancement, glory, and enrichment. For years these men had been chasing him. And now at the end of the chase they had him cornered, they had forced him to dismount, compelled him at last to turn and face them. He had won, all the prizes of the race were his, he held in his proud hands the chief trophy of all, India. There had been no umpire to decide if the race was being fairly run. But now they had found a court of appeal, they had made themselves members of it, they had put themselves on terms of equality with their successful rival. They could not take his chief trophy away from him—he had presented it to the nation—but they could at least dim its lustre, show that it had been won by foul means ; they might even succeed in taking away his wealth, reducing him to General Lawrence's condition—for who can doubt that the thought of the ripe old veteran living in quiet retirement upon his small pension was often in their minds ? They were envious, rancorous, unscrupulous, merciless. There was not a generous impulse among them.

But Clive proved, as he had always proved, too clever, too great a quarry to be caught by them. Never was his superiority over his enemies and rivals, a superiority of mind, character, intelligence, natural abilities, better displayed than in this final reckoning with them. They had a case of sorts, but they ruined it by allowing rancour to run away with their judgment, by manufacturing charges against him in a way that has disgusted the world ever since, by miscalculating their ground and the temper of the House of Commons, by thinking that they could get the national court of appeal to accept a vindictive act of private revenge as an act of substantial justice. They should have seen that, however legitimate and understandable their private sense of grievance was, it could not be translated into terms of public law and morality and be made the basis for a criminal prosecution. They failed and, as we have said, they most emphatically deserved to fail.

But they obtained their revenge nevertheless, the only revenge possible. They obtained it through the popular obloquy that had descended upon him, which no resolution of the House of Commons could remove, and the acute suffering that it caused him. The resolution was an utterly inadequate sop to his pride. He had always expected more in the way of gratitude and recognition than he had received. What could he think now, what could he feel when he heard that even the King—of all persons in the kingdom !—had expressed regret at the passing of that saving resolution, had expressed the greatest satisfaction that his minister had voted with the minority, had written : " I own I am amazed that private interest could make so many forget what they owe their country and come to a resolution that seems to approve of Lord Clive's rapine " ?

Rapine ! The King thought *that* of him ! If he had cut his throat then and there, it would not have been surprising ! And, whenever he ventured abroad, what could have been his feelings when he found that everyone, even his neighbours, echoed the cry ? Here was victory enough for his enemies. It was more than enough.

IV

He had one last service to render India, and it was a service that forms a sad epilogue to his life : the gift of the Triumvirate that was to ruin the fair promise of Warren Hastings's administration. For Clive has to share with Lord North the responsibility of what was to happen in India with the setting up of the new government appointed by the Regulating Act : the rule of the majority in the Supreme Council, Clavering, Monson, and

Francis, over the minority, Warren Hastings, the Governor-General, and Barwell, with all the evil consequences that it entailed.

It is a responsibility that goes deep, extending from his disapproval of Hastings's departure from his system to deliberate inoculation of Francis with his ideas. His connection with the party opposing Hastings was suspiciously close and intimate. When we find, for instance, the family connection between him and Joseph Fowke, it is hard not to suspect that the opposition party was really born at Walcot.

Fowke, a private merchant of Calcutta, was the man who went down the river to meet the arriving councillors and give them " some useful lights into the state of affairs and character of persons " ; in other words, he was the man who, bearing a grudge against the Governor-General, instilled in their minds suspicions of Hastings's integrity and later became one of the chief conspirators.[217] He was John Walsh's brother-in-law, and Walsh, let us remember, was not only Clive's agent but Lady Clive's cousin. The Fowke papers make the connection even clearer. They contain evidence that Lady Clive was on terms of warm affection with female members of the Fowke family, that another member of the Fowke family, Arthur, was a frequent visitor at Walcot, as was also Clavering, whose special *protégé* Joseph Fowke became. They also contain a letter from Walsh to his nephew Francis Fowke, Joseph's son, in which he says (March 30, 1774) : " General Clavering and Mr. Francis, the son of the translator of Horace, are particular friends of ours and will be ready to render you any service in their power." Clavering and Francis met at Clive's house.[218]

If it was Fowke who instilled into the minds of his arriving friends doubts of Hastings's integrity, it was certainly Clive with the aid of his secretary Strachey who instilled doubts, and more than doubts, of the wisdom of his policy. And the two doubts when combined and solidified into convictions, as happened so easily with the aid of personal pride and ambition, were quite enough to launch the new councillors upon their career of ruining Hastings and hamstringing his administration. Whether Clive was acquainted with Francis before his appointment or had anything to do with obtaining it for him is doubtful, though they had political connections in common. But after his appointment Francis made haste to attach himself to Clive and freely imbibed his views, while Clive for his part did his best to mould Francis's views upon his own, sending him elaborate data and memoranda. (Strachey to Francis, 1776 : "I gave you in writing a faithful abstract of every measure of his [Clive's] Government. If you cannot form a better system, dare to recommend it as the best.") [219] With so much effect did he do this that six months before the new councillors sailed Burke reported to Rockingham (October 20, 1773) : "I find that this Mr. Francis is entirely in the interests of Lord Clive. Everything contributes to the greatness of that man who, whether government or the Company prevails, will go near to govern India." [220]

It is not a little strange that no one has pointed out the extraordinarily close resemblance that exists between the conduct immediately upon arrival of Clive and his Select Committee and that of Clavering, Monson, and Francis. In the speed with which the latter made up their minds that they were confronted with another Augean stable (which they described in similar terms), in the kind of language they employed against the members of the previous administration, and the charges of bribery and corruption they brought against them, in the way they proceeded to take matters entirely into their own hands and reverse political arrangements already made, it can only seem that Clavering and Francis were paying their mentor the great compliment of imitating him. It is seldom that history repeats itself exactly, but it is very clear that Francis wanted the world to believe that in this case it had, even to his willingness and ability to play the martyred role of Clive. Dr. Sophia Weitzman, in her study of *Warren Hastings and Philip Francis*, shows that he took over Clive's ideas, prejudices, and policies in their entirety, using them as the main stick with which to beat Hastings.

Light on Clive's mind is forthcoming from Francis's sycophancy. When a man set himself to work on another man's mind as deliberately and as cleverly as Francis tried to work on Clive's (and later on Burke's), and when he shows as much skill both in reading that mind and the character that goes with it and utilizing the knowledge for his own ends as Francis displayed (he saw smouldering in Burke's the fanatical fires of enthusiasm for the cause of justice and humanity and hatred of oppression, and he fanned those fires and directed them against Hastings), we are likely to find that knowledge instructive. Francis found that the largest place in Clive's mind was occupied by his *jaghire*, that the surest way he could arouse his interest in what was happening in Bengal and enlist his support against Hastings was by arousing his fears for the *jaghire's* safety. This he did by constantly proclaiming the fact that Hastings had utterly ruined Bengal and all its revenues. Evidently Francis had read enough of the Bible to know that " Where thy treasure is, there shall thy heart be also." He might have succeeded in his endeavour if it had not been for the fact that before even the first letter was written Clive was already dead.

CONCLUSION

"Can a man take fire in his bosom and his clothes not be burned?"
Book of Proverbs

THERE IS LITTLE MORE TO ADD. When the biographer of Oliver Cromwell is just beginning his story, the biographer of Robert Clive is ending his.

Life for Clive had become unbearable. Who is to say that in those last days of torment he lacked fortitude? "How miserable is my condition! I have a disease which makes life unsupportable, but which doctors tell me won't shorten it an hour." Could he have borne up if his pride, his most vulnerable possession, had not been mortally wounded? He had so many ills to contend with, physical, mental, spiritual. During that last year he was sunk in gloom. The building of his great new mansion at Claremont gave him no pleasure; nothing could longer give him that, and Margaret tried everything she could think of to divert him. All in vain. The great world outside his gates was torn in strife; England's colonies were on the verge of open revolt, but he was past caring. Was there a wistful hope on the part of some who were still his admirers that he might accept the command of the British forces in America? If so, it must have died as soon as uttered. England was fated to meet this great crisis in her history without a single man in her ranks of statesmen or soldiers equal to it. Pain and opium taken to relieve it had effectively removed Lord Clive from contact with the world of affairs.

At last there came the tragic day, November 22, 1774. It happened as the family were making ready to leave the house in Berkeley Square for Bath. They heard a heavy fall in the next room, and rushing in they found Lord Clive lying dead on the floor.

Some uncertainty surrounds the precise manner of his going. The family, naturally anxious to hush it up as much as possible, gave out that it had been accidental and caused by an overdose of opium. The general belief is that he cut his own throat. There seems no sufficiently strong reason for thinking that this belief is incorrect. But whether it was the poison or the razor that was the actual cause, his death was not, one feels certain, accidental ; it was written in his stars that when life became insupportable he would take it.

At dead of night they removed his body to the country, burying it in the little church of Moreton Say just outside the gates of Styche Park, leaving the world to speculate as it pleased about the manner of his sudden decease. But they left no stone to mark the place where they laid him. As he had been in the beginning, a lonely, unhappy exile, so he was now at the end.

We set ourselves a task at the outset of this book. We have now completed it. We have seen the hero emerge out of the situation created by Dupleix ; we have seen him rise to great heights ; and then, even while still rising, gradually fade away, not having the necessary qualities to sustain the part. As he faded we have also seen him moving steadily towards his predestined, tragic end, a victim of circumstances interwoven with his own unfortunate nature, a man too much blessed for a time with good fortune, then inevitably deserted by it. Not two men, but one born under stars that were both lucky and unlucky.

If we would sum him up in a few words we would say that he was a law unto himself, a man who followed the devices and desires of his own nature wherever they led him, regardless of consequences either to himself or to others, reckless of everyone else's feelings and interests, isolated curiously from everybody and unable long to remain in harness or even friendship with his associates, once the friend and later the enemy of Sulivan, Vansittart, Hastings, Spencer, Sumner, Rous.[1] A man whose decisions were his own and taken in secret, and who in only one or two special crises is ever known to have sought advice.

Partly in consequence of this, few men have exposed less of themselves to the common view. He kept no diary, left no memoirs. Like Marlborough's, his correspondence deals strictly with the matter in hand refraining from discursive remarks ; but unlike Marlborough's, his letters even to his wife reveal very little of himself, his expressions of love being few and stilted. If he knew doubt, discouragement, uncertainty, genuine anguish of soul, he generally kept the fact to himself, leaving us to guess at

[1] A paraphrase of words applied by T. P. O'Connor to Lord Carson.

what went on within himself. Was that cold, almost inhuman firmness of will and purpose, keeping its own counsel and requiring no outside aid whether of God or man to inform, guide, or sustain it—was it a mask or was it his real self? Both to his contemporaries and to us he seemed made of energy and ambition, restless, dæmonic, volcanic alike in their source and manifestations.

We have been able to give practically no intimate pictures of him because such pictures do not exist. A few of his intimates may have penetrated his wall of reserve, but what they found there, other than apparently genuinely agreeable qualities, we do not know. He was well and faithfully served by his secretaries Walsh and Strachey, who appear to have been devoted to him, and it may be that when the private papers of the latter are explored to the bottom and published by their present owner they will be found to contain all the evidence required to establish Clive's character as " a man of the kindest affections and every social virtue." It will still remain true, however, that he never appeared in that guise to the world at large.

One thing he lacked above everything else : magnanimity. He lacked much else of the finer, warmer human qualities, but it was that lack, pitiful at times in its utterness, that more than any thing chills our feeling for him and forces disapproving words and harsh judgment to our lips. If he had only had a spark of that nobility of soul of Robert E. Lee, for example, how much greater a man he would have been, how much more sympathetic and admirable !

His essential fame as the acquirer of an Indian empire for Britain remains untouched. In fact, it has if anything been enlarged by a close study of his conflict with Sulivan. The overcoming of the opposition at home to the acquisition of an empire was as necessary to its establishment as the military victory itself. Plassey, the overthrow of Sulivan, the acquisition of the *dewani* were the three main steps in the process, and for each of them Clive was singly responsible. But that is the limit we place to his achievement. Just as the Roman Empire was the work of Augustus rather than of Julius, the Mogul Empire of Akbar rather than of Babar, and no Greek Empire followed the conquests of Alexander, so the British Empire in India was not the work of Clive but of the men who followed him, Warren Hastings most of all, and but for them his achievement would not have endured. His gifts were too limited for that larger task. He had not the sympathy, nor the imagination, nor the knowledge, nor the understanding, nor the patience, nor the endurance necessary for the setting up of a great new system of government or for administering it when set up. His mind was too centred upon himself, his personal ambitions, his ease and comfort and the state of his health for him ever to have achieved anything of permanent worth in that direction. The task required self-sacrifice above everything else, unending toil in the hot season as well as in the cool; it required men who would think first of India, who would take the time to know its people and their languages, habits, needs, and problems, and who would be charitable and tolerant in their judgments of men as well as firm and just in their dealings with them; who would devote themselves unsparingly to their work and not think about retirement until it was done; and who would have that greater love that Hastings acknowledged when he confessed loving India a little more than his own country. Such men there were to be in plenty; and whatever one may think of the empire that they served or of the methods by which it was achieved or of the man who acquired it, their fame is noble and deathless; they took the impure work of Clive's hands and purified it, so far as they could, by the blood and sweat of their toil.

APPENDICES

2 I

A

HOW PITT AND THE DIRECTORS DEALT WITH THE "COLONEL PROBLEM"

COLONEL ADLERCRON's behaviour in withholding his regiment, the 39th, from the Bengal expedition forced the Home Government to ask the question, What is the use of sending British regiments to India if their colonels are able to prevent them from serving under the Company's orders? The answer was, clearly none. Yet the solution that was found to the problem was of a kind that can only be labelled "typically British" and "typically eighteenth-century." Was Parliament appealed to to solve it by legislation? Certainly not! That would have been undue interference with the rights of private property!

Pitt, whose greatness was never better shown than in his insistence on the oneness of the British effort, found for the distracted Directors a much better and cleverer solution. He ordered that the 39th Regiment of Foot should be disbanded and its colonel recalled to England. Sad fate, indeed, for a regiment that bears on its colours the proud motto "Primus in Indis"! The order was contained in a letter from the Court of Directors to the Select Committee at Fort St. George dated February 1, 1757. But there was a catch in it! The disbandment of a regiment was not the same as its being ordered home. The idea was that by throwing the King's officers and men out of employment while still in India they would be forced to seek fresh employment out there in the Company's service. Every encouragement, in fact, was to be given them to do so. If any of the officers refused the bait, they had to be accommodated with a return passage; but no obligation rested on the Company to provide shipping for the enlisted men.

Thus Colonel Adlercron paid the penalty for his undue insistence on his rights. In October 1757 eight of his officers sailed for home, others followed later, and the rest exchanged the King's service for the Company's, whilst the Company obtained a whole regiment of enlisted men for its service without any trouble or expense. But the Colonel himself, though bereft of his regiment, refused at first to go. When it was suggested to him that he might like to take passage on the first ship, he gallantly declared it to be his "indispensable duty to be the last man of my regiment that embarks"; "he will," Edmund Maskelyne told Clive, "stay to the last to plague our gentry."

Pitt, however, still had to solve the difficulty of getting fresh troops to India without having the same difficulty arising each time. The Company badly wanted soldiers, its own attempts to recruit them in competition with the

Crown having proved entirely unsuccessful ; it wanted the King's men without the King's colonels ! Accordingly, Pitt proposed to the King that a battalion from each of the new regiments that were then being raised should be " loaned " to the Company without its field officers, so that they could be placed under the orders of Lawrence and Clive without any possibility of a clash of authority. This was done, and in this way the Company obtained the army that was required to consolidate Clive's gains and repel Lally's attack.

The debt, therefore, that the Company owed to Pitt was great. It was suitably acknowledged by Sulivan, who wrote to the minister that the Company " not only owed their present glorious situation but their very existence to his generous protection."

B

SUMMARY OF WILL OF LORD ROBERT CLIVE [1]

" Baron of Plassey in the Kingdom of Ireland."

ALL castles, manors, messuages, tenements, real estates, etc. unto and to the use of my cousin George Clive of Fleet Street, London, banker, my friends John Walsh of Chesterfield Street, Mayffair in the county of Middlesex, Esqr., Henry Strachey of Park Street near Grosvenor Square, Middx., Esq., and Christopher D'Oyly of Charles Street near Berkeley Square, Middx., Esq., and their heirs and assigns, upon trusts.

Manor of Styche, Salop, and messuages, lands, etc. in " Woodland Newstead Lane Warrenshall Morton Sea old ffields Betchley Longslow and Drayton in the county of Salop " upon trust to

	second son	—Robert Clive [under 21 years of age] with
remainder to eldest	„	—Edward „	
do.	brother	—William „	
do.	cousin	—Robert „	Archdeacon of Salop
do.	„	—George „	of Fleet St., London, banker.
do.		—Edward Bolton Clive, son of George [above].
do.	eldest daughter	—Rebecca Clive	
do.	second „	—Charlotte „	
do.	third „	—Margaret „	

Wife—Lady Clive, to receive annual sum of £2000 as a satisfaction for " all dower or thirds she may be entitled to out of my real estates."

cousin, Henry Clive to receive £100 annually

„ Charles „ „ „ £50 „

aunt, Ann Clive „ „ £25 „

Henry Strachey „ „ £400 „

Arrabella Ashley " in case she shall be in my ffamily at my decease "—£50 annually.

Isaac Talboys £30 annually on same condition.

Benjamin Hudson £15 „ „ „

" The sword set with diamonds which was presented to me by the East India Company and my diamond badge belonging to me as Knight of the Bath " and all plate, books, etc. upon trust for son Edward Clive " at his age of twenty one years."

[1] P.C.C. 426 Bargrave.

Leasehold house in Berkeley Square, " where I now live " upon trust for wife's use and after her death to be made over to son Edward or " to such person as shall then be entitled to the present estate. . . ."

" Capital houses at Walcot Oakley Park Styche and Clermont " referred to.

Out of the " growing payments from the East India Company on account of my Jaghire " funeral expenses and other debts to be paid.

 £500 to each Trustee of the will.

 £100 to each sister and their respective husbands.

 £50 to each of collateral relations of name of Clive.

£10,000 to wife.

£10,000 to brother William Clive.

£30,000 to son Robert Clive on attaining 25 years of age.

£30,000 to each other son do. do. do.

£20,000 to each daughter, Rebecca, Charlotte, Margaret Clive on attaining 21 years of age.

Executors—George Clive, cousin.

  John Walsh.

  Henry Strachey.

  Christopher D'Oyly.

Wife and executors to be guardians of the children.

Provisions made for all children during their minority.

Date of will—24 November 1773.

Proved—At London, 13 December 1774 ; all executors present.

C

THE LIFE OF ROBERT, LORD CLIVE, BY CHARLES CARACCIOLI

THIS curious publication, which appeared three years after Clive's death, is on all counts the most ill-arranged, unreadable, hopelessly compiled, and for the most part unreliable work of biography that has ever come off a groaning and abused printing-press ! I have not calculated its length, but it cannot be far short of, and may exceed a million words. Because of its character it is doubtful whether anyone paid much attention to it at the time of its publication, let alone read it with any closeness, and it is even more to be doubted whether anyone from that day to this has had the necessary fortitude, patience, and endurance to wade through it. Historians and biographers have of necessity included it in their lists of sources, but they have done so with the air of " holding their noses ! " If it is an " authority " it surely must be among the worst on record. In it is to be found one of the richest collections of foul stories about a man in the whole realm of historical literature. Clive, if Mr. Caraccioli is to be believed, put Don Juan and Casanova entirely to shame, even at the time when as an invalid he had gone with Margaret to the south of France.

Professor H. H. Dodwell is the most recent scholar to have dipped into this extraordinary work—and he does not mince his words, describing it as " a piece of hack-work manifestly inspired and paid for by Clive's enemies," therefore, " worthless and contemptible." There is no question at all that it is such a piece of work, and for a historian's purpose it *is* worthless. But is it equally worthless from a biographer's standpoint ?

I asked myself that question as I waded through its pages, and I came at length to a somewhat different conclusion. A biographer must be concerned with more than concrete facts that can pass a scientific test. A historian is justified in throwing out of court a work that can make the statement that Stringer Lawrence was *not* presented with a sword set with diamonds as Clive was, because he is practically certain the statement is untrue.[1] A biographer, however, fully as much interested as he is in states of mind as in facts, is justified in probing deeper, and any work that seems to throw light on the state of mind and the causes of it of his subject's enemies is worthy of his attention. For it is axiomatic in biography that a man to be properly known must be seen through the eyes of his enemies as well as of his admirers.

---

[1] I say " practically certain " because though we know that the Court of Directors voted him the sword and he wrote expressing his thanks, we have no actual record of his receipt of it.

Caraccioli's book has value for a biographer if only because it enables him to gauge the warmth of feeling that Clive stirred up against himself. It is astonishing, when one comes to think of it, that anyone should have gone to the labour and expense of compiling and publishing such a book merely in order to blacken the reputation of a man already in his grave. The fact suggests a ferocity of hatred quite unusual. But there is more to be gleaned from it than that.

It is a curious production in more ways than one. It is fairly obviously a compilation from many different sources. Charles Caraccioli—if he existed at all, and we know nothing whatever about him—was at most its editor or compiler, and a glance is enough to reveal his entire incompetence for the job. The various contributions, many of them repetitions, are strung together without regard for order, sequence, consistency, accuracy, or any other literary or historical value. One does not always begin where another leaves off—it may be injected into the middle without anything to indicate the fact. Scant attention is paid to quotation marks and not the slightest to whether the statement is fact or opinion. It is such a complete potpourri that although it is in the main virulently hostile to Clive one occasionally finds a passage that is actually favourable to him (*i.e.* a Clive-ish account of Plassey, Vol. I, pp. 307–19). One infers that such a passage must have got in by accident owing to the editor's carelessness !

The literary incompetence displayed in it is, indeed, something to be marvelled at and pitied, but not necessarily to be wholly derided. The contributors are anonymous, but as much of their material deals with military matters one judges that many of them may have been military gentlemen, among whom no doubt were the officers whom Clive from time to time angered. So that one gets the feeling that the literary incompetence displayed here is the kind common, as Orme noted, to most soldiers ; in this instance being more marked because they are venting their spleen instead of employing their reason. Even when they are on their own professional ground they are unable to say clearly and simply what they mean ; they are so busy hurling their shafts at Clive with blood in their eye and vigour, if not skill, in their arm, that sober argument is beyond them.

Yet there are times when what passes for argument seems to have definite point and their anger to have some understandable quality behind it. One of those times is when they compare Lawrence and Clive as objects of their country's admiration and military men's regard. It becomes clear then that their affection for Lawrence was quite as strong as their dislike for Clive. In their clumsy way they try to tell us that there is more to war than heroic exploits : there is the organization, training, and disciplining of an army, its wise leadership, and its need of a commander that has its confidence. So we read this eulogy of Lawrence :

" No commanding officer in India did more real service to the Company, was more active in the field, more careful of the life and welfare of the soldier, more affable to the inferior officers, and at the same time more exact in the military discipline. Ever since this excellent officer retired his un-spotted honour, his disinterestedness, his moderation, his justice, during twenty years of toil and fatigues in Indostan, made him beloved, esteemed and revered by the army, the presidencies and the natives. He died lately, at the age of 78, in peace with his conscience, full of years, and leaving a name equally respected in Europe and in Indostan " (I, 222).

The tribute has a ring of genuine sincerity.

The rest of their point of view may be gathered from the contrast they draw between Clive obtaining his *jaghire* in Bengal and Colonels Lawrence and Drapier and the army gallantly and ably defending Madras, Coote winning the battle of Wandewash and taking Pondichéry, and Forde conquering the Circars, all of these being " soldiers who fought for glory, not for plunder." Clive, they say, abandoned the field to officers who had not acquired a military renown by the pillage and slaughter of timid Asiatics, but in obstinate battles and sieges against warlike and disciplined veterans. . . . " During these glorious achievements Mr. Clive pampered at Bengal in the affluence and luxury of an eastern potentate, sedulous to accumulate by lawless exactions and monopolies his ill-gotten treasure " (I, 65).

The work contains much else, including an excellent description of India and the Mogul constitution. But I have indicated enough of its contents to show that it cannot be dismissed as entirely worthless by anyone trying to judge Clive's career impartially and understand all its aspects.

D

WARREN HASTINGS, MAKER OF BRITISH INDIA—AN IMPORTANT CORRECTION

ON p. 150 (p. 124 of American edition) of the above work there appears an elaborate argument based upon words reputed to have been used by Edmund Burke showing that his astigmatic hostility to Warren Hastings dated as early as 1773. I gave as my authority for this " discovery " the biography of Burke by the Rev. Dr. R. H. Murray (Oxford University Press, 1931). I am afraid, however, this is another time that Homer has nodded ! For when one examines what Burke actually said one finds that his meaning was precisely opposite from what it would appear from the passages abstracted from their context ! I humbly confess that until Dr. Weitzman pointed out the blunder to me I had not consulted the original source for myself. I am deeply grateful to her for enabling me to make this belated correction.

The source is as Dr. Murray gave it, *i.e.* Sir Henry Cavendish's *Debates of the House of Commons*, Vol. XXXVI. ; Egerton MSS., Vol. 250. Burke in the speech in question is arguing that ministers have violated public faith by breaking the East India Company's charter, the ground for their action being that the Company's powers are insufficient to prevent the abuses which have prevailed in the government of Bengal. But, he proceeds,

" Parliament after abusing the powers of the East India Company is obliged to resort to them. . . . You have got no new powers for your officers by the breach of your charter. You have got no new instructions. If there are no new powers, if no new instructions, let us see who are the instructors."

He points out that the Directors are the same.

" Since the powers are the same, since the instructors and instructions are the same, what remains but to make it a question of men ? The men are the same, the very men. *Mr. Hastings is to have the casting vote, a man nominated by this Parliament. If the insinuations of the Committee of Secrecy, if the speeches to-day are true, this man is guilty of everything charged—this man is to be first President, he is even given a controlling power in the Council.* Who is the next ? Mr. Barwell. If it be true that no obedience is paid to its orders, I do not believe you will have much obedience paid to your own Direction, whom you have so blackened. These are the men you have got in Asia, with only the addition of three from Europe, I mean General Clavering, Monson and Francis. With regard to the first, I will be bold to say, because he has been

named and approved by [defective manuscript] character stands high, a
very respectable person, the next for many reasons *the*
third I know *some personal character. If appointed legally,*
and constitutionally, I know no person fitter for his place. But I cannot be wiser
than the law. I shall always think whatever talents a man has about him, the man
who is legally appointed to his office is the fittest. I am obliged to know the law.
I am not obliged to know men : I am obliged to adhere to them." [1]

So Burke asked, " for what purpose and gain do you break charters ? " He
defends the Company's government. He points to its army

" growing more strong and powerful, what reflection is this upon any C.
[? Council] as to the interior disorders. I take it from the secret Committee.
Not a word that does not show a constant struggle to redress those disorders.
Every capital disorder has been either redressed or is going to be so. The
great questions of presents are few. The business of monopoly and oppressive trade is almost knocked on the head. The anarchy of the Company the
greatest grievance is reformed by the beginning of a system one of the most
beautiful ever seen established in any place. . . . Some disorders still prevail
—which I pray to God you may not find more subsisting under your new
government. What is it you did for 7 years together ? You have complained since 1767 of these disorders ; while they were rising to the height
the House never attempted to apply a remedy. Now the fire is got under,
we are by a little belated wisdom, trying to put a little credit . . ." (The
meaning of the rest of the passage is obscure.)

From this it will be seen that Burke was using an involved line of argument
to defend the Company against the reproach implied in the Regulating Bill,
this being his consistent attitude at that time and therefore what we might
expect. So far from attacking Hastings, he was actually by implication
defending him as the Company's chosen servant and the originator of the
reforms ! In consequence, Burke's subsequent reversal of his position becomes
all the sharper by contrast. Here he even speaks of Hastings's new system of
government as " one of the most beautiful ever seen established in any
place " !

That seems a fact of some importance to the historian and to biographers of
Hastings and Burke.

[1] The italicized passages are those quoted by Dr. Murray and myself.

NOTES AND REFERENCES

NOTE : I have restricted these references for the most part to manuscript and less obvious published sources. The vast majority of the documents relating to Clive having already been published by Sir John Malcolm and Sir George Forrest and by S. C. Hill in *Bengal in 1756-1757*, I have made no reference to them. The references to Orme are to the O.V. MSS. except where otherwise stated.

1. Orme and Clive were appointed writers the same day, December 15, 1742 : Auber, I, 5.
2. Orme MSS. 288, 36.
3. *Ibid.*, 17, 13 (4) : Orme to Lord Holdernesse, November 15, 1757 : " Colonel Clive has made his fortune at Bengal, and writes me that he is no longer a cross to my views in the succession to this government."
4. Most of Clive's memos. were written in 1763.
5. Orme MSS. 293, 10.
6. See Orme MSS. 222, 149.
7. H. D. LOVE, *Vestiges of Old Madras*, vol. II, p. 513. He was found guilty by the Court of Directors, but his guilt is doubtful. He retired a poor man with an income of £400.
8. Letter to Colonel Richard Smith, February 1, 1766—Orme MSS. 222, 149.
9. S. C. HILL, *Catalogue of the Orme MSS.*, p. xxix. ; Orme MSS. 23, 26.
10. Letter to Colonel Richard Smith, November 18, 1767—Orme MSS. 222, 189.
11. G. W. FORREST, Preface to *Life of Clive*.
12. Shropshire Parish Records, vol. 8.
13. R. J. MINNEY, *Clive*, p. 8.
14. Transactions of the Shropshire Archæological Society.
15. *Biographia Britannica* (2nd Ed.), p. 645.
16. WILLIAM BOYD, *History of Western Education* (1921), p. 297.
17. *Johnson's England*, vol. II, p. 219.
18. Court Minutes, LX, 182, 202.
19. I.O., Madras European Inhabitants, 1702–80, vol. 8.
20. I.O., Records of Fort St. George, Despatches to England, 1746–51, 86.
21. *A Voyage to India in 1761 : Bengal Past and Present*, vol. XLV, p. 99.
22. H. H. DODWELL, *The Nabobs of Madras* (1926), p. 26.
23. *Ibid.*, p. 228.
24. THOMAS AUDEN, *Memorials of Old Shropshire* (1906), p. 220.
25. VIRGINIA M. THOMPSON, *Dupleix and His Letters* (1933), p. 101.

26. VIRGINIA M. THOMPSON, *Dupleix and His Letters* (1933), p. 102.
27. H. H. DODWELL, *Dupleix and Clive* (1920), p. 7.
28. CHARLES DALTON, *Memoir of Captain Dalton* (1886), p. 51.
29. DODWELL, *The Nabobs of Madras*, p. 62.
30. VIRGINIA M. THOMPSON, *op. cit.*, p. 178.
31. *Ibid.*, pp. 179–80.
32. *Ibid.*, p. 181.
33. HAVELOCK ELLIS, *A Study of British Genius*.
34. THOMPSON, *op. cit.*, p. 188 ; *Diary of Ananda Ranga Pillai*, vol. IV, p. 328.
35. DODWELL, *The Nabobs of Madras*, p. 41.
36. DODWELL, *Calendar of Madras Despatches 1744–55*, p. 108.
37. L. B. NAMIER, *England in the Age of the American Revolution*, p. 20.
38. ORME, *India*, i, pp. 219 *et seq.*
39. DODWELL, *Madras Despatches*, p. 14.
40. *Ibid.*, p. 81.
41. LOVE, *Vestiges of Old Madras*, vol. II, p. 489.
42. DODWELL, *Madras Despatches*, p. 140.
43. ORME, O.V. 287, 395 ; 288, 203.
44. *Ananda Ranga Pillai*, vol. VII, p. 438.
45. DODWELL, *Madras Despatches*, p. 141.
46. ORME, O.V. 287, 135.
47. *Ibid.*
48. *Ibid.*, 87–89.
49. *Ibid.*, 157.
50. *Ibid.*, *India*, cxi, 521.
51. I.O., Home Miscellaneous Series, 806.
52. ORME, 287, 169.
53. DODWELL, *Madras Despatches*, p. 148.
54. ORME, *India*, ii, 277–92.
55. THOMPSON, *op. cit.*, pp. 439, 441.
56. ORME, 287, 177.
57. THOMPSON, *op. cit.*, pp. 342 *et seq.*
58. CARACCIOLI, C., *Life of Robert, Lord Clive* (1777), vol. I, p. 188.
59. THOMPSON, *op. cit.*, p. 352.
60. ORME, *India*, i, 178.
61. *Ibid.*, ii, 462.
62. *Ibid.*
63. *Ibid.*, ii, 478.
64. *Ananda Ranga Pillai*, vol. VIII, p. 114.
65. *Ibid.*, p. 177.
66. THOMPSON, *op. cit.*, p. 439.
67. ORME, *India*, ii, 233.
68. THOMPSON, *op. cit.*, pp. 433 *et seq.*
69. R. O. CAMBRIDGE, *Account of War in India*, p. 35 ; THOMPSON, *op. cit.*, p. 381.

70. DALTON, *Memoir of Captain Dalton*, p. 215.

71. THOMPSON, *op. cit., passim.*

72. *Cambridge History of British Empire*, vol. IV, p. 134.

73. W. H. DAGLIESH, *The Company of the Indies in the Days of Dupleix* (1933), pp. 182–5.

74. DODWELL, *Nabobs of Madras*, pp. 182, 198.

75. DAGLIESH, *op. cit.*, p. 162.

76. ORME, *India*, ii, 490.

77. *Ibid., India*, ii, 472.

78. *Ibid.*, 288, 123.

79. *Ibid., India*, ii, 474.

80. *Ibid.*, 287, 363.

81. *Ibid.*, 288, 101.

82. *Ibid., India*, ii, 49.

83. *Ibid.*, 288, 37.

84. *Ibid.*, 288, 109.

85. L. B. NAMIER, *Structure of Politics at the Accession of George III*, vol. I, p. 37.

86. ORME, 28, II (4).

87. *Ibid.*, 289, 22.

88. Home Misc. Ser., 806, 319.

89. The material for this and the succeeding chapters is taken largely from *Bengal in 1756–7* (edited by S. C. Hill), to which no further reference seems necessary.

90. ORME, 19, 1.

91. ORME, *History*, vol. II, pp. 123–134.

92. ORME, 28, 10. See also J. W. THOMPSON and S. K. PADOVER, *Secret Diplomacy*, 1500–1815, Chap. 7. *The Perfect Technique* (1937).

93. ORME, 27, 10.

94. SURGEON IVES, *Voyage to India* (1773), p. 153.

95. ORME, Various, 164A, 115 : The MSS. contains this passage, and the one following, which were omitted from the work (2nd Volume of Orme's *History*) published in 1778. The presumption is that after Clive's death Orme carefully edited his account of Plassey and omitted such passages as appeared derogatory to Clive's character.

96. FORREST omits those for the 1st Battalion (*Life*, vol. I, p. 459).

97. *Life of Clive*, vol. I, p. 273.

98. ORME, 20, 10.

99. S. C. HILL, *Catalogue to Orme Collection*, p. 36.

100. IVES, *Voyage*, 153 :
　　"I have been more minute in the description of this battle of Plassey than was Mr. Scrafton, because some persons have taken great pains to misrepresent it, with a view to tarnish the glory of Colonel Clive on that important victory ; pretending that their accounts were taken *verbatim* from Sir Eyre Coote's journal, as read by him to the Select

Committee of the House of Commons, which sat the preceding sessions on East India affairs. Having, therefore, been lately favoured with the perusal of Sir Eyre Coote's journal, I can aver that the several publications alluded to are totally devoid of truth ; and the public may be assured that the description given here of the battle corresponds in every *material* particular with that journal. Sir Eyre Coote himself, also, in a late conversation with me, declared, ' that the publications before mentioned were absolutely false ; that any person might be convinced thereof, by appealing to the minutes of the Committee of the House of Commons, where what was delivered by him on his examinations, was committed to paper.' He also authorized me publicly to declare ' that he has on all occasions been ever ready to do justice to Lord Clive's merit.' "

Ives adds that Coote did all the service that was in his power.

101. WYLLY, *Life of Sir Eyre Coote*, p. 58.
102. ORME, 293, 31.
103. Home Misc., 808.
104. *Ibid.*, 808, 91–93.
105. I.O., Bengal Papers.
106. Home Misc., 808, 105–115.
107. *Ibid.*, 809.
108. *Bengal Past and Present*, vol. LII, p. 84.
109. Home Misc., 809.
110. J. LONG, *Selections from Unpublished Records of Government*, 1748–67 (1869) ; No. 417.
111. *Chatham Correspondence*, vol. I, p. 341.
112. I.O., Misc. Letters Rec'd, XL, 222.
113. LONG, *op. cit.*, No. 367.
114. DODWELL, *Dupleix and Clive*, p. 157.
115. Home Misc. 808(1).
116. *Cambridge History of British Empire*, vol. IV.
117. Records of the Genealogical Society of London.
118. T. G. P. SPEAR, *The Nabobs*, p. 68.
119. I.O., Bengal Despatches, 1753–9, I.
120. General Letter to Bengal, March 23, 1759.
121. FORREST, *Life*, vol. II, p. 176.
122. Home Misc. 809.
123. *Ibid.*
124. WYLLY, *op. cit.*, p. 88.
125. JAMES MILL, *History of British India*, vol. III, p. 260.
126. FORREST, *Life*, vol. II, p. 152.
127. *Ibid.*, 150.
128. HILL, *Introduction to Orme Catalogue*, p. xxv.
129. Home Misc., 807.
130. I.O., East Indian Tracts, CXVII, No. I.

131. See, *inter alia*, N. CHATTERJI, *Mir Qasim, Nawab of Bengal,* 1760–63 (Allahabad).

132. H. VANSITTART, *Letter to the Proprietors,* p. 109.

133. The First Report of the Committee.

134. DODWELL, *Dupleix and Clive,* p. 193.

135. *D. N. B.,* Article on Henry Vansittart.

136. The Committee's Third Report, Appendix, 80.

137. *The Annual Register,* 1760, p. 120.

138. NAMIER, *Structure of Politics,* p. 69.

139. Home Misc., 808.

140. The full facts of Clive's election dealings and relations with Newcastle, Powis, Sandwich, etc., are to be found in Namier's *Structure of Politics,* to which I am indebted for this account.

141. General Letters of the Court to Bengal, January 21, 1761.

142. Letter of March 16, 1761.

143. Chatham MSS., 60, Sulivan to Pitt, February 5, 1761 ; Basil Williams, *Life of Wm. Pitt, Earl of Chatham,* vol. II, p. 28.

144. Letter to Peter Amyatt, February 27, 1762.

145. These two letters were included by Malcolm (*Life,* vol. II, pp. 190–2), but omitted by Forrest.

146. EDWARD THOMPSON and G. T. GARRATT, *Rise and Fulfilment of British Rule in India,* p. 6.

147. Chatham MSS. 60.

148. S. SUTHERLAND, *E. H. R.,* July 1934.

149. NAMIER, *Structure of Politics,* p. 357.

150. I.O., *Tracts,* CCXX, Part 3.

151. *Grenville Papers,* vol. II, p. 160.

152. *Ibid.,* vol. IV, p. 14.

153. *Ibid.,* vol. II, pp. 180–3.

154. *Ibid.,* vol. II, p. 184.

155. I.O., Misc. Letters Rec'd, XLVI (1764), No. 134A.

156. *Grenville Papers,* vol. II, p. 301 ; Clive to Grenville, February 29, 1764.

157. Letter to the Court, April 27, 1764.

158. *Grenville Papers,* vol. II, pp. 301, 307.

159. Chatham MSS. 60.

160. *Grenville Papers,* vol. II, p. 309.

161. *Bengal Past and Present,* vol. LI, p. 172.

162. *Grenville Papers,* vol. II, p. 310.

163. Orme 21, 25.

164. DODWELL, *Dupleix and Clive,* p. 229.

165. H. VANSITTART, *Letter to the Proprietors,* p. 99.

166. The Letters of Richard Barwell, *Bengal Past and Present,* vol. VIII, p. 187.

167. *A Letter to the Proprietors of East India Stock from John Johnstone, Esq.,* London, 1776 ; I.O., Tracts, L, No. 1.

168. MILL, *History,* Book IV, Chap. 7.

169. Forrest omits this passage ; it comes after the words " their Principle and Manners "—see *Life*, vol. II, p. 311.
170. Home Misc. 809 (3).
171. CARACCIOLI, *op. cit.*, vol. I, p. 140.
172. Letter from Clive to the Company, May 23, 1769 (published in London, 1806).
173. M. E. MONCKTON-JONES, *Warren Hastings in Bengal*, 1772–74, p. 85.
174. See Barwell's letters, *Bengal Past and Present*.
175. Home Misc. 808 (3).
176. *Ibid.*, 809 (3).
177. *Ibid.*, Letter of April 5.
178. CARACCIOLI, *op. cit.*, vol. I, p. 405.
179. Letter to Court of September 30, 1765.
180. Mr. Dodwell is of the same opinion, see *Dupleix and Clive*, p. 254 (note).
181. BOLTS, W., *Considerations on Indian Affairs* (1772–75), vol. II, pp. 28–39 ; Proceedings of House of Commons Committee on Clive's letter of April 17, 1765.
182. Clive to Sir Joseph York, November 7, 1765, Bolts, vol. II, p. 40.
183. *I.e.* Barwell's words ; see his letters.
184. For Munro and Carnac cases, see First Report of House of Commons Committee.
185. Clive to Fletcher, August 6, 1765, Home Misc. 809 (3).
186. See Fifth Report of Committee.
187. See Third Report of Committee.
188. Letter to Court of April 27, 1764.
189. *Letter to the Proprietors*, p. 136.
190. Barwell's Letters, *Bengal Past and Present*, vol. IV, p. 118.
191. The account given here is based principally on Strachey's *Narrative*.
192. CARACCIOLI, *op. cit.*, vol. I, pp. 222–63.
193. This letter does not appear in Forrest.
194. Letter to the Rev. Gilbert Burrington, March 10, 1767 ; Home Misc. Series, 765, 167.
195. I.O., Tracts, L., No. 3 ; *Grenville Papers*, vol. III, p. 323.
196. BASIL WILLIAMS, *op. cit.*, vol. II, p. 233.
197. *Grenville Papers*, vol. III, p. 325.
198. I.O., Tracts, vol. 378, part I.
199. H.M.C., 10th Report, p. 410.
200. H.M.C., Report on the Palk MSS. p. 157 : " Sulivan comes in singly with the consent of all parties. I should have thought, after all that is passed and in such times as these, he had better have relinquished so troublesome and, to him, so very unprofitable an employ. However, it is to him the *summum bonum* " (Letter of Palk, April 1771).
201. *Ibid.*, 116. Hastings wrote from Madras : " It gave me an unspeakable pleasure to hear of the new commission granted to Mr. Van, and to find such a man as Colonel Forde joined with him. I cannot say I was

so well pleased to see Scrafton's name with theirs, but a further reflection has reconciled me to it. All parties will be better pleased with the measures taken by the Commissioners than if Mr. Van alone, or joined only with his friends, had formed them : and Scrafton is neither ill-natured nor hard to manage when he has not troublesome people about him. Forde will, if I mistake not, have a great ascendant over him. He is a reasonable and steady man, and Mr. Van, from his superior abilities and knowledge of the methodical part of business, in which I believe the others are deficient, will certainly take the lead in everything. I suppose the Commission will last during the period of Cartier's government, and our friend return to his former station. I know no other recompense the Company can make him for his trouble and the odium which the execution of such a trust will unavoidably draw on him. Bengal certainly requires such a ruler. The Company's affairs there have been declining very fast, and for their sake more than that of this Presidency, which stands in great need of such a reforming power also, I am most heartily glad the Company have adopted so wise a plan, the wisest they ever thought of."

202. See W. W. HUNTER, *Annals of Rural Bengal* (1872), pp. 19–40.
203. H.M.C., Palk Papers, p. 117.
204. *Ibid.*, p. 50.
205. ORME, 222, 189.
206. *Ibid.*, 37, 18.
207. *Ibid.*, 202, 17, 36.
208. Letter to Sir Horace Mann, July 19, 1769.
209. *Warren Hastings, Maker of British India*, p. 67.
210. S. WEITZMAN, *Warren Hastings and Philip Francis*, p. 204.
211. *Ibid.*, p. 206.
212. A copy of the memorandum is among the Francis MSS., India Office, vol. 46.
213. MALCOLM, *Life*, vol. III, p. 329.
214. *Ibid.*
215. MACAULAY, *Essay on Clive*.
216. P. E. ROBERTS, *A Historical Geography of British Dependencies*, vol. VII, India, part 1 : "It is usually said by Clive's biographers that these Committees were inspired solely by animus against him . . . but there is little evidence of any unnecessary bias in the Reports themselves, and they are a valuable storehouse of facts for the history of the East India Company."
217. WEITZMAN, *op. cit.*, p. 297.
218. I.O., Fowke MSS.
219. WEITZMAN, *op. cit.*, p. 284.
220. *Burke's Correspondence*, vol. I, p. 446.

INDEX

2 K*